ALA GUIDE TO

MEDICAL &
HEALTH SCIENCES

REFERENCE

ALA Editions purchases fund advocacy, awareness,
and accreditation programs for library professionals worldwide.

ALA GUIDE TO
MEDICAL & HEALTH SCIENCES
REFERENCE

American Library Association

Chicago / 2011

Printed in the United States of America

15 14 13 12 11   5 4 3 2 1

While extensive effort has gone into ensuring the reliability of the information in this book, the publisher makes no warranty, express or implied, with respect to the material contained herein.

ISBN: 978-0-8389-1023-8

Library of Congress Cataloging-in-Publication Data
ALA guide to medical & health sciences reference.
   p. ; cm.
 Includes bibliographical references and indexes.
 ISBN 978-0-8389-1023-8 (alk. paper)
 1. Medicine—Information services—United States. 2. Medicine—Reference books—United States. I. American Library Association. II. Title: Guide to medical & health sciences reference. III. Title: ALA guide to medical and health sciences reference.
 [DNLM: 1. Medicine—United States—Abstracts. 2. Medicine—United States—Resource Guides. 3. Information Services—United States—Abstracts. 4. Information Services—United States—Resource Guides. 5. Reference Books, Medical—United States—Abstracts. 6. Reference Books, Medical—United States—Resource Guides. ZWB 100]
 R118.4.U6A43 2011
 610—dc22

                                                                        2011009719

Book design by Karen Sheets de Gracia in Helvetica and Melior.

♾This paper meets the requirements of ANSI/NISO Z39.48-1992 (Permanence of Paper).

ALA Editions also publishes its books in a variety of electronic formats. For more information, visit the ALA Store atalastore.ala.org and select eEditions.

CONTENTS

series introduction   *xi*

contributors   *xiii*

Editors' Guide   *1*

one   **MEDICINE**   *5*

Bibliography   *7*
  Audiovisual materials   *17*
  Government publications   *17*
  Incunabula   *18*
  Periodicals   *19*
Biography   *23*
  Bibliography   *25*
  Great Britain   *27*
  International   *29*
  United States   *34*
Classification   *36*
Dictionaries   *45*
  Abbreviations   *54*
  Multilingual   *56*
  Specialized and specialist dictionaries   *61*
Directories   *75*
  Canada   *76*
  Great Britain   *80*
  International   *82*
  United States   *85*
Encyclopedias   *96*
Guides   *120*
Handbooks   *125*
Histories   *145*
  Bibliography   *156*
  Directories   *166*
  Historical surveys   *167*

Indexes; Abstract journals; Databases   *174*
   Specialized indexes   *187*
Internet resources   *192*
Library catalogs   *207*
Medical illustration and images   *210*
Quotations   *218*
Statistics   *219*
Style manuals   *244*
Thesauruses   *250*

two **BIOETHICS**   *252*

Bibliography   *252*
Dictionaries   *254*
Directories   *254*
Encyclopedias   *255*
Guides   *256*
Handbooks   *256*
Indexes; Abstract journals; Databases   *264*
Internet resources   *266*

three **CONSUMER HEALTH**   *275*

Dictionaries   *283*
Directories   *286*
Encyclopedias   *288*
Guides   *306*
Handbooks   *320*
Indexes; Abstract journals; Databases   *323*
Internet resources   *325*

four **DENTISTRY**   *342*

Bibliography   *343*
Biography   *343*
Classification   *343*
Dictionaries   *344*
Directories   *348*
Encyclopedias   *350*
Guides   *351*

Handbooks   *351*
Histories   *355*
Indexes; Abstract journals; Databases   *358*
Internet resources   *361*

five   **HEALTH CARE**   *363*

Bibliography   *365*
Dictionaries   *368*
Directories   *371*
Encyclopedias   *373*
Guides   *374*
Handbooks   *376*
Indexes; Abstract journals; Databases   *382*
Internet resources   *386*
Statistics   *396*

six   **INTERNATIONAL AND GLOBAL HEALTH**   *406*

Dictionaries   *407*
Directories   *407*
Encyclopedias   *408*
Handbooks   *409*
Histories   *414*
Indexes; Abstract journals; Databases   *415*
Internet resources   *418*
Statistics   *425*

seven   **MEDICAL JURISPRUDENCE**   *432*

Bibliography   *432*
Dictionaries   *433*
Directories   *435*
Encyclopedias   *436*
Guides   *437*
Handbooks   *437*
Indexes; Abstract journals; Databases   *446*
Internet resources   *450*
Statistics   456

eight NURSING   *457*

Bibliography   *457*
Biography   *460*
Dictionaries   *461*
Directories   *467*
Encyclopedias   *469*
Handbooks   *471*
Histories   *479*
Indexes; Abstract journals; Databases   *483*
Internet resources   *488*
Statistics   *490*
Thesauruses   *490*

nine NUTRITION   *491*

Bibliography   *492*
Dictionaries   *493*
Directories   *496*
Encyclopedias   *496*
Guides   *500*
Handbooks   *501*
Indexes; Abstract journals; Databases   *511*
Internet resources   *516*
Tables   *518*

**ten PHARMACOLOGY AND PHARMACEUTICAL
      SCIENCES**   *519*

Bibliography   *521*
Dictionaries   *522*
Directories   *527*
Dispensatories and pharmacopoeias   *528*
Encyclopedias   *534*
Guides   *538*
Handbooks   *540*
Histories   *569*
Indexes; Abstract journals; Databases   *574*
Internet resources   *579*
Thesauruses   *583*

eleven **PSYCHIATRY** *584*

Bibliography *584*
Classification *585*
Dictionaries *587*
Directories *593*
Encyclopedias *594*
Guides *601*
Handbooks *602*
Histories *618*
Indexes; Abstract journals; Databases *623*
Internet resources *625*
Statistics *627*
Treatises *627*

twelve **PUBLIC HEALTH** *628*

Bibliography *632*
Dictionaries *634*
Directories *638*
Encyclopedias *640*
Guides *645*
Handbooks *647*
Histories *659*
Indexes; Abstract journals; Databases *661*
Internet resources *666*
Statistics *682*

thirteen **TOXICOLOGY** *688*

Dictionaries *689*
Directories *690*
Encyclopedias *691*
Guides *694*
Handbooks *694*
Indexes; Abstract journals; Databases *703*
Internet resources *711*

SERIES INTRODUCTION

AS THE PUBLISHER of the essential *Guide to Reference Books*, first printed more than a century ago, as well as *Reference Sources for Small and Medium-Sized Libraries* and *Fundamental Reference Sources*, the American Library Association has long been a source for authoritative bibliographies of the reference literature for practicing librarians, library educators, and reference service trainers. The ALA Guide to Reference series continues that tradition with expertly compiled, discipline-specific, annotated bibliographies of reference works. The volumes in the series draw their content from the successor to *Guide to Reference Books*, the online *Guide to Reference* (www.guidetoreference.org), and thus serve as snapshots of the evolving content of the online *Guide*.

Although compiled in North America for use largely in North American libraries serving institutions of higher education, the series volumes will also be valuable to public and school librarians, independent researchers, publishers, and book dealers, as well as librarians outside North America, for identifying sources that will answer questions, directing researchers, creating local instructional materials, educating and training LIS students and reference staff, and inventorying and developing reference collections. Because these guides provide a usably comprehensive, rather than exhaustive, repertory of sources as the foundation for reference and information services in today's North American higher education research settings, English-language works figure prominently. Works in other languages are included, however, as categories require them and as higher education curricula in North American colleges and universities suggest their inclusion.

The reader will find entries for works that are, for the most part, broadly focused; works on individual persons or works that are narrowly focused geographically or chronologically are not included. Selection criteria favored titles published in the last fifteen years; the reader will want to consult earlier printed bibliographies and indexes, such as the numerous print editions of *Guide to Reference Books*, for many earlier and still important works.

Together, the volumes in this series include works that can most usefully satisfy the vast majority of demands made on a reference service, while not altogether excluding "exotic" or little-known works that will meet only the unusual need. The hope is that the works included will directly meet 80 percent of the needs that librarians have for reference sources and, in the remaining 20 percent of cases, will lead to other works that will suffice.

Librarians today have a broader definition of that much-mooted and ambiguous term *reference work* than ever before. The volumes in this series therefore include the traditional array of encyclopedic, bibliographic, and compendious works as well as websites, search engines, and full-text databases. Because of current reference practice and user preferences, the bibliographies in the series include those online sources that have replaced their printed versions for most librarians under most circumstances. The annotations for such sources describe the relationships between online and print versions.

In addition to providing classified annotated bibliographies, every volume includes editors' guides that orient readers to each discipline, its scope and concerns, and the kinds of sources available for working in it. The editors' guides will be useful, therefore, to the generalist librarian and LIS student as background to the bibliographies or as intellectual frameworks for addressing reference questions.

We at ALA Publishing hope you find the series helpful and welcome your comments at guidetoreference@ala.org. To get the full benefit of the comprehensive compilation in a wide range of subject areas, we also encourage you to subscribe to the online *Guide*, where you have access to updated entries (especially current Web resources), annotations, and user comments.

CONTRIBUTORS

UNDER THE DIRECTION of general editors Robert Kieft (2000–2009) and Denise Bennett (2009–), many librarians have contributed their time and their knowledge of reference literature to this series. A comprehensive list of these contributors appears under the About section of the online *Guide to Reference* (www.guidetoreference.org).

EDITOR'S GUIDE

THE MEDICAL AND Health Sciences category provides an annotated list of print and electronic biomedical and health-related reference sources, including Internet resources and digital image collections. The original purpose of the *Guide* remains (i.e., to provide a wide selection of bibliographic and information resources relevant to the provision of reference services in a biomedical library). It is intended to help users find relevant research, clinical, and consumer health information resources. As with previous editions of the *Guide*, the current edition cannot claim to be exhaustive in coverage; coverage in the medical section/subsections remains rather selective. Following previous editions of the *Guide*, some of the resources in this section are not strictly reference materials in the traditional sense. Emphasis is on U.S. resources, with a few representative examples from other countries. With few exceptions, materials in the medicine section would generally be found in the Library of Congress classification R. The intended audience is biomedical researchers, clinicians, and allied health professionals, as well as health consumers and the general public.

The medical subsections of the previous edition of the *Guide* were retained. Three new subsections were added in this edition. The subsections are Medicine, Bioethics, Consumer Health (new), Dentistry, Health Care (new), International and Global Health (new), Medical Jurisprudence, Nursing, Nutrition, Pharmacology and Pharmaceutical Sciences, Psychiatry, Public Health, and Toxicology. Also retained was the taxonomy within the different subsections. A new subcategory for Internet resources was added to all subsections.

The majority of reference resources included in this edition have been published between 1995 and 2007. Some of the selections were retained from the previous edition of the *Guide*, regardless of publication date; others are updated to the most recent editions. For older editions that have not been updated, an attempt was made to locate and substitute web-based resources with similar content. Print indexing and abstracting services have largely been replaced with online services, and *Guide* entries for bibliographic databases and digital database resources reflect this trend. Highly specialized databases have been kept to a minimum. Information on several high-profile print indexes is still included, but in summary format rather than with the full description found in the 11th edition of the *Guide*.

As a result of the rapid growth of the Internet, increased focus is on electronic resources, with inclusion of many relevant web-based electronic-only resources. The large number of biomedical websites dictates selective coverage. As a leading provider of information and information resources, the National Library of Medicine (NLM) and the National Center for Biotechnology Information (NCBI) have set the tone with the provision of a large number of highly useful web-based resources. Other U.S. government agencies, the World Health Organization (WHO), the Pan American Health Organization (PAHO), and professional and other noncommercial medical organizations also provide many relevant web-based reference sources.

Though it appears that Internet access is the preferred way for users to access biomedical reference materials, print reference collections continue to play a role at this time. In many cases, reference sources are published both in print and as an e-book. Electronic-only resources are currently fewer than expected, but will most likely appear in steadily rising numbers. Though online reference is the desired future, much of the information that is needed today is still located in "trusted" print reference resources. The trend, however, is toward online reference resources.

—CHRISTA MARIA MODSCHIEDLER, EDITOR

1 > MEDICINE

1   **American Cancer Society [homepage].** American Cancer Society. 1990s–. Atlanta: American Cancer Society. http://www.cancer.org.

RC261

Cancer information presented for health professionals, patients, and other health consumers. Includes the full text of *Cancer facts and figures* (515) and other statistics, providing incidence and trends of the major types of cancer survival rates and distribution of cancer by race and ethnicity. Also includes support programs and services, resources for healthy living, clinical trials, treatment decisions, tools to understand treatment options (including alternative treatments, and possible side effects), and an online glossary of cancer-related terms. Information in English and Spanish. Also contains Asian-language cancer education materials.

2   **Encyclopedia of immunology.** 2nd ed. Peter J. Delves, Ivan M. Roitt. 4 v., ill. (some color). San Diego, Calif.: Academic Press, 1998. ISBN: 0122267656.

616.07903   QR180.4.E53

1st ed., 1992.

While due for an update, the 2nd ed. of the encyclopedia expanded from three to four volumes. Provides comprehensive coverage of the field of immunology with significant additions to the 1st ed., including sections of color photographs and more figures and illustrations. Each volume includes a glossary from Roitt's 1997 text *Essential immunology*. Available as an e-book. Appropriate for research libraries.

pamphlets, broadsides, and articles in periodical publications relating to the medical sciences—medicine, surgery, pharmacy, dentistry, and veterinary medicine—printed in the present territory of the United States of America during British dominion and the Revolutionary War. Francisco Guerra. 885 p., facsims. New York: L.C. Harper, 1962.

016.61   Z6659.G8

Half-title: *American medical bibliography, colonial period and Revolutionary War, 1639–1783.*

(Yale University. Dept. of the History of Science and Medicine. Publication; 40).

In three sections: (1) books, pamphlets, broadsides; (2) almanacs; and (3) periodical publications (magazines and newspapers). Gives detailed bibliographical information, with references to other historical sources. "Bibliographies," p. 776–784; "References in text," p. 785–810.

8   **American medical imprints, 1820–1910: A checklist of publications illustrating the history and progress of medical science, medical education, and the healing arts in the United States: a preliminary contribution.** Francesco Cordasco. 2 v. Totowa, N.J.; Fairview, N.J.: Rowman and Littlefield; Junius-Vaughn Press, 1985. ISBN: 0847673383.

016.610973   Z6661.U5C67; R152

Continues *Early American medical imprints: A guide to works printed in the United States, 1668–1820* (15). A "systematic and enumerative bibliography intended as a functional checklist" that includes "any item which could legitimately be related to the medical arts and their progress in the U.S."—*Introd.* Contains 36,612 entries arranged chronologically by decade of publication. Each entry includes a transcription of the work's title page; for most items, only the principal pagination is given. Shows one to four library locations. Some items are annotated, and there is an index of names. Introductory material includes "A handlist of selected bibliographies, catalogues, and related reference materials." An appendix, "Wood's library of standard medical authors" (a checklist of 100 medical textbooks published in New York by William Wood and Co. from the 1870s to the 1890s), was originally published by *AB bookman's weekly* 73 (1984): 3333–56.

9   **ARBA in-depth: Health and medicine.** Martin Dillon, Shannon Graff Hysell. xiii, 252 p. Westport, Conn.: Libraries Unlimited, 2004.

016.61   Z6658.A648; R129

(ARBA in-depth series)

Contains 473 signed reviews for health-related and medical reference titles, taken from the last six editions of *American reference books annual (ARBA)*. Includes reviews of print and Internet sites. Detailed table of contents, author/title, and subject indexes. Also available online. Intended for "reference librarians, collection development specialists, scholar, researcher, and patron."—*Cover*. Online version available via ARBAonline (http://www.arbaonline.com/).

10 **Bibliography of the history of medicine.** National Library of Medicine (U.S.), United States; Public Health Service. 28 v. Bethesda, Md.; Washington: U.S. Dept. of Health and Human Services, Public Health Service, National Institutes of Health, National Library of Medicine; For sale by the Supt. of Docs., U.S. G.P.O., 1966–[1994]. ISSN: 0067-7280.

016.6109   Z6660.B582

Produced by National Library of Medicine (NLM) (427). Annual, each 5th issue being a quinquennial cumulation. Cumulations: 1964/69 (publ. 1972. 1475 p.); 1970/74 (1976. 1069 p.); 1975/79 (1980. 924 p.); 1980/84 (1985. 1300 p.); 1985/89 (1990. 1454 p.). Supt. of Docs. classification: HE 20.3615. Consists of citations drawn from NLM's now discontinued HISTLINE database (cf. "FAQ Retired Databases" http://www.nlm.nih.gov/services/pastdatabases.html) monographs, analytic entries for symposia, congresses, etc., and chapters in general monographs. Works on the general history and philosophy of science are largely excluded. Attempts to avoid extensive duplication of topics regularly covered in "Critical bibliographies" section of *Isis* (now merged into History of Science, Technology and Medicine Database [Mountain View, Calif.: Research Libraries Group], but there is considerable duplication with *Current work in the history of medicine* [later called *Wellcome bibliography for the history of medicine* [386].] Subject and author listings. Remains useful for pre-1993 material. NLM's History of Medicine Historical Collection webpages, "Books and Journals" [http://www.nlm.nih.gov/hmd/collections/books/index.html] and "Printed Catalogs and Guides" [http://www.nlm.nih.gov/hmd/help/printed/index.html] provide further help in searching the literature in the history of medicine.

11 **A catalogue of seventeenth century printed books in the National Library of Medicine.** Peter Krivatsy, National Library of Medicine (U.S.). xiv, 1315 p. Bethesda, Md.: U.S. Dept. of Health and Human Services, Public Health Service, National Institutes of Health, National Library of Medicine, 1989.

016.6109032   Z6659.N38; R128.7

Shipping list no.: 89-261-P. Item 508-F.

For some 13,300 books printed 1601–1700, "monographs, dissertations and corresponding program disputations, broadsides, pamphlets and serials" (*Introd.*), provides title page transcription, physical description, and reference to standard bibliographies. Entries are alphabetical by author, editor, compiler, occasionally by corporate body, and in a few instances by title. Most authors' names are in vernacular form with cross-references to latinized or other names. There is no index, but the National Library of Medicine's (427) History of Medicine Division maintains indexes of printers, publishers, and vernacular imprints.

Complements earlier catalogs of pre–19th-century holdings of NLM: *A catalogue of incunabula and manuscripts in the Army Medical Library*, by Dorothy M. Schullian and Francis E. Sommer, ([1948?]); *A catalogue of sixteenth century printed books in the National Library of Medicine*, comp. by Richard J. Durling (1967); *A catalogue of incunabula and sixteenth century books in the National Library of Medicine: first supplement*, comp. by Peter Krivatsy (1971); and *A short title catalogue of eighteenth century printed books in the National Library of Medicine*, comp. by John Ballard Blake (1979).

12   **The development of medical bibliography.** Estelle Brodman. ix, 226 p., ports., diagrs. [Washington]: Medical Library Association, 1954.

016.61   Z6658.B7

(Publication [Medical Library Association]; no. 1)

Comprehensive survey of medical bibliography since 1500, covering printed medical bibliographies in Western languages that pertain to medicine in general rather than to its subdivisions or specialties. Personal bibliographies and bibliographies that do not make up the main portion of a work have been excluded, as have catalogs (with the exception of the *Index-catalogue of the Library of the Surgeon General's Office*). No distinction made between indexes and abstracts as bibliographies.

"For each bibliography discussed there is a biographical sketch of the compiler, a description of the work emphasizing advances in technique, and a discussion of the importance of the work in the history of medical bibliography."—*Introd.*

Appendix 1 lists references; appendix 2 lists medical bibliographies since 1500 which were not discussed in the body of the text, arranged by century. General and author indexes. A digitized version of this book is available at http://www.nlm.nih.gov/hmd/collections/digital/brodman/brodman.html as part of the National Library of Medicine's History of

Medicine digital collections. Like this work, *The great medical bibliographers: A study in humanism*, by John F. Fulton, identifies important medical bibliographies and bio-bibliographies.

13 Disease and destiny: A bibliography of medical references to the famous. Judson Bennett Gilbert. 535 p. London: Dawsons of Pall Mall, 1962.

016.92   Z6664.A1G5

Drawn largely from *Index-catalogue of the library of the Surgeon General's Office* (IndexCat [479]), *Index medicus* (420), and *Quarterly cumulative index medicus.*

A bibliography of writings that treat the medical history of famous people in history, the humanities, and the arts and sciences in all countries from ancient to modern times. Personalities are listed alphabetically and identified by dates of birth and death and a brief descriptive phrase. Books and papers about them are listed in chronological order. Introduction contains a bibliography of monographic literature of medicobiographical writing.

14 Doody's review service. Doody Enterprises, Inc. 2006–. Chicago: Doody Enterprises, Inc. http://www.doody.com/drs/.

Database of expert reviews of books and software in the health sciences (basic science, clinical medicine, nursing, allied health, and other health-related disciplines), with bibliographic information, a weekly literature update with timely reviews by professionals at major North American academic institutions, and ratings (Doody's Star Rating®) of newly published titles. Integrates the annually updated list of "Doody's Core Titles in the Health Sciences (DCT)" which "distills the perspectives of academic healthcare professionals and health sciences librarians into a core list."—*Publ. website.* DCT, first issued in Dec. 2004, is a useful collection development and management tool that is being used by many librarians in place of the recently discontinued "Brandon/Hill Selected Lists" (1965–2004 compiled by librarians, Al Brandon, Dorothy R. Hill, Henry N. Stickell, and others), publ. periodically in the *Bulletin of the Medical Library Association*, its later title, *Journal of the Medical Library Association*, and *Nursing outlook*. Overview and history of the Brandon/Hill lists can be found at http://library.mssm.edu/brandon-hill/history.shtml, provided by Levy Library, Mount Sinai Medical Center, 2007.

15 Early American medical imprints: A guide to works printed in the United States, 1668–1820. Robert B. Austin National Library of Medicine (U.S.). x, 240 p. Washington: U.S. Dept. of Health, Education, and Welfare, Public Health Service, 1961.

016.610973   Z6661.U5A44

At head of title: *National Library of Medicine.*

Alphabetical author listing of more than 2,100 separately published items, including books, pamphlets, theses, broadsides, and selected periodicals, with full bibliographical information and many annotations. Library holdings are indicated for 67 libraries. Appendixes include a chronological index and a list of 74 items in Charles Evans's *American bibliography, 1639–1729,* which are not included because copies could not be located or because they could not be verified as having been printed.

16   **Grey literature report.** New York Academy of Medicine
        Library. [1999]–. [New York, N.Y.]: New York Academy of
        Medicine. ISSN: 1931-7050. http://www.nyam.org/library/pages/
        grey_literature_report.

362.1

A publication of the New York Academy of Medicine Library (http://www. nyam.org/library/).

Grey literature is defined as "that which is produced on all levels of government, academics, business and industry in print and electronic formats, but which is not controlled by commercial publishers" (cf. *Website,* New York Academy of Medicine "What is Grey Literature?" http://www. nyam.org/library/pages/what_is_grey_literature).

Considered an alerting service to new grey literature in health services research and various public health topics, assisting researchers and librarians with the identification of this literature for both reference and collection development purposes. The Academy's entire Grey Literature Collection can be searched by keyword(s). The Academy's collection policy for grey literature is found at http://www.nyam.org/library/ pages/grey_literature_collection_developme nt_policy#conditions. Also included on the website is an A–Z list of grey literature producing organizations, including nonprofit and government agencies (http://www. nyam.org/library/pages/grey_literature_producing_organizations). The publications are cataloged in the New York Academy of Medicine Library Online Catalog (475).

The New York Academy of Medicine Library website provides links to its online library catalog (New York Academy of Medicine Library Online Catalog [475]), and its historical and other collections.

17   Health science books, 1876–1982. R.R. Bowker Co. 4 v. (xi, 4601
       p.). New York: R.R. Bowker Co., 1982. ISBN: 0835214478.
016.61   Z6658.H4; R129

Prepared by the R.R. Bowker Company's Dept. of Bibliography in collaboration with the Publications Systems Dept. Includes indexes.
       Contents: v. 1–3, Subject index; v. 4, Author index.
       Arranged by Library of Congress subject headings, the entries provide
complete LC entry with tracings, call number, and ISBN. Includes a guide
to MeSH/LC equivalents and a guide to LC/MeSH equivalents for the
health sciences.

18   **History and bibliography of artistic anatomy: Didactics
       for depicting the human figure.** Boris Röhrl. xx, 493 p., ill.
       Hildesheim, Germany: Olms, 2000. ISBN: 3487110741.
743.49   NC760.R65

Contents: pt. 1, History: ch. 1, Introd., ch. 2, Anatomy in the art of the
Ancient World and the Middle Ages; ch. 3, From the 13th to the 15th cent.;
ch. 4, 16th cent.; ch. 5, 17th cent.; ch. 6, 18th cent.; ch. 7, 19th cent.; ch. 8,
20th cent.; ch. 9, Definition of genres; pt. 2, Bibliography: (1) Bibliography
and description of books A–Z; (2) Appendices: Selected list of secondary
literature; Index of ill.; Index of persons; Index of places and schools of art.
       Considered a reference book which contains the didactical structure
and content of specific teaching manuals. Presents the different subgroups
of medically oriented teaching and how anatomy was taught in schools.
Includes, for example, Leonardo da Vinci's anatomical sketchbooks. The
bibliography in pt. 2 contains "books on osteology, myology, morphology,
and locomotion for artists. Treatises accompanying écorchés and theoretical essays. Manuals on proportions, expression and portrait drawing."—*t.p.*

19   **Institute of Medicine (IOM).** Institute of Medicine. 1998–.
     Washington: National Academy of Sciences. http://www.iom.edu/.

The Institute of Medicine (IOM), one of the U.S. National Academies,
has the mission to "serve as adviser to the nation to improve health" and
"provides independent, objective, evidence-based advice to policymakers, health professionals, the private sector, and the public."—*Main page.*
Offers a list of all publications by the IOM since 1970 (http://www.iom.
edu/CMS/2955.aspx), which cover a broad range of topics, including
aging, child health, a variety of diseases, global health, health care quality, minority health, nutrition, public health, public policy, preventive
medicine, women's health, and many other areas. The National Academies

MEDICINE

13

Press (http://www.nap.edu) provides online access to the publications of the four National Academies, i.e., National Academy of Sciences, National Academy of Engineering, IOM, and National Research Council.

20   Medical and health care books and serials in print. R. R. Bowker Co. New York: Bowker, c1985–. ISSN: 0000085X.

016.61   Z6658.B65R129

Medical and Health Care Books and Serials in Print. Title varies: 1972–77, *Bowker's medical books in print*; 1978–84, *Medical books and serials in print: An index to literature in the health sciences.* Derived from *Books in print, Ulrich's periodicals directory* (New Providence, N.J.: R. R. Bowker, 2001–), and related Bowker databases.

Description based on the 2007 ed. (2 v.).

A comprehensive and authoritative source for information on 109,000 books, including 3,500 new book titles, and 22,600 U.S. and foreign serials, with full ordering and publisher information. The available books in medicine, psychiatry, dentistry, veterinary medicine are classified in 6,000 subject categories. Indexed by author and title.

21   Medicine: A bibliography of bibliographies. Theodore Besterman. 409 p. Totowa, N.J.: Rowman and Littlefield, 1971. ISBN: 0874710502.

016.01661   Z6658.A1B4

Rather than listing citations alphabetically as they were in the parent publication, this source lists them topically as follows: medicine, anatomy, hygiene, pharmacology, pharmaceutics, psychiatry, and special subjects such as adrenal glands, balneology, and yaws. "Useful to those who seek primary signposts to information in varied fields of inquiry."—*Pref.* Wide subject and language coverage.

22   Medicine, health, and bioethics: Essential primary sources. K. Lee Lerner, Brenda Wilmoth Lerner. lvii, 513 p., ill. Detroit: Thomson/Gale, 2006. ISBN: 1414406231.

174.2   R724.M313

(Series: Social issues primary sources collection.)

Contains complete primary sources or excerpts of documents and publications published 1823–2006, illustrating major biomedical issues. Each entry includes the complete text or an excerpt with complete original citation, subject area, historical context, significance. For students, health professionals, and also general readers. Also available as an e-book.

23   **National academies press.** National Academies Press (U.S.). 1999–.
      Washington: National Academies Press. www.nap.edu/.

                                                          Z1217.N37

Contains free online access to over 3,700 monographs, mainly reports of
the academy on issues of importance to the science community and society—for example, future trends in employment opportunities in different fields, analyses of discrepancies in gender/racial makeup of scientists
in discplines, as well as the prospects of scientific projects or programs.
Overall, it provides a wealth of information on the state of science. The
National Academies are made up of the National Academy of Sciences,
National Academy of Engineering, the Institute of Medicine, and the
National Research Council.

24   **Recent dissertations in the medical humanities.** Jonathon Erlen,
      University of Pittsburgh Health Sciences Library System. 2001–.
      Pittsburgh: Health Sciences Library, University of Pittsburgh
      Medical Center. http://www.hsls.pitt.edu/guides/histmed/
      researchresources/dissertations/.

Provides a monthly current awareness service for selected recent medical
dissertation and theses. Arranged by topics, currently covers the following
areas: AIDS (social and historical contexts); alternative medicine (social
and historical contexts); art and medicine; biomedical ethics; history of
medicine prior to 1800; history of medicine and health care; history of
science and technology; literature/theater and medicine; nursing history;
pharmacy/pharmacology and history; philosophy and medicine; psychia-
try/psychology and history; public health/international health; religion
and medicine; women's health and history. To view complete citations,
abstracts, and full-text of dissertations requires a subscription to Proquest
Dissertations and Theses (PQDT) (Ann Arbor, Mich.: ProQuest).

25   **Repertorium commentationum a societatibus litterariis
      editarum.** Jeremias David Reuss. 16 v. New York: B. Franklin, 1961.

                                                          Z5051.R44

Originally publ. 1801–21; repr., 1961. Contents: (1) Historia naturalis,
generalis et zoologia; (2) Botanica et mineralogia; (3) Chemia et res metal-
lica; (4) Physica; (5) Astronomia; (6) Oeconomia; (7) Mathesis, mechanica,
hydrostatica, hydraulica, hydrotechnia, aerostatica, pnevmatica, technolo-
gia, architectura civilis, scientia navalis, scientia militaris; (8) Historia; (9)
Philologia, linguae, scriptures graeci, scriptores latini, litterae elegaritiores,

poesis, rhetorica, ars antiqua, pictura, musica; (10-16) Scientia et ars medica et chirurgica.

A very valuable index to the publ. of the learned societies of various countries from the time of the founding of each society to 1800, thus preceding the Royal Society of London's Catalogue of scientific papers. Sections are arranged topically and include an author index. Freely available online at http://www-gdz.sub.uni-goettingen.de/cgi-bin/digbib.cgi?PPN366452967.

26 **Thornton's medical books, libraries, and collectors: A study of bibliography and the book trade in relation to the medical sciences.** 3rd rev. ed. John Leonard Thornton, Alain Besson. xxi, 417 p., ill. Aldershot, Hants, U.K.; Brookfield, Vt.: Gower, 1990. ISBN: 0566054817.

381.45002   Z286.M4T47

1st ed., 1949, and 2nd ed., 1966, had title: *Medical books, libraries and collectors: A study of bibliography and the book trade in relation to the medical sciences.*

An introductory history of the literature of medicine from the earliest times through the 19th century. A separate chapter treats medical writings before the invention of printing. Medical literature of the 20th century is included in chapters on growth of the medical periodical literature and medical libraries of today. Intends "to record the chief writings of every prominent author and to chart the growth and development of ancillary subjects such as periodicals, bibliographies and libraries."—*Introd.*

Includes a bibliography and indexes of personal and institutional names, journal titles, and subjects.

27 **Women in medicine: A bibliography of the literature on women physicians.** Sandra L. Chaff. Metuchen, N.J.: Scarecrow Press, 1977–. ISBN: 0810810565.

016.6106952   Z7963.M43W65; R692

"Comprehensive coverage of the literature about women physicians in all parts of the world."—*Introd.* Includes 4,000 citations (books, medical and nonmedical journal articles, alumnae and alumni magazine articles, doctoral dissertations), representing the literature from 1750 through 1975. Entries provide bibliographical information and annotation. Author, subject, and personal name indexes; appendixes of directories and special library collections.

Audiovisual Materials

28 Fact sheet, access to audiovisual materials. National Library of Medicine (U.S.). 2001–. Bethesda, Md.: National Library of Medicine. http://www.nlm.nih.gov/pubs/factsheets/lrc.html.

Provides a description of NLM's audiovisual collection covering biomedical subjects: "60,000 audiovisual programs in almost 40 formats, over 3,500 of historical interest."—*Main page.* Includes instructions for on-site access, copyright restrictions for audiovisual materials, and other information. Online catalog access to identify audiovisual materials via LocatorPlus (480).

29 Videos of surgical procedures (MedlinePlus). National Library of Medicine (U.S.). 2004?–. Bethesda, Md.: National Library of Medicine, National Institutes of Health, U.S. Dept. of Health and Human Services. http://www.nlm.nih.gov/medlineplus/surgeryvideos.html.

Pt. of MedlinePlus® (463). Provides links to prerecorded webcasts of surgical procedures, that is, actual operations performed at medical centers in the U.S. since Jan. 2004. Intended for educational purposes.

Government Publications

30 Current bibliographies in medicine. National Library of Medicine (U.S.); Reference Section. 1996–. Bethesda, Md.: U.S. Dept. of Health & Human Services, National Institutes of Health, National Library of Medicine, Reference Section. http://www.nlm.nih.gov/pubs/resources.html.

Publ. in print format between 1988–97, continuing in part *Literature search* of the National Library of Medicine (NLM) (427) which ceased in 1988. In 1989, absorbed NLM's "Specialized bibliography series." Selected bibliographies also published in online format under title *NLM resource lists and bibliographies: Current bibliographies in medicine* 1992–?

Bibliographies prepared in support of National Institutes of Health Consensus Development Conferences (cf. website). Each bibliography covers a subject area of biomedicine of current popular interest. 2000–. Offered in both HTM and PDF formats. Also referred to as CBM.

31 GPO access. U.S. Government Printing Office. 1995. Washington: U.S. Government Printing Office. http://www.gpoaccess.gov.

JK468.A8

and online database. These versions are searchable by title, abbreviated title, keyword in title, CODEN, ISSN, ISBN, meeting data, source information, holdings information, and publication details.

35   Directory of open access journals. Lund University Libraries. 2003–. Lund, Sweden: Lund University Libraries. http://www.doaj. org.
011.34

Directory of free, full-text, scholarly journals in all subjects and languages. Journals must be peer reviewed or have an editorial review board. The database includes more than 2,800 journals, 860 of which are searchable at the article level. Browsable by title and subject tree. Entries link out to full-text content at the journal's homepage; records include title, subject, ISSN, publisher, language, related keywords, and year of first online issue available.

36   EMBASE list of journals indexed. Excerpta Medica. Amsterdam, The Netherlands: Elsevier Science, 1979–. ISSN: 0929-3302.
Previous title, 1979–82: *Excerpta medica: List of journals abstracted*; 1983–92: *List of journals abstracted*.
Description based on 2006 ed.
Complete list of journals (more than 5,000) indexed in EMBASE (414) and its print equivalent, *Excerpta medica*. Provides information on new, changed, and discontinued titles. Arranged in alphabetical order by full journal title, with ISSN, CODEN, the abbreviated journal title, and an indication if the journal is indexed cover-to-cover or selectively and if it is a "priority journal" (currently 1,835 titles are considered the most important in biomedicine by the publisher). Also provides several other listings: number of journals per classification; list of journals per subject classification; number of journals per country of publication; list of journals per country of publication.
"EMBASE Active Journals (June 2007)" in pdf format at http://info. embase.com/embase_suite/content/journals/embase_active_jou rnals.pdf.

37   List of journals indexed for MEDLINE. National Library of Medicine (U.S.). 2005–. Bethesda, Md.: National Library of Medicine, National Institutes of Health. ISSN: 1932-3212. http:// purl.access.gpo.gov/GPO/LPS68116.
615   Z6660.L775

Supersedes *List of journals indexed in Index medicus*, 1960–2004. Updated annually.

Description based on the 2007 ed. Provides bibliographic information for 5,164 journals indexed. Titles are listed in four sections: (1) Alphabetic listing by abbreviated title; (2) Alphabetic listing by full title, followed by abbreviated title; (3) Alphabetic list by subject field; (4) Alphabetic list by country of publication. Also includes separate listings of titles added, title changes during the preceding year, and titles no longer indexed. More detailed bibliographic information about serials indexed in MEDLINE® (425) can be found in LocatorPlus (480)™. Available in PDF format. Also published as a print edition. A related title is *List of serials indexed for online users* (38).

38   **List of serials indexed for online users.** National Library of Medicine (U.S.). [2000]–. Bethesda, Md.: National Library of Medicine. ISSN: 1555-2403. http://purl.access.gpo.gov/GPO/ LPS8318.

016.6105   Z6660.L56

1983–2005 print ed. (2002–5 publ. by Bernan, Lanham, Md.). Continues: *List of serials and monographs indexed for online users* (publ. 1980–2). Also called LSIOU. Updated annually. Description based on the 2007 ed.

   Arranged alphabetically by abbreviated title followed by full title, with bibliographic information for serials which are indexed with MeSH® (575) terms and cited in MEDLINE® (425)/PubMed® (432). The 2007 list contains 12,493 serial titles, including 5,164 titles currently indexed for MEDLINE. Indicates titles which are selectively indexed (symbol used: "s") and "core clinical journals" subset limit (symbol used: "*"). Further bibliographic information can be found via LocatorPlus® (480). Information about available formats at http://www.nlm.nih.gov/tsd/serials/ terms_cond.html.

   A separate list is available for the 5,164 titles indexed for MEDLINE in 2007, entitled *List of journals indexed for MEDLINE* (425).

39   **Public library of science (PLoS).** Public Library of Science. 2000–. [San Francisco]: Public Library of Science. http://www. publiclibraryofscience.org/.

PLoS is a non-profit organization of scientists and physicians who are committed to promote free and timely online access to the international scientific and medical literature. Since 2003 a nonprofit scientific and medical publishing venture. Publishes high-profile open-access journals (e.g., *PLoS biology*, *PLoS medicine*, *PLoS ONE*, and several others), funded

Potter's disease, Thomas's splint. Includes a list of biographies for additional reading. Indexed.

45   Blacks in science and medicine. Vivian O. Sammons. xii, 293 p.
      New York: Hemisphere, 1990. ISBN: 0891166653.
509.22B   Q141.B58

Presents biographical information, based on published sources, for more than 1,500 living and deceased individuals who have contributed to the development of science, medicine, and technology, focusing on contributions by African Americans in the United States. Entries are brief, in who's-who style, but include citations to the source material. Extensive bibliography. A very useful index to biographees is arranged by such categories as occupation, discipline, and invention and notes "first black" and "first (black or white)" achievements.

46   Doctors and discoveries: Lives that created today's medicine.
      John Galbraith Simmons. xx, 459 p., ill. Boston: Houghton Mifflin,
      2002. ISBN: 0618152768.
610.922B   R134.5.S56

Profiles 86 individuals who are considered important and influential to contemporary medicine. In addition to the "figures of constant reference" (pt. III) from the past, also includes contemporary researchers. Source notes, bibliography, and index.

47   Doctors: The biography of medicine. 1st ed. Sherwin B. Nuland.
      xxi, 519 p., ill. New York: Knopf, 1988. ISBN: 0394551303.
610.922B   R134.N85

Traces the development of modern medicine through the lives of famous physician-scientists (e.g., Hippocrates, Galen, Andreas Vesalius, Ambroise Paré, William Harvey, Giovanni Morgagni, and others) and discoveries and inventions (e.g., stethoscope, anesthesia, microscope, antiseptic surgery, "blue-baby" operation, heart transplantation, and others). Includes "anecdotes and colorful episodes."—*Introd.* Bibliography; index.

48   Profiles in science. National Library of Medicine (U.S.). 1998–.
      Bethesda, Md.: U.S. National Library of Medicine. http://www.
      profiles.nlm.nih.gov.
509.20904   Q141.P76

Profiles in Science® (National Library of Medicine), a collaboration of NLM's Lister Hill National Center for Biomedical Communications (http://lhncbc.nlm.nih.gov/lhc/servlet/Turbine) and NLM's History of Medicine Division (http://www.nlm.nih.gov/hmd/).

Includes a growing number of scientists, physicians, and other leaders in biomedical research and health, providing access to the digitized archival collections of the papers, and other published and unpublished materials of the individual scientists. Further information at http://profiles.nlm. nih.gov/Help/About/.

49   Women and medicine. 3rd ed. Beatrice Levin. x, 205 p., ill.
Lanham, Md.: Scarecrow Press, 2002. ISBN: 0810842386.
610.820973   R692.L49

1st ed., 1980; 2nd ed., 1988.

Contents: The dinosaur is twitching: famous firsts; To be a doctor in America: overcoming obstacles; Shattering the glass ceiling: surgeons general and presidents' doctors; Historical perspectives: midwives and doctors around the globe; Women on the march: civil war heroines; Pioneers, o pioneers!: then and now; One university's contributions: those remarkable Johns Hopkins women; Oh, brave new world: Nobel Prize winners in medicine; Women's proper place: our biological selves; A peaceful revolution: the fight for birth control; What was the doctor wearing?: from white coats to space suits.

Comprehensive history of women experiencing and overcoming sexism in medical schools and the medical profession. Biographical chapters on many famous women in medicine, for example, on Elizabeth Blackwell, Janet Travell, Mary Putnam Jacobi, Marie Curie, and also other Nobel Prize winners.

Bibliography

50   A bibliography of medical and biomedical biography. 3rd ed.
Leslie T. Morton, Robert J. Moore. xi, 425 p. Aldershot, England;
Burlington, Vt.: Ashgate, 2005. ISBN: 0754650693.
016.610922   Z6660.5.M67; R134

1st ed., 1989; 2nd ed., 1994.

1st ed., 1989 (begun as a 3rd ed. of John L. Thornton's *A select bibliography of medical biography* [68]); 2nd ed., 1994.

Includes biographical references to 3,740 individuals in the biomedical sciences as well as in clinical medicine and surgery. Lists only English-language publications and provides references to biographies published in book form, among others to entries in *Dictionary of scientific biography*

(64), *Biographical memoirs of fellows of the Royal Society* (54); *Obituary notices of fellows of the Royal Society*, Biographical memoirs of the National Academy of Sciences (71), and selected periodical references. An initial section of individual biographies is alphabetic by biographee, giving nationality, field, and notable accomplishments; location of archival materials is also indicated. A list of collective biographies follows, usually giving a brief description of the work, while a third section provides a short list of books on the history of medicine and related works, arranged by subject. Indexed by discipline; biographees are listed within each discipline by birth date. This edition also includes the names of individuals listed in Morton and Moore's *Chronology of medicine and related sciences* (Aldershot, U.K.; Bookfield, Vt.: Scolar Press; Ashgate Publ. Co., 1997).

51   The development of medical bibliography. Estelle Brodman. ix, 226 p., ports., diagrs. [Washington]: Medical Library Association, 1954.

016.61   Z6658.B7

(Publication [Medical Library Association]; no. 1)

Comprehensive survey of medical bibliography since 1500, covering printed medical bibliographies in Western languages that pertain to medicine in general rather than to its subdivisions or specialties. Personal bibliographies and bibliographies that do not make up the main portion of a work have been excluded, as have catalogs (with the exception of the *Index-catalogue of the Library of the Surgeon General's Office*). No distinction made between indexes and abstracts as bibliographies.

"For each bibliography discussed there is a biographical sketch of the compiler, a description of the work emphasizing advances in technique, and a discussion of the importance of the work in the history of medical bibliography."—*Introd.*

Appendix 1 lists references; appendix 2 lists medical bibliographies since 1500 which were not discussed in the body of the text, arranged by century. General and author indexes. A digitized version of this book is available at http://www.nlm.nih.gov/hmd/collections/digital/brodman/brodman.html as part of the National Library of Medicine's History of Medicine digital collections. Like this work, *The great medical bibliographers: A study in humanism*, by John F. Fulton, identifies important medical bibliographies and bio-bibliographies.

52   Disease and destiny: A bibliography of medical references to the famous. Judson Bennett Gilbert. 535 p. London: Dawsons of Pall Mall, 1962.

016.92   Z6664.A1G5

Drawn largely from *Index-catalogue of the library of the Surgeon General's Office* (IndexCat [479]), *Index medicus* (420), and *Quarterly cumulative index medicus.*

A bibliography of writings that treat the medical history of famous people in history, the humanities, and the arts and sciences in all countries from ancient to modern times. Personalities are listed alphabetically and identified by dates of birth and death and a brief descriptive phrase. Books and papers about them are listed in chronological order. Introduction contains a bibliography of monographic literature of medicobiographical writing.

53   **Doctors, nurses, and medical practitioners: A bio-bibliographical sourcebook.** Lois N. Magner. xiii, 371 p. Westport, Conn.: Greenwood Press, 1997. ISBN: 0313294526.

610.922B   R153.D63

Biographical information on 56 "significant but lesser known individuals, outside their own country, extraordinary, yet unsung" (*Introd.*), covering the time period 1710–1924, with essays focusing on the life and career. Bibliographic references include archival materials and works written by and about the particular individual. Appendixes: (A), Listing by occupations and special interests; (B), Listing by date of birth; (C), Listing by place of birth; (D), Listing of women practitioners. Intended for students and scholars.

Great Britain

54   **Biographical memoirs of fellows of the Royal Society.** Royal Society (Great Britain). 49+ vols., ill. London: Royal Society, 1955–. ISSN: 0080-4606.

Q41.L8476

Continues *Obituary notices of fellows of the Royal Society* (1932–54), and previous notices were published in *Proceedings of the Royal Society.* Vol. 75 (1905) of the *Proceedings* contained obituaries of deceased fellows chiefly for 1898–1904 with a general index to previous notices from 1860–99. Contains long biographical articles with excellent autographed ports. of deceased members of the Royal Society, including foreign members. Usually includes bibliographies, some quite extensive. Also available online through JSTOR (New York: JSTOR, 1995?–).

55   **Plarr's lives of the fellows of the Royal College of Surgeons of England.** Victor Plarr. 2 v. Bristol; London: Printed and publ. for the Royal College of Surgeons by J. Wright & Sons Ltd.; London, Simpkin, Marshall Ltd., 1930.

R489.A1P5

At head of title: *Thelwall Thomas memorial.*

Biographies of fellows from those elected in 1843 (founding date of the fellowship) through those who died before 1930. Much of the information was obtained from obituary notices or from friends and relatives of the fellows. For each fellow, includes references to publications sufficient to indicate the subjects in which each was interested.

Continued by: Sir D'Arcy Power and William Richard Le Fanu, *Lives of the fellows of the Royal College of Surgeons of England, 1930–1951*, publ. 1953 (biographies of fellows who died from 1930 to the end of 1951, including some who died before 1930 but were omitted from Plarr's list; includes lists of publications); R.H.O.B. Robinson and W.R. Le Fanu, *Lives of the fellows of the Royal College of Surgeons of England, 1952–1964*, publ. 1970; James Paterson Ross and W.R. Le Fanu, *Lives of the fellows of the Royal College of Surgeons of England, 1965–1973*, publ. 1981; *Lives of the fellows of the Royal College of Surgeons of England, 1983–1990*, ed. by Ian Lyle and Selwyn Taylor, publ. 1995; John P. Blandy, *Lives of the fellows of the Royal College of Surgeons of England, 1991–1996*, publ. 2000; *Lives of the fellows of the Royal College of Surgeons of England, 1997–2002* (with a cumulated index to the previous volumes).

56 **The roll of the Royal College of Physicians of London: Comprising biographical sketches of all the eminent physicians whose names are recorded in the Annals.** 2d ed., rev. and enl. ed. William Munk, G. H. Brown, Richard Robertson Trail, Royal College of Physicians of London. 1878–.

R773.R75

Vols. 4–. have title: *Lives of the fellows.*

Contents: v. 1, 1518–1700; v. 2, 1701–1800; v. 3, 1801–1825; v. 4, 1826–1925; v. 5, Continued to 1965 (ed. by R. R. Trail); v. 6, Continued to 1975 (ed. by G. Wolstenholme); v. 7, Continued to 1983 (ed. by G. Wolstenholme).

Vols. 1–3 have subtitle: *Comprising biographical sketches of all eminent physicians, whose names are recorded in the Annals from the foundation of the College in 1518 to its removal in 1825 from Warwick Lane to Pall Mall East.*

Vol. 4 contains short biographies of 874 fellows elected between 1826 and 1925 who died before Jan. 1, 1954.

Vol. 5 contains biographies of 422 fellows who died since the end of 1953 or who died earlier but were not included in the previous volume because they were elected to the Fellowship after 1925. Arranged alphabetically. Also designated as "Munk's roll, v. 5."

International

57   Bio-bibliographisches Verzeichnis jüdischer Doktoren im 17.
und 18. Jahrhundert. Manfred Komorowski. 128 p., ill. München;
New York: Saur, 1991. ISBN: 3598109806.

R512.A1K65

(Bibliographien zur deutsch-jüdischen Geschichte; Bd. 3) A chronological list, 1624–1799, of 412 Jewish physicians who completed their medical
education at European universities. A typical entry includes name, home
town, location of the university, brief Latin title of the dissertation, date
pertaining to the completion of the dissertation ("Promotionsdatum"),
and reference(s) to biographical works and sources where further information about the physician can be found. Indexed.

58   **Biographical dictionary of medicine.** Jessica Bendiner, Elmer
Bendiner. 284 p. New York: Facts On File, 1990. ISBN: 0816018642.
610.922B   R134.B455

Subjects are included on the basis of their importance to the history of
medicine. Entries vary in length from one paragraph to several pages.
Includes a chronology of important events in the history of medicine and
a brief bibliography. Separate name and subject indexes.

59   **A biographical dictionary of women healers: Midwives, nurses,
and physicians.** Laurie Scrivener, J. Suzanne Barnes. x, 340 p.,
ports. Westport, Conn.: Oryx Press, 2002. ISBN: 157356219X.
610.820922B21   R692.S38

Alphabetically-arranged brief entries include names, dates, education, professional organizations, etc., from Colonial times to the present. Includes
240 American and Canadian women. Appendix 1 is a listing of individuals
by occupation (nurses, midwives, physicians); appendix 2 provides a time
line of events and the historical context in which women practiced. Provides a starting point for further research. *Dictionary of American nursing
biography* (1027), *Women in medicine: An encyclopedia* (70), and *American
midwives: 1860 to the present* provide added information on women in the
health professions.

60   **Biographisches Lexikon der hervorragenden Ärzte aller Zeiten
und Völker.** 2. Aufl. ed. August Hirsch, Ernst Julius Gurlt, A.
Wernich. 5 v., ports. Berlin, Wien: Urban & Schwarzenberg,
1929–1934.
016.61   Z6658.B61

MEDICINE

29

Wayne Hafner, Fred W. Hunter, E. Michael Tarpey, American Medical Association. 2 v., ill. Chicago: American Medical Association, 1993. ISBN: 0899705278.

610.92273   R712.A1D47

Provides brief entries, with name, birth and death dates, place of birth, type of practice, practice and board specialties, license, hospital affiliation, *JAMA* citation for obituary notice, death notice information, etc. Includes indexes to African-American female and male practitioners, female practitioners, self-designated homeopathic, and osteopathic practitioners. L. Holloway's *Medical obituaries: American physicians' biographical notices in selected medical journals before 1907* provides additional useful information.

76   **Who's who in medicine and healthcare.** New Providence, N.J.: Marquis Who's Who, c1996–. ISSN: 0000-1708.

R153.W43

Description based on 6th ed. (2006–07). Compilation of biographical information on medical professionals, including administrators, educators, researchers, clinicians, and other medical and healthcare personnel. Listings include full name, occupation, date/place of birth, family background, education summary, writings, and association memberships and awards. Includes a section on "Ten who made a difference." Also available online on Who's Who on the Web (http://www.marquiswhoswho.com).

Classification

77   **AJCC cancer staging manual.** 6th ed. Frederick L. Greene, American Joint Committee on Cancer, American Cancer Society. xiv, 421 p., ill. New York: Springer-Verlag, 2002. ISBN: 0387952713.

616.9940012   RC258.M36

1st ed.–4th ed. (1977–92) had title: *Manual for staging of cancer*; 5th ed., 1997.

Prepared by the American Joint Committee on Cancer (AJCC), first organized in 1959 as the American Joint Committee for Cancer Staging and End-Results Reporting (AJC), in cooperation with the UICC (Union internationale contre le cancer = International Union against Cancer). "Since the 1980s, worldwide agreement for cancer staging has culminated in the simultaneous publication of the *TNM classification of malignant tumors* by the UICC and the *Cancer staging manual* by the AJCC."—*Pref.*

A historical overview, with information on the founding organizations, is provided in the introduction. "Milestones in UICC TNM History" can be found at http://www.uicc.org/index.php?id=1156. Designed to facilitate uniform classification ("taxonomy of cancer" [*Pref.*]) and description of cancer and information on staging cancer at various anatomic sites. Allows comparison of statistics reported from various institutions worldwide. Organized into 48 chapters, with changes since the previous edition at the beginning of each chapter. Illustrated with line drawings. Index. Available online via STAT!Ref (Teton Data Systems, http://www.tetondata.com/index.htm). *The AJCC cancer staging atlas*, by Frederick L. Greene, is a companion volume, with approx. 400 black-and-white illustrations which "... depict the anatomic extent of disease for tumor (T), regional lymph node (N), and distinct metastasis (M) for multiple sites. and allow the reader to visualize the progressive extent of malignant disease."— *Publ. note.* Includes new or revised classifications for tumor staging for melanoma and breast, bone, kidney, prostate, and thyroid cancer. Related classifications and publications include the World Health Organization classification of tumours series, publ. by IARC since 2000, which is a continuation of the International histological classification of tumours series, publ. between 1967–99 (commonly referred to as "Blue Books"), with definitions, descriptions, and illustrations of tumor types and proposed nomenclature; WHO's International classification of diseases for oncology: ICD-O (81), a numerical coding system for neoplasms; *TNM: Classification of malignant tumours*; *TNM atlas: Illustrated guide to the TNM classification of malignant tumours*; and *UICC manual of clinical oncology*.

78   **Application of the international classification of diseases to neurology: ICD-NA.** 2nd ed. World Health Organization. xi, 574 p., ill. Geneva, [Switzerland]: World Health Organization, 1997. ISBN: 924154502X.

616.80012   RC346.A66

1st ed., 1987 (developed in 1984–85) related to the International Classification of Diseases (ICD)-9.

One of the adaptations of the Tenth Revision of the International Statistical Classification of Diseases and Related Health Problems (ICD-10), developed "to respond to the needs of specialist disciplines such as neurology."—*Pref.* Contains outline of the history and structure of the ICD and ICD-NA, and the "ICD Family of Classifications." Other specialty-based adaptations of the ICD include oncology (*International classification of diseases for oncology: ICD-O* [81], dentistry [*Application of the international classification of diseases to dentistry and stomatology: ICD-DA* [776], dermatology, psychiatry [*The ICD-10*

82   **International classification of diseases, ninth revision, clinical
      modification.** National Center for Health Statistics (U.S.). 199?–.
      Hyattsville, Md.: U.S. Dept. of Health and Human Services,
      Centers for Disease Control and Prevention, National Center for
      Health Statistics. http://www.cdc.gov/nchs/icd9.htm.

Contents: v. 1, Tabular list of diseases and external injuries; v. 2, Alphabetical index to diseases; v. 3, Tabular list of procedures.

ICD-9-CM is based on the World Health Organization (951)'s (WHO) *International classification of diseases, ninth revision (ICD-9)*, "designed to promote international comparability in the collection, processing, classification, and presentation of mortality statistics."—*Website.* In addition it also provides morbidity detail for indexing of medical records and health statistics and for assigning codes to diagnoses associated with inpatient, outpatient, and physician utilization in the U.S. ICD-9-CM is considered the official system for assigning codes to diagnoses and procedures associated with hospital (inpatient and outpatient) and physician office utilization in the U.S. The National Center for Health Statistics (NCHS) (539) and the Centers for Medicare and Medicaid Services are responsible for all changes to the ICD-9-CM.

A prerelease version of ICD-10-CM (June 2003) is available at http://www.cdc.gov/nchs/about/otheract/icd9/icd10cm.htm.

Previously available in various print and CD-ROM editions.

83   **International classification of functioning, disability and health
      (ICF).** World Health Organizations. 2001–. Geneva, Switzerland:
      World Health Organization (WHO). http://www.who.int/
      classifications/icf/en/index.html.

World Health Organization (WHO); International Classification of Functioning, Disability and Health (ICF).

"Describes how people live with their health condition. ICF is a classification of health and health related domains that describe body functions and structures, activities and participation. The domains are classified from body, individual and societal perspectives. Since an individual's functioning and disability occurs in a context, ICF also includes a list of environmental factors. ICF is useful to understand and measure health outcomes. It can be used in clinical settings, health services or surveys at the individual or population level."—*Website.* ICF complements the *International statistical classification of diseases and related health problems* (ICD-10) (80) and is part of the WHO Family of International

Classifications: WHO-FIC (90) website which provides access to WHO's reference and other classifications.

84   International statistical classification of diseases and related health problems. World Health Organization. 1994–2007. Geneva, Switzerland: World Health Organization. http://www.who.int/ classifications/apps/icd/icd10online/.

Title varies: International Classification of Diseases; ICD-10. The original three-volume print version, publ. 1992–94, has title *International statistical classification of diseases and related health problems* (v. 1, *Tabular list*; v. 2, *Instruction manual*; v. 3, *Alphabetical index*).

Contents: ch. 1, "Certain infectious and parasitic diseases"; ch. 2, "Neoplasms"; ch. 3, "Diseases of the blood and blood-forming organs and certain disorders involving the immune mechanism"; ch. 4, "Endocrine, nutritional and metabolic diseases"; ch. 5, "Mental and behavioural disorders"; ch. 6, "Diseases of the nervous system"; ch. 7, "Diseases of the eye and adnexa"; ch. 8, "Diseases of the ear and mastoid process"; ch. 9, "Diseases of the circulatory system"; ch. 10, "Diseases of the respiratory system"; ch. 11, "Diseases of the digestive system"; ch. 12, "Diseases of the skin and subcutaneous tissue"; ch. 13, "Diseases of the musculoskeletal system and connective tissue"; ch. 14, "Diseases of the genitourinary system"; ch. 15, "Pregnancy, childbirth and the puerperium"; ch. 16, "Certain conditions originating in the perinatal period"; ch. 17, "Congenital malformations, deformations and chromosomal abnormalities"; ch. 18, "Symptoms, signs and abnormal clinical and laboratory findings, not elsewhere classified"; ch. 19, "Injury, poisoning and certain other consequences of external causes"; ch. 20, "External causes of morbidity and mortality"; ch. 21, "Factors influencing health status and contact with health services"; ch. 22, "Codes for special purposes."

"Standard diagnostic classification for all general epidemiological and many health management purposes used to classify diseases and other health problems recorded on many types of health and vital records including death certificates and hospital records [and] provide the basis for the compilation of national mortality and morbidity statistics by WHO member states."— *WHO summary* (http://www.who.int/classifications/icd/en/). Additional information and links to several full-text ICD publications, updates, and ICD adaptations can be found, e.g., *Application of the International Classification of Diseases to dentistry and stomatology* (776), *International classification of functioning, disability and health* (83), *International Classification* its SNOMED international division and offer services and products for the adoption and use of SNOMED CT. Detailed information about SNOMED CT is provided at both the IHTSDO (http://www.ihtsdo. org/about-ihtsdo/faq/) and CAP websites (http://www.cap.org/apps/cap. portal?_nfpb=true&_pageLabel=snomed_page).

The National Library of Medicine (NLM) is the U.S. member of IHTSDO. NLM's Unified Medical Language System (UMLS) (89), a metathesaurus containing biomedical concepts and terms from many controlled vocabularies and classifications, includes SNOMED CT FAQs at http://www.nlm.nih.gov/research/umls/Snomed/snomed_faq.html.

89 **Unified medical language system (UMLS).** National Library of Medicine (U.S.). 1999–. Bethesda, Md.: National Library of Medicine. http://purl.access.gpo.gov/GPO/LPS2400.

The purpose of the UMLS is to facilitate the development of computer systems concerned with the use of the biomedical and health-related language. NLM produces and distributes the UMLS Knowledge Sources (Metathesaurus [http://www.nlm.nih.gov/pubs/factsheets/umlsmeta. html], the Semantic Network [http://www.nlm.nih.gov/pubs/factsheets/ umlssemn.html], and the SPECIALIST lexicon [http://www.nlm.nih.gov/ pubs/factsheets/umlslex.html]) and associated software tools and programs for the use of various systems developers in building or enhancing electronic information systems (e.g., electronic patient records, public health data, scientific literature, etc.) and informatics research. The lexical tools work in combination with the UMLS Knowledge Sources but can also be used independently. The UMLS Fact Sheet (http://www.nlm.nih. gov/pubs/factsheets/umls.html) provides further detailed information and explanation. Questions concerning the inclusion of SNOMED CT: Systematized Nomenclature of Medicine—Clinical Terms (88) in UMLS are answered in FAQs: SNOMED CT in the UMLS (http://www.nlm.nih. gov/research/umls/Snomed/snomed_faq.html).

90 **WHO family of international classifications.** World Health Organization. 2007. Geneva, [Switzerland]: World Health Organization. http://www.who.int/classifications/en/.

Provides information and explanation on various internationally recognized and endorsed reference classifications and links to their full text: International statistical classification of diseases and related health problems (ICD) (84), International classification of functioning, disability and health (ICF)

(83), and International classification of health interventions (ICHI) (http://www.who.int/classifications/ichi/en/index.html), currently under development. Also provides information about or links to full-text and updates for WHO's derived and related classifications and terminologies.

Derived classifications include International classification of diseases for oncology (ICD-O-3) (81); The ICD-10 classification of mental and behavioural disorders: Clinical descriptions and diagnostic guidelines (80); Application of the international classification of diseases to dentistry and stomatology (ICD-DA) (776); Application of the international classification of diseases to neurology (ICD-10-NA) (78).

Related classifications include: International classification of primary care (ICPC); International classification of external causes of injury (ICECI); Anatomical, therapeutic, chemical (ATC) classification system with Defined Daily Doses (DDDs); ISO 9999 Technical aids for persons with disabilities—classification and terminology.

Volumes tracing the history of disease classification 1903–38 are available at http://www.who.int/library/collections/historical/en/index1.html as part of the WHO Library Historical Collection.

The North American Collaborating Center (NACC), part of the National Center for Health Statistics (539), serves as WHO's Collaborating Center for the Family of International Classifications for North America (http://www.cdc.gov/nchs/about/otheract/icd9/nacc.htm).

Dictionaries

91 **The American Heritage medical dictionary.** xxxii, 909 p., ill.
Boston: Houghton Mifflin, 2007. ISBN: 0618824359.

610.3   R121.A4446

1st ed., 1995, to 2nd ed., 2004, had title *The American Heritage Stedman's medical dictionary*; 2007 ed. is rev. ed. of the 2nd ed.

Provides clear definitions for approx. 45,000 medical words and phrases, including tests, diseases, treatments, technology, and prescription and nonprescription drugs. Also includes health policy terms. Intended for health care consumers, students, and health professionals. Also available online via Credo Reference (London; Boston: Credo Reference).

92 **Black's medical dictionary.** 41st ed. Harvey Marcovitch. viii, 814 p., 16 p. of plates, ill. London: A. and C. Black, 2005.

610.3

1st ed., 1906. 40th ed., 2002.

A standard dictionary of British terminology, with clear explanation of medical terms. Frequently updated. The 41st ed. includes 5,000 medical terms, including new terms and concepts (e.g., new diagnostic imaging techniques, minimally invasive surgery, gene therapy) and revisions. Many cross-references. Several appendixes provide information on subjects such as first aid, travel and health, health economics, Great Britain's National Health Service, and international organizations. Intended for nurses, healthcare professionals, students, and consumers. Available online via Credo Reference (London; Boston: Credo Reference).

93 **The Cambridge historical dictionary of disease.** Kenneth F. Kiple. xiii, 412 p.; 25 cm. Cambridge, U.K.; New York: Cambridge University Press, 2003. ISBN: 0521808340.

616.009 RC41.C365

International and interdisciplinary resource for medical history of human disease, originally published as pt. VIII of the *Cambridge world history of human disease* (337), rewrites and edits essays into shorter and up-to-date entries and also takes information from other parts of the original publication. Available online via Gale Virtual Reference Library (Farmington Hills, Mich.: Gale Cengage Learning, 2002–).

94 **Concise dictionary of modern medicine.** Joseph C. Segen. xix, 765 p. New York: McGraw-Hill, 2006. ISBN: 0838515355.

R121.S42

A revision of J.C. Segen's 1995 ed. of *Current med talk: A dictionary of medical terms, slang, and jargon.*

Illustrated dictionary, with 20,000 current medical terms, covering clinical and basic science aspects, also jargon and casual speech not necessarily found in other reference sources. Intended to supplement standard medical dictionaries. Also available in a 2002 ed. with the same title and as *Dictionary of modern medicine*, published in 2002, which contains 40,000 entries.

95 **Dictionary of biomedical sciences.** Peter J. Gosling. 444 p. London; New York: Taylor & Francis, 2002. ISBN: 0415241383.

610.3 R121.G623

Concise guide to a wide range of technical terms, abbreviations, and acronyms in the biomedical sciences and related disciplines. Not intended to be a dictionary of medical laboratory scientific techniques (cf. *Pref.*). American spelling where it differs from current use in the U.K. Cross-references. Several appendixes, covering reference ranges of blood and urinary constituents, metric conversions, biomedical science organizations, a select bibliography and further reading. Entries in alphabetical order, with no inverted headings.

96   **A dictionary of the history of medicine.** Anton Sebastian.
vi, 781 p., ill. New York: Parthenon Publ. Group, 1999. ISBN: 1850700214.

610.9   R121.S398

This illustrated medical history dictionary, a scholarly work, includes terms, with Latin and Greek origins of terms, brief biographies of notable people in medicine, eponymic information, important events, conditions, procedures, and other historical information for a broad range of subjects. Includes anecdotes and background material on both well- and little-known facts of medical history. Drawings and photographs of antique medical instruments and rare medical conditions. A negative review (*Journal of the history of medicine and allied sciences* 56, no. 2 [2001]: 182–83) cites factual errors, omissions, and "overly broad coverage." Users are cautioned to double check facts in other sources.

By the same author, *Dates in medicine: A chronological record of medical progress over three millennia* provides important milestones in the development of medicine. It is part of the Landmarks in Medicine series (publ. 2000–2002 by Parthenon), which also includes several other titles, including *Dates in ophthalmology: A chronological record of progress in ophthalmology over the last millennium*, by Daniel Albert, and several other titles by Helen S. J. Lee: *Dates in cardiology, Dates in gastroenterology, Dates in infectious disease, Dates in obstetrics and gynecology, Dates in neurology, Dates in oncology*, and *Dates in urology*, all with the subtitle *A chronological record of progress over the last millennium.*

97   **Dorland's illustrated medical dictionary.** 31st ed. W. A. Newman
Dorland. xxvii, 2175 p., ill. (some color). Philadelphia: W.B. Saunders, 2007. ISBN: 9781416023647.

R121.D73

1st–22nd ed., 1900–51 had title: *The American illustrated medical dictionary*; 30th ed., c2003.

Designed to satisfy the conventional use of a dictionary; that is, to discover spelling, meaning, and derivation of specific terms and to assist

MEDICINE

in the creation of words by defining prefixes, suffixes, and stems. Includes a section on "Fundamentals of medical etymology." Reflects standard and current terminology, with official nomenclatures from various fields, for example, NLM's MeSH: Medical Subject Headings (575), Terminologia Anatomica (1998), and several others. Also includes eponyms, acronyms, abbreviations, pronunciation, cross-references, etc. Illustrated throughout. In this ed., several appendixes have been updated and reorganized (for example, the tables of weights and measures and conversion tables) and a new appendix provides a list of phobias. For health professionals and students in medicine, nursing, and allied health. CD-ROM includes *Dorland's pocket medical dictionary* for PDA and download access to *Dorland's electronic medical speller*. Internet access for subscribers at http://www.dorlands.com/wsearch.jsp. Also available online via Credo Reference (London; Boston: Credo Reference).

98   Encyclopedia and dictionary of medicine, nursing, and allied health. 7th ed. Benjamin Frank Miller. xxxi, 2262 p., [40] p. of plates, ill. (chiefly color). Philadelphia: Saunders, 2003. ISBN: 0721697917.

610.3   R121.M65

1st ed. (1972) had title *Encyclopedia and dictionary of medicine and nursing*; 6th ed. (1997) had title *Miller-Keane encyclopedia and dictionary of medicine, nursing, and allied health.*

A concise work intended for students and workers in the nursing and allied health fields. Clear definitions and and explanations of the current multidisciplinary terminology. This edition has 3,900 new terms, including the "latest changes for diagnosis-related groups, nursing diagnoses, and key nursing taxonomies."—*Foreword*; for example, definitions are provided for the complete vocabulary of the Unified Nursing Language System. Pronunciation guides; a list of stems, prefixes, and suffixes; and 32 page color atlas of human anatomy.

The print resource is supplemented by a CD-ROM that contains spellchecker software, derived from *Dorland's medical speller* 3.0, and also by a website where updates relating to major changes in health professional vocabularies are posted (http://evolve.elsevier.com/millerkeane/)—cf. *Foreword*.

99   Encyclopedic reference of genomics and proteomics in molecular medicine. Detlev Ganten, Klaus Ruckpaul. New York: Springer, 2005. ISBN: 3540442448.

An effective blend of dictionary and encyclopedia formats, this two-volume set covers the proliferating terminology in the fields of genomics and proteomics, elucidating how these fields relate to molecular medicine. Some entries explain familiar terms in this context (e.g., addiction, gene, informed consent). Definition entries are short, provide thorough explanations, and list cross-references to related entries or, in the case of acronyms, to the full term or phrase. This title is also available online.

Article-length encyclopedic entries are signed and provide author affiliation and contact information. All articles include synonyms and definition sections followed by material appropriate to the topic, such as characteristics, description, clinical applications, clinical relevance, molecular interactions, regulatory mechanisms, therapeutic consequences, and more specific subheadings as appropriate. Cross-references enhance articles' interrelationships. Articles are beautifully illustrated with figures, tables, and photographs, many in color. All articles list references and many include Internet resources.

Most appropriate for academic libraries, especially those supporting molecular biology and medical research. Public libraries might find the *Encyclopedic dictionary of genetics, genomics, and proteomics* (Hoboken, N.J.: Wiley-Liss, 2003) a sufficient alternative.

100 **Medical dictionary (MedlinePlus).** National Library of Medicine (U.S.). 2002–. Bethesda, Md.: National Library of Medicine. http://www.nlm.nih.gov/medlineplus/mplusdictionary.html.

R121

Part of MedlinePlus (463). This online dictionary, based on *Merriam-Webster's medical dictionary,* can be searched from the MedlinePlus home page (via "Dictionary" tab). Contains definitions for words and phrases used by health care professionals, a pronunciation guide, and brief biographies of individuals (after whom particular diseases are named). Most MedlinePlus Health Topics pages contain a link or links to additional online dictionaries and/or glossaries from various sources.

Numerous online medical dictionaries and glossaries are also available from many other sources. They include titles made available from various government agencies, organizations, and commercial publishers. Some examples include online medical dictionaries accessible via Credo Reference (currently 24 titles) [London; Boston: Credo Reference], Deciphering Medspeak [http://www.mlanet.org/resources/medspeak/; MLANET [465]], Diabetes Dictionary [http://diabetes.niddk.nih.gov/dm/pubs/dictionary/index.htm; National Institute of Diabetes and Digestive and Kidney Diseases], Dictionary of Cancer Terms [National Cancer Institute] [143], mediLexicon [http://www.medilexicon.com; MedicineNet], On-line Medical Dictionary [http://cancerweb.ncl.ac.uk/omd/index.html; by Dr. Graham Clark], Talking Glossary of Genetics Terms [http://www.nhgri.nih.gov/glossary.cfm; National Human Genome Research Institute], and many others.

101   **Medical phrase index: A comprehensive reference to the terminology of medicine.** 5th ed. Jean A. Lorenzini, Laura Lorenzini Ley. Los Angeles: Practice Management Information Corp. (PMIC), 2006.

1st ed., 1978; 4th ed., 2001.

"For medical transcribers, medical records librarians, medical assistants, legal secretaries, insurance claims examiners–for anyone who must capture medical terminology accurately and quickly."—*Publ. notes.* Includes both formal and informal phrases which are cross-indexed for each major word. Entries are arranged alphabetically. For words with more than one spelling, gives directions to common usage; sound-alikes are indicated.

102   **Melloni's illustrated medical dictionary.** 4th ed. Ida Dox, Biagio John Melloni, Ida Dox. xiii, 764 p., ill. (some color). New York: Parthenon, 2002. ISBN: 185070094X.

610.3   R121.D76

1st ed., 1979; rev. ed. of: *Melloni's illustrated medical dictionary*, Ida G. Dox, B. John Melloni, Gilbert M. Eisner. 3rd ed. 1993.

Includes 30,000 terms, with 4,000 new terms in this rev. ed. More than 3,000 color ill. are keyed to terms, with color coordination between the illustration and the specific term. Phonetic pronunciations are included in a separate list at the front of the book, also a list of abbreviations, prefixes, suffixes, and combining form. Fewer entries but more ill. than *Dorland's illustrated medical dictionary* (97). For students in the health sciences. Also available in a "pocket" version entitled *Melloni's pocket medical dictionary: Illustrated* (Parthenon, 2004).

103   **Merriam-Webster's medical dictionary.** Enl. print ed. Merriam-Webster. Springfield, Mass.: Merriam-Webster, 2007. ISBN: 9780877796.

610.3   R121.M565

Abridged version of *Merriam-Webster's medical desk dictionary*.

Brief definitions for medical and scientific terms, including definitions of diseases, medical tests, and popular medical terms. Also includes eponyms and short biographies of famous doctors. No illustrations. Available online via Medical Dictionary (MedlinePlus) (463) and Credo Reference (London; Boston: Credo Reference). A related title is *Webster's New World medical dictionary* (111).

104 Mosby's dictionary of medicine, nursing and health professions. 7th ed. Mosby, Inc. xiv, 43, 2247 p., color ill. St. Louis: Mosby Elsevier, 2006. ISBN: 0323035620.

610.3   R121.M89

1st ed., 1982, and 2nd ed., 1986, had title: *Mosby's medical and nursing dictionary*; 3rd ed., 1990, and 4th ed., 2002, had title: *Mosby's medical, nursing, and allied health dictionary*; 5th ed., 1998, and 6th ed., 2001, had title: *Mosby's medical, nursing, and allied health dictionary*.

This updated edition reflects recent developments in medical and healthcare terminology. Encyclopedic-style definitions and approx. 2,450 color illustrations, photographs, and a "color atlas of human anatomy," organized by organ system. Appendixes include, e.g., reference information such as normal laboratory values for children and adults, units of measurement, dietary guide and U.S. dietary reference intakes, complementary and alternative medicine, herbs and natural supplements, American Sign Language guidelines, and three major nursing classifications. A website is provided for purchasers on Mosby's Electronic Resource Links and Information Network (MERLIN), with links to medical, nursing, and allied health organizations (cf. *Foreword*).

Available online via Credo Reference (London; Boston: Credo Reference).

MEDICINE

51

105 PDR medical dictionary. Medical Economics Company. v, ill. Montvale, N.J.: Medical Economics, c1995–. ISSN: 1094-4176.

616   R121.P275

Description based on 3rd ed., 2006. Contains terms and definitions for the medical and health science specialties, images and illustrations, and color anatomical plates with Latin and English anatomical terms for gross anatomy and neuroanatomy. Also contains a cross-reference table of generic drugs and brand-name drugs, and other reference charts (e.g., metric and SI units, temperature equivalents, and weights and measures).

106 Sloane's medical word book: A spelling and vocabulary guide to medical transcription. 4th ed. Ellen Drake, Sheila B. Sloane. xii, 1501 p., color ill. Philadelphia: Saunders, 2002. ISBN: 072167626X.

610.14   R123.S57

1st ed., 1973; 3rd ed., 1991, had title: *Medical word book: A spelling and vocabulary guide to medical transcription.*

Designed for purposes of medical transcription, providing lists of terms without definitions. In three major parts: pt. 1, a list of general medical terms, general surgical terms, and laboratory, pathology, and chemistry terminology; pt. 2, terms associated with 18 specialties; pt. 3, abbreviations and symbols, anatomy plates, a list combining forms, and rules for forming plurals in medical terminology. Appendix contains table of elements and table of weights and measures.

107 Stedman's medical dictionary. 28th ed. Thomas Lathrop Stedman. 1 v. (various pagings); 1 CD-ROM, ill. (chiefly color). Baltimore: Lippincott, Williams & Wilkins, 2006. ISBN: 0781733901.

610.3   R121.S8

1st ed., 1911, titled *A practical medical dictionary*; title of later editions varies slightly. 27th ed., 2000.

A standard work, frequently revised. Offers approx. 107,000 terms and definitions (5,000 terms new in this edition) and 1,500 images. Many color illustrations, including a 40-page anatomy atlas. Contains "extensive system of usage notes, alerting users to common errors of sense, spelling, and pronunciation, including confusion between words of similar form or meaning."—*Pref.* Appendixes include cancer classification systems, body mass and body surface calculations, abbreviations to use in medication orders, and others. This ed. includes CD-ROM, including the "Stedman's plus spellchecker 2006" and 300 LifeArt® medical clipart four-color images. Also available online via Credo Reference (London; Boston: Credo Reference).

Recent editions of other Stedman's dictionaries include *Stedman's medical dictionary for the health professions and nursing* (6th ed., 2008) (108); *The American Heritage medical dictionary* (2007 ed.) (91), formerly titled *The American Heritage Stedman's medical dictionary*; and *Stedman's medical abbreviations, acronyms and symbols* (4th ed., 2008) (117).

108 **Stedman's medical dictionary for the health professions and nursing: Illustrated.** 6th ed. Thomas Lathrop Stedman. xl, 1696, 589 p., ill. (some color), 1 CD-ROM. Philadelphia: Wolters Kluwer Health/Lippincott, Williams and Wilkins, 2008. ISBN: 9780781776189.

610.3   R121.S8

Title varies. 1st ed., 1986, had title *Stedman's pocket medical dictionary*; 2nd ed., 1994, *Stedman's concise medical dictionary*; 3rd ed., 1997, *Stedman's concise medical dictionary: Illustrated*; 4th ed., 2001, *Stedman's concise medical dictionary for the health professions*; 5th ed., 2005, *Stedman's medical dictionary for the health professions and nursing*.

This revised edition provides concise definitions with pronunciation keys. Contains 54,000 entries, 68 appendixes with extensive information (e.g., nursing classifications), and many color and black-and-white illustrations. Accompanying CD-ROM contains the full text of the print edition, with audio-pronunciation, anatomy animations, various images, and medical/pharmaceutical spellchecker.

Recent editions of other Stedman's dictionaries include, for example, *Stedman's medical dictionary* (Baltimore: Lippincott, Williams & Wilkins, 2006) (28th ed., 2006); *The American Heritage medical dictionary* (2007 ed.) (91), formerly titled *The American Heritage Stedman's medical dictionary*; and *Stedman's medical abbreviations, acronyms and symbols* (4th ed., 2008) (117).

109 **Stedman's medical eponyms.** 2nd ed. Susan L. Bartolucci, Thomas Lathrop Stedman, Pat Forbis. xix, 899 p. Baltimore: Lippincott, Williams & Wilkins, 2005. ISBN: 0781754437.

610.148   R121.F67

1st ed., 1998.

Developed from entries found in *Stedman's medical dictionary* (107) and supplemented with terminology found in the current medical literature. Provides concise definitions of approx. 18,000 terms "to both frequently encountered and hard-to-find eponyms."—*Publ. notes.* Entries include biographical information (e.g., nationality, specialty, and birth/death dates) in most cases. Included are equipment names, diagnostic and therapeutic procedures, operations, techniques and maneuvers, incisions, methods and approaches, syndromes and diseases, anatomic terms, and more. Intended for health care professionals, students, transcriptionists,

MEDICINE

53

116   **Melloni's illustrated dictionary of medical abbreviations.** Biagio John Melloni, June L. Melloni. 485 p., ill. New York: Parthenon Publ. Group, 1998. ISBN: 1850707081.

610.148   R121.M539

Abbreviations compiled from recent medical texts and journals. Approx. 15,000 entries and 150 ill. A–Z arrangement.

117   **Stedman's medical abbreviations, acronyms and symbols.** 4th ed. Thomas Lathrop Stedman. xxviii, 875, 214 p. Baltimore: Wolters Kluwer Health/Lippincott Williams & Wilkins, 2008. ISBN: 9780781772.

610.148   R123.S69

Title varies: 1st ed., 1992, had title *Stedman's abbreviations: Abbreviations, acronyms and symbols*; 2nd ed., 1999, *Stedman's abbreviations, acronyms, and symbols*; 3rd ed., 2003, *Stedman's abbrev.: Abbreviations, acronyms and symbols.*

This updated edition contains approx. 75,000 abbreviations, acronyms, and symbols for medical, health, and nursing professionals, medical transcriptionists, medical editors and copy editors, and others. Abbreviations in boldface; multiple meanings listed alphabetically, with explanatory material in parentheses. Includes "do not use" abbreviations. Fourteen appendixes. Also available as a CD-ROM and a downloadable file.

Recent editions of other Stedman's dictionaries include *Stedman's medical dictionary* (Baltimore: Lippincott, Williams & Wilkins, 2006) (28th ed., 2006), *Stedman's medical dictionary for the health professions and nursing* (6th ed., 2008) (108), and *The American Heritage medical dictionary* (2007 ed.) (91), formerly titled *The American Heritage Stedman's medical dictionary.*

Multilingual

118   **Dictionary of medicine = Dictionnaire de médecine: French–English with English–French glossary = Français–anglais avec glossaire anglais–français.** 2nd rev. ed. Svetolik P. Djordjevic. xi, 1103 p. Rockville, Md.: Schreiber, 2004. ISBN: 1887563849.

610.3   R121.D59

1st ed., 2000.

Revised edition, with a wide range of biomedical terms and their definitions, acronyms, abbreviations, eponyms, and proprietary drugs. Also includes adverbial phrases. Medical specialist listings for many acronyms, indicating specialty in which a particular acronym is used.

119 Dictionnaire français-anglais anglais-français des termes médicaux et biologiques et des médicaments = French-English English-French dictionary of medical and biological terms and medications. Gary S. Hill. xii, 939, lxii p. Paris: Flammarion Médecine-Sciences, 2005. ISBN: 2257101693.

The title is descriptive of its content. Another French-English, English-French dictionary is *Dictionary of medicine, French-English with English-French glossary* (Rockville, Md.: Schreiber, 2004). Pierre Lépine's *Dictionnaire français-anglais, anglais-français des termes médicaux et biologiques* remains an important dictionary despite its 1974 publ. date.

120 Elsevier's dictionary of medicine and biology: In English, Greek, German, Italian, and Latin. Giannis Konstantinidis, Stavroula Tsiantoula. Amsterdam, [The Netherlands]; Boston: Elsevier, 2005. ISBN: 0444514406.

610.3   R121.E47

In 2 v. Contents: pt. 1, basic table: English and Latin; pt. 2, indexes: Greek, Italian, and German.

Covers the life sciences, with emphasis on "cell biology, biochemistry, molecular biology, immunology, developmental biology, microbiology, genetics, and also the fields of human anatomy, histology, pathology, physiology, zoology, and botany" (*Pref.*) and other fields. The basic table is "an active English to target languages dictionary" (*Note to the reader*) and also includes Latin terms; pt. 2 contains Greek, Italian, and German indexes with reference numbers to the English terms contained in pt. 1. Contains approx. 27,500 main English entries and more than 130,000 translations. All main entries are followed by grammatical information. For scientists, teachers, and students. Pt. 1 is available online via netLibrary.

121 Elsevier's dictionary of medicine: Spanish–English and English–Spanish. Ana Hidalgo-Simón. viii, 763 p. Amsterdam, [The Netherlands]; Boston: Elsevier, 2004. ISBN: 0444507345.

610.3   R121.H478

Bilingual dictionary with the modern terminology of medicine and the biomedical sciences currently in use. Older and obsolete terms have been omitted. Includes both American and British medical English.

information on Hispanic culture and popular health beliefs. For health-care workers who communicate with Spanish-speaking patients. Alphabetical word index; phrase and sentence index. Includes audio CD.

129 **Southwestern medical dictionary: Spanish-English, English-Spanish.** 2nd ed. Margarita Artschwager Kay. xxi, 308 p., ill. Tucson: University of Arizona Press, 2001. ISBN: 0816521557.
610.3   R121.K238
1st ed., 1977.

Contents: pt. I, Spanish to English; pt. II, English to Spanish. Appendix (A) Food items; (B) Kinship terms; (C) Plants reported to the Arizona Poison and Drug Information Center; (D) Anatomical illustrations with bilingual labels.

Brief definitions for standard Spanish terminology and for words relating to medicine and current health-related problems, with examples on how a word is used in a sentence, with translation.

130 **Spanish-English, English-Spanish medical dictionary = Diccionario médico español-inglés, inglés-español.** 3rd ed. Onyria Herrera McElroy, Lola L. Grabb. 769 p. Philadelphia: Lippincott, Williams & Wilkins, 2005. ISBN: 0781750113.
610.3   R121.M488
1st ed., 1992; 2nd ed., 1996. Imprint varies.

Covers approx. 20,000 terms, medical phrases, and idiomatic expressions to communicate effectively with patients in medical office settings. Contains signs and symptoms, tests, surgical procedures, and treatments; etiology of common diseases, translation of consent form, living will, rights of the patient, etc.; also abbreviations, conversion tables, pronunciation, and simplified Spanish and English grammar guide and glossary. Also includes a review of body systems and associated anatomy terms in English and Spanish. Another title, Glenn T. Roger's pocket-sized *English-Spanish, Spanish-English medical dictionary = Diccionario médico, inglés-español, español-inglés* (3rd ed., 2007), "contains virtually all health-related terms likely to occur in a conversation between a health worker and a Spanish-speaking patient, including common colloquialisms and slang terms not found in similar dictionaries."—*Publ. notes*

131   **Standard acupuncture nomenclature.** World Health Organization. 1993. Manila, Philippines: World Health Organization, Regional Office for the Western Pacific. http://whqlibdoc.who.int/wpro/-1993/9290611057.pdf.

1st print ed., 1984. Description based on the web PDF edition.

"Efforts to develop a uniform nomenclature have been going on for some time with a view to achieving global agreement on a standard acupuncture nomenclature."—*Introd.* Entry for each of the classical acupuncture points has three parts: (1) the standardized name of the classical point, (2) a brief explanation of the name of the point, and (3) a multilingual comparative list of the names of the point.

Specialized and Specialist Dictionaries

132   **The cancer dictionary.** 3rd ed. Michael J. Sarg, Ann D. Gross, Roberta Altman. xv, 416 p., ill. New York: Facts On File, 2007. ISBN: 0816064113.

616.994003   RC262

1st ed., 1992; [2nd] rev. ed., 2000.

Designed for general readers, attempts to provide definitions for every term connected with cancer, with many new terms, drugs, and treatments since the previous edition. Includes many cross-references, and capitalized terms within a definition have their own entry. Appendixes include websites of national cancer and AIDS organizations, and listings of both comprehensive and clinical cancer centers by state. Includes bibliographic references and index. Also available as an e-book.

133   **Churchill Livingstone's international dictionary of homeopathy.** Jeremy Swayne, Faculty of Homoeopathy (London); Homoeopathic Trust, Homoeopathic Trust (London). xix, 251 p., ill. Edinburgh, [Scotland]; New York: Churchill Livingstone, 2000. ISBN: 0443060096.

615.53203   RX41.C48

Provides definitions and explanations of terms and concepts related to the principles and practice of homeopathy. Includes bibliographic references (p. [232]–233) and index. Available online via Credo Reference (London; Boston: Credo Reference) as *International dictionary of homeopathy.*

134 **A clinician's dictionary of pathogenic microorganisms.** James H. Jorgensen, Michael A. Pfaller. viii, 273 p. Washington, D.C.: ASM Press, 2004. ISBN: 1555812805.

616.904103   QR81.J67

"This booklet catalogues the current state of microbial taxonomy as of mid-2003."—*Pref.* Concise reference for pathogenic microorganisms (bacteria, fungi, parasites, and viruses) that affect humans. Entries include common and also less frequent pathogens. Reflects current microbial taxonomy and covers recent changes in terminology. Old and obsolete species names are included, with cross-references to older terms. Also available in PDA format and as e-book from publisher at http://www.asm.org.

135 **Companion to clinical neurology.** 3rd ed. William Pryse-Phillips. xvi, 1214 p., ill. Oxford; New York: Oxford University Press, 2009. ISBN: 9780195367720.

616.8003   RC334.P79

1st ed., 1995; 2nd ed., 2003.

Alphabetically arranged terms and definitions used in neurology. Includes accepted diagnostic criteria, assessment tools, descriptions, eponymic disorders, Internet sites, etc. Also contains brief biographies and portraits of well-known neurologists. Contains extensive list of bibliographical references.

Also available as an e-book via netLibrary.

An older edition (Oxford; New York: Oxford University Press, 2003) of this work was previously included in *Guide to reference.*

136 **Comprehensive dictionary of audiology, illustrated.** 2nd ed. Brad A. Stach. xvi, 363 p., ill. Clifton Park, N.Y.: Thomson/Delmar Learning, 2003. ISBN: 1401848265.

617.8003   RF291.S73

1st ed., 1997.

Described as a source of terminology for the profession, practice, and science of audiology. This expanded ed. contains 7,000 terms, abbreviations, acronyms, and cross-references, including many older terms ("if they are generic enough to stand the test of time"—*Pref.*), but emphasizing modern terminology concerning hearing disorders and diseases or disorders affecting the auditory system and speech. Cross-references, tables, and illustrations. Several appendixes include, for example, audiometric symbols, list of toxins which can affect hearing, a glossary with codes for report writing, and associations and other organizations.

137 Comprehensive tumour terminology handbook. Phillip H.
McKee, C. J. M. de Wolf International Union against Cancer. xx,
362 p. New York: Wiley, 2001. ISBN: 0471184853.
616.9920014   RC254.6.C66

Includes synonyms, eponyms, and pathologic descriptions to classify tumors. Organized in 44 sections; each section provides the tumor terminology related to one organ or organ system of the human body. Follows a consistent tabular format in all sections. Tumor terminology is presented in three columns: preferred and recommended terms (shown in bold), synonyms, and comments. Useful as a reference for researchers, health professionals, and patients.

138 Concise dictionary of biomedicine and molecular biology. 2nd
ed. Pei-Show Juo. 1154 p., ill. Boca Raton, [Fla.]: CRC Press, 2002.
ISBN: 0849309409.
610.3   R121.J86

1st ed., 1996.
Includes terminology commonly used in biomedicine, biotechnology, biochemistry, molecular biology, and related fields. 30,000 entries in this edition. Includes definitions, chemical structures, abbreviations, equations of enzymatic reactions and restriction endonucleases, and integrates "terminology and abbreviations from a variety of disciplines. and fill the need for a handy reference volume."—*Pref.* Useful for students and professionals in the allied health fields. Online version available via netLibrary.

MEDICINE
63

139 Dermatology lexicon project. Art Papier, Lowell Goldsmith,
University of Rochester, Dept. of Dermatology. 2005–. Rochester,
N.Y.: University of Rochester. http://www.dermatologylexicon.org/.

International online open-source project with the goal of creating a standardized and reliable dermatology vocabulary. Provides diagnostic concepts, definitions, morphologic terminology, with illustrations and interactive animations. Includes dermatologic diagnoses and their synonyms, therapies, procedures, lab tests, etc. Also provides links to lexical/medical informatics resources, dermatology research, and organizations as well as patient information.

140   **Dermatology therapy: A–Z essentials.** Norman Levine, Carol C.
       Levine. 639 p., color ill. Berlin; New York: Springer, 2004. ISBN:
       3540008640.

615.778   RL801.D475

Concise entries describing more than 800 skin conditions, giving definition and synonyms, pathogenesis, clinical manifestation, and differential diagnosis and therapy. Preferred treatment is indicated with a blue
star. Includes drugs commonly used in dermatology, giving trade name,
generic availability, side effects, drugs interactions, etc. Color photos. Written for an academic audience.

141   **Dictionary for clinical trials.** 2nd ed. Simon Day. xii, 249 p., ill.
       Chichester, U.K.; Hoboken, N.J.: John Wiley & Sons, 2007. ISBN:
       0470058161.

610.724   R853.C55D39

1st ed., 1999.

     This rev. and expanded ed. includes definitions for terms and short
phrases from a variety of fields (e.g., medicine, statistics, epidemiology,
ethics, and others) and from publications related to clinical trials, such as
trial protocols, regulatory guidelines, reports, etc. Cross-references, line
figures, and graphs. Available online via netLibrary.

142   **Dictionary of alternative medicine.** J. C. Segen. vi, 407 p., ill.
       Stamford, Conn.: Appleton & Lange, 1998. ISBN: 0838516203.

615.503   R733.S44

Derived, in part from *Dictionary of modern medicine*, publ. 1992, and *Current MedTalk*, publ. 1995.

     Defines and describes the alternative and complementary medicine
terminology, including slang, acronyms, synonyms, and cross-references.
Bibliographical references (p. 406–407).

     Other recent titles in this subject area include *Mosby's dictionary of
complementary and alternative medicine*, publ. 2005, which covers the
terminology of alternative healthcare systems, mind-body interventions,
biologically based therapies, manipulative and body-based health methods, and energy therapies, with 24 appendixes (Acupuncture–Yoga) and
bibliography (available in print and online via Credo [London; Boston:
Credo Reference]), and *Stedman's alternative & complementary medicine
words*, (2nd ed., 2005), an A–Z list of 53,000 words intended for medical
transcriptionists, medical editors, and others.

143 **Dictionary of cancer terms.** National Cancer Institute, National Institutes of Health. Bethesda, Md.: National Cancer Institute. http://www.cancer.gov/dictionary/.

Contains more than 4,000 terms related to cancer and medicine. Available in both English and Spanish. Detailed instructions on how to search this dictionary are available on the website. Other cancer vocabulary resources include the NCI Thesaurus, NCI Metathesaurus, and NCI Terminology Browser, made available via NCI Enterprise Vocabulary Services (EVS) at http://evs.nci.nih.gov.

144 **Dictionary of developmental disabilities terminology.** 2nd ed. Pasquale J. Accardo, Barbara Y. Whitman, Shirley K. Behr, Tony Stubblefield. xxiv, 451 p., ill. Baltimore, Md.: Paul H. Brooks Publ., 2002. ISBN: 155766594X.

618.9285889003   RJ135.A26

1st ed., 1996.

Interdisciplinary resource, with terminology from medicine, genetics, mental retardation, pediatrics, psychology, social work, physical therapy, and others. Provides concise definitions for neurodevelopmental disorders and developmental disabilities, with brief descriptions of medical syndromes. Includes tests and published instruments, key legislation, associations and organizations, and public laws relating to disabilities. Synonyms and and acronyms, with cross-references to full name of acronym. Includes bibliographical references.

145 **Dictionary of environmental and occupational medicine: Wörterbuch Umwelt- und Arbeitsmedizin.** Karl-Heinz Ohrbach. 551 p. Weinheim, [Germany]; New York: Wiley-VCH, 2001. ISBN: 3527303537.

616.9800321; 616.98003   RC963.A3.O37

Includes approx. 15,000 terms and phrases (English/German and German/English) describing environmental factors and their impact on human health, safety, and preventive medicine, with focus on the workplace. For physicians, scientists, and translators.

146 **Dictionary of environmental health.** David Worthington. New York: Spon Press, 2002. ISBN: 0415267242.

616.9803   RA566.W68

(Clay's library of health and the environment)

"Provides a one-stop reference to over 3,000 common and not so

MEDICINE

common terms, concepts, abbreviations, acronyms, and a wealth of supporting data. suitable for. environmental and public health practitioners and students."—*Publ. description.* Appendix I: Units and measurements; Appendix II: Abbreviations and acronyms. Cross-references, bibliographical references, and index. Available as an e-book.

147 **Dictionary of eye terminology.** 4th ed. Barbara Cassin, Melvin L. Rubin. 286 p., ill. Gainesville, Fla.: Triad, 2001. ISBN: 0937404632.
617.7003   RE21.C37
1st ed., 1984; 3rd ed., 1997.

Brief definitions, with pronunciation guides only for difficult words. Each term is also assigned a general category—e.g., pathologic condition, optical device, or surgical procedure—which provides a context for each definition. This edition includes new surgical techniques, new laser technology, a larger number of drugs, and systemic diseases with ocular manifestations. Includes approx. 5,000 terms and 1,000 abbreviations. Intended to make ophthalmic terminology understandable to those not familiar with the field. For students and health professionals.

148 **A dictionary of genetics.** 7th ed. Robert C. King, William D. Stansfield, Pamela Khipple Mulligan. New York: Oxford University Press, 2006. ISBN: 9780195307627.
576.503   QH427.K55

This edition of a respected dictionary presents expanded information in the rapidly changing field of genetics and includes valuable supplementary material. Entries include acronyms and common words adopted by geneticists; entries for organisms include scientific and common names and explain their economic importance or advantageous use for elucidating genetic phenomena. Appendixes add value to the dictionary by providing a list of the scientific names of 240 domesticated species grouped by common name; a table showing genome size and gene numbers of organisms and organelles included in the dictionary; recommended Internet sites; 512 periodicals relevant to genetics; a bibliography of 140 books; a chronology of genetics from 1590 to 2001; and a list of Nobel Prize winners in the field with references to their key publications. Available as an e-book.

149 **The dictionary of health economics.** Anthony J. Culyer. Northampton, Mass.: Edward Elgar, 2005. ISBN: 1843762080.
362.103   RA410.A3C85

Definitions of terms, concepts, and methods from the field of health economics and related fields, such as epidemiology, pharmacoeconomics, medical sociology, medical statistics, and others. Alphabetical arrangement. Personal names are included only when they are part of a headword. Also includes health economists' professional organizations, but no government agencies or research groups in universities (cf. *Pref.*). For health services researchers and professionals. Also available as an e-book. A similar title is *Dictionary of health economics and finance* (150).

150　**Dictionary of health economics and finance.** David E. Marcinko, Hope R. Hetico. 436 p. New York: Springer Publ., 2006. ISBN: 0826102549.

338.47362103　　　　　　　　　　　　　　　RA410.A3D53

Definitions, abbreviations and acronyms, and eponyms of medical economics and health care sector terminology. Bibliography. A similar title is *The dictionary of health economics* (149).

151　**Dictionary of health insurance and managed care.** David Edward Marcinko. New York: Springer, 2006. ISBN: 0826149944.

368.382003　　　　　　　　　　　　　　　　RA413.D53

Up-to-date health insurance, managed care plans and programs, health care industry terminology and definitions, abbreviatons, and acronyms. Available online via netLibrary.

152　**Dictionary of medical eponyms.** 2nd ed. Barry G. Firkin, Judith A. Whitworth. viii, 443 p., ill., ports. New York: Parthenon Publ. Group, 1995. ISBN: 1850704775.

610.3　　　　　　　　　　　　　　　　　　R121.F535

1st ed., 1987.

　　This corrected edition offers explanations of approx. 2,300 eponyms currently used in internal medicine; in general, eponymous terms from subspecialties have been excluded. Alphabetical arrangement. Each entry includes a brief definition of the term, and provides biographical information about the person from whom the term is derived; some entries include a photograph or a portrait. Although the orientation is Australian, these terms are used in most English-speaking countries. Includes some cross-references, but there is no index. The introduction provides a brief list of reference sources, but individual entries do not provide bibliographic citations. Not as comprehensive and a work in progress is an

online resource entitled Who Named It? (http://www.whonamedit.com/), a
biographical dictionary of medical eponyms.

153 Dictionary of medical sociology. William C. Cockerham, Ferris
Joseph Ritchey. xxvi, 169 p. Westport, Conn.: Greenwood Press,
1997. ISBN: 0313292698.

306.46103   RA418.C655

Positioned at the intersection of arguably the softest of the soft sciences
(sociology) and the hardest of the hard sciences (medicine), medical
sociology has developed at a rapid pace over the last two decades to richly
inform both of its parent disciplines. This dictionary from 1997 defines
key terms from the newly-emerging field at that time, but also demonstrates how each discipline informs and expands the other. A useful reference tool, and also an informal guide to the newly-created field. Includes
bibliographical references and index.

154 Dictionary of medical syndromes. 4th ed. Sergio I. Magalini,
Sabina C. Magalini. vii, 960 p. Philadelphia: Lippincott-Raven,
1997. ISBN: 0397584180.

616.003   RC69.M33

1st ed. 1997; 3rd ed., 1990.

Alphabetical arrangement by name of syndrome, giving for each as
appropriate: synonyms, symptoms and signs, etiology, pathology, diagnostic procedures, therapy, prognosis, and bibliography. Index (p. 865–960).
Less inclusive, the *Dictionary of syndromes and inherited disorders* by Patricia Gilbert (3rd ed.) is written in nontechnical language.

155 Dictionary of ophthalmology. Michel Millodot, Daniel M.
Laby. xx, 313 p., ill. (chiefly color). Oxford; Boston: Butterworth-
Heinemann, 2002. ISBN: 0750647973.

617.7003

Alphabetical arrangement of approx. 4,000 key terms and definitions
on eye diseases and related ophthalmic vocabulary. Includes synonyms,
cross-references, and color illustrations. Another title by the same author
is *Dictionary of optometry and visual science* (156).

156 Dictionary of optometry and visual science. 6th ed. Michel
Millodot. xxi, 347 p., ill. Edinburgh, [U.K.]; New York:
Butterworth-Heinemann, 2004. ISBN: 0750688084.

617.75003   RE939.7.M54

1st–4th eds. (1986–97) had title *Dictionary of optometry*; 5th ed., 2000. Rev. ed.

This edition contains 4,900 terms, 83 tables, and 192 illustrations. In concise entries, defines terms commonly used in optometry, ocular pathology, ocular pharmacology and therapeutics, and other visual science terminology. All definitions from previous editions have been revised and in many cases expanded. Many cross-references. Available online via Credo Reference (London; Boston: Credo Reference). Another title by the same author is *Dictionary of ophthalmology* (155).

157 **Dictionary of visual science and related clinical terms.** 5th ed. Henry W. Hofstetter. xviii, 630 p., ill. Boston: Butterworth-Heinemann, 2000. ISBN: 0750671319.

617.7003   RE21.D42

1st ed. (1960) through 4th ed. (1989) had title *Dictionary of visual science.*

A comprehensive dictionary providing succinct definitions for terms in all fields of visual science, including anatomy and physiology of the eye, optics, and ocular pharmacology. Includes entries for syndromes with ocular manifestations. In this edition, expanded coverage of ocular disease and therapeutic pharmacologic agents, and 400 new terms on optics and refractive surgery. Compound and eponymous terms are listed alphabetically under the noun, and pronunciation is given for more difficult terms. An appendix lists terms, symbols, and abbreviations, and there are reference tables related to visual science. Includes CD-ROM.

158 **Illustrated dictionary of immunology.** 2nd ed. Julius M. Cruse, R. E. Lewis. 675 p., ill. Boca Raton, Fla.: CRC Press, 2003. ISBN: 0849319358.

616.07903   QR180.4C78

1st ed., 1995.

Updated ed., with many new entries from the contemporary literature of immunology and its subspecialties (for example, autoimmunity, immunopathology, transplantation). Concise definitions of current terms and approx. 1,200 illustrations of various kinds provide an understanding of current immunologic vocabulary and concepts. Includes photographs of historical figures. Alphabetical arrangement. Intended for both immunologists and non-immunologists. Available online via CRCnetBASE (Boca Raton, Fla.; London: CRC Press; Taylor and Francis).

159   **Jablonski's dictionary of syndromes and eponymic diseases.** 2nd
      ed. Stanley Jablonski. ix, 665 p., ill. Malabar, Fla.: Krieger, 1991.
      ISBN: 0894642243.

616.003   R121.J24

Rev. ed. of *Illustrated dictionary of eponymic syndromes and diseases and
their synonyms*, 1969.

   Entries under personal names may provide brief biographical information. Many cross-references, and some entries include references.

160   **Lewis' dictionary of occupational and environmental safety and
      health.** Jeffrey W. Vincoli. 1093 p., ill. Boca Raton, Fla.: Lewis,
      2000. ISBN: 1566703999.

363.1103   T55.L468

Comprehensive resource for the terminology of the interdisciplinary area
of industrial safety and environmental health. Includes approx. 25,000
definitions.

   Available online via CRCnetBASE (Boca Raton, Fla.; London: CRC
Press; Taylor and Francis).

161   **The managed health care dictionary.** 2nd ed. Richard
      Rognehaugh. xii, 261 p. Gaithersburg, Md.: Aspen Publ., 1998.
      ISBN: 0834211440.

362.10425803   RA413.R58

1st ed., 1996.

   Includes over 1,000 terms with definitions, including slang, acronyms, etc.,
many with cross-references. Does not include medical specialties and health
professions. Intended for health professionals, patients, and others. Another
more recent title is *Dictionary of health insurance and managed care* (151).

162   **A manual of orthopaedic terminology.** 7th ed. Fred R. T. Nelson,
      Carolyn Taliaferro Blauvelt. 496 p. Philadelphia: Mosby/Elsevier,
      2007. ISBN: 0323045030.

616.70014   RD723.B53

1st ed., 1977; 6th ed., 1998.

   Contents: (1) Classifications of fractures, dislocations, and sports-
related injuries; (2) Musculoskeletal diseases and related terms; (3) Imaging techniques; (4) Orthopaedic tests, signs, and maneuvers; (5) Laboratory
evaluations; (6) Casts, splints, dressings, and traction; (7) Prosthetics and
orthotics; (8) Anatomy and orthopaedic surgery; (9) The spine; (10) The

hand and wrist; (11) The foot and ankle; (12) Physical medicine and rehabilitation: physical therapy and occupational therapy; (13) Musculoskeletal research. Appendixes: (A) Orthopaedic abbreviations and acronyms;
(B) Anatomic positions and directions; (C) Etymology of orthopaedics;
(D) ICD codes for eponymic musculoskeletal disease terms.

Vocabulary of orthopedics, with brief definitions. Arranged in 13 topical chapters and various appendixes. Bibliographic references and index.
Also available from publisher in a searchable web version.

163   Medical meanings: A glossary of word origins. 2nd ed. William
S. Haubrich. Philadelphia: American College of Physicians, 2003.
ISBN: 1930513496.

610.14   R123.H29

1st ed., 1984; rev. and expanded ed., 1997.

An etymological dictionary of medical terms, relating word origins to
their current meaning. Cross-reference index.

164   Melloni's illustrated dictionary of obstetrics and gynecology.
June L. Melloni, Ida Dox, Harrison H. Sheld. 401 p., ill. (some color).
New York: Parthenon Publ. Group, 2000. ISBN: 1850707103.

618.03   RG45.M45

Contains over 15,000 concise definitions, including terms from other disciplines that are related to female health. Includes 280 ill., with color correlation of a defined term and its illustration. Cross-references, pronunciation
guide, and relevant abbreviations. For health professionals and students.

165   Melloni's illustrated dictionary of the musculoskeletal system.
Biagio John Melloni. 308 p., ill. New York: Parthenon Publ. Group,
1998. ISBN: 1850706670.

611.703   QM100.M44

Dictionary with 4,600 terms and definitions, with color illustrations, covering the musculoskeletal system. Contains tables of the muscles and bones
of the human body, with description of each bone and insertion and action
of each muscle. For physical therapy and occupational therapy students.

166   National Cancer Institute. National Cancer Institute. Bethesda,
Md.: National Cancer Institute. http://www.cancer.gov/.

Website created by the National Cancer Institute (NCI), a division of the
National Institutes of Health (NIH).

MEDICINE

71

Contents: NCI Home, Cancer Topics, Clinical Trials, Cancer Statistics, Research and Funding, News, About NCI.

Links to cancer-related information for health professionals, medical students, and patients. Provides guidance to searching the cancer literature in PubMed (432) by searching the "cancer subset" and access to already prepared searches on more than 100 different topics. Non-PubMed citations previously found in CANCERLIT, a database no longer being maintained, consist primarily of meeting abstracts from the annual meetings of the American Society of Clinical Oncology (ASCO) and the American Association for Cancer Research (AACR). ASCO abstracts for recent years are available via http://www.asco.org, AACR abstracts at http://aacrmeetingabstracts.org/. Also provides access to PDQ: Physician Data Query (http://www.cancer.gov/cancertopics/pdq), a database with the latest information about cancer treatment, screening, prevention, genetics, etc.

The NCI website includes descriptions of various types of cancer (A–Z List of Cancers: http://www.cancer.gov/cancertopics/alphalist/) and related topics, with links to diagnosis and treatment information and supportive care, information on clinical trials, cancer prevention, cancer statistics (e.g., SEER Cancer Statistics Review [547]), cancer statistics tools, cancer mortality maps and graphs, and related NCI websites. Links to the Dictionary of Cancer Terms (143) and various cancer vocabulary resources (e.g., NCI Thesaurus, NCI Metathesaurus, and NCI Terminology Browser), NCI Drug Dictionary, NCI publications, etc. Available both in English and Spanish.

167 Neurological eponyms. Peter J. Koehler, G. W. Bruyn, John Pearce. xiv, 386 p., ill. Oxford; New York: Oxford University Press, 2000. ISBN: 0195133668.

616.8014   RC343.N434

Collection of short essays that describe the derivations of many common neurological eponyms, derived from *Eponyms in neurological examination* (Netherlands Society of Neurology, 1995), but revised and expanded (*Pref.*).

Contents: Pt. I, Structures and processes (ch. 1–10); pt. II, Symptoms and signs (ch. 11–17); pt. III, Reflexes and other tests (ch. 18–27); pt. IV, Syndromes (ch. 28–39); pt. V, Diseases and defects (ch. 40–55). Each chapter deals with one or two people's association with the eponym, with brief biography and reference to the publication important for the naming of a particular syndrome. For medical professionals and others with an interest in medical history. Includes bibliographical references and index.

168 **Ophthalmic eponyms: An encyclopedia of named signs, syndromes, and diseases in ophthalmology.** Spencer P. Thornton. ix, 324 p. Birmingham, Ala.: Aesculapius, [1967].

617.7003   RE21.T54

In two sections: (1) "Signs, syndromes, and diseases in medical, pediatric, and neuro-ophthalmology"; and (2) "Eponyms in ophthalmic surgery." Arrangement is alphabetical within each section. Bibliographic references are included with most entries.

169 **Oxford dictionary of medical quotations.** Peter McDonald. 212 p. Oxford; New York: Oxford University Press, 2004. ISBN: 0192630474.

610   R705.S565

Source of quotations (mostly from the English-speaking countries: Great Britain, Ireland, and North America, with just a few from other countries) from books, plays, poems, ballads, etc., covering a variety of topics related to medicine, "selected on the basis of their usefulness to modern medical authors, journalists, politicians, nurses, physios, lecturers, and even health managers, something for everyone within these pages."—*Pref.* Quotations are listed under author (with biographical information in many cases) in alphabetical order, reference to the source when possible, and an index of keywords. "How to Use the Dictionary" provides further helpful information. Available online via netLibrary.

170 **The Oxford dictionary of sports science and medicine.** 3rd ed. Michael Kent. vii, 612 p., ill. Oxford; New York: Oxford University Press, 2006. ISBN: 9780198568506.

617.102703   RC1206.O94

Includes clearly written, scientific definitions of nearly 8,000 terms related to sports medicine and sports science. Offers updated entries of terms covering sports nutrition, drug and doping regulations, and gene technology. Illustrated with drawings and photographs. Electronic version via Oxford Reference Online (Oxford; New York: Oxford University Press, 2002–).

171 **The progressive era's health reform movement: A historical dictionary.** Ruth C. Engs. xxii, 419 p. Westport, Conn.: Praeger, 2003. ISBN: 0275979326.

362.1097303   RA395.A3E547

Covers 1880–1925, the time period labeled the Progressive era of the United States. Entries cover individuals (biographical information/assessment of historical importance), events, crusades (e.g., exercise, vegetarian diets, alternative health care), legislation, publications, and terms. Includes entries on the health reform movement and campaigns against alcohol, tobacco, drugs, and sexuality. For scholars, students, and general readers. "Selected chronology" (p. [371]–407), bibliographical references, and index. Available online via netLibrary.

172 **Slee's health care terms.** 5th ed. Debora A. Slee, Vergil N. Slee, H. Joachim Schmidt. 700 p. Sudbury, Mass.: Jones and Bartlett Publ., 2007. ISBN: 9780763746155.

362.103 RA423.S55

1st ed., 1986; 4th ed., 2001. Also called *Health care terms*.

Provides concise definitions for terms from a wide range of disciplines in the healthcare field, including administration, organization, finance, statistics, law, and governmental regulation. Many cross-references. Pays particular attention to acronyms. Terms used in definitions are italicized to indicate the term is defined elsewhere in the dictionary; related terms may be grouped together under one term, such as the many entries under the term "hospital." Intended for all types of healthcare consumers.

173 **Standard acupuncture nomenclature.** World Health Organization. 1993. Manila, Philippines: World Health Organization, Regional Office for the Western Pacific. http://whqlibdoc.who.int/wpro/-1993/9290611057.pdf.

1st print ed., 1984. Description based on the web PDF edition.

"Efforts to develop a uniform nomenclature have been going on for some time with a view to achieving global agreement on a standard acupuncture nomenclature."—*Introd.* Entry for each of the classical acupuncture points has three parts: (1) the standardized name of the classical point, (2) a brief explanation of the name of the point, and (3) a multilingual comparative list of the names of the point.

174 **Terminology of communication disorders: Speech-language-hearing.** 5th ed. Lucille Nicolosi, Elizabeth Harryman, Janet Kresheck. Baltimore: Lippincott, Williams & Wilkins, 2004. ISBN: 0781741963.

616.855003 RC423.N52

1st ed., 1978; 4th ed., 1996.

Updated ed., intended as a comprehensive dictionary and sourcebook for the terminology of speech, language, and hearing disorders. Alphabetical arrangement, brief definitions, illustrations, many cross-references for synonyms and related terms. Includes charts, lists, tables, and several appendixes.

175 **The words of medicine: Sources, meanings, and delights.** Robert Fortuine. xvi, 434 p. Springfield, Ill.: Charles C. Thomas, 2001. ISBN: 0398071322.

610.14   R123.F64

Provides a brief history of the English medical vocabulary from its Indo-European roots to the modern era. Addresses medical word formation from Greek and Latin roots, prefixes, suffixes, Latin and Greek verbs and adjectives, spelling, euphemisms, etc. Contains several chapters on "word-imagery" (*Introd.*), including obsolete words still encountered in literary works and historical documents, "loan words" borrowed from other languages, and historical and modern terms (for example, drug names, managed care, and medical genetics). Also contains chapters on eponyms, folk etymology, and acronyms. "Not considered a handbook for learning terminology, nor a word list, nor a dictionary." Although the book is not in dictionary format, it provides succinct, accurate definitions for many of the words discussed. Intended for physicians and other health professionals who are already familiar with most of the terms discussed.

Directories

176 **The directory of complementary and alternative medicine.** Hugh P. Greeley, Anne M. Banas. xxi, 530 p. Marblehead, Mass.: Opus Communications, 2000. ISBN: 1578390656.

615.5   R733.D563

Contents: (1) Mind-body medicine (Mind-body methods, Religious healing and spirituality, Social and contextual areas); (2) Alternative medical systems (Oriental medicine and acupuncture, Traditional indigenous systems/folk medicine, Unconventional Western systems, Naturopathic medicine/naturopathy); (3) Lifestyle and disease prevention therapies (Clinical preventive practices, Lifestyle therapies); (4) Biologically based therapies (Herbal medicine and phytotherapy, Special diet therapies, Orthomolecular medicine, Pharmacological, biological, and instrumental interventions); (5) Manipulation and body-based systems (Chiropractic medicine, Massage and bodywork, Naprapathy, Osteopathic medicine,

Unconventional physical therapies); (6) Biofield therapeutics/vibrational medicine; (7) Therapies for specific health conditions. Appendix: International CAM organization. Index.

Organization of this directory is based on the classification scheme of the National Institutes of Health's (NIH) (470) Center for Complementary and Alternative Medicine (NCCAM), which groups CAM practices into seven major categories. Entries include description, title, education and training requirements, licensing, certification, professional associations, and practice sites.

Canada

177   **AAMC curriculum directory.** Association of American Medical Colleges. 2002–. Washington: Association of American Medical Colleges. http://services.aamc.org/currdir/.

Print version ceased with 2000 ed. Title varies: also called *Curriculum directory*.

Online edition generated from the AAMC's Curriculum Management and Information Tool (CurrMIT), which allows each medical school to manage its curriculum locally. Selected data from CurrMIT are available to the public in the *AAMC curriculum directory*.

Describes medical student education programs and institutional characteristics at 125 medical schools in the United States and 17 schools in Canada. Presents comparable data about required courses, U.S. Medical Licensing Exams, clerkships, electives, and combined degree programs (course details search at http://services.aamc.org/currdir/section4/start.cfm), and describes educational methods and current trends in curricular and instructional innovation (http://services.aamc.org/currdir/section1/innovations.cfm). Also provides a graphic representation of each medical school program. A list of AAMC member medical schools can be found at http://www.aamc.org/medicalschools.htm. Related titles, also published by the AAMC, are *Directory of American medical education* (181) and *Medical school admission requirements, U.S.A. and Canada* (184).

178   **Annual statistics of medical school libraries in the United States and Canada: Compiled by Houston Academy of Medicine– Texas Medical Center Library.** Gary Byrd, Eric Albright, Barbara Epstein, Cynthia Henderson, Mary Moore, Connie Poole, Susan Starr, Laurie Thompson, Houston Academy of Medicine-Texas Medical Center Library, Association of Academic Health Sciences

Library Directors (U.S.). Houston, Tex.: Houston Academy of
Medicine–Texas Medical Center Library, 1978–. ISSN: 0196-6448.
026.610973   Z675.M4A6

Assoc. of Academic Health Sciences Libraries (AAHSL); Assoc. of Academic Health Sciences Library Directors; AAHSL Assessment and Statistics Committee.

Description based on 29th ed., 2005/2006. Also publ. at the AAHSL website (http://www.aahsl.org/), but accessible only to AAHSL members.

Contents: The Composite health sciences library, 2005–2006; Survey highlights, 2005–2006; Five-year trends, 2001–2002 to 2005–2006; General tables; Salary tables; Appendixes.

Based on annual survey of AAHSL libraries. Of a potential 160 institutions, 125 completed the general survey. "AAHSL comprises the libraries serving the accredited U.S. and Canadian medical schools belonging to or affiliated with the Association of American Medical Colleges. It includes other related libraries and organizations that lead in resolving information and knowledge management problems in the health care environment."—*Pref.*

Comparative data on significant characteristics of collections, (including electronic monograph and serial titles), expenditures (including expenditures for access to and purchase of electronic resources), personnel, and services in academic health sciences libraries in the Unites States and Canada.

MEDICINE

77

179 **Best medical schools.** Princeton Review (Firm). New York:
Random House, 2004–. ISSN: 1553-8761.
610.13   R745.C875

Title varies. 1997–1999: *The best medical schools*; 2000–2003: *Complete book of medical schools*.

Description based on 2006 ed. (2005).

Based on student input regarding the curriculum, teaching, and student life, rates accredited medical and osteopathic schools, 126 allopathic schools in the U.S. and 16 in Canada, and 20 osteopathic schools. Provides profiles and statistical data (student body, admissions, cost, and aid) for the different schools. Alphabetical index and index by location.

180 **Canadian medical directory.** Don Mills, Ont.: Seccombe House.
ISSN: 0068-9203.
610.695202571   R713.01.C3

Imprint varies. Description based on 52nd ed., 2006.

Brief biographical information for Canadian physicians; alphabetical arrangement, with address, telephone number, medical school and year of degree, professional memberships, position, and hospital affiliation. Separate listings provide names of physicians by geographic location, certified specialists, and expert medical witnesses with physicians' area of medical expertise. Also includes section of related miscellaneous information, such as listings of hospitals and Canadian healthcare associations and government agencies. Also includes a section "Year in Review" with a summary of major medical news from the *Canadian Medical Association Journal*. More detailed information on hospitals, long-term care facilities, medical clinics, and laboratories can be found in its annual companion volume, *Canadian health facilities directory*. Both publications are available both in print and as a CD-ROM.

181 **Directory of American medical education.** Association of American Medical Colleges. Washington, D.C: Association of American Medical Colleges, 1995–.

610.71173   R712.A1A8

Title varies: 1951/52–1966/67, *Association of American Medical Colleges. directory*; 1968–1995, *AAMC directory of American medical education.* Description based on 2006/07 ed.

Provides alphabetical and geographical listings of U.S. medical schools and Canadian affiliate institutional members, and information on AAMC's organizational structure, activities, and its various member organizations. Related titles, also published by the AAMC, are *AAMC curriculum directory* (177) and *Medical school admission requirements, U.S.A. and Canada* (184).

182 **Find a library (MedlinePlus).** National Library of Medicine (U.S.). 200?–. Bethesda, Md.: National Library of Medicine. http://www.nlm.nih.gov/medlineplus/libraries.html.

Part of Directories (MedlinePlus) (204).

Clickable map of the United States and Canada for locating health sciences/medical libraries. Medical/Health Sciences Libraries on the Web (196) provides further information for finding medical libraries internationally.

183 **Guide to Canadian health care facilities: Guide des établissements de santé du Canada.** Canadian Hospital Association. Ottawa: Canadian Hospital Association = Association des hôpitaux du Canada, 1993–. ISSN: 1195-0110.

362.1102571   RA978.C2G85

Formed by the merger of: *Canadian hospital directory* and *Directory of long term care centres in Canada*. 1953–92, *Canadian hospital directory* = *Annuaire des hôpitaux du Canada*; 1980–90s, *Directory of long term care centres in Canada* = *Répertoire des centres de soins de longue durée au Canada*; subtitle varies.

Description based on v. 14 (2006–07). Text in English and French.

Comprehensive information in standardized format on Canadian healthcare facilities, including outpatient health services centers and nursing stations. Lists medical staff with contact information for CEOs, directors of medicine, and other key professionals and services. Includes section for the provincial regional health boards and regional health authority restructuring. Also includes closed or merged hospitals and health facilities. Index of hospitals, nursing homes, long-term care facilities, health associations, provincial and territorial hospital and health organizations, provincial and federal government departments hospital equipment and medical suppliers.

184 **Medical school admission requirements, U.S.A. and Canada.**
Association of American Medical Colleges. Evanston, Ill.:
Association of American Medical Colleges, 1964–. ISSN:
0738-6060.

R745.A8

1st–14th ed., 1947–63: *Admission requirements of American medical colleges*. Title varies.

2006–07 ed. has title: *Medical school admission requirements (MSAR™)*.

Contents of 2006–07 ed.: ch. 1, Medicine as a career; ch. 2, The process of medical education; ch. 3, Undergraduate premedical preparation; ch. 4, The application process; ch. 5, Applicant and accepted applicant data; ch. 6, Increasing diversity in medical school; ch. 7, Selection; ch. 8, Acceptance; ch. 9, Financing a medical education; ch. 10, Information on combined college/MD programs for high school students; ch. 11, Training of physician-scientists: MD-PhD programs; ch. 12, Information about U.S. medical schools; ch. 13, Information about Canadian medical schools.

A website, maintained by the AAMC, "tomorrow's doctors.org" (http://www.aamc.org/students/start.htm), provides related online information for people interested in a medical career and prospective medical students, and various resources for medical students and residents.

The annual *Directory of American medical education* (title varies) (181) lists member institutions, with information on their facilities and administration.

185   Peterson's graduate programs in business, education, health,
      information studies, law and social work. Peterson's (Firm). ill.
      Princeton, N.J.: Peterson's, 1997–. ISSN: 1088-9442.
378.15530257   L901.P459

The standard guide to graduate schools, with information on programs
offered; degree requirements; number and gender of faculty; number, gender, and ethnicity of students; average student age; percentage of students
accepted; entrance requirements; application deadlines; application fee;
costs; and financial aid. Also available online.

186   Research centers directory. Gale Research Co. Detroit: Gale
      Research, 1965–. ISSN: 0080-1518.
001   AS25.D5

(Based on 34th ed.) This annual publ. contains listings of more than 14,300
North American laboratories, including full contact information, e-mail,
and URLs, when available. Listings also include short descriptive statements about the laboratories. Divided by subject category, the first part
contains the descriptive listings, while the second part consists of subject,
geographic, personal name, and master indexes. Available as an e-book.

Great Britain

187   Directory of health library and information services in the
      United Kingdom and the Republic of Ireland. 11th ed. Library
      Association. London: Library Association, 2002–.
                                                                 Z675.M4

1st ed. (1957) through 4th ed. (1976) had title *Directory of medical libraries in the British Isles*; 5th ed. (1982) through 10th ed. (1997–98) *Directory
of medical and health care libraries in the United Kingdon and Republic of
Ireland*.
    "Compiled for the Health Libraries Group of the Library Association."
    Alphabetical arrangement by name of library and various other
information services (e.g., NHS Direct Online). For each library or other
service listed gives, as appropriate, location, stack policy, hours, holdings,
classifications, computer facilities and availability, and user accessibility.
Three indexes: index by towns, index of personal names, and a general
index. Glossary of acronyms and abbreviations.

188 **Guide to libraries and information sources in medicine and health care.** 3rd ed. Peter Dale. 209 p. London: British Library, Science Reference & Information Service, 2000. ISBN: 0712308563. 026.610941

1st ed., 1995; 2nd ed., 1997; 3rd paperback ed., 2002.

"Aims to provide useful and informative coverage of leading sources of information in order to facilitate the work of librarians, information workers, and researchers [and] covers those libraries and information services which are prepared to accept serious enquiries from outside."—*Pref.* The various organizations are listed alphabetically. Entries provide detailed contact information, summary of the purpose of the organization, subject coverage, and services. Appendix provides medical Internet resources. Organisation acronym index; organisation index; subject index.

189 **List of registered medical practitioners.** General Medical Council. 2005–. London: General Medical Council. http://www.gmc-uk.org/register/search/index.asp.

General Medical Council (Great Britain). Pub. in print format as *Medical register*, 1859–2004; 2005–. Also available on CD-ROM.

Provides access to a list of registered medical practitioners, a listing of all doctors who are registered to practice in the United Kingdom, with the doctor's reference number, name, any former name, gender, year and place of primary medical degree, registration status, date of registration, entry in GP/Specialist Register, and any publicly available fitness-to-practice history since October 20, 2005.

190 **The Medical directory: London, provinces, Wales, Scotland, Ireland, abroad, Navy, Army & Air Force.** London: J. & A. Churchill Ltd., 1845–. ISSN: 0305-3342.

R713.29.M4

Publ. varies. Publ. in association with the Royal Society of Medicine (RSM). Description based on ed. 162, 2006, 2 v.; publ. in paper and CD-ROM formats.

Contains a listing of registered medical practitioners in the U.K., giving brief biographical information. Also provides information on U.K. healthcare organizations, including an alphabetical listing of all NHS trusts and hospitals, educational institutions, medical associations, and medical societies.

International

191   ClinicalTrials.gov. National Institutes of Health, National Library of Medicine (U.S.), United States. 2000–. Bethesda, Md.: National Institutes of Health. http://clinicaltrials.gov.

R853.C55

Provides information about federally and privately funded research in human volunteers for patients, their families and other consumers, and health care professionals. Contents include clinical trials, experimental treatments, experimental and new diagnostic procedures, patient enrollment and recruitment, and all study phases. Explains who may participate, location (U.S. and other countries), and contact information. Searchable by key terms, disease, location, treatment, age group, study phase, etc. Trial listings by condition, sponsor, and status. For additional information and various links to related websites, consult the NLM fact sheet on Clinical-Trials.gov at http://www.nlm.nih.gov/pubs/factsheets/clintrial.html.

192   Directory of special libraries and information centers. Gale Research. Detroit: Gale Research, 1963–. ISSN: 0731-633X.
026.0002573   Z731.D56

Subtitle: *A guide to special libraries, research libraries, information centers, archives, and data centers maintained by government agencies, business, industry, newspapers, educational institutions, nonprofit organizations, and societies in the field of science and engineering, medicine, law, art, religion, the social sciences and humanities.* The 33rd ed. (2007) lists more than 35,000 special libraries worldwide. Provides address, phone and fax numbers, contact person, e-mail address, URL, and founding date, plus brief information on collections, staffing, and services.

In v. 1, libraries are listed by name, sponsoring body, or institution in a single alphabetical sequence spanning three physical parts, with a subject index in pt. 3. Appendixes list networks and consortia; libraries for the blind and physically handicapped; and depository libraries for U.S. patents and trademarks, U.S. government documents, and publications of the U.N., World Bank, and European Community. Vol. 2 offers geographic and personnel indexes. Vol. 3, issued mid-year with the title *New special libraries* (1971–), lists new or previously overlooked libraries. A complementary annual publication, *Subject directory of special libraries and information centers* (Detroit: Gale Research, 1975–), presents the same entries in a subject arrangement. Also available as an e-book.

193 **Directory of the Medical Library Association.** Medical Library Association. Hampden, Conn.: Shoe String Press, 1959–. ISSN: 0543-2774.

026   WMLCL833577

Produced by Medical Library Association (MLA).

Publ. in print 1959–2001; title and imprint vary. From 2002 on, available only online in PDF format. The online MLA Membership Directory, searchable by name and location, is accessible to MLA members from the MLA website via user name and password.

Description based 2005–06 PDF version (http://www.mlanet.org/ order/store/cat/product_info.php?products_id=101). Users can sign up for updates to this edition.

Contents: "Board of directors"; "Headquarters staff"; "Representatives to allied organizations"; "Committee rosters"; "Task force rosters"; "Section council"; "Section officers"; "Section rosters" (alphabetical by section; names only); "Special interest group (SIG) conveners"; "Chapter council"; "Chapter officers"; "Member listings: Individual members and institutional representatives"; "Institutional members, United States"; "Institutional members, Canada"; "Institutional members, other international."

Provides general information about the association and a listing of members. Further information about MLANet/MLA at MLANET: The Medical Library Association's Network of Health Information Professionals (465).

194 **GeneTests.** Children's Hospital and Medical Center (Seattle, Wash.). 1993–. Seattle, Wash.: Univ. of Washington. http://www. genetests.org/.

Contents: Home page; About GeneTests; GeneReviews; Laboratory directory; Clinic directory; Educational materials.

Provides authoritative information on genetic testing and its use in diagnosis, disease management, and genetic counseling. Promotes use of genetic services in patient care and decision making by individuals. GeneReviews and Laboratory directory can be searched by disease, gene symbol, protein name, etc. Contains context-sensitive illustrated glossary, teaching tools, and other resources.

195 **International research centers directory.** Detroit: Gale Research, 1981–. ISSN: 0278-2731.

001.4025   Q179.98.I58

"*International Research Centers Directory* provides unparalleled access to government, university, independent, nonprofit, and commercial research and development activities in countries worldwide. Entries include English and foreign name of center, full mail and electronic address, personal contact, organizational affiliates, staff, description of research program, publications, services, and more. Master, subject, personal name, and country indexes are provided."—*Publ. website*

196   Medical/health sciences libraries on the Web. Eric Rumsey, Hardin Library of the Health Sciences, University of Iowa. 1997–. Iowa City, Iowa: Hardin Library of the Health Sciences, University of Iowa. http://www.lib.uiowa.edu/hardin/hslibs.html. 026.61

Part of Hardin MD (457).

Geographical arrangement. Provides links to the websites of individual libraries in the United States, Canada, Australia, Germany, the United Kingdom, and others. List does not claim to be complete and allows for individual libraries not currently on the list to be added.

Other medical libraries directories include, for example, *Directory of health library and information services in the United Kingdom and the Republic of Ireland*, 2003–. The World Health Organization (WHO) (951) Library and Information Networks for Knowledge (LNK) is in the process of compiling World Directory of Medical Libraries (http://www.who.int/ghl/directory/en/), part of a WHO initiative, Global Health Library, which is in progress and, when completed, will provide a comprehensive listing of medical/health libraries worldwide.

197   World directory of medical schools. World Health Organization. 1953–. Geneva, Switzerland: World Health Organization. http://www.who.int/hrh/wdms/en/index.html.

Print editions: 1st ed., 1953; 7th ed., 2000.

In the process of being updated, it "will be a Web-based database with comprehensive information on health training institutions worldwide, including schools of medicine, dentistry, nursing, midwifery, public health, pharmacy, and rehabilitation."—*Main page*

Print edition arranged by country, lists institutions of basic medical education in 157 countries and also provides information on obtaining a license to practice medicine in 14 countries that do not have medical schools. Provides name and address, year instruction started, language used in teaching, and duration of medical education to obtain a degree, including practical training.

United States

198 AAMC curriculum directory. Association of American Medical Colleges. 2002–. Washington: Association of American Medical Colleges. http://services.aamc.org/currdir/.

Print version ceased with 2000 ed. Title varies: also called *Curriculum directory*.

Online edition generated from the AAMC's Curriculum Management and Information Tool (CurrMIT), which allows each medical school to manage its curriculum locally. Selected data from CurrMIT are available to the public in the *AAMC curriculum directory*.

Describes medical student education programs and institutional characteristics at 125 medical schools in the United States and 17 schools in Canada. Presents comparable data about required courses, U.S. Medical Licensing Exams, clerkships, electives, and combined degree programs (course details search at http://services.aamc.org/currdir/section4/start. cfm), and describes educational methods and current trends in curricular and instructional innovation (http://services.aamc.org/currdir/section1/innovations.cfm). Also provides a graphic representation of each medical school program. A list of AAMC member medical schools can be found at http://www.aamc.org/medicalschools.htm. Related titles, also published by the AAMC, are *Directory of American medical education* (181) and *Medical school admission requirements, U.S.A. and Canada* (184).

199 AHA guide to the health care field. American Hospital Association. Chicago: Healthcare Infosource, Inc., 1997–.

RA977.A1A46; RA977. A44

Title varies: 1949–71, pt. 2 of Aug. issue (called "Guide issue," 1956–70) of *Hospitals*, which superseded *American hospital directory* (1945–48); 1972–73, *The AHA guide to the health care field*; 1974–96, *American Hospital Association guide to the health care field*.

"America's directory of hospitals and health care systems."—*Cover* Description based on 2006–07 ed.

"Provides basic data reflecting the delivery of health care in the United States and associated territories."—*Introd.* Four major sections, each with table of contents and explanatory information: (A) Hospitals, institutional, and associate members; (B) networks, health care systems, and alliances; (C) lists of health organizations, agencies, and providers; and (D) indexes. Current edition also available in CD-ROM format.

Statistical information concerning hospitals is published in *AHA hospital statistics* (508).

200   **Annual statistics of medical school libraries in the United States and Canada: Compiled by Houston Academy of Medicine–Texas Medical Center Library.** Gary Byrd, Eric Albright, Barbara Epstein, Cynthia Henderson, Mary Moore, Connie Poole, Susan Starr, Laurie Thompson, Houston Academy of Medicine-Texas Medical Center Library, Association of Academic Health Sciences Library Directors (U.S.). Houston, Tex.: Houston Academy of Medicine–Texas Medical Center Library, 1978–. ISSN: 0196-6448.
026.610973   Z675.M4A6

Assoc. of Academic Health Sciences Libraries (AAHSL); Assoc. of Academic Health Sciences Library Directors; AAHSL Assessment and Statistics Committee.

Description based on 29th ed., 2005/2006. Also publ. at the AAHSL website (http://www.aahsl.org/), but accessible only to AAHSL members.

Contents: The Composite health sciences library, 2005–2006; Survey highlights, 2005–2006; Five-year trends, 2001–2002 to 2005–2006; General tables; Salary tables; Appendixes.

Based on annual survey of AAHSL libraries. Of a potential 160 institutions, 125 completed the general survey. "AAHSL comprises the libraries serving the accredited U.S. and Canadian medical schools belonging to or affiliated with the Association of American Medical Colleges. It includes other related libraries and organizations that lead in resolving information and knowledge management problems in the health care environment."—*Pref.*

Comparative data on significant characteristics of collections, (including electronic monograph and serial titles), expenditures (including expenditures for access to and purchase of electronic resources), personnel, and services in academic health sciences libraries in the Unites States and Canada.

201   **AOA yearbook and directory.** American Osteopathic Association. 2003–. Chicago: American Osteopathic Association. http://www.osteopathic.org/index.cfm?PageID=ps_yearbook.

Contains information formerly included in the print version, *Directory of osteopathic physicians*, 1899–1951, and *Yearbook and directory of osteopathic physicians*, 1952–2000, plus additional information.

Website contents: AOA directory; AOA organization; AOA membership; Accredited healthcare facilities; Requirements for certification; Osteopathic research; Continuing medical education; AOA documents and data; Component societies—State and specialty societies; Licensing; Predoctoral education; Postdoctoral education; Glossary of osteopathic terminology; Osteopathic coding.

In addition to extensive information about the AOA, provides links to the AOA directory Find an Osteopathic Physician (http://www.osteopathic.org/directory.cfm), and several other directories (http://www.osteopathic.org/index.cfm?PageID=aoa_dir). AOA members also have access to the online Directory of the Osteopathic Profession. Offers links to a variety of consumer health and patient resources (http://www.osteopathic.org/index.cfm?PageID=you_main).

202 **Barron's guide to medical and dental schools.** 11th ed. Saul Witschnitzer, Edith Wischnitzer. Hauppauge, N.Y.: Barron's, 2006. ISBN: 9780764133.

610.71173   R690.W558

1st ed., 1982 (based on *Barron's guide to medical, dental, and allied health science careers* [1974], and its updated versions, published in 1975 and 1977); 10th ed., 2003.

Contents: pt.1. Medicine; pt. 2. Dentistry.

Intended as a guidance manual for pre-professional students. Presents basic data and detailed information for accredited medical, dental, and osteopathic schools in the U.S. and Canada, such as admissions requirements, curriculum, grading and promotion policies, facilities and special features of an institution, etc. Includes a full-length model Medical College Admission Test (MCAT) with answers, and selected questions from recent Dental College Admission Tests (DAT), sample essays for medical student applications, and other advice for students considering a medical or dental career. Separate chapter on opportunities for women and minorities.

203 **Best medical schools.** Princeton Review (Firm). New York: Random House, 2004–. ISSN: 1553-8761.

610.13   R745.C875

Title varies. 1997–1999: *The best medical schools*; 2000–2003: *Complete book of medical schools.*

Description based on 2006 ed. (2005).

Based on student input regarding the curriculum, teaching, and student life, rates accredited medical and osteopathic schools, 126 allopathic schools in the U.S. and 16 in Canada, and 20 osteopathic schools. Provides profiles and statistical data (student body, admissions, cost, and aid) for the different schools. Alphabetical index and index by location.

204   Directories (MedlinePlus). National Library of Medicine (U.S.), National Institutes of Health (U.S.). 200?–. Bethesda, Md.: U.S. National Library of Medicine, National Institutes of Health, Dept. of Health and Human Services. http://www.nlm.nih.gov/medlineplus/directories.html.

RC48

Pt. of MedlinePlus (463).

Contents: Doctors and dentists—general; Hospital and clinics—general; Doctors and dentists—specialists; Other healthcare providers; Hospitals and clinics—specialized; Other healthcare facilities and services; Libraries.

Links to directories to help find health professionals, services, and facilities. Includes, for example, access to the American Medical Association's DoctorFinder (209), how to find a dentist, a Medicare participants physicians directory, and many others.

205   Directory of American medical education. Association of American Medical Colleges. Washington, D.C: Association of American Medical Colleges, 1995–.

610.71173   R712.A1A8

Title varies: 1951/52–1966/67, *Association of American Medical Colleges. directory*; 1968–1995, *AAMC directory of American medical education.* Description based on 2006/07 ed.

Provides alphabetical and geographical listings of U.S. medical schools and Canadian affiliate institutional members, and information on AAMC's organizational structure, activities, and its various member organizations. Related titles, also published by the AAMC, are *AAMC curriculum directory* (177) and *Medical school admission requirements, U.S.A. and Canada* (184).

206 Directory of deceased American physicians, 1804–1929: A genealogical guide to over 149,000 medical practitioners providing brief biographical sketches drawn from the American Medical Association's Deceased Physician Masterfile. Arthur Wayne Hafner, Fred W. Hunter, E. Michael Tarpey, American Medical Association. 2 v., ill. Chicago: American Medical Association, 1993. ISBN: 0899705278.

610.92273   R712.A1D47

Provides brief entries, with name, birth and death dates, place of birth, type of practice, practice and board specialties, license, hospital affiliation, *JAMA* citation for obituary notice, death notice information, etc. Includes indexes to African-American female and male practitioners, female practitioners, self-designated homeopathic, and osteopathic practitioners. L. Holloway's *Medical obituaries: American physicians' biographical notices in selected medical journals before 1907* provides additional useful information.

207 **Directory of physicians in the United States.** American Medical Association; Survey & Data Resources. Chicago: American Medical Association, Div. of Survey and Data Resources, 1992–. ISSN: 10963588.

610.257   R712.A1A6

Continues: *American medical directory*, 1st ed. (1906)–32nd ed. (1990). 33rd ed.–issued in four vols.: v. 1, Alphabetical index of physicians; v. 2–4, Geographical register of physicians.

Also issued in a CD-ROM version.

Description based on 40th ed., 2007.

For 924,081 physicians, gives school and year of graduation, practice specialties, type of practice, and licensing and American Board of Specialties (ABMS) certification information. Also includes administrators, teachers, residents, researchers, and retired physicians. The CD-ROM version provides additional functionality and search capabilities.

208 **DIRLINE.** National Institutes of Health (U.S.). [1983?–.] Bethesda, Md.: U.S. National Institutes of Health, Dept. of Health and Human Services. http://dirline.nlm.nih.gov/.

DIRLINE® (Directory of Information Resources Online), maintained by the National Library of Medicine (NLM) (427).

Online annotated directory of organizations, research resources, projects, databases, and other information resources concerned with health and biomedicine from a variety of sources, including federal, state, and local government agencies, academic and research institutions, and also consumer health-related resources such as self-help groups and health hotlines. Resources are mostly from the U.S. but also include some international resources. Currently contains over 8,000 entries, with topics on most diseases and conditions and health services research and technology assessment. Can be searched using MeSH® (Medical Subject Headings) (575), keywords, or by name and location of a resource. Detailed information on DIRLINE can be found via a fact sheet prepared by NLM: http://www.nlm.nih.gov/pubs/factsheets/dirlinfs.html.

209 **DoctorFinder.** American Medical Association. 1997–. Chicago: American Medical Association. http://www.ama-assn.org/aps/amahg.htm.

R712.A1

Also called AMA Doctor Finder; earlier title was AMA Physician Select: On-Line Doctor Finder.

Tool for locating licensed physicians (doctors of medicine [MD] and doctors of osteopathy [DO]) in the United States and information about them. Can be searched by physician name or medical specialty. Listings include address, medical school and year of graduation, residency training, primary practice, specialty, and indication of AMA membership. AMA member listings generally include more information.

Other sites to find doctors include, for example, a search engine created by the Administrators In Medicine (AIM) National Organization for State Medical and Osteopathic Board Executive Directors, entitled Docfinder Searches (http://www.docboard.org/) and links identified through Healthfinder.gov (706).

210 **Encyclopedia of medical organizations and agencies: A subject guide to organizations, foundations, federal and state government agencies, research centers, and medical and allied health schools.** Donna Batten. Detroit: Gale Research Co., 1983–. ISSN: 0743-4510.

362.102573

R712.A1E53

1st ed., 1983; 15th ed., 2005. Subtitle varies. Description based on 16th ed., 2006.

Arranged by medical subjects, in 69 chapters. Major divisions include national and international associations, state and federal agencies, research centers, and computer-based information and database services. Entries provide contact and descriptive information, such as the organization's name, address, website, telephone number, key officials, founding year, number of members, number of employees, and publications. Includes websites and e-mail addresses. Name, keyword, and subject indexes. Derived from *Encyclopedia of associations* (Detroit: Gale Research, 1987).

211   Find a library (MedlinePlus). National Library of Medicine (U.S.). 200?–. Bethesda, Md.: National Library of Medicine. http://www.nlm.nih.gov/medlineplus/libraries.html.

Part of Directories (MedlinePlus) (463).

Clickable map of the United States and Canada for locating health sciences/medical libraries. Medical/Health Sciences Libraries on the Web (196) provides further information for finding medical libraries internationally.

212   FREIDA online. American Medical Association, Accreditation Council for Graduate Medical Education (U.S.). 1997–. Chicago: American Medical Association. http://www.ama-assn.org/ama/pub/category/2997.html.

FREIDA Online®: Fellowship and Residency Electronic Interactive Database. Online version of the *Graduate medical education directory* (213).

Online database containing graduate medical education programs accredited by the Accreditation Council for Graduate Medical Education, as well as combined specialty programs. Allows a search of programs and a comparison of programs regarding length of training, program size, number of faculty, etc. Provides graduates' career plan statistics and links to related resources.

213   Graduate medical education directory. American Medical Association, Accreditation Council for Graduate Medical Education (U.S.). Chicago: American Medical Association, 1993–. ISSN: 1079-0519.

610   R840.D56

Title varies: 1948–51, *Approved internships and residencies in the United States*; 1952–73/74, *Directory of approved internships and residencies*; 1974–75, *Directory of approved residencies*; 1975/76–77/78, *Directory of accredited residencies*; 1978/79–86/87, *Directory of residency programs accredited by the Liaison Committee on Graduate Medical Education*; 1987/88–92/93, *Directory of graduate medical education programs*. Also known as "The green book." Description based on 91st ed., 2006–07. "Including programs accredited by the Accreditation Council for Graduate Medical Education."—*Cover.* The Web-based version has title: FREIDA Online (Fellowship and Residency Electronic Interactive Database Access) (212), made available by the American Medical Association. Provides essential information on residency programs. Contains information on the Electronic Residency Application Service (ERAS provided by the AAMC: American Association of Medical Colleges), National Resident Matching Program (http://www.nrmp.org/), and the Educational Commission for Foreign Medical Graduates (http://www.ecfmg.org/). Has sections for: (1) Graduate medical education information; (2) Specialty/subspecialty information and data; (3) Accredited graduate medical education programs; (4) New and withdrawn programs; (5) Graduate medical education teaching institutions. Appendixes: A, Combined specialty programs; B, Medical Specialty Board certification requirements; C, Medical schools in the United States; D, Graduate medical education glossary; E, Listings of subspecialty and fellowship programs; F, Medical licensure information; G, Accredited residency programs. A companion publication, *GMED companion: An insider's guide on selecting a residency program*, also published by the American Medical Association, contains supplemental data on specialty and subspecialty programs and several appendixes listing medical specialty websites, core competencies in genetics, medical licensure information, and a glossary.

214 **Health professions career and education directory.** American
Medical Association. Chicago: American Medical Association,
2000–. ISSN: 1545-2964.

R847.D57; R735.A1H43

Title varies: *Directory of accredited allied medical education programs,* 1969/70; *Directory of approved allied medical education programs,* 1971; *Allied medical education directory,* 1972–76; 7th ed. (1978)– *Allied health education directory*; 24th ed. (1996–97) *Allied health and rehabilitation professions*; 25th–27th ed., 1997/98–1999/2000 *Health professions education directory.*

Updated annually; 28th ed., 2000–.
Description based on 34th ed. (2006/07).

Contains information on educational programs in health care occupations, and data from accrediting agencies, including licensure, certification, and registration for practicing in a particular profession. Educational programs are listed alphabetically by state and by city, with contact information, annual class capacity, program length, tuition cost, etc. Provides details on the history and development of the various health professions.

215 **Health professions education standards.** American Medical Association. Chicago: American Medical Association, 1999. ISBN: 0899709885.

Provides details for educational standards and guidelines for accredited programs of the professions listed in the companion *Health professions career and education directory* (214). Includes mission statements, policies, professional ethics and responsibilities, etc.—*Publ. notes*

Another American Medical Association publication, *Health professions library: Educational programs, standards, and careers,* 2001–02 (publ. 2001 on CD-ROM), provides similar and additional information on 6,100 programs in 52 health professions.

216 **Medical and health information directory.** Anthony Thomas Kruzas. Detroit: Gale Research Co., 1977–. ISSN: 0749-9973.
610.72073   R118.4.U6M43

Ed. varies. Description based on 19th ed., 2007. Ed. by Donna Batten (project ed.).

Subtitle: *A guide to organizations, agencies, institutions, programs, publications, services, and other resources concerned with clinical medicine, basic biomedical sciences and the technological and socioeconomic aspects of health care.*

Contents: v. 1, Organizations, agencies, and institutions; v. 2, Publications, libraries, and other information resources; v. 3, Health services; Alphabetical name and keyword index (with all resources included in this directory as well as former or alternate names of resources).

Entries include name, address, including e-mail and website information, if available, membership, the year when a particular organization was founded, purpose, meeting, and publications.

217 **Medical school admission requirements, U.S.A. and Canada.** Association of American Medical Colleges. Evanston, Ill.: Association of American Medical Colleges, 1964–. ISSN: 0738-6060.

R745.A8

MEDICINE

1st–14th ed., 1947–63: *Admission requirements of American medical colleges.* Title varies.

2006–07 ed. has title: *Medical school admission requirements (MSAR™).* Contents of 2006–07 ed.: ch. 1, Medicine as a career; ch. 2, The process of medical education; ch. 3, Undergraduate premedical preparation; ch. 4, The application process; ch. 5, Applicant and accepted applicant data; ch. 6, Increasing diversity in medical school; ch. 7, Selection; ch. 8, Acceptance; ch. 9, Financing a medical education; ch. 10, Information on combined college/MD programs for high school students; ch. 11, Training of physician-scientists: MD-PhD programs; ch. 12, Information about U.S. medical schools; ch. 13, Information about Canadian medical schools.

A website, maintained by the AAMC, "tomorrow's doctors.org" (http://www.aamc.org/students/start.htm), provides related online information for people interested in a medical career and prospective medical students, and various resources for medical students and residents.

The annual *Directory of American medical education* (title varies) (181) lists member institutions, with information on their facilities and administration.

218 The official ABMS directory of board certified medical specialists. American Board of Medical Specialties. New Providence, N.J.: Marquis Who's Who, 1993–. ISSN: 0000-1732.
610.695202573   R712.A1O335

Formed by the merger of *Directory of medical specialists* (16th ed. [1974/75]–25th ed. [1991/92]. Chicago: Marquis Who's Who, 1975–92), assuming its edition numbering, and *ABMS compendium of certified medical specialists*, ed. 1–4 (1987–92/93). Ed. 4 had title: *The official American Board of Medical Specialties (ABMS) directory of board certified medical specialists.* Imprint varies. Currently publ. by Elsevier in cooperation with the American Board of Medical Specialties (ABMS). Description based on the 38th ed., 2006. 4 v.

Lists over 650,000 certified physicians (practicing, retired, and newly certified specialists). Arranged by U.S. Medical Specialty Boards in alphabetical order, then by states, cities, and towns. Coverage of 36 specialties and 90 subspecialties and outline of certification requirements for each specialty. For each physician, lists name, certification(s), type of practice, birth date and place, education, career history, teaching positions, professional memberships, office address and phone number. Personal name index. The specialty in which the person's full biographical sketch is found is printed in bold face. Foreign medical degrees appear in shortened form in the biographical sketches, but are shown in full in the index. Also available on CD-ROM and in online format through subscription at http://www.BoardCertifiedDocs.com.

219 **Peterson's graduate programs in business, education, health, information studies, law and social work.** Peterson's (Firm). ill. Princeton, N.J.: Peterson's, 1997–. ISSN: 1088-9442.

378.15530257   L901.P459

The standard guide to graduate schools, with information on programs offered; degree requirements; number and gender of faculty; number, gender, and ethnicity of students; average student age; percentage of students accepted; entrance requirements; application deadlines; application fee; costs; and financial aid. Also available online.

220 **Research centers directory.** Gale Research Co. Detroit: Gale Research, 1965–. ISSN: 0080-1518.

001   AS25.D5

(Based on 34th ed.) This annual publ. contains listings of more than 14,300 North American laboratories, including full contact information, e-mail, and URLs, when available. Listings also include short descriptive statements about the laboratories. Divided by subject category, the first part contains the descriptive listings, while the second part consists of subject, geographic, personal name, and master indexes. Available as an e-book.

221 **Who's who in medicine and healthcare.** New Providence, N.J.: Marquis Who's Who, c1996–. ISSN: 0000-1708.

R153.W43

Description based on 6th ed. (2006–07). Compilation of biographical information on medical professionals, including administrators, educators, researchers, clinicians, and other medical and healthcare personnel. Listings include full name, occupation, date/place of birth, family background, education summary, writings, and association memberships and awards. Includes a section on "Ten who made a difference." Also available online on Who's Who on the Web (http://www.marquiswhoswho.com).

222   **www.health.gov.** Office of Disease Prevention and Health
      Promotion. Washington: U.S. Department of Health and Human
      Services. http://www.health.gov/.

Coordinated by the Office of Disease Prevention and Health Promotion,
Office of Public Health Service, U.S. Dept. of Health and Human Services
(HHS).

"Portal to the Web sites of a number of multi-agency health initiatives and activities of the U.S. Department of Health and Human Services (HHS) and other Federal departments and agencies."—*Main page.*
Provides links to general health information (e.g., Healthfinder [706],
National Health Information Center [http://www.health.gov/nhic/], MedlinePlus [463], and others), special initiatives (e.g., Healthy People 2010
[530], Dietary Guidelines for Americans 2005 [Washington: U.S. Dept.of
Health and Human Services; U.S. Dept. of Agriculture, 2005], and others),
health news, the major federal agencies (U.S. Dept. of Health and Human
Services [894] and its agencies, Office of Public Health and Science [http://
www.osophs.dhhs.gov/ophs/], Office of the Surgeon General [http://www.
surgeongeneral.gov/]), and other key government agencies with "direct
health responsibilities" (e.g., Dept. of Defense [DoD], Environmental Protection Agency [EPA], Dept. of Veterans Affairs [VA], Occupational Safety
and Health Administration [OSHA], and others).

Encyclopedias

223   **Current medical diagnosis and treatment.** Marcus A. Krupp,
      Milton J. Chatton, Lawrence M. Tierney, Stephen J. McPhee, Maxine
      A. Papadakis. ill. New York: McGraw-Hill, 1974–. ISSN: 0092-8682.
616.07505   RC71.A14

Imprint varies: 1962–86 publ. by Lange Medical Publ.; 1987–2003, Appleton and Lange. Supersedes: *Current diagnosis and treatment* (1962–73).
Also known as *CMDT.*

Description based on 45th ed., 2006, ed. by Lawrence M. Tierney, Stephen J. McPhee, and Maxine A. Papadakis. Also available on CD-ROM and
online (via McGraw-Hill's AccessMedicine at http://www.accessmedicine.
com/resourceTOC.aspx?resourceID=1).

Provides concise and up-to-date information on diseases and disorders and widely accepted methods currently available for diagnosis and
treatment. Covers internal medicine, gynecology/obstetrics, dermatology, ophthalmology, otolaryngology, psychiatry, neurology, and imaging
procedures. Includes information on nutrition, medical genetics, and an

annual update on HIV infection and AIDS. Several chapters are available only online: "Diagnostic testing and medical decision making"; "Basic genetics"; "Basic immunology"; and "Information technology in patient care: The Internet, telemedicine, and clinical decision support." An appendix provides therapeutic drug monitoring and laboratory reference ranges. Index. For health professionals and also general readers seeking information on specific diseases and their diagnosis and treatment.

224 Encyclopedia of aging. 4th ed. Richard Schulz. 2 v., 720 p. New York: Springer, 2006. ISBN: 0826148433.

305.2603   HQ1061.E53

From the 1st ed. in 1987, this encyclopedia has provided a thorough presentation of a wide range of items, issues, and facts dealing with aging. Now in its 4th ed., it documents in thoughtful essays many aspects of the lives of older persons, as well as issues and services for the elderly. Made up of some 600 essays, including 200 that are entirely new, with others significantly updated. Multidisciplinary, covering relevant materials from biology, physiology, genetics, medicine, psychology, nursing, social services, sociology, economics, technology, and political science. Extensive listing of further resources, cross-references, and thorough index. Definitive work on gerontology and geriatrics. A must-have reference title for general and research collections. Available as an e-book.

225 Encyclopedia of aging and public health. Sana Loue, Martha Sajatovic. 843 p. New York: Springer, 2007. ISBN: 0387337539.

Interdisciplinary resource for professionals in the fields of public health and geriatrics. Contains entries on health and diseases of adults as they age, and quality and accessibility of care for an aging population. Includes biological, psychosocial, historical, ethical, and legal aspects. Entries include references and resource lists. Available as an e-book as part of Springer eReference.

226 Encyclopedia of aging. David J. Ekerdt. 4 v., ill. New York: Macmillan Reference USA, 2002. ISBN: 0028654722.

305.2603   HQ1061.E534

A basic, interdisciplinary gerontology encyclopedia for general readers. Entries cover a broad range of sociological, psychological, legal, economic, medical, biological, and public policy subjects. Includes source documents, cross-references, bibliographies at the end of each article, and a list of articles grouped by topical areas. Not so comprehensive as to be overwhelming, this is a basic resource which can serve as a good starting point for some researchers, even for middle and high school students, as well as for older levels. Available as an e-book.

227 Encyclopedia of AIDS: A social, political, cultural, and scientific record of the HIV epidemic. Raymond A. Smith. xli, 601 p., ill., ports. Chicago: Fitzroy Dearborn, 1998. ISBN: 1579580076.
362.1969792003   RA644.A25E5276

Covers the time period 1981–96 of the AIDS epidemic, with particular focus on 1991–96. Information is presented in eight major areas: basic science and epidemiology; transmission and prevention; pathology and treatment; impacted populations; policy and law; politics and activism; culture and society; and the global epidemic. Contains 250 entries listed in alphabetical order, with keywords helpful in searching the literature, and references for further reading, and also a resource guide pointing to a variety of additional resources. For undergraduate and graduate students, health professionals, and general readers. Available online via netLibrary.

Another resource in this subject area for general readers is *The encyclopedia of HIV and AIDS* (247).

Current HIV/AIDS literature citations can be accessed via MEDLINE® (425)/PubMed® (AIDS subset) (432).

228 The encyclopedia of Alzheimer's disease. Carol Turkington. xvi, 286 p., ill. New York: Facts On File, 2003. ISBN: 0816048185.
616.831003   RC523.T87

Part of *Facts On File library of health and living series* (678); also available online via Health Reference Center (Facts On File, Inc.) (418). Alphabetically arranged entries discuss Alzheimer's disease, its causes, symptoms, treatments, related conditions, both physical and emotional, sufferers, and more. Several appendixes list resources, associations, legal and financial issues, clinical trials, etc. Includes cross-references, glossary, bibliography, and index. For general readers, but also useful for health professionals. Another encyclopedia on Alzheimer's disease is Elaine A. Moore's *Encyclopedia of Alzheimer's disease: With directories of research, treatment, and care facilities* (Jefferson, N.C.: McFarland, 2003).

229 Encyclopedia of Alzheimer's disease: With directories of research, treatment, and care facilities. Elaine A. Moore, Lisa Moore. xi, 401 p., ill. Jefferson, N.C.: McFarland, 2003. ISBN: 0786414383.
616.831003   RC523.M665

"Comprehensive reference guide intended for anyone involved in the care, treatment, and day-to-day concerns of patients with Alzheimer's disease and related disorders, for anyone who is interested in learning more about the genetic and environmental factors that contribute to both early onset and late onset Alzheimer's disease."—*Pref.* Entries on the different basic science and medical aspects of this disease, research and treatment, caregiving, and many other topics. Contains sections on long-term and day-care treatment centers, arranged by state and city, research facilities by state, listing of resources (books, booklets, pamphlets, caregiver resources, legal assistance, Internet support groups, etc.). For public, academic, and medical libraries. Another encyclopedia on Alzheimer's disease is Carol Turkington's *The encyclopedia of Alzheimer's disease* (228).

230 Encyclopedia of biomaterials and biomedical engineering. Gary E. Wnek, Gary L. Bowlin. 2 v., ill. New York: Marcel Dekker, 2004. ISBN: 0824755626.

610.2803   R857.M3E53

Describes applications "utilizing traditional engineering approaches to analyze and solve problems in life sciences in medicine" (*Pref.*), such as biosensors, implants, orthopedic devices, and tissue engineering. Intended to be multidisciplinary and comprehensive. Contains more than 175 articles averaging about ten pages in length. Articles are signed. Contributors (more than 400, largely from the U.S.) are predominantly from academia, but some are from industry. Arranged alphabetically. Includes brief contents (inside front cover), table of contents, cross-references, article references, and index.

2nd ed. (New York: Informa Healthcare USA, 2008) will be published in 2008 in both print and online formats.

231 The encyclopedia of blindness and vision impairment. 2nd ed. Jill Sardegna. xiii, 333 p., ill. New York: Facts On File, 2002. ISBN: 0816042802.

362.4103   RE91.S27

1st ed., 1991.

Treats all aspects of blindness, including health issues, education, legal questions, and organizations. This updated ed. contains over 500 entries, with more than 100 updated entries and revised appendixes that reflect new developments and information (cf. *Pref.* to the 2nd ed.). Includes both brief definitions and main articles (1–2 pages in length), some of which include a short list of references. Twelve appendixes list updated information, including websites for relevant companies, organizations, schools, federal agencies, publications, and services related to blindness and vision impairment. Bibliography and index. Also available online via netLibrary.

232 **Encyclopedia of cancer.** 2nd ed. Joseph R. Bertino. 4 v., ill. (some color). San Diego, Calif.: Academic Press, 2002. ISBN: 0122275551.
616.994003 RC262.E558
1st ed., 1996.

Vol. 1, A–Cm; v. 2, Co–K; v. 3, L–Q; v. 4, R–Z, Index.

This enl. ed. covers a broad range of cancer-related topics from both basic science and clinical science. Includes recent advances in the etiology, prevention, and the various imaging modalities and treatments currently available. Extensive cross-referencing.

An online version of the Encyclopedia of Cancer is available via Elsevier ScienceDirect at http://www.sciencedirect.com/science/referenceworks/ 0122275551

233 **Encyclopedia of cancer and society.** Graham A. Colditz. 3 v., ill. (some color). Thousand Oaks, Calif.: Sage, 2007. ISBN: 9781412949.
616.994003 RC254.5.E48

Addresses the issues surrounding cancer and its effects on society. Describes the different types of cancer; possible causes; suspected carcinogens; cancer treatments, including alternative treatments and diets; and controversies in treatment and research. Contains information on the relationship between race and ethnicity and cancer risk, socioeconomic factors, cancer researchers, cancer associations, hospitals and treatment centers, health and medical policy issues, cancer incidence rates for other countries, and many other related topics. Includes a chronology of cancer from 3000 BCE to the present as well as an "Atlas of cancer" (p. A1–A16). Intended for students, practitioners, and researchers.

234 **The encyclopedia of complementary and alternative medicine.** Tova Navarra, Adam Perlman. xxiii, 276 p., ill. New York: Facts On File, 2004. ISBN: 0816049971.
615.503 R733.N38

Provides information concerning medicines and treatments that may supplement Western medical practices. Approx. 400 entries and appendixes, with lists of organizations, herbs, and a historic timeline of complementary and alternative therapies. Glossary, bibliography, and index.

Pt. of *Facts On File library of health and living series* (678); also available online via Health Reference Center (Facts On File, Inc.) (689) and netLibrary.

235 Encyclopedia of complementary health practice. Carolyn Chambers Clark, Rena J. Gordon, Barbara Harris. xxi, 638 p., ill. New York: Springer, 1999. ISBN: 0826112390.

615.503   R733.E525

"Comprehensive, authoritative, and concise information in the application of complementary health practices that supplement traditional medical procedure as a vehicle for communication across traditional and complementary disciplines."—*Pref.* Divided into four parts: pt. I, Contemporary issues in complementary health practices; pt. II, Conditions; pt. III, Influential substances; pt. IV, Practices and treatments. Cross-references, contributor directory, resource directory, and extensive references. Subject index and contributor index.

236 Encyclopedia of disability. Gary L. Albrecht. 5 v., ill. Thousand Oaks, Calif.: Sage Publications, 2006. ISBN: 0761925651.

362.403   HV1568.E528

"Conceived as an effort to bring current knowledge of and experience with disability across a wide variety of places, conditions, and cultures to both the general reader and the specialist."—*Introd.* In the first four volumes of this landmark new reference work, more than 500 scholars have contributed some 1,000 entries, which span history far back into antiquity up to the present time, cover cultures and peoples from all over the world, and delve into topics both expected and unexpected, with clarity, insight, and extensive documentation. Entries range from one paragraph to ten pages, and conclude with a bibliography of both print and electronic resources. The fifth and final volume includes a wealth of primary documents drawn from religious texts, including the Bible, literature and poetry, medicine, diaries, and legislation, all divided into three time periods: the ancient world; historical time from 1500 to 1800; and the modern era from 1945 to the present. Documents are annotated and lavishly illustrated. A superb resource at both basic and advanced levels. Available as an e-book.

237 Encyclopedia of drugs, alcohol and addictive behavior. 2nd ed. Rosalyn Carson-DeWitt. 4 v. (lx, 1863 p.), ill. New York: Macmillan Reference USA, 2001. ISBN: 0028655419.

362.2903   HV5804.E53

This 2nd ed. of the 1995 landmark encyclopedia on alcoholism and drug abuse updates information found there, and also has added entries on addictive behaviors such as eating disorders and compulsive gambling. Definitive and comprehensive, with signed entries usually from two to four pages in length, with bibliographies. Multidisciplinary perspective includes behavioral and pharmacological aspects, as well as legal issues. Discusses drug abuse and the economics of production, trade, and sales in various countries. In addition, there are extensive listings of organizations that deal with various aspects of alcoholism, drug abuse, and addictive behaviors. The sweeping coverage and certain authority of the 1st ed. have been preserved and enhanced. Available as an e-book.

238   **Encyclopedia of endocrine diseases.** Luciano Martini. 4 v. (xxxiv, 2400 p.), ill. Amsterdam, [The Netherlands]; Boston: Elsevier Academic Press, 2004. ISBN: 0124755704.

616.4003   RC649.E476

Contents: v. 1. A–D; v. 2. E–Im; v. 3. In–Pl; v. 4. Po–Z, Index.

"Intended to provide a comprehensive reference work on the extensive spectrum of diseases and disorders that can occur within the endocrine system."—*Pref.* Approx. 500 topics. Each entry begins with a defining paragraph and has cross-references listed at the end of each article. Further readings and subject index. Written to be accessible to both the health professional and general reader.

Also available online via Elsevier Science Direct http://www.info. sciencedirect.com/content/books/ref_works/

239   **Encyclopedia of folk medicine: Old world and new world traditions.** Gabrielle Hatfield. xx, 392 p, ill. Santa Barbara, Calif.: ABC-CLIO, 2004. ISBN: 1576078744.

615.8803   R733.H376

Collection of folk medicine and remedies derived from animals, plants, and minerals; themes and contributions from many cultures and disciplines with examples from Britain, Ireland, and North America. Each entry includes a bibliography of selected books and journal articles. Cross-references to related subjects. Index. Available online via netLibrary.

240   **Encyclopedia of gastroenterology.** Leonard R. Johnson. 3 v., ill. (some color). Amsterdam, [The Netherlands]; Boston: Academic Press, 2004. ISBN: 0123868602.

616.33003   RC802.E513

Contents: v. 1, A–E; v. 2, F–N; v. 3, O–Z.

Articles covering various aspects of gastroenterology and hepatology in both the basic sciences and the clinical areas. Articles have been classified into 25 different subject areas. Entries on specific diseases and their treatment, including nutritional aspects and specific anatomical sites (e.g., esophagus, stomach, and liver). 477 entries. Each entry begins with a glossary of cross-referenced terms and an abstract and has a list of references for further reading. Subject index. Clinical and academic audiences. Available online from publisher at http://www.sciencedirect.com/science/referenceworks/0123868602/

241   The encyclopedia of genetic disorders and birth defects. 2nd ed. James Wynbrandt, Mark D. Ludman. 474 p. New York: Facts On File, 2000. ISBN: 0816039895.

616.04203   RB155.5

1st ed., 1991; 2nd ed., 2000 (description based on 2nd ed.); 3rd ed. due Oct. 2007.

Presents some 1,000 articles written for both health-care professionals and general readers. Entries for disorders, selected on the basis of incidence and historical and clinical importance, discuss prognosis, prevalence, mode of inheritance, and the availability of both carrier screening and prenatal diagnosis; many include addresses of private organizations which can provide further information. Also included are brief discussions of subjects and terminology related to genetic disorders and congenital anomalies. If known, the biochemical and molecular basis of a disease is given. The introduction provides a brief history of human genetics. Numerous cross-references. Appendixes provide statistics and tables on congenital malformations and infant mortality, directory information for private and government organizations, and selected Web resources. Bibliography; subject and name index.

Part of *Facts On File library of health and living series* (678). Also available online via Health Reference Center (Facts On File, Inc.) (689).

242   Encyclopedia of genetics. Sydney Brenner, Jeffrey H. Miller, William Broughton. 4 v. (lxx, 2257 p.), ill. San Diego, Calif.: Academic Press, 2002. ISBN: 0122270800.

576.503   QH427.E532

More than 700 expert authors contributed articles (arranged alphabetically) that range from glossary items, definitions, and short articles to full articles of five pages or longer (many with further reading lists). Many entries are accessible to nonspecialists, while others are written for expert researchers. Cross-references and liberal inclusion of figures and tables enhance the text. A thorough table of contents provides an overview of the set's coverage, while a more detailed index is also available. Appropriate for academic and large public libraries, this title has an online edition available for an added fee.

243 **Encyclopedia of genetics, genomics, proteomics, and bioinformatics.** Lynn B. Jorde. 8 v. Hoboken, N.J.: John Wiley & Sons, 2005. ISBN: 9780470849743.

599.935   QH431.E62

Each of the four two-volume pairs of this work is devoted to one of the main topics in the title; the review articles are categorized as introductory, specialist, or basic techniques and approaches. A sampling of the many broad topics includes gene mapping, complex traits and diseases, genetic medicine and clinical genetics, structuring and integrating data, and modern programming paradigms in biology. Studies in human and mouse genomes predominate, although other model eukaryotes and some pathogenic bacteria are also presented thoroughly. An online edition is available from the publisher for an additional fee.

244 **Encyclopedia of gerontology.** 2nd ed. James E. Birren. 2 v. Oxford, U.K.; San Diego, Calif.: Academic Press/Elsevier, 2007. ISBN: 0123705304.

RC952.5.E58

1st ed., 1996.

Alphabetical arrangement of 181 articles on all aspects of aging, the aged, old age, with topics such as theories of aging, biological, behavioral, social, and environmental influences on aging, etc. Written in a standard format, each chapter includes a brief table of contents, a glossary of words with definitions as used in the chapter, and brief bibliography. Cross-references; subject index. Intended for students and professionals.

Other well-regarded, but less recent or comprehensive gerontology encyclopedias are Ekerdt's 2002 *Encyclopedia of aging,* or Schulz's 2006 *Encyclopedia of aging* (4th ed., 2006).

245 **Encyclopedia of health and aging.** Kyriakos S. Markides. 650 p. Thousand Oaks, Calif.: Sage Publications, 2007. ISBN: 9781412909495.

613.043803   RA777.6.E534

Resource on health and aging in the United States and abroad. "Reader's Guide" lists entries by key themes and topics, with entries contributed from different disciplines (e.g., biology, epidemiology, health psychology, public policy, sociology, and others) related to health and aging: aging and the brain; diseases and medical conditions; drug-related issues; function and syndromes; mental health and psychology; nutritional issues; physical status; prevention and health behaviors; sociodemographic and cultural issues; studies of aging and systems of care. Also addresses economic issues and provides recent research results and facts on health and aging. Includes further readings, bibliographical references, a list of online resources, and index. Appropriate for academic, various types of health sciences libraries, and public libraries.

246   Encyclopedia of health and behavior. Norman B. Anderson. 2 v. Thousand Oaks, Calif.: Sage, 2004. ISBN: 0761923608.

610.3   R726.5.E53

Contents: v. 1, A–G; v. 2, H–W.

Health and behavior as an area of study can be defined as an interdisciplinary field of health science, health care, and public health that focuses on the interaction of behavioral, psychological, emotional, social, cultural, and biological factors with physical health outcomes. Approx. 200 entries such as stress and health, pain management, social support, health, smoking, health promotion and disease prevention, and HIV/AIDS. Includes policy and organizational issues, including health care costs. Cross-references. Appendix with online resources and an annotated listing of organizations. Author and subject indexes. For scholars, health professionals, and also general readers. Available online through http://www.gale.com.

247   The encyclopedia of HIV and AIDS. 2nd ed. Sarah Watstein, Stephen E. Stratton. xii, 660 p. New York: Facts On File, 2003. ISBN: 0816048088.

616.9792003   RC606.6.W385

1st ed. (1998) had title: *The AIDS dictionary*.

Rev. entries from the previous ed. and many new entries covering the medical conditions and drugs associated with HIV/AIDS, its science aspects, and vaccine development. Also includes cultural and social sciences topics. Appendixes with a glossary of frequently used abbreviations, HIV/AIDS statistics in the U.S. and worldwide by country, and other selected resources, including a list of World Wide Web sites. Includes bibliography and index. For general readers.

Part of the *Facts On File library of health and living series* (678). Available online via Health Reference Center (Facts On File, Inc.) (689) and also netLibrary.

Another resource in this subject area for general readers is Encyclopedia of AIDS: A social, political, cultural, and scientific record of the HIV epidemic (227).

248 **Encyclopedia of hormones.** Helen L. Henry, Anthony W. Norman. 3 v., ill. Amsterdam, [The Netherlands]; Boston: Academic Press, 2003. ISBN: 0123411033.

571.7403   QP571.E52

This set presents 300 articles, six to eight pages long, that cover topics in plant and animal (vertebrate and invertebrate) hormones, growth factors, interleukins, and hormone receptors and action mechanisms. Aspects of hormones presented include chemical structure and biological synthesis; major physiological systems in which they operate; cellular and subcellular sites of their action; nature of signal transduction mechanisms in hormone action; and biological consequences of an excess or deficiency of specific hormones. Articles begin with a topical outline, abstract, and glossary of key terms. They provide cross-references and list of suggested readings.

Each volume contains the table of contents, foreword, preface, and guide to using the entire set as well as the individual volume's contents. Vol. 3 provides a glossary containing nearly all terms defined in individual articles and an alphabetical index of broad subjects and more specific keywords. Appropriate for academic and research libraries.

Also available online from publisher for an additional fee.

249 **Encyclopedia of infectious diseases: Modern methodologies.** Michel Tibayrenc. 747 p., [24] p. of plates, ill. (some color), maps (some color). Hoboken, N.J.: Wiley-Liss, 2007. ISBN: 0471657328.

362.1969003   RA643.E53

Provides coverage of modern multidisciplinary approaches and applications of newly developed technologies to the study of infectious diseases and their surveillance and control. Emphasis is on medical applications. Articles on AIDS, malaria, SARS and influenza, evolution of pathogens and the relationship between human genetic diversity and the spread of infectious diseases, uses of various technologies, and various specialized topics (e.g., bioterrorism, antibiotics, using a geographic information system to spatially investigate infectious disease, representation of infectious diseases in art, and others). Includes list of web resources. For an academic audience. Available online via NetLibrary.

Carol Turkington and Bonnie Lee Ashby's *Encyclopedia of infectious diseases*, 3rd ed., 2007 (part of the Facts On File library of health and living series [678]), is also a useful resource, intended for health professionals, general readers, and public libraries.

250   **Encyclopedia of life sciences.** 2nd ed. Anne O'Daly. 13 v. (1872 p.), ill. (some color), color maps. Tarrytown, N.Y.: Marshall Cavendish, 2004. ISBN: 0761474420.

570.3   QH302.5.E53

Written to appeal to those lacking strong scientific backgrounds, this revised 2nd ed. is accessible to middle school readers and above. The 13-volume set is rich with illustrations, color photographs and diagrams, and color-coded sidebars. The sidebars expand on content of the articles featuring facts to add depth to some topics, biographical highlights about scientists, tidbits from evolutionary history, alerts to risks arising from pollution, threats to species, and explanations of how topics in life science relate to industry, medicine, and human activity. Many topics that surface frequently in introductory high school and college biology classes receive thorough treatment (e.g., abortion, animal experimentation, and recycling). An index appears in each volume. Vol. 13 has a comprehensive index, indexes by broad subtopics such as botany and medicine, a bibliography, and glossary. Articles provide recommendations for further reading, cross-references among keywords and topics, and explicit connections to interdisciplinary concepts. Valuable for high school, public, and undergraduate library collections.

251   **Encyclopedia of life sciences.** Nature Publishing Group. 20 v., ill. (some color), maps, color plates. London; New York: Nature Publishing Group, 2002. ISBN: 1561592749.

QH302.5.E525

Aimed at academic libraries, this comprehensive encyclopedia has 20 volumes, including an index volume. Topic areas with thorough coverage include molecular biology, physiology, evolution, and ecology; however, treatment of descriptive biology on animals and plants is minimal. Several articles address medical subjects but agriculture and biotechnology are excluded. The 3,300 articles are categorized by the specificity of material presented; designations are elementary, secondary (more specialized), and supplementary, which cover special topics. Detailed index volume includes a list of articles in alphabetical order and classified by topic. Each article begins with a short definition. Cross-references appear at the paragraph level, and each article includes further reading recommendations and bibliographies of material current as of 2002. Most articles have illustrations, though color images are limited to a section of plates in each volume. The online edition is not regularly updated, but the graphics and navigation enhance the content. Six additional volumes published by Wiley in 2007 (v. 21–26), with index in v. 26 to the new material. The publisher will integrate this title with *Encyclopedia of the human genome* (London; New York: Nature Publishing Group, 2003).

252 **Encyclopedia of medical anthropology: Health and illness in the world's cultures.** Carol R. Ember, Melvin Ember. 2 v. (xliv, 1071 p.), ill. New York: Kluwer Academic/Plenum, 2004. ISBN: 0306477548.

362.103   RA418.E354

Medical anthropology as part of cultural anthropology is concerned with the application of anthropological and social science theories and methods to questions about health, illness and healing. Vol. 1, "Health and illness in the world's cultures," contains essays grouped into five sections: general concepts and perspectives; medical systems; political, economic, and social issues; sexuality, reproduction, and the life cycle; and health conditions and diseases. Vol. 2, "Cultures" describe the state of health and illness around the world. Subject index.

253 **Encyclopedia of medical devices and instrumentation.** 2nd ed. John G. Webster. Hoboken, N.J.: Wiley, 2006. ISBN: 0471263583.

610.2803   R856.A3E53

1st ed., 1988, 4 v.

Contents: v. 1, Alloys, shape memory—Brachytherapy, Intravascular; v. 2, Capacitive microsensors for biomedical applications–Drug infusion systems; v. 3, Echocardiography and Doppler echocardiography–Human spine, biomechanics of; v. 4, Hydrocephalus, tools for diagnosis and treatment of–Monoclonal antibodies; v. 5, Nanoparticles–Radiotherapy accessories; v. 6, Radiotherapy, heavy ion–X-rays, production of.

An alphabetically arranged collection of approx. 300 articles by experts, providing a comprehensive treatment of the contributions of engineering, physics, and computer science to the various areas of medicine. Discusses function and use of diagnostic and therapeutic devices. Articles include many illustrations and substantial bibliographies of the primary literature. Cross-references; index.

Available online from Wiley Interscience.

254   Encyclopedia of medical genomics and proteomics. Jürgen Fuchs, Maurizio Podda. 2 v. (xxviii, 1359 p., xxix), ill. New York: Dekker, 2005. ISBN: 0824755022.

616.04203   RB155.E54

Presents an overview of medical applications of current nucleic acid and protein technology for diagnosis, treatment, and management of human diseases, including infections, neoplastic, and genetic diseases. Contains 400 entries, with figures and tables. Topics include, among others, diagnostic microbiology, genetic testing, genomic and proteomic medicine, pharmacogenetics, and tissue and cell typing. Bibliographic references, including website references, and index. For researchers, clinicians, science and medical students, and general readers. Also available in a continually updated online edition.

255   Encyclopedia of molecular cell biology and molecular medicine. 2nd ed. Robert A. Meyers. 16 v., ill. (some color). Weinheim, [Germany]: Wiley-VCH Verlag, 2004–2005. ISBN: 3527305432.

572.803   QH506.E534

1st ed., 1996–97 (6 v.).

Contents: Vol. 1, adipocytes to biological regulation by protein phosphorylation; v. 2, bioorganic chemistry to chamydomonas; v. 3, chromosome organization within the nucleus to e-cell: computer simulation of the cell; v. 4, electric and magnetic field reception to FTIR of biomolecules; v. 5, fungal biotechnology to growth factors; v. 6, growth factors and oncogenes in gastrointestinal cancers to informatics (computational biology); v. 7, innate immunity to mass spectrometry, high speed DNA fragment sizing; v. 8, mass spectrometry-based methods of proteome analysis to mucoviscidosis (cystic fibrosis), molecular cell biology of; v. 9, mutagenesis, malignancy, and genome instability to organic cofactors as coenzymes; v. 10, origins of life, molecular basis of to programmed cell death; v. 11, proteasomes to receptor, transporter, and ion channel diseases; v. 12, recombination and genome rearrangements to serial analysis of gene expression; v. 13, sex hormones (male): analogs and antagonists to synchrotron infrared microspectroscopy; v. 14, syngamy and cell cycle control to triacylglyerol storage and mobilization, regulation of; v. 15, triplet repeat diseases to zebrafish (Danio rerio) genome and genetics; v. 16, index (including acronyms, cross-references, organizations, and some species names), cumulative table of contents, and list of authors.

Considered an interdisciplinary authoritative, peer-reviewed encyclopedic reference work with comprehensive treatment of molecular biology, cell biology, molecular genetics, and molecular medicine topics, with focus on molecular medicine. This edition has 150 new articles and 250 from the first edition. Each article begins with a keyword section, including definitions, and references to the primary and secondary literature. Articles are organized by the following broad, primary topical categories: nucleic acids; structure determination technologies for biomolecules; biochemistry; proteins, peptides, and amino acids; biomolecular interactions; cell biology; molecular cell biology of specific organisms, organs, or systems, and diseases; pharmacology; and biotechnology. Articles vary in length, typically ten to forty pages, most with an extensive list of references. Cross-references help the reader to find relevant entries. Each volume has a section of color plates, a glossary, figures depicting DNA base pairing, and tables listing the amino acids with their chemical structures, abbreviated names, and RNA codes, and the same glossary that appears in all volumes. Aimed at specialists and investigators in other disciplines who are interested in this field, the work is edited by 15 international experts, including ten Nobel Prize winners.

Appropriate for academic and other research library collections. Also available online.

256 Encyclopedia of neuroscience. 3rd ed., rev. and enl. ed. George Adelman, Barry H. Smith. 1 CD-ROM. Amsterdam, The Netherlands: Elsevier BV, 2004. ISBN: 0444514325.

612.803   RC334.E53

Print editions: 1st ed., 1987, supplemented by *Neuroscience year: Supplement. to the Encyclopedia of neuroscience*, v. 1–3, 1989–93; 2nd rev. and enl. ed., 2 v., 1999; 3rd ed., 2004, not issued in print, only CD-ROM. CD-ROM editions: 2nd rev. and enl. ed. (e.g., [1st] CD-ROM ed., 1997); 3rd rev. and enl. ed. (e.g., [2nd] CD-ROM ed.), 2004.

Description based on the 2nd rev. and enl. CD-ROM ed. (1997) and 2nd rev. print ed. (1999).

Contains alphabetically arranged articles covering clinical and basic aspects of neuroscience, its many subfields, new research findings, and many recently developed tools and techniques such as neuroimaging and functional imaging. Both volumes begin with a list of all entries and end with a subject index. Vol. 2 contains two appendixes: I. "Concise biographies of contributors to neuroscience, 300 B.C. to 1960 A.D.," and II. "Society for neuroscience policies on the use of animals and human subjects in neuroscience." The 2nd ed. was originally published in CD-ROM format, with 800 contributions, over 14,000 EMBASE (414) abstracts, and direct access to relevant websites, illustrations, animations, and videos. Readers are encouraged to use the CD-ROM edition with its additional capabilities. It is viewed by the publisher "as the foundation of a revisable and updatable neuroscience database."—*Pref.*

257   Encyclopedia of obesity and eating disorders. 3rd ed. Dana K. Cassell, David H. Gleaves. 362 p. New York: Facts On File, 2006. ISBN: 0816061971.
616.8526003   RC552.E18.C37

1st ed., 1994; 2nd ed., 2000.

Provides concise entries on the causes, symptoms, and treatments, including pharmacotherapy, of obesity and the various eating disorders (e.g., anorexia nervosa, bulimia, etc.). Lists sources of information, websites, audiovisuals, and other resources. Bibliography and index. For general readers and health professionals.

Part of *Facts On File library of health and living* (678) series. Available online via Health Reference Center (689).

258   Encyclopedia of obesity. Kathleen Keller. 2 v., ill., port. Los Angeles: Sage, 2008. ISBN: 9781412952385.
362.196398003   RC628.E53

"Reader's guide" topics: biological or genetic contributions to obesity; children and obesity; dietary interventions to treat obesity; disordered eating and obesity; environmental contributions to obesity; health implications of obesity; medical treatments for obesity; new research frontiers on obesity; obesity and ethnicity/race; obesity and the brain or obesity and behavior; obesity as a public health crisis; psychological influences and outcomes of obesity; societal influences and outcomes of obesity; women and obesity; worldwide prevalence of obesity.

This interdisciplinary resource explores a variety of topics on obesity, health conditions, and issues related to obesity. Written in nontechnical

MEDICINE

111

language and intended as a starting point for different audiences, from scholars to the general public. References at the end of each entry. Glossary and index in both volumes. Available online via Sage eReference.

259 **Encyclopedia of pain.** Robert F. Schmidt, William D. Willis. 3 v., ill. (some color). Berlin; New York: Springer, 2007. ISBN: 9783540439578.

616.047203   RB127.E523

Contents: v. 1, A–G; v. 2, H–O; v. 3, P–Z.

Approx. 3,000 alphabetically arranged entries, with color images and figures as appropriate, on all aspects of pain and pain management. Includes bibliographic references and A–Z listing of entries at the end of each volume. No index. Online ed. (http://www.springer.com) provides keyword searching. For academic health sciences libraries.

260 **Encyclopedia of respiratory medicine.** 4 v. Amsterdam, [The Netherlands]; Boston: Academic Press, 2006. ISBN: 0124383602.

RC732

In 4 v. Covers various aspects of respiratory medicine, including basic science and clinical aspects, and treatment of diseases that affect the respiratory system. Uniform layout of entries. Written for students, researchers, and health professionals. Diagrams and illustrations. Subject index. Available online via Elsevier Reference Works on Science Direct (http://www.info.sciencedirect.com/content/books/ref_works/).

261 **Encyclopedia of stress.** 2nd ed. George Fink. Boston: Elsevier, 2007. ISBN: 0120885034.

1st ed., 2000.

"Comprehensive reference source on stressors, the biological mechanisms involved in the stress response, the effects of activating the stress response mechanisms, and the disorders that may arise as a consequence of acute or chronic stress. Includes a wide range of related topics such as neuroimmune interactions, cytokines, enzymatic disorders, effects on the cardiovascular system, immunity and inflammation, and physical illnesses. It also goes beyond the biological aspects of stress to cover topics such as stress and behavior, psychiatric and psychosomatic disorders, workplace stress, post-traumatic stress, stress-reduction techniques, and current therapies."—*Publ. notes.* For researchers, clinicians, professionals, and students. Available online via Elsevier ScienceDirect.

Ada P. Kahn's *The encyclopedia of stress and stress-related diseases*, part of the *Facts On File library of health and living series* (678) and available online via Health Reference Center (Facts On File, Inc.) (689), provides accessible content on stress and stress-related diseases for all types of readers and libraries.

262   Encyclopedia of the human brain. V. S. Ramachandran. 4 v., xxxv, 903 p., ill. San Diego, Calif.: Academic Press, 2002. ISBN: 0122272102.

612.8303   QP376.E586

More than 220 signed entries authored by leaders in neuroscience and psychology cover topics ranging from anatomy, physiology, neuropsychology, and clinical neurology to neuropharmacology, evolutionary biology, genetics, and behavioral science. Each entry consists of an outline and definition paragraph, glossary, cross-references, and a list of suggested readings. Detailed subject index is the main point of access. Valuable for life sciences collections and academic libraries. Available as an online database.

263   Encyclopedia of the neurological sciences. Michael J. Aminoff, Robert B. Daroff. 4 v., ill. (some color). Amsterdam, [The Netherlands]; Boston: Academic Press, 2003. ISBN: 0122268709.

612.803   RC334.E535

v. 1, A–De; v. 2, Di–L; v. 3, M–Ph; v. 4, Pi–Z, index.

Approx. 1,000 concise entries in 32 subject areas deal with basic science aspects and clinical issues of the neurological sciences, including neurology, neuroanatomy, neurobiology, neurosurgery, psychiatry, and other related areas. Alphabetical sequence by title, with groupings according to specific discipline. Suggestions for further reading at the end of each entry. Includes biographies of famous neuroscientists. Some graphics. Outline of contents in v. 4. Extensive cross-references. Subject index. Written for readers from other disciplines, not necessarily for the specialist. Also available online via ScienceDirect.

264   Encyclopedia of women's health. Sana Loue, Martha Sajatovic, Keith B. Armitage. vii, 710 p. New York: Kluwer Academic/Plenum, 2004. ISBN: 0306480735.

613.04244   RA778.E5825

Covers the history of women's health as well as current topics and issues. Interdisciplinary resource, including topics from medicine, psychology, law, and other areas and perspectives. Also includes alternative and complementary health topics. Suggested readings. Written for both general readers and health professionals. Available online via Springer eReference.

265   **The encyclopedia of women's health.** 5th ed. Christine Ammer.
xii, 434 p., ill. New York: Facts On File, 2005. ISBN: 0816057907.
613.0424403   RA778.A494

1st ed. (1983) has title *A to Z of women's health*; [2nd] ed. (1989) through 4th ed. (2000) have title *The new A to Z of women's health*. Title for 5th ed. varies; issued both as *The new A to Z of women's health: A concise encyclopedia* and *The encyclopedia of women's health*. Pt. of *Facts On File library of health and living series* (New York: Facts On File, 1999–).

   Entries cover a broad range of women's health issues and changing health needs during the different stages of their lives. Also gives attention to social and emotional issues. Appendix, topically arranged, provides contact information for associations and organizations. Alphabetical arrangement, cross-references, and index.

266   **Encyclopedia of women's health issues.** Kathlyn Gay. xvii, 300 p.,
ill. Westport, Conn.: Oryx Press, 2002. ISBN: 157356303X.
613.0424403   RA778.G39

Goes beyond the description of the various health problems and diseases that women experience and also includes social, political, legal, economic, and ethical aspects of women's health. Treats contemporary issues and also provides a historical perspective when appropriate. Can serve as a starting point for research on gender issues in health care policy and politics. Alphabetical arrangement, bibliography, and a selection of websites. Index. For an academic audience and also general readers.

267   **Encyclopedic reference of cancer.** Manfred Schwab. xxiii, 992 p.,
ill. Berlin; New York: Springer, 2001. ISBN: 3540665277.
616.994003   RC254.5.S393

Keyword definitions and short essays trying to close the language gap between clinical and basic science. The ultimate goal to apply the nomenclature of the Human Genome Organisation (HUGO) has, however, not been fully realized (cf. *Pref.*). Includes information on syndromes, genes, molecules, and methods. Cross-references. Also available as part of Springer eReference works.

268 **Encyclopedic reference of immunotoxicology.** Hans-Werner Vohr. xxi, 730 p., ill. (some color). Berlin; New York: Springer, 2005. ISBN: 3540441727.

616.07903   QR180.4.E55

"Immunotoxicology focuses on the undesirable effects of chemicals on the immune system. The exposure of humans to such agents may be intentional (drugs) or unintentional (environment). The side effects may lead to over-activation of the immune system, or equally to immunosuppression. The end points of dysregulation therefore also varies: allergies, cancer, autoimmunity, poor resistance to infection."—*Pref.* Intended for scientists and advanced students. Also available online.

269 **French's index of differential diagnosis: An A–Z.** 14th ed. Herbert French, Mark T. Kinirons, Harold Ellis. xiv, 831 p. ill. (some color). London; New York: Hodder Arnold, 2005. ISBN: 0340810475.

616.07503   RC71.5.F74

1st ed., 1912: *An index of differential diagnosis of main symptoms*; 13th ed., 1996.

Based on symptoms patients might present to their physicians, offers a description of the different diagnoses, supported in many cases by illustrations, lists, and tables. Diagnoses are described in order of importance, with emphasis on the more common diagnoses. Intended to provide decision support for clinicians.

270 **The Gale encyclopedia of alternative medicine.** 2nd ed. Jacqueline L. Longe. 4 v. (xxii, 2411 p.), ill. (some color). Detroit: Thomson/ Gale, 2005. ISBN: 0787674249.

615.503   R733.G34

1st ed., 2001.

Contents: v. 1, A–C; v. 2, D–K; v. 3, L–R; v. 4, S–Z.

Presents information and covers all aspects of alternative and complementary practices, therapies, and remedies, and their effect on various diseases and disorders. Alphabetically arranged entries, side bar glossary of key terms, websites, suggestions for further readings, list of selected organizations, etc. Each volume contains a list of all entries in the set. General index. Available online in the Gale Virtual Reference Library (Farmington Hills, Mich.: Gale Cengage Learning, 2002–).

271   The Gale encyclopedia of cancer: A guide to cancer and its
       treatments. 2nd ed. Jacqueline L. Longe. 2 v. (xxxvii, 1419 p.),
       color ill. Detroit: Thomson/Gale, 2005. ISBN: 1414403623.
616.994003   RC254.5.G353
1st ed., 2002.
       Contents: v. 1, A–K; v. 2, L–Z.
       Survey of 120 cancers. Following a standardized format, entries on a
variety of cancers, treatments, diagnostic procedures, cancer drugs and
their side effects, also on cancer biology, carcinogenesis, and cancer genetics. Entries for cancer types include definition, description, demographics, causes and symptoms, diagnosis, clinical staging, treatments and
treatment team, prognosis, coping with cancer treatment, clinical trials,
prevention, special concerns, and resources. For cancer drugs: definition,
purpose, description, recommended dosage, precautions, side effects,
and drug interactions are included, also traditional and alternative treatments and information on clinical trials. A resources section provides
additional information. Contact information for organizations and support groups in an appendix at the back of v. 2. Alphabetical arrangement,
cross-references, color images for many malignancies, and anatomical
illustrations. List of contents; general index. The online version is part of
Gale Virtual Reference Library (Farmington Hills, Mich.: Gale Cengage
Learning, 2002–).

272   **The Gale encyclopedia of genetic disorders.** 2nd ed. Brigham
       Narins. 2 v., color ill. Detroit: Thomson/Gale, 2005. ISBN:
       1414403658.
616.04203   RB155.5.G35
1st ed., 2002.
       Contents: v. 1, A–L; v. 2, M–Z.
       Signed entries with detailed information for genetic diseases, dis-
orders, and conditions. A standardized format provides for each entry
as appropriate: definitions, description, genetic profile, demographics,
signs and symptoms, diagnosis, treatment and management, prognosis,
resources, and key terms. Available as an e-book.

273   **The Gale encyclopedia of medicine.** 3rd ed. Jacqueline L.
       Longe, Gale Group. Detroit: Thomson; Gale Group, 2005. ISBN:
       1414403682.
616.003   RC41.G35

1st ed., 1999; 2nd ed., 2002.

"Medical information on common medical disorders, conditions, tests, and treatment fills a gap between basic consumer health resources and highly professional materials. Articles follow a standardized format that provides information at a glance. Designed with ready reference in mind— alphabetical arrangement, definitions of key terms, contact information for organizations and support groups, resources section for additional information, illustrations, and general index."—*Introd.* Encyclopedias in other medical subjects published by Gale also following this type of arrangement and a standardized format include *The Gale encyclopedia of alternative medicine* (2nd ed., 2005) (270), *The Gale encyclopedia of cancer: A guide to cancer and its treatments* (2nd., 2005) (271), *The Gale encyclopedia of genetic disorders* (2nd ed., 2005) (272), *The Gale encyclopedia of mental disorders* (Detroit: Thomson Gale, 2008) (2003), and *The Gale encyclopedia of nursing and allied health* (2nd ed., 2007) (1049). Available as an e-book.

274 Macmillan encyclopedia of death and dying. Robert Kastenbaum. 2 v. (xxi, 1017 p.). New York: Macmillan Reference USA, 2003. ISBN: 002865689X.

306.9   HQ1073.M33

Scholarly multidisciplinary resource on all aspects of death and dying and also related contemporary psychosocial issues, such as bereavement, grief and mourning across cultures, etc. Alphabetically arranged signed entries. Useful resource for health professionals and also for general readers. Suitable for academic library collections and large public libraries. An appendix provides information on organizations. Illustrations, bibliographies and index. Also available as an e-book through netLibrary and Gale Virtual Reference Library (Farmington Hills, Mich.: Gale Cengage Learning, 2002–).

Similar recent titles include *Encyclopedia of death and dying* (London; New York: Routledge, 2002), ed. by Glennys Howarth and Oliver Leaman, publ. 2002, and *Handbook of death and dying* (Thousand Oaks, Calif.: Sage, 2003), ed. by Clifton D. Bryant, publ. 2003.

275 Medical encyclopedia (MedlinePlus). National Library of Medicine (U.S.). 1999–. [Atlanta]; Bethesda, Md.: A.D.A.M.; National Library of Medicine. http://www.nlm.nih.gov/ medlineplus/encyclopedia.html.

RC81.A2

Title varies: A.D.A.M. Medical Encyclopedia; MedlinePlus, Medical Encyclopedia.

Articles about diseases and conditions, injuries, nutrition, poisons, surgeries, symptoms, tests, and other special topics. Contains medical illustrations and images. Accessible via "Medical Encyclopedia" tab from MedlinePlus (463).

276   **Medicine, literature and eponyms: An encyclopedia of medical eponyms derived from literary characters.** Alvin E. Rodin, Jack D. Key. xxii, 345 p., ill. Malabar, Fla.: R.E. Krieger, 1989. ISBN: 0894642774.

610.321   R121.R62

Defines more than 350 medical eponyms derived from literary characters; among the sources are mythology, fables, and cartoons. Each entry includes a synopsis of the medical condition, a description of the associated literary character and of how specific characteristics correspond to symptoms of the condition, further literary references to the medical state, and other related material. A list of references to both the literary character and the medical condition appear with each entry. Subject index.

277   **The MIT encyclopedia of communication disorders.** Raymond D. Kent, Massachusetts Institute of Technology. vii, 618 p., ill. Cambridge, Mass.: MIT Press, 2004. ISBN: 0262112787.

616.855003   RC423.M56

Areas covered include audiology, speech-language pathology, communication sciences and various disorders (such as hearing, language, speech), and voice abnormalities. With basic science entries (normal anatomy and physiology, physics, psychology, psychophysics, linguistics), disorders entries (specific disorders, methods for the identification and assessment of disorders), and clinical management entries (behavioral, pharmacological, surgical, prosthetic) (cf. *Introd.*). Separate chapters for adults and children for many topics. References, further reading, and bibliographies. For health professionals, researchers, students, and educated laypersons. Online access via MIT CogNet (Cambridge, Mass.: MIT Press, 2000?–) and netLibrary.

278   **Nature encyclopedia of the human genome.** David N. Cooper, Nature Publishing Group. 5 v., ill. (some color). London; New York: Nature Publishing Group, 2003. ISBN: 0333803868.

611.0181603   QH447.N38

Designed not only for researchers but also for teachers and students, this broad-ranging treatment provides an important overview of a field that is highly technical and subject to rapid change. A topical outline of all the peer-reviewed articles in the five volumes serves as a beefed-up table of contents. Some of the areas covered include structural and functional genomics; proteomics; bioinformatics; ethical, legal, and social issues; mathematical and population genetics; and history. Articles are labeled as introductory, intermediate, and advanced; each begins with a box showing article contents. All provide references, most have cross-references, and some offer suggested further reading and links to websites. Blind entries help the reader find articles (e.g., chimpanzee nucleotide diversity redirects to human and chimpanzee nucleotide diversity). The table of contents and indexing are thorough; the glossary in the final volume is useful. Excellent illustrations and sections of color plates enhance the text. Soon to be integrated with *Encyclopedia of life sciences* (250). Important for academic and medical library collections.

279 **The Oxford companion to the body.** Colin Blakemore, Sheila Jennett, Alan Cuthbert. xii, 753 p., ill. (some color). Oxford; New York: Oxford University Press, 2001. ISBN: 019852403X.
612.003   QM7.O96

Interdisciplinary treatment of the human body in a single-volume encyclopedia with more than 350 articles by experts recruited by the Physiological Society of the United Kingdom, representing research in medicine, social sciences, and the humanities. Entertaining and informative, articles explore human anatomy from artistic, cultural, historical, and religious points of view, emphasizing normal function of the human body with some entries about disease and treatment important in social or medical history. "From conception to resurrection, kiss to orgasm, codpieces to pubic wigs, blood clotting to blood letting, from fasting to farting. All human life is here!"— *Pref.* Somewhat under-illustrated, though color plates of human anatomy follow the index. Appropriate for public and academic libraries. Also available as an e-book. Electronic version via Oxford Reference Online (Oxford; New York: Oxford University Press, 2002–).

280 **The Oxford illustrated companion to medicine.** 3rd ed. Stephen Lock, John M. Last, George Dunea. xiv, 889 p., ill. Oxford; New York: Oxford University Press, 2001. ISBN: 0192629506.
610/.3   R121.O884

Title varies. 1st ed., 1986 had title: *The Oxford companion to medicine*; 2nd ed., 1994 had title: *The Oxford medical companion.*

Restructures, updates, and revises information originally published in the *Oxford medical companion.*

Not entirely alphabetic arrangement. Entries cover both historical and contemporary topics in the medical, nursing, and allied health sciences. Four indexes: Topics, grouped under major headings (p. 879–81); alphabetic "List of Individual Conditions and Diseases" (p. 883–4); "People Index"— inclusion in this list of deceased persons implies a separate biography (page no. in bold face) or a substantial mention in the text. Includes bibliographical references. Large number of illustrations and color plates. General index of alphabetically arr. broader topics. For general readers and professionals. Electronic version via Oxford Reference Online (Oxford; New York: Oxford University Press, 2002–) has title: *The Oxford companion to medicine.*

281   Wiley encyclopedia of biomedical engineering. Metin Akay.
Hoboken, N.J.: Wiley, 2006. ISBN: 047124967X.
610.2803   R856.A3.W55

Approx. 350 alphabetically arranged signed articles in 6 v., with tables, figures, and illustrations. Covers areas such as biochemical engineering, biomedical devices and instrumentation, rehabilitation and orthopedic engineering, and biomedical education (including Internet learning and distance education). Also available in electronic format, with some of the color graphics only available in the online ed. A similar earlier title is *Encyclopedia of biomaterials and biomedical engineering.*

282   Wiley encyclopedia of molecular medicine. Haig H. Kazazian.
John Wiley & Sons. 5 v. (xxix, 3699 p.), ill. New York: John Wiley & Sons, 2002. ISBN: 0471374946.
572.803   QH506.W535

Comprehensive resource in molecular medicine, with coverage "ranging from the organ to the cell to the molecular."—*Publ. notes.* Considered an essential resource for geneticists, biochemists, molecular biologists, medical researchers, and clinicians. Available online via Knovel (Norwich, N.Y.: Knovel, 2003–).

Guides

283   Alternative medicine. Christine A. Larson. xv, 215 p. Westport, Conn.: Greenwood Press, 2007. ISBN: 0313337187.
610   R733.L37

Contents: "The origins of alternative medicine"; "The theories underlying alternative medicine"; "The business of alternative medicine"; "Why consumers seek alternative treatments"; "Do alternative therapies work?"; "Should alternative medicine be regulated by the government?"; "Should managed care provide coverage for alternative therapies?"; "Pharmaceuticals versus alternative therapies"; "Culture and health: Who bears responsibility for health and healthcare?"; "The future of health and healthcare."

Guide to alternative medicine, covering practical and also controversial issues, with recommendations on using safe alternative medicine practices together with Western medicine. Annotated primary source documents, alternative medicine timeline, and glossary. Includes bibliographical references (p. [201]–208) and index. For researchers, clinicians, consumers, and academic and medical libraries. Also available as an e-book.

284 Alternative medicine resource guide. Francine Feuerman, Marsha J. Handel. 335 p. Lanham, Md.: Medical Library Association, 1997. ISBN: 0810832844.

615.5   R733.F48

Provides information on alternative systems of medicine—Ayurvedic, Chinese, and herbal medicine, homeopathy, naturopathy—and various manipulative (e.g., chiropractic and osteopathy) and other therapies, such as biofeedback and sensory therapies. Organized into two main sections: pt. I, a resource guide with reference information on specific services and products, organizations, and companies; pt. II, a selective, evaluative, annotated bibliography of books, journals, and newsletters, limited to English-language print sources published in the U.S. since 1988. Appendix lists book publishers. Index.

285 Current practice in health sciences librarianship. Alison Bunting, Medical Library Association. 8 v., ill. Chicago; New York: Medical Library Association; Forbes Custom Publishing, 1994–2001.

1st ed. (1943)–4th ed. (1982–1988) had title *Handbook of medical library practice*, 3 v.

Rev. ed. in 8 v.

Contents: v. 1 (1994), *Reference and information services in health sciences libraries*, ed. M. Sandra Wood; v. 2 (1995), *Educational services in health sciences libraries*, ed. F. Allegri; v. 3 (1996), *Information access and delivery in health sciences libraries*, ed. Carolyn E. Lipscomb; v. 4 (1997), *Collection development and assessment in health sciences libraries*, ed. Daniel T. Richards and Dottie Eakin; v. 5 (1996), *Acquisitions in health sciences libraries*, ed. David H. Morse; v. 6 (2001), *Bibliographic management of information resources in health sciences libraries*, ed. Laurie L. Thomson; v. 7 (1999), *Health sciences environment and librarianship in health sciences libraries*, ed. Lucretia W. McClure; v. 8 (2001), *Administration and management in health sciences libraries*, ed. Rick B. Forsman.

A guide to library standards, practices, policies, and institutional issues in biomedical libraries, written by library specialists.

286   **Doody's review service.** Doody Enterprises, Inc. 2006–. Chicago: Doody Enterprises, Inc. http://www.doody.com/drs/.

Database of expert reviews of books and software in the health sciences (basic science, clinical medicine, nursing, allied health, and other health-related disciplines), with bibliographic information, a weekly literature update with timely reviews by professionals at major North American academic institutions, and ratings (Doody's Star Rating®) of newly published titles. Integrates the annually updated list of "Doody's Core Titles in the Health Sciences (DCT)" which "distills the perspectives of academic healthcare professionals and health sciences librarians into a core list."— *Publ. website.* DCT, first issued in Dec. 2004, is a useful collection development and management tool that is being used by many librarians in place of the recently discontinued "Brandon/Hill Selected Lists" (1965–2004 compiled by librarians, Al Brandon, Dorothy R. Hill, Henry N. Stickell, and others), publ. periodically in the *Bulletin of the Medical Library Association*, its later title, *Journal of the Medical Library Association*, and *Nursing outlook*. Overview and history of the Brandon/Hill lists can be found at http://library.mssm.edu/brandon-hill/history.shtml, provided by Levy Library, Mount Sinai Medical Center, 2007.

287   **Introduction to reference sources in the health sciences.** 5th ed. Jeffrey T. Huber, Jo Anne Boorkman, Jean C. Blackwell. 386 p. New York: Neal-Schuman, 2008. ISBN: 9781555706364.

016.61072   Z6658.I54; R118.6

1st ed., 1980; 4th ed., 2004.

Contents: pt. 1, "The reference collection" (ch. 1); pt. 2, "Bibliographic sources" (ch. 2–6); pt. 3, "Information sources" (ch. 7–14).

Discusses various types of bibliographic and information sources, both print and electronic, and their use in reference work. Written for library school students, practicing librarians, and health science library users. Each of the chapters covers specialized topics such as building, organizing, and managing a reference collection; bibliographic sources for monographs and periodicals; indexing, abstracting, and digital databases; terminology; medical and health statistics; history sources; and additional relevant areas. Contains figures and tables. Includes bibliographical references and index.

An older edition (Oxford; New York: Oxford University Press, 2003) was previously included in *Guide to reference*.

288   **The Medical Library Association encyclopedic guide to searching and finding health information on the Web.** P. F. Anderson, Nancy J. Allee. 3 v. New York: Neal-Schuman Publ., 2004. ISBN: 1555704948.

025.0661   R859.7.I58M436

Contents: v. 1, Search strategies/quick reference guide; v. 2, Diseases and disorders/mental health and mental disorders; v. 3, Health and wellness/ life stages and reproduction, and cumulative index. A comprehensive guide written by experienced health sciences librarians. Recommends search terms, search strategies, and search engines for checking the Internet for answers to health-related questions. Useful for both health care consumers and librarians involved in teaching health information literacy. Companion website at http://www-personal.umich.edu/~pfa/mlaguide/ indextest.html. Also available on CD-ROM, with search capability and links to over 11,000 websites.

289   **Medical reference works, 1679–1966: A selected bibliography.** John Ballard Blake, Charles Roos, National Library of Medicine (U.S.). viii, 343 p. Chicago: Medical Library Association, 1967.

016.61   Z6658.B63

Supersedes the bibliographies published as part of the Medical Library Association's *Handbook of medical library practice*, 1943 and 1956. Prep. by the staff of the National Library of Medicine.

Lists more than 2,700 titles in classed arrangement within three main sections: Medicine, general; History of medicine; and Special subjects. Titles have been selected for their usefulness in answering questions in biomedical libraries; titles especially useful for smaller medical libraries are marked with an asterisk. "Handbooks and treatises in the basic sciences and clinical medicine have only rarely been included."—*Pref.* Brief annotations.

Three supplements: *Medical reference works, 1679–1966: A selected bibliography.* Supplement (290). Suppl. 1 (more than 300 references with the emphasis on works published 1967–68); suppl. 2–3 add about 750 citations for the periods 1969–72 and 1973–74.

290 **Medical reference works, 1679–1966: A selected bibliography. Supplement.** Mary Virginia Clark, Joy S. Martyniuk, John Ballard, Blake Medical Library Association. v. 1–3. Chicago: Medical Library Association, 1970–1975.

016.61   Z6658.B63 Suppl.; R129

(Medical Library Association publication no. 3). Suppl., 1 comp. by Mary Virgina Clark; suppl. 2–3, comp. by Joy S. Richmond.

The 1st suppl. follows the pattern of the main work (*Medical reference works, 1679–1966: A selected bibliography* [289]) but excludes references on the history of medicine "since material of this sort is listed in the annual *Bibliography of the history of medicine,*"—*Pref.* Includes more than 300 references with the emphasis on works published 1967–68. The 2nd and 3rd suppl. are computer-produced from the National Library of Medicine's *Current catalog*; therefore, these citations are arranged by author and subject. "General historical works, pharmacopoeias, reviews, and popular works have been excluded" (*Pref.*), suppl. 2. A total of about 750 citations are added for the periods 1969–72 and 1973–74. Most references of the suppl. are annotated.

291 **National Library of Medicine guide to finding health information.** National Library of Medicine. 2001–. Bethesda, Md.: National Institutes of Health. http://www.nlm.nih.gov/services/guide.html.

Contents: How Can the National Library of Medicine Help Me with My Research?; Why Should I Go to a Public Library, and What Can I Find There?; What Other Resources Can I Find at a Medical Library, and How Do I Find One That Is Open to Me?; How Can I Get Information From Other Government or Health-Related Organizations?; How Do I Search for Other Medical Information on the Web?; How Do I Evaluate the Information I Find?

Overview and starting points for researchers concerning services provided by the National Library of Medicine, other government agencies, and health-related organizations. Provides links to consumer health information resources and professional health literature resources.

292 **The new Walford guide to reference resources: Volume 1: Science, technology, and medicine.** 9th ed. Ray Lester. xix, 827 p., ill. London: Facet, 2005–. ISBN: 1856044955.

011.02   Z1035.1

"This book is the first volume of a series that succeeds *Walford's guide to reference material* (London: Library Association, 1999–2000), published 1959 and 2000 by Library Association Publishing." The scope and format of this guide is much different from the "old Walford," and thus it would behoove librarians to keep both eds. on the shelf. This version concentrates on websites and on general interest resources, including many that aren't specific to science and technology. Includes current awareness sources and many monographs that aren't traditional reference sources, but rather are popular introductions to topics.

Volume 2: The social sciences (London: Facet, 2008) was published Jan. 2008; and *Volume 3: Arts, humanities, and general reference* is expected in 2009. For more information, see publisher's page at http://www.facetpublishing.co.uk/newwalford/index.shtml.

293 **Science.gov.** U.S. Department of Energy, Office of Scientific and Technical Information. 2002–. Oak Ridge, Tenn.: U.S. Dept. of Energy, Office of Scientific and Technical Information. http://www.science.gov/.

"Science.gov is a gateway to over 50 million pages of authoritative selected science information provided by U.S. government agencies, including research and development results."—*Website.* Provides a single interface for searching major government-sponsored indexes; for example, NTIS (Washington: National Technical Information Service, 1964–), AGRICOLA (1141), PubMed (432), STINET (http://stinet.dtic.mil/), and United States Patents. Also searches science-related websites of federal agencies. One can browse by major discplines and subjects or search one or all areas of Science.gov. A very good portal to government information.

Handbooks

294 **Atlas of cancer.** Maurie Markman. xii, 628 p., ill. (some color). Philadelphia: Lippincott, Williams & Wilkins, 2003. ISBN: 1573401927.

616.994   RC262.A846

Contents: (I) Head and neck; (II) Gynecologic cancer; (III) Lung cancer; (IV) Upper gastrointestinal cancers; (V) Lower gastrointestinal cancers; (VI) Leukemia; (VII) Lymphoma; (VIII) Sarcoma; (IX) Breast cancer; (X) Genitourinary cancers; (XI) Skin cancer; (XII) Neuro-oncology.

"Highlights the major features of current cancer management, both diagnostic and therapeutic, and clearly lays out fundamental facts regarding our understanding of the etiology and pathophysiology of malignant disease."—*Pref.* Each section provides a summary introduction to a particular cancer, with U.S. statistics, epidemiology and etiology, histology, genetics, staging, major risk factors, imaging, surgical management, treatment modalities, prevention, and other information as appropriate to the specific cancer. Each chapter includes a list of references. Index.

295   Bergey's manual of systematic bacteriology. 2nd ed. David R. Boone, Richard W. Castenholz, George M. Garrity. v. 1–2 in 4, ill. New York: Springer, 2001–2005. ISBN: 0387987711.

579.3012   QR81.B46

The most comprehensive work in the field of bacterial taxonomy, this extensive revision of this authoritative manual is ongoing. The 2nd ed. will comprise five volumes when complete. The Bergey's Manual Trust is working with more than 150 international authorities to expand and update content. This new edition will reflect growth in the field; more than 2,200 new species and 390 new genera have been described since the 1st ed. was published in 1984. Advances in molecular sequencing techniques have generated this new information, and elucidation of genes in highly conserved regions of the prokaryotic genome lead to a natural classification reflective of the evolutionary history of bacteria and archaea. The 2nd ed. presents bacterial taxonomy following a phylogenetic organizational scheme. Volumes of the 2nd ed. will be available individually and, eventually, as a complete set.

296   The biomedical engineering handbook. 3rd ed. Joseph D. Bronzino. 3 v., ill. Boca Raton, Fla.: CRC/Taylor and Francis, 2006. ISBN: 0849321247.

610.28   R856.B513

1st ed., 1995; 2nd ed., 2000.

Contents: v. 1, Biomedical engineering fundamentals; v. 2, Medical devices and systems; v. 3, Tissue engineering and artificial organs.

Provides a comprehensive overview of the field of biomedical engineering, with many revisions from the previous edition, reflecting technological changes in recent years. Includes new sections, for example, on biomimetrics (defined as the imitation of biological processes), ethical issues associated with medical technology, and a new chapter on virtual instrumentation. Includes bibliographical references and index.

May be available online, in whole or in part, via http://www.crcnetbase.com/.

297 **Biomedical informatics: Computer applications in health care and biomedicine.** 3rd ed. Edward Hance Shortliffe, James J. Cimino. xxvi, 1037 p., ill. New York: Springer, 2006. ISBN: 9780387289861.

610.28   R858.M397

1st ed., 1990 (Reading, Mass.: Addison-Wesley) had title *Medical informatics: Computer applications in health care*; 2nd ed., 2001, *Medical informatics: Computer applications in health care and biomedicine.*

(Health informatics series.)

"The field of biomedical informatics sits at the crossroads of computer science, decision science, cognitive science, and biomedicine, [and this book] provides the conceptual framework and practical know-how to navigate this integral discipline."—*Cover*

Provides an overview of concepts in biomedical informatics and biomedical information management. Bibliography, glossary, name index, and subject index. Available online via Springer eBooks and netLibrary.

298 **The bioterrorism sourcebook.** Michael R. Grey, Kenneth R. Spaeth. xxxiii, 549 p., ill. New York: McGraw-Hill Medical Publ. Div., 2006. ISBN: 0071440860.

303.625   RC88.9.T47; G746

Contents: section I, Clinical principles and practices (ch. 1–9); section II, Infectious agents (ch. 10–16); section III, Biotoxins and category B and C agents (ch. 17–20); section IV, Chemical weapons (ch. 21–26); section V, Nuclear and radiation syndromes (ch. 27–30).

Clinical and public health guidance preparing for and responding to immediate and long-term bioterrorism-related conditions. Provides concise and essential information on the various aspects and agents of a bioterrorist attack and the expected consequences, with synopses, illustrations, tables, charts, and practical tips. Selected bibliography; index. Available online via McGraw-Hill's AccessMedicine.

The CDC's (1485) "Emergency Preparedness and Response" site, "intended to increase the nation's ability to prepare for and respond to public health emergencies" (http://www.bt.cdc.gov/) provides extensive information resources for bioterrorism, chemical, and radiation emergencies, natural disasters, and other threats.

AHRQ's (Agency for Healthcare Research and Quality) (872) "Public Health Preparedness" (http://www.ahrq.gov/prep/) provides a wide variety of tools, resources, and resource links.

Additional resources in this area include, for example, *Bioterrorism and public health* (2002), available in print and also online via Thomson's eMedguides (http://www.eMedguides.com/bioterrorism), *Bioterrorism preparedness* (2006), also available in print and online, and others.

299 **The cancer handbook.** 2nd ed. Malcolm Alison. 2 v. Chichester, England; Hoboken, N.J.: John Wiley & Sons, 2007. ISBN: 9780470018521.

616.994 RC263.C29168

1st ed., 2002.

Contents: pt. I, The molecular and cellular basis of cancer; pt. II, The causation and prevention of cancer; pt. III, Systematic oncology; pt. IV, Pre-clinical models for human cancer; pt. V, The treatment of cancer.

Overview of scientific and clinical information of all the major areas in cancer research and oncology. Glossary of terms, extensive cross-referencing, references, further readings, black-and-white illustrations and color plates, tables, and figures. Resource for medical and life sciences students, researchers, clinicians, and scientists. Online access via Wiley Interscience (http://www.interscience.wiley.com) is restricted to subscribers.

300 **Catalog of human cancer genes: McKusick's Mendelian inheritance in man for clinical and research oncologists (onco-MIM).** John J. Mulvihill. xxv, 646 p. Baltimore, Md.: Johns Hopkins University Press, 1999. ISBN: 0801847990.

616.994042 RC268.42.M84

Provides a subset of cancer-related (or "neoplasia" in Mendelian inheritance in man [MIM] nomenclature) citations selected from McKusick's *Mendelian inheritance in man: catalog of autosomal dominant, autosomal recessive, and x-linked phenotypes.* Includes entries on phenotypes, disorders and conditions, discussion of genes and proteins, etc. Entries grouped by organ system. Considered a valuable starting point in research, but needs to be supplemented with more recent citations from OMIM: Online Mendelian Inheritance in Man (Bethesda, Md.: National Center for Biotechnology Information, 2000–) and PubMed (432). Of interest to health professionals.

301 **Codes of professional responsibility: Ethics standards in business, health, and law.** 4th ed. Rena A. Gorlin. xvii, 1149 p. Washington: Bureau of National Affairs, 1999. ISBN: 1570181489.

174 BJ1725.C57

Collects some 60 codes of ethics or similar documents ("statements of principles," "ethical guidelines," etc.) of North American organizations within the three domains listed in the subtitle. Construing these domains broadly, it embraces, e.g., professions such as engineering, computing, and journalism under "business," and mental health and social work under "health." Also includes directory of U.S. and worldwide organizations and programs concerned with professional responsibility and an extensive guide to information resources including periodicals, reference works, and websites. Indexes of issues, professions, and organizations. Serving a similar function for the U.K., *Professional codes of conduct in the United Kingdom* (London; New York: Mansell, 1996), 2nd ed., presents an even broader range of codes, numbering around 200 reproduced in full, plus summary descriptions of some 300 more.

An extensive web-based collection, "Codes of Ethics Online," is among the resources offered at the Center for the Study of Ethics in the Profession at IIT website (http://ethics.iit.edu/), which also provides links to other ethics centers and the catalog of CSEP's extensive library—a virtual bibliography of the field of professional ethics.

302   The complete writing guide to NIH behavioral science grants.
Lawrence M. Scheier, William L. Dewey. 506 p. New York: Oxford University Press, 2007. ISBN: 9780195320275.
362.1079   RA11.D6C65

Contents: ch. 1, Peer review at the National Institutes of Health; ch. 2, Drug abuse research collaboration in the 21st century; ch. 3, A brief guide to the essentials of grant writing; ch. 4, Sample size, detectable difference, and power; ch. 5, Exploratory/developmental and small grant award mechanisms; ch. 6, Funding your future: What you need to know to develop a pre- or postdoctoral training application; ch. 7, Unique funding opportunities for underrepresented minorities and international researchers; ch. 8, R01 grants: The investigator-initiated cornerstone of biomedical research; ch. 9, P50 research center grants; ch. 10, P20 and P30 center grants: Developmental mechanisms; ch. 11, The K award: An important part of the NIH funding alphabet soup; ch. 12, T32 grants at the NIH: Tips for success; ch. 13, SBIR funding: A unique opportunity for the entrepreneurial researchers; ch. 14, Federal grants and contracts outside of NIH; ch. 15, The financing and cost accounting of science: Budgets and budget administration; ch. 16, Documenting human subjects protections and procedures; ch. 17, Navigating the maze: Electronic submission;

ch. 18, Revisions and resubmissions; ch. 19, Concluding remarks: The bottom line. Appendix 1: The NIH Web sites; Appendix 2: NIH institutes, centers, and their websites.

Presents important considerations in developing research proposals and funding mechanisms for both junior and established researchers. Provides practical information on how to construct and write successful grants, electronic grant submission, revising research proposals, etc. Useful to researchers, clinicians, and educators in a wide variety of subject areas who are interested in submitting grants to the NIH.

303   Conn's current therapy. Howard F. Conn, Robert E. Rakel. ill.
Philadelphia: W. B. Saunders, 1984–. ISSN: 8755-8823.

615.505   RM101.C87

Title varies: 1949–1983, *Current therapy*. 1949–1983 ed. Howard F. Conn; 1984–. ed. Robert E. Rakel.

Description based on 58th ed., 2006.

Presents authoritative, current advances and methods of therapeutics and diagnostics. Arranged in 19 sections offering broad coverage of diseases (e.g., infectious diseases, diseases of allergy) and disorders of the various organ systems (e.g., respiratory system, cardiovascular system). Each section contains articles by specialists on more specific topics. List of approx. ten references for each chapter. Several appendixes and index. This edition provides a website containing the book and some additional features (e.g., calculators and drug reference). Any content can be downloaded to a handheld device. License and access to the online version are restricted to individuals (cf. *Pref.*). Electronic full-text available via Elsevier's MD Consult (http://home.mdconsult.com/).

304   Encyclopedic reference of traditional Chinese medicine: [A manual from A–Z, symptoms, therapy, and herbal remedies].
Xinrong Yang. 660 p., color ill. Berlin; New York: Springer, 2003.
ISBN: 3540428461.

610.951   R601.D538

Introduction to traditional Chinese medicine with its long history. "Owing to the Traditional Chinese Medicine literatures were written in the classical literary style and the translation into English of most of their terms was not standardized and normalized, the translation of these terms remains to be discussed by specialists and linguists. Many terms of diseases in this book have to use the terms of Western Medicine in Latin. Some terms have to be transliterated into English."—*Pref.* Acupuncture terms from WHO's 1984 publication on "Standard Acupuncture Nomenclature" (1993 ed. of *Standard acupuncture nomenclature: A brief explanation of 361 classical acupuncture point names and their multilingual comparative list* is available at http://whqlibdoc.who.int/wpro/-1993/9290611057.pdf).

Provides 5,000 entries with concise annotations, listing, as appropriate for a particular entry, symptoms, pathogenesis, diseases, therapeutic principle, herbal and other drugs. Alphabetical arrangement. Color ill.

305   The enzyme reference: A comprehensive guidebook to enzyme nomenclature, reactions, and methods. Daniel L. Purich, R. Donald Allison. ix, 929 p., ill. San Diego, Calif.: Academic Press, 2002. ISBN: 0125680414.

572.7   QP601.P87

"The aim of this work is to provide a fuller spectrum of information in a single source on enzyme-catalyzed reactions than is currently available in any published reference work or as part of any Internet database."–*Publ. notes*

Enzymes chosen for inclusion are those classified by the Enzyme Commission and others for which the chemical reaction is known. Includes 6,000 enzyme reactions (with Enzyme Commission numbers, alternative names, substrates, products, alternative substrates, and properties) and chemical structures of key metabolites and cofactors. Describes catalyzed reactions, reaction stoichiometry, and cofactors. Provides extensive references to literature and the most comprehensive index available to *Methods in enzymology* (New York: Academic Press, 1955–). The index lists enzyme names. Appropriate for academic, medical, and other special libraries. Also available online via netLibrary.

306   The essential guide to aging in the twenty-first century: Mind, body, and behavior. [3rd ed.] Donald H. Kausler, Barry C. Kausler, Jill A. Krupsaw. xiii, 516 p. Columbia, [Mo.]: University of Missouri Press, 2007. ISBN: 9780826217073.

305.2603   HQ1064.U5K30

Really the 3rd ed. of the *Graying of America* (Champaign, Ill.: University of Illinois Press, 2001), this volume builds on the strengths of that former title, presenting the biological and psychological aspects of aging in a concise and non-technical way that is still clear and takes the reader seriously. Includes nearly 588 entries, including 172 new ones and 150 which have been substantially revised. This volume has added important research from the last five years, for example, the interaction of health issues (such as hearing) on the health of a spouse or partner, the importance of getting enough sunlight and sleep, and what makes a quality nursing home. Includes bibliographical references and indexes. A comprehensive handbook to growing old with strength and grace. Available as an e-book.

307 **The family practice desk reference.** 4th ed. Charles E. Driscoll, Edward T. Bope. xi, 1035 p., ill. Chicago: AMA Press, 2003. ISBN: 1579471900.

610   RC55.F22

1st ed., 1986 had title: *Handbook of family practice*; 3rd ed., 1996.

Includes aspects of health and illness management for common conditions and diseases encountered by family physicians. Organized by "life-cycle approach" (*Pref.*), e.g., care of children, maternity care, women's health, men's health, and by body system (e.g., cardiovascular, respiratory, gastrointestinal, etc.). Entries in standardized format, each with a table of contents and list of references, and organized by conditions. Each chapter presents symptoms using differential diagnosis tables, laboratory values, and diagnostics.

308 **First aid manual.** 2nd American ed., fully rev. and updated ed. Jon R. Krohmer, Michael Webb, Michael R. Bond, American College of Emergency Physicians. 288 p., ill. New York: DK Publ., 2004. ISBN: 0756601959.

616.0252   RC86.8.F565

Published by American College of Emergency Physicians® (ACEP)

Contents: (1) What is first aid?; (2) Action at an emergency; (3) The practice of first aid; (4) Resuscitation; (5) Disorders of the respiratory system; (6) Disorders of the circulation ssytem; (7) Wounds and bleeding; (8) Disorders of consciousness; (9) Bone, joint, and muscle injuries; (10) Burns and scalds; (11) Effects of heat and cold; (12) Foreign bodies; (13) Poisoning; (14) Bites and stings; (15) Emergency childbirth; (16) Miscellaneous conditions; (17) Dressings and bandages; (18) Handling and transport; (19) Emergency first aid. Index.

"A comprehensive guide to treating emergency victims of all ages in any situation."—*Cover.* Step-by-step explanation and color photographs of life-saving procedures (e.g., cardiopulmonary resuscitation, treatment of blocked airway, etc.), treatments and techniques, following current

MEDICAL & HEALTH SCIENCES

first-aid guidelines. Section for the most critical emergencies at the end of the book.

309 **GeneTests.** Children's Hospital and Medical Center (Seattle, Wash.). 1993–. Seattle, Wash.: Univ. of Washington. http://www. genetests.org/.

Contents: Home page; About GeneTests; GeneReviews; Laboratory directory; Clinic directory; Educational materials.

Provides authoritative information on genetic testing and its use in diagnosis, disease management, and genetic counseling. Promotes use of genetic services in patient care and decision making by individuals. GeneReviews and Laboratory directory can be searched by disease, gene symbol, protein name, etc. Contains context-sensitive illustrated glossary, teaching tools, and other resources.

310 **Guides to the evaluation of permanent impairment.** 6th ed. Robert D. Rondinelli, Elizabeth Genovese, Christopher R. Brigham, American Medical Association. xxiv, 634 p., ill. [Chicago]: American Medical Association, 2008. ISBN: 9781579478.

614.1   RA1055.5.G85

1st ed., 1965 (repr. *Journal of the American Medical Assoc.*, Feb. 15, 1958, special ed.); 5th ed., 2001.

Contents: ch. 1, "Conceptual foundations and philosophy"; ch. 2, "Practical application of the guides"; ch. 3, "Pain-related impairment"; ch. 4, "The cardiovascular system"; ch. 5, "The pulmonary system"; ch. 6, "The digestive system"; ch. 7, "The urinary and reproductive systems"; ch. 8, "The skin"; ch. 9, "The hematopoietic system"; ch. 10, "The endocrine system"; ch. 11, "Ear, nose, throat, and related structures"; ch. 12, "The visual system"; ch. 13, "The central and peripheral nervous system"; ch. 14, "Mental and behavioral disorders"; ch. 15, "The upper extremities"; ch. 16, "The lower extremities"; ch. 17, "The spine and pelvis"; appendix; glossary; index.

"Defines an innovative new international standard for impairment assessment … The goal is to provide an impairment rating guide that is authoritative, fair, and equitable to all parties"… *(Pref.)*, applying terminology and a framework based on the World Health Organization's International Classification of Functioning, Disability, and Health (ICF) (83). Five impairment classes allow patient rating from no impairment to impairment considered most severe. Also includes diagnosis-based grids for each organ system. Employs a peer-review process, with guidance from an editorial panel and input from state medical associations and national medical specialty societies.

311 Handbook of environmental health. 4th ed. Herman Koren, Michael S. Bisesi. 2 v., ill. Boca Raton, Fla.: Lewis Publ., 2003. ISBN: 1566705363.

363.7   RA565.K67

1st ed., 1980; 3rd ed., 1996.

Contents: v. 1, Biological, chemical, and physical agents of environmental related disease; v. 2, Pollutant interactions in air, water, and soil.

Includes various environmental health topics, issues, and hazards such as emerging infectious diseases and microorganisms, air quality and its effect on ecosystems, toxicology, and effects of the environment on humans. Describes interactions between humans and the environment and how they affect health and welfare of individuals. Comprehensive bibliography (v. 1, p. 647–702) and indexes. Available online via netLibrary.

312 Handbook of health behavior research. David S. Gochman. 4 v., ill. New York: Plenum Press, 1997. ISBN: 0306454432.

613   RA776.9.H363

Contents: (I) Personal and social determinants; (II) Provider determinants; (III) Demography, development, and diversity; (IV) Relevance for professionals and issues for the future.

Interdisciplinary resource, presenting and explaining health behavior concepts and research findings. Includes a glossary, bibliographical references, and index. For an academic audience.

313 Handbook of neurologic rating scales. 2nd ed. Robert M. Herndon. xiv, 441 p. New York: Demos Medical Publ., 2006. ISBN: 1888799927.

616.80475   RC348.H296

1st ed., 1997.

Contents: ch. 1, Introduction to clinical neurologic scales (Robert M. Herndon and Gary Cutter); ch. 2, Generic and general use scales (Robert M. Herndon); ch. 3, Pediatric developmental scales (Roger A. Brumback); ch. 4, Pediatric neurologic and rehabilitation rating scales (Raphael Corcoran Sneed, Edward L. Manning, and Cathy F. Hansen); ch. 5, Amyotrophic lateral sclerosis clinimetric scales: Guidelines for administration and scoring (Benjamin Rix Brooks); ch. 6, Scales for the assessment of movement disorders (Stephen T. Gancher); ch. 7, Multiple sclerosis and demyelinating diseases (Robert M. Herndon and Jeffrey I. Greenstein); ch. 8, Assessment of the elderly with dementia (Richard Camicioli and Katherine Wild); ch. 9, Clinical stroke scales (Wayne M. Clark and J. Maurice Hourihane); ch. 10, Peripheral neuropathy and pain scales (Robert M. Herndon); ch. 11, Diagnostic headache criteria and instruments (Elcio J. Piovesan and Stephen D. Silberstein); ch. 12, Scales for assessment of ataxia (Robert M. Herndon); ch. 13, Assessment of traumatic brain injury (Risa Nakase-Richardson, Frances Spinosa, Charles F. Swearingen, and Domenic Esposito); ch. 14, Health-related quality-of-life scales for epilepsy (James J. Cereghino); ch. 15, Rehabilitation outcome measures (Samuel T. Gontkovsky and Risa Nakase-Richardson); ch. 16, Human immunodeficiency virus-associated cognitive impairment (Giovanni Schifitto and Michelle D. Gaugh); ch. 17, Summary and conclusions (Robert M. Herndon).

Reference source on methods of measurement and rating scales used in neurology to assess neurologic disease. Useful in the design of clinical trials and for interpreting the literature of clinical trials in neurology.

314 HIV InSite knowledge base. Laurence Peiperl, Paul Volberding, P. T. Cohen, University of California, San Francisco. 1996(?)–. San Francisco: University of California. http://hivinsite.ucsf.edu/InSite. jsp?page=KB.
025.174; 616.9792; 362.1969792; 616.979201

Online adaptation of *The AIDS knowledge base* (AKB), which appeared in several print editions (1st ed., 1990; 2nd ed., 1994; 3rd ed., 1999).

Contents: Epidemiology of HIV; Natural Science of HIV; Diagnosis and Clinical Management of HIV; Clinical Manifestations of HIV; Infections Associated with HIV; Malignancies Associated with HIV; Transmission and Prevention of HIV; HIV Policy.

Continually updated online resource covering HIV/AIDS clinical topics and also access to selected related materials (e.g., guidelines, fact sheets, journal articles, etc.), including both links within the HIV InSite and outside resources. For academic libraries.

315 Interpretation of diagnostic tests. 8th ed. Jacques B Wallach. Philadelphia: Wolters Kluwer Health/Lippincott, Williams & Wilkins, 2007. ISBN: 9780781730.
616.0756   RB38.2.W35

1st ed., 1970; 7th ed., 2000. Also available online via Ovid.

Information about tests and diseases, also new technologies and techniques used in testing (e.g., genetic testing, DNA probes, and monoclonal antibodies). Includes sections on normal values, specific laboratory examinations, diseases of organ systems, and drugs and laboratory test values; also on bioterrorism. Appendixes include a list of abbreviations and acronyms, and a table of conversion factors. Subject index. Designed for clinicians, but also useful for health consumers. Available online via Books@Ovid.

Similar print titles include *Laboratory tests and diagnostic procedures* (318), *Mosby's manual of diagnostic and laboratory tests* (325), and *Tietz clinical guide to laboratory tests* (334); a web-based resource is *Lab tests online: A public resource on clinical lab testing from the laboratory professionals who do the testing* (Washington: American Association for Clinical Chemistry, 2001–).

316 Interpreting the medical literature. 5th ed. Stephen H. Gehlbach. x, 293 p., ill. New York: McGraw-Hill, 2006. ISBN: 0071437894.

610.7222   R118.6.G43

1st ed., 1982; 4th ed., 2002.

Contents: ch. 1, "Tasting an article"; ch. 2, "Study design: General considerations"; ch. 3, "Study design: The case-control approach"; ch. 4, "Study design: The cross-sectional and follow-up approaches"; ch. 5, "Study design: The experimental approach"; ch. 6, "Study design: Variations"; ch. 7, "Making measurements"; ch. 8, "Analysis: Statistical significance"; ch. 9, "Analysis: Some statistical tests"; ch. 10, "Interpretation: Sensitivity, specificity, and predictive value"; ch. 11, "Interpretation: Risk"; ch. 12, "Interpretation: Causes"; ch. 13, "Cases series, editorials, and reviews"; ch. 14, "A final word"; Index.

Assists with understanding and utilizing the information presented in medical studies and reports and also with the critical reading and interpretation of conflicting studies. Provides clinical examples from the published medical and public health literature.

317 Introduction to health sciences librarianship. M. Sandra Wood. xvii, 494 p., ill. (some color). Binghamton, N.Y.: Haworth Information Press, 2008. ISBN: 9780789035.

026.61   Z675.M4.I58

Contents: sec. 1, "Introduction/overview"; sec. 2, "Technical services"; sec. 3, "Public services"; sec. 4, "Administration"; sec. 5, "Special topics."

Overview of health sciences librarianship and the different types of health sciences libraries, reflecting current trends in the health care field;

the important influence of many organizations, particularly the Medical Library Association (MLA), the Association of Academic Health Sciences Libraries (AAHSL), and the National Library of Medicine (NLM); and the pervasive role of advances in information technology. Addresses concepts such as information literacy, evidence-based librarianship, and health informatics. Glossary; index.

318 **Laboratory tests and diagnostic procedures.** 4th ed. xii, 1184 p., ill. Philadelphia: Saunders, 2004. ISBN: 0721603882.

RB38.2.L33

1st ed., 1993; 3rd ed., 2001.

Pt. 1, "Diseases, conditions, and symptoms," contains an alphabetical list of diseases and conditions, with mention of the appropriate test and/ or procedure for each disease. Pt. 2 lists laboratory and diagnostic procedures in alphabetical order, norms for different age groups and all known national and international units, usage of a particular test for a specific condition, causes of abnormal laboratory test results, and a description of the test or procedure with an interpretation of test results and post-procedure care. Mentions medico-legal implications and need for informed consent. An appendix lists reportable diseases. Index. Similar print titles include *Interpretation of diagnostic tests* (315), *Mosby's manual of diagnostic and laboratory tests* (325), and *Tietz clinical guide to laboratory tests* (334); a web-based resource is *Lab tests online: A public resource on clinical lab testing from the laboratory professionals who do the testing* (Washington: American Association for Clinical Chemistry, 2001–).

319 **Lab tests online.** American Association for Clinical Chemistry. 2001–. Washington: American Association for Clinical Chemistry. http://www.labtestsonline.org.

Produced and maintained by the American Association for Clinical Chemistry, in collaboration with several other professional societies.

Provides patients and other health consumers with reliable information on clinical laboratory tests that are commonly used to diagnose various diseases and conditions and their interpretation. Also provides links to additional resources and websites.

Print titles containing information about lab tests include *Interpretation of diagnostic tests* (315), *Laboratory tests and diagnostic procedures* (318) *Mosby's manual of diagnostic and laboratory tests* (325), and *Tietz clinical guide to laboratory tests* (334).

320 **Measuring health: A guide to rating scales and questionnaires.**
3rd ed. Ian McDowell. xvi, 748 p., ill. Oxford; New York: Oxford
University Press, 2006. ISBN: 9780195165.

614.42   RA408.5.M38

1st ed., 1987; 2nd ed., 1996.

Overview of the field of health measurement, with in-depth information on selected commonly-used instruments (e.g., measurement of pain, general health status, quality of life, mental status, etc.) with the purpose of measuring health status in research studies. Provides description of methods, comparisons, and critical reviews of health measurement instruments or scales and their quality, indicating purpose, conceptual basis, reliability, validity, etc. This edition includes 104 scales. For health care researchers, epidemiologists, and social scientists. Index. Available as an e-book via netLibrary.

321 **The Medical Library Association guide to managing health care libraries.** Ruth Holst, Sharon A. Phillips, Karen McNally Bensing, Medical Library Association. xi, 371 p., ill. Chicago; New York: Medical Library Association; Neal-Schuman Publ., 2000. ISBN: 1555703976.

026.61   Z675.M4M5

Based on *Hospital library management*, 1983.

Contents: ch. 1, Libraries in health care settings: An introduction (Ruth Holst); ch. 2, The health care environment (Eloise C. Foster, Gail L. Warden); ch. 3, Administrative issues (Ruth Holst, Sharon A. Phillips); ch. 4, Planning and marketing (Beth A. Salzwedel, Ellen Wilson Green); ch. 5, Quality improvement (Nardina Nameth Mein); ch. 6, Financial management (Sharon A. Phillips); ch. 7, Human resources management (Holly Shipp Buchanan); ch. 8, Space planning (Rosanne Labree); ch. 9, Managing the one person library (Judith M. Topper, Karen McNally Bensing); ch. 10, Information and educational services (Jacqueline D. Doyle, Kay E. Wellik); ch. 11, Information resources (Susan F. Anderson, Michelynn McKnight); ch. 12, Collection development (Ruth Holst, Elaine Noonan Skopelja); ch. 13, Access to library resources (Kimberley M. Granath, Marlene S. Englander, Gretchen A. Hallerberg); ch. 14, Document delivery (Ruth Holst, Karen McNelly Bensing); ch. 15, Managing audiovisual services (Sharon A. Phillips, Larry D. Weitkemper); ch. 16, Health Information for patients and consumers (Margaret Bandy).

Resource and practical guide for librarians in different types of healthcare libraries, and students. Presents an overview of the medical library profession, challenges resulting from the current healthcare environment, and new roles which librarians need to assume in this new environment.

322 MEDLINE: A guide to effective searching in PubMed and other interfaces. 2nd ed. Brian S. Katcher. xi, 136 p., ill. San Francisco: Ashbury Press, 2006. ISBN: 0967344514.

025.0661   Z699.5.M39K373

1st ed., 1999.

Contents: ch. 1, Origins of MEDLINE and why it works the way it does; ch. 2, Working in MEDLINE; ch. 3, Medical subject headings (MeSH); ch. 4, Publication types and other limiting strategies; ch. 5, Framing questions and other practical tips; Appendix A: MEDLINE interfaces and related resources on the World Wide Web; Appendix B: Journals in the Abridged Index Medicus (AIM); Index.

A medical informatics resource for librarians, students, and others to become more informed about MEDLINE® (425) searching via PubMed® (432) and additional interfaces (e.g., Ovid, Medscape, Infotrieve, Paperchase, and others). Includes step-by-step examples for effective searching.

323 The Merck manual of diagnosis and therapy. Merck & Co. Rahway, N.J: Merck, 1950–. ISSN: 0076-6526.

615.5805   RC55.M4

Title varies: *Merck's manual of the materia medica* (varies slightly), 1899–1940. 17th ed., 1999; 18th ed., 2006.

Also issued 1987– as two soft cover vols: *Merck manual of diagnosis and therapy*. Vol. I, General medicine; and *Merck manual of diagnosis and therapy*. Vol. II, Gynecology, obstetrics, pediatrics, genetics.

Periodically revised to provide up-to-date medical information that will facilitate accurate diagnosis and promote effective treatment. Most entries include a definition or description, etiology, symptoms and signs, diagnosis, prognosis, and treatment. Surgical procedures are rarely described. Includes tables and ill. Indexed. The current ed. is also available online (http://www.merck.com/mmpe/index.html).

The Merck Manuals (324) page provides further information about this and several other Merck publications.

324 The Merck manuals. Merck and Co. 1995–. Whitehouse Station, N.J.: Merck and Co. http://www.merck.com/pubs/.

"A trusted source for medical information."—*Website*

Contents: pt. 1, The Databases; pt. 2, Data Flow and Processing; pt. 3, Querying and Linking the Data; pt. 4, User Support. Glossary.

In-depth guide to NCBI bioinformatics resources, including a variety of databases and search engines. Describes both well-known (e.g., GenBank [415], PubMed [432], OMIM [330], and others) and also less well-known NCBI databases (e.g., the macromolecular structure databases, GEO, and many others) and gives details on how they work. Intended for biomedical researchers, health professionals, and students.

328 **NLM training manuals and resources.** National Library of Medicine (U.S.). 2003–. Bethesda, Md.: National Library of Medicine. http://www.nlm.nih.gov/pubs/web_based.html.

Produced by National Library of Medicine (NLM) (427).

Provides access to online training materials used in conjunction with classes and courses offered by the National Training Center and Clearinghouse (NTCC), e.g., for PubMed (432), NLM Gateway (429), ClinicalTrials.gov (191), TOXNET (1580), Unified Medical Language System (UMLS) (89), and others.

329 **NORD guide to rare disorders.** National Organization for Rare Disorders. lxiv, 895 p., [16] p. of plates, ill. (some color). Philadelphia: Lippincott, Williams & Wilkins, 2003. ISBN: 0781730635.

616   RC48.8.N385

NORD (National Organization for Rare Disorders) is "a non-profit voluntary health agency dedicated to the identification, treatment, and cure of all orphan diseases."—*Pref.*

Contents: ch. 1, Autoimmune & connective tissue disorders; ch. 2, Cardiovascular disorders; ch. 3, Chromosomal disorders; ch. 4, Dermatologic disorders; ch. 5, Dysmorphic disorders; ch. 6, Emerging/infectious diseases; ch. 7, Endocrine disorders; ch. 8, Gastroenterologic disorders; ch. 9, Hematologic/oncologic disorders; ch. 10, Inborn errors of metabolism; ch. 11, Neurologic disorders; ch. 12, Neuromuscular disorders; ch. 13, Ophthalmologic disorders; ch. 14, Pulmonary disorders; ch. 15, Renal disorders; ch. 16, Skeletal disorders.

At what point a disease is considered rare differs among countries. In the U.S., a disease is considered a rare or an "orphan" disease if it is a low-incidence disease that affects fewer than 200,000 people. This resource "covers about 800 of the estimated 6,000 rare diseases [and] presents many of the signs and symptoms that can be an aid in the diagnosis and differentiation of rare diseases in addition to possible treatment."—*Foreword*. Lists resources which provide help to patients and families affected by a rare disorder. Includes a "List of Orphan Products Approved for Marketing." Index. For physicians and other health professionals, patients, and students. Other resources in this area can be located via National Organization for Rare Disorders, Inc. (428) and NIH's Office of Rare Diseases (476).

330 **OMIM.** Victor A. McKusick, National Center for Biotechnology Information. 2000–. Bethesda, Md.: National Center for Biotechnology Information. http://www.ncbi.nlm.nih.gov/omim/.

OMIM and Online Mendelian Inheritance in Man are trademarks of the Johns Hopkins University (JHU); OMIM is a continuously updated catalog of human genes and genetic disorders compiled by Dr. Victor A. McKusick and colleagues at JHU and developed for the Web by the National Center for Biotechnology Information (NCBI) (6). OMIM has its origins in the print *Mendelian inheritance in man: Catalogs of autosomal dominant, autosomal recessive, and X-linked phenotypes*. A related title is John J. Mulvihill's *Catalog of human cancer genes: McKusick's Mendelian inheritance in man for clinical and research oncologists* (300).

The OMIM help document (http://www.ncbi.nlm.nih.gov/Omim/omimhelp.html) provides guidance for basic and advanced searches. OMIM FAQs (http://www.ncbi.nlm.nih.gov/Omim/omimfaq.html) explain the OMIM numbering system and symbols and the OMIM gene map and morbid map, as well as provide answers to a variety of specific questions.

Records provide descriptions of genetic traits, references to the literature, and extensive links to MEDLINE (425), protein, and DNA sequence records in NCBI's Entrez (3) system and from other data repositories. "OMIM is intended for use primarily by physicians and other professionals concerned with genetic disorders, by genetics researchers, and by advanced students in science and medicine. While the OMIM database is open to the public, users seeking information about a personal medical or genetic condition are urged to consult with a qualified physician for diagnosis and for answers to personal questions."—*Website*

331 **Oxford desk reference: Clinical genetics.** Helen V. Firth, Jane A. Hurst, Judith G. Hall. xliii, 708 p., ill. Oxford; New York: Oxford University Press, 2005. ISBN: 0192628968.

616.042   RB155.F55

MEDICINE

143

Contents: ch. 1, Introduction; ch. 2, Clinical approach; ch. 3, Common consultations; ch. 4, Cancer; ch. 5, Chromosomes; ch. 6, Pregnancy and fertility; Appendix; Index.

Covers Mendelian disorders, chromosomal aberrations, congenital anomalies, and syndromes. Also mentions familial cancers and genetic predisposition to disease, pregnancy-related topics, and diagnostic criteria for specific conditions. Bibliography, glossaries of terms used in genetics and dysmorphology, and a list of abbreviations. Written for health professionals.

332 **Professional guide to signs and symptoms.** 5th ed. Lippincott, Williams & Wilkins. x, 918 p., ill. Philadelphia: Lippincott, Williams & Wilkins, 2007. ISBN: 1582555109.

616.047   RC69.P77

1st ed., 1993; 4th ed., 2003.

Alphabetically organized reference tool helpful for identification and interpretation of selected signs and symptoms of various diseases, agents of bioterrorism, signs and symptoms associated with herbs, and laboratory test results. This edition also contains advice on how to conduct a patient history and a table of English-Spanish translations. Selected references and index. Also available online via Books@Ovid. A related title, *Professional guide to diseases*, has been regularly updated since 1981, with the 8th ed. published in 2005.

333 **The SAGE handbook of health psychology.** Stephen Sutton, Andrew Baum, Marie Johnston. xiii, 432 p., ill. Thousand Oaks, Calif: SAGE Publ., 2004. ISBN: 0761968490.

616.0019   R726.7.S24

Contents: ch. 1, Context and perspectives in health psychology; ch. 2, Epidemiology of health and illness: A socio-psycho-physiological perspective; ch. 3, Biological mechanisms of health and disease; ch. 4, Determinants of health-related behaviours: Theoretical and methodological issues; ch. 5, Health-related cognitions; ch. 6, Individual differences, health and illness: The role of emotional traits and generalized expectancies; ch. 7, Stress, health and illness; ch. 8, Living with chronic illness: A contextualized, self-regulation approach; ch. 9, Lifespan, gender and cross-cultural perspectives in health psychology; ch. 10, Communicating about health threats and treatments; ch. 11, Applications in health psychology: How effective are interventions?; ch. 12, Research methods in health psychology; ch. 13,

Assessment and measurement in health psychology; ch. 14, Professional issues in health psychology.

Comprehensive interdisciplinary handbook reflecting international health psychology research and issues. For advanced students, researchers, and practitioners. Includes bibliographical references and index.

334 Tietz clinical guide to laboratory tests. 4th ed. Alan H. B. Wu li, 1798 p. St. Louis: Saunders/Elsevier, 2006. ISBN: 0721679757.

616.075   RB38.2.C55

1st ed., 1983–3rd ed., 1995 had title: *Clinical guide to laboratory tests.*

Contents: section 1, Preanalytical aspects; section 2, General clinical tests; section 3, Molecular diagnostics; section 4, Therapeutic drugs and drugs of abuse; section 5, Clinical microbiology; section 6, Immunophenotyping markers; section 7, Pharmacogenomics; section 8, Allergy testing; Test index; Disease index.

Presents diagnostic information on commonly used tests as well as specialized tests and procedures, with discussion of biological variables and drug interferences that may affect test results. Provides reference ranges for most laboratory tests and clinical interpretation of laboratory data. For health professionals. Similar print titles include *Interpretation of diagnostic tests (709), Laboratory tests and diagnostic procedures* (318), *Mosby's manual of diagnostic and laboratory tests* (325); a web-based resource is *Lab tests online: A public resource on clinical lab testing from the laboratory professionals who do the testing* (Washington: American Association for Clinical Chemistry, 2001–).

Histories

335 American surgery: An illustrated history. Ira M. Rutkow, Stanley B. Burns. xiv, 638 p., ill. (some color), color map. Philadelphia: Lippincott-Raven Publ., 1998. ISBN: 0316763527.

617.0973   RD27.3.U6R87

Contents: ch. 1, Native American surgery; ch. 2, Surgical practice in colonial America, 1607–1783; ch. 3, English and French influences, 1784–1845; ch. 4, Surgical anesthesia, 1846–1860; ch. 5, Civil War surgery, 1861–1865; ch. 6, Professionalization and antisepsis, 1866–1889; ch. 7, German authority and scientific advancement, 1890–1916; ch. 8, World War I surgery, 1917–1918; ch. 9, Consolidation and specialization, 1919–1940;

ch. 10, World War II surgery, 1941–1945; ch. 11, American surgical supremacy, 1946–1974; ch. 12, Socioeconomic and political transformation, 1975–1997; Surgical specialties and biographies; ch. 13, General surgery; ch. 14, Cardiothoracic surgery; ch. 15, Colorectal surgery; ch. 16, Gynecologic surgery; ch. 17, Neurologic surgery; ch. 18, Ophthalmologic surgery; ch. 19, Orthopedic surgery; ch. 20, Otorhinolaryngologic surgery; ch. 21, Plastic surgery; ch. 22, Urologic surgery; References; Index.

Chronological arrangement, describing the development of American surgery, starting with Native American surgery and a description of practices of the various tribes. Includes biographies of important figures for the different time periods. Describes the development of the surgical subspecialties. Other titles by Ira Rutkow include *History of surgery in the United States* (San Francisco: Norman Publ., 1988–92) and *Surgery: An illustrated history* (St. Louis: Published by Mosby-Year Book Inc. in collaboration with Norman Publ., 1993).

336   **The Cambridge historical dictionary of disease.** Kenneth F.
Kiple. xiii, 412 p.; 25 cm. Cambridge, U.K.; New York: Cambridge
University Press, 2003. ISBN: 0521808340.
616.009   RC41.C365

International and interdisciplinary resource for medical history of human disease, originally published as pt. VIII of the *Cambridge world history of human disease* (337), rewrites and edits essays into shorter and up-to-date entries and also takes information from other parts of the original publication. Available online via Gale Virtual Reference Library (Farmington Hills, Mich.: Gale Cengage Learning, 2002–).

337   **The Cambridge world history of human disease.** Kenneth F.
Kiple, Rachael Rockwell Graham. xxiv, 1176 p., ill. Cambridge;
New York: Cambridge University Press, 1993. ISBN: 0521332869.
610.9   R131.C233

Repr., 2001.

Modeled to a certain extent after *Handbook of geographical and historical pathology* by A. Hirsch (London: New Sydenham Soc., 1883–86), tr. by Charles Creighton from the 2nd German ed. of *Handbuch der historisch-geographischen Pathologie* (2 v., Stuttgart: Enke, 1881–86). A major work, the result of the Cambridge History and Geography of Human Disease project which began in late 1985. Pt. I covers the "major historical roots and branches of medical thought from ancient times to the twentieth century," while pt. II "deals with concepts of disease in the East and West, as well as with concepts of complex physical and mental ailments."— *Introd*. Other sections treat medical specialties and disease prevention, the measurement of health, the history of human disease in Asia and elsewhere, and the geography of human disease. The final section, pt. VIII (rewritten into shorter and up-to-date entries in *Cambridge historical dictionary of disease* [93]), covers major human diseases, past and present. A list of tables, figures, and maps is provided, and also a bibliography for each topic covered. Names index includes proper names, dates, and brief biographical sketches of all historical figures in medicine mentioned by more than one author.

338 **Companion encyclopedia of the history of medicine.** W. F. Bynum, Roy Porter. 2 v., ill. London; New York: Routledge, 1993. ISBN: 0415047714.

610.9   R133.E5

1997, 1993 1st. paperback ed.

Contents: pt. 1, The place of medicine; pt. 2, Body systems; pt. 3, Theories of life, health and disease; pt. 4, Understanding disease; pt. 5, Clinical medicine; pt. 6, Medicine in society; pt. 7, Medicine, ideas, and culture. Comprehensive survey of all aspects of the history of medicine. Includes 72 essays on the development of medical science, the medical profession and institutions, and medicine's interrelationship with society, culture, religion, etc. Bibliographical notes for each article. Cross-references and index.

339 **A dictionary of the history of medicine.** Anton Sebastian. vi, 781 p., ill. New York: Parthenon Publ. Group, 1999. ISBN: 1850700214.

610.9   R121.S398

This illustrated medical history dictionary, a scholarly work, includes terms, with Latin and Greek origins of terms, brief biographies of notable people in medicine, eponymic information, important events, conditions, procedures, and other historical information for a broad range of subjects. Includes anecdotes and background material on both well- and little-known facts of medical history. Drawings and photographs of antique medical instruments and rare medical conditions. A negative review (*Journal of the history of medicine and allied sciences* 56, no. 2 [2001]: 182–83) cites factual errors, omissions, and "overly broad coverage." Users are cautioned to double check facts in other sources.

By the same author, *Dates in medicine: A chronological record of medical progress over three millennia* provides important milestones in the development of medicine. It is part of the Landmarks in Medicine series (publ. 2000–2002 by Parthenon), which also includes several other titles, including *Dates in ophthalmology: A chronological record of progress in ophthalmology over the last millennium,* by Daniel Albert, and several other titles by Helen S. J. Lee: *Dates in cardiology, Dates in gastroenterology, Dates in infectious disease, Dates in obstetrics and gynecology, Dates in neurology, Dates in oncology,* and *Dates in urology,* all with the subtitle *A chronological record of progress over the last millennium.*

340   The DOs: Osteopathic medicine in America. 2nd ed. Norman Gevitz. xiv, 242 p., ill., map. Baltimore: Johns Hopkins University Press, 2004. ISBN: 0801878330.

615.5330973   RZ325.U6G48

1st ed., 1982.

A history of osteopathic medicine, from its beginning in the 19th century to the present, detailing its philosophy, practice, and relationship with the medical profession. This rev. ed. has 11 chapters, with two new chapters on recent developments and growth of the profession. Includes bibliographic notes and index.

341   Encyclopaedia of the history of science, technology, and medicine in non-Western cultures. Helaine Selin. xxvii, 1117 p., ill., maps (some color). Dordrecht, [The Netherlands]; Boston: Kluwer Academic, 1997. ISBN: 0792340663.

509   Q124.8.E53

Contains 600 signed entries with references. Includes major topics (e.g., agriculture, maps, and medicine) in several cultures/geographic areas. Also includes famous scientists. List of entries, index, list of authors.

342   Encyclopedia of medical history. Roderick E. McGrew, Margaret P. McGrew. xiv, 400 p. New York: McGraw-Hill, 1985. ISBN: 0070450870.

610.9   R133.M34

Intends "to provide an easily accessible historical treatment of important medical topics."—*Pref.* Includes 103 essays, each with a bibliography of additional readings. Topical entries are arranged in alphabetical order. No biographical articles, but individuals' contributions to medical science are discussed in the essays. Index.

343   Encyclopedia of plague and pestilence: From ancient times to the present. 3rd ed. George C. Kohn. New York: Facts On File, 2007. ISBN: 9780816069354; 0816069352.

614.403   RA649.E53

1st ed., 1995; rev. ed., 2001. Description based on 2001 rev. ed.

Alphabetical listing by geographical location of major epidemic diseases (700 main entries), with the exception for names in common use (e.g., black death, HIV/AIDS epidemic, etc.). Same name but different dates are listed in chronological order. Cross-references. Further reading at the end of entry. Bibliography of selected secondary sources; index. Appendix 1: Entries by disease; Appendix 2: Geographical list of entries; Appendix 3: Timetable of plague and pestilence. Intended for general readers. *The Cambridge world history of human disease* (337) provides further and more scholarly information in this subject area.

344   The evolution of surgical instruments: An illustrated history from ancient times to the twentieth century. John Kirkup. xviii, 510 p., [16] p. of plates, ill. (some color). Novato, Calif.: Historyofscience.com, 2006. ISBN: 0930405862.

617.917809   RD71.K53

Norman surgery series, no. 13; Norman science and technology series, no. 8; Norman science technology series, no. 8.

Contents: (1) Historical introduction; (2) Materials; (3) Structure & form; (4) Applied instrumentation.

General illustrated history of surgical instruments and apparatus. Instruments are grouped by forms and use. Each chapter covers the history of the instrument category up to the present time, identifying the surgeons and technology that made each advance possible. Illustrations are mostly black-and-white; section with color plates. Appendix provides a list of museums worldwide exhibiting surgical instruments. Bibliographical references (p. 449–465). Index.

Earlier titles on the subject include C. J. S. Thompson's *The history and evolution of surgical instruments*, Elisabeth's Bennion's *Antique medical instruments*, with focus on the aesthetic aspects of medical surgical instruments to 1879, and *American surgical instruments: The history of their manufacture and a directory of instrument makers to 1900.—Publ. notes Smith's reference and illustrated guide to surgical instruments* is the result of a review of manufacturers' catalogs and contains "2,397 competitive pattern instruments with 7,560 variations and 2,210 exclusive pattern instruments. and over 140,000 entries of information" (*Pref.*) in use at the time.

345   **Fact sheet, access to audiovisual materials.** National Library of Medicine (U.S.). 2001–. Bethesda, Md.: National Library of Medicine. http://www.nlm.nih.gov/pubs/factsheets/lrc.html.

Provides a description of NLM's audiovisual collection covering biomedical subjects: "60,000 audiovisual programs in almost 40 formats, over 3,500 of historical interest."—*Main page.* Includes instructions for on-site access, copyright restrictions for audiovisual materials, and other information. Online catalog access to identify audiovisual materials via LocatorPlus (480).

346   **History of medicine.** Karolinska Institutet Library. Stockholm, Sweden: Karolinska Institutet Library. http://www.mic.ki.se/ History.html.

Contents: General–Museums, Libraries, and Special Collections; Indigenous Cultures; Mesopotamian Medicine; Ancient Egyptian Medicine; Traditional Chinese Medicine; Traditional Indian Medicine; Classical Islamic Medicine; Western Medicine (divided into Ancient Period, up to 499 CE; Medieval Period, 500–1450; Early Modern Period, 1451–1600; and Modern Period, 1601–Present); History of Diseases.

Provides selected links to information sources on the history of biomedicine, with text and images in many cases. Also provides access to museums, libraries, special collections, and the Karolinska Institute, Stockholm, Sweden.

347   **History of medicine.** National Library of Medicine (U.S.). Bethesda, Md.: National Library of Medicine. http://www.nlm.nih. gov/hmd/index.html.

"The National Library of Medicine (NLM) (427) houses one of the world's largest history of medicine collections and makes available print and non-print materials that document the history of medicine, health, and disease in all time periods and cultures."—*About Us page.* This website provides access to many full-text digitized books, images (Images from the History of Medicine [352]), and manuscripts (Digital Manuscripts Program) from

MEDICAL & HEALTH SCIENCES

its collections. Also provides quick links to NLM's catalogs (LocatorPlus [480], NLM catalog [Entrez] [3], IndexCat [479]), MEDLINE (425)/ PubMed (432), Profiles in Science (48), manuscript finding aids (http:// www.nlm.nih.gov/hmd/manuscripts/alpha.html), online exhibitions, Directory of History of Medicine Collections (388), and other resources. For scholars, researchers, and the general public.

348   **The history of surgery in the United States, 1775–1900.** Ira M. Rutkow. v. 1–, ill. San Francisco: Norman Publ., 1988–92. ISBN: 0930405021.

016.6170973   Z6666.R87; RD27.3.U

(Norman bibliography series; no. 2, 5).

2 v.: v. 1 (1988); v. 2 (1992); also part of Norman surgery series; no. 2, no. 4.

Contents: v. 1, Textbooks, monographs, and treatises; v. 2, Periodicals and pamphlets.

Vol. 1 lists 552 works "written by surgeons living in the U.S."—*Introd.* Most entries are either first editions of textbooks or the initial printing of a treatise or monograph. Each entry includes a summary. Brief biographical sketches of authors. Includes 130 reproductions from various cited works and a short-title list of all items found in the volume. Vol. 2 provides a survey and analysis of the early American surgical periodical and pamphlet literature, by American surgeons. Bibliographical indexes; name index and subject index. Both volumes are arranged by surgical specialties and within each surgical specialty in chronological order.

Other titles by Ira M. Rutkow include *American surgery: An illustrated history* (335) and *Surgery: An illustrated history* (361).

Other titles in the Norman surgery series include: no. 1: Charles Truax, *The mechanics of surgery*; no. 3: Leonard F. Peltier, *Fractures: A history and iconography of their treatment*, which is also part of another series, entitled Norman orthopedic series no. 1; no. 5: Leonard F. Peltier, *Orthopedics: A history of iconography.*

349   **History of the health sciences World Wide Web links.** Patricia Gallagher, Stephen Greenberg, Medical Library Association, History of Medicine Section. [Chicago?]: Medical Library Association. http://www.mla-hhss.org/histlink.htm.

Electronic access to the resources listed in ch. 4 ("What a tangled Web: World Wide Web resources in the history of the health sciences") of the print edition of *History of the health sciences* (Chicago: Medical Library

Association, 2002), under the following headings: "Organizations in the history of the health sciences," "History of the health sciences library collections," "History of the health sciences educational programs," "Organizations and museums with history of the health sciences interests," "Important figures in medicine—their lives and works," "Databases," "Link pages," "Oaths, prayers and declarations," "For children," "The history of diseases," "Bibliographies/chronologies/histories," "Listservs and newsgroups," and "Journals."

350   A history of the National Library of Medicine: The nation's treasury of medical knowledge. Wyndham D. Miles, National Library of Medicine (U.S.). viii, 531 p., ill., ports. Bethesda, Md.; Washington: U.S. Dept. of Health and Human Services, Public Health Service, National Institutes of Health, National Library of Medicine; For sale by the Supt. of Docs., U.S. G.P.O, 1982.
026.610975284   Z733.N3M54

Presents a detailed history of the NLM (or its earlier official name, the Library of the Office of the Surgeon General, United States Army) from its beginnings in 1818 to the early 1980s, with chapters, for example, on the development of the Library during the Civil War, biographies of John Shaw Billings and Fielding Garrison, the beginning of indexing, the Index-catalogue and Index Medicus, the Library during WWI and WWII, modernizing the library and its services, and many others. Several appendixes include, for example, members of the Board of Regents, a selected chronology, biographies of staff members, etc. This title is also available online in a PDF edition at http://www.nlm.nih.gov/hmd/manuscripts/miles/miles.html.

A website, "The story of the NLM historical collections" (http://www.nlm.nih.gov/hmd/about/collectionhistory.html), provides related information.

351   The illustrated history of surgery. 2nd rev. and updated ed. Knut Hæger. 295 p., ill. (some color). London; Chicago: Fitzroy Dearborn Publ., 2000. ISBN: 1579583199.
617.09   RD19.H34

Contents: ch. 1, The beginnings of medicine; ch. 2, The rise of Western surgery; ch. 3, Medieval medicine; ch. 4, Surgery in the Renaissance; ch. 5, Medicine becomes a science; ch. 6, The surgeons of the Enlightenment; v. 7, Surgery in the Age of Revolutions; ch. 8, The human face of surgery; ch. 9,

The triumph of complex operations; ch. 10, The world of modern surgery. Detailed contents: http://www.loc.gov/catdir/toc/fy031/2001268056.html

Survey of the development of surgery and the profession of surgery, from prehistoric to modern times. Includes information on herbal remedies, early anesthetics and procedures related to surgery, and the use of drugs. Includes portraits of famous surgeons. Contains approx. 200 color illustrations. Chronological table; bibliography; illustration sources; index. For specialists and general readers.

352 **Images from the history of medicine.** National Library of Medicine (U.S.). Bethesda, Md.: National Library of Medicine. http://wwwihm.nlm.nih.gov/.

Images from the History of Medicine (IHM): "Database of over 60,000 images in the National Library of Medicine's (NLM) (427) historical prints and photographs collection. The collection of portraits, photographs, fine prints, caricatures, genre scenes, posters, and other graphic art illustrates the social and historical aspects of medicine from the Middle ages to the present."—*IHM Fact Sheet* (http://www.nlm.nih.gov/pubs/factsheets/ihmfact.html). The IHM database can be searched by keyword or by browsing a list of terms. Further details via the IHM fact sheet.

353 **Information sources in the history of science and medicine.** Pietro Corsi, Paul Weindling. xvi, 531 p., ill. London; Boston: Butterworth Scientific, 1983. ISBN: 0408107642.

509   Q125.I46

Consists of 23 topical chapters (e.g., "The history of technology," "Scientific instruments," "Medicine since 1500") written by authorities. Each chapter includes background and history, a discussion of the literature, and an extensive list of references. Remains the best guide and overview of the field. Indexed.

354 **MedHist.** Wellcome Library for the History and Understanding of Medicine. London: Wellcome Library for the History and Understanding of Medicine. http://medhist.ac.uk/.

Developed and managed by the Wellcome Library for the History and Understanding of Medicine (483) and affiliated with Intute (http://www.intute.ac.uk/), a service created by a network of U.K. universities and partners to access Web resources.

MEDICINE

153

Searchable catalog of evaluated Internet resources and websites relating to the history of medicine. Covers all aspects of the history of health and development of medical knowledge. For students and faculty as well as general readers.

355 **Medical discoveries: Who and when; a dictionary listing thousands of medical and related scientific discoveries in alphabetical order, giving in each case the name of the discoverer, his profession, nationality, and floruit, and the date of the discovery.** J. E. Schmidt. ix, 555 p. Springfield, Ill.: Thomas, [1959].

610.9   R131.S35

Lists biomedical and related scientific discoveries. Each entry contains the elements listed in the descriptive subtitle. Information found in this resource could possibly be supplemented by *Medical firsts: From Hippocrates to the human genome* (356) and *Medical discoveries: Medical breakthroughs and the people who developed them*, written in nontechnical language.

356 **Medical firsts: From Hippocrates to the human genome.** Robert E. Adler. vii, 232 p., ill. Hoboken, N.J.: John Wiley & Sons, 2004. ISBN: 0471401757.

610.9   R133.A43

Contents: Hippocrates: A principle and a method; Herophilus and Erasistratus: The light that failed; Marcus Varro: The germ of an idea; Dioscorides: The herb man of Anazarbus; Soranus: The birthing doctor; Galen of Pergamon: Combative genius; The enlightened mind of Abu Bakr al-Razi; Ibn al-Nafis, Galen's nemesis; Fracastoro: The poet of pestilence; Paracelsus, Renaissance rebel; Andreas Vesalius, driven to dissection; Johann Weyer, a voice of sanity in an insane world; William Harvey and the movements of the heart; Edward Jenner, a friend of humanity; Such stuff as dreams are made of: The discovery of anesthesia; Antisepsis: Awakening from a nightmare; The quiet Dr. Snow; Pasteur and the germ theory of disease; Out of the corner of his eye: Roentgen discovers x-rays; Sigmund Freud's dynamic unconscious; Beyond bacteria: Ivanovsky's discovery of viruses; The prepared mind of Alexander Fleming; Margaret Sanger and the pill; Organ transplantation, a legacy of life; A baby's cry: The birth of in vitro fertilization; Humanity eradicates a disease—smallpox—for the first time; Cannibals, kuru and mad cows: A new kind of plague; Self, non-self and danger: Deciphering the immune system; Discovery can't wait—cracking the human genome; Into the future.

Presents medical discoveries and the famous and also less well-known individuals associated with these "medical firsts." Organized chronologically. Illustrations; references and further reading; index. Available online via Questia.

357   Medicine: An illustrated history. Albert S. Lyons, R. Joseph Petrucelli. 616 p., ill. New York: H. N. Abrams, [1978]. ISBN: 0810910543.

610.9   R131.L95

Reprint, ©1987.

Contents: Early types of medicine; Ancient civilizations; Greece and Rome; Medieval medicine; The fifteenth and sixteenth centuries; The seventeenth century; The eighteenth century; The nineteenth century (The beginnings of modern medicine); The twentieth century. Bibliography, p. 604–607.

Approx. 1,000 photographs from ancient to modern times, with explanatory text. Includes works of art, archaeological discoveries, mummies, portraits of famous physicians and scientists, and 19th and 20th century medical discoveries and developments.

358   Medicine in America: A short history. James H. Cassedy. xi, 187 p. Baltimore: Johns Hopkins University Press, 1991. ISBN: 0801842077.

610.973   R151.C375

Overview of the history of medicine and health care in America (colonial period through the 1980s), with broad coverage and emphasis on social history and medical developments being presented in their social and political context. Chronological arrangement. Bibliographical essay, arranged by subject headings, which includes only monographs. Index. For health professionals and also general readers, and considered a good starting point for students.

359   Medieval science, technology, and medicine: An encyclopedia. Thomas F. Glick, Steven John Livesey, Faith Wallis. xxv, 598 p., ill. New York: Routledge, 2005. ISBN: 0415969301.

509.02   Q124.97.M43

Entries range from one to a few pages, focusing on European and Islamic topics. Entries include bibliographies and cross-references. A unique resource for this slice of science and technology development. One section of the *Routledge encyclopedias of the middle ages* series.

360 **The progressive era's health reform movement: A historical dictionary.** Ruth C. Engs. xxii, 419 p. Westport, Conn.: Praeger, 2003. ISBN: 0275979326.

362.1097303   RA395.A3E547

Covers 1880–1925, the time period labeled the Progressive era of the United States. Entries cover individuals (biographical information/assessment of historical importance), events, crusades (e.g., exercise, vegetarian diets, alternative health care), legislation, publications, and terms. Includes entries on the health reform movement and campaigns against alcohol, tobacco, drugs, and sexuality. For scholars, students, and general readers. "Selected chronology" (p. [371]–407), bibliographical references, and index. Available online via netLibrary.

361 **Surgery: An illustrated history.** Ira M. Rutkow. xiii, 550 p., ill. (some color), color maps. St. Louis: Published by Mosby-Year Book Inc. in collaboration with Norman Publ., 1993. ISBN: 0801660785.

617.09   RD19.R88

Pictorial record of the history of surgery. Traces the development of surgery from its primitive beginnings. Includes brief biographies of famous surgeons, charts, and timelines. Other titles by Ira Rutkow include *American surgery: An illustrated history* (335) and *The history of surgery in the United States, 1775–1900* (348).

362 **Turning the pages online.** Lister Hill National Center for Biomedical Communications. 2003–. Bethesda, Md.: National Library of Medicine. http://archive.nlm.nih.gov/proj/ttp/intro.htm.

Produced by National Library of Medicine (NLM).

Turning the Pages Information System (TTPI), initially created by the British Library. TTP at NLM is the result of collaboration between the British Library and NLM, with refinement of the original technology. Detailed information about research, design, system development, software, and content available on website.

Web version provides access to the digitized images of rare historic books in the biomedical sciences. Includes many important and influential works in the history of medicine. Provides the ability to browse titles and bibliographic information, to turn the pages, and to use zoom images.

Bibliography

363 **An annotated catalogue of medical Americana in the Library of the Wellcome Institute for the History of Medicine: Books**

and printed documents, 1557–1821, from Latin America and the Caribbean Islands and manuscripts from the Americas, **1575–1927.** Robin Price, Wellcome Institute for the History of Medicine Library. xix, 319 p., ill. London: The Institute, 1983. ISBN: 0854840400.

016.61098   Z6661.A45W44; R150

Spine title: *A catalogue of medical Americana in the Wellcome Institute Library.* Title on ser. t.p.: *Medical Americana in the Wellcome Institute Library.*

(Publications of the Wellcome Institute for the History of Medicine. Catalogue series Amer.; 1).

This historical bibliography covers all the American manuscripts, including those relating to North America. Also includes a selection of printed materials for Latin America to 1821. Index of authors, persons mentioned in notes, and titles of anonymous works. Bibliography: p. 293–303. Includes index.

364   Arabic medical manuscripts of the Wellcome Library: A descriptive catalogue of the Hadd d Collection (WMS 401– 487). Nikolaj Serikoff Wellcome Library for the History and Understanding of Medicine. xiii, 553 p., [10] p. of plates, ill. Leiden [The Netherlands]; Boston: Brill, 2005. ISBN: 9004147985.

016.61011.3109421   Z6621.W383.A73

Sir Henry Wellcome Asian series, v. 6.

Precursor: "*Index of the Arabic medical books preserved at the library of Dr. Sāmi Ibrahām Haddād,* published in Arabic in 1984 by Farid Haddād and Hans Hinrich Biesterfeld."—*Acknowledgements*

This catalog provides a detailed description of the collection of Arabic medical manuscripts and related subjects preserved in the Wellcome Library for the History and Understanding of Medicine (London) (483) and serves as a guide to this collection. Text in English and Arabic. Divided into three parts: Haddād collection; Iskander collection; and collection of fragments, new acquisitions, and other uncataloged codexes. The introduction of the catalog describes characteristics of entries and their arrangement and codicology (e.g., shelf number, physical description, ink, paper, watermarks content, etc.). CD-ROM with digitized images of the manuscripts and details of their bindings. Several appendixes and detailed indexes for the whole collection. Considered a research tool for "librarians, historians, paleographers, art historians, conservators."—*Publisher's description.* The electronic version of this catalog is part of the Wellcome collection and accessible at http://library.wellcome.ac.uk/doc_ WTL038891.html. "Islamic culture and the medical arts" (http://www.

nlm.nih.gov/exhibition/islamic_medical/islamic_00.html) provides access to many Arabic medical manuscripts in the collections of the National Library of Medicine (427).

365 Bibliography of the history of medicine of the United States and Canada, 1939–1960. Genevieve Miller. xvi, 428 p. Baltimore: Johns Hopkins Press, [1964].

016.61097   Z6661.U5M52

Repr.: N.Y.: Arno Pr., 1979.

A consolidation of the annual bibliographies reprinted from the *Bulletin of the history of medicine*, covering the years 1939–1960. Classified arrangement; author index. A section, "Biography," p. 1–26, lists books and periodical articles about persons under the names of the biographees.

366 A bibliography of the writings of Dr. William Harvey, 1578–1657. 3rd ed. Geoffrey Keynes, Gweneth Whitteridge, Christine English. xvi, 136 p., [8] p. of plates, ill., ports. San Francisco; Winchester, Hampshire, U.K.: St. Paul's Bibliographies, 1989. ISBN: 9780906795149.

1st ed., 1928 had title: *A bibliography of the writings of William Harvey, MD, discoverer of the circulation of the blood, 1628–1928*; 2nd ed., 1953.

Rev. ed. of the bibliography of Harvey's works, with a new introduction and revised holdings and locations. Editions of Harvey's works published since 1953 have been added.

367 Bibliotheca Osleriana a catalogue of books illustrating the history of medicine and science. Sir William Osler, Osler Library. xli, 792 p. Montreal: McGill-Queen's University Press, 1969. ISBN: 0773590501.

016.61   Z6676.O86

Catalog of the Osler Library. An earlier version (Oxford: Clarendon Pr., 1929) described the basic collection and had nearly as many entries as the 1969 ed. Some 8,000 entries in classed arrangement with index. Particularly valuable for its annotations.

368 A catalogue of printed books in the Wellcome Historical Medical Library. Wellcome Historical Medical Library. 5 v. London: Wellcome Historical Medical Library, 1962–2007. ISBN: 1888262044 (set).

016.61   Z6676.W4

(Publications of the Wellcome Historical Medical Library. Catalogue series.)

Complete in 5 v. Spine title of v. 1–4, *A catalogue of printed books in the Wellcome Historical Library*, v. 5, *A catalogue of printed books in the Wellcome Library*.

Contents: v. 1, Books printed before 1641 (publ. 1962); v. 2, Books printed from 1641 to 1850 A–E (publ. 1966); v. 3, Books printed from 1641 to 1850 F–L (publ. 1976); v. 4, Books printed from 1641 to 1850 M–R (publ. 1995); v. 5, Books printed from 1641 to 1850 S–Z (publ. 2007).

Catalog of early printed books in the Wellcome Library. Reference source for medical historians and bibliographers.

369   **A catalogue of seventeenth century printed books in the National Library of Medicine.** Peter Krivatsy, National Library of Medicine (U.S.). xiv, 1315 p. Bethesda, Md.: U.S. Dept. of Health and Human Services, Public Health Service, National Institutes of Health, National Library of Medicine, 1989.

016.6109032   Z6659.N38; R128.7

Shipping list no.: 89-261-P. Item 508-F.

For some 13,300 books printed 1601–1700, "monographs, dissertations and corresponding program disputations, broadsides, pamphlets and serials" (*Introd.*), provides title page transcription, physical description, and reference to standard bibliographies. Entries are alphabetical by author, editor, compiler, occasionally by corporate body, and in a few instances by title. Most authors' names are in vernacular form with cross-references to latinized or other names. There is no index, but the National Library of Medicine's (427) History of Medicine Division maintains indexes of printers, publishers, and vernacular imprints.

Complements earlier catalogs of pre–19th-century holdings of NLM: *A catalogue of incunabula and manuscripts in the Army Medical Library*, by Dorothy M. Schullian and Francis E. Sommer, ([1948?]); *A catalogue of sixteenth century printed books in the National Library of Medicine*, comp. by Richard J. Durling (1967); *A catalogue of incunabula and sixteenth century books in the National Library of Medicine: first supplement*, comp. by Peter Krivatsy (1971); and *A short title catalogue of eighteenth century printed books in the National Library of Medicine*, comp. by John Ballard Blake (1979).

370   **Catalogue of Western manuscripts on medicine and science in the Wellcome Historical Medical Library.** S. A. J. Moorat, Wellcome Historical Medical Library. 2 v. in 3, color front. London: Wellcome Historical Medical Library, 1962–1973.

016.61   Z6611.M5W44

MEDICINE

159

(Publications of the Wellcome Historical Medical Library; Catalogue series; MS1–MS3).

Contents: v. 1, Mss. written before 1650 A.D.; v. 2, Mss. written after 1650 A.D. (2 v.).

A group of titles not included in *A catalogue of printed books in the Wellcome Historical Medical Library (370). Catalogue of Western manuscripts in the Wellcome Library for the history and understanding of medicine: Western manuscripts 5120–6244,* publ. in 1999 and curated by Richard Palmer, is a continuation of the original two volumes.

371 **A chronology of medicine and related sciences.** Leslie T. Morton, Robert J. Moore. 784 p. Aldershot, U.K.; Bookfield, Vt.: Scolar Press; Ashgate Publ. Co., 1997. ISBN: 1859282156.

610.9   R133.M717

"Does not claim to be exhaustive but aims to portray the broad development of a wide field over a long period."—*Introd.* Each year's entries are divided into three groups: a) Events (e.g., Nobel Prizes, the establishment of institutions, hospitals, etc., significant publications), b) Births: descriptive biographical entries for individuals; c) Deaths: name, year of birth, and subject keywords. Entries in groups a and b include a brief annotation and a bibliographic reference, and when available the citation number of Morton's medical bibliography (382). Index of personal names (listing of birth entry); subject index (subjects and corporate/institutional names); journal code list.

372 **The Cole Library of early medicine and zoology: Catalogue of books and pamphlets.** Nellie B. Eales. pl., facsim. Oxford: Alden P. [for] the University of Reading Library, 1969–1975.

016.59   Z6676.R35

Contents: v. 1, 1472–1800; v. 2, 1800 to present day and supplement to v. 1.

A descriptive catalog of a distinguished collection. Chronological arrangement, with subject and author indexes.

373 **A commentary on the medical writings of Rudolf Virchow: Based on Schwalbe's Virchow-Bibliographie, 1843–1901.** L. J. Rather, Rudolf Ludwig, Karl Virchow, J. Schwalbe. xi, 236 p., ill. San Francisco, Calif.: Norman Publ., 1991. ISBN: 0930405196.

616.07092B   Z8943.5.S393R37; RB24

(Norman bibliography series; no. 3).

An annotated bibliography that lists in chronological order Virchow's publications in pathology, parasitology, epidemiology, social medicine, public health and sanitation, medical history and philosophy, forensic medicine, military medicine, school hygiene, and medical therapy. "Commentary touches on most of the more important items in Schwalbe's first list."—*Pref.* Entries are numbered. Name and subject indexes.

374 **Encyclopedia of medical sources.** Emerson Crosby Kelly. 476 p. Baltimore: Williams & Wilkins Co., 1948.

016.61   Z6658.K4

The author "kept a list of references to medical eponyms and original works. A search for the earliest or best article has been conducted and great care has been exercised in copying the correct title with exact reference."—*Pref.* This bibliography of first-to-publish articles is arranged alphabetically by investigator/author and gives the contribution with its citation in the literature. Includes an index to the specific condition, disease, medication, treatment, test, etc.

375 **Health and British magazines in the nineteenth century.** E. M. Palmegiano. ix, 282 p. Lanham, Md.: Scarecrow Press, 1998. ISBN: 0810834863.

016.6   Z6673.P288; RA776.5

Bibliography of 2,604 entries based on headlines and captions in major British Victorian serials (selected mainly from the *Wellesley index to Victorian periodicals 1824–1900* [Ann Arbor, Mich.: ProQuest Information and Learning Company]), providing a synopsis of health issues during this period that demonstrates "the evolution of popular thinking about the practice of human health and outlines major concepts and investigates the formation of essential categories still in use, such as ideas of wellness and unwellness, the meaning of care and care-givers, and the productive status of being healthy."—*Publ. notes.* Indexed by author and subject.

376 **Health of black Americans from post reconstruction to integration, 1871–1960: An annotated bibliography of contemporary sources.** Mitchell F. Rice, Woodrow Jones. xxiii, 206 p. New York: Greenwood Press, 1990. ISBN: 0313263140.

016.362108996073   RA448.5.N4.R52

No. 26 of *Bibliographies and indexes in Afro-American and African studies* series.

A comprehensive annotated bibliography of the literature on "the condition of blacks [including] patterns of mortality, morbidity and utilization behaviors of blacks from slavery to the mid-20th century" that aims to provide "a fuller understanding of the history of health care inequities in the U.S."—*Introd.* In three chapters: 1871–1919, 1920–50, 1951–60. Entries give full bibliographic information. Subject and author indexes.

A companion volume by the same compilers, *Black American health: An annotated bibliography*, treats the literature of the 1970s and 1980s.

377 **History of science, technology, and medicine database.** History of Science Society, Society for the History of Technology, Istituto e museo di storia della scienza (Italy), Wellcome Library for the History and Understanding of Medicine, Research Libraries Group. Mountain View, Calif.: Research Libraries Group. http://www.hssonline.org/teaching/teaching_database.html.

"*History of Science, Technology, and Medicine* is the definitive international bibliography on the development and influence of science, from prehistory to the present. It integrates four premier tools for historians: *Isis Current Bibliography of the History of Science, Current Bibliography in the History of Technology, Bibliografia Italiana di Storia della Scienza*, and citations from the Wellcome Library for the History and Understanding of Medicine (incorporating the former Wellcome Bibliography for the History of Medicine [386])."—*Publisher website.* Contains over 250,000 records, indexing journals since 1975.

378 **The history of the health care sciences and health care, 1700–1980: A selective annotated bibliography.** Jonathon Erlen. xvi, 1028 p. New York: Garland, 1984. ISBN: 0824091663.
016.610903   Z6660.8.E74; R148

(Garland reference library of the humanities; v. 398).

Contains 5,004 entries with descriptive annotations; arranged alphabetically by topic. Includes English-language books, journal articles, government documents, unpublished masters' theses, and PhD dissertations. Index. Intended for researchers and students.

379 **History of the health sciences.** 2nd rev. ed. Stephen J. Greenberg, Patricia E. Gallagher. 142 p. Chicago: Medical Library Association, 2002.

Z6660.8.G74

1st ed. (1999) has title: *Bibkit: History of the health sciences.*
(MLA BibKit; no. 5).

Contents: ch. 1, In case of emergency, break glass: Ready reference sources in the history of the health sciences; ch. 2, Medicine's greatest hits: Primary sources in the history of the health sciences; ch. 3, Knowledge is of two kinds: Secondary sources in the history of health sciences; ch. 4, What a tangled web: World wide web resources in the history of the health sciences: section 1, Organizations in the history of the health sciences; section 2, History of the health sciences library collections; section 3, History of the health sciences educational programs; section 4, Organizations and museums with history of the health sciences interests; section 5, Important figures in medicine—their lives and works; section 6, Databases; section 7, Link pages; section 8, Oaths, prayers and declarations; section 9, For children; section 10, The history of diseases; section 11, Bibliographies/chronologies/histories; section 12, Listservs and newsgroups; section 13, Journals.

Collaboration of a librarian and a historian in compiling this resource. Includes resources in medicine, nursing, and the allied sciences. Intended for reference librarians and library users, but not necessarily for history of medicine specialists. Accompanying computer disk provides links to the websites listed in ch. 4. *History of the health sciences world wide web links* (Chicago?: Medical Library Association), a continually updated website, also provides electronic access to the resources listed in ch. 4.

MEDICINE

163

380   Homoeopathy in the United States: A bibliography of homoeopathic medical imprints, 1825–1925. Francesco Cordasco. xx, 231 p. Fairview, N.J.: Junius-Vaughn Press, 1991. ISBN: 094019807X.

016.6155320973   Z6675.H7C67; RX71

Intended in part to replace Thomas Lindsley Bradford's *Homoeopathic bibliography of the United States, from the year 1825 to the year 1891, inclusive* (Philadelphia: Boericke & Tafel, 1892). Divided into three chronological periods, 1825–59, 1860–89, and 1890–1925, which correspond to periods in the history of the field. Historical and biographical works are included, while association and periodicals literature are not. Includes bibliographical references (p. [203]–211) and index.

381   Medicine in Great Britain from the Restoration to the nineteenth century, 1660–1800: An annotated bibliography. Samuel J. Rogal. x, 258 p. New York: Greenwood Press, 1992. ISBN: 0313281157.

016.61094109033   Z6661.G7R63; R486

(Bibliographies and indexes in medical studies, no. 8.)

Provides bibliographic citations, with brief descriptions, to more than 2,000 references published in "medical tracts, treatises, narratives, guides and references published in England, Ireland, Scotland and Wales during one of the most significant periods in the overall history of science in the Western world."—*Pref.* Entries may also provide brief biographical information about the author. References are arranged by topics: general subject, diseases, or anatomical region. Subject and name indexes.

382 **Morton's medical bibliography: An annotated check-list of texts illustrating the history of medicine (Garrison and Morton).** 5th ed. Leslie T. Morton, Jeremy M. Norman. xxiv, 1243 p. Aldershot, Hants, U.K.; Brookfield, Vt.: Scolar Press; Gower, 1991. ISBN: 0859678970.

016.61   Z6660.8.M67; R131

1st ed., 1943; 4th ed., 1983. Title varies.

A major revision of this classic work. A bibliography of 8,927 books and periodical articles in various languages and periods, early times to the present. Classed arrangement with brief annotations indicating the significance of the work in the history and development of the medical sciences; chronological arrangement within each subject category. Name and subject index.

383 **Recent dissertations in the medical humanities.** Jonathon Erlen, University of Pittsburgh Health Sciences Library System. 2001–. Pittsburgh: Health Sciences Library, University of Pittsburgh Medical Center. http://www.hsls.pitt.edu/guides/histmed/ researchresources/dissertations/.

Provides a monthly current awareness service for selected recent medical dissertation and theses. Arranged by topics, currently covers the following areas: AIDS (social and historical contexts); alternative medicine (social and historical contexts); art and medicine; biomedical ethics; history of medicine prior to 1800; history of medicine and health care; history of science and technology; literature/theater and medicine; nursing history; pharmacy/pharmacology and history; philosophy and medicine; psychiatry/psychology and history; public health/international health; religion and medicine; women's health and history. To view complete citations, abstracts, and full-text of dissertations requires a subscription to Proquest Dissertations and Theses (PQDT) (Ann Arbor, Mich.: ProQuest).

384 **Secondary sources in the history of Canadian medicine: A bibliography.** Charles G. Roland. xxiii, 190 p. Waterloo, Ont.: Hannah Institute for the History of Medicine, 1984–2000. ISBN: 088920182X.

016.610971   Z6661.C3R64; R461

Vol. 2 has special title: *Bibliographie de l'histoire de la médecine*. Publ. varies.

Broad, enumerative retrospective bibliography, categorized by biographical listing, subject entries, and author listing. Contains published sources about events or persons. Entries do not contain annotations or library location(s). Further inclusions, exclusions, and omissions are mentioned in the introduction. Bibliographic references, list of journal abbreviations. Vol. 2 continues and also expands v. 1. It includes 1984–98 publications, and also many pre-1984 publications not included in v. 1. Vol. 2 contains more French-language material.

Continuously maintained data files are available to scholars at McMaster University.

385 **Sir William Osler: An annotated bibliography with illustrations.** Richard L. Golden, Charles G. Roland. xv, 214 p., ill. San Francisco: Norman Publ., 1988. ISBN: 0930405005.

016.61   Z8647.8.S55; R464

(Norman bibliography series; no. 1.)

Revised and updated ed. of Maude E. Abbott's *Classified and annotated bibliography of Sir William Osler's publications*, 2nd ed. (Montreal: The Medical Museum, McGill Univ., 1939).

Contains 1,493 citations, some with annotations, arranged chronologically in 11 categories. This ed. includes a checklist of Osler's papers published under his pseudonym (Egerton Yorrick Davis) and a list of editions, printings, and translations of *The principles of medicine*. Supplemented by *Addenda to Sir William Osler: An annotated bibliography with illustrations*, ed. by Richard L. Golden ([s.n.], Huntington, N.Y., 1997), with addenda and its index limited to new and revised entries.

386 **Wellcome bibliography for the history of medicine.** Wellcome Library for the History and Understanding of Medicine. 2003–Jun. 2004. [London]: Wellcome Library for the History and Understanding of Medicine. http://bibpurl.oclc.org/web/24.

Publ. from May 2003 (no issues Jan.–Apr. 2003) until it ceased in Jul. 2004.

Continues: *Current work in the history of medicine,* publ. 1954–99. 1991–99, available both in print and online and continued as online publication with the same title, 2000–Dec. 2002.

Index of articles on the history of medicine, arranged by subject, with international coverage. Wellcome bibliography archive files (May 2000–Jun. 2004) are freely available via the Wellcome Library website, as will the entries created in the Library catalogue (cf. Wellcome website).

387   WHO historical collection. World Health Organization. 2000s–. Geneva, Switzerland: World Health Organization. http://www.who. int/library/collections/historical/en/print.html.

Produced by World Health Organization (WHO) (951); part of WHO Library and Information Networks for Knowledge (LNK).

Covers conferences before the founding of the WHO, WHO official records, International Sanitary Conventions (since 1851), and official records, reports, and other published materials from the Office International d'Hygiène Publique (OIHP), the health organization of the League of Nations (UNRRA). Includes materials on plague, cholera, and yellow fever, and also more recent epidemics; international classifications and nomenclatures of diseases; and public health and medicine monographs on public health in different countries and languages. Related links are, for example, WHOLIS: World Health Organization Library Database (484) and WHO Archives (http://www.who.int/archives/en/index.html). The distinctions between the WHO library, the WHO archives, and WHO records are described at http://www.who.int/archives/fonds_collections/ partners/en/index.html.

Directories

388   Directory of history of medicine collections. Crystal Smith, National Library of Medicine (U.S.), History of Medicine Division. 2006. Bethesda, Md.: U.S. Dept. of Health & Human Services, National Institutes of Health, National Libray of Medicine, History of Medicine Division. http://www.nlm.nih.gov/hmd/directory/ directoryhome.html.

"2007 Directory of History of Medicine Collections," developed by the History of Medicine Division (HMD) (Bethesda, Md.: National Library of Medicine) of the the National Library of Medicine (NLM) (427).

History of medicine component of DIRLINE® (Directory of

Information Resources Online) (208). Contains locations and descriptions of medical history collections in the U.S., Canada, and other parts of the world. Includes medicine, dentistry, nursing, and veterinary medicine. Helpful to researchers in identifying medical history collections throughout the world. Further details about this directory at http://www.nlm.nih.gov/hmd/directory/about.html. Also available as a print edition.

Historical Surveys

389   **The Cambridge illustrated history of medicine.** Roy Porter. 400 p., ill. (some color), color maps. Cambridge; New York: Cambridge University Press, 1996. ISBN: 0521442117.

610.9   R131.C232

A history of Western medicine from antiquity to the present in ten chapters. Includes a brief reference guide with chronology, major human diseases (in tabular format, listing disease, cause, and means of transmission), notes, further reading, and index of medical personalities. Illustrated with prints, paintings, photographs, diagrams, maps, and tables. Written for general readers. *The Cambridge history of medicine* (Cambridge, 2006), also ed. by Roy Porter, contains a ten-page update, with the same text as the 1996 ed. but no ill.

390   **Chiropractic: History and evolution of a new profession.** Walter I. Wardwell. xv, 358 p., ill. St. Louis: Mosby-Year Book, 1992. ISBN: 0801668832.

615.5340973   RZ225.U6W37

Includes bibliographical references (p. 289–340) and index.

Scholarly work on the history of chiropractic since its beginning in 1895, with chapters on the early leaders in the field, their schools, the struggle for licensing legislation and resulting medical opposition, and acceptance of chiropractic. Other titles in the history of chiropractic include J. Stuart Moore's *Chiropractic in America: The history of a medical alternative, Chiropractic: An illustrated history,* and *A history of chiropractic education in North America: Report to the Council on Chiropractic Education* (396).

391   **Fragments of neurological history.** John Pearce. xvii, 633 p., ill., ports. London: Imperial College Press, 2003.

616.809   RC338.P436

A collection of articles in the history of neurology and medicine. Includes, for example, biographical reviews (e.g., Galen and Vesalius), chapter entitled "Illness of the famous, and some medical truants," and chapters on anatomical and neurophysiological phenomena, dementias, headaches, cranial nerve and various other neurological disorders, and the origins of insulin and aspirin. For neurologists, neuroscientists, physicians, and general readers. Includes bibliographical references and index.

392 **The genesis of neuroscience.** A. Walker, Edward Laws, George Udvarhelyi, American Association of Neurological Surgeons. [Park Ridge, Ill.]: American Association of Neurological Surgeons, 1998. ISBN: 1879284626.

616.8009 QP353

Contents: ch. 1, Origins of neuroscience; ch. 2, From Galen through the 18th century: An overview; ch. 3, The evolution of encephalization; ch. 4, The spinal cord; ch. 5, The peripheral nerves; ch. 6, Clinical and pathological examination of patients with neurological disorders; ch. 7, Manifestation of cerebral disorders: Headache, epilepsy, sleep disorders, and cerebrovascular disease; ch. 8, Congenital anomalies of the nervous system; ch. 9, Infections and inflammatory involvement of the central nervous system; ch. 10, The evolution of neurosurgery; ch. 11, Neuroscience comes of age. Appendixes (A) The arts in the evolution of neuroscience; (B) Medical fees throughout the ages; (C) Historical glossary of neurological syndromes; (D) Bibliography of writings by A. Earl Walker; Index.

Describes the origins of neurology and neurosurgery from prehistoric times until the 19th century. Includes portraits of many neurologists and neurosurgeons. Other titles in this area include *Fragments of neurological history* (391) and *History of neurology* (400).

393 **The greatest benefit to mankind: A medical history of humanity.** 1st American ed. Roy Porter. xvi, 831 p., ill. New York: W. W. Norton, 1998. ISBN: 0393046346.

610.9 R131.P59

British ed. publ. with subtitle: *A medical history of humanity from antiquity to the present.*

Contents: (I) Introduction; (II) The roots of medicine; (III) Antiquity; (IV) Medicine and faith; (V) The Medieval west; (VI) Indian medicine; (VII) Chinese medicine; (VIII) Renaissance; (IX) The new science; (X) Enlightenment; (XI) Scientific medicine in the nineteenth century; (XII)

Nineteenth-century medical care; (XIII) Public medicine; (XIV) From Pasteur to penicillin; (XV) Tropical medicine, world diseases; (XVI) Psychiatry; (XVII) Medical research; (XVIII) Clinical science; (XIX) Surgery; (XX) Medicine, state and society; (XXI) Medicine and the people; (XXII) The past, the present and the future.

Explores the evolution of medicine through the ages and the development of medical specialties and medical practice. While viewpoint is global, emphasis is on Western medicine. Chronological table of contents, illustrations, bibliographical references (p. 719–764), and index.

394   Guardians of medical knowledge: The genesis of the Medical Library Association. Jennifer Connor. xi, 190 p., ill. [Chicago, Ill.]; Lanham, Md.: Medical Library Association; Scarecrow Press, 2000. ISBN: 0810834707.

026.6106073   Z673.M5C66

Medical Library Association (MLA), established in 1898.

Focuses on the early history of MLA and the physicians who founded and led the MLA. "Portrays the genesis of the Medical Library Association (MLA) through analysis of its origins, its dominant medical culture, and its intricate network of physician leaders."—*Author's descr.* Includes a listing of MLA presidents, 1898–1998, officers of national associations, and other tables. Ill. Includes bibliographical references (p. [153]–180) and index.

395   The history of American homeopathy: The academic years, 1820–1935. John S. Haller. xiv, 444 p., ill. New York: Pharmaceutical Products Press, 2005. ISBN: 0789026597.

615.5320973   RX51.H34

Describes the life of the founder of homeopathy, Samuel Hahnemann (1755–1843), homeopathy in Europe and the U.S., and the controversies homeopathic medicine created until its demise. Includes works of American homeopathic physicians, a list of homeopathic journals, and homeopathic medical colleges.

396   A history of chiropractic education in North America: Report to the Council on Chiropractic Education. Joseph C. Keating, Alana K. Callender, Carl Service, Cleveland Association for the History of Chiropractic. ix, 516 p., ill., ports. [Davenport, Iowa]: The Association, 1998. ISBN: 0965913112.

615.534071173   RZ225.U6K425

"The story of the Council on Chiropractic Education (CCE) is an important piece of the saga of chiropractic education" (*Foreword*) and its struggles and successes in the development of the profession, quality education and training of doctors, and standard-setting and recognized accreditation. *Chronology of events and activities related to the application for correspondent status of the Sherman College of Chiropractic*: p. 471–472. Includes bibliographical references (p. 473–494) and index.

397   A history of medicine. 2nd ed. Lois N. Magner. xii, 611 p., ill. Boca Raton, Fla.: Taylor & Francis, 2005. ISBN: 0824740742.

610.9   R131.M179

1st ed., 1992.

Contents: Paleopathology and paleomedicine; Medicine in ancient civilizations: Mesopotamia and Egypt; The medical traditions of India and China; Greco-Roman medicine; The Middle Ages; The Renaissance and the scientific revolution; Native civilizations and cultures of the Americas; The Americanization of old world medicine; Clinical and preventive medicine; The medical counterculture: Unorthodox and alternative medicine; Women and medicine; The art and science of surgery; Medical microbiology and public health; Diagnostics and therapeutics.

Survey of the major areas, themes, and important events of medicine and its famous men and women. Useful for students and general readers. Online ed. available via netLibrary.

398   A history of medicine. 2d ed., rev. and enl. ed. Arturo Castiglioni, E. B. Krumbhaar. xxx, 1192, lxi p., illus., ports. New York: Knopf, 1947.

610.9   R131.C272

Translation of: *Storia della medicina* (rev. and enl. ed. Milan: A. Mondadori, 1936).

A comprehensive and readable source, especially strong in coverage of Greek and Roman history of medicine. Includes a useful bibliography (p. 1147–1192) arranged by subject. Index of subjects and index of names. Serves to supplement Fielding H. Garrison's *Introduction to the history of medicine* (402).

399   History of medicine in the United States. Francis R. Packard, Robert P. Parsons. 2 v., front., ill., plates, ports., facsims. New York: P. B. Hoeber, Inc., 1931 [i.e., 1932].

R151.P12

Repr.: N.Y.: Hafner, 1963.

An enlargement of the author's earlier work (1901). Contains much useful reference material, in both text and ill., on American medical history, biography, and bibliography. Gives a bibliography of pre-Revolutionary medical publications and a general bibliography.

400   History of neurology. Fielding H. Garrison, Lawrence C. McHenry. xv, 552 p., ill., facsims., ports. Springfield, Ill.: Thomas, [1969].

616.809   RC338.G36

Contents: ch. 1, Ancient origins; ch. 2, "The Middle Ages and the Renaissance"; ch. 3, "The seventeenth century"; ch. 4, "The eighteenth century"; ch. 5, "The nineteenth century: Neuroanatomy"; ch. 6, "The nineteenth century: Neurophysiology"; ch. 7, "The nineteenth century: Neurochemistry"; ch. 8, "The nineteenth century: Neuropathology"; ch. 9, "Clinical neurology"; ch. 10, "The neurological examination"; ch. 11, "Neurological diseases."

A re-publication of Garrison's *History of neurology*, previously published in 1925 as a historical chapter in Charles L. Dana's *Textbook of nervous diseases*.

Presents a broad survey of neurology from antiquity to the beginning of the 20th century. Other more recent titles in the history of neurology are, for example, *A short history of neurology: The British contribution* (404), *The genesis of neuroscience* (392), and *Fragments of neurological history* (391), to name a few.

401   Illustrated history of medicine. Jean-Charles Sournia. 585 p., ill. London: Harold Starke Publ., 1992. ISBN: 1872457053.

610.9   R131

Engl. language ed. of *Histoire de la médecine et des médecins* by Jean-Charles Sournia.

Contents: ch. I, The diseases of prehistory; ch. II, The continued existence of ethnomedicine; ch. III, The archaeology of medicine; ch. IV, The Greeks establish our system of medicine; ch. V, The Middle Ages in the Mediterranean countries; ch. VI, Different types of medicine; ch. VII, Anatomy in the Renaissance; ch. VIII, The seventeenth century and the Age of Reason; ch. IX, Medicine in the Age of the Enlightenment; ch. X, Conversion to clinical medicine; ch. XI, Laboratory medicine; ch. XII, From X-rays to penicillin; ch. XIII, The explosion of knowledge and techniques; Appendixes.

Extensive pictorial history of medicine. Includes bibliographical references (p. 562–63) and index.

402 **An introduction to the history of medicine: With medical chronology, suggestions for study and bibliographic data.**
4th ed., rev. and enl. ed. Fielding H. Garrison. 996 p., ill., ports. Philadelphia: W.B. Saunders, 1929. ISBN: 0721640303.

R131.G3

Errata slip tipped in after t.p. Repr., 1967. 1st ed., 1913; 3rd ed., 1921.

Valuable reference history, covering the whole history of medicine from the earliest times to the 1920s. Much biography and bibliography are included for every period. Appendixes include: a chronology of medicine and public hygiene; hints on the study of medical history; bibliographic notes for collateral reading including histories of medicine, medical biography, and histories of medical subjects. Index of personal names and index of subjects.

403 **Science and technology in medicine: An illustrated account based on ninety-nine landmark publications from five centuries.**
Andras Gedeon. vii, 551 p., ill. (some color). New York: Springer, 2006. ISBN: 0387278745.

610   R131.G43

Each of the 99 essays ("landmark publications") includes a brief biographical sketch, a description of the particular scientific and technological discovery, excerpts, and a summary of the original publication. Explains the significance and gives historical perspective and background for many medical techniques, 1528 to the present. Includes bibliography and timeline. Index of personal names.

404 **A short history of neurology: The British contribution, 1660–1910.** F. Clifford Rose. ix, 282 p., ill. Oxford; Boston: Butterworth-Heinemann, 1999. ISBN: 0750641657.

616.80941   RC339.G7R68

Concise history of British neurology, with contributions from neurologists, neuroscientists, neurosurgeons, and medical historians. Includes chapters on Thomas Willis (1621–75) and other famous neuroscientists, the evolution of British neurology in comparison to other countries, neurological texts, and other important areas in the development of neurology. Includes bibliographical references and index.

405   **Two centuries of American medicine, 1776–1976.** James III
Bordley, A. McGehee Harvey. xv, 844 p., ill. Philadelphia: Saunders,
1976. ISBN: 0721618731.

610.973   R151.B58

Contents: pt. 1, The first century—1776–1876; pt. 2, Period of scientific advance—1887–1946; pt. 3, Period of explosive growth—1946–76;
Appendix A, Population figures; Appendix B, Chronological summary of
major events in American medical history.

The purpose is "to relate in language that can be understood by interested laymen, as well as the physician, an account of the extraordinary
advances in medical education and in the prevention and treatment of disease that have taken place during the two centuries of this nation's political
independence."—*Pref.* Includes bibliography and index.

406   **The Western medical tradition: 800 B.C.–1800 A.D.** Lawrence I.
Conrad, Wellcome Institute for the History of Medicine. xiv, 556
p., ill. Cambridge; New York: Cambridge University Press, 1995.
ISBN: 0521381355.

610.94   R131.W47

Contents: ch. 1, Medicine in the Greek world, 800–50 BC; ch. 2, Roman
medicine, 250 BC–200 AD; ch. 3, Medicine in late antiquity and the early
Middle Ages; ch. 4, The Arab-Islamic medical tradition; ch. 5, Medicine
in Medieval Western Europe, 1000–1500; ch. 6, Medicine in early modern
Europe, 1500–1700; ch. 7, The eighteenth century; ch. 8, Conclusion.

Survey of the history of Western medicine, with ill. from the Wellcome
collection. Selected bibliographies for each chapter and general bibliography at the end of the vol. Written for scholars. A companion vol. is *The
Western medical tradition 1800 to 2000* (New York: Cambridge University
Press, 2006).

407   **The Western medical tradition: 1800 to 2000.** W. F. Bynum,
Anne Hardy, Stephen Jacyna. xiii, 614 p., ill. New York: Cambridge
University Press, 2006. ISBN: 0521475244.

610   R131.W472

Contents: ch. 1, Medicine in transformation, 1800–49 (Stephen Jacyna);
ch. 2, The rise of science in medicine, 1850–1913 (W. F. Bynum); ch. 3,
Continuity in crisis: Medicine, 1914–45 (Christopher Lawrence); ch. 4,
Medical enterprise and global response, 1945–2000 (Anne Hardy and E.
M. Tansey).

"Gives an account of the last two centuries of the development of 'Western' medicine [and a description of] important people, events, and transformations, [and] explanations for why medicine developed as it did. It contains historical summaries of the development of medicine after the Second World War."—*Introd.* Considered a companion vol. to *The Western medical tradition, 800 B.C. to A.D. 1800* (Cambridge; New York: Cambridge University Press, 1995).

408   **Western medicine: An illustrated history.** Irvine Loudon. xvi, 347 p., [24] p. of plates, ill. (some color), facsims. (some color), maps, ports. (some color). Oxford; New York: Oxford University Press, 1997. ISBN: 0198205090.

610.9   R131.W47

Emphasis on art and visual representation. The Wellcome Iconographic Collections videodisc, containing 56,000 images on the history of medicine, was used in designing this resource. Videodisc was made from 1990–93 at the Wellcome Institute for the History of Medicine, which was dissolved as of Oct. 2000 and is now called The Wellcome Library for the History and Understanding of Medicine (483). Ranging from "Medicine in the classical world" to "Medicine in the second half of the twentieth century," with coverage of various medical themes related to the social history of medicine, medical education, the medical profession, public health, medical genetics, and molecular medicine. Further reading, chronology, glossary, and list of ill. sources. Index.

409   **Women, health, and medicine in America: A historical handbook.** Rima D. Apple. xxii, 580 p., ill. New York: Garland Publ., 1990. ISBN: 0824084470.

610.82   RA564.85.W664

Includes chapters on a wide variety of subjects, including Childbirth in America, 1650–1990; Historical perspectives on women and mental illness; and Race as a factor in health. Extensive bibliography and index.

Indexes; Abstract journals; Databases

410   **BIOSIS previews.** Thomson Reuters, Biological Abstracts, Inc. Philadelphia: Thomson Reuters. http://www.thomsonreuters.com/ products_services/scientific/Biological_Abstracts.

QH301

Online edition of *Biological abstracts*, BIOSIS Previews includes *Biological abstracts/RRM*, which stands for reports, reviews, and meetings. Long regarded as the most thorough source for indexing in all areas of biology and biomedicine, BIOSIS Previews covers research reports in journals and other publications, reviews, books, and conference papers. Over the years, coverage has expanded to include interdisciplinary fields of biochemistry, biotechnology, genetics, and molecular biology. Nearly 6,000 journals and 1,500 international meetings are indexed. Online subscriptions are available from various providers; most content is updated weekly, and backfiles are available from 1926 to the present. Database available through several vendors.

411　**CAM on PubMed.** Alternative Medicine, National Library of Medicine. Bethesda, Md.: National Center for Complementary and Alternative Medicine; National Library of Medicine. http://nccam. nih.gov/camonpubmed/.

CAM (Complementary and Alternative Medicine) is jointly developed by the National Library of Medicine (NLM) (427) and the National Center for Complementary and Alternative Medicine (NCCAM). "NCCAM defines complementary and alternative medicine (CAM) as those health care practices not currently considered an integral part of conventional medicine. It covers a broad range of healing therapies, approaches, and systems. Some examples of CAM include acupuncture, herbs, homeopathy, chiropractic, hypnosis, and traditional Oriental medicine."—*NCCAM website.* CAM can be searched either as a subset of PubMed (432), which provides citations to the journal literature of complementary and alternative medicine, or from the NCCAM website (http://nccam.nih.gov/), with citations back to 1966, including different CAM therapies and therapeutic systems.

412　**The Cochrane Library.** Cochrane Collaboration. 1996–. Hoboken, N.J.: Wiley Interscience. ISSN: 1465-1858. http://www3. interscience.wiley.com/cgi-bin/mrwhome/106568753/HOME.

R723.7

Acronyms: Evidence-based medicine (EBM); Evidence-based Health Care (EBHC).

Imprint varies: 1996–2003, Update Software Ltd., Oxford, U.K.; publ. by Wiley Interscience 2004–. Produced by contributors to the Cochrane Collaboration (founded in 1993 and named after the British epidemiologist, Archie Cochrane) and consists of a group of experts in the various clinical specialties who apply EBM criteria to the review and selection of studies, perform meta-analyses, and then write detailed topical reviews.

The Cochrane Library consists of several online databases that provide systematic reviews, meta-analyses of the literature, and randomized clinical trials: Cochrane Database of Systematic Reviews (CDSR)—Cochrane Reviews and protocols; Database of Abstracts of Reviews of Effectiveness (DARE)—Other Reviews; Cochrane Central Register of Controlled Trials (CENTRAL)—Clinical Trials; Cochrane Methodology Register (CMR)—Methods Studies; Health Technology Assessment Database (HT)—Health Technology; and NHS Economic Evaluation Database (NHSEED). Further detailed descriptions can be found at http://www3.interscience.wiley.com/cgi-bin/mrwhome/106568753/ProductDescriptions.html. Also available via Ovid and EBSCO.

The major product of the Cochrane Collaboration is the Cochrane Database of Systematic Reviews, prepared mostly by healthcare professionals who work as volunteers in one of the many Cochrane Review Groups. Editorial teams oversee the preparation and updating of the reviews and applying quality standards. Provides access to full-text review articles reviewing the effects of health care.

Other examples of EBM and EBHC resources include ACP Journal Club and ACP PIER (American College of Physicians), Clinical Evidence (BMJ), DynaMed (EBSCO), InfoRetriever/InfoPOEMS (http://www.InfoPOEMS.com), Evidence Matters, PubMed (432)/PubMed Clinical Queries (systematic reviews and meta-analyses [http://www.ncbi.nlm.nih.gov/entrez/query/static/clinical.shtml]), Turning Research Into Practice [TRIP] database, Health Services Technology Assessment Text [HSTAT] [419], NLM gateway [429], searching across several government information systems [e.g., PubMed [432], ClinicalTrials.gov [191], HSRProj, etc.], National Guideline Clearinghouse [326], and others.

Many websites from various organizations and universities provide EBM and EBHC-related subject guides, e.g., EBM Resource Center, New York Academy of Medicine [http://www.ebmny.org/], "Evidence-Based Practice" subject guide [Hardin Library for the Health Sciences, The University of Iowa http://www.lib.uiowa.edu/hardin/eb.html], "Evidence Based Medicine" [Welch Medical Library, Johns Hopkins University http://www.welch.jhu.edu/internet/ebr.html], and many others.

Print EBM/EBHC resources are, for example, Sharon E. Strauss and R. Brian Haynes' *Evidence-based medicine: How to practice and teach EBM*

[3rd ed., 2005; author varies: 1st and 2nd ed. by David L. Sackett] and *Clinical epidemiology: How to do clinical practice research* [3rd ed., 2006], by R. Brian Haynes.

413   CRISP. National Institutes of Health. 1998–. Bethesda, Md.: National Institutes of Health. http://purl.access.gpo.gov/GPO/ LPS1687.

Produced by National Institutes of Health (NIH) (470).

"Searchable database of federally funded biomedical research projects conducted at universities, hospitals, and other research institutions."—*Main page.* Extensive help pages for effective use of the database are provided at http://crisp.cit.nih.gov/crisp/crisp_help.help. *The CRISP thesaurus* (http://crisp.cit.nih.gov/Thesaurus/index.htm), until 1999 also available in print format, is a controlled vocabulary used to assign indexing terms and keywords to research projects and is also useful for searching this database.

414   EMBASE. Elsevier Science. 1974–. Amsterdam, The Netherlands: Elsevier Science. http://www.embase.com/.

EMBASE.com (originally launched in 1999, now release 6.0) is a biomedical and pharmaceutical database containing bibliographic records with abstracts from EMBASE (1974–present) and MEDLINE (1966–present, deduplicated and searchable with EMTREE) (574). Indexes 7,000 journals. About half of records have full-text links.

EMBASE is the online version of *Excerpta Medica: The international medical abstracting service*, an abstracting journal with approx. 52 subsections (44 currently in use), providing author and subject access to the biomedical literature and published since 1947, searchable in EMBASE since 1974. With few exceptions, EMBASE section headings correspond to the titles of the *Excerpta Medica* abstract journals. Information about EMBASE Classic (backfile 1947–73), available at http://www.info.embase-classic.com/ and factsheet at http://www.info.embaseclassic.com/pdfs/factsheet.pdf.

Bibliographic database for the biomedical literature, with extensive coverage of pharmacology, drug research, and toxicology; also covers veterinary medicine, dentistry, and nursing. Indexes more than 4,000 journals. Titles indexed are listed in the *EMBASE list of journals indexed* (36). International in scope, with coverage of unique titles not indexed in MEDLINE. *EMTREE thesaurus* (574) provides a controlled vocabulary for

EMBASE, with all MeSH (575) terms having been converted to EMTREE index terms. Records contain bibliographic information, controlled terms (EMTREE medical and drug descriptors, EMTREE codes), drug trade names and manufacturers, and medical device trade names and manufacturers. Most records include abstracts, and many include a CAS registry number. Also available from several commercial vendors.

415   GenBank. National Center for Biotechnology Information (U.S.). 1990s–. Bethesda, Md.: National Center for Biotechnology Information, National Library of Medicine, National Institutes of Health, U.S. Dept. of Health and Human Services. http://www. ncbi.nlm.nih.gov/Genbank/.

Genetic sequence database, an annotated collection of all publicly available nucleotide (DNA and RNA) sequences and their protein translations. Laboratories around the world contribute sequence data to GenBank, and more than 100,000 organisms are represented. The overview gives current status of number of records and nucleic acid bases in the database and also instructions for submitting, revising, or updating sequence data. Maintained by NCBI, GenBank joins the DNA Databank of Japan (DDBJ) and the European Molecular Biology Laboratory (EMBL) in forming the International Nucleotide Sequence Database Collaboration (INSCD, http://www.insdc.org/), based on continual exchange of data among these organizations.

Searchable from NCBI's Entrez (3) browser or the BLAST (basic local alignment search tool) system, which uses software algorithms to find regions of local similarity between nucleic acid sequences. Important for libraries supporting genetics and molecular biology teaching and research.

416   GeneTests. Children's Hospital and Medical Center (Seattle, Wash.). 1993–. Seattle, Wash.: Univ. of Washington. http://www. genetests.org/.

Contents: Home page; About GeneTests; GeneReviews; Laboratory directory; Clinic directory; Educational materials.

Provides authoritative information on genetic testing and its use in diagnosis, disease management, and genetic counseling. Promotes use of genetic services in patient care and decision making by individuals. GeneReviews and Laboratory directory can be searched by disease, gene symbol, protein name, etc. Contains context-sensitive illustrated glossary, teaching tools, and other resources.

417 **Global Index Medicus.** World Health Organization. 2005?–. Geneva, Switzerland: World Health Organization. http://www.who. int/ghl/medicus/en/.

Produced by World Health Organization (WHO) (951); publ. under the auspices of WHO Regional Offices.

Intended to complement the internationally known biomedical bibliographic indexes. Although most of the significant medical periodicals published in the developed countries are indexed in MEDLINE (425) and other databases, there is still a considerable amount of important and highly relevant medical and health documentation from developing countries that is not included.

418 **Health reference center—academic.** Gale Group. 1999–. Farmington Hills, Mich.: Gale; Cengage Learning. http://www. galegroup.com.

R11

Available on either InfoTrac or Powersearch platform (customer must choose).

A multisource database and integrated collection of nursing, allied health, and medicine journals; consumer health magazines; newsletters; newspaper articles; pamphlets; and reference books. Records are available in a combination of indexing, abstract, and full-text formats. Designed for nursing and allied health students as well as consumer health researchers.

Other Gale resources include a consumer health resource, Health and Wellness Resource Center (632), and Gale Virtual Reference Library (Farmington Hills, Mich.: Gale Cengage Learning, 2002–).

419 **Health Services Technology Assessment Texts (HSTAT).** National Library of Medicine (U.S.). 1994?–. Bethesda, Md.: National Library of Medicine (U.S.), National Institutes of Health, Dept. of Health and Human Services. http://hstat.nlm.nih.gov.

Coordinated by the National Library of Medicine's National Information Center on Health Services Research and Health Care Technology (NICHSR). Part of the "NCBI Bookshelf" (http://www.ncbi.nlm.nih.gov/sites/entrez?db=Books).

Searchable collection of full-text documents containing results of health services research, evidence reports and technology assessments, consensus conference reports, clinical practice guidelines (e.g., HIV/AIDS approved guidelines and information), reports of the Surgeon General, and other health information in support of health care decision making.

Intended for health care providers, health service researchers, policy makers, payers, consumers, and information professionals. Further details in the *HSTAT fact sheet* (http://www.nlm.nih.gov/pubs/factsheets/hstat.html).

420 **Index medicus.** U.S. Dept. of Health, Education and Welfare, Public Health Service, National Institutes of Health, National Library of Medicine. Bethesda, Md.: U.S. Dept. of Health, Education and Welfare; Public Health Service; National Institutes of Health; National Library of Medicine, 1960–2004. ISSN: 0019-3879.

016.61 Z6660.I42

Title varies; imprint varies. *Index medicus*: series I, 1879–99; series II, 1903–20; series III, 1921–27; 1916–26, *Quarterly cumulative index to current medical literature*, publ. by the American Medical Association (AMA); 1927–56, *Quarterly cumulative index medicus* (AMA) and *Cumulated index medicus* (AMA); 1941–59, *Current list of medical literature* (Army Medical Library, now National Library of Medicine [NLM] [427]); 1960–2004 again called *Index medicus* (n.s., cumulated annually as *Cumulated index medicus* until 2000), available online as PubMed® (432)/MEDLINE® (425) and currently used exclusively in its online version. For a review of the scope of coverage for *Index medicus*–related titles see *Introduction to reference sources in the health sciences* (287).

Provides subject and author access. Remains useful for researching the biomedical, healthcare, and related literature from other disciplines for which online access is not yet available in PubMed/MEDLINE.

Related titles: *Bibliographia medica (Index Medicus): Receuil mensuel* (Institut de Bibliographie, Paris), by Marcel Baudouin, publ. 1900–02 while publication of *Index medicus* was temporarily suspended; IndexCat (479), the online version of *Index catalogue of the Library of the Surgeon-General's Office*: 1st series, 1880–95; 2nd series, 1896–1916; 3rd series, 1918–32; 4th series A–Mez, 1936–48; 4th series Mh–MN, 1955; 5th series, 1959–61; *Bibliography of medical reviews* (separate publication, 1955–67; 1968–77 publ. separately and also as pt. of *Index medicus*; 1978–. publ. only as pt. of *Index medicus*); 1970–97, *Abridged index medicus* (NLM), intended for individual physicians and small libraries. "Index Medicus Chronology" (http://www.nlm.nih.gov/services/indexmedicus.html) provides further details.

421 **International clinical trials registry platform search portal (ICTRP).** World Health Organization. 200?–. Geneva, [Switzerland]: World Health Organization. http://www.who.int/trialsearch/.

Produced by World Health Organization (WHO) (951).

Database to locate information about clinical trials. Described by Tim Evans (WHO) as a "collaborative international initiative led by WHO that facilitates the identification of all clinical trials, regardless of whether or not they have been published." For health care researchers.

422 ISI web of knowledge. Thomson Reuters. 2002–. Philadelphia: Thomson Reuters. http://www.isiwebofknowledge.com/.

Z5321

Platform for proprietary databases such as ISI Web of Science (423), Journal Citation Reports (Philadelphia: Thomson Reuters, 1994–), ISI Essential Science Indicators, ISI Current Contents Connect, ISI Proceedings, ISI Chemistry, BIOSIS Previews (410), and Zoological Record (Philadelphia: Thomson Reuters, 199?–); tools such as Index to Organism Names, ISI-HighlyCited.com, ScienceWatch.com; and many other nonproprietary databases, including MEDLINE (425) and CAB Abstracts (1143). Includes access to EndNote Web bibliographic management software. Permits cross searching of all subscribed databases.

423 ISI web of science. Thomson Reuters. 2002. Philadelphia: Thomson Reuters. http://www.thomsonreuters.com/ products_services/scientific/Web_of_Science.

Web of Science is the citation indexing component of ISI's suite of databases, now unified under the name ISI Web of Knowledge (422). Includes the Science Citation Index, the Social Sciences Citation Index (Stamford, Conn.?: Thomson Reuters), and the Arts and Humanities Citation Index (Stamford, Conn.?: Thomson Reuters). Allows for searches of a cited reference as well as general search options. Includes the ability to search for "related records" that have similar common citations, even though the items do not actually cite each other. Coverage currently goes back to 1900.

424 Literature, arts, and medicine database. New York University School of Medicine. 1993–. New York: New York University School of Medicine. http://litmed.med.nyu.edu/Main?action=new.

Part of Medical Humanities, New York University (NYU) School of Medicine (http://medhum.med.nyu.edu), Division of Educational Informatics (DEI). Previously part of the Hippocrates Project (NYU School of Medicine), a media laboratory that applies information technology to medical education. Established 1993 in Gopher; Web-based since 1994.

Contains selected annotations for works of literature, art, and performing arts pertaining to the illness experience, medical education, and medical practice, i.e., their placement in a medical context. Each annotation provides a summary, including a description for works of art, critical commentary, publishing information, and relevant keywords. Provides a "viewing room" (for digital resources), a "listening room" (for literary texts), and a "screening room" (excerpts of videos or theater productions). Annotations are searchable by words or phrases, title, work category (art, film, literature, theater), art form, genre, or medium; also provides search capability for people, keyword, annotator, and free text. Intended for an academic audience. This website also provides links to syllabi in medical humanities from other institutions as well as a directory (organized by country, state, and institution) of individuals engaged in various aspects of medical humanities work.

425 **MEDLINE.** National Library of Medicine (U.S.). 1900s–. Bethesda, Md.: National Library of Medicine (U.S.). http://purl.access.gpo. gov/GPO/LPS4708.

MEDLINE®—Medical Literature Analysis and Retrieval System Online (National Library of Medicine®—NLM), primary subset of PubMed® (432) and part of the Entrez (3) databases provided by the National Center for Biotechnology Information (NCBI). Coverage extends back to 1950, with some older material (cf. http://www.nlm.nih.gov/services/oldmed. html).

Bibliographic database, providing comprehensive access to the international biomedical literature from the fields of medicine, nursing, dentistry, veterinary medicine, allied health, and the preclinical sciences. It is also a primary source of information from the international literature on biomedicine, including the following topics as they relate to biomedicine and health care: Biology, environmental science, marine biology, plant and animal science, biophysics, and chemistry. For indexing articles, NLM uses Medical Subject Headings MeSH® (575), a controlled vocabulary of biomedical terms. MEDLINE can also be searched via the NLM Gateway (429). An increasing number of MEDLINE citations contain a link to the free full-text articles.

The MEDLINE database is the electronic counterpart of *Index Medicus®* (420), *Index to dental literature* (811), and the *International nursing index* (1081).

For detailed information, see the MEDLINE fact sheet at http://www. nlm.nih.gov/pubs/factsheets/medline.html.

426   **National Center for Biotechnology Information.** National
      Center for Biotechnology Information. 1995(?)–. [Rockville, Md.]:
      National Center for Biotechnology Information. http://www.ncbi.
      nlm.nih.gov.

660.6; 574.873282   TP248.2

The National Center for Biotechnology Information (NCBI) "dissemi-
nates biomedical information—all for the better understanding of molecular processes affecting human health and disease."—*Main page.* Its main
page provides links to NCBI's literature databases, molecular databases,
genomic resources, and tools for data mining as well as information about
the work of the NCBI. Major examples are the Entrez (3) retrieval system
and PubMed (432). Provides a resource guide (http://www.ncbi.nlm.
nih.gov/Sitemap/ResourceGuide.html) with each link leading to a brief
description of the resource on this page, then to the resource itself. Also
includes a graphical site map and an "alphabetical quicklinks table" that
provide direct links to resources.

427   **National Library of Medicine.** National Library of Medicine
      (U.S.), National Institutes of Health. 1993–. Bethesda, Md.:
      National Library of Medicine. http://www.nlm.nih.gov/.

Homepage of the U.S. National Library of Medicine (NLM). Contains
information about NLM's databases and other electronic resources, e.g.,
PubMed (432)/MEDLINE (425), ClinicalTrials.gov (191), Entrez (3),
LocatorPlus (480), MedlinePlus (463), MeSH (575), NLM Catalog (482),
NLM Classification (85), NLM Gateway (429), TOXNET (1580), Unified
Medical Language System (UMLS) (89), and the Visible Human Project
(502), to name a few of NLM's important resources. An annotated list
of NLM databases and electronic resources (http://www.nlm.nih.gov/
databases/) provides access to additional resources. Also includes a link to
NLM's numerous "retired databases" (http://www.nlm.nih.gov/services/
pastdatabases.html). Health information and NLM's products and services are presented for several different user groups: the public, health care
professionals, researchers, librarians, and publishers. A listing and link to
NIH A Clinical Alerts, which are "provided to expedite the release of findings from the NIH-funded clinical trials where such release could significantly affect morbidity and mortality" (*Clinical Alerts and Advisories page*)
are available at http://www.nlm.nih.gov/databases/alerts/clinical_alerts.
html#advisories. Milestones in NLM History (http://www.nlm.nih.gov/
about/nlmhistory.html) and the NLM Fact Sheets (http://www.nlm.nih.
gov/pubs/factsheets/nlm.html) provide further information.

428   National Organization for Rare Disorders, Inc. National
Organization for Rare Disorders. 1999–. Danbury, Conn.: National
Organization for Rare Disorders. http://www.rarediseases.org/.

RC48

The National Organization for Rare Disorders (NORD) provides alphabetical Index of Rare Diseases and several searchable databases—namely,
Rare Disease Database, Index of Organizations (list of organizations), and
Organizational Database (patient organizations)—as well as advice on
how to interpret search results. Other resources in this area can be located
via *NORD guide to rare disorders* (329) and NIH's Office of Rare Diseases
(476).

429   NLM gateway. National Library of Medicine (U.S.). 2000–.
Bethesda, Md.: National Library of Medicine. http://gateway.nlm.
nih.gov/.

RA11

Allows simultaneous searching of information resources at the National
Library of Medicine (NLM). Databases include MEDLINE (425)/PubMed
(432) and the NLM Catalog (482) as well as other resources, including
information on current clinical trials and consumer health information
(MedlinePlus [463]). Currently provides access to 21 databases and other
information resources (for a complete list of databases and other details,
see http://www.nlm.nih.gov/pubs/factsheets/gateway.html). An overview of
the search results is presented in several categories (bibliographic resources,
consumer health resources, and other information), with a listing of the
individual databases and the number of results within these categories.

430   OLDMEDLINE data. National Library of Medicine (U.S.). 2003–.
Bethesda, Md.: National Library of Medicine. http://www.nlm.nih.
gov/databases/databases_oldmedline.html.

Journal article citations from *Cumulated index medicus* and the *Current list
of medical literature* (see *Index medicus* [420]), covering medicine, preclinical sciences, and allied health sciences from 1949 through 1965. Most of
these OLDMEDLINE records are included in the MEDLINE (425) database and can be searched via PubMed (432) or the NLM Gateway (429).

A chart is provided for the OLDMEDLINE data. It contains information
on date added, citations added, and the title and year of the printed index.
Website also provides a brief history of NLM's use of MEDLARS (Medical
Literature Analysis and Retrieval System) and introduction of Medline.

431   Public library of science (PLoS). Public Library of Science. 2000–. [San Francisco]: Public Library of Science. http://www. publiclibraryofscience.org/.

PLoS is a non-profit organization of scientists and physicians who are committed to promote free and timely online access to the international scientific and medical literature. Since 2003 a nonprofit scientific and medical publishing venture. Publishes high-profile open-access journals (e.g., *PLoS biology*, *PLoS medicine*, *PLoS ONE*, and several others), funded by authors and participating institutions. The full content of every PLoS issue is placed into PubMed Central (PMC) (40). PLoS titles can also be accessed via Directory of Open Access Journals: DoAJ (35).

432   PubMed. U.S. National Center for Biotechnology Information, National Library of Medicine, National Institutes of Health. 1996–. Bethesda, Md.: U.S. National Center for Biotechnology Information. http://www.ncbi.nlm.nih.gov/sites/entrez/.

PubMed®, developed and maintained by the National Center for Biotechnology Information (NCBI) at the National Library of Medicine® (NLM) (427). It is available via the NCBI Entrez (3) retrieval system. PubMed also provides access to the other Entrez molecular biology resources (*PubMed Overview*). Starting May 23, 2007, NCBI is changing to a new version of Entrez in a phased implementation (cf. Nahin AM. New and Improved PubMed®/Entrez and New URL *NLM tech. bull.*, 2007 May–Jun.; [356]: http://www.nlm.nih.gov/pubs/techbull/mj07/mj07_issue_cover.html).

Provides a search interface for more than 16 million bibliographic citations and abstracts in the fields of medicine, nursing, dentistry, veterinary medicine, health care systems, and preclinical sciences. It provides access to articles indexed for MEDLINE® (425) and for selected life sciences journals. PubMed subsets found under the "Limits" tab are: MEDLINE and PubMed Central®, several journal groups (i.e., core clinical journals, dental journals, and nursing journals), and topical subsets (AIDS, bioethics, cancer, complementary medicine, history of medicine, space life sciences, systematic reviews, and toxicology). "Linkout" provides access to full-text articles.

For detailed information see the PubMed fact sheet at http://www.nlm.nih.gov/pubs/factsheets/pubmed.html. For a brief overview of searching PubMed, see the PubMed Quick Start at http://www.ncbi.nlm.nih.gov/books/bv.fcgi?rid=helppubmed.section.pubmedhelp.

PubMed_Quick_Start. For details on the now completed OLDMEDLINE retrospective conversion projects, see http://www.nlm.nih.gov/pubs/tech-bull/so06/so06_oldmedline_status.html.

433   PubMed central. National Library of Medicine. 2000–. Bethesda, Md.: National Center for Biotechnology Information. http://www. pubmedcentral.nih.gov.

025174570610.7   R11

Produced by National Library of Medicine (NLM) and National Institutes of Health (NIH); developed and managed by NIH's National Center for Biotechnology Information (NCBI).

NLM's free and open-access online digital archive of peer-reviewed full-text research papers in the medical and life sciences. The continuously growing PMC journals list (http://www.pubmedcentral.nih.gov/fprender.fcgi) includes, for example, titles from the Public Library of Science (PLoS) (39) and BioMed Central (BMC) (http://www.biomedcentral.com/), publishers of many open-access journals. Also includes the complete back files of many important medical journals that NLM has digitized in collaboration with the Wellcome Trust and the Joint Informations Systems Committee (JISC). The list is alphabetically arranged and available as a full or tabbed list, used to find journals added to PMC in the last 60 days. Other helpful links are provided, e.g., NIH Public Access (http://publicaccess.nih.gov/) and NIH Manuscript Submission System (http://www.nihms.nih.gov/). Further information at PMC Frequently Asked Questions (http://www.pubmedcentral.nih.gov/about/faq.html).

434   SciFinder. Chemical Abstracts Service. 1998?–. Columbus, Ohio: Chemical Abstracts Service. http://www.cas.org/products/scifindr/.

QD9

SciFinder and its academic version SciFinder Scholar have become the primary searching interfaces for the Chemical Abstracts Service (CAS) databases: Chemical Abstracts (34); the CAS Registry file of over 33 million substances, many with structural and property information; CASREACT, a file of over 14 million single and multistep reaction sequences; CHEMLIST, about 250,000 regulated chemicals; CHEMCATS, sources of over 17 million commercially available chemicals; MARPAT, a patent file of over 750,000 searchable Markush structures. In addition to the CAS databases, SciFinder also provides access to MEDLINE (425). The client software will be replaced by SciFinder Web in 2011.

The SciFinder searching interface allows exploring by natural language query, author or organizational name, chemical structure/substructure, or molecular formula. Specific literature queries can be done using bibliographic details, patent number, or CA abstract number. Specific substances can be located using the CAS Registry number. Text search results can be further analyzed, refined, or categorized by a variety of criteria. Structure searches are carried out graphically, and the results can also be refined in a variety of ways.

435 **Scirus.** Elsevier Science (Firm). 2001–. [s.l.]: Elsevier B. V. http://www.scirus.com/.

Scirus is a freely available search engine that focuses on scientific information. It indexes more than 300 million Web pages as well as several e-print repositories, open source journals, patents, and the full text of journal articles from participating publishers, such as SIAM, ScienceDirect, and Scitation. It filters out nonscience websites and documents, and allows for search refinement by suggesting related terms to the search terms entered. Overall, Scirus provides a lot of power for a free search engine; and although a substantial number of journals are searched by this database, users should be cautioned that the searches are by no means comprehensive.

436 **Scopus.** Elsevier Science Publishers. [s.l.]: Elsevier B. V. http://www.scopus.com/.

Scopus provides powerful, user-friendly searching of the STM journal literature (15,000 titles), as well as websites (265 million pages), patents (18 million), conference proceedings, and book series. It rivals the ISI Web of Science (423) in its breadth of coverage of the current journal literature. Scopus does not replace the ISI Web of Science, due to its lack of consistent citation searching before 1996, but it does provide a large database of quality resources from many fields in many formats. Scopus uses the Scirus (435) database to search the Web, patents, and preprint servers.

Specialized Indexes

437 **Aerospace medicine and biology.** United States National Aeronautics and Space Administration, Scientific and Technical Information Branch. 1964–2000? Washington, D.C.: Scientific and Technical Information Branch, National Aeronautics and Space Administration. http://purl.access.gpo.gov/GPO/LPS1988.

MEDICINE

Supersedes an earlier publication of the same title, issued 1952–63 (1952–53 called *Aviation medicine*). Supt. of Docs. classification: NAS 1.21:7011 (NASA-SP-7011). 1964-2000 distr. to depository libraries in microfiche. Sep. 1995–Jul. 12, 1999 accessible via the Internet. Current research in this subject area (i.e., biological and physiological effects of atmospheric and space flight on humans) can be located via the NASA technical reports server (Hampton, Va.: National Aeronautics and Space Administration, 1994–).

A selection of annotated references to unclassified reports and journal articles that were introduced into the NASA Scientific and Technical Information System and announced in *Scientific and technical aerospace reports (STAR)* (http://www.sti.nasa.gov/Pubs/star/star.html) and *International aerospace abstracts (IAA)*. Although emphasis is placed on applied research, references to fundamental studies are also included. International coverage; signed annotations in English.

438 Cancer.gov. National Cancer Institute. 1990s–. Bethesda, Md.: National Cancer Institute. http://www.cancer.gov/.

A metasite for cancer information for health care professionals as well as patients. Provides extensive information on all aspects of cancer as a disease and current cancer treatment, including, for example, complementary and alternative medicine, screening, prevention, and genetics. Links for searching the PubMed (432) cancer literature subset and PDQ Query at http://www.cancer.gov/cancertopics/pdq/cancerdatabase.

439 CINAHL. Cinahl Information Systems, EBSCO. 1982–. Ipswich, Mass.: EBSCO. http://www.ebscohost.com/cinahl/.

CINAHL® [database]. Title varies. Online version: 1984–1992 (with coverage 1982–.), publ. by Cinahl Information Systems; 1993–., publ. jointly by EBSCO and Cinahl Information Systems. Also available in different enhanced versions: CINAHL® with Full Text, CINAHL® Plus™, and CINAHL® Plus with Full Text. Comparisons of the different versions at http://www.ebscohost.com/uploads/thisTopic-dbTopic-592.pdf.

Print version: 1956–76 entitled: *Cumulative index to nursing and allied health literature*; 1977–. *Cumulative index to nursing and allied health literature*® (continues to be published in print).

Authoritative database for the professional literature of nursing and allied health. Provides references to journal articles, books, book chapters, pamphlets, audiovisual materials, dissertations, educational software, selected conference proceedings, standards of professional practice, and more. Some full-text material is included. Currently indexes a large number of journals, as well as publications from the American Nurses' Association and the National League for Nursing. Allows for application of specific interest category filter, e.g., evidence-based practice, informatics, patient safety, public health, women's health, and others. Subject access is provided by *CINAHL subject heading list: Alphabetic list, tree structures, permuted list* (1093). Complements *International nursing index* (1081), publ. 1966–2000.

440 HealthSTAR (Ovid). National Library of Medicine (U.S.). 2000–. Sandy, Utah: Ovid Technologies. http://www.ovid.com/site/ products/ovidguide/hstrdb.htm.

Ovid HealthSTAR (HSTR); HealthSTAR (Health Services Technology, Administration, and Research).

"Comprised of data from the National Library of Medicine's (NLM) MEDLINE and former HealthSTAR databases. contains citations to the published literature on health services, technology, administration, and research. It focuses on both the clinical and non-clinical aspects of health care delivery. Offered by Ovid as a continuation of NLM's now-defunct HealthSTAR database. Retains all existing backfile citations and is updated with new journal citations culled from MEDLINE. Contains citations and abstracts (when available) to journal articles, monographs, technical reports, meeting abstracts and papers, book chapters, government documents, and newspaper articles from 1975 to the present."—*Publ. notes.* A list of NLM's retired databases, including the original HealthSTAR database, can be found at http://www.nlm.nih.gov/services/pastdatabases.html.

Relevant content on health services research, health technology, health administration, health policy, health economics, etc., can also be found in MEDLINE® (425)/PubMed® (432), NLM® Gateway (429), and also CINAHL® (439).

441 Hospital and health administration index. American Hospital Association.; Resource Center, National Library of Medicine (U.S.). Chicago: American Hospital Association, 1995–1999. ISSN: 1077-1719.

016.36211   Z6675.H75H67; RA963

1945–54, *Index of current hospital literature*; 1955–57, *Hospital periodical literature index*; 1957–94, *Hospital literature index*, cumulated at five-year intervals for the 1945–77 volumes as *Cumulative index of hospital literature*. Discontinued; last published in 1999. Described as a "primary guide to literature on hospital and other health care facility administration, including multi-institutional systems, health policy and planning, and the administrative aspects of health care delivery. Special emphasis is given to the theory of health care systems in general; health care in industrialized countries, primarily in the United States; and provision of health care both inside and outside of health care facilities."—*Introd.* A separate online database, HealthSTAR (Health Services Technology, Administration, and Research) for this literature, previously maintained by NLM, is no longer available (cf. list of NLM's retired databases at http://www.nlm.nih.gov/services/pastdatabases.html). Relevant content is available via MEDLINE (425)/PubMed (432) or HealthSTAR (Ovid) (440), and also CINAHL (439).

442   **Nutrition abstracts and reviews series A.** CAB International. 1990–. [Wallingford, England, U.K.]: CAB International. http://www.cabi.org/AbstractDatabases.asp?SubjectArea=&PID=79.

Vol. 1 (Oct. 1931) through v. 46 (1976), *Nutrition abstracts and reviews* (NARA), Commonwealth Agricultural Bureau (CAB) International (CABI). Split into ser. A (Human and Experimental) and ser. B (Livestock Feeds and Feeding). Since 1977, available in print. A searchable online back file, derived from *CAB abstracts*, is available going back to 1990; also included in the full CAB Abstracts (1143) database, available though multiple vendors.

A searchable international abstract database that includes a variety of biomedical and agricultural subject areas, with papers relevant to all aspects of human nutrition selected from approx. 1,000 journals, books, reports, and conferences. Covers techniques (analytical methodologies for carbohydrates, fiber, lipids, proteins, etc.); foods (functional foods, food additives, supplements; beverages, food processing, food contamination, etc.); physiological and biochemical aspects (endocrinology and nutritional immunology, fasting, vitamins, phytochemicals, minerals, etc.); nutrition and health (diet studies, infant feeding, sports nutrition, nutritional status, etc.); clinical nutrition (e.g., malnutrition, obesity, food allergies, cancer, etc.); and many other subjects.

443   **POPLINE.** Johns Hopkins University Bloomberg School of Public Health. Baltimore: Johns Hopkins University Bloomberg School of Public Health. http://db.jhuccp.org/ics-wpd/popweb/.

HQ766

POPLINE (Population Information Online) is a database on reproductive health with international coverage. Provides bibliographic citations with abstracts to English-language published and unpublished biomedical and social science literature on population research, demography, family planning, and related health issues. Includes links to full-text documents, RSS feeds for topical searches, and other special features. Detailed list of subjects covered internationally and in reference to developing countries at http://db.jhuccp.org/ics-wpd/popweb/aboutpl.html.

444   PubChem. National Center for Biotechnology Information. Bethesda, Md.: National Center for Biotechnology Information; National Library of Medicine. http://purl.access.gpo.gov/GPO/ LPS61236.

Public Cheminformatics Database (PubChem), pt. of NIH's Molecular Libraries Roadmap Initiative (http://www.mli.nih.gov/).

Three databases, integrated with Entrez [browser]: The Life Sciences Search Engine (3), provide information on the biological activities of small molecules: bioactivity data (PubChem BioAssay); compound structures (PubChem Compound); and substance information (PubChem Substance). PubChem Compound and PubChem Substance databases, where possible, provide links to bioassay description, literature, references, and assay data points. The PubChem BioAssay database also includes links back to the substance and compound databases. Also provides compound neighboring, substructure, superstructure, similarity structure, bioactivity data, and other search features (cf. http://pubchem.ncbi.nlm.nih.gov/ help.html#PubChem_Overview). Further detailed information is found at http://pubchem.ncbi.nlm.nih.gov/help.html.

445   SPORTDiscus. Sport Information Resource Centre. Ipswich, Mass.: EBSCO. http://search.epnet.com.

See http://www.ebscohost.com for information on product without subscription.

Produced by Sport Information Resource Centre, Ottawa (SIRC); and SPORTDiscus via EBSCOhost platform.

Multidisciplinary full-text database, with comprehensive bibliographic coverage of sports, fitness, and related disciplines. Includes monographic literature dating back to 1949, journal coverage back to 1975. References from journal and magazine articles, books, book chapters, conference proceedings, dissertations, theses, and websites. Useful research tool for health professionals researching the sports medicine literature. Training documentation and help guides available.

MEDICINE

Internet Resources

446 **AEGiS.** AEGiS. 1990–. San Juan Capistrano, Calif.: AEGiS. http://www.aegis.com/.

AIDS Education Global Information System (AEGiS) is a nonprofit organization.

This frequently updated resource provides the latest international HIV/AIDS news, clinical information, legal information about HIV-related cases, a conference database, links to relevant U.S. government sites and other websites, and HIV/AIDS-related publications (e.g., activist, general, patient-oriented, and professional) available via the Internet. Also provides a timeline and HIV/AIDS statistics.

447 **AIDSinfo.** U.S. Department of Health and Human Services, National Institutes of Health (U.S.), AIDS Clinical Trials Information Service. Bethesda, Md.: National Institutes of Health. http://www.aidsinfo.nih.gov.

RA643.8

Result of merging two previous U.S. Dept. of Health and Human Services (DHHS) projects. Supersedes the AIDS Clinical Trials Information Service (ACTIS) and the HIV/AIDS Treatment Information Service (ATIS).

Resource for current information on federally and privately funded clinical trials for AIDS patients and HIV-infected persons, federally approved HIV treatment and prevention guidelines, and medical practice guidelines. Provides access to a searchable HIV/AIDS drugs database (via "Drugs" tab) that includes approved and investigational anti-HIV medications, including side effects, dosages, and interactions with other drugs or food; also access to brochures, fact sheets, and other Web resources on HIV/AIDS, current and archived versions of DHHS guidelines, and a searchable HIV glossary (English and Spanish). For HIV/AIDS patients, the general public, health care providers, and researchers.

Additional major HIV/AIDS resources can be accessed via the following sites: Fact sheet, AIDS Information Resources (http://www.nlm.nih.gov/pubs/factsheets/aidsinfs.html), Specialized Information Services: HIV/AIDS Information (http://sis.nlm.nih.gov/hiv.html), CDC National Prevention Information Network (NPIN) (http://www.cdcnpin.org/scripts/hiv/index.asp), UNAIDS: Joint United National Programming on HIV/AIDS (http://www.unaids.org/en/), and AIDS Treatment Data Network (http://www.atdn.org/).

448 **American Academy of Family Physicians [homepage].** American Academy of Family Physicians. 1998–. Leawood, Kans: American Academy of Family Physicians. http://www.aafp.org/online/en/home.html.

616.007; 610.9206   R130.3

Searchable website with resources for AAFP (American Academy of Family Physicians) members, residents, students, patients, and the general public. Contains information, software, photographs, graphics, and other materials, providing access to information on a variety of clinical and research resources for medical and healthcare topics. Examples are "Familydoctor.org" (http://familydoctor.org/online/famdocen/home.html), an online "Dictionary of common Medical Terms," health trackers, health calculators, how to find a family doctor (http://familydoctor.org/cgi-bin/memdir.pl), and "Conditions A to Z" (http://familydoctor.org/online/famdocen/home/common.html), also available as (*AAFP conditions A to Z* via STAT!Ref). Also provides public health resources on various topics (http://www.aafp.org/online/en/home/clinical/publichealth.html) e.g., cultural proficiency, health disparities/minority health, disease prevention, etc.

449 **American Academy of Pediatrics.** American Academy of Pediatrics. 1995–. Elk Grove Village, Ill.: American Academy of Pediatrics. http://www.aap.org/.

610.9206; 618.92

American Academy of Pediatrics (AAP) official website.

This searchable website provides information for health consumers on various topics of concern to parents relating to the health and safety of children (e.g., finding a pediatrician, various diseases and conditions, immunization, behavioral and mental health topics, car safety seats, Internet safety, toy safety resources, and many others). Also provides information for AAP members and other medical professionals, such as links to AAP policy statements and clinical practice guidelines, and access to Red Book® Online which includes the latest clinically tested guidelines of approx. 200 conditions. Also provides information on professional education, research, clinical and technical reports by or endorsed by the AAP, other AAP publications, etc.

450 **American Cancer Society [homepage].** American Cancer Society. 1990s–. Atlanta: American Cancer Society. http://www.cancer.org.

RC261

Cancer information presented for health professionals, patients, and other health consumers. Includes the full text of *Cancer facts and figures* (515) and other statistics, providing incidence and trends of the major types of cancer survival rates and distribution of cancer by race and ethnicity. Also includes support programs and services, resources for healthy living, clinical trials, treatment decisions, tools to understand treatment options (including alternative treatments, and possible side effects), and an online glossary of cancer-related terms. Information in English and Spanish. Also contains Asian-language cancer education materials.

451   American Medical Association. American Medical Association. 1995–. Chicago: American Medical Association. http://www.ama-assn.org/.

This searchable website provides a variety of professional resources and standards for AMA members, including, for example, information sources on medical ethics, public health (e.g., eliminating health disparities, health preparedness, disaster response, obesity), medical science, legal issues, and AMA history (with timeline and highlights of AMA history). Also provides information on medical education and licensure as well as online resources and other links for medical school students and residents. Includes a section for patients, with access to patient education resources.

Other useful AMA-related links include, for example, DoctorFinder (209) and PolicyFinder (http://www.ama-assn.org/ama/noindex/category/11760.html), *Code of medical ethics, current opinions with annotations* (Chicago: American Medical Association), *Current procedural terminology: CPT* (853), FREIDA (212), *Graduate medical education directory* (213), *Health professions career and education directory* (214), and *State medical licensure requirements and statistics* (548). Many of these resources have general reference value in academic and public libraries.

452   amfAR. American Foundation for AIDS Research. 1999–. New York; Washington: American Foundation for AIDS Research. http://www.amfar.org.

"amfAR™, the Foundation for AIDS Research, is one of the world's leading nonprofit organizations dedicated to the support of AIDS research, HIV prevention, treatment education, and the advocacy of sound AIDS-related public policy."—*Website*

Provides basic HIV/AIDS facts and statistics, HIV testing, information about various therapies (approved or under development), young people and HIV/AIDS, women and HIV/AIDS, global initiatives, and many other related topics and links.

"amfAR global links," formerly know as *HIV/AIDS treatment directory*, and "HIV/AIDS treatment insider," available 2000-5, have ceased publication. *The AmFAR AIDS handbook: The complete guide to understanding HIV and AIDS*, a comprehensive guide to help readers understand HIV/ AIDS, treatment options, and how treatment decisions are made, has not been updated since 1999.

453   **Association of American Medical Colleges (AAMC).** Association of American Medical Colleges (AAMC). 1995–. Washington: Association of American Medical Colleges (AAMC). http://www. aamc.org/.

610.71106; 610.07

Not-for-profit association representing U.S. and Canadian medical schools; teaching hospitals and health systems; and academic and professional societies. Intends to "serve as the voice and advocate for academic medicine and medical education, research and health care" (*main page*), with its priorities outlined in "Learn, serve, lead: the mission and vision and strategic priorities of the AAMC" (http://www.aamc.org/about/learn-servelead.pdf). Links to related member groups, e.g., Council of Academic Societies, Council of Deans, Group on Resident Affairs, Group on Student Affairs, Women in Medicine, and others. AAMC publications and projects include *AAMC data book* (507), *Directory of American medical education* (181), *Medical school admission requirements, U.S.A. and Canada* (184), MedEdPORTAL (461), and others.

454   **Cancer.gov.** National Cancer Institute. 1990s–. Bethesda, Md.: National Cancer Institute. http://www.cancer.gov/.

A metasite for cancer information for health care professionals as well as patients. Provides extensive information on all aspects of cancer as a disease and current cancer treatment, including, for example, complementary and alternative medicine, screening, prevention, and genetics. Links for searching the PubMed (432) cancer literature subset and PDQ Query at http://www.cancer.gov/cancertopics/pdq/cancerdatabase.

455   **DermAtlas.** Bernard A. Cohen, Christoph U. Lehmann, Johns Hopkins University. 2000–. Baltimore: Johns Hopkins University. http://www.dermatlas.org.

International collaborative project providing access to a growing collection of dermatology images. As of Mar. 2010, contains more than 11,550 images by more than 500 contributors. Searchable by keywords, diagnosis, category of disease, body site, and pigmentation. Also provides links to other dermatology websites. For health care professionals, patients, and other health care consumers.

DermIS (http://www.dermis.net/dermisroot/en/home/index.htm) is another example of an online collection of dermatology images and links to related information from various academic institutions worldwide.

456   **GeneTests.** Children's Hospital and Medical Center (Seattle, Wash.). 1993–. Seattle, Wash.: University of Washington. http://www.genetests.org/.

Contents: Home page; About GeneTests; GeneReviews; Laboratory directory; Clinic directory; Educational materials.

Provides authoritative information on genetic testing and its use in diagnosis, disease management, and genetic counseling. Promotes use of genetic services in patient care and decision making by individuals. GeneReviews and Laboratory directory can be searched by disease, gene symbol, protein name, etc. Contains context-sensitive illustrated glossary, teaching tools, and other resources.

457   **Hardin MD (Hardin meta directory of Internet health sources).** Hardin Library for the Health Sciences. 1996–. Iowa City, Iowa: Hardin Library for the Health Sciences, University of Iowa. http://www.lib.uiowa.edu/hardin/md/.

004.67025; 610.02   RC81.H37

Listing of websites from a variety of sources, covering diseases and conditions and, in many cases, providing links to illustrations for diseases. Provides a good starting point for basic medical and health information. A related site by the Hardin Library is Medical/Health Sciences Libraries on the Web (196).

458   **Health education assets library (HEAL).** Sharon E. Dennis, Chris Candler, Sebastian Uijtdehaage, University of California, University of Utah, University of Oklahoma. 2000–. Los Angeles; Salt Lake City, Utah; Oklahoma City, Okla.: University of California; University of Utah; University of Oklahoma. http://www.healcentral.org.

HEAL is a collaborative multi-institutional project, "building a multimedia resource management system that allows faculty to build, manage, and distribute personal collections of digital multimedia resources."—*HEAL local page*. It is a repository of health sciences images, videos, and audio files from different authoritative collections. Users can search, browse, download, and contribute their own files. The resources are described with metadata, including medical subject headings (MeSH [575]), for easy and accurate browsing and searching. For a quick overview of HEAL and its recent statistics, see "HEAL at a glance" at http://www.healcentral. org/about/HEAL_at_a_Glance.pdf. Copyright information is provided at http://www.healcentral.org/copyrights.jsp.

HEAL is part of the National Science Digital Library (Boulder, Colo.: National Science Digital Library), a project funded by the National Science Foundation. "NSDL is the Nation's online library for education and research in Science, Technology, Engineering, and Mathematics."—*NDSL website*. Since the fall of 2000, the National Library of Medicine (Office of High Performance Computing and Communications) (427) has collaborated with HEAL. The Association of American Medical Colleges (AAMC) also endorses the project and provides assistance. Further background information is provided at http://www.healcentral.org/about/aboutHistory.jsp.

Another major project, MedEdPortal (AAMC) (461), provides a growing number of online resources for use in medical education.

459   Human Genome Project information. U.S. Department of Energy Office of Science. 1990s–. Oak Ridge, Tenn.: Oak Ridge National Laboratory, U.S. Department of Energy. http://www.ornl.gov/sci/ techresources/Human_Genome/home.shtml.

QH447

Website sponsored by the U.S. Dept. of Energy Office of Science, Office of Biological and Environmental Research, Human Genome Program; website maintained by the Human Genome Management Information System (HGMIS) at Oak Ridge National Laboratory for the U.S. Department of Energy Human Genome Program.

Contents: About HGP (Goals; Progress; History; Benefits; ELSI; Genetics 101; FAQ); Research (Mapping; Sequencing; Technology; Bioinformatics; Gene Function; ELSI; Microbes); Education Resources (Teachers; Students; Careers; Webcasts; Images; Videos; Presentation); Ethical, Legal, and Social Issues (ELSI); Medicine and the New Genetics (Gene Testing; Gene Therapy; Pharmaceuticals; Genetic Counseling; Diseases); Media.

"Begun formally in 1990, the U.S. Human Genome Project was a 13-year effort coordinated by the U.S. Department of Energy and the National Institutes of Health. The project originally was planned to last 15 years, but rapid technological advances accelerated the completion date to 2003."—*About the Human Genome Project page.* This website provides a multitude of annotated links to resources on all aspects of the HPG. Articles analyzing the genome continue to be published, with further information presented at Post–Human Genome Project Progress and Resources (http://www.ornl.gov/sci/techresources/Human_Genome/project/progress.sh tml). Information for Genetic Professionals (http://www.kumc.edu/gec/geneinfo.html), a clinical-genetics site by Debra Collins, Genetics Education Center, University of Kansas Medical Center, provides further information in this area.

460   Institute of Medicine (IOM). Institute of Medicine. 1998–. Washington: National Academy of Sciences. http://www.iom.edu/.

The Institute of Medicine (IOM), one of the U.S. National Academies, has the mission to "serve as adviser to the nation to improve health" and "provides independent, objective, evidence-based advice to policymakers, health professionals, the private sector, and the public."—*Main page.* Offers a list of all publications by the IOM since 1970 (http://www.iom.edu/CMS/2955.aspx), which cover a broad range of topics, including aging, child health, a variety of diseases, global health, health care quality, minority health, nutrition, public health, public policy, preventive medicine, women's health, and many other areas. The National Academies Press (http://www.nap.edu) provides online access to the publications of the four National Academies, i.e., National Academy of Sciences, National Academy of Engineering, IOM, and National Research Council.

461   MedEdPORTAL. Association of American Medical Colleges. 2006–. Washington: Association of American Medical Colleges. http://www.aamc.org/mededportal/.

Description based on MedEdPORTAL (version 1.4).

A project by the Association of American Medical Colleges (AAMC) that provides access to teaching resources used in medical education. Designed to help faculty publish and share educational resources. MedEdPORTAL staff review submissions for relevance and appropriateness before they are published on the site. Includes a user review feature. All approved user reviews are listed at the end of each published resource's details page. Information about copyright and copyright symbols can be found in the "Overview" section of the website.

MedEdPORTAL publications are cataloged using medical subject headings (MeSH: Medical Subject Headings [575]). Currently includes over 100 Virtual Patients (VPs), "interactive programs that simulate real-life clinical scenarios."—*Publisher's description.* To locate these and other resources, MedEdPORTAL can be browsed by discipline (list of subject areas and number of available resources within each category). Also searchable by keyword.

AAMC also participates in Health Education Assets Library (HEAL) (458), a repository of health sciences images, videos, and audio files from different collections.

462 **Medical images and illustrations.** Karolinska Intitutet. 1999–. Stockholm, Sweden: Karolinska Institutet. http://www.mic.ki.se/ MEDIMAGES.html.

Contents: Cardiovascular System; Dermatology; Endocrinology; Gastroenterology; Hematology; Histology; Neurology; Pathology; Pediatrics; General; Anatomy and Orthopedics; Visible Human Project (502); Dentistry and Oral Health; Eye, Ear-Nose-Throat and Respiratory System; Gynecology and Obstetrics; Microbiology, Infectious; Oncology; Radiology, Radiography, Nuclear Medicine and Ultrasonography; Surgery/Anesthesiology; Urogenital.

Contains links to Internet pages and sites, offering biomedical images (photos, illustrations, etc.), with copyright information. Arranged by topics and also alphabetically. This page is part of the library at Karolinska Institutet's Directory of Quality Controlled Links (http://www.mic.ki.se/ Other.html), which provides a large number of biomedical links, diseases and disorders links, clinical case studies, etc.

463 **MedlinePlus.** U.S. National Library of Medicine. 1998–. Bethesda, Md.: U.S. Dept. of Health and Human Services, National Library of Medicine. http://medlineplus.gov/.

025.04; 651.504261; 613   RA776.5

MedlinePlus®

A consumer health reference database with information from the National Library of Medicine (NLM) (427), the National Institutes of Health (NIH) (470), other government agencies, and various health-related organizations. A continually expanding and updated resource. Information on over 700 diseases and conditions, as well as drug information (prescription, nonprescription), herbs and supplements, an illustrated medical encyclopedia and dictionary, interactive patient tutorials, lists of hospitals, physicians, and dentists, and health news. Provides preformulated MEDLINE (425)/PubMed® (432) searches for recent articles. Includes *NIH*

MedlinePlus Magazine, a new quarterly guide for patients and their families, providing authoritative medical and healthcare information. "MedlinePlus en español" toggles between English and Spanish. Provides links to browse selected health information in multiple languages other than English and Spanish at http://www.nlm.nih.gov/medlineplus/languages/languages. html. "Go Local" links users to relevant health information in their own city, county, and state. Detailed descriptive information is available at http://www.nlm.nih.gov/pubs/factsheets/medlineplus.html.

464   Men's health (MedlinePlus). National Library of Medicine (U.S.). 200?–. Bethesda, Md.: National Library of Medicine, National Institutes of Health, Dept. of Health and Human Services. http:// www.nlm.nih.gov/medlineplus/menshealth.html.

RA777.8

A MedlinePlus® (425) Health Topic. Collection of links for a variety of resources on men's health (e.g., specific conditions, treatments, prevention/screening, etc.) and also related issues and topics.

465   MLANET. Medical Library Association. 1998–. Chicago: Medical Library Association (MLA). http://www.mlanet.org/.

Medical Library Association (MLA), since 1889, "a nonprofit, educational organization of more than 1,100 institutions and 3,600 individual members in the health sciences information field, committed to educating health information professionals, supporting health information research, promoting access to the world's health sciences information, and working to ensure that the best health information is available to all."—*MLA website*

Searchable home page for MLA which provides a variety of resources for its members, such as professional standards and practices, discussion of information issues and policy, career information resources, professional credentialing, publications, etc. Also provides resources for health consumers, e.g., "A User's guide to finding and evaluating health information on the Web" (http://www.mlanet.org/resources/userguide. html), including "Deciphering MedSpeak," and MLA's guidelines on finding quality information on the Internet. Provides links to websites considered quality sites ("top ten") by MLA: Cancer.gov (438), Centers for Disease Control (CDC) (940), familydoctor.org (http://familydoctor. org/online/famdocen/home.html), healthfinder® (706); HIV InSite (314), Kidshealth® (http://www.kidshealth.org/), Mayo Clinic (Rochester, Minn.:

Mayo Foundation for Medical Education and Research, 1998–), MEDEM: An information partnership of medical societies (http://medem.com/ MedLB/medlib_entry.cfm), MedlinePlus (463), and NOAH: New York Online Access to Health (http://www.noah-health.org/).

Currently 23 different MLA sections have their own webpages (http:// www.mlanet.org/sections/sections.html). A prominent example of a section website is the Consumer and Patient Information Section of the Medical Library Association (CAPHIS) (625).

466　National academies press. National Academies Press (U.S.). 1999–. Washington: National Academies Press. www.nap.edu/.

Z1217.N37

Contains free online access to over 3,700 monographs, mainly reports of the academy on issues of importance to the science community and society—for example, future trends in employment opportunities in different fields, analyses of discrepancies in gender/racial makeup of scientists in discplines, as well as the prospects of scientific projects or programs. Overall, it provides a wealth of information on the state of science. The National Academies are made up of the National Academy of Sciences, National Academy of Engineering, the Institute of Medicine, and the National Research Council.

467　National Cancer Institute. National Cancer Institute. Bethesda, Md.: National Cancer Institute. http://www.cancer.gov/.

Website created by the National Cancer Institute (NCI), a division of the National Institutes of Health (NIH).

Contents: NCI Home, Cancer Topics, Clinical Trials, Cancer Statistics, Research and Funding, News, About NCI.

Links to cancer-related information for health professionals, medical students, and patients. Provides guidance to searching the cancer literature in PubMed (432) by searching the "cancer subset" and access to already prepared searches on more than 100 different topics. Non-PubMed citations previously found in CANCERLIT, a database no longer being maintained, consist primarily of meeting abstracts from the annual meetings of the American Society of Clinical Oncology (ASCO) and the American Association for Cancer Research (AACR). ASCO abstracts for recent years are available via http://www.asco.org, AACR abstracts at http://aacrmeetingabstracts.org/. Also provides access to PDQ: Physician Data Query (http://www.cancer.gov/cancertopics/pdq), a database with the latest information about cancer treatment, screening, prevention, genetics, etc.

The NCI website includes descriptions of various types of cancer (A–Z List of Cancers: http://www.cancer.gov/cancertopics/alphalist/) and related topics, with links to diagnosis and treatment information and supportive care, information on clinical trials, cancer prevention, cancer statistics (e.g., SEER Cancer Statistics Review [547]), cancer statistics tools, cancer mortality maps and graphs, and related NCI websites. Links to the Dictionary of Cancer Terms (143) and various cancer vocabulary resources (e.g., NCI Thesaurus, NCI Metathesaurus, and NCI Terminology Browser), NCI Drug Dictionary, NCI publications, etc. Available both in English and Spanish.

468 **National Center for Complementary and Alternative Medicine.**
National Center for Complementary and Alternative Medicine. 2000–. Silver Spring, Md.: National Center for Complementary and Alternative Medicine. http://nccam.nih.gov.

RC271.A62

National Center for Complementary and Alternative Medicine (NCCAM), established in 1998. Part of the National Institutes of Health (NIH) (470).

Explores complementary and alternative medicine (CAM), providing research opportunities in clinical and basic science and research training. Operates an information clearinghouse to answer requests for information and is considered the public's point of contact for scientifically based information on CAM and for information about NCCAM. Provides a variety of publications and extensive online health information (http://nccam.nih.gov/health/), links to clinical trials, popular health topics, diseases, conditions, treatments, and therapies for both health professionals and consumers. Also provides links to other organizations, including MedlinePlus (463): Alternative Medicine, MedlinePlus: Herbs and Supplements, NIH Office of Dietary Supplements (468), and other organizations that provide CAM information. Website is searchable at http://nccam.nih.gov/htdig/search.html. NCCAM and the National Library of Medicine (NLM) (427) have collaborated to create CAM on PubMed (432).

469 **National Human Genome Research Institute (U.S.).** National Human Genome Research Institute. 1995–. Bethesda, Md.: National Human Genome Research Institute, National Institutes of Health, U.S. Dept. of Health and Human Services. http://genome.gov/.

QH445.2

National Human Genome Research Institute (NHGRI), previously known as National Center for Human Genome Research (NCHGR), which was established in 1989 because of the Human Genome Project (HGP), since 1990 is a collaborative project of the U.S. Dept. of Energy (DOE) and National Institutes of Health (NIH) to map the human genome; and since HGP's completion in 1993, to apply genome technologies to the study of specific diseases. In 1996, the Center for Inherited Disease Research (CIDR) was also established (cofunded by eight NIH institutes and centers) to study the genetic components of complex disorders. A timeline, 1988 to the present, provides further details about HPG, its completion in 2003, associated events, research, and relevant publications at http://genome.gov/10001763.

Provides access to information, databases, and links to other resources concerning research, grants, health, policy and ethics, educational resources, etc. Some examples include the NHGRI Policy and Legislation Database http://genome.gov/PolicyEthics/LegDatabase/pubsearch.cfm, Online Bioethics Resources (620), the Ethical, Legal and Social Implications (ELSI) Research Program, and Initiatives and Resources for Minority and Special Populations (http://genome.gov/10001192), information on current research projects (e.g., the ENCODE Project [ENCyclopedia Of DNA Elements], a pilot project for testing and comparing new methods to identify functional sequences in DNA), model organisms, creation of Centers of Excellence in Genomic Science, the Genetics Variation Program, the Haplotype Map, gene discovery and technology development, establishment of the Center for Inherited Disease Research, and much more.

470 **National Institutes of Health (NIH).** National Institutes of Health. 1995–. Bethesda, Md.: National Institutes of Health. http://www.nih.gov/.

Portal to information about NIH's organization, its programs for conducting and supporting medical research, and links to other U.S. government information. Includes information and scientific advances, with listings, descriptions, and quick links to the 28 individual NIH institutes, centers, and offices, at http://www.nih.gov/icd/, including the National Library of Medicine (NLM) (427). Functions as an online medical reference tool to access health-related information of various kinds (for example, Health Topics A–Z). Includes, for example, research training and scientific resources at NIH facilities, hospitals, and laboratories supported by NIH; Nobel Prize winners among NIH scientists; information resources provided by NLM; information on NIH news and events; health information, research, grants and contracts, scientists, scientific resources, institutes, and offices. An overview of the NIH Roadmap for Medical Research, a major initiative to identify "major opportunities and gaps in biomedical research in the 21st century" (*NIH Roadmap page*) and related links are provided at http://nihroadmap.nih.gov/overview.asp.

471   **National Library of Medicine.** National Library of Medicine (U.S.), National Institutes of Health. 1993–. Bethesda, Md.: National Library of Medicine. http://www.nlm.nih.gov/.

Homepage of the U.S. National Library of Medicine (NLM). Contains information about NLM's databases and other electronic resources, e.g., PubMed (432)/MEDLINE (425), ClinicalTrials.gov (191), Entrez (3), LocatorPlus (480), MedlinePlus (463), MeSH (575), NLM Catalog (482), NLM Classification (85), NLM Gateway (429), TOXNET (1580), Unified Medical Language System (UMLS) (89), and the Visible Human Project (502), to name a few of NLM's important resources. An annotated list of NLM databases and electronic resources (http://www.nlm.nih.gov/databases/) provides access to additional resources. Also includes a link to NLM's numerous "retired databases" (http://www.nlm.nih.gov/services/pastdatabases.html). Health information and NLM's products and services are presented for several different user groups: the public, health care professionals, researchers, librarians, and publishers. A listing and link to NIH A Clinical Alerts, which are "provided to expedite the release of findings from the NIH-funded clinical trials where such release could significantly affect morbidity and mortality" (*Clinical Alerts and Advisories page*) are available at http://www.nlm.nih.gov/databases/alerts/clinical_alerts. html#advisories. Milestones in NLM History (http://www.nlm.nih.gov/about/nlmhistory.html) and the NLM Fact Sheets (http://www.nlm.nih.gov/pubs/factsheets/nlm.html) provide further information.

472   **National Network of Libraries of Medicine (NN/LM).** National Library of Medicine (U.S.). 2001–. Bethesda, Md.: National Library of Medicine. http://nnlm.gov/.

Coordinated by the National Library of Medicine (NLM). Searchable website, with informative sections on member services, outreach, resource sharing, document delivery, funding, training, and other educational opportunities. The Health Information on the Web tab provides "links to web resources from the National Library of Medicine that Network members may share with health professionals and the public."—*Health*

Information on the Web page. Several NN/LM National Centers, i.e., National Training Center and Clearinghouse (NTCC), Outreach Evaluation Resource Center (OERC), and Web Services Technology Operations Center (Web STOC), are important components. The National Network of Libraries of Medicine Fact Sheet (http://www.nlm.nih.gov/pubs/fact-sheets/nnlm.html) and National Network of Libraries of Medicine Membership Program Fact Sheet (http://www.nlm.nih.gov/pubs/factsheets/nnlmem.html) provide additional information.

473 **National Organization for Rare Disorders, Inc.** National
     Organization for Rare Disorders. 1999–. Danbury, Conn.: National
     Organization for Rare Disorders. http://www.rarediseases.org/.

RC48

The National Organization for Rare Disorders (NORD) provides alphabetical Index of Rare Diseases and several searchable databases—namely, Rare Disease Database, Index of Organizations (list of organizations), and Organizational Database (patient organizations)—as well as advice on how to interpret search results. Other resources in this area can be located via *NORD guide to rare disorders* (329) and NIH's Office of Rare Diseases (476).

474 **National Women's Health Information Center.** National Women's
     Health Information Center. 1990s–. Fairfax, Va.: U.S. Department
     of Health and Human Services. http://www.4woman.gov/.
613.04240285; 615.507; 305.40285

National Women's Health Information Center (NWHIC) is a federal government resource for women's health information. Presents reliable information on women's health concerns and issues for health professionals and health consumers. Links to organizations concerned with women's health, health tools, health topics, publications of interest and concern to women of all ages, and statistics via Quick Health Data Online (http://www.4woman.gov/quickhealthdata/). Link to girlshealth.gov with health information for young girls and educators.

Other examples of Internet resources with valuable information for health consumers, health professionals, and researchers include Women's Health (MedlinePlus) (http://www.nlm.nih.gov/medlineplus/women-shealth.html); Women's Health (General), National Institutes of Health (http://health.nih.gov/result.asp/729); and Women's Health (NIH) (http://health.nih.gov/search.asp/28).

MEDICINE

205

475 **New York Academy of Medicine Library online catalog.** New York Academy of Medicine. New York: New York Academy of Medicine. http://www.nyam.org/library/pages/online_library_catalog.

Z680.3

Contains materials acquired after 1972, the library's complete journal collection, and portions of rare books, manuscript collections, and government documents. For older materials, the New York Academy of Medicine's card catalog or printed catalogs (images of all cards filed in the card catalog through approx. 1970) still need to be consulted. They include *Subject catalog of the library* (1969; 34 v. and 4-v. supplement), *Author catalog of the library* (1969; 43 v. and 5-v. supplement), *Illustration catalog* (1976), and *Portrait catalog* (5 v., 1960).

Other titles publ. by the New York Academy of Medicine include, for example, *Grey literature report* (16), NOAH: New York Online Access to Health (http://www.nyam.org/library/pages/noah_ny_online_access_to_health1), "a gateway to freely available online resources related to public health preparedness, expert guidelines, factsheets, websites, research reports, articles, and other tools aimed at the public health community. All resources are cataloged and may be searched by keyword or browsed by topic through the database."—*Main page*

476 **Office of Rare Diseases.** National Institutes of Health (U.S.). 2002–. Bethesda, Md.: National Institutes of Health. http://rarediseases.info.nih.gov.

Answers questions about rare diseases for patients and other health consumers, healthcare providers, researchers, educators, students, and others interested in rare diseases. Links to definitions, causes, treatments, and publications about rare diseases, provides resources on genetic information, genetic research, genetic testing laboratories and clinics, genetic counseling services, and patient support groups. Also includes information on rare diseases research and research resources. Other reference sources in this area include, for example, National Organization for Rare Disorders, Inc. (428) and *NORD guide to rare disorders* (329).

477 **OncoLink.** Abramson Cancer Center of the University of Pennsylvania. 1994–. Philadelphia: University of Pennsylvania. http://cancer.med.upenn.edu/.

615.507; 616.992; 616.994

Contents: Types of cancer; Cancer treatment information; Coping with cancer; Cancer resources and news; Ask the cancer expert; OncoLink Library.

Designed for educational purposes to help cancer patients, families, health care professionals, and the general public to get accurate cancer-related information. Provides comprehensive information about specific types of cancer, updates on cancer treatment, and news about research advances, with information provided at various levels, from introductory to in-depth.

Library Catalogs

478   **The Cole Library of early medicine and zoology: Catalogue of books and pamphlets.** Nellie B. Eales. pl., facsim. Oxford: Alden P. [for] the University of Reading Library, 1969–1975.
016.59   Z6676.R35

Contents: v. 1, 1472–1800; v. 2, 1800 to present day and supplement to v. 1.

A descriptive catalog of a distinguished collection. Chronological arrangement, with subject and author indexes.

479   **IndexCat.** U.S. National Library of Medicine, Library of the Surgeon-General's Office, Army Medical Library, Armed Forces Medical Library, National Library of Medicine. Bethesda, Md.: U.S. National Library of Medicine, National Institutes of Health, Health and Human Services. http://indexcat.nlm.nih.gov.

IndexCat™ is the digitized version of the *Index-catalogue of the library of the Surgeon General's Office* (Army Medical Library), ser. 1–5, 61 v. Washington: U.S. Govt. Printing Office, 1880–1961. Ser. 1, A–Z (1880–95); ser. 2, A–Z (1896–1916); ser. 3, A–Z (1918–32); ser. 4. v. 1–11, A–Mn (1936–55); ser. 4 is incomplete, last half was never published; 5th series (1959–61).

"A collaborative project initiated by the American Association for the History of Medicine with support from the Wellcome Trust, the Burroughs Wellcome Fund, and the U.S. National Library of Medicine (427)."—*Website*

Content and coverage is the same as the printed catalog, e.g., from early times through 1950 imprints. Includes journal titles and articles, also news articles, letters, biographical, and obituary articles, dissertations and theses, books, pamphlets, reports, and portraits. Subject headings in

IndexCat do not conform to the Medical subject headings (MeSH®) (575). Searchable by keywords (subject, author, title, journal title, note content, and by year of publication). Further information about *IndexCat* at http://www.nlm.nih.gov/hmd/indexcat/aboutic.html.

IndexCat and LocatorPlus (480)™, NLM's online public catalog, may be searched at the same time. LocatorPlus contains NLM holdings and current information for books, pamphlets, dissertations, and journal titles.

480   **LocatorPlus.** National Library of Medicine (U.S.). 1998–.
        Bethesda, Md.: National Library of Medicine. http://purl.access.
        gpo.gov/GPO/LPS4582.

LocatorPlus is the National Library of Medicine (NLM) continuously updated online public catalog. Includes catalog records for books, journals, audiovisuals, and other materials in NLM's collections. Provides holdings information for journals and other materials; links from catalog records to Internet resources, including online journals; and access to other NLM resources. Can be searched by keyword, author, title, journal title, MeSH (575), call number, etc. See LocatorPlus fact sheet at http://www.nlm.nih.gov/pubs/factsheets/locatorplus.html for additional information. The NLM Catalog (482) provides another search interface to NLM bibliographic records for journals, books, audiovisuals, electronic resources, etc.

481   **New York Academy of Medicine Library online catalog.** New York
        Academy of Medicine. New York: New York Academy of Medicine.
        http://www.nyam.org/library/pages/online_library_catalog.

                                                                    Z680.3

Contains materials acquired after 1972, the library's complete journal collection, and portions of rare books, manuscript collections, and government documents. For older materials, the New York Academy of Medicine's card catalog or printed catalogs (images of all cards filed in the card catalog through approx. 1970) still need to be consulted. They include *Subject catalog of the library* (1969; 34 v. and 4-v. supplement), *Author catalog of the library* (1969; 43 v. and 5-v. supplement), *Illustration catalog* (1976), and *Portrait catalog* (5 v., 1960).

Other titles publ. by the New York Academy of Medicine include, for example, *Grey literature report* (16), NOAH: New York Online Access to Health (http://www.nyam.org/library/pages/noah_ny_online_access_to_health1), "a gateway to freely available online resources related to public health preparedness, expert guidelines, factsheets, websites, research reports, articles, and other tools aimed at the public health community.

All resources are cataloged and may be searched by keyword or browsed by topic through the database."—*Main page*

482   NLM catalog (Entrez). National Library of Medicine (U.S.). 2004–. Bethesda, Md.: National Library of Medicine. http://www. ncbi.nlm.nih.gov/entrez/query.fcgi?db=nlmcatalog.

"The NLM Catalog provides access to NLM bibliographic data for journals, books, audiovisuals, computer software, electronic resources and other materials. Links to the library's holdings in LocatorPlus (480), NLM's online public access catalog, are also provided."—*Main page*

483   The Wellcome Library for the History and Understanding of Medicine. Wellcome Library for the History of Medicine. London: Wellcome Library for the History of Medicine. http://library. wellcome.ac.uk/.

The Wellcome Library website provides several links to its holdings. The online library catalog contains records for all Wellcome Library collections in all formats, covering both the history of medicine and current biomedical topics. It also provides access to the growing Wellcome Images (503), with more than 160,000 images; Moving Image and Sound Collections, Iconographic Collections (more than 100,000 prints, drawings, paintings, photographs, and other media); and Archives and Manuscripts of persons and organizations in medical science and health care. Links to MetaFind, which allows cross-searching of various catalogs and databases, and Med-Hist (354).

MEDICINE

209

484   WHOLIS. World Health Organization. Geneva, Switzerland: World Health Organization. http://www.who.int/library/databases/en/.

Title varies: WHOLIS; WHOLIS Webcat. Formerly known as World Health Organization Library Catalogue; WHO Library Catalogue; World Health Organization Library Catalog; WHO Library Catalog.

The WHO LNK (http://www.who.int/library/en/) offers worldwide online access to WHOLIS, WHO's online catalog. "WHOLIS indexes all WHO publications from 1948 onwards and articles from WHO-produced journals and technical documents from 1985 to the present. An on-site card catalogue provides access to the pre-1986 technical documents. It contains bibliographic information with subject headings and, for some records, abstracts. For some records, full text links are available. An online tutorial for guidance in using WHOLIS is available."—*Main page*

Medical Illustration and Images

485 **De humani corporis fabrica.** Andreas Vesalius, Daniel Garrison, Malcolm Hast, Northwestern University (Evanston, Ill.), Dept. of Classics. 2003–. Evanston, Ill.: Northwestern University. http://vesalius.northwestern.edu/.

Collaborative project of faculty members of Northwestern University Weinberg College of Arts and Sciences and Feinberg School of Medicine, library administrators of Galter Health Sciences Library and Northwestern University Library, and Northwestern University Academic Technologies to translate and annotate Vesalius's work *De humani corporis fabrica.* English translation has title *On the fabric of the human body: An annotated translation of the 1543 and 1555 editions of Andreas Vesalius's De Humani Corporis Fabrica.*

This website provides access to the complete annotated text of the first book of the atlas. The translated text contains many bibliographic citations. The online edition of the atlas includes modern anatomical names (*nomina anatomica*) for all parts of the body and provides the ability to search text, reference figures, and anatomical terms. Also includes 272 anatomical woodcut drawings and diagrams, "applying 21st century computer technology to sixteenth century images, the online Fabrica's illustrations have been edited and enhanced for better viewing."—*Press release.* Images can be browsed by name and by body location. Notes on the graphical editing are provided on the website.

Translation of all seven books of the original anatomical atlas and its revisions is in progress and will eventually appear on this website. A listing of the titles of Books 1–7, a fact sheet, and other help pages found on the website provide further detailed information.

486 **DermAtlas.** Bernard A. Cohen, Christoph U. Lehmann, Johns Hopkins University. 2000–. Baltimore: Johns Hopkins University. http://www.dermatlas.org.

International collaborative project providing access to a growing collection of dermatology images. As of Mar. 2010, contains more than 11,550 images by more than 500 contributors. Searchable by keywords, diagnosis, category of disease, body site, and pigmentation. Also provides links to other dermatology websites. For health care professionals, patients, and other health care consumers.

DermIS (http://www.dermis.net/dermisroot/en/home/index.htm) is another example of an online collection of dermatology images and links to related information from various academic institutions worldwide.

487 **Dermatology lexicon project.** Art Papier, Lowell Goldsmith, University of Rochester, Dept. of Dermatology. 2005–. Rochester, N.Y.: University of Rochester. http://www.dermatologylexicon.org/.

International online open-source project with the goal of creating a standardized and reliable dermatology vocabulary. Provides diagnostic concepts, definitions, morphologic terminology, with illustrations and interactive animations. Includes dermatologic diagnoses and their synonyms, therapies, procedures, lab tests, etc. Also provides links to lexical/medical informatics resources, dermatology research, and organizations as well as patient information.

488 **Hardin MD (Hardin meta directory of Internet health sources).** Hardin Library for the Health Sciences. 1996–. Iowa City, Iowa: Hardin Library for the Health Sciences, University of Iowa. http://www.lib.uiowa.edu/hardin/md/.
004.67025; 610.02 RC81.H37

Listing of websites from a variety of sources, covering diseases and conditions and, in many cases, providing links to illustrations for diseases. Provides a good starting point for basic medical and health information. A related site by the Hardin Library is Medical/Health Sciences Libraries on the Web (196).

489 **Health on the Net Foundation (HON).** Health on the Net Foundation. 1995–. Geneva, [Switzerland]: Health on the Net Foundation (HON). http://www.hon.ch/.
R859.7.E43

Health on the Net Foundation (HON) is a nonprofit, nongovernmental organization known for its HONcode, which defines rules and ethical standards for website developers on how information is provided in terms of the source and data provided. The HONcode is not considered an award or quality rating system for websites.

Provides a "portal to medical information on the Internet."—*Website.* Searchable website provides access to resources for individuals/patients and medical professionals. Includes HON's history and current contact information, access to listservs, newsgroups, and FAQs. For medical and health queries, HON's MedHunt© (http://www.hon.ch/HONHunt/AdvHONHunt.html) and HONselect© (http://www.hon.ch/HONselect/) help locate quality websites and support groups, medical terminology, journal articles, and healthcare news. HONmedia (http://www.hon.ch/HONmedia/) is a growing and searchable repository of medical images and videos (currently contains 6,800 medical images and videos, pertaining to 1,700 topics and themes).

490   Historical anatomies on the Web. National Library of Medicine (U.S.). 2003–. Bethesda, Md.: National Library of Medicine. http:// www.nlm.nih.gov/exhibition/historicalanatomies/home.html.

NC760

Digital project designed to provide access to selected high-quality images (not the entire books) from important anatomical atlases in NLM's collection, with author and title description, the artist, and illustration technique. Emphasis on the images, not the text. Examples include Albrecht Dürer's *Vier Bücher von menschlicher Proportion* (1528) and Andreas Vesalius's *De humani corporis fabrica libri septem* (1543).

491   History and bibliography of artistic anatomy: Didactics for depicting the human figure. Boris Röhrl. xx, 493 p., ill. Hildesheim, Germany: Olms, 2000. ISBN: 3487110741.

743.49   NC760.R65

Contents: pt. 1, History: ch. 1, Introd., ch. 2, Anatomy in the art of the Ancient World and the Middle Ages; ch. 3, From the 13th to the 15th cent.; ch. 4, 16th cent.; ch. 5, 17th cent.; ch. 6, 18th cent.; ch. 7, 19th cent.; ch. 8, 20th cent.; ch. 9, Definition of genres; pt. 2, Bibliography: (1) Bibliography and description of books A–Z; (2) Appendices: Selected list of secondary literature; Index of ill.; Index of persons; Index of places and schools of art.

Considered a reference book which contains the didactical structure and content of specific teaching manuals. Presents the different subgroups of medically oriented teaching and how anatomy was taught in schools. Includes, for example, Leonardo da Vinci's anatomical sketchbooks. The bibliography in pt. 2 contains "books on osteology, myology, morphology, and locomotion for artists. Treatises accompanying écorchés and theoretical essays. Manuals on proportions, expression and portrait drawing."—*t.p.*

492   Human anatomy: From the Renaissance to the digital age. Benjamin A. Rifkin, Michael J. Ackerman. 343 p., ill. (some color). New York: Abrams, 2006. ISBN: 0810955458.

743.49   NC760.R54

History of artistic anatomy, with anatomic art and ill. from the Middle Ages to the computerized images of modern times. Contains biographies of famous anatomists and reproductions of their work. For artists, physicians, medical students, and also general readers.

493 MedEdPORTAL. Association of American Medical Colleges. 2006–. Washington: Association of American Medical Colleges. http://www.aamc.org/mededportal/.

Description based on MedEdPORTAL (version 1.4).

A project by the Association of American Medical Colleges (AAMC) that provides access to teaching resources used in medical education. Designed to help faculty publish and share educational resources. MedEdPORTAL staff review submissions for relevance and appropriateness before they are published on the site. Includes a user review feature. All approved user reviews are listed at the end of each published resource's details page. Information about copyright and copyright symbols can be found in the "Overview" section of the website.

MedEdPORTAL publications are cataloged using medical subject headings (MeSH: Medical Subject Headings [575]). Currently includes over 100 Virtual Patients (VPs), "interactive programs that simulate real-life clinical scenarios."—*Publisher's description.* To locate these and other resources, MedEdPORTAL can be browsed by discipline (list of subject areas and number of available resources within each category). Also searchable by keyword.

AAMC also participates in Health Education Assets Library (HEAL) (458), a repository of health sciences images, videos, and audio files from different collections.

494 Medical encyclopedia (MedlinePlus). National Library of Medicine (U.S.). 1999–. [Atlanta]; Bethesda, Md.: A.D.A.M.; National Library of Medicine. http://www.nlm.nih.gov/medlineplus/encyclopedia. html.

RC81.A2

Title varies: A.D.A.M. Medical Encyclopedia; MedlinePlus, Medical Encyclopedia.

Articles about diseases and conditions, injuries, nutrition, poisons, surgeries, symptoms, tests, and other special topics. Contains medical illustrations and images. Accessible via "Medical Encyclopedia" tab from MedlinePlus (463).

495 Medical images and illustrations. Karolinska Intitutet. 1999–. Stockholm, Sweden: Karolinska Institutet. http://www.mic.ki.se/ MEDIMAGES.html.

Contents: Cardiovascular System; Dermatology; Endocrinology; Gastro-enterology; Hematology; Histology; Neurology; Pathology; Pediatrics;

MEDICINE

213

General; Anatomy and Orthopedics; Visible Human Project (502); Dentistry and Oral Health; Eye, Ear-Nose-Throat and Respiratory System; Gynecology and Obstetrics; Microbiology, Infectious; Oncology; Radiology, Radiography, Nuclear Medicine and Ultrasonography; Surgery/Anesthesiology; Urogenital.

Contains links to Internet pages and sites, offering biomedical images (photos, illustrations, etc.), with copyright information. Arranged by topics and also alphabetically. This page is part of the library at Karolinska Institutet's Directory of Quality Controlled Links (http://www.mic.ki.se/Other.html), which provides a large number of biomedical links, diseases and disorders links, clinical case studies, etc.

496   **NCI visuals online.** National Cancer Institute. 200?–. Bethesda, Md.: National Cancer Institute. http://visualsonline.cancer.gov/.

Produced by National Cancer Institute (NCI) (166), Office of Communication and Education; NCI Office of Media Relations.

Contains images from the NCI collections, e.g., general biomedical and science-related images, cancer-specific scientific and patient care-related images, portraits of NCI directors and staff, etc. Can be searched (http://visualsonline.cancer.gov/search.cfm) and browsed (http://visualsonline.cancer.gov/browse.cfm). All images are in the public domain and may be used, linked, or reproduced without permission, but credit should be given to the listed source and/or author.

497   **NetAnatomy.** Raymond J. Walsh, Stephen P. Raskin, Scholar Educational Systems, Inc. 2001–. Crofton, Md.: Scholar Educational Systems, Inc. http://www.NetAnatomy.com/.

QM23.2

Produced by Scholar Educational Systems (SES). "This website contains content that addresses three of the major anatomical disciplines, including radiographic anatomy, cross-sectional anatomy, and human gross anatomy."—*Publ. notes.* For educators and students in the health professions. Available only through institutional subscription.

498   **The Netter Collection of medical illustrations.** Frank H. Netter, Ernst Oppenheimer. v. 2, 3, pt. 1, 6, 8, pt. 3, ill (some color). Summit, N.J.: Novartis, 1997–. ISBN: 0914168754.

616.070222

RB33.N48

(Netter clinical science).

Anatomical and pathological color ill., with explanatory text, of the major organ systems of the human body as well as diagnostic and surgical procedures. Available in a variety of educational products in various formats, including books, charts, and software (e.g., The Netter Presenter™— Human Anatomy). Individual volumes in this new series are listed at http://www.elsevier.com/wps/find/bookseriesdescription.cws_home/BS_NCS CI/description?navopenmenu=1.

Based on and continues *The Ciba collection of medical illustrations: A compilation of pathological and anatomical paintings*, prepared by Frank H. Netter, publ. 1953–94. Contents: Digestive system: pt. I, Upper digestive tract (1954); pt. II, Lower digestive tract (1959); pt. III, Liver, biliary tract and pancreas (1964); Endocrine system (1965); Heart (1969); Kidneys, ureters and urinary bladder (1973); Musculoskeletal system: pt. I, Anatomy, physiology, and metabolic disorders (1994); pt. II, Developmental disorders, tumors, rheumatic diseases and joint replacements (1994); pt. III, Trauma, evaluation and management (1988); Nervous system: pt. I, Anatomy and physiology (1984); pt. II, Neurologic and neuromuscular disorders (1987); Respiratory system (1979).

499   Public health image library (PHIL). Centers for Disease Control and Prevention. [1998]–. Atlanta: Centers for Disease Control and Prevention. http://phil.cdc.gov/Phil/.

Public Health Image Library (PHIL), created by a working group at the Centers for Disease Control and Prevention (CDC) (940); National Library of Medicine (NLM) (427).

Collection of a variety of single images, image sets, multimedia files, etc., with current and historical content about people, places, scientific subjects, etc. FAQ section (http://phil.cdc.gov/Phil/faq.asp) provides detailed information. Useful for public health professionals, scientists, librarians, teachers, and students.

This website also provides links to other CDC and NLM image libraries (e.g., Images from the History of Medicine [352] and Visible Human [502]). Complements other medical image collections such as Health Education Assets Library (HEAL) (458) and ImagesMD (http://www.images.md).

500   The sourcebook of medical illustration: Over 900 anatomical, medical, and scientific illustrations available for general re-use

and adaptation free of normal copyright restrictions. Peter Cull. xxiii, 481 p., chiefly ill. Carnforth, U.K.; Park Ridge, N.J.: Parthenon Pub. Group, 1989. ISBN: 0940813726.

611.00222   QM25.S677

A collection of line drawings, simple medical ill., and graphics designed to assist in the communication of medical and scientific information. Sections include body outlines and all anatomical features, as well as illustrations relating to obstetrics, anesthesia, cells and tissues, bacteria, yeasts, protozoans, helminths, viruses, arthropods, scientific symbols, and maps.

501   Turning the pages online. Lister Hill National Center for Biomedical Communications. 2003–. Bethesda, Md.: National Library of Medicine. http://archive.nlm.nih.gov/proj/ttp/intro.htm.

Produced by National Library of Medicine (NLM).

Turning the Pages Information System (TTPI), initially created by the British Library. TTP at NLM is the result of collaboration between the British Library and NLM, with refinement of the original technology. Detailed information about research, design, system development, software, and content available on website.

Web version provides access to the digitized images of rare historic books in the biomedical sciences. Includes many important and influential works in the history of medicine. Provides the ability to browse titles and bibliographic information, to turn the pages, and to use zoom images.

502   The Visible Human Project. National Library of Medicine (U.S.). 1994–. Bethesda, Md.: U.S. National Library of Medicine. http://www.nlm.nih.gov/research/visible/visible_human.html.

The Visible Human Project® (VHP) was established in 1989. The Visible Human Male data set was released in Nov. 1994, the Visible Human Female data set in Nov. 1995.

Presents "anatomically detailed, three-dimensional representations of the normal male and female human bodies."—*Website.* Consists of MRI (magnetic resonance imaging), CT (computed tomography), and cryosection images of cadavers, intended "as a reference for the study of human anatomy and to serve as test bed and model for the construction of network-accessible image libraries. Data sets have been applied to a wide range of educational, diagnostic, treatment planning, virtual reality, artistic, mathematical, and industrial uses" (*Website*) and other applications by NLM and by a large number of licensees worldwide. The applications developed by or under the direction of NLM include, for example, "Anat-Quest", "Atlas of Functional Human Anatomy," and other projects of electronically representing images in clinical medicine and biomedical research. A project overview and links to related information can be found at http://www.nlm.nih.gov/research/visible/visible_human.html. Useful mainly for graduate students and faculty.

503 **Wellcome images.** Wellcome Library. 2007–. London: Wellcome Library. http://medphoto.wellcome.ac.uk/indexplus/page/Home. html.

R133

Previously known as the Wellcome Trust Medical Photographic Library. Part of the Wellcome Collection (http://www.wellcomecollection.org/sitemap/index.htm) developed by the Wellcome Trust (http://www.wellcomecollection.org/aboutus/WTD027244.htm), linked from the Wellcome Library for the History and Understanding of Medicine (483) website.

Allows access to images, manuscripts, and illustrations on the medical and social history of medicine, modern biomedical science, clinical medicine from antiquity to the present, molecular models, portraits, depiction of medical practice, etc. All content made available under a Creative Commons License, which allows users to copy, distribute, and display the image, provided the source is fully attributed and it is used for noncommercial purposes. A valuable aid for teachers and researchers.

504 **The whole brain atlas.** Keith A. Johnson, J. Alex Becker, Harvard University School of Medicine. Cambridge, Mass.: Harvard Medical School. http://www.med.harvard.edu/AANLIB/home. html.

RC386.6

Sponsored in part by the "Depts. of Radiology and Neurology at Brigham and Women's Hospital, Harvard Medical School, the Countway Library of Medicine, and the American Academy of Neurology."—*Sponsors*

Contents: Normal Brain; Cerebrovascular Disease (Stroke or "Brain Attack"); Neoplastic Disease (Brain Tumor); Degenerative Disease; Inflammatory or Infectious Disease.

Atlas of the human brain in health and disease, providing a resource for central nervous system imaging. Includes magnetic resonance, x-ray computed tomography, and nuclear medicine images. Contains normal and pathologic structure images and multiplanar and vascular anatomy.

Quotations

505   The quotable Osler. William Osler, Mark E. Silverman, T. J. Murray, American College of Physicians—American Society of Internal Medicine. xxxv, 283 p., ill. Philadelphia: American College of Physicians—American Society of Internal Medicine, 2002. ISBN: 1930513348.

610   R705.O83

Contents: (1) Personal qualities; (2) The art and practice of medicine; (3) The medical profession; (4) Diagnosis; (5) Disease, specific illnesses, lifestyle, drugs; (6) Medical education; (7) Men and women, aging, history; (8) Science and truth; (9) Faith, religion, melancholy, death.

"Filled with Osler's best sayings and writings, provides a comprehensive view of Osler's wisdom for an audience of the 21st century."—*Publ. notes.* "Brief remarks or aphorisms rather than lengthy quotations" (*Foreword*) and proverbs, organized by topics. Bibliography and index. A rev. 2008 ed. (Philadelphia: American College of Physicians, 2008) is available.

Sir William Osler: An annotated bibliography with illustrations (San Francisco: Norman Publ., 1998), supplemented by addenda in 1997, provides details on Osler's extensive writings.

506   The Yale book of quotations. Fred R. Shapiro, Joseph Epstein. xxiv, 1067 p., ports. New Haven, Conn.: Yale University Press, 2006. ISBN: 0300107986.

082   PN6081.Y35

Compiler of the *Oxford dictionary of American legal quotations* (New York: Oxford University Press, 1993) and profiled in the *Wall Street Journal* (Jan. 22, 1997) for his indefatigable research on legal footnotes, the Yale librarian Fred Shapiro has ascended to the highest ranks of quotation mavens.

Modeled on the *Oxford English dictionary* approach to documenting first word use, this work serves as an outstanding historical dictionary of quotations. Besides including quotations omitted from many classic works, *The Yale book of quotations* includes modern American popular culture, children's literature, sports, and computers among its 12,000 entries. Shapiro used eclectic sources to find and verify entries, including databases, the Internet, hundreds of quotation books, and the American Dialect Society e-mail list.

He relied on the "indispensable" *Oxford dictionary of quotations* (Oxford; New York: Oxford University Press, 2004) for pre-1800 citations; post-1800 quotations were rechecked and verified.

Arranged alphabetically by author or specific category (e.g., modern proverbs, radio and television catchphrases). Keyword index.

Other important sources that involved extensive research on quotation origins include *Quote verifer* (New York: St. Martin's Press, 2006) and *Brewer's quotations* (London; New York: Cassell; Distributed in the United States by Sterling Pub., 1995).

Statistics

507　**AAMC data book: Medical schools and teaching hospitals by the numbers.** Association of American Medical Colleges, Division of Medical School Services and Studies, AAMC Data Services. 1 v. Washington: Association of American Medical Colleges, 2007. ISBN: 1577540662.

R745

Publ. since 1990; subtitle varies.

Contents: (A) Accredited U.S. medical schools; (B) U.S. medical school applicants and students; (C) U.S. medical school faculty; (D) U.S. medical school revenue; (E) U.S. medical school tuition, financial aid, and student debt; (F) U.S. graduate medical education; (G) U.S. teaching hospitals; (H) Health care financing; (I) Biomedical research; (J) Physicians in the U.S.; (K) U.S. medical school faculty compensation; (L) Price indices and federal expenditures; Supplemental section: census data tables.

Provides current and historical statistical information on U.S. medical schools and teaching hospitals, with revisions posted to the Association of American Medical Colleges (AAMC) (453) website.

508　**AHA hospital statistics.** American Hospital Association. Chicago: Health Forum, 2005–. ISSN: 0090-6662.

RA981.A2A6234

Title varies: Prior to 1971 issued as part 1 of the annual guide issue of *Hospitals*; 1971–90, *Hospital statistics*; 1991–97, *American Hospital Association hospital statistics*; 1998–2004, *Hospital statistics*. Editions starting in

1998 draw data from the 1996– AHA annual survey of hospitals. Statistical complement to the *AHA guide to the health care field* (199). Description based on 2006 ed. Subtitle: *The comprehensive reference source for analysis and comparison of hospital trends*. Reference source for analysis and comparison of hospital trends. Recent additions include community health indicators, utilization, personnel, and finance by all metropolitan statistical areas (MSAs), five-year trend data, breakdowns between inpatient and outpatient care, facilities and services information. Includes "Historical trends in utilization, personnel, and finances for selected years from 1946-2004." A glossary (p. 199–210) explains specific terms used in the tables and text of this volume. Hospitals included are not necessarily identical to those included in the *AHA guide to the health care field* (199).

509 American health: Demographics and spending of health care consumers. New Strategist Publications, Inc. xvi, 504 p., ill. Ithaca, N.Y.: New Strategist Publications, 2005–. ISBN: 1885070748.
614.4273   RA445.A442

Publ. 1998–2000 as *Best of health: Demographics of health care consumers*. (American consumer series).
Description based on 1st, 2005 ed.; 2nd ed., 2007.
Contents: ch. 1, Addictions; ch. 2, Aging; ch. 3, Alternative medicine; ch. 4, Attitudes towards health care; ch. 5, Births; ch. 6, Health care coverage and cost; ch. 7, Deaths; ch. 8, Disability; ch. 9, Diseases and conditions; ch. 10, Health care visits; ch. 11, Hospital care; ch. 12, Mental health; ch. 13, Sexual attitudes and behavior; ch. 14, Weight and exercise. Detailed table of contents: http://www.loc.gov/catdir/toc/fy0606/2005284141.html.

Data on health care consumers from many different sources, including information from the federal government (e.g., National Center for Health Statistics [539], incl. *Health, United States* [529], Consumer Expenditure Survey [http://www.bls.gov/cex/], MEPS Medical Expenditure Panel Survey [886], to name a few). Contains 300 tables, graphs, a glossary, bibliographical references (p. 493–495) and index. Available online via netLibrary.

510 American Hospital Association. American Hospital Association. Chicago: American Hospital Association. http://www.aha.org/aha_app/index.jsp.

Founded in 1898, the association represents hospitals, health care networks, and their consumers. The website provides "Fast Facts on U.S. Hospitals," reports and studies, trends, testimony, regulations, and a section for members only. Some information is only available for a fee.

511 **Atlas of cancer.** Maurie Markman. xii, 628 p., ill. (some color). Philadelphia: Lippincott, Williams & Wilkins, 2003. ISBN: 1573401927.

616.994   RC262.A846

Contents: (I) Head and neck; (II) Gynecologic cancer; (III) Lung cancer; (IV) Upper gastrointestinal cancers; (V) Lower gastrointestinal cancers; (VI) Leukemia; (VII) Lymphoma; (VIII) Sarcoma; (IX) Breast cancer; (X) Genitourinary cancers; (XI) Skin cancer; (XII) Neuro-oncology.

"Highlights the major features of current cancer management, both diagnostic and therapeutic, and clearly lays out fundamental facts regarding our understanding of the etiology and pathophysiology of malignant disease."—*Pref.* Each section provides a summary introduction to a particular cancer, with U.S. statistics, epidemiology and etiology, histology, genetics, staging, major risk factors, imaging, surgical management, treatment modalities, prevention, and other information as appropriate to the specific cancer. Each chapter includes a list of references. Index.

512 **Atlas of cancer mortality in the United States, 1950–94.** Susan S. Devesa, National Cancer Institute (U.S.). 1 atlas (367 p.), color maps. [Bethesda, Md.]: National Institute of Health, National Cancer Institute, 1999.

614.599940223   G1201.E51A8

Utilizes 1950–94 mortality data from the National Center for Health Statistics (539) and population estimates from the Census Bureau to calculate age-adjusted cancer mortality rates of 40 forms of cancer. Includes computerized color-coded maps showing geographic patterns and summary tables, figures, and text, suggesting explanations for the variations in cancer rates. Supplemented by two websites—one that contains the entire text of the atlas (http://www3.cancer.gov/atlasplus/new.html), and another that provides various options for viewing the maps (http://www3.cancer.gov/atlasplus).

513 **The Cambridge dictionary of statistics.** 3rd ed. Brian S. Everitt. ix, 432 p., ill. Cambridge, [England, U.K.]: Cambridge University Press, 2006. ISBN: 0521690277.

                                                             QA276.15.E84

Includes 3,600 entries. Covers medical, survey, theoretical, and applied statistics, including computational aspects, and standard and specialized statistical software. Also includes brief biographies of more than 100 noteworthy statisticians. Definitions include mathematical detail and graphical material for completeness and clarity. Many definitions include references to other books and articles for further information. Useful for specialist and nonspecialist alike.

514   The Cambridge dictionary of statistics in the medical sciences.
Brian Everitt. 274 p., ill. Cambridge; New York: Cambridge University Press, 1995. ISBN: 0521473829.

610.21   RA407.E94

Concise definitions and brief explanations of approx. 2,000 statistical terms and concepts used in the biomedical sciences. Also includes relevant mathematical, computing, and genetic terms. Graphical illustrations and numeric examples. *The Cambridge dictionary of statistics* (3rd ed., 2006) (513) by the same author also covers medical statistics.

515   Cancer facts and figures. American Cancer Society. 1997–. Atlanta: American Cancer Society. http://www.cancer.org/docroot/STT/ content/STT_1x_Cancer_Facts__Figures_2007.asp.

Part of the services provided by American Cancer Society (ACS) (1), a nationwide, community-based voluntary health organization. Also publ. in print format since 1956.

Description based on 2007 ed.

Contents: Cancer: Basic Facts; Selected Cancers; Special Section: Cancer-Related Pain; Cancer in Racial and Ethnic Minorities; Tobacco Use; Nutrition and Physical Activity; Environmental Cancer Risks; The International Fight against Cancer; The American Cancer Society; Sources of Statistics; Factors That Influence Cancer Rates.

Provides basic facts and data about cancer in general and selected cancers, cancer incidence, risk factors, mortality, and survival. Annual estimates of expected new cases and deaths. Each issue also has a special section that addresses different topics (e.g., 2007, cancer-related pain; 2006, environmental pollutants and cancer; 2005, cancers linked to infectious diseases; 2004, cancer disparities, etc.). Also includes, for example, trends in cigarette smoking, fruit and vegetable consumption, physical inactivity, overweight and obesity, and screening exams. Additional statistics on various topics and estimates of new cases and a glossary of cancer-related terms are provided at http://www.cancer.org/docroot/stt/stt_0.asp.

SEER cancer statistics review (547) and the National Cancer Institute's SEER (Surveillance Epidemiology and End Results) program (http://seer.

cancer.gov) are other sources for authoritative information on cancer statistics.

516   DHHS Data Council gateway to data and statistics. U.S. Department of Health and Human Services. 200?–. Washington: U.S. Department of Health and Human Services. http://www.hhs-stat.net/about.htm.

RA407.3

Provides access to key health and human services data and statistics. Covers information sponsored by federal, state, and local governments. Complements other government resources such as FirstGov (http://www.usa.gov/) and FedStats (519). Links to health and human services surveys and data systems sponsored by Federal agencies. Datafinder leads to websites that contain statistics and data. The MetaDirectory is a comprehensive list and description of the statistical and surveillance systems supported by HHS agencies. Other key resources links lead to additional information.

517   Encyclopedia of statistical sciences. 2nd ed. Samuel Kotz, N. Balakrishnan, Campbell B. Read. v. 1–14, ill. Hoboken, N.J.: Wiley-Interscience, 2006. ISBN: 9780471150442.
519.503   QA276.14.E5

The 2nd ed. is expanded by about 50 percent over the 1st ed. and encompasses materials included in supplement and update volumes issued between editions. Entries are signed, most include bibliographies, and most are multipage. Over 600 contributors. Includes some biographical articles. Aim is to provide articles that are accessible to the student and the nonspecialist. Enough depth to impart basic understanding and facilitate rudimentary application of the concepts with references to more detailed readings. Good, broad coverage of the mathematical aspects of statistical theory and the application of statistical methods. Appropriate for collections supporting instruction and research in statistics as well as those supporting users in other disciplines who use statistical methods in their research.

Also available in an online edition through Wiley InterScience.

518   Faststats A to Z. National Center for Health Statistics (NCHS). Hyattsville, Md.: U.S. Dept. of Health and Human Services, Centers for Disease Control and Prevention, National Center for Health Statistics. http://www.cdc.gov/nchs/fastats/Default.htm.

Provides topic-appropriate public health statistics (e.g., birth data, morbidity and mortality statistics, and health care use) and relevant links to further information and publications. Includes state and territorial data, with clickable map for individual state data. Also includes data derived from the "Behavioral Risk Factor Surveillance System (BRFSS)," which compiles data for 16 negative behaviors.

519 FedStats. U.S. Federal Interagency Council on Statistical Policy. [Washington, D.C.]: Interagency Council on Statistical Policy. http://www.fedstats.gov/.

HA37.U55

FedStats provides a portal to publicly available statistics produced by more than 100 U.S. government agencies, including agriculture, census, education, health and human services, interior, justice, labor, transportation, and the treasury. It permits several access points to the agency sites, including an A–Z subject index, keyword searching, and federated searching across agency websites. This outstanding resource also provides a link to online versions of frequently requested publications such as the *Statistical abstract of the United States* and the *State and metropolitan area data book*.

520 Finding and using health statistics. National Information Center on Health Services Research and Health Care Technology, National Library of Medicine (U.S.). 2008–. Bethesda, Md.: National Library of Medicine. http://www.nlm.nih.gov/nichsr/usestats/.

Contents: "Introduction"; "About health statistics" ("Importance"; "Uses"; "Sources"; "Health statistics enterprise"); "Finding health statistics" ("Challenges"; "Natural structure"; "Strategies"; "Internet strategies"); "Supporting material" (including a glossary, exercises, and examples).

"This course describes the range of available health statistics, identifies their sources and helps you understand how to use information about their structure as you search."—*Main page*

Reviews various approaches to finding health statistics and provides help with developing search strategies. Links to numerous relevant examples of statistical web resources and portals from federal and state governments, universities, and private organizations. Provides a good introduction and overviews for health professionals, students, and reference librarians.

521 The global burden of disease: A comprehensive assessment of mortality and disability from diseases, injuries, and risk factors

in 1990 and projected to 2020. Christopher J. L. Murray, Alan D. Lopez, Harvard School of Public Health. xxxii, 990 p. Cambridge, Mass.: Publ. by the Harvard School of Public Health on behalf of the World Health Organization and the World Bank, 1996. ISBN: 0674354486.

614.42   RA441.G56

(Global burden of disease and injury series; v. 1) "The Global Burden of Disease Series provides, on a global and regional level, a detailed and internally consistent approach to meeting information needs concerning epidemiological conditions and disease burden."—*Foreword.* GDB is considered to have set new standards for measuring population health. It also attempts to provide a comparative index of the burden of each disease or injury, i.e., the number of disability-adjusted life years lost as a result of either premature death or years lived with disability. The findings attempt to provide a comprehensive assessment of the health of populations. Results are only approximate, with the reliability of data considered poor for some regions of the world; with estimates of causes of death, incidence and prevalence of disease, injury, and disability, measures and projections of disease burden, and measures of risk factors. Other titles in this series include, e.g., *Global health statistics: A compendium of incidence, prevalence, and mortality estimates for over 200 conditions* (524), *Health dimensions of sex and reproduction: The global burden of sexually transmitted diseases, HIV, maternal conditions, perinatal disorders, and congenital anomalies*, and *The global epidemiology of infectious diseases*. Another related title is *Global burden of disease and risk factors* (521) and the World Health Organization's "Global burden of disease estimates" website (http://www.who.int/healthinfo/bodestimates/en/index.html), with recent results and links.

522   Global burden of disease and risk factors. Alan D. Lopez, Disease Control Priorities Project. xxix, 475 p., ill. [New York]: Washington: Oxford University Press; World Bank, 2006. ISBN: 9780821362.

362.1   RA441.G5613

Disease Control Priorities Project is a partnership of the Fogarty International Center (U.S. National Institutes of Health), the World Bank, The World Health Organization, and the Population Reference Bureau.

Contents: ch. 1, Measuring the Global Burden of Disease and risk factors, 1990–2001; ch. 2, Demographic and epidemiological characteristics of major regions, 1990–2001; ch. 3, The burden of disease and mortality by condition: data, methods, and results for 2001; ch. 4, Comparative quantification of mortality and burden of disease attributable to selected risk factors; ch. 5, Sensitivity and uncertainty analyses for burden of disease and risk factor estimates; ch. 6, Incorporating deaths near the time of birth into estimates of the Global Burden of Disease.

Presents the results of the "Global Burden of Disease Study" (quantification of the impact of diseases, injuries, and risk factors on population health) and the CEA (Cost-Effectiveness Analysis) Study and a description of the global epidemiology of diseases, injuries, and risk factors. Resource for researchers interested in the development of methods to measure disease burden and in global and regional health policy.

Related titles are, e.g., *The global burden of disease: A comprehensive assessment of mortality and disability from diseases, injuries, and risk factors* (955), *Global health statistics: A compendium of incidence, prevalence, and mortality estimates for over 200 conditions* (524), and the World Health Organization's "Global burden of disease estimates" website (http://www.who.int/healthinfo/bodestimates/en/index.html), with recent results and links.

Available online at http://bibpurl.oclc.org/web/13502.

523   **Globalhealth.gov.** U.S. Dept. of Health and Human Services.
        1990s–. Washington: U.S. Dept. of Health and Human Services.
        http://globalhealth.gov/index.html.

Produced by HHS Office of Global Health Affairs (OGHA). Title varies: Global Health.gov; GlobalHealth.

Provides access to information about major global health topics, such as avian influenza, HIV/AIDS, malaria, etc. and links to partner organizations (e.g., WHO [951], PAHO [950], and others) and information on international travel, health regulation, refugee health, and related areas. CDC's (940) Coordinating Office for Global Health (http://www.cdc.gov/cogh/) provides additional information and resources.

524   **Global health statistics: A compendium of incidence, prevalence, and mortality estimates for over 200 conditions.** Christopher
        J. L. Murray, Alan D. Lopez, World Health Organization. vii, 906
        p. Boston; Cambridge, Mass.: Publ. by The Harvard School of
        Public Health on behalf of the World Health Organization and the
        World Bank; Distributed by Harvard University Press, 1996. ISBN:
        0674354494.

614.42   RA407.M87

(Global burden of disease and injury series; 2)

Provides information on the underlying epidemiological statistics for over 200 conditions and several chapters with detailed data for each condition.

Part of the Global burden of disease series which "provides, on a global and regional level, a detailed and internally consistent approach to meeting information needs concerning epidemiological conditions and disease burden. Volumes summarize epidemiological knowledge about all major conditions and most risk factors."—*Foreword*

Other titles in this series include, for example, the *Global burden of disease: A comprehensive assessment of mortality and disability from diseases, injuries, and risk factors in 1990 and projected to 2020* (955), *Health dimensions of sex and reproduction: The global burden of sexually transmitted diseases, HIV, maternal conditions, perinatal disorders, and congenital anomalies,* and *The global epidemiology of infectious diseases.* Other related titles are *Global burden of disease and risk factors* (522) and the World Health Organization's "Global burden of disease estimates" website (http://www.who.int/healthinfo/bodestimates/en/index.html), with recent results and links.

525 Health and healthcare in the United States: County and metro area data. NationsHealth Corporation. 2 v., maps. Lanham, Md.: Bernan Press, c1999–c2001. ISSN: 1526-1573.

362   RA407.3.H415

1st ed., 1999–2nd ed., 2000; 2nd ed. technical consultant, Russell G. Bruce.

Compendium of health-related statistics and reference maps for each of the 3,000 counties and the 80 metropolitan areas in the U.S.—demographics, vital statistics, healthcare resources, and Medicare data. Based on information from the National Center for Health Statistics (539) and the U.S. Bureau of the Census. Accompanying CD-ROMs make it possible to manipulate the data.

526 Health data for all ages (HDAA). National Center for Health Statistics. 200?–. Atlanta: National Center for Health Statistics. http://www.cdc.gov/nchs/health_data_for_all_ages.htm.

Searchable website presents tables that provide Centers for Disease Control and Prevention (CDC) (940) health statistics for infants, children, adolescents, adults, and older adults. Table topics include pregnancy and birth, health conditions/risk factors, health care access and use, mortality, and others, and topics can be customized with characteristics such as age, gender, race/ethnicity, and geographic location.

527 **Health statistics: An annotated bibliographic guide to information resources.** 2nd ed. Frieda Weise. x, 178 p. Lanham, Md.: Medical Library Association and Scarecrow Press, 1997. ISBN: 0810830566.

016.36210973021   Z7553.M43W444; RA407.3

1st ed., ©1980.

Rev. ed. Contents: Ch. 1, General references; ch. 2, Compilations of health statistics; ch. 3, Vital statistics; ch. 4, Morbidity; ch. 5, Health resources; ch. 6, Health services utilization; ch. 7, Health care costs and expenditures; ch. 8, Population characteristics; Appendixes A–D; Glossary; Index.

Annotated bibliography of basic vital and health statistics. "Health statistics include a wide spectrum of information: vital statistics (birth, death, marriage, and divorce); morbidity and other measures of health status; health care facilities, health personnel and health professions education; use of health care services; and health care costs and expenditures, linked to population and demographic data."—*Pref.* Contains mostly print, but also electronic resources. Several appendixes include, for example, newsletters and journals, lists of government agencies, and private associations from which information can be obtained.

528 **Health statistics (MedlinePlus).** National Library of Medicine (U.S.). 2000–. Bethesda, Md.: National Library of Medicine. http://www.nlm.nih.gov/medlineplus/healthstatistics.html.

Part of MedlinePlus (463); National Library of Medicine (NLM) (427).

Contents: Overviews; Latest News; Related Issues; Research; Journal Articles; Directories; Organizations; Newsletters/Print Publications; Law and Policy; Children; Teenagers; Men; Women; Seniors.

Provides helpful links to various types of health and vital statistics for consumers and health professionals. FAQ Statistics (http://www.nlm.nih.gov/services/statistics.html) is another website made available by NLM that answers questions on how to find statistics for U.S. and global health and medicine topics.

529 **Health, United States.** National Center for Health Statistics. 1975–. Rockville, Md.: National Center for Health Statistics. http://purl.access.gpo.gov/GPO/LPS2649.

Description based on the 2006 ed. (30th annual report). Subtitle of this edition: With Chartbook on Trends in the Health of Americans with Special Feature on Pain.

"An annual report on trends in health statistics. The report consists of two main sections: a chartbook containing text and figures that illustrates major trends in the health of Americans; and a trend tables section that contains 147 detailed data tables. The two main components are supplemented by an executive summary, a highlights section, an extensive appendix and reference section, and an index."—*NCHS website.* Hyperlinks to tables and graphs. Also provides easy access to other online resources provided by NCHS, for example, Faststats A–Z (518), Healthy People 2010 (530), and other websites.

530   **Healthy People 2010.** National Center for Health Statistics (NCHS). Hyattsville, Md.: Centers for Disease Control (U.S.), National Center for Health Statistics. http://www.cdc.gov/nchs/hphome.htm.

RA395.A3

Contents: Healthy people 2010: Understanding and improving health; Healthy people 2010: Objectives for improving health; Appendixes; Tracking healthy people 2010.

Described as a "national initiative of the U.S. Dept. of Health and Human Services [HHS] that brings together national, state, and local organizations, businesses, communities, and individuals to improve the health of all Americans, eliminate disparities in health, and improve years and quality of life. Since its inception in 1979, it has been coordinated by the Office of Disease Prevention and Health Promotion."—*Website.* Represents the third time that HHS has developed ten-year health objectives for the nation. Previous reports include *Healthy people 2000* (http://purl.access.gpo.gov/GPO/LPS3745) and *Healthy people: The Surgeon General's report on health promotion and disease prevention: Background papers: Report to the Surgeon General on health promotion and disease prevention* (Washington, D.C.: Institute of Medicine, 1979). "Healthy People DATA 2010," an interactive database system accessible via CDC WONDER (1399) provides various reports and data. A search interface providing searches for published literature related to the Healthy People 2010 was added to the "special queries" section of PubMed (432).

Also available in print format: *Tracking healthy people 2010: Healthy people 2010* (Washington, D.C.: U.S. Dept. of Health and Human Services, 2000 [Nov. 2000 version]), which supersedes the conference edition, entitled *Healthy people 2010* (Washington, D.C.: U.S. Dept. of Health and Human Services, 2000 [Jan. 2000]).

531 **Healthy women.** Centers for Disease Control and Prevention (U.S.), National Center for Health Statistics (U.S.). 2004. Hyattsville, Md.: National Center for Health Statistics; Centers for Disease Control and Prevention; U.S. Dept. of Health and Human Services. http://www.cdc.gov/nchs/datawh/statab/chartbook.htm.
RA408.W65

Title varies: Suggested title for website: Healthy Women: State Trends in Health and Mortality; suggested citation for print version, publ. in 2004 as *Women's health and mortality chartbook* by K. M. Brett and Suzanne G. Hayes.

Provides access to the PDF version of *Women's health and mortality chartbook*, developed by NCHS with support from the Office on Women's Health. It describes the health of people in each state in the U.S. by sex, race, and age by reporting current data on critical issues of relevance to women. Because of the large file size, this report has been broken into four accessible PDF files. Users may also download the entire report. Website provides help for using tables.

Other publications in this area include *Women's health data book: A profile of women's health in the United States,* ed. by D. Misra, a collaborative publication by the Jacobs Institute of Women's Health and the Henry J. Kaiser Family Foundation (Kaiser Family Foundation [884]) since 1992, complemented by *State profiles on women's health: Women's health issues,* publ. since 1998.

532 **Historical statistics of the United States.** Richard Sutch, Susan B. Carter. New York: Cambridge University Press. http://hsus.cambridge.org/.

Standard source for American historical data. No uniform end date for tables, but many end in the late 1990s. Examples of tables include population, work, labor, education, health, and government finance. Tables are easily searched and can be downloaded into Excel or CSV formats. Also in print as a 5-vol. set.

533 **How to report statistics in medicine: Annotated guidelines for authors, editors, and reviewers.** 2nd ed. Thomas A. Lang, Michelle Secic. New York: American College of Physicians, 2006. ISBN: 1930513690.
610.72   RA409.L357

1st ed., 1997.

Rev. ed., with new and updated content. Considered a standard guide to interpreting and reporting statistics in scientific and medical writing. Provides guidelines for reporting statistical analyses, research, and trial design used in biological sciences and medical research, how to display data, and explanation of statistical terms and tests.

534 **Injury data and resources.** National Center for Health Statistics. Atlanta: National Center for Health Statistics. http://www.cdc.gov/nchs/injury.htm.

"The purpose of this Web site is to provide an overview of injury morbidity and mortality data and statistics available from the National Center for Health Statistics (NCHS) (539) and other sources and to provide details on injury surveillance methodology and tools to assist in data analysis."— *Main page*. Provides links to a variety of resources, including the International Collaborative Effort (ICE) on Injury Statistics (http://www.cdc.gov/nchs/advice.htm), relevant coding schemes, and additional resources (e.g., WISQARS: Web-based Injury Statistics Query and Reporting System [1404], CDC WONDER [1399], Faststats [518], and others).

535 **International health data reference guide.** National Center for Health Statistics (U.S.). ill. Hyattsville, Md.: U.S. Dept. of Health and Human Services, Public Health Service, National Center for Health Statistics, [1984?]–.

362.1021   RA407.A58

Description based on 11th ed., 2003.

"Provides information collected in 2003 on the availability of selected national vital, hospital, health personnel resources, and population-based health survey statistics. Information for 40 nations. Main purpose is to provide information not readily available in published form. It is not designed to provide information on the availability of measures such as crude birth and death rates or life expectancy at birth."—*Pref*. Biennial. Also available online on the National Center for Health Statistics (NCHS) (539) website at http://purl.access.gpo.gov/GPO/LPS24629.

536 **Medical statistics from A to Z.** 2nd ed. Brian Everitt. vi, 248 p., ill. Cambridge; New York: Cambridge University Press, 2006. ISBN: 0521867630.

610.727   RA407.E943

1st ed., 2003.

Contains approx. 1,500 terms with definitions and references for further reading. Written in non-technical language. For health professionals and students.

537 **MEPS Medical Expenditure Panel Survey.** U.S. Agency for Healthcare Research and Quality. 1996–. Bethesda, Md.: Agency for Healthcare Research and Quality. http://www.meps.ahrq.gov/mepsweb/.

RA408.5

Produced by Agency for Health Care Research and Quality (AHRQ) (733).

"Set of large-scale surveys of families and individuals, their medical providers (doctors, hospitals, pharmacies, etc.), and employers across the United States. MEPS collects data on the specific health services that Americans use, how frequently they use them, the cost of these services, and how they are paid for, as well as data on the cost, scope, and breadth of health insurance held by and available to U.S. workers."—*Website.* Provides information on health expenditures, utilization of health services, health insurance, and nursing homes, and reimbursement mechanisms. MEPS topics include access to health care, children's health, children's insurance coverage, health care disparities, mental health, minority health, the uninsured, and other topics. Further details concerning the survey background, data overview, and frequently asked questions are provided at the website. Provides full-text access to MEPS publications: highlights, research findings, statistical briefs, etc.

538 **National Cancer Institute.** National Cancer Institute. Bethesda, Md.: National Cancer Institute. http://www.cancer.gov/.

Website created by the National Cancer Institute (NCI), a division of the National Institutes of Health (NIH).

Contents: NCI Home, Cancer Topics, Clinical Trials, Cancer Statistics, Research and Funding, News, About NCI.

Links to cancer-related information for health professionals, medical students, and patients. Provides guidance to searching the cancer literature in PubMed (432) by searching the "cancer subset" and access to already prepared searches on more than 100 different topics. Non-PubMed citations previously found in CANCERLIT, a database no longer being maintained, consist primarily of meeting abstracts from the annual meetings of the American Society of Clinical Oncology (ASCO) and the American Association for Cancer Research (AACR). ASCO abstracts for recent years are available via http://www.asco.org, AACR abstracts at http://aacrmeetingabstracts.org/. Also provides access to PDQ: Physician Data Query (http://www.cancer.gov/cancertopics/pdq), a database with the latest information about cancer treatment, screening, prevention, genetics, etc.

The NCI website includes descriptions of various types of cancer (A–Z List of Cancers: http://www.cancer.gov/cancertopics/alphalist/) and related topics, with links to diagnosis and treatment information and supportive care, information on clinical trials, cancer prevention, cancer statistics (e.g., SEER Cancer Statistics Review [547]), cancer statistics tools, cancer mortality maps and graphs, and related NCI websites. Links to the Dictionary of Cancer Terms (143) and various cancer vocabulary resources (e.g., NCI Thesaurus, NCI Metathesaurus, and NCI Terminology Browser), NCI Drug Dictionary, NCI publications, etc. Available both in English and Spanish.

539   National Center for Health Statistics (NCHS). National Center
      for Health Statistics (U.S.). 1990s–. Hyattsville, Md.: Centers for
      Disease Control and Prevention. http://www.cdc.gov/nchs/.

RA409

NCHS is the primary agency for compiling and making available American health and vital statistics and data sets. Searchable website, with topically arranged site index. Its home page provides links to various resources in several categories, including What's New; Health E-stats; Information Showcase; Top 10 Links; surveys and data collection systems (data collected through personal interviews and systems based on records, with data from vital and medical records); and microdata access (including links to NCHS public-use data files and documentation and state data). Surveys and data collection systems include the National Health and Nutrition Examination Survey (NHANES), National Health Care Survey (NHCS), National Health Interview Survey (NHIS), National Immunization Survey (NIS), Longitudinal Studies of Aging (LSOAs), National Vital Statistics System (NSS), and Injury Statistics Query and Reporting System. Examples of linked resources include *Faststats A to Z* (518) and Health,

United States (529). Details on NCHS publications and information products are provided at http://www.cdc.gov/nchs/products.htm.

NCHS serves as the World Health Organization's (WHO's) Collaborating Center for the Family of International Classifications for North America (North American Collaborating Center [NACC] established in 1976) and is responsible for coordinating all official disease classification activities in the United States, in close cooperation with the Canadian Institute for Health Information (CIHI), Statistics Canada, and the Pan American Health Organization. A portal to the disease classifications in North America (e.g., International Classification of Diseases, Ninth Revision, Clinical Modification: ICD-9-CM [82] and International Classification of Functioning, Disability, and Health [ICF] [83]) is provided at http://www.cdc.gov/nchs/icd9.htm.

540   National vital statistics system (NVSS). National Center for Health Statistics. 2000s–. Hyattsville, Md.: National Center for Health Statistics. http://www.cdc.gov/nchs/nvss.htm.

NVSS is a unit of the National Center for Health Statistics (539), which is responsible for the official vital statistics of the United States: births, deaths (annual mortality data, monthly provisional mortality data, cause-of-death data by age, race, sex, etc.), marriages, divorces, and fetal deaths. Provides access to a vital-statistics information sources portal (http://www.cdc.gov/nchs/about/major/dvs/Vitalstatsonline.htm), with links to publications and information products (http://www.cdc.gov/nchs/products.htm), including Advance Data, Vital and Health Statistics Series (also referred to as "series reports" and "rainbow series"; http://www.cdc.gov/nchs/products/pubs/pubd/series/ser.htm), Vital Statistics of the United States (http://www.cdc.gov/nchs/products/pubs/pubd/vsus/vsus.htm), and many others that can be identified via a helpful site index at http://www.cdc.gov/nchs/siteindex.htm or via NCHS Web Search (http://www.cdc.gov/nchs/search/search.htm).

541   OECD health data. Organisation for Economic Co-operation and Development. Paris: Organisation for Economic Co-operation and Development. http://www.oecd.org/health/healthdata.

Title varies: SourceOECD Health Data.

Part of SourceOECD (Organisation for Economic Co-operation and Development, [Paris, France]: OECD), which contains publications (monographs, periodicals, and statistical databases) issued by the OECD.

Interactive database and source of statistics on health and health care systems of the OECD member states. Allows cross-country comparisons of national health care systems. Includes, for example, health status, health care resources, health care utilization, expenditure on health, and health care financing. Available in online and CD-ROM formats.

542   Physician characteristics and distribution in the U.S. American Medical Association. Chicago: Survey & Data Resources, American Medical Association, 1982–. ISSN: 0731-0315.

331.119161069520973   RA410.7.D47

Earlier titles: 1963–69, *Distribution of physicians, hospitals, and hospital beds in the U.S.*; 1970–73, *Distribution of physicians in the U.S.*; 1974–81, *Physician distribution and medical licensure in the U.S.* No issue publ. in 1989. Data derived from the American Medical Association's (AMA) Physician Masterfile, originally established in 1906 as a record-keeping system for physician membership and mailing purposes.—*Foreword*

Description based on 2006 ed.

Contents: Five chapters: 1. Physician characteristics for age, sex, major professional activity, specialty, and race; 2. Physician distribution (i.e., geographical distribution by state); 3. Analysis of professional activity by specialty and geographic region; 4. Primary care specialties (including trends, age, sex, board certification, school and year of graduation, state location and metro area); 5. Physician trends (trend data for specialty, major professional activity, age, and sex); Appendices A–F (self-designated practice specialties, American Specialty Boards, Metropolitan Statistical Areas [MSAs], etc.) and index.

Current, historical, and comparative data on U.S. physicians, with both summary and detailed statistical information and tabulations. Describes professional and individual characteristics of physicians and provides information on their geographical location. Census summary data by state, age, gender, and specialty.

543   Physician compensation and production survey. Medical Group Management Association. Englewood, Colo: Center for Research in Ambulatory Health Care Administration, 1992–. ISSN: 1064-4563.

331   R728.5.P48152

Description based on 2007 report, with data from 2006 survey.

Contents: section 1, Key findings and demographics; section 2, Physician compensation and benefits; section 3, Physician productivity;

section 4, Physician time worked; section 5, Summary tables; section 6, Nonphysician providers; section 7, Physician placement starting salaries.

"Data on compensation for healthcare professionals and on medical group practices and financial operations will assist in evaluating the ranges of compensation and productivity for both. physicians and nonphysician providers."—*Publ. notes.* The Bureau of Labor Statistics website "Sector 62—Health Care and Social Assistance" (http://www.bls.gov/oes/current/oessrci.htm#62) also provides extensive information in this area as part of its occupational employment and wage estimates.

Physician socioeconomic statistics (formed by the union of *Physician marketplace statistics* and *Socioeconomic characteristics of medical practice*), publ. by the American Medical Association, was discontinued in 2003.

544   Portrait of health in the United States. Daniel Melnick, Beatrice A. Rouse. xxi, 376 p., ill. Lanham, Md: Bernan, 2001. ISBN: 089059189X.

614.4273   RA410.53.P675

"Major statistical trends & guide to resources."—*Cover*

"Presents a picture of American health using a variety of measures ranging from self-perceived health status and reported acute and chronic health conditions to more objective measures such as life expectancy, medical diagnosis, hospitalization, and death rates. Data not found easily elsewhere are included."—*Pref.* Compiled from results reported by federal and public health agencies. Includes, for example, societal trends, health outcomes, leading chronic and acute health conditions and causes of death, incidence, mortality and survival rates of various illnesses, access to care, insurance and costs, life expectancy, quality of life issues, and other relevant information. Also available online via netLibrary.

545   Publications from the National Center for Health Statistics for the period 1898–2004 on DVD. Centers for Disease Control and Prevention (U.S.), National Center for Health Statistics (U.S.). 2 DVD-ROMs, color [Rockville, Md.]: U.S. Dept. of Health and Human Services, Centers for Disease Control, National Center for Health Statistics, 2004.

RA407.3

National Center for Health Statistics (NCHS) (539); National Office of Vital Statistics; U.S. Census Bureau. Compilation of most of the NCHS publications and selected data products. Disk 1 includes Advance data reports; Vital and health statistics series reports; Monthly vital statistics report summaries and supplements; Health, United States; and other miscellaneous reports. Disk 2 includes Vital statistics of the United States and Life tables published by NCHS, the National Office of Vital Statistics, and the U.S. Census Bureau.

546   Secondary data sources for public health: A practical guide.
Sarah Boslaugh. x, 152 p. Cambridge, [England, U.K.]; New York: Cambridge University Press, 2007. ISBN: 052169023.
362.10727   RA409.B66
Part of Practical Guides to Biostatistics and Epidemiology.

Contents: ch. 1, "An introduction to secondary analysis"; ch. 2, "Health services utilization data"; ch. 3, "Health behaviors and risk factors data"; ch. 4, "Data on multiple health topics"; ch. 5, "Fertility and mortality data"; ch. 6, "Medicare and Medicaid data"; ch. 7, "Other sources of data"; appendixes: I, "Acronyms"; II, "Summary of data sets and years available"; III, "Data import and transfer".

This guide lists the major sources of secondary data for health-related subjects that are important in epidemiology and public health research. They are often stored in different locations and not necessarily easily accessible. Examples include the National Hospital Discharge Survey, the Healthcare Cost Utilization Project, the Behavioral Risk Factor Surveillance System, the National Health and Nutrition Survey, Medicare Public Use Files, Web portals to statistical data, etc. Description of each resource includes title, focus, core section, data collection, and information on accessing data and ancillary materials. Includes bibliography and index.

MEDICINE

237

547   SEER cancer statistics review 1975–2004. National Cancer Institute (U.S.). 1973–. Bethesda, Md.: National Cancer Institute.
http://purl.access.gpo.gov/GPO/LPS3349.
362.19699400973021   RA645.C3.A65
National Cancer Institute (NCI); SEER (Surveillance Epidemiology and End Results).

Titles of print and online products vary, including *Cancer statistics review* (CSR), published annually by the Cancer Statistics Branch of the NCI. Description based on the 1975–2004 online ed. Contents at http://seer.cancer.gov/csr/1975_2004/sections.html.

CSR is "a report of the most recent cancer incidence, mortality, survival, prevalence, and lifetime risk statistics."—*Main page*

NCI's SEER Program (http://seer.cancer.gov) is an authoritative source of information on cancer incidence and survival in the United States. Overview of the SEER program can be found at http://seer.cancer.gov/about/. The SEER website provides a wide array of additional cancer statistics resources, including a glossary of statistical terms, cancer statistics fact sheets, state cancer profiles, statistical reports and monographs, etc.

548   **State medical licensure requirements and statistics.** American Medical Association. Chicago: American Medical Association, 1999–. ISSN: 1549-4055.

362.172   RA396.A3U2

1999/2000–. (publ. 2000)–

1982–98: *U.S. medical licensure statistics and licensure requirements* (title varies). Description based on 2007 ed.

Contents: Licensure policies and regulations of state medical/osteopathic boards; Statistics of state medical licensing boards; Medical licensing examinations and organizations; Information for international medical graduates; Federal and national programs and activities; Other organizations and programs; Appendixes (including a "Glossary of Medical Licensure Terms").

"Presents current information and statistics on licensure in the United States and possessions. Data were obtained from a number of sources, including state boards of medical examiners, the Federation of State Medical Boards, National Board of Medical Examiners, Educational Commission for Foreign Graduates, and the United States Medical Licensing Examination."—*Foreword*. Includes 54 allopathic and 14 osteopathic boards of medical examiners.

A related Internet resource on medical licensure is found at http://www.ama-assn.org/go/licensure.

549   **Statistical abstract of the United States.** U.S. Dept. of the Treasury, Bureau of Statistics, U.S. Dept. of Commerce and Labor, U.S. Bureau of Foreign and Domestic Commerce, U.S. Bureau of the Census. ill. Washington: U.S. G.P.O., 1878–. ISSN: 0081-4741.

317.3   HA202

A single-volume work presenting quantitative summary statistics on the political, social, and economic organization of the United States. Statistics given in the tables cover a period of several years. Indispensable in any library: it serves not only as a first source for statistics of national importance but also as a guide to further information, as references are given to the sources of all tables. Includes a table of contents arranged by broad subject areas and a detailed alphabetical index. Also available online from the Census Bureau at http://www.census.gov/compendia/statab/.

Supplement: *County and city data book* (Washington: U.S. Dept. of Commerce, Bureau of the Census, 1949–).

550 Statistical handbook on infectious diseases. Sarah Watstein, John Jovanovic. xxiii, 321 p., ill., maps. Westport, Conn.: Greenwood Press, 2003. ISBN: 1573563757.

614.0727   RA643.W33

Contents: (A) Nationally notifiable diseases; (B) Human Immunoficiency Virus (HIV) and Acquired Immunodeficiency Syndrome (AIDS); (C) Malaria; (D) Sexually transmitted diseases; (E) Tuberculosis; (F) Foodborne diseases; (G) Waterborne diseases; (H) Infectious disease worldwide: present issues, emerging concerns; (I) Vaccine-preventable diseases; (J) Infectious disease elimination and eradication; (K) Bioterrorism and biological warfare; Appendix: World Health Organization (WHO) regions. Glossary.

"Comprehensive statistical overview of the status of infectious disease worldwide, often hard to find, or difficult to interpret. A carefully selected array of tables and charts of authoritative statistical information, placing valuable statistics into context with introductory text."—*Publ. notes.* Selection from a variety of print and web-based sources. Includes bibliographical references (p. [315]–318) and index. For general readers and students as a good starting point for research. Available online via the Greenwood Digital Collection (http://ebooks.greenwood.com/).

551 Statistical methods for health care research. 5th ed. Barbara Hazard Munro. xiii, 494 p., ill. Philadelphia: Lippincott, Williams & Wilkins, 2005. ISBN: 0781748402.

610.727   RT81.5.M86

1st ed. 1986; 4th ed., 2000.

Contents: http://www.loc.gov/catdir/toc/ecip0416/2004007098.html. Explains statistical methods frequently used in the health care literature. Includes charts, graphs, and examples from the literature. New material on regression diagnostics has been added. Associated website.

MEDICINE

239

552 **Statistical record of health and medicine.** Gale Research Inc. 2 v.
Detroit: Gale Research Inc., c1995–c1998. ISSN: 1078-6961.
362.10973021   RA407.3.S732

Description based on 2nd ed., 1998.

Compilation of U.S. national, state, and municipal health and medical statistics from a variety of sources. Provides statistics on health status of Americans, health insurance, health care costs and expenditures, medical professions, international rankings and comparisons, etc. Further detailed notes on scope and coverage in the introduction and the sources from which the information is drawn. Keyword index.

Can be supplemented by more recent resources, for example, *Chronology of public health in the United Sates* (Jefferson, N.C.: McFarland, 2005), which covers events back to 1796, but mainly since 1900, as well as various government websites containing health and medical statistics.

553 **WHO child growth standards.** World Health Organization. 2006.
Geneva, Switzerland: World Health Organization. http://www.who.int/childgrowth/en/index.html.

Since the late 1970s, the National Center for Health Statistics (539)/WHO (951) growth reference has been in use to chart children's growth. It was based on data from a limited sample of children from the United States and is now considered less adequate for international comparisons. In 1997, WHO, in collaboration with the United Nations University, undertook the Multicentre Growth Reference Study (MGRS), which is a community-based, multicountry project with more than 8,000 children from Brazil, Ghana, India, Norway, Oman, and the United States. The new standards are the result of this study, which had as its goal "to develop a new international standard for assessing the physical growth, nutritional status and motor development in all children from birth to age five."—*Press release.* The first new growth charts released (Apr. 2007) include weight-for-age, length/height-for-age, and weight-for-length/height growth indicators as well as a Body Mass Index (BMI) standard for children up to age 5, and standards for sitting, standing, walking, and several other key motor developments.

The title of the print version is *WHO child growth standards: Length/height-for-age, weight-for-age, weight-for-length, weight-for-height and body mass index–for–age: Methods and development.*

554 **WHO global infobase.** World Health Organization. 2000s?–.
Geneva, Switzerland: World Health Organization. http://www.who.int/infobase.

Produced by World Health Organization (WHO) (951).

Title varies: also called WHO Global InfoBase Online.

"Data warehouse that collects, stores and displays information on chronic diseases and their risk factors for all WHO member states."— *Main page.* Provides information on health topics, e.g., alcohol and its relationship to disease and injury, blood pressure, cholesterol, diet, overweight and obesity, physical activity, tobacco, diabetes, oral health, visual impairment, and other topics, such as mortality estimates. Information comes from various national surveys, and WHO collaborates with its regional offices to keep information up to date. Provides individual country pages, allows comparison of countries, and displays comparable risk factor data. Extensive help pages include glossary, FAQ page, definitions of terms used, etc.

555 WHO mortality database. World Health Organization. 2005–. Geneva, Switzerland: World Health Organization. http://www.who.int/whosis/mort.

Part of WHOSIS (WHO Statistical Information System): A Guide to Health and Health-Related Statistical Information (556).

Contains mortality data officially reported by WHO member states. It includes cause-of-death statistics coded according to the ninth and tenth revision of the ICD (International Statistical Classification of Diseases and Related Health Problems: Tabular List of Inclusions and Four-Character Subcategories [84]), i.e., data on registered deaths by age group, sex, year, and cause of death. These files are not considered user-friendly since they consist of raw data files. However, the necessary instructions are provided.

556 WHOSIS. World Health Organization. [1994]–. Geneva, [Switzerland]: World Health Organization. http://www.who.int/whosis/.

Published by World Health Organization (WHO).

Provides description and online access to statistical and epidemiological information, data, and tools available from WHO and other sites: mortality and health status, disease statistics, health systems statistics, risk factors and health services, and inequities in health. Provides links to several databases: WHOSIS database, with the latest "core health indicators" from WHO sources (including *The world health report* [559] and *World health statistics* [560]), which make it possible to construct tables for any combination of countries, indicators and years, Causes of Death database,

WHO Global InfoBase Online, Global Health Atlas, and Reproductive Health Indicators database.

557   **WISQARS.** National Center for Injury Prevention and Control. 2000–. Atlanta: National Center for Injury Prevention and Control. http://www.cdc.gov/ncipc/wisqars.

HB1323.A2

WISQARS (Web-Based Injury Statistics Query and Reporting System), National Center for Injury Prevention and Control of the U.S. Centers for Disease Control and Prevention (940); CDC Injury Center.

Described as "an interactive database system that provides customized reports of injury-related data."—*Main page.* Injury statistics presented in two categories, i.e., fatal U.S. injury statistics and national estimates of nonfatal injuries treated in U.S. hospital emergency departments, each with links to tables, charts, tutorial, help, and FAQs. CDC's Injury Center (http://www.cdc.gov/ncipc/cmprfact.htm) provides links to a variety of injury related topics, fact sheets, Injury Fact Book (http://www.cdc.gov/ncipc/fact_book/factbook.htm), and overviews on injury response, violence prevention, and prevention of unintentional injuries.

The National Center for Health Statistics (NCHS) (539) also makes a variety of injury data and resources available at http://www.cdc.gov/nchs/injury.htm.

558   **Women's health USA.** U.S. Dept. of Health and Human Services, Maternal and Child Health Bureau. 2002–. Rockville, Md.: U.S. Dept. of Health and Human Services, Maternal and Child Health Bureau. http://purl.access.gpo.gov/GPO/LPS21379.

Part of Health Resources and Services Administration (HRSA) (877), within the U.S. Dept. of Health and Human Services (HHS) (894).

Description based on 5th online ed., 2006.

Contents: Population Characteristics; Health Status; Health Services Utilization; Indicators in Previous Editions; Site Map.

Collection of current and historical data on health challenges facing women, with information on life expectancy and addressing topics such as postpartum depression, smoking, alcohol, illicit drug use, etc. Brings together the latest available information from various government agencies (HHS, U.S. Dept. of Agriculture, U.S. Dept. of Labor, U.S. Dept. of Justice).

National Women's Health Information Center, Womenshealth.gov (http://www.womenshealth.gov/), provides extensive further information.

559 **The world health report.** World Health Organization. 1995–. Geneva, [Switzerland]: World Health Organization. ISSN: 1020-3311. http://www.who.int/whr/.

614.405   RA8.A265

Pt. of WHOSIS (WHO Statistical Information System) a guide to statistical information (556). Description based on the 2006 online ed., has subtitle: "working together for health." Also available in print format. 2007 ed. ("promoting international health security") due Aug. 2007.

"Every year. takes a new and expert look at global health, focusing on a specific theme, while assessing the current global situation. Using the latest data gathered and validated by WHO, each report paints a picture of the changing world."—*Website*. Website also provides links to the full-text reports 1995–2005, each with focus on a special theme: 1995, "bridging the gaps"; 1996, "fighting disease, fostering development"; 1997 "conquering suffering, enriching humanity"; 1998, "life in the 21st century: a vision for all"; 1999, "making a difference"; 2000, "health systems: improving performance"; 2001, "mental health: new understanding, new hope"; 2002, "reducing risks, promoting healthy life"; 2003, "shaping the future"; 2004, "changing history"; 2005, "make every mother and child count;" 2006, "working together for health."

560 **World health statistics.** World Health Organization. 2005–. Geneva, Switzerland: World Health Organization. http://www.who.int/healthinfo/statistics/en/.

1939/46–96 publ. as *World health statistics annual = Annuaire de statistiques sanitaires mondiales* (print version).

Part of WHOSIS: WHO Statistical Information System (556).

Description based on online 3rd ed., 2007 ed. (http://www.who.int/whosis/whostat2007.pdf).

Contents: pt. 1, "Ten statistical highlights in global public health." Pt. 2, "World health statistics": "Health status: Mortality"; "Health status: Morbidity"; "Health services coverage"; "Risk factors"; "Health systems"; "Inequities in health"; "Demographic and socioeconomic statistics."

"Presents the most recent health statistics for WHO's 193 Member States. collated from publications and databases produced by WHO's technical programmes and regional offices. Selected on the basis of their relevance to global health, the availability and quality of the data, and the accuracy and comparability of estimates. The statistics for the indicators are derived from an interactive process of data collection, compilation, quality assessment and estimation occurring among WHO's technical programmes and its Member States."—*Introd.* Print version also available.

Style Manuals

561 AMA manual of style: A guide for authors and editors. 10th ed. Cheryl Iverson, American Medical Association. New York: Oxford University Press, 2007. ISBN: 9780195176339.

808.06661   R119.A533

Title varies: 1st ed., 1962, called *AMA stylebook*; 6th ed., 1976, called *Stylebook: Editorial manual*; 7th ed., 1981, called *Manual for authors and editors*; 8th ed., 1989, called *American Medical Association manual of style*; 9th ed., 1998, called *American Medical Association manual of style: A guide for authors and editors.* Comp. varies.

Contents: Section 1, Preparing an article for publication; Section 2, Style; Section 3, Terminology; Section 4, Measurements and quantitation; Section 5, Technical information. Index.

Presents guidelines for medical authors and editors in writing and preparing manuscripts for publication. Offers advice on style, usage, nomenclature, statistics, and mathematical composition; also considers types of articles, fraud and plagiarism, inclusive language, grammar, and the publishing process, with information on electronic publishing, style recommendations for electronic references, and copyright issues. Ch. 24 is a "Glossary of Publishing Terms."

562 Citing medicine. Karen Patrias, Dan Wendling, National Library of Medicine (U.S.), National Center for Biotechnology Information. 2007. Bethesda, Md.: National Library of Medicine. http://www.nlm.nih.gov/citingmedicine.

R119

Updates and supersedes *National Library of Medicine recommended format for bibliographic citation*, publ. 1991; National Library of Medicine Recommended Formats for Bibliographic Citation: Internet Supplement, publ. 2001.

Contents: Citing Published Print Documents; Citing Unpublished Material; Citing Audio and Visual Media (Audio Cassettes, Video Cassettes, Slides, Photographs, Etc.); Citing Material on CD-ROM, DVD, or Disk; Citing Material on the Internet. Appendixes: (A) Abbreviations for

Commonly Used English Words in Journal Titles; (B) Additional Sources for Journal Title Abbreviations; (C) Abbreviations for Commonly Used English Words in Bibliographic Description; (D) ISO Country Codes for Selected Countries; (E) Two-Letter Abbreviations for Canadian Provinces and U.S. States and Territories; (F) Notes for Citing MEDLINE/PubMed.

Provides information on how to construct and format citations. Describes rules and exceptions for specific citations, as well as recent rule changes. Includes examples.

Part of the NCBI Bookshelf (http://www.ncbi.nlm.nih.gov/sites/entrez?db=books), a searchable, growing collection of online books.

563   The clinician's guide to medical writing. Robert B. Taylor. xiv, 266 p., ill. New York: Springer, 2005. ISBN: 0387222499.
808.06661   R119.T395

Contents: (1) Getting started in medical writing; (2) Basic writing skills; (3) From page one to the end; (4) Technical issues in medical writing; (5) What's special about medical writing?; (6) How to write a review article; (7) Case reports, editorials, letters to the editor, book reviews, and other publication models; (8) Writing book chapters and books; (9) How to write a report of a clinical study; (10) Getting your writing published; Appendix 1, Glossary of terms used in medical writing; Appendix 2, Commonly used proofreader's marks; Appendix 3, Commonly used medical abbreviations; Appendix 4, Normal laboratory values for adult patients; Index.

The author provides a brief introduction, practical advice, and various models and examples for medical writing. Intended to teach clinicians about the basics of medical writing and publishing. Also available as an e-book.

564   The complete guide to medical writing. Mark Stuart. 491 p.
London; Chicago: Pharmaceutical Press, 2007. ISBN: 0853696675.
808.06661   R119

Contents: sec. 1, "Medical writing essentials"; sec. 2, "Reviews and reports"; sec. 3, "Medical journalism and mass media"; sec. 4, "Medical writing in education"; sec. 5, "Medical writing for medical professionals"; sec. 6, "Medical publishing"; appendixes: (1) "Common medical abbreviations"; (2) "Measurements"; (3) "Normal values for common laboratory tests"; (4) "Proof correction marks"; (5) "A to Z of medical terms in plain English."

Covers aspects of scientific and medical writing, medical journalism, and medical publishing. Resource for medical professionals and students to provide help with writing, communicating, and presenting scientific and medical information clearly and accurately, with examples from the pharmaceutical sciences. Covers copyright and patient confidentiality. For authors and editors.

565   The complete writing guide to NIH behavioral science grants.
Lawrence M. Scheier, William L. Dewey. 506 p. New York: Oxford University Press, 2007. ISBN: 9780195320275.
362.1079   RA11.D6C65

Contents: ch. 1, Peer review at the National Institutes of Health; ch. 2, Drug abuse research collaboration in the 21st century; ch. 3, A brief guide to the essentials of grant writing; ch. 4, Sample size, detectable difference, and power; ch. 5, Exploratory/developmental and small grant award mechanisms; ch. 6, Funding your future: What you need to know to develop a pre- or postdoctoral, training application; ch. 7, Unique funding opportunities for underrepresented minorities and international researchers; ch. 8, R01 grants: The investigator-initiated cornerstone of biomedical research; ch. 9, P50 research center grants; ch. 10, P20 and P30 center grants: Developmental mechanisms; ch. 11, The K award: An important part of the NIH funding alphabet soup; ch. 12, T32 grants at the NIH: Tips for success; ch. 13, SBIR funding: A unique opportunity for the entrepreneurial researchers; ch. 14, Federal grants and contracts outside of NIH; ch. 15, The financing and cost accounting of science: Budgets and budget administration; ch. 16, Documenting human subjects protections and procedures; ch. 17, Navigating the maze: Electronic submission; ch. 18, Revisions and resubmissions; ch. 19, Concluding remarks: The bottom line. Appendix 1: The NIH Web sites; Appendix 2: NIH institutes, centers, and their websites.

Presents important considerations in developing research proposals and funding mechanisms for both junior and established researchers. Provides practical information on how to construct and write successful grants, electronic grant submission, revising research proposals, etc. Useful to researchers, clinicians, and educators in a wide variety of subject areas who are interested in submitting grants to the NIH.

566   Health professionals style manual. Shirley H. Fondiller, Barbara J. Nerone. New York: Springer, 2006. ISBN: 0826102077.
808.06661   R119.F66

Rev. ed. of *Health professionals stylebook*, 1993.

Contents: ch. 1, "Style and substance: The dynamic duo"; ch. 2, "From principles to practice: The art of effective writing"; ch. 3, "Understanding usage: An alphabetical guide to specific writing tips and pitfalls"; ch. 4, "Be clear and direct: How to avoid redundancies, euphemisms, and cliches"; ch. 5, "Harness the potential of computers and the Internet." Appendixes: A, "Common abbreviations and acronyms in health care"; B, "Commonly misspelled words"; C, "Using prefixes and suffixes"; D, "Common proof-reader's marks"; E, "Electronic resources"; F, "Referencing." Includes references for further reading and index.

Provides guidelines about writing clearly and effectively, covering American usage only. Addresses style, style errors, English grammar, composition techniques, and other areas of technical writing. Can be used as a supplement to other style manuals. For researchers and students in the various health professions.

567 How to report statistics in medicine: Annotated guidelines for authors, editors, and reviewers. 2nd ed. Thomas A. Lang, Michelle Secic. New York: American College of Physicians, 2006. ISBN: 1930513690.

610.72   RA409.L357

1st ed., 1997.

Rev. ed., with new and updated content. Considered a standard guide to interpreting and reporting statistics in scientific and medical writing. Provides guidelines for reporting statistical analyses, research, and trial design used in biological sciences and medical research, how to display data, and explanation of statistical terms and tests.

568 How to write and publish a scientific paper. 6th ed. Robert A. Day, Barbara Gastel. xv, 302 p., ill. Westport, Conn.: Greenwood Press, 2006. ISBN: 0313330271.

808.0665   T11.D33

Contents: pt. I, Some preliminaries; pt. II, Preparing the text; pt. III, Preparing the tables and figures; pt. IV, Publishing the paper; pt. V, Doing other writing for publication; pt. VI, Conference communications; pt. VII, Scientific style; pt. VIII, Other topics in scientific communication; Appendixes (1) Selected journal title word abbreviations, (2) Words and expressions to avoid, (3) SI (Système International) prefixes and their abbreviations; Glossary of technical terms; references; index.

"The main purpose of this book is to help scientists and students of the sciences in all disciplines to prepare manuscripts that will have a high probability of being accepted for publication and of being completely understood when they are published."—*Pref.* This updated ed. reflects new developments in scientific publishing for beginning students and researchers.

569　**A manual for writers of research papers, theses, and dissertations: Chicago style for students and researchers.** 7th ed. Kate L. Turabian, Wayne C. Booth, Gregory G. Colomb. xviii, 466 p., ill. Chicago: University of Chicago Press, 2007. ISBN: 9780226823362.

808.02   LB2369.T8

Presents the "Chicago style" for formal papers; a significant revision of previous editions. In three parts: pt. I, adapted from *The craft of research* (Chicago: University of Chicago Press, 2003) (2003), provides practical advice on the research and writing process; pt. II covers citation forms (including those for electronic materials); and pt. III covers writing mechanics (punctuation, capitalization, quotations, etc.). Appendix gives general guidelines for formatting and submitting dissertations. Bibliography lists sources on finding and presenting information.

Revised to be in conformity with the 15th ed. of *The Chicago manual of style* (Chicago: University of Chicago Press, 2003). Standard source to consult before using the *Manual*.

570　**Scientific style and format: The CSE manual for authors, editors, and publishers.** 7th ed. Council of Science Editors. xvi, 658 p., ill. Reston, Va.: Council of Science Editors; Rockefeller University Press, 2006. ISBN: 097796650X.

808.066   T11.S386

Desk reference useful to anyone writing, editing, publishing, or peer reviewing scientific disciplines. Content reflects the interdisciplinary relationships among many scientific fields and discusses print and electronic publishing and basics of copyright. Explains conventions of punctuation, abbreviation, capitalization, symbols, and required format and contents of citations to references. Chapters address electromagnetic spectrum; chemical names, elements, and formulas; drugs, cells, chromosomes, and genes; viruses, bacteria, taxonomy, and nomenclature; the earth; and astronomical objects and time systems. Gives rules for abbreviating journal titles and publisher names, and an annotated bibliography of other style manuals, dictionaries, handbooks, and guides to word usage and prose style. Discusses technical elements of publishing books, journal articles, conference papers and proceedings, technical reports, and other types of monographs in science. Useful to authors, editors, publishers, students, and translators, this title is appropriate for academic libraries.

571   **Uniform requirements for manuscripts submitted to biomedical journals.** International Committee of Medical Journal Editors. 1997–. Philadelphia: International Committee of Medical Journal Editors. http://www.icmje.org/index.html.

International Committee of Medical Journal Editors (ICMJE), originally established in 1978 by a group of editors, known as the Vancouver Group. Title varies; first published in 1979, with multiple updated versions since then published in *Annals of internal medicine*. Most recently updated in Oct. 2007.

Contents: (I) Statement of Purpose; (II) Ethical Considerations in the Conduct and Reporting of Research; (III) Publishing and Editorial Issues Related to Publication in Biomedical Journals; (IV) Manuscript Preparation and Submission; (V) References; (VI) About the International Committee of Medical Journal Editors; (VII) Authors of the Uniform Requirements; (VIII) Use, Distribution, and Translation of the Uniform Requirements; (IX) Inquiries. Provides guidelines and helpful recommendations for the format of manuscripts submitted to journals that agree to use the Uniform Requirements. Answers to frequently asked questions are provided at http://www.icmje.org/faq.pdf. Links to journals that have requested inclusion on the list of publications that follow the ICJMJE's *Uniform requirements for manuscripts submitted to biomedical journals* (http://www.icmje.org/jrnlist.html).

572   **Writing and publishing in medicine.** 3rd ed. Edward J. Huth. ix, 348 p. Baltimore: Williams & Wilkins, 1999. ISBN: 0683404474.
808.06661   R119.H87

1st ed., 1982 and 2nd ed., 1990 had title: *How to write and publish papers in medicine.*

This rev. and reorganized ed. details the steps in writing and publishing a paper and offers specific suggestions on content likely to be needed in papers reporting several types of research: in clinical trials, observational studies, and reports of laboratory research (cf. *Introd.*).

Provides information on punctuation, abbreviation, citation, formats for references, etc. Follows recommendations from an earlier version of the *Uniform requirements for manuscripts submitted to biomedical journals* (571).

Thesauruses

573 **Current procedural terminology: CPT.** Standard ed. American Medical Association. Chicago: American Medical Association, 1966–. ISSN: 0276-8283.

616.0014   RB115.C17

1st ed., 1966 and 2nd ed., 1970 had title: *Current procedural terminology.* Vols. for 1999–. publ. as a revision of the 4th ed. of *Physicians' current procedural terminology,* originally publ. in 1977. Description based on 2005 ed.

"Set of codes, descriptions, and guidelines intended to describe procedures and services performed by physicians and other health care providers. Each procedure or service is identified with a five-digit code. The use of CPT® codes simplifies the reporting of services."—*Foreword.* Listed in six sections: Evaluation and management; Anesthesiology; Surgery; Radiology (including nuclear medicine and diagnostic ultrasound); Pathology and laboratory; Medicine. CPT 2005 procedure codes and descriptions are also available on CD-ROM and electronic software, as are CPT changes from previous and current editions. For detailed information on CPT codes see http://www.ama-assn.org/ama/pub/category/3113.html.

574 **EMTREE thesaurus.** Excerpta Medica (Firm). Amsterdam, [The Netherlands]; New York: Excerpta Medica, 1991–. ISSN: 09293299.

Z699.5.M39E49

Developed from 1974–90, *Master list of medical indexing terms (MALI-MET)*; EMTAGS (discont. in 1998) and EMCLAS (i.e., the original subject classification system for EMBASE [414]) integration into EMTREE (1988–91). Annual updates.

Description based on 2006 ed.

Cover title: *EMTREE: The life science thesaurus.* Contents: v. 1, Alphabetical index; v. 2, Tree structure; v. 3, Permuted term index.

Hierarchically structured drug and disease controlled vocabulary used for subject indexing and for searching the biomedical literature (e.g.,

EMBASE, with "preferred terms" [i.e., drug and medical terms]), synonyms, and MeSH®: Medical Subject Headings (575). Contains a list of EMBASE section headings which, with a few exceptions, correspond to the titles of the Excerpta Medica abstract journals, published since 1947, and searchable in EMBASE since 1974. Also available online.

575   **MeSH.** U.S. National Library of Medicine. 1975–. Bethesda, Md.:
       U.S. National Library of Medicine. http://www.nlm.nih.gov/mesh/
       MBrowser.html.

MeSH®; MeSH Browser; National Library of Medicine (NLM) (427)

"MeSH is the National Library of Medicine's controlled vocabulary thesaurus. It consists of sets of terms naming descriptors in a hierarchical structure that permits searching at various levels of specificity. MeSH descriptors are arranged in both an alphabetic and a hierarchical structure. 22,997 descriptors in MeSH and 151,000 headings called 'Supplementary Concept Records' (formerly 'Supplementary Chemical Records') within a separate thesaurus. Many cross-references help in locating the most appropriate MeSH heading."—*MeSH Fact Sheet* (http://www.nlm.nih. gov/pubs/factsheets/mesh.html). MeSH is used for indexing, cataloging, and searching biomedical and health-related information and documents.

Access points to MeSH are available via the MeSH Browser, which contains the full contents of the vocabulary and the MeSH website (http:// www.nlm.nih.gov/mesh), which provides additional information about MeSH and for obtaining MeSH in different electronic formats.

MeSH subject descriptors appear in MEDLINE® (425)/PubMed® (432), the NLM catalog, and in other Entrez databases (Entrez [browser]: The Life Sciences Search Engine [http://www.ncbi.nlm.nih.gov/sites/ gquery]). Related pages are the Unified Medical Language System (ULMS®) and the NLM classification.

Supplement to Index Medicus®, commonly known as "Black and White" MeSH, combines the alphabetic arrangement and the tree structures in a single publication. It was published in print format each Jan., with the 2007 issue being the last issue since the decision was made to discontinue the printed edition. Other separate MeSH publications (*Annotated alphabetic MeSH*, the *MeSH trees structures*, and the *Permuted MeSH*) ceased publication in 2004. A brief history of MeSH and other introductory material can be found at http://www.nlm.nih.gov/mesh/ intro_preface2007.html.

2 > BIOETHICS

576   **Thesaurus ethics in the life sciences.** German Reference Centre
for Ethics in the Life Sciences (DRZE). 1999–. Bonn, Germany:
Deutsches Referenzzentrum für Ethik in den Biowissenschaften
(DRZE). http://www.drze.de/BELIT/thesaurus?la=en.

Description based on 4th ed., 2007. Publ. in English, German, and French.
Joint project of the German Reference Centre for Ethics in the Life Sci
ences (DRZE), Centre de documentation en éthique des sciences de la vie
et de la santé, Information and Documentation Centre for Ethics in Medicine, Interdepartmental Centre for Ethics in the Sciences and Humanities,
and Library and Information Services, Kennedy Institute of Ethics.

Contents: (I) Ethics, Philosophy, Theology; (II) Society, Politics,
Economics, Law, Education, Media; (III) Science, Research, Technology
and Technology Assessment; (IV) Biology; (V) Medicine and Care; (VI)
Transplantation and Transfusion; (VII) Prolongation of Life, Dying and
Death; (VIII) Health Care and Health Economics; (IX) Genetics, Human
Reproduction and Sexuality; (X) Environment, Landscape and Ecosphere;
(XI) Agriculture and Forestry, Animal Husbandry and Food; (XII General
Terms; [XIII] Geographic Names; [XIV] Personal Names.

Controlled indexing and research tool to include established and also
new fields of bioethics which previously were treated either marginally
or not at all. For researchers [both experts and interested members of
the public], librarians, and information specialists indexing bioethical
literature and documents.

Bibliography

577   **Bibliography of bioethics.** LeRoy Walters, Tamar Joy Kahn,
Kennedy Institute. Washington: Kennedy Institute of Ethics, 1975–.
ISSN: 0363-0161.

016.1742   Z6675.E8B53; R724; QH332

"An ongoing research project of the Kennedy Institute, Center for Bioethics at Georgetown University."

- Imprint varies: 1975–80, Detroit: Gale Research; 1981–83, New
  York: Free Press. 1984–. Washington: Kennedy Institute of Ethics.
- Vol. 1–10, ed. by LeRoy Walters; v. 10–, LeRoy Walters and Tamar
  Joy Kahn.

- Includes as a section: "Bioethics thesaurus," which is also published separately.
- Description based on v. 32 (2006).

Section I: Periodical literature and essays—subject entries; Section II: Periodical literature and essays—author index; Section III: Monographs— title index.

A subject bibliography listing journal and newspaper articles, books and book chapters, government reports, and reports of international organizations and Web documents selected for indexing for the bioethics subset of MEDLINE® (425) and for the National Library of Medicine's NLM catalog (Entrez) (3). Concerned with ethical and public policy aspects, for example, assisted suicide, new reproductive technologies, cloning, human experimentation, genetic engineering, informed consent, organ donation, and transplantation, managed care, and other concerns in the allocation of health care resources. Vol. 32 (2006) indexes material acquired by the National Reference Center for Bioethics Literature (NRCBL) (618) in 2005 and selected for indexing for the MEDLINE bioethics subset. In addition to PubMed® (432) and the NLM Catalog and using NLM's Medical Subject Headings (MeSH® [575]), citations are also available via the databases maintained by NRCBL, ETHXWeb (603), and GenETHX (604), and also via the Kennedy Institute of Ethics Web gateway at http://bioethics.georgetown.edu.

BIOETHICS

253

578 Medicine, health, and bioethics: Essential primary sources.
K. Lee Lerner, Brenda Wilmoth Lerner. lvii, 513 p., ill. Detroit: Thomson/Gale, 2006. ISBN: 1414406231.

174.2   R724.M313

(Series: Social issues primary sources collection.)

Contains complete primary sources or excerpts of documents and publications published 1823–2006, illustrating major biomedical issues. Each entry includes the complete text or an excerpt with complete original citation, subject area, historical context, significance. For students, health professionals, and also general readers. Also available as an e-book.

579 Recent dissertations in the medical humanities. Jonathon Erlen, University of Pittsburgh Health Sciences Library System. 2001–. Pittsburgh: Health Sciences Library, University of Pittsburgh Medical Center. http://www.hsls.pitt.edu/guides/histmed/researchresources/dissertations/.

Provides a monthly current awareness service for selected recent medical dissertation and theses. Arranged by topics, currently covers the following areas: AIDS (social and historical contexts); alternative medicine (social and historical contexts); art and medicine; biomedical ethics; history of medicine prior to 1800; history of medicine and health care; history of science and technology; literature/theater and medicine; nursing history; pharmacy/pharmacology and history; philosophy and medicine; psychiatry/psychology and history; public health/international health; religion and medicine; women's health and history. To view complete citations, abstracts, and full-text of dissertations requires a subscription to Proquest Dissertations and Theses (PQDT) (Ann Arbor, Mich.: ProQuest).

Dictionaries

580   **The new dictionary of medical ethics.** [New ed.] Kenneth M. Boyd, Roger Higgs, A. J. Pinching. xii, 285 p. London: BMJ Publ., 1997. ISBN: 0727910019.

1st ed., 1977; rev. ed., 1981 had title *Dictionary of medical ethics*, A. S. Duncan, G. R. Dunstan, R. B. Welbourn, eds. "Differs in many ways from the earlier work. Contains 700 concise entries on the most important ethical issues in medicine today. Contributed by leading experts and practitioners in medicine, nursing, allied professions, health policy, anthropology, law, philosophy, and theology."—*Publ. description.* Short essays on major topics and brief explanation of key terms and concepts, e.g., doctor-patient relationship, controversial issues such as abortion, euthanasia, xenografts, etc., "inevitably treating these illustratively rather than comprehensively."—*Pref.* Cross-references to related ethical issues. Brief bibliography; index of entries. A few of the contributors are from the U.S.; most are from the U.K.

Directories

581   **DIRLINE.** National Institutes of Health (U.S.). [1983?–.] Bethesda, Md.: U.S. National Institutes of Health, Dept. of Health and Human Services. http://dirline.nlm.nih.gov/.

DIRLINE® (Directory of Information Resources Online), maintained by the National Library of Medicine (NLM) (427).

Online annotated directory of organizations, research resources, projects, databases, and other information resources concerned with health and biomedicine from a variety of sources, including federal, state, and local government agencies, academic and research institutions, and also consumer health-related resources such as self-help groups and health hotlines. Resources are mostly from the U.S. but also include some international resources. Currently contains over 8,000 entries, with topics on most diseases and conditions and health services research and technology assessment. Can be searched using MeSH® (Medical Subject Headings) (575), keywords, or by name and location of a resource. Detailed information on DIRLINE can be found via a fact sheet prepared by NLM: http://www.nlm.nih.gov/pubs/factsheets/dirlinfs.html.

Encyclopedias

582   **Encyclopedia of bioethics.** 3rd ed. Stephen Garrard Post. New
      York: Macmillan Reference USA, 2003. ISBN: 0028657748.
174.95703   QH332.E52

1st ed., 1978; 2nd ed., 1995.

The definition of bioethics as "the systematic study of the moral dimensions—including moral vision, decisions, conduct, and politics—of the life sciences and health care, employing a variety of ethical methodologies in a interdisciplinary setting"—(*Introd.* to the 1995 ed.) also "shapes [this revised edition], which continues the broad topical range of earlier editions."—*Introd.* Approx. 450 original, signed articles focus on the core areas of bioethics. Articles are arranged alphabetically, with numerous cross-references. Most articles have extensive bibliographies. Significant revisions, updates, and new entries (e.g., bioterrorism, cloning, health policy, and stem cell research) since the last edition. Topical outline of entries and index. The appendix, a collection of primary documents, gives the text of codes and various policy and ethical statements related to medical ethics. It also includes an annotated bibliography on literature and medicine and an annotated bibliography on law and medicine. Previous editions are still considered useful for anyone interested in the history of bioethics. For researchers, students, and general readers. Available online via Gale and netLibrary.

583   **Encyclopedia of science, technology, and ethics.** Carl Mitcham.
      4 v., cxiv, 2378 p., ill., maps. Detroit: Macmillan Reference USA,
      2005. ISBN: 0028658310.
503   Q175.35.E53

Over 670 articles exploring issues, technologies, or other concepts in science and technology. Includes description of the technologies or scienctific principles involved, relevant social institutions and organizations, and social perspectives surrounding the technology. Entries have bibliographies and are referenced in the text. Some entries can be strident and opinionated, but all are well referenced. Available as an e-book.

Guides

584 **The Blackwell guide to medical ethics.** Rosamond Rhodes, Leslie
Francis, Anita Silvers. 435 p. Malden, Mass.: Blackwell Publ., 2007.
ISBN: 9781405125833.

174.2   R724.B515

(Blackwell philosophy guides; 21.)

Contents: part I, Individual decisions about clinical issues: (1) Patient decisions; (2) Individual decisions of physicians and other health care professionals; part II, Legislative and judicial decisions about social policy: (1) Liberty; (2) Justice.

"Helpful tool for navigating the complex literature and diverse views on the key issues in medical ethics. Employing crucial distinctions between the personal decisions of patients, the professional decisions of individual health care providers, and political decisions about public policy, the chapters in the volume address the most central and controversial topics in medical ethics."—*Publ. notes.* Includes bibliographical references and index.

Handbooks

585 **BioLaw: A legal and ethical reporter on medicine, health care,
and bioengineering.** James F. Childress. (loose-leaf). Frederick,
Md.: University Publications of America, 1986–.

1983–1985 had title: *Bioethics reporter.*

Editors: 1986–. James F. Childress et al.

Loose-leaf; updated between editions. Has supplement: Biolaw. microfiche supplement.

Each annual consists of 2 v.: v. 1, Resource manual, contains essays on biological, medical, and health care issues with ethical and legal implications; v. 2, includes updates on many previously published topics and special sections on laws, regulations, court cases, etc. Each update comes with a cumulative subject index covering both volumes and a cumulative index to court cases.

586   **Codes of professional responsibility: Ethics standards in business, health, and law.** 4th ed. Rena A. Gorlin. xvii, 1149 p. Washington: Bureau of National Affairs, 1999. ISBN: 1570181489.

174   BJ1725.C57

Collects some 60 codes of ethics or similar documents ("statements of principles," "ethical guidelines," etc.) of North American organizations within the three domains listed in the subtitle. Construing these domains broadly, it embraces, e.g., professions such as engineering, computing, and journalism under "business," and mental health and social work under "health." Also includes directory of U.S. and worldwide organizations and programs concerned with professional responsibility and an extensive guide to information resources including periodicals, reference works, and websites. Indexes of issues, professions, and organizations. Serving a similar function for the U.K., *Professional codes of conduct in the United Kingdom* (London; New York: Mansell, 1996), 2nd ed., presents an even broader range of codes, numbering around 200 reproduced in full, plus summary descriptions of some 300 more.

An extensive web-based collection, "Codes of Ethics Online," is among the resources offered at the Center for the Study of Ethics in the Profession at IIT website (http://ethics.iit.edu/), which also provides links to other ethics centers and the catalog of CSEP's extensive library—a virtual bibliography of the field of professional ethics.

587   **Contemporary issues in healthcare law and ethics.** 3rd ed. Dean M. Harris. 377 p. Chicago; Washington: Health Administration Press; AUPHA Press, 2007. ISBN: 9781567932.

344.730321   KF3825.Z9.H3

1st ed., 1999, had title *Healthcare law and ethics: Issues for the age of managed care*; 2nd ed., 2003.

Contents: (1) "The role of law in the U.S. healthcare system"; (2) "Managing and regulating the healthcare system"; (3) "Patient care issues"; (4) "Legal and ethical issues in health insurance and managed care"; table of cases; table of statutes; table of regulations; index.

This revised and updated edition presents essential information and examines legal and ethical issues in health care. Includes, for example, the U.S. Supreme Court's decisions on physician-assisted suicide, partial-birth abortion, issues in emergency contraception, HIPAA Privacy Rule, medical malpractice, reporting of medical errors, and other topics. Also available as e-book via netLibrary.

BIOETHICS

257

588 **Ethics.** American Psychiatric Association. Arlington, Va.: American Psychiatric Association. http://www.psych.org/psych_pract/ethics/ethics.cfm.

Produced by the American Psychiatric Association (APA) (1390).

Provides online access to APA's ethics-related publications, originally published in print version in 2001: *Opinions of the Ethics Committee on the principles of medical ethics: With annotations especially applicable to psychiatry*, which includes the APA's procedures for handling complaints of unethical conduct, and *Ethics primer of the American Psychiatric Association.*

589 **Guide to the code of ethics for nurses: Interpretation and application.** Marsha Diane Mary Fowler, American Nurses Association. 176 p. Silver Spring, Md.: American Nurses Association, 2008. ISBN: 9781558102.

174.2 RT85.G85

Produced by American Nurses Association (ANA).

Intended as a guide to the *Code of ethics for nurses with interpretive statements* (Washington, D.C.: American Nurses Association, 2001) on how to apply ethical standards and values in nursing practice. Each chapter discusses a single code provision and provides the text of the code of ethics, the history, purpose, theory, application, case studies, and examples. Includes bibliographical references and index.

590 **Handbook for health care ethics committees.** Linda Farber Post, Jeffrey Blustein, Nancy N. Dubler. xiii, 327 p. Baltimore: Johns Hopkins University Press, 2007. ISBN: 0801884489.

610 R725.3.P67

Contents: (I) Curriculum for ethics committees; (II) Clinical ethics consultation; (III) White papers, memoranda, guidelines, and protocols; (IV) Sample policies and procedures; (V) Institutional code of ethics; (VI) Key legal cases in bioethics; (VII) An ethics committee meeting. "A handbook. that distills the important information and presents basic foundation of bioethical theory and its practical application in clinical and organizational settings."—*Pref.* Contains chapters on ethical foundations of clinical practice, decision making, informed consent and refusal, truth telling, disclosure and confidentiality, special decision-making concerns of minors, end-of-life issues, palliation, justice, access to care, and organizational ethics, clinical ethics consultation, white papers, memoranda, guidelines and protocols, and sample policies and procedures.

591 Handbook of bioethics and religion. David E. Guinn. xv, 437 p., ill. Oxford; New York: Oxford University Press, 2006. ISBN: 0195178734.

174.957   R725.55.H36

Contents: pt. I, Historical perspectives; pt. II, Religion and the terrain of public discourse; pt. III, Religion and bioethics in the public square; pt. IV, Religion and official discourse; pt. V, Religion an ethical praxis; pt. VI, Instrumentalizing religion; pt. VII, Institutional religion. Presents the "important question of *how* religion plays a role and normatively what *should be* its role in public bioethics" against the background of those who object to any "religious engagement in the formation of public bio-ethical policy," and who were unwilling to contribute to this publication. Contributors approach "the issue from a non-absolutist position (i.e., that religion should or should not participate in public bioethics)."—*Introd.* Includes bibliographical references and index. Also available as an e-book from publisher.

592 Handbook of bioethics: Taking stock of the field from a philosophical perspective. George Khushf. vi, 568 p. Dordrecht; Boston: Kluwer Academic, 2004. ISBN: 1402018703.

174.957   R725.5.H36

(Philosophy and medicine; v. 78). Contents: section I, The emergence of bioethics; section II, Bioethical theory; section III, Core concepts in clinical ethics; section IV, The public policy context; section V, Foundations of the health professions. "This volume takes stock of bioethics from a philosoph-ical perspective. Twenty-six essays provide a survey of the most important theoretical and practical areas of bioethics. Each essay reviews the extant literature on the topic, identifying the important philosophical themes and resources. Each sketches important areas where future research needs to be conducted and where valuable collaboration can take place with those doing more traditional philosophical research on topics such as personal identity, moral theory, or the nature of scientific judgment."—*Introd.* Includes bibliographical references and index. Also available as an e-book.

593 History of AMA ethics. American Medical Association (AMA). 1995?–. [Chicago]: American Medical Association (AMA). http://www.ama-assn.org/ama/pub/category/1930.html.

Provides links to various resources such as the Code of medical ethics history, the Council on Ethical and Judicial Affairs' *AMA code of medical*

BIOETHICS

ethics, digitized versions of different editions (1903, 1957, 1980, and 2001 versions) of AMA's *Principles of medical ethics* and timelines "tracing AMA's work in medical ethics."—*Website*

594   International guidelines on HIV/AIDS and human rights. Office of the United Nations High Commissioner for Human Rights (OHCHR); UNAIDS Joint United Nations Programme on HIV/AIDS. 2006 Geneva, [Switzerland]: United Nations OHCHR. http://www.ohchr.org/english/issues/hiv/guidelines.htm.

Organized jointly by the Office of the United Nations High Commissioner for Human Rights (OHCHR) and the UNAIDS Joint United Nations Programme on HIV/AIDS.

2006 consolidated version of the Second (Geneva, 23–25 Sep. 1996) and Third (Geneva, 25–26 July 2002) International Consultation on HIV/AIDS and Human Rights.

Contents: (I) Guidelines for state action: (A) Institutional responsibilities and processes; (B) Law review, reform and support services; (C) Promotion of a supportive and enabling environment; (II) Recommendations for dissemination and implementation of the guidelines on HIV/AIDS and human rights: (A) States; (B) United Nationals system and regional intergovernmental bodies; (C) Nongovernmental organizations; (III) International human rights obligations and HIV: (A) Human rights standards and the nature of State obligations; (B) Restrictions and limitations; (C) The application of specific human rights in the context of the HIV epidemic; Annex 1, History of the recognition of the importance of human rights in the context of HIV; Annex 2, List of participants at the Second International Consultation on HIV/AIDS and Human Rights; Annex 3, List of participants at the Third International Consultation on HIV/AIDS and Human Rights.

"A tool for States in designing, co-ordinating and implementing effective national HIV/AIDS policies and strategies. Human rights standards apply in the context of HIV/AIDS and translating them into practical measures that should be undertaken at the national level, based on three broad approaches: improvement of government capacity for multi-sectoral coordination and accountability; reform of laws and legal support services, with a focus on anti-discrimination, protection of public health, and improvement of the status of women, children and marginalized groups; and support and increased private sector and community participation to respond ethically and effectively to HIV/AIDS.

OHCHR encourages governments, national human rights institutions, non-governmental organizations and people living with HIV and AIDS to use the Guidelines for training, policy formulation, advocacy, and the development of legislation on HIV/AIDS-related human rights."—*Website*

595 Law, liability, and ethics for medical office professionals. 4th ed. Myrtle Flight. x, 350 p. Clifton Park, N.Y.: Thomson/Delmar Learning, c2004. ISBN: 1401840337.

344.730411   KF2905.F58

1st ed., 1988; 3rd ed., 1998.

Contents: ch. 1, From examining room to courtroom; ch. 2, Functioning within the legal system; ch. 3, Intent makes the difference; ch. 4, Your words may form a contract; ch. 5, Anatomy of a medical malpractice case; ch. 6, Health care is big business; ch. 7, The medical record: the medical assistant's responsibility; ch. 8, Introduction to ethics; ch. 9, Privacy, confidentiality, privileged communication: the nexus of law and ethics; ch. 10, Birth and the beginning of life; ch. 11, Professional ethics and the living; ch. 12, Ethics: death and dying; Appendixes: (A) The civil and criminal case processes; (B) Answers to cases for discussion; Glossary; Bibliography; Index.

Provides basic information in medical law and ethics for medical professionals and helps with understanding their rights and the rights of the patients.

Another legal resource, designed for dental professionals, is *Law and risk management in dental practice* (986).

596 Legal and ethical issues for health professionals. George D. Pozgar. xii, 378 p. Boston: Jones and Bartlett Publ., 2005. ISBN: 0763726338.

174.2   KF3821.P68

Contents: ch. 1, Introduction to ethics; ch. 2, Contemporary ethical dilemmas; ch. 3, Health Care Ethics Committee; ch. 4, End-of-life dilemmas; ch. 5, Development of law; ch. 6, Introduction to law; ch. 7, Government, ethics, and the law; ch. 8, Organizational ethics and the law; ch. 9, Health care professionals' ethical and legal issues; ch. 10, Physicians' ethical and legal issues; ch. 11, Employee rights and responsibilities; ch. 12, Patient consent; ch. 13, Patient abuse; ch. 14, Patient rights and responsibilities.

Overview of the ethical and legal issues and their interrelationship in the health care field. Guide to additional resources. Includes glossary, bibliographical references, and index.

597 **Medical ethics: Codes, opinions, and statements.** Baruch A. Brody. xxxix, 1074 p., ill. Washington: Bureau of National Affairs, 2000. ISBN: 1570181004.

174.2   R725.M117

Compilation of documents of medical ethics standards and policy positions of the major medical organizations in the U.S., including both usual and controversial issues. Includes bibliographical references and index. Another title by the same author, *Medical ethics: Analysis of the issues raised by the codes, opinions, and statements*, complements this resource.

598 **Medical records and the law.** 4th ed. William H. Roach, American Health Information Management Association. xix, 591 p. Sudbury, Mass.: Jones and Bartlett Publ., 2006. ISBN: 0763734454.

344.73041   KF3827.R4R63

1st ed., 1985; 3rd ed., 1998.

Contents: ch. 1, Introduction to the American legal system; ch. 2, Medical records and managed care; ch. 3, Medical record requirements; ch. 4, Medical records entries; ch. 5, Documenting consent to treatment; ch. 6, Access to health information; ch. 7, Reporting and disclosure requirements; ch. 8, Documentation and disclosure: special areas of concern; ch. 9, HIV/AIDS: mandatory reporting and confidentiality; ch. 10, Discovery and admissibility of medical records; ch. 11, Legal theories in improper disclosure cases; ch. 12, Risk management and quality management; ch. 13, Electronic health records; ch. 14, Health information in medical research; Index. Provides information on the growth of electronic health record systems and electronic data networks. Addresses the issues related to medical research involving human subjects and how patient information can be used.

599 **The Oxford handbook of bioethics.** Bonnie Steinbock. Oxford: Oxford University Press, 2007.

Contents: pt. I, Theoretical and methodological issues; pt. II, Justice and policy; pt. III, Bodies and bodily parts; pt. IV, End of life; pt. V, Reproduction and cloning; pt. VI, Genetics and enhancement; pt. VII, Research ethics; pt. VIII, Public and global health. Contains a selection and discussion of central issues in contemporary bioethics, with original essays reflective of a particular author's interpretation of a bioethical issue. Includes bibliographical references and index. Online edition available via netLibrary.

600   **The rights of patients: The authoritative ACLU guide to the rights of patients.** 3rd ed. George J. Annas. xxi, 387 p. Carbondale, Ill.: Southern Illinois University Press, 2004. ISBN: 0809325152.

344.7303211   KF3823.A96

Title varies: 1st ed., 1975, had title: *The rights of hospital patients: The basic ACLU guide to a hospital patient's rights*; 2nd ed., 1989, had title: *The rights of patients: The basic ACLU guide to patient rights.*

American Civil Liberties Union (ACLU).

(ACLU handbook series).

Contents: (I) Patient rights; (II) The patient rights advocate; (III) Reforming American medicine; (IV) Hospitals; (V) Emergency medicine; (VI) Informed choice; (VII) Choices about surgery and children's care; (VIII) Reproductive health; (IX) Research; (X) Medical records; (XI) Privacy and confidentiality; (XII) Care of the dying; (XIII) Suffering, pain, and suicide; (XIV) Death, organ donation, and autopsy; (XV) Patient safety and medical malpractice. Appendixes: (A) Internet resources; (B) Convention on human rights and biomedicine; (C) Childbearing patient bill of rights. Index.

"Offers fully documented exposition and explanation of the rights of patients from birth to death. A resource not only for patients and their families but also for physicians, hospital administrators, medical and nursing students, and other health care workers."—*Publ. notes.* Emphasizes the importance of having a patient rights advocate, with a section "tips for advocates" in most chapters.

601   **Source book in bioethics.** Albert R. Jonsen, Robert M. Veatch, LeRoy Walters. ix, 510 p. Washington: Georgetown University Press, 1998. ISBN: 0878406832.

174.209   R724.S599

Contents: Ethics of research with human subjects; A short history; Ethics of death and dying; Changing attitudes toward death and medicine; Ethical issues in human genetics; Issues in genetics; Ethical issues arising from human reproductive technologies and arrangements; Readings on human reproduction; Ethical issues in the changing health care system; The changing health care scene. Collection of significant documents in bioethics and social ethics, covering the time period from 1947–95, with original text reprinted either in full or abridged format, presenting a historical survey of bioethics and major ethical issues in healthcare and key bioethical decisions. Includes legislative documents and reports by various organizations and governments. Bibliographical references and index.

Indexes; Abstract journals; Databases

602   Bibliography of bioethics. LeRoy Walters, Tamar Joy Kahn, Kennedy Institute. Washington: Kennedy Institute of Ethics, 1975–. ISSN: 0363-0161.

016.1742   Z6675.E8B53; R724; QH332

"An ongoing research project of the Kennedy Institute, Center for Bioethics at Georgetown University."

Imprint varies: 1975–80, Detroit: Gale Research; 1981–83, New York: Free Press. 1984–. Washington: Kennedy Institute of Ethics.

Vol. 1–10, ed. by LeRoy Walters; v. 10–, LeRoy Walters and Tamar Joy Kahn.

Includes as a section: "Bioethics thesaurus," which is also published separately.

Description based on v. 32 (2006).

Section I: Periodical literature and essays—subject entries; Section II: Periodical literature and essays—author index; Section III: Monographs—title index.

A subject bibliography listing journal and newspaper articles, books and book chapters, government reports, and reports of international organizations and Web documents selected for indexing for the bioethics subset of MEDLINE® (425) and for the National Library of Medicine's NLM catalog (Entrez) (3). Concerned with ethical and public policy aspects, for example, assisted suicide, new reproductive technologies, cloning, human experimentation, genetic engineering, informed consent, organ donation, and transplantation, managed care, and other concerns in the allocation of health care resources. Vol. 32 (2006) indexes material acquired by the National Reference Center for Bioethics Literature (NRCBL) (618) in 2005 and selected for indexing for the MEDLINE bioethics subset. In addition to PubMed® (432) and the NLM Catalog and using NLM's Medical Subject Headings (MeSH® [575]), citations are also available via the databases maintained by NRCBL, ETHXWeb (603), and GenETHX (604), and also via the Kennedy Institute of Ethics Web gateway at http://bioethics.georgetown.edu.

603   ETHXWeb. National Reference Center for Bioethics Literature, Library and Information Services, Kennedy Institute of Ethics, Georgetown University. 2000–. Washington: National Reference Center for Bioethics Literature, Library and Information Services, Kennedy Institute of Ethics, Georgetown University. http:// bioethics.georgetown.edu/databases/ETHXWeb/basice.htm.

"A Bibliographic Database on Bioethics and Professional Ethics" produced by National Reference Center for Bioethics Literature (NRCBL) (618); Kennedy Institute of Ethics, Georgetown University.

Indexes journal articles, books and book chapters, bills, laws, court decisions, reports, news articles, audiovisuals relating to bioethics and professional ethics (*cf. Website*). Allows for basic, advanced (with links to a subject list of phrases and the NRCBL classification scheme), and Boolean search (with links to database fields list, subject list, and the NRCBL classification scheme). Search tips are provided. The same search interface is used for GenETHX (604), another bibliographic database from the NRCBL. NRCBL's "Search Databases on the Web" (http://bioethics.george-town.edu/databases/index.htm) provides links to search the bioethics literature in the NRCBL and NLM® databases.

604   GenETHX. National Information Resource on Ethics and Human Genetics, Library and Information Services, Kennedy Institute of Ethics, Georgetown University. 2003–. Washington: National Information Resource on Ethics and Human Genetics, Library and Information Services, Kennedy Institute of Ethics, Georgetown University. http://bioethics.georgetown.edu/databases/GenETHX/ basicg.htm.

Produced by National Information Resource on Ethics and Human Genetics (NIREHG) (616); Kennedy Institute of Ethics Library and Information Services (http://bioethics.georgetown.edu/); National Reference Center for Bioethics Literature (NRCBL) (618).

Indexes journal articles, books and book chapters, bills, laws, court decisions, reports, news articles, and audiovisuals relating to ethics and public policy issues in genetics. Allows for basic, advanced, and Boolean searches. Provides search tips, links to "NRCBL classification scheme," "Thesaurus keywords for genetics," and various other related information resources. Another database from NRCBL is ETHXWeb (603). NRCBL's databases page (http://bioethics.georgetown.edu/databases/index.htm)

provides various additional links for searching the bioethics literature in the NRCBL, the National Library of Medicine (427) databases, and other related databases.

605   PubMed. U.S. National Center for Biotechnology Information, National Library of Medicine, National Institutes of Health. 1996–. Bethesda, Md.: U.S. National Center for Biotechnology Information. http://www.ncbi.nlm.nih.gov/sites/entrez/.

PubMed®, developed and maintained by the National Center for Biotechnology Information (NCBI) at the National Library of Medicine® (NLM) (427). It is available via the NCBI Entrez (3) retrieval system. PubMed also provides access to the other Entrez molecular biology resources (*PubMed Overview*). Starting May 23, 2007, NCBI is changing to a new version of Entrez in a phased implementation (cf. Nahin AM. New and Improved PubMed®/Entrez and New URL *NLM tech. bull.*, 2007 May–Jun.; [356]: http://www.nlm.nih.gov/pubs/techbull/mj07/mj07_issue_cover.html).

    Provides a search interface for more than 16 million bibliographic citations and abstracts in the fields of medicine, nursing, dentistry, veterinary medicine, health care systems, and preclinical sciences. It provides access to articles indexed for MEDLINE® (425) and for selected life sciences journals. PubMed subsets found under the "Limits" tab are: MEDLINE and PubMed Central®, several journal groups (i.e., core clinical journals, dental journals, and nursing journals), and topical subsets (AIDS, bioethics, cancer, complementary medicine, history of medicine, space life sciences, systematic reviews, and toxicology). "Linkout" provides access to full-text articles.

    For detailed information see the PubMed fact sheet at http://www.nlm.nih.gov/pubs/factsheets/pubmed.html. For a brief overview of searching PubMed, see the PubMed Quick Start at http://www.ncbi.nlm.nih.gov/books/bv.fcgi?rid=helppubmed.section.pubmedhelp.PubMed_Quick_Start. For details on the now completed OLDMEDLINE retrospective conversion projects, see http://www.nlm.nih.gov/pubs/techbull/so06/so06_oldmedline_status.html.

Internet Resources

606   ACP Center for Ethics and Professionalism. American College of Physicians (ACP). 1996–. Philadelphia: American College of Physicians. http://www.acponline.org/ethics/.

As part of the American College of Physicians (ACP), "the nation's largest medical specialty society." Its mission is to enhance the quality and effectiveness of health care by fostering excellence and professionalism in the practice of medicine (http://www.acponline.org/college/aboutacp/aboutacp.htm?hp) [and] "devoted to policy development and implementation on issues related to medical ethics and professionalism, and as a resource for ACP members and the public."—*Website.* Includes ethics and human rights, end-of-life care, managed care ethics, and other issues. The Center develops position papers on current topics, case studies that explore common ethical dilemmas for patients and physicians, educational programs and resources, and performs advocacy and outreach efforts. Provides online access to its "Ethics Manual" (http://www.acponline.org/ethics/ethics_man.htm) and ACP's ethics policy statements (http://www.acponline.org/ethics/policy_statements.htm).

607 American Medical Association. American Medical Association. 1995–. Chicago: American Medical Association. http://www.ama-assn.org/.

This searchable website provides a variety of professional resources and standards for AMA members, including, for example, information sources on medical ethics, public health (e.g., eliminating health disparities, health preparedness, disaster response, obesity), medical science, legal issues, and AMA history (with timeline and highlights of AMA history). Also provides information on medical education and licensure as well as online resources and other links for medical school students and residents. Includes a section for patients, with access to patient education resources.

Other useful AMA-related links include, for example, DoctorFinder (209) and PolicyFinder (http://www.ama-assn.org/ama/noindex/category/11760.html), *Code of medical ethics, current opinions with annotations* (Chicago: American Medical Association), *Current procedural terminology: CPT* (853), FREIDA (212), *Graduate medical education directory* (213), *Health professions career and education directory* (214), and *State medical licensure requirements and statistics* (548). Many of these resources have general reference value in academic and public libraries.

608 Bioethics information resources. National Library of Medicine (U.S.). 2007–. Bethesda, Md.: U.S. National Library of Medicine, National Institutes of Health, Dept. of Health and Human Services. http://www.nlm.nih.gov/bsd/bioethics.html.

Resource to assist users (specialists, researchers, clinicians, and the general public) in finding bioethics information. Provides, for example, bioethics-filtered search boxes for MEDLINE® (425), PubMed® (432), NLM catalog (Entrez) (482), and links to other National Library of Medicine (427) databases or information resources (e.g., Genetics home reference [703], MedlinePlus® [463], NLM gateway [429], NIH's Bioethics resources on the Web [609] and other bioethics-related websites such as the President's Council on Bioethics [National Bioethics Advisory Committee] [621], and the Kennedy Institute of Ethics' National Reference Center for Bioethics Literature [NRCBL] [618], and others).

609 **Bioethics resources on the web.** National Institutes of Health (U.S.). 2000–. [Bethesda, Md.]: National Institutes of Health (NIH), Office of Extramural Research (OER), Inter-Institute Bioethics Groups (BIG). http://purl.access.gpo.gov/GPO/ LPS55764.

Web page sponsored by the NIH Office of Science Policy (OSP) and the NIH Inter-Institute Bioethics Interest Group in cooperation with the NIH Office of Extramural Research (OER).

Annotated list of resources and web links that provide access to NIH and other federal resources, relevant organizations, documents, background information, and various positions on bioethical issues, with emphasis on research ethics, genetics, and medicine and healthcare topics. A link to "Health Law Resources" is provided at http://bioethics.od.nih. gov/legal.html.

610 **Bioethicsweb.** Wellcome Trust. London: Wellcome Trust. http:// bioethicsweb.ac.uk/.

A joint project by the Joint Information Committee (JISC), the University of Nottingham, and the Wellcome Trust.

"BioethicsWeb offers free access to a searchable catalogue of Internet sites and resources covering biomedical ethics."—*Website*. Managed by Intute (http://www.intute.ac.uk/), a free online service which evolved from the Resource Discovery Network (RDN) and launched in July 2006, created by a network of U.K. universities and partners. Provides access to Internet resources selected by subject specialists for education and research, with a broad selection of websites with content that addresses ethical, legal, public policy, and social questions and issues.

611   Ethics and health [Internet resource]. World Health Organization (WHO). 2002–. Geneva, [Switzerland]: World Health Organization. http://www.who.int/ethics/en/.

World Health Organization (WHO) Dept. of Ethics, Trade, Human Rights and Health Law (ETH); WHO Dept. Sustainable Development and Environmental Health (SDE); WHO Research Ethics Review Committee; U.N. Inter-Agency Committee on Bioethics; National Bioethics Commissions.

"This site has been created as an aid to persons, both inside and outside WHO, seeking information about bioethics, including the ethical aspects of healthcare delivery and planning as well as the ethics of clinical care, research, and biotechnology [with] information about a range of topics in ethics."—*Website.* Reflects various collaborative projects within WHO and also other agencies and provides links to various bioethics topics, full text of ethics publications, ethical considerations and guidelines for research and good clinical practice.

612   Genomic Resource Centre. World Health Organization, Human Genetics Programme. 2003–. Geneva, [Switzerland]: World Health Organization. http://www.who.int/genomics/en/.

Genomic Resource Centre (GRC), developed by the World Health Organization (WHO) (951), addresses the ethical, legal, and social implications (ELSI) of human genomics.

"The GRC serves as a platform to highlight the latest scientific research as well as practical health care applications of human genomics and its ethical, social and legal implications."—*Website.* Addresses areas of medical genetics, such as genetic counselling, presymptomatic diagnosis, population genetics, and ethics and genomics. "ELSI genetics resource directory" (http://www.who.int/genomics/elsi/regulatory_data/en/index.html) provides online resources on ELSI of human genetics, ethics organizations, guidelines, codes, declarations, legislations, etc. For health professionals, policy makers, patients and their families, and the general public.

613   The Hastings Center. Hastings Center. 1999–. Garrison, N.Y.: The Hastings Center. http://bibpurl.oclc.org/web/6093.

"The Hastings Center is an independent, nonpartisan, and nonprofit bioethics research institute founded in 1969 to explore fundamental and emerging questions in health care, biotechnology, and the environment."—*Web page.* Its home page provides a description of the Hastings Center activities, including biomedical research projects, studies, and updates, as well as links to various scholarly resources (e.g., "Bioethics forum: diverse commentary on issues in bioethics") and selected online publications. Site index.

614 **Human Genome Project information.** U.S. Department of Energy Office of Science. 1990s–. Oak Ridge, Tenn.: Oak Ridge National Laboratory, U.S. Department of Energy. http://www.ornl.gov/sci/ techresources/Human_Genome/home.shtml.

QH447

Website sponsored by the U.S. Dept. of Energy Office of Science, Office of Biological and Environmental Research, Human Genome Program; website maintained by the Human Genome Management Information System (HGMIS) at Oak Ridge National Laboratory for the U.S. Department of Energy Human Genome Program.

Contents: About HGP (Goals; Progress; History; Benefits; ELSI; Genetics 101; FAQ); Research (Mapping; Sequencing; Technology; Bioinformatics; Gene Function; ELSI; Microbes); Education Resources (Teachers; Students; Careers; Webcasts; Images; Videos; Presentation); Ethical, Legal, and Social Issues (ELSI); Medicine and the New Genetics (Gene Testing; Gene Therapy; Pharmaceuticals; Genetic Counseling; Diseases); Media.

"Begun formally in 1990, the U.S. Human Genome Project was a 13-year effort coordinated by the U.S. Department of Energy and the National Institutes of Health. The project originally was planned to last 15 years, but rapid technological advances accelerated the completion date to 2003."—*About the Human Genome Project page.* This website provides a multitude of annotated links to resources on all aspects of the HPG. Articles analyzing the genome continue to be published, with further information presented at Post–Human Genome Project Progress and Resources (http://www.ornl.gov/sci/techresources/Human_Genome/project/progress.sh tml). Information for Genetic Professionals (http://www.kumc.edu/gec/geneinfo.html), a clinical-genetics site by Debra Collins, Genetics Education Center, University of Kansas Medical Center, provides further information in this area.

615 **National Human Genome Research Institute (U.S.).** National Human Genome Research Institute. 1995–. Bethesda, Md.: National Human Genome Research Institute, National Institutes of Health, U.S. Dept. of Health and Human Services. http://genome.gov/.

QH445.2

National Human Genome Research Institute (NHGRI), previously known as National Center for Human Genome Research (NCHGR), which was established in 1989 because of the Human Genome Project (HGP), since 1990 is a collaborative project of the U.S. Dept. of Energy (DOE) and National Institutes of Health (NIH) to map the human genome; and since HGP's completion in 1993, to apply genome technologies to the study of specific diseases. In 1996, the Center for Inherited Disease Research (CIDR) was also established (cofunded by eight NIH institutes and centers) to study the genetic components of complex disorders. A timeline, 1988 to the present, provides further details about HPG, its completion in 2003, associated events, research, and relevant publications at http://genome.gov/10001763.

Provides access to information, databases, and links to other resources concerning research, grants, health, policy and ethics, educational resources, etc. Some examples include the NHGRI Policy and Legislation Database http://genome.gov/PolicyEthics/LegDatabase/pubsearch.cfm, Online Bioethics Resources (620), the Ethical, Legal and Social Implications (ELSI) Research Program, and Initiatives and Resources for Minority and Special Populations (http://genome.gov/10001192), information on current research projects (e.g., the ENCODE Project [ENCyclopedia Of DNA Elements], a pilot project for testing and comparing new methods to identify functional sequences in DNA), model organisms, creation of Centers of Excellence in Genomic Science, the Genetics Variation Program, the Haplotype Map, gene discovery and technology development, establishment of the Center for Inherited Disease Research, and much more.

BIOETHICS

271

616   National information resource on ethics and human genetics.
Library and Information Services, Kennedy Institute of Ethics, Georgetown University. Washington: Kennedy Institute of Ethics, Georgetown University. http://bioethics.georgetown.edu/nirehg/index.htm.

The National Information Resource on Ethics and Human Genetics (NIREHG) is funded by the National Human Genome Research Institute (469), National Institutes of Health (NIH) (470); part of Kennedy Institute of Ethics Library and Information Services (http://bioethics.georgetown.edu/).

Contents: GenETHX (604) Database; Request a Bibliographic Search; About the NIREHG Project; Annotated Bibliographies: Scope Note Series; Books on Ethics and Genetics: Online Catalog; Digital Collection Projects; DNA Patents Database; Genetics Links; Genetics Organizations; Genetics

QuickBibs; Genetics Syllabi; Send Comments; National Reference Center for Bioethics Literature (618).

Provides a variety of information resources on ethics and human genetics, including bibliographic databases, online bibliographies, and print publications.

617 **National Institute of Environmental Health Sciences.** National Institute of Environmental Health Sciences. 1994?–. Research Triangle Park, N.C.: National Institute of Environmental Health Sciences. http://www.niehs.nih.gov.

RA565

Website of National Institute of Environmental Health Sciences (NIEHS). Contents: Health and Education; Research; Funding Opportunities; Careers and Training; News and Events; About NIEHS.

Presents information and resources for several user groups, including health professionals, research scientists, teachers, children, and the general public. Includes a list of environmental health topics (i.e., A–Z List of Conditions and Diseases Linked to Environmental Exposures), access to specialized databases and software, resources of the NIEHS Library and Information Services (http://www.niehs.nih.gov/research/resources/library/index.cfm), NIEHS bioethics resources (http://www.niehs.nih.gov/research/resources/bioethics/index.cfm), and other information resources.

618 **National Reference Center for Bioethics Literature.** National Reference Center for Bioethics Literature, Library and Information Services, Kennedy Institute of Ethics, Georgetown University. Washington: Library and Information Services, Kennedy Institute of Ethics, Georgetown University. http://bioethics.georgetown.edu/nrc/.

378.04   R724

National Reference Center for Bioethics Literature (NRCBL), produced by the Kennedy Institute of Ethics at Georgetown University (http://kennedyinstitute.georgetown.edu/index.htm).

Contents: Request a bibliographic search; New resources in bioethics; About the NRCBL; Education/teaching resources; Links/organizations; Publications; Search catalogs; Search databases on the web; Special collections; Visit the NRCBL; Site index; Site map; National Information Research on Ethics and Human Genetics.

Homepage of the NRCBL, "a specialized collection of books, journals, newspaper articles, legal materials, regulations, codes, government publications, and other relevant documents concerned with issues in biomedical and professional ethics. The library holdings represent the world's largest collection related to ethical issues in medicine and biomedical research. This collection functions both as a reference library for the public and as an in depth research resource for scholars from the U.S. and abroad."—*Website*. Its "Search Databases on the Web" page (http://bioethics.georgetown.edu/databases/index.htm) provides access to NRCBL's bibliographic databases (ETHXWeb [603] and GenETHX [604]) and also National Library of Medicine® resources relating to bioethics: PubMed® [432], NLM Catalog [482], and LocatorPlus™ [480]. Includes a link to the "digital archive on the protection of human subjects," a collaborative project of the Office for Human Research Protections [OHRP], part of the U.S. Dept. of Health and Human Services.

NRCBL's "Bioethics Resources on the Web," publ. as *Scope note* no. 38 [http://bioethics.georgetown.edu/publications/scopenotes/sn38.htm] provides an extensive bibliography of directories, electronic journals, full-text documents, news, current awareness, and teaching resources.

A major print resource, *Bibliography of bioethics* [577], is published by the Center for Bioethics at the Kennedy Institute of Ethics in cooperation with the National Library of Medicine®.

BIOETHICS

273

619   NLM gateway. National Library of Medicine (U.S.). 2000–. Bethesda, Md.: National Library of Medicine. http://gateway.nlm. nih.gov/.

RA11

Allows simultaneous searching of information resources at the National Library of Medicine (NLM). Databases include MEDLINE (425)/PubMed (432) and the NLM Catalog (482) as well as other resources, including information on current clinical trials and consumer health information (MedlinePlus [463]). Currently provides access to 21 databases and other information resources (for a complete list of databases and other details, see http://www.nlm.nih.gov/pubs/factsheets/gateway.html). An overview of the search results is presented in several categories (bibliographic resources, consumer health resources, and other information), with a listing of the individual databases and the number of results within these categories.

620 Online bioethics resources. National Human Genome Research
Institute (U.S.). 2000s–. Bethesda, Md.: National Institutes of
Health. http://genome.gov/10001744.

Produced by National Human Genome Research Institute (NHGRI),
which includes the Ethical, Legal and Social Issues (ELSI) Program.

Provides information about the ELSI research program (http://
genome.gov/10001618) and an extensive collection of selected online
bioethics resources, including ELSI websites, programs, and reports from
NHGRI, National Institutes of Health (NIH) (470), U.S. Dept. of Health
and Human Services (HHS), Bioethics Resources on the Web (609), U.S.
Dept. of Energy (DOE), and other resources.

Also provides access to the "NHGRI Policy and Legislation Database,"
which contains federal and state laws/statutes; federal legislative materials;
and federal administrative and executive materials, including regulations,
institutional policies, and executive orders, with focus on subject areas
such as privacy of genetic information and confidentiality, informed
consent, insurance and employment discrimination, genetic testing and
counseling, and commercialization and patenting.

621 President's Council on Bioethics. President's Council on Bioethics
(U.S.). [2002?–. Washington: [Executive Office of the President,
Council on Bioethics]. http://www.bioethics.gov.

"Advising the President on ethical issues related to advances in biomedical science and technology."—*Website.* Searchable website. Includes
transcripts of meetings by topics (e.g., aging and end-of-life, bioethics in
literature, cloning, health care, nanotechnology, organ transplantation,
stem cells, and many other bioethical subjects), background materials,
bookshelf, and links to related national and international sites.

622 Quackwatch. Stephen Barrett. [1996]–. [Allentown, Pa.]: Stephen
Barrett, MD http://www.quackwatch.org.

615.8   R730

Founded in 1969 as the Lehigh Valley Committee Against Health Fraud,
incorporated in 1970. Assumed its current name in 1997. Maintained by
Dr. S. Barrett and a network of volunteers and expert advisors. Affiliated
with the National Council Against Health Fraud (http://www.ncahf.com/)
and Bioethics Watch (http://www.bioethicswatch.org/).

"Nonprofit corporation whose purpose is to combat health-related
frauds, myths, fads, fallacies, and misconduct. Its primary focus is
on quackery-related information that is difficult or impossible to get

elsewhere. Activities include: Investigating questionable claims; Answering inquiries about products and services; Advising quackery victims; Distributing reliable publications; Debunking pseudoscientific claims; Reporting illegal marketing; Assisting or generating consumer-protection lawsuits; Improving the quality of health information on the Internet; Attacking misleading advertising on the Internet."—*Website*

In addition, includes a list of websites that provide access to 21 special areas—autism, chiropractic, dentistry, diet and nutrition, mental health, and other topics of interest to consumers. Its "Internet Health Pilot" site provides links to many other reliable health sites; its "Casewatch" site contains legal matters and regulatory issues. The contents of all sites can be searched simultaneously or individually (http://www.quackwatch.org/wgsearch.html).

623 **World Medical Association Ethics Unit.** World Medical Association. 2003–. Ferney-Voltaire, France: World Medical Association. http://www.wma.net/e/ethicsunit/.

Produced by World Medical Association (WMA).

Coordinates the WMA's ethics policies with the goal "to establish and promote the highest possible standards of ethical behavior and care by physicians."—*About* (http://www.wma.net/e/ethicsunit/index.htm). Serves as a clearinghouse of ethics information resources for national medical associations and physicians, develops new resources, and collaborates with other international organizations involved in medical ethics and health and human rights. Makes accessible the online version of John R. Williams's *Medical ethics manual* (http://www.wma.net/e/ethicsunit/resources.htm), a list of codes and declarations of adopted ethics policies and declarations in order of their date of first adoption and amendments, including the International Code of Medical Ethics and Declaration of Helsinki: Ethical Principles for Medical Research Involving Human Subjects, as well as many others. Also provides a list of health and human rights organizations and resources.

3 > CONSUMER HEALTH

624 **Academy of General Dentistry.** 1996–. Chicago: Academy of General Dentistry. http://www.agd.org/.

Academy of General Dentistry (AGD), a nonprofit organization of more than 35,000 general dentists, founded in 1952.

In addition to professional resources for dentists, website also provides consumer-oriented oral health resources—e.g., help with finding a dentist (http://www.agd.org/findadentist/default.asp); A–Z list of oral health resources, including an oral health glossary (http://www.agd.org/public/oralhealth/).

625 Consumer and Patient Health Information Section of the Medical Library Association (CAPHIS). Medical Library Association. 2001–. [Chicago, Ill.]: Medical Library Association. http://caphis.mlanet.org.

RA393

CAPHIS (Consumer and Patient Health Information Section) of the Medical Library Association (MLANET: the Medical Library Association's network of health information professionals [465]).

"Tailored to the professional needs and interests of consumer health information specialists" (*Publ. notes*), the CAPHIS portal provides selected consumer health information sources and practical tools provided for librarians and health care consumers: CAPHIS discussion list, *Consumer connections* (an online newsletter), a consumer health library directory, collection development tools, the official MLA policy statement "The Librarian's Role in the Provision of Consumer Health Information and Patient Education," list of health topics ("CAPHIS top 100 list: Web sites you can trust"), and other useful resources.

626 DailyMed. National Library of Medicine (U.S.). [2005]–. Bethesda, Md.: U.S. National Library of Medicine, National Institutes of Health; Health and Human Services. http://dailymed.nlm.nih.gov/.

A searchable website with growing content, providing health consumers, students, and health professionals with online information on prescription medications and labeling from FDA-approved medication package inserts. Each entry gives a description of the medication, its clinical pharmacology, indications and usage, warnings and precautions, dosage and administration, adverse reactions, etc.

Additional consumer health information about U.S. drugs provided by NLM can be found in MedlinePlus (463) under headings such as drugs, supplements, and herbal information, drug safety, medicines, over-the-counter medicines, pain relievers, and possibly others. PubMed (432) and its MEDLINE (425) subset and TOXLINE (1578), can be searched for references to professional journal articles.

627   Drugs in pregnancy and lactation. Gerald G. Briggs. Baltimore: Williams and Wilkins, 1983–. ISSN: 0897-6112.

618.32071   RG627.6.D79D798

Triennial. Description based on 8th ed., 2008.

This updated edition summarizes data on specific drugs. Arranged in alphabetical order, each drug monograph provides the U.S. generic name, pharmacologic class, risk factor, fetal risk summary, breast feeding summary, and references where available. An appendix arranges the drugs by pharmacologic category, allowing comparison of drugs within the same pharmacologic class to determine different risk factors. Written for clinicians caring for pregnant women. Another print resource is *Drugs for pregnant and lactating women* (Philadelphia: Saunders/Elsevier, 2009) by Carl P. Weiner and Catalin Buhimschi. An online resource, LactMed (part of TOXNET [1580]), is a web-based peer-reviewed database with information on drugs and lactation.

628   First aid manual. 2nd American ed., fully rev. and updated ed. Jon R. Krohmer, Michael Webb, Michael R. Bond, American College of Emergency Physicians. 288 p., ill. New York: DK Publ., 2004. ISBN: 0756601959.

616.0252   RC86.8.F565

Published by American College of Emergency Physicians® (ACEP)

Contents: (1) What is first aid?; (2) Action at an emergency; (3) The practice of first aid; (4) Resuscitation; (5) Disorders of the respiratory system; (6) Disorders of the circulation system; (7) Wounds and bleeding; (8) Disorders of consciousness; (9) Bone, joint, and muscle injuries; (10) Burns and scalds; (11) Effects of heat and cold; (12) Foreign bodies; (13) Poisoning; (14) Bites and stings; (15) Emergency childbirth; (16) Miscellaneous conditions; (17) Dressings and bandages; (18) Handling and transport; (19) Emergency first aid. Index.

"A comprehensive guide to treating emergency victims of all ages in any situation."—*Cover.* Step-by-step explanation and color photographs of life-saving procedures (e.g., cardiopulmonary resuscitation, treatment of blocked airway, etc.), treatments and techniques, following current first-aid guidelines. Section for the most critical emergencies at the end of the book.

629 The 5-minute herb and dietary supplement consult. Adriane Fugh-Berman. xv, 475 p. Philadelphia: Lippincott, Williams & Wilkins, 2003. ISBN: 0683302736.

615.321   RM666.H33.F835

Ready-reference resource, arranged alphabetically by botanical or dietary supplement, with Latin and biological names. Entries include concise description, appropriate dosage, pharmacokinetics, drug interactions, risks, etc. For academic, medical, and public libraries.

630 Food and Drug Administration. Food and Drug Administration. [2005]. [Washington, D.C.]: The Office. http://www.fda.gov/.

The FDA's site has a wide range of information for the consumer and the researcher, including: Enforcement Activities (clinical trials, enforcement reports, product recalls and alerts); Products Regulated by FDA (animal drugs and food, aquaculture, bioengineered food, biologics, gene therapy, mobile phones, sunlamps, tattoos, food, drugs, xenotransplantation); news; hot topics; publications; major initiatives/activities (advisory committees, bar coding, buying medical products online, Data Council, Facts@FDA) and Food Industry (Prior Notice of Imports, Registration of Food Facilities).

631 Food and Nutrition Information Center. Food and Nutrition Information Center. Beltsville, Md.: Food and Nutrition Information Center. http://www.nal.usda.gov/fnic/.

351; 640.73; 371.7; 612.3; 641.3   RA784

The Food and Nutrition Information Center (FNIC), located at the National Agricultural Library (NAL) of the U.S. Dept. of Agriculture (USDA), provides online global nutrition information. The FNIC website contains multiple links to reliable food and nutrition and metabolism information for consumers and nutrition professionals. The A–Z list (http://www.nal.usda.gov/fnic/topics_a-z.shtml) includes important topics (e.g., infant nutrition, childhood obesity, weight control, etc.), or browse by subject for dietary guidance, food labeling, and many other major categories. Also included are links to resource lists for specific nutrition topics (http://www.nal.usda.gov/fnic/resource_lists.shtml) and to FNIC and other nutrition-related databases (http://www.nal.usda.gov/fnic/databases.shtml).

632 Health and wellness resource center. Gale Group. 2001–. Farmington Hills, Mich.: Gale; Cengage Learning. http://www.gale.com/HealthRC/.

Provides access to a collection of Gale reference titles (e.g., *Gale encyclopedia of cancer* [Detroit: Thomson/Gale, 2005], *Gale encyclopedia of childhood and adolescence* [Detroit: Gale, 1998], *Gale encyclopedia of genetic disorders* [Detroit: Thomson/Gale, 2005], *Gale encyclopedia of medicine* [Detroit: Thomson; Gale Group, 2005], *Medical and health information directory* [216]), and others; access to full-text articles from the periodical literature; pamphlets; news; and other content, such as access to selected health websites. Also makes available add-on modules [e.g., Alternative Health Module with, for example, the *Gale encyclopedia of alternative medicine* [Detroit: Thomson/Gale, 2005], and the Disease Profiler Module with health statistics]. "Ever-growing electronic resource center for all levels of health research" (*Publ. notes*), particularly for nursing and allied health professionals and consumer health, public, and health science libraries.

Other Gale resources include Health Reference Center—Academic [418] and Gale Virtual Reference Library [Farmington Hills, Mich.: Gale Cengage Learning, 2002–].

633 **Health information for international travel.** Phyllis E. Kozarsky, Paul M. Arguin, Ava W. Navin, U.S. Centers for Disease Control and Prevention. 1974–. Atlanta: U.S. Dept. of Health and Human Services, Centers for Disease Control and Prevention. http://purl. access.gpo.gov/GPO/LPS3580.

Part of the Centers for Disease Control (CDC) (940) Travelers' Health website (http://wwwn.cdc.gov/travel/default.aspx). Also called "Yellow book" or "CDC yellow book." Description based on the 2008 ed., also issued in print with title *CDC health information for international travel 2008* (Philadelphia, Pa.: Elsevier Mosby, 2007). Previous print eds. issued since 1989 as a serial, *International travel health guide*.

Contents: ch. 1, "Introduction"; ch. 2, "Pre- and posttravel general health recommendations"; ch. 3, "Geographic distribution of potential health hazards to travelers"; ch. 4, "Prevention of specific infectious diseases"; ch. 5, "Yellow fever vaccine requirements and information on malaria risk and prophylaxis, by country"; ch. 6, "Noninfectious risks during travel"; ch. 7, "Conveyance and transportation issues"; ch. 8, "International travel with infants and young children"; ch. 9, "Advising travelers with specific needs."

Provides comprehensive information on vaccination requirements and recommendations for international travelers concerning health risks.

The World Health Organization's website, International Travel and Health (1451), also offers extensive travel information.

634   **Health on the Net Foundation (HON).** Health on the Net
       Foundation. 1995–. Geneva, [Switzerland]: Health on the Net
       Foundation (HON). http://www.hon.ch/.

R859.7.E43

Health on the Net Foundation (HON) is a nonprofit, nongovernmental organization known for its HONcode, which defines rules and ethical standards for website developers on how information is provided in terms of the source and data provided. The HONcode is not considered an award or quality rating system for websites.

Provides a "portal to medical information on the Internet."—*Website.* Searchable website provides access to resources for individuals/patients and medical professionals. Includes HON's history and current contact information, access to listservs, newsgroups, and FAQs. For medical and health queries, HON's MedHunt© (http://www.hon.ch/HONHunt/ AdvHONHunt.html) and HONselect© (http://www.hon.ch/HONselect/) help locate quality websites and support groups, medical terminology, journal articles, and healthcare news. HONmedia (http://www.hon.ch/ HONmedia/) is a growing and searchable repository of medical images and videos (currently contains 6,800 medical images and videos, pertaining to 1,700 topics and themes).

635   **Household products database.** Specialized Information Services,
       National Library of Medicine (U.S.). Bethesda, Md: Specialized
       Information Services, U.S. National Library of Medicine, National
       Institutes of Health, Dept. of Health & Human Services. http://
       householdproducts.nlm.nih.gov/.

TS175

Part of TOXNET® (1580).

Provides information on potential health effects and composition of chemicals contained in common household products. Includes reference to health effects information contained in Material Safety Data Sheets (MSDS). Products can also be searched by type, manufacturer, product ingredient/chemical name, and by health effects. Additional details concerning this resource can be found via TOXNET fact sheet at http://www. nlm.nih.gov/pubs/factsheets/toxnetfs.html.

636 MLANET. Medical Library Association. 1998–. Chicago: Medical Library Association (MLA). http://www.mlanet.org/.

Medical Library Association (MLA), since 1889, "a nonprofit, educational organization of more than 1,100 institutions and 3,600 individual members in the health sciences information field, committed to educating health information professionals, supporting health information research, promoting access to the world's health sciences information, and working to ensure that the best health information is available to all."—*MLA website*

Searchable home page for MLA which provides a variety of resources for its members, such as professional standards and practices, discussion of information issues and policy, career information resources, professional credentialing, publications, etc. Also provides resources for health consumers, e.g., "A User's guide to finding and evaluating health information on the Web" (http://www.mlanet.org/resources/userguide. html), including "Deciphering MedSpeak," and MLA's guidelines on finding quality information on the Internet. Provides links to websites considered quality sites ("top ten") by MLA: Cancer.gov (438), Centers for Disease Control (CDC) (940), familydoctor.org (http://familydoctor.org/online/famdocen/home.html), Healthfinder® (706); HIV InSite (314), Kidshealth® (http://www.kidshealth.org/), Mayo Clinic (Rochester, Minn.: Mayo Foundation for Medical Education and Research, 1998–), MEDEM: An information partnership of medical societies (http://medem.com/MedLB/medlib_entry.cfm), MedlinePlus (463), and NOAH: New York Online Access to Health (http://www.noah-health.org/).

Currently 23 different MLA sections have their own webpages (http://www.mlanet.org/sections/sections.html). A prominent example of a section website is the Consumer and Patient Health Information Section of the Medical Library Association (CAPHIS) (625).

637 Natural medicines comprehensive database. Jeff M. Jellin, Therapeutic Research Faculty. 1999–. Stockton, Calif.: Therapeutic Research Faculty. http://www.naturaldatabase.com/.

RM258.5

Available in a professional and a consumer version. Publication varies.

Compilation of natural medicines distributed in the U.S. Contains up-to-date clinical and research information for natural (i.e., herbal and

CONSUMER HEALTH

281

and nonherbal) medicines and dietary supplements distributed in the U.S. Products can be found by most commonly used name, brand name (with editor's comments as appropriate or necessary), ingredient names, scientific names (botanical names), or popular names, with search features to find the safe use (with safety ratings based on evidence: likely safe; possibly safe; possibly unsafe; likely unsafe; unsafe), adverse effects (between natural and pharmaceutical products), interactions ("natural product/drug interaction checker"); also a "natural product effectiveness checker" for each natural medicine. Suitable for pharmacists, physicians, and students in the healthcare field, all types of medical libraries, and also for consumers. Also available in print version since 1999 (11th ed., 2009). Everything in the book is also contained in the web version, which has important added features, such as daily updates, additional search capabilities, patient education handouts, and hyperlinked references, to name a few.

638 **NLM gateway.** National Library of Medicine (U.S.). 2000–.
Bethesda, Md.: National Library of Medicine. http://gateway.nlm.
nih.gov/.

RA11

Allows simultaneous searching of information resources at the National Library of Medicine (NLM). Databases include MEDLINE (425)/PubMed (432) and the NLM Catalog (482) as well as other resources, including information on current clinical trials and consumer health information (MedlinePlus [463]). Currently provides access to 21 databases and other information resources (for a complete list of databases and other details, see http://www.nlm.nih.gov/pubs/factsheets/gateway.html). An overview of the search results is presented in several categories (bibliographic resources, consumer health resources, and other information), with a listing of the individual databases and the number of results within these categories.

639 **patientINFORM.org.** patientINFORM. 2005–. [s.l.]:
patientINFORM. http://www.patientinform.org/.

Online service that provides patients and their caregivers access to the latest research findings and important advances in regard to the diagnosis and treatment of specific diseases, with initial focus on cancer, diabetes, and heart disease. Current participants are the American Cancer Society (ACS), American Diabetes Association (ADA), American Heart

Association (AHA), and the National Organization for Rare Disorders (NORD), approx. 20 publishers, the International Association of STM Publishers, MedlinePlus (463), the Welch Medical Library at Johns Hopkins, and others. Publishers provide these organizations with online access to their peer-reviewed biomedical journals of newly-published articles and also to the backfiles of these journals. These organizations, in turn, provide consumers with links to the full text of selected journal articles and create additional patient-oriented information on their own websites. FAQ index (http://www.patientinform.com/faq-index/) provides further information.

640   Tyler's honest herbal: A sensible guide to the use of herbs and related remedies. 4th ed. Steven Foster, Varro E. Tyler. xxi, 442 p. New York: Haworth Herbal Press, 1999. ISBN: 0789007053.

615.321   RM666.H33T94

Title varies: 1st ed. (1981) had title *The honest herbal*; 2nd ed. (1987), *The new honest herbal*; 3rd ed., 1993. Provides references and peer-reviewed scientific data on the uses of herbs and herbal remedies. Includes approx. 100 herbs. Arranged in alphabetical order by common name, each entry describes the plant with the appropriate nomenclature, botanical information, the chemistry and pharmacology of its active ingredients, its traditional uses, positive and negative features when used for therapeutic purposes, folklore, and other facts. An evaluation by the author based on available evidence follows for each herb. Mentions possible safety concerns. Includes a chapter on laws and regulations. References to the literature. For general readers and as a starting point for scientists; index. *Tyler's herbs of choice* (re-issued in 1999 as *Tyler's herbs of choice: The therapeutic use of phytomedicinals*) provides related information.

Dictionaries

641   The American Heritage medical dictionary. xxxii, 909 p., ill. Boston: Houghton Mifflin, 2007. ISBN: 0618824359.

610.3   R121.A4446

1st ed., 1995, to 2nd ed., 2004, had title *The American Heritage Stedman's medical dictionary*; 2007 ed. is rev. ed. of the 2nd ed.

Provides clear definitions for approx. 45,000 medical words and phrases, including tests, diseases, treatments, technology, and prescription and nonprescription drugs. Also includes health policy terms. Intended for health care consumers, students, and health professionals. Also available online via Credo Reference (London; Boston: Credo Reference).

642   The cancer dictionary. 3rd ed. Michael J. Sarg, Ann D. Gross, Roberta Altman. xv, 416 p., ill. New York: Facts On File, 2007. ISBN: 0816064113.

616.994003   RC262

1st ed., 1992; [2nd] rev. ed., 2000.

Designed for general readers, attempts to provide definitions for every term connected with cancer, with many new terms, drugs, and treatments since the previous edition. Includes many cross-references, and capitalized terms within a definition have their own entry. Appendixes include websites of national cancer and AIDS organizations, and listings of both comprehensive and clinical cancer centers by state. Includes bibliographic references and index. Also available as an e-book.

643   Dictionary of cancer terms. National Cancer Institute, National Institutes of Health. Bethesda, Md.: National Cancer Institute. http://www.cancer.gov/dictionary/.

Contains more than 4,000 terms related to cancer and medicine. Available in both English and Spanish. Detailed instructions on how to search this dictionary are available on the website. Other cancer vocabulary resources include the NCI Thesaurus, NCI Metathesaurus, and NCI Terminology Browser, made available via NCI Enterprise Vocabulary Services (EVS) at http://evs.nci.nih.gov.

644   Medical dictionary (MedlinePlus). National Library of Medicine (U.S.). 2002–. Bethesda, Md.: National Library of Medicine. http://www.nlm.nih.gov/medlineplus/mplusdictionary.html.

R121

Part of MedlinePlus (463). This online dictionary, based on *Merriam-Webster's medical dictionary*, can be searched from the MedlinePlus home page (via "Dictionary" tab). Contains definitions for words and phrases used by health care professionals, a pronunciation guide, and brief biographies of individuals (after whom particular diseases are named). Most MedlinePlus Health Topics pages contain a link or links to additional online dictionaries and/or glossaries from various sources.

Numerous online medical dictionaries and glossaries are also available from many other sources. They include titles made available from various government agencies, organizations, and commercial publishers. Some examples include online medical dictionaries accessible via Credo Reference (currently 24 titles) [London; Boston: Credo Reference], Deciphering Medspeak [http://www.mlanet.org/resources/medspeak/; MLANET [465]], Diabetes Dictionary [http://diabetes.niddk.nih.gov/dm/pubs/dictionary/index.htm; National Institute of Diabetes and Digestive and Kidney Diseases], Dictionary of Cancer Terms [National Cancer Institute] [143], mediLexicon [http://www.medilexicon.com; MedicineNet], On-line Medical Dictionary [http://cancerweb.ncl.ac.uk/omd/index.html; by Dr. Graham Clark], Talking Glossary of Genetics Terms [http://www.nhgri.nih.gov/glossary.cfm; National Human Genome Research Institute], and many others.

645   Mosby's dental drug reference. 8th ed. Arthur H. Jeske. 1415 p. St. Louis: Mosby, Inc., an affiliate of Elsevier, Inc., 2007. ISBN: 9780323052665.

RK701

1st ed., 1994; 7th ed., 2005.

Alphabetical arrangement of drugs that dental patients may be taking, listed by generic name and indexed by brand name, with drug monograph information presented in a consistent format. Provides information on side effects, precautions, contraindications, and drug interactions. Also includes alternative therapies. Therapeutic and pharmacologic index. Accompanied by CD-ROM that contains color images of conditions resulting from drugs patients are taking, and also customizable patient handouts. Intended for dental professionals, but also useful for health consumers.

646   Webster's new world medical dictionary. 2nd ed. MedicineNet. com. 441 p., 1 CD-ROM. New York: Wiley, 2003. ISBN: 0764524615.

610.3   R121.W3585

1st ed., 2000.

This second edition provides definitions of more than 8,000 medical terms, including diseases, treatments, scientific terms, abbreviations and acronyms, pharmaceuticals, herbal supplements, etc. Accompanying CD-ROM contains the complete text of this dictionary in searchable format. Online access via MedicineNet.com's MedTerms dictionary (http://www.medterms.com/) and via Credo Reference (London; Boston: Credo Reference).

Directories

647   **AOA yearbook and directory.** American Osteopathic Association. 2003–. Chicago: American Osteopathic Association. http://www. osteopathic.org/index.cfm?PageID=ps_yearbook.

Contains information formerly included in the print version, *Directory of osteopathic physicians*, 1899–1951, and *Yearbook and directory of osteopathic physicians*, 1952–2000, plus additional information.

Website contents: AOA directory; AOA organization; AOA membership; Accredited healthcare facilities; Requirements for certification; Osteopathic research; Continuing medical education; AOA documents and data; Component societies—State and specialty societies; Licensing; Predoctoral education; Postdoctoral education; Glossary of osteopathic terminology; Osteopathic coding.

In addition to extensive information about the AOA, provides links to the AOA directory Find an Osteopathic Physician (http://www.osteopathic.org/directory.cfm), and several other directories (http://www. osteopathic.org/index.cfm?PageID=aoa_dir). AOA members also have access to the online Directory of the Osteopathic Profession. Offers links to a variety of consumer health and patient resources (http://www.osteopathic.org/index.cfm?PageID=you_main).

648   **ClinicalTrials.gov.** National Institutes of Health, National Library of Medicine (U.S.), United States. 2000–. Bethesda, Md.: National Institutes of Health. http://clinicaltrials.gov.

R853.C55

Provides information about federally and privately funded research in human volunteers for patients, their families and other consumers, and health care professionals. Contents include clinical trials, experimental treatments, experimental and new diagnostic procedures, patient enrollment and recruitment, and all study phases. Explains who may participate, location (U.S. and other countries), and contact information. Searchable by key terms, disease, location, treatment, age group, study phase, etc. Trial listings by condition, sponsor, and status. For additional information and various links to related websites, consult the NLM fact sheet on Clinical-Trials.gov at http://www.nlm.nih.gov/pubs/factsheets/clintrial.html.

649   **Directories (MedlinePlus).** National Library of Medicine (U.S.), National Institutes of Health (U.S.). 200?–. Bethesda, Md.: U.S.

National Library of Medicine, National Institutes of Health, Dept. of Health and Human Services. http://www.nlm.nih.gov/medlineplus/directories.html.

RC48

Pt. of MedlinePlus (463).

Contents: Doctors and dentists—general; Hospital and clinics—general; Doctors and dentists—specialists; Other healthcare providers; Hospitals and clinics—specialized; Other healthcare facilities and services; Libraries.

Links to directories to help find health professionals, services, and facilities. Includes, for example, access to the American Medical Association's DoctorFinder (209), how to find a dentist, a Medicare participants physicians directory, and many others.

650 DIRLINE. National Institutes of Health (U.S.). [1983?–.] Bethesda, Md.: U.S. National Institutes of Health, Dept. of Health and Human Services. http://dirline.nlm.nih.gov/.

DIRLINE® (Directory of Information Resources Online), maintained by the National Library of Medicine (NLM) (427).

Online annotated directory of organizations, research resources, projects, databases, and other information resources concerned with health and biomedicine from a variety of sources, including federal, state, and local government agencies, academic and research institutions, and also consumer health-related resources such as self-help groups and health hotlines. Resources are mostly from the U.S. but also include some international resources. Currently contains over 8,000 entries, with topics on most diseases and conditions and health services research and technology assessment. Can be searched using MeSH® (Medical Subject Headings) (575), keywords, or by name and location of a resource. Detailed information on DIRLINE can be found via a fact sheet prepared by NLM: http://www.nlm.nih.gov/pubs/factsheets/dirlinfs.html.

651 DoctorFinder. American Medical Association. 1997–. Chicago: American Medical Association. http://www.ama-assn.org/aps/amahg.htm.

R712.A1

Also called AMA DoctorFinder; earlier title was AMA Physician Select: On-Line Doctor Finder.

Tool for locating licensed physicians (doctors of medicine [MD] and doctors of osteopathy [DO]) in the United States and information about them. Can be searched by physician name or medical specialty. Listings include address, medical school and year of graduation, residency training, primary practice, specialty, and indication of AMA membership. AMA member listings generally include more information.

Other sites to find doctors include, for example, a search engine created by the Administrators In Medicine (AIM) National Organization for State Medical and Osteopathic Board Executive Directors, entitled Docfinder Searches (http://www.docboard.org/) and links identified through Healthfinder.gov (706).

Encyclopedias

652   American Medical Association complete medical encyclopedia.
American Medical Association. 1408 p., ill. (some color). New
York: Random House Reference, 2003. ISBN: 0812991001.

610.3   RC81.A2A497

Organized in A–Z format, includes medical terms for diseases and disorders, explanations for tests, surgical procedures and imaging techniques, drugs, drug treatments and their potential side effects, preventive medicine, and food and nutrition. Includes information on various issues of current concern and interest, such as alternative medicine and bioterrorism, and a chapter on "Twenty-First Century Medicine" describing advances in genetic research, stem cell research, biomedical imaging, bionic people, and virtual surgery. Supplemented by symptom charts (p. 12–64), an atlas of the body (p. 65–72), first aid treatment (p. 1312–1333), sample legal forms (p. 1335–43), a list of self-help organizations (p. 1344–46), and HIPAA (Health Insurance Portability and Accountability Act) and confidentiality of patients' health information. Cross-references. General index.

**653   American Medical Association handbook of first aid and
emergency care.** Rev. ed. Jerrold B. Leikin, Bernard J. Feldman,
American Medical Association. xvi, 352 p., ill. New York: Random
House, 2000. ISBN: 0375754865.

616.0252   RC86.8.A426

1st ed., 1980; rev. ed., 1990.

Updated ed., with the organization of the book retained from the previous ed. Pt. 1 helps readers prepare for emergency situations, pt. 2 provides an alphabetical listing of injuries and illnesses, designed to be consulted at the time of an emergency, and pt. 3 deals with common sports injuries. Subject index.

654 **The complete reference guide to medicine and health.** Richard
J. Wagman. 4 v., ill. (some color). New York: Facts On File, 2005.
ISBN: 0816061440.

610   RC81.C7174

Encyclopedic set, with information on the human body and how to keep it healthy. Addresses physical and mental illnesses and disorders, their causes, symptoms, and treatment, and surgical operations and procedures. Contains sections on drug addiction and alcohol abuse, nutrition, health, physical fitness, and the different stages of life and death. Photographs, illustrations, and diagrams. Glossary and general index in v. 4. Written for general readers, students, and medical and health practitioners. For public library collections.

655 **Current medical diagnosis and treatment.** Marcus A. Krupp,
Milton J. Chatton, Lawrence M. Tierney, Stephen J. McPhee,
Maxine A. Papadakis. ill. New York: McGraw-Hill, 1974–. ISSN:
0092-8682.

616.07505   RC71.A14

Imprint varies: 1962–86 publ. by Lange Medical Publ.; 1987–2003, Appleton and Lange. Supersedes: *Current diagnosis and treatment* (1962–73). Also known as *CMDT*.

Description based on 45th ed., 2006, ed. by Lawrence M. Tierney, Stephen J. McPhee, and Maxine A. Papadakis. Also available on CD-ROM and online (via McGraw-Hill's AccessMedicine at http://www.accessmedicine. com/resourceTOC.aspx?resourceID=1).

Provides concise and up-to-date information on diseases and disorders and widely accepted methods currently available for diagnosis and treatment. Covers internal medicine, gynecology/obstetrics, dermatology, ophthalmology, otolaryngology, psychiatry, neurology, and imaging procedures. Includes information on nutrition, medical genetics, and an annual update on HIV infection and AIDS. Several chapters are available only online: "Diagnostic testing and medical decision making"; "Basic genetics"; "Basic immunology"; and "Information

CONSUMER HEALTH

technology in patient care: The Internet, telemedicine, and clinical decision support." An appendix provides therapeutic drug monitoring and laboratory reference ranges. Index. For health professionals and also general readers seeking information on specific diseases and their diagnosis and treatment.

656   The encyclopedia of addictive drugs. Richard Lawrence Miller. 491 p. Westport, Conn.: Greenwood Press, 2002. ISBN: 0313318077.

615.78   RM316.M555

Contents: Introduction; Drug types; Alphabetical listing of drugs; Sources for more information; Drug name index; Subject index. Provides non-technical description of approx. 130 addictive drugs, including both pharmaceutical and natural products and aspects of drug abuse. Alphabetical listing of substances, with pronunciation, alternative names (including street names), legal status (federal schedule status; discussion of schedules and scheduling), historical and present uses and misuses, abuse factors, interactions with other drugs, and findings of cancer risks and birth defects. Also includes a section on drug types in general categories. List of print and electronic sources with further information. For general readers.

Available online via netLibrary.

657   Encyclopedia of aging. David J. Ekerdt. 4 v., ill. New York: Macmillan Reference USA, 2002. ISBN: 0028654722.

305.2603   HQ1061.E534

A basic, interdisciplinary gerontology encyclopedia for general readers. Entries cover a broad range of sociological, psychological, legal, economic, medical, biological, and public policy subjects. Includes source documents, cross-references, bibliographies at the end of each article, and a list of articles grouped by topical areas. Not so comprehensive as to be overwhelming, this is a basic resource which can serve as a good starting point for some researchers, even for middle and high school students, as well as for older levels. Available as an e-book.

658   The encyclopedia of Alzheimer's disease. Carol Turkington. xvi, 286 p., ill. New York: Facts On File, 2003. ISBN: 0816048185.

616.831003   RC523.T87

Part of *Facts On File library of health and living series* (678); also available online via Health Reference Center (Facts on File, Inc.) (689).

Alphabetically arranged entries discuss Alzheimer's disease, its causes, symptoms, treatments, related conditions, both physical and emotional, sufferers, and more. Several appendixes list resources, associations, legal and financial issues, clinical trials, etc. Includes cross-references, glossary, bibliography, and index. For general readers, but also useful for health professionals. Another encyclopedia on Alzheimer's disease is Elaine A. Moore's *Encyclopedia of Alzheimer's disease: With directories of research, treatment, and care facilities* (Jefferson, N.C.: McFarland, 2003).

659 **Encyclopedia of Alzheimer's disease: With directories of research, treatment, and care facilities.** Elaine A. Moore, Lisa Moore. xi, 401 p., ill. Jefferson, N.C.: McFarland, 2003. ISBN: 0786414383.

616.831003   RC523.M665

"Comprehensive reference guide intended for anyone involved in the care, treatment, and day-to-day concerns of patients with Alzheimer's disease and related disorders, for anyone who is interested in learning more about the genetic and environmental factors that contribute to both early onset and late onset Alzheimer's disease."—*Pref.* Entries on the different basic science and medical aspects of this disease, research and treatment, caregiving, and many other topics. Contains sections on long-term and day-care treatment centers, arranged by state and city, research facilities by state, listing of resources (books, booklets, pamphlets, caregiver resources, legal assistance, Internet support groups, etc.). For public, academic, and medical libraries. Another encyclopedia on Alzheimer's disease is Carol Turkington's *The encyclopedia of Alzheimer's disease* (228).

660 **The encyclopedia of complementary and alternative medicine.** Tova Navarra, Adam Perlman. xxiii, 276 p., ill. New York: Facts On File, 2004. ISBN: 0816049971.

615.503   R733.N38

Provides information concerning medicines and treatments that may supplement Western medical practices. Approx. 400 entries and appendixes, with lists of organizations, herbs, and a historic timeline of complementary and alternative therapies. Glossary, bibliography, and index.

Pt. of *Facts On File library of health and living series* (678); also available online via Health Reference Center (Facts On File, Inc.) (689) and netLibrary.

661 **Encyclopedia of complementary health practice.** Carolyn
Chambers Clark, Rena J. Gordon, Barbara Harris. xxi, 638 p., ill.
New York: Springer, 1999. ISBN: 0826112390.

615.503   R733.E525

"Comprehensive, authoritative, and concise information in the application of complementary health practices that supplement traditional
medical procedure as a vehicle for communication across traditional and
complementary disciplines."—*Pref.* Divided into four parts: pt. I, Contemporary issues in complementary health practices; pt. II, Conditions; pt. III,
Influential substances; pt. IV, Practices and treatments. Cross-references,
contributor directory, resource directory, and extensive references. Subject
index and contributor index.

662 **The encyclopedia of depression.** 2nd ed. Roberta Roesch. ix, 278
p., ill. New York: Facts On File, 2001. ISBN: 0816040478.

616.8527003   RC537.R63

1st ed., 1991.

An alphabetic listing of entries that vary in length from 50 to 1,000
words and treat all aspects (biological, psychological, etc.) related to
depression. New subjects in this edition include alternative therapies, new
treatments, and the potential benefits of the Human Genome Project.
Appendixes provide statistics, psychiatric drug information, and information sources (including selected treatment centers, self-help groups,
publications, and an extensive bibliography). Numerous cross-references;
subject index. Intended for general readers.

Part of *Facts On File library of health and living series* (678). Also available online via Health Reference Center. (689)

663 **Encyclopedia of dietary supplements.** Paul M. Coates. xviii, 819
p., ill. New York: Marcel Dekker, 2005. ISBN: 0824755049.

613.2   RM258.5.E53

"The goal is to provide readers with comprehensive yet accessible, information on the current state of science for individual supplement ingredients
and extracts."—*Pref.* Includes commonly used supplements, including
vitamins, minerals, and other ingredients found in foods, and also natural
products, such as herb extracts. Alphabetically-arranged entries include
basic information about each substance and its regulatory status. References to the scientific literature or evidence to support claims of benefit are

provided. For clinicians, researchers, health care professionals, and consumers. Available both in print and online, with updates at the publisher's website. Other titles, for example, *Guide to understanding dietary supplements* (New York: Haworth Press, 2003), *Mosby's handbook of herbs and natural supplements* (St. Louis: Mosby, 2004), and *PDR for nutritional supplements* (1246), may also be useful to health professionals and consumers.

664 **Encyclopedia of diet fads.** Marjolijn Bijlefeld, Sharon K. Zoumbaris. xv, 242 p., ill. Westport, Conn.: Greenwood Press, 2003. ISBN: 0313322236.

613.2503   RM222.2.B535

Entries for various kinds of diets and major weight loss programs, with appropriate comments, criticisms, and suggested dietary guidelines. Additional entries and information on nutrition in health and illness, vitamins, etc. Introduction includes a brief history of dieting and fad diets. Annotated list of websites and several other appendixes. For general readers and allied health professionals.

665 **The encyclopedia of elder care: The comprehensive resource on geriatric and social care.** 2nd ed. Liz Capezuti, Eugenia L. Siegler, Mathy Doval Mezey. xxxvii, 860 p. New York: Springer, 2008. ISBN: 9780826102.

362.19897003   RC954.E53

1st ed., 2001.

"Designed to encapsulate all aspects of care for an aging population: a comprehensive, multidisciplinary compilation of topics that reflects the breadth and depth of issues of concerns to those who care for older individuals—from individual to society, from patient to professional, from symptom to treatment."—*Pref.* Entries address elder care in the areas of society, community, caregiving, and the individual. Intended for professionals from a variety of health professions and for students. Organized alphabetically by topic, with listing of Internet resources and bibliographic references. Electronic edition available from netLibrary.

666 **Encyclopedia of family health.** 3rd ed. David B. Jacoby, R. M. Youngson, Marshall Cavendish Corporation. Tarrytown, N.Y.: Marshall Cavendish, 2005. ISBN: 0761474862.

610.3   RC81.A2E5

1st ed., 1998.

Covers general health topics, physical and mental diseases and their treatment, etc. List of organizations; index. Intended for general readers and useful for undergraduate students.

667   **Encyclopedia of foods: A guide to healthy nutrition.** Mayo Clinic. xi, 516 p., color ill. San Diego, Calif.: Academic Press, 2002. ISBN: 0122198034.

641.3003   TX349.E475

Contents: pt. 1, "A guide to healthy nutrition: Optimizing health"; "Nutrients and other food substances"; "Food-health connection"; "Planning meals: Selecting healthful foods, plus two weeks of menus"; "Preparing healthful meals"; pt. 2, "Encyclopedia of foods"; "Fruits"; "Vegetables"; "Grains"; "Dairy goods"; "Meat and other high-protein foods"; "Fats, oils, and sweets"; "Others."

Contains discussion of dietary guidelines and the relationship between diet and various diseases. Appendix includes reading list, selected websites, charts of dietary reference intakes, and information about nutrients in foods, vitamins, and minerals. Color photographs, diagrams, and other illustrations. Useful for public and academic libraries.

668   **The encyclopedia of genetic disorders and birth defects.** 2nd ed. James Wynbrandt, Mark D. Ludman. 474 p. New York: Facts On File, 2000. ISBN: 0816039895.

616.04203   RB155.5

1st ed., 1991; 2nd ed., 2000 (description based on 2nd ed.); 3rd ed. due Oct. 2007.

Presents some 1,000 articles written for both health-care professionals and general readers. Entries for disorders, selected on the basis of incidence and historical and clinical importance, discuss prognosis, prevalence, mode of inheritance, and the availability of both carrier screening and prenatal diagnosis; many include addresses of private organizations which can provide further information. Also included are brief discussions of subjects and terminology related to genetic disorders and congenital anomalies. If known, the biochemical and molecular basis of a disease is given. The introduction provides a brief history of human genetics. Numerous cross-references. Appendixes provide statistics and tables on congenital malformations and infant mortality, directory information for private and government organizations, and selected Web resources. Bibliography; subject and name index.

Part of *Facts On File library of health and living series* (678). Also available online via Health Reference Center (Facts On File, Inc.) (689).

669   **Encyclopedia of health and aging.** Kyriakos S. Markides.
650 p. Thousand Oaks, Calif: Sage Publications, 2007. ISBN: 9781412909495.
613.043803   RA777.6.E534

Resource on health and aging in the United States and abroad. "Reader's Guide" lists entries by key themes and topics, with entries contributed from different disciplines (e.g., biology, epidemiology, health psychology, public policy, sociology, and others) related to health and aging: aging and the brain; diseases and medical conditions; drug-related issues; function and syndromes; mental health and psychology; nutritional issues; physical status; prevention and health behaviors; sociodemographic and cultural issues; studies of aging and systems of care. Also addresses economic issues and provides recent research results and facts on health and aging. Includes further readings, bibliographical references, a list of online resources, and index. Appropriate for academic, various types of health sciences libraries, and public libraries.

670   **The encyclopedia of HIV and AIDS.** 2nd ed. Sarah Watstein, Stephen E. Stratton. xii, 660 p. New York: Facts On File, 2003. ISBN: 0816048088.
616.9792003   RC606.6.W385

1st ed. (1998) had title: *The AIDS dictionary.*
Rev. entries from the previous ed. and many new entries covering the medical conditions and drugs associated with HIV/AIDS, its science aspects, and vaccine development. Also includes cultural and social sciences topics. Appendixes with a glossary of frequently used abbreviations, HIV/AIDS statistics in the U.S. and worldwide by country, and other selected resources, including a list of World Wide Web sites. Includes bibliography and index. For general readers.

Part of the *Facts On File library of health and living series* (678). Available online via Health Reference Center (Facts On File, Inc.) (689) and also netLibrary.

Another resource in this subject area for general readers is Encyclopedia of AIDS: A social, political, cultural, and scientific record of the HIV epidemic (227).

671 **Encyclopedia of mental health.** Howard S. Friedman. 3 v., ill. San Diego, Calif.: Academic Press, 1998. ISBN: 0122266757.

616.89003   RA790.5.E53

Contents: v. 1, A–Di; v. 2, Do–N; v. 3, O–Z, index. "Taking into account new knowledge about the genetic, biological, developmental, social, societal and cultural nature of human beings, bring[s] together emerging trends of mental health, validity (or invalidity) of psychiatric diagnosis (and DSM IV), including standards for psychotherapy, models of normality, and psychiatric epidemiology."—*Pref.* Each article contains an outline, a glossary, cross-references, and a bibliography. Aimed at a wide range of users, including students, researchers, and allied health professionals. Another encyclopedia with the same title by Ada P. Kahn is part of the *Facts On File Library of health and living series* (678), a collection of titles on medical subjects for general readers which is also available online via Health Reference Center (Facts On File, Inc.) (689).

672 **Encyclopedia of obesity and eating disorders.** 3rd ed. Dana K. Cassell, David H. Gleaves. 362 p. New York: Facts On File, 2006. ISBN: 0816061971.

616.8526003   RC552.E18.C37

1st ed., 1994; 2nd ed., 2000.

Provides concise entries on the causes, symptoms, and treatments, including pharmacotherapy, of obesity and the various eating disorders (e.g., anorexia nervosa, bulimia, etc.). Lists sources of information, websites, audiovisuals, and other resources. Bibliography and index. For general readers and health professionals.

Part of *Facts On File library of health and living* (678) series. Available online via Health Reference Center (689).

673 **Encyclopedia of obesity.** Kathleen Keller. 2 v., ill., port. Los Angeles: Sage, 2008. ISBN: 9781412952385.

362.196398003   RC628.E53

"Reader's guide" topics: biological or genetic contributions to obesity; children and obesity; dietary interventions to treat obesity; disordered eating and obesity; environmental contributions to obesity; health implications of obesity; medical treatments for obesity; new research frontiers on obesity; obesity and ethnicity/race; obesity and the brain or obesity and behavior; obesity as a public health crisis; psychological influences and outcomes of obesity; societal influences and outcomes of obesity; women and obesity; worldwide prevalence of obesity.

This interdisciplinary resource explores a variety of topics on obesity, health conditions, and issues related to obesity. Written in nontechnical language and intended as a starting point for different audiences, from scholars to the general public. References at the end of each entry. Glossary and index in both volumes. Available online via Sage eReference.

674 **The encyclopedia of the brain and brain disorders.** 2nd ed. Carol Turkington, Joseph R. Harris. ix, 369 p. New York: Facts On File, 2002. ISBN: 081604774X.

612.8203   QP376.T87

Accessible reference about the brain and brain disorders from a medical writer for general readers. More than 800 clear, concise entries; also includes three directories (of self-help, professional, and governmental organizations), a glossary, an extensive list of references, and an index to a wide range of terms. The 1st ed., called *The brain encyclopedia*, was published in 1996. Part of the *Facts On File library of health and living series* (New York: Facts On File, 1999–). Available online via Health Reference Center (689).

675 **The encyclopedia of women's health.** 5th ed. Christine Ammer. xii, 434 p., ill. New York: Facts On File, 2005. ISBN: 0816057907.

613.0424403   RA778.A494

1st ed. (1983) has title *A to Z of women's health*; [2nd] ed. (1989) through 4th ed. (2000) have title *The new A to Z of women's health*. Title for 5th ed. varies; issued both as *The new A to Z of women's health: A concise encyclopedia* and *The encyclopedia of women's health*. Pt. of *Facts On File library of health and living series* (New York: Facts On File, 1999–).

Entries cover a broad range of women's health issues and changing health needs during the different stages of their lives. Also gives attention to social and emotional issues. Appendix, topically arranged, provides contact information for associations and organizations. Alphabetical arrangement, cross-references, and index.

676 **Encyclopedia of women's health issues.** Kathlyn Gay. xvii, 300 p., ill. Westport, Conn.: Oryx Press, 2002. ISBN: 157356303X.

613.0424403   RA778.G39

Goes beyond the description of the various health problems and diseases that women experience and also includes social, political, legal, economic, and ethical aspects of women's health. Treats contemporary issues and also provides a historical perspective when appropriate. Can serve as a starting point for research on gender issues in health care policy and politics.

Alphabetical arrangement, bibliography, and a selection of websites. Index. For an academic audience and also general readers.

677 **The Facts On File encyclopedia of health and medicine.** Glenn S. Rothfeld, Deborah S. Romaine. Facts On File, Inc. New York: Facts On File, 2006. ISBN: 0816060630.

610.3   R125.R68

Provides health and medical information in a concise format, intended for general readers. Body systems and general health problems and topics are interconnected; e.g., each section begins with an overview of a system, related medical breakthroughs, and an A-to-Z listing of disorders and topics relating to the particular system. Index is essential for any topic not commonly known to relate to a particular body system. Vol. 4 provides a cumulative bibliography. A resource section lists URLs for various healthcare organizations; several appendixes, with medical abbreviations and symbols, a listing of Nobel Prize winners for physiology or medicine, and recommended immunization and routine exam schedules. Another resource for general readers by the same publisher is Richard J. Wagman's 2005 *The complete reference guide to medicine and health*.

678 **Facts On File library of health and living series.** Facts On File. New York: Facts On File, 1999–. ISBN: 0816074364.

This series is a growing collection of titles on medical subjects that provide an overview and help for understanding specific health conditions and health care issues. Contains different encyclopedias on a variety of diseases, conditions, and health issues. Each typically contains an A-to-Z section that defines the causes, cures, key research, medical terms, symptoms, treatments, and trends; appendixes with statistical information; bibliographies for further research; directory of organizations, associations, support groups, etc. Written for general readers but also useful to health professionals.

Encyclopedias for the following subjects are available: addictions and addictive behaviors; adoption; allergies; Alzheimer's disease (*The encyclopedia of Alzheimer's disease* [228]); arthritis; asthma and respiratory disorders; autism spectrum disorders; autoimmune diseases; back and spine systems and disorders; blindness and vision impairment; brain and brain disorders (*The encyclopedia of the brain and brain disorders* [674]); breast cancer; cancer; child abuse; children's health and wellness; complementary and alternative medicine (*The encyclopedia of complementary and alternative medicine* [234]); deafness and hearing disorders; death and dying; digestive system and digestive disorders; depression (*The encyclopedia of depression* [662]); endocrine diseases and disorders; genetic disorders and birth defects (*The encyclopedia of genetic disorders and birth defects* [241]); heart and heart disease; hepatitis and other liver diseases; HIV and AIDS (*The encyclopedia of HIV and AIDS* [247]); infectious diseases; learning disabilities; memory and memory disorders; men's health; mental health; multiple sclerosis; muscle and skeletal systems and disorders; nutrition and good health; obesity and eating disorders (*The encyclopedia of obesity and eating disorders* [New York: Facts On File, 2006]); Parkinson's disease; schizophrenia and other psychotic disorders; senior health and well-being; sexually transmitted diseases; skin and skin disorders; sleep disorders; sports medicine; stress and stress-related diseases; suicide; vitamins, minerals, and supplements; women's health (*The encyclopedia of women's health* [265]); women's reproductive cancer; work-related illnesses, injuries, and health.

Available online via Health Reference Center (689).

679   The Gale encyclopedia of alternative medicine. 2nd ed. Jacqueline L. Longe. 4 v. (xxii, 2411 p.), ill. (some color). Detroit: Thomson/ Gale, 2005. ISBN: 0787674249.

615.503   R733.G34

1st ed., 2001.

Contents: v. 1, A–C; v. 2, D–K; v. 3, L–R; v. 4, S–Z.

Presents information and covers all aspects of alternative and complementary practices, therapies, and remedies, and their effect on various diseases and disorders. Alphabetically arranged entries, side bar glossary of key terms, websites, suggestions for further readings, list of selected organizations, etc. Each volume contains a list of all entries in the set. General index. Available online in the Gale Virtual Reference Library (Farmington Hills, Mich.: Gale Cengage Learning, 2002–).

680   The Gale encyclopedia of cancer: A guide to cancer and its treatments. 2nd ed. Jacqueline L. Longe. 2 v. (xxxvii, 1419 p.), color ill. Detroit: Thomson/Gale, 2005. ISBN: 1414403623.

616.994003   RC254.5.G353

1st ed., 2002.

Contents: v. 1, A–K; v. 2, L–Z.

Survey of 120 cancers. Following a standardized format, entries on a variety of cancers, treatments, diagnostic procedures, cancer drugs and their side effects, also on cancer biology, carcinogenesis, and cancer genetics. Entries for cancer types include definition, description, demographics, causes and symptoms, diagnosis, clinical staging, treatments and treatment team, prognosis, coping with cancer treatment, clinical trials, prevention, special concerns, and resources. For cancer drugs: definition, purpose, description, recommended dosage, precautions, side effects, and drug interactions are included, also traditional and alternative treatments and information on clinical trials. A resources section provides additional information. Contact information for organizations and support groups in an appendix at the back of v. 2. Alphabetical arrangement, cross-references, color images for many malignancies, and anatomical illustrations. List of contents; general index. The online version is part of Gale Virtual Reference Library (Farmington Hills, Mich.: Gale Cengage Learning, 2002–).

681   The Gale encyclopedia of children's health: Infancy through adolescence. Kristine M. Krapp, Jeffrey Wilson, Gale Group. 4 v. (xix, 2178 p.), color ill. Detroit: Thomson; Gale Group, 2005. ISBN: 0787692417.

618.920003   RJ26.G35

Vol. 1, A–C; v. 2, D–K; v. 3, L–R; v. 4, S–Z.

Includes approx. 600 articles, presented in a standardized format. Each entry provides definition and description of various diseases, disorders and other problems, their causes, symptoms, diagnosis, treatment, prognosis, etc. Glossary, color photos, illustrations, charts (growth charts), tables, childhood medications, and resources for further reading and study. General index. For use by general readers and health professionals. Available as an e-book.

682   The Gale encyclopedia of diets: A guide to health and nutrition. Jacqueline L. Longe, Thomson Gale (Firm). 2 v. Detroit: Thomson Gale, 2007. ISBN: 9781414429.

613.203   RA784.G345

Addresses a wide range of diets and related health and nutrition issues, with the intent to supplement advice given by health professionals. Signed articles include a list of additional resources, with definitions of terms, cross-references, and "see also" references. Index. Written for health consumers and general readers. For public, academic, and health science libraries. Available electronically through Gale Virtual Reference Library (Farmington Hills, Mich.: Gale Cengage Learning, 2002–).

Other resources providing information on diets include, for example, *Encyclopedia of human nutrition* (682) and *Encyclopedia of nutrition and good health*, published in various editions since 1997.

683   The Gale encyclopedia of genetic disorders. 2nd ed. Brigham
Narins. 2 v., color ill. Detroit: Thomson/Gale, 2005. ISBN:
1414403658.
616.04203   RB155.5.G35
1st ed., 2002.
  Contents: v. 1, A–L; v. 2, M–Z.
  Signed entries with detailed information for genetic diseases, disorders, and conditions. A standardized format provides for each entry as appropriate: definitions, description, genetic profile, demographics, signs and symptoms, diagnosis, treatment and management, prognosis, resources, and key terms. Available as an e-book.

684   The Gale encyclopedia of medicine. 3rd ed. Jacqueline L.
Longe, Gale Group. Detroit: Thomson; Gale Group, 2005. ISBN:
1414403682.
616.003   RC41.G35
1st ed., 1999; 2nd ed., 2002.
  "Medical information on common medical disorders, conditions, tests, and treatment fills a gap between basic consumer health resources and highly professional materials. Articles follow a standardized format that provides information at a glance. Designed with ready reference in mind—alphabetical arrangement, definitions of key terms, contact information for organizations and support groups, resources section for additional information, illustrations, and general index."—*Introd.* Encyclopedias in other medical subjects published by Gale also following this type of arrangement and a standardized format include *The Gale encyclopedia of alternative medicine* (2nd ed., 2005) (270), *The Gale encyclopedia of cancer: A guide to cancer and its treatments* (2nd., 2005) (271), *The Gale encyclopedia of genetic disorders* (2nd ed., 2005) (272), *The Gale encyclopedia of mental disorders* (Detroit: Thomson Gale, 2008) (2003), and *The Gale encyclopedia of nursing and allied health* (2nd ed., 2007) (1049). Available as an e-book.

685   The Gale encyclopedia of mental health. 2nd ed. Laurie J.
Fundukian, Jeffrey Wilson. 2 v., color ill. Detroit: Thomson Gale,
2008. ISBN: 9781414429878.
616.89003   RC437.G35

1st ed., 2003, had title *The Gale encyclopedia of mental disorders.*

Provides an overview of mental health and illness, diagnostic procedures, psychotherapy, and various other treatments, including drugs, herbal preparations, and alternative therapies. Includes mostly disorders recognized by the American Psychiatric Association, but also mentions some not formally recognized as distinct disorders. Disease and medication entries are in a standardized format. Diseases include definition, description, causes and symptoms, demographics, diagnosis, treatment, prognosis, prevention, and resources. Medications include definition, purpose, description, recommended dosage, precautions, side effects, interactions, and resources.

Available electronically through Gale Virtual Reference Library (Farmington Hills, Mich.: Gale Cengage Learning, 2002–).

686 **The Gale encyclopedia of neurological disorders.** Stacey L. Chamberlin, Brigham Narins, Gale Group. 2 v., ill. Detroit: Thomson Gale, 2005. ISBN: 078769150X.

616.8003   RC334.G34

Contents: v. 1, A–L; v. 2, M–Z, glossary, index. Information on disorders of the nervous system, with articles on neurological diseases, disorders and syndromes, tests, treatments, diagnostic equipment, and medications. A typical entry for a disease includes, e.g., definition, description, demographics, causes and symptoms, diagnosis, treatment team, treatment, recovery and rehabilitation, clinical trials, prognosis, special concerns, resources, and key terms. Intended for patients, their families, allied health students, and general readers. Drug and treatment data also provide structured entries, with definition, purpose, description, recommended dosage, precautions, side effects, interactions, resources, and key terms. Available online in the Gale Virtual Reference Library (Farmington Hills, Mich.: Gale Cengage Learning, 2002–).

687 **The Gale encyclopedia of surgery: A guide for patients and caregivers.** Anthony J. Senagore. 3 v. (xvii, 1724 p.), color ill. Detroit: Gale, 2004. ISBN: 0787677213.

617.91003   RD17.G34

Contents: v. 1, A–F; v. 2, G–O; v. 3, P–Z.

Approx. 475 alphabetically-arranged entries, with definitions of key terms and articles of varying length. Explains 250 surgical procedures, following a consistent format, with step-by-step illustrations for many of them. Appendixes list centers for specific surgical specialties, national organizations, and support groups for patients. Bibliographies for further reading; glossary of medical terms; index. Available as an e-book.

688   **The Harvard Medical School family health guide.** 1st Free Press trade paperback ed. Anthony L. Komaroff, Harvard Medical School. 1312 p., ill. (some color). New York: Free Press, 2005. ISBN: 0684863731.

610   RC81.H38

[1st ed.], 1999.

Contents: Navigating the health care system; Taking charge of your health; How your body works; Diagnosing disease; Symptom charts; Brain and nervous system; Behavioral and emotional disorders; Eyes; Ears, nose, and throat; Teeth, mouth, and gums; Lungs; Skin, hair, and nails; Color guide to visual diagnosis; Cosmetic and reconstructive surgery; Bones, joints, and muscles; Blood disorders; Digestive system; Urinary system; Hormonal disorders; Infections and immune system diseases; Infertility, pregnancy, and childbirth; Health of infants and children; Health of adolescents; Health of women; Health of men; Health of seniors; Caregiving and eldercare; Death and dying; Medicines; First aid and emergency care; Replaceable parts of irreplaceable you. Updated edition. Comprehensive, easy-to-understand guide to information about the diagnosis, treatment, and prevention of disease. Helpful to health consumers in finding good medical care and in evaluating the care they receive. Kept up-to-date by an associated searchable website.

689   **Health reference center (Facts On File, Inc.).** Facts On File, Inc. 2005–. New York: Facts On File. http://www.factsonfile.com/ newfacts/DataDetail.asp?SidText=0816046964&Pagevalue=Online.

Database containing full-text encyclopedic information (drawn from titles in the Facts On File library of health and living series [678]) on a wide variety of health topics and related social issues, mental health, health and wellness, and topics about body systems and related diseases and conditions. Written in nontechnical language. Hyperlinked entries. Glossary.

690   **Magill's medical guide.** 3rd rev. ed. Anne Chang. 4 v. (xviii, 2938 p.), ill. Pasadena, Calif.: Salem Press, 2005. ISBN: 1587651599.

610.3   RC41.M34

1st ed., 1995–96; 2nd rev. ed., 2002.

    Contents: v. 1. Abdomen–Domestic violence; v. 2. Down syndrome–Laser use in surgery; v. 3. Law and medicine-Rheumatology; v. 4. Rhinoplasty and submucous resection–Zoonoses. Index. This revised edition includes 960 articles (with "89 new topics and 148 newly commissioned articles."—*Publ. notes.* Arranged alphabetically, with cross-references, describes diseases and disorders, also surgical and nonsurgical procedures. Entries include information on human genetics, human anatomy, human physiology, and microbiology as appropriate, and also the medical/surgical specialties involved. Bibliographies, including references to websites. Several appendixes, for example, "Diseases and Other Medical Conditions," with a listing of approx. 800 diseases, disorders, symptoms, etc. with definitions. Glossary. Alphabetical list of contents, lists of entries arranged by anatomy or system affected, and entries arranged by specialties and related fields at the end of each volume.

    An extensively revised 4th ed. [Pasadena, Calif.: Salem Press, 2008] was published in Nov. 2007 and includes a three-year subscription to the e-version.

691   **Mayo Clinic family health book. 3rd ed.** Scott C. Litin Mayo Clinic. xvi, 1448 p., ill. (some color). New York: HarperResource, 2003. ISBN: 0060002506.

613   RC81.M473

1st ed., 1990; 2nd ed., 1996.

    Contents: pt. I, Living well; pt. II, Common conditions and concerns through life's stages; pt. III, Making sense of your symptoms; pt. IV, First aid and emergency care; pt. V, Diseases and disorders; pt. VI, Tests and treatments. Described as "a classic home medical reference with a strong emphasis on self-care."—*Publ. notes.* Another title, *Mayo Clinic book of alternative medicine* (2007), provides information on using natural therapies in conjunction with conventional medicine. A related web resource is MayoClinic.com: reliable information for a healthier life (710).

692   **Medical encyclopedia (MedlinePlus).** National Library of Medicine (U.S.). 1999–. [Atlanta]; Bethesda, Md.: A.D.A.M.; National Library of Medicine. http://www.nlm.nih.gov/ medlineplus/encyclopedia.html.

                                                          RC81.A2

Title varies: A.D.A.M. Medical Encyclopedia; MedlinePlus, Medical Encyclopedia.

Articles about diseases and conditions, injuries, nutrition, poisons, surgeries, symptoms, tests, and other special topics. Contains medical illustrations and images. Accessible via "Medical Encyclopedia" tab from MedlinePlus (463).

693 **The Merck manual of medical information.** 2nd home ed., [all new & completely rev.] ed. Mark H. Beers, Andrew J. Fletcher. xxxviii, 1907 p., ill. (some color). Whitehouse Station, N.J.: Merck Research Laboratories, 2003.

616   RC81.M535

Author varies: 1st ed., 1997, by Robert Berkow et al.

Contents: section (1) Fundamentals; (2) Drugs; (3) Heart and blood vessel disorders; (4) Lung and airway disorders; (5) Bone, joint, and muscle disorders; (6) Brain and nerve disorders; (7) Mental health disorders; (8) Mouth and dental disorders; (9) Digestive disorders; (10) Liver and gallbladder disorders; (11) Kidney and urinary tract disorders; (12) Disorders of nutrition and metabolism; (13) Hormonal disorders; (14) Blood disorders; (15) Cancer; (16) Immune disorders; (17) Infections; (18) Skin disorders; (19) Ears, nose, and throat disorders; (20) Eye disorders; (21) Men's health issues; (22) Women's health issues; (23) Children's health issues; (24) Accidents and injuries; (25) Special subjects. Appendixes: (I) Weights and measures; (II) Common medical tests; (III) Drug names: generic and trade; (IV) Resources for help and information. Index. "Source of accurate, reliable information that should stimulate better communication between patients and their doctors."—*Pref.* Based on the *Merck manual of diagnosis and therapy* (Rahway, N.J.: Merck, 1950–), this title transforms the language of the professional version into commonly used English while retaining the information about diseases, diagnosis, prevention, and treatment. Available in two versions: the original print version and an online version, made accessible via the Merck Manuals (324) online page (http://www.merck.com/pubs/), which also provides information and access to several other Merck publications.

694 **World of health.** Brigham Narins. viii, 1424 p., ill. Detroit: Gale Group, 2000. ISBN: 0787636495.

610   R130.5.W67

Overview of the medical sciences and health-related disciplines, covering significant discoveries and brief biographies of important persons related to these discoveries and other historical events, disorders, therapies, procedures, devices, etc. Alphabetical arrangement, cross-references,

CONSUMER HEALTH

305

bibliographical references (p. 1277–1281), a chronology 5000 BCE–1999, and index. Written in concise language for students and general readers. Useful for public libraries.

Guides

695 AIDSinfo. U.S. Department of Health and Human Services, National Institutes of Health (U.S.), AIDS Clinical Trials Information Service. Bethesda, Md.: National Institutes of Health. http://www.aidsinfo.nih.gov.

RA643.8

Result of merging two previous U.S. Dept. of Health and Human Services (DHHS) projects. Supersedes the AIDS Clinical Trials Information Service (ACTIS) and the HIV/AIDS Treatment Information Service (ATIS).

Resource for current information on federally and privately funded clinical trials for AIDS patients and HIV-infected persons, federally approved HIV treatment and prevention guidelines, and medical practice guidelines. Provides access to a searchable HIV/AIDS drugs database (via "Drugs" tab) that includes approved and investigational anti-HIV medications, including side effects, dosages, and interactions with other drugs or food; also access to brochures, fact sheets, and other Web resources on HIV/AIDS, current and archived versions of DHHS guidelines, and a searchable HIV glossary (English and Spanish). For HIV/AIDS patients, the general public, health care providers, and researchers.

Additional major HIV/AIDS resources can be accessed via the following sites: Fact sheet, AIDS Information Resources (http://www.nlm.nih.gov/pubs/factsheets/aidsinfs.html), Specialized Information Services: HIV/AIDS Information (http://sis.nlm.nih.gov/hiv.html), CDC National Prevention Information Network (NPIN) (http://www.cdcnpin.org/scripts/hiv/index.asp), UNAIDS: Joint United National Programming on HIV/AIDS (http://www.unaids.org/en/), and AIDS Treatment Data Network (http://www.atdn.org/).

696 Alternative medicine. Christine A. Larson. xv, 215 p. Westport, Conn.: Greenwood Press, 2007. ISBN: 0313337187.

610   R733.L37

Contents: "The origins of alternative medicine"; "The theories underlying alternative medicine"; "The business of alternative medicine"; "Why consumers seek alternative treatments"; "Do alternative therapies work?";

"Should alternative medicine be regulated by the government?"; "Should managed care provide coverage for alternative therapies?"; "Pharmaceuticals versus alternative therapies"; "Culture and health: Who bears responsibility for health and healthcare?"; "The future of health and healthcare."

Guide to alternative medicine, covering practical and also controversial issues, with recommendations on using safe alternative medicine practices together with Western medicine. Annotated primary source documents, alternative medicine timeline, and glossary. Includes bibliographical references (p. [201]–208) and index. For researchers, clinicians, consumers, and academic and medical libraries. Also available as an e-book.

697 **American Medical Association family medical guide.** 4th ed., completely rev. and updated ed. American Medical Association. xiv, 1184 p., ill. (some color). Hoboken, N.J.: John Wiley & Sons, 2004. ISBN: 0471269115.

613   RC81.A543

1st ed., 1982; 2nd ed., 1987; 3rd ed. (print), 1994; computer disk, 1995.

Aimed at general readers, this guide presents a general discussion of the healthy body, self-diagnosis symptom charts with visual aids to diagnosis, diseases and other disorders and problems, preventive health care practices, and caring for the sick. Includes a section on accidents and emergencies. Glossary and subject index.

698 **The complementary and alternative medicine information source book.** Alan M. Rees. x, 229 p., ill. [Phoenix, Ariz.]: Oryx Press, 2001. ISBN: 1573563889.

615.5   R733.C65285

Contents: (1) Complementary and alternative medicine: A new dimension in medical consumerism; (2) The best of complementary and alternative medicine information resources; (3) Complementary and alternative medicine organizations; (4) Complementary and alternative medicine magazines and newsletters; (5) Pamphlet materials; (6) Professional literature; (7) CD-ROM information products; (8) Complementary and alternative medicine sources on the Internet (Tom Flemming); (9) Popular books on complementary and alternative medicine. Appendixes: (1) General information about CAM and the NCCAM; (2) Major domains of complementary and alternative medical practices; (3) Frequently asked questions (about CAM); (4) Considering CAM?; (5) NCCAM CAM research centers; (6) Want information about alternative medicine?; (7)

MEDLINE and related databases (and alternative medicine). Author, title, and subject indexes.

Intended as a companion volume to the *Consumer health information source book* (700) and as a "supplement by providing in depth access to the growing literature relating to complementary and alternative medicine."—*Pref.* For patients, other health consumers, and librarians in both public and academic libraries.

Available online via Gale's Health and Wellness Resource Center.

699 Consumer health: A guide to Internet information resources.
2nd rev. ed. Jana Liebermann, Cecilia Durkin, Medical Library Association. 213+ p. Chicago, Ill: Medical Library Association, 2004. ISBN: 0912176520; 9780912176529.

RA773.6

1st ed., 2001; (MLA BibKit; no. 7).

Contents: ch. 1, Quality matters; ch. 2, Gateways to health information on the Internet; ch. 3, Electronic libraries; ch. 4, Diseases and conditions; ch. 5, Family health issues; ch. 6, Special populations; ch. 7, Drug information sources; ch. 8, Mental health and substance abuse; ch. 9, Complementary and alternative therapies; ch. 10, Wellness and prevention; ch. 11, Health care providers; ch. 12, Hot health topics—medical news sites; Conclusion: surviving Internet overload. Designed to assist librarians in identifying quality consumer-oriented websites which are considered to be useful for patients, caregivers, and other health care consumers to better understand diseases, treatments, and healthcare issues. Includes annotated entries for a variety of resources (e.g., online guides and tutorials, medical search engines, quality filters, international gateways, electronic libraries, subject-specific websites, medical news, etc.). A chapter focuses on special populations (e.g., senior citizens, minorities, and disabled individuals). Eight appendixes: (1) Savvy health surfing; (2) Quality filters for medical websites; (3) Medical and health information databases and directories; (4) Medical dictionaries and glossaries; (5) Selected health books and pamphlets; (6) Health materials in multiple languages; (7) Easy-to-read/easy-to-understand/low literacy consumer health materials; (8) Quick guide to Internet drug information sources. Includes bibliographical references (p. 182–206) and index.

700 Consumer health information source book. 7th ed. Alan M. Rees. Westport, Conn.: Greenwood Press, 2003. ISBN: 1573565091.

016.613   Z6673.R43; RA766

A guide to popular health information in both print and electronic format on a wide variety of topics. Provides brief annotations and evaluations of approx. 2,000 selected consumer health publications in a variety of formats: books, home medical guides, popular health magazines, and newsletters. English- and Spanish-language pamphlets, and websites. Also includes information on clearinghouses and centers, toll-free hotlines, and health organizations that provide information to the general public. Contains chapters on recent developments in consumer health information on the Internet with a ranking of websites, and a description of 12 innovative libraries considered "models of excellence." Author, title, and subject indexes. Has a companion volume, T*he complementary and alternative medicine information source book* (698). Intended for consumers and reference and collection development librarians. Also available as an e-book.

701   A consumer's guide to dentistry. 2nd ed. Gordon J. Christensen. x, 214 p., color ill. St. Louis: Mosby, 2002. ISBN: 0323014836.

617.6   RK61.C57

1st ed., 1994.

Contents: Ch. 1 "How to use this book," finding solutions to your oral problems; ch. 2 "Divisions in dentistry," types of dentists; ch. 3 "Finding the right dentist," what to consider in your choice of dentists; ch. 4 "Managed care," managed care programs in dentistry; ch. 5 "Pain control," controlling pain in dentistry; ch. 6 "Infection control," infection control in the dental office; ch. 7 "Endodontics," root canals, dead teeth, inside of teeth; ch. 8 "Esthetic dentistry," cosmetic dentistry, improving your smile; ch. 9 "Geriatric dentistry," dentistry for mature people; ch. 10 "Implant dentistry," substitutes for tooth roots placed into your jaw; ch. 11 "Occlusion," your bite, the way your teeth come together, temporomandibular joints, temporomandibular dysfunction; ch. 12 "Oral and maxillofacial surgery," oral pathology, oral medicine diseases, and surgery related to the oral and facial areas; ch. 13 "Orthodontics," straightening teeth; ch. 14 "Pediatric dentistry," dentistry for children; ch. 15 "Periodontics," gums and bone surrounding teeth, ch. 16 "Prosthodontics," fixed crowns or bridges cemented onto teeth; ch. 17 "Prosthodontics," removable dentures replacing all or some teeth; ch. 18 "Restorative or operative dentistry," fillings for teeth; ch. 19 "Preventing the need for dental treatment"; ch. 20 "Additional sources of information."

Written for the dental patient, provides information about dental health and various treatment options for dental problems. Illustrations.

702 Dietary guidelines for Americans, 2005. U.S. Department of
Health [2005.] Washington: U.S. Dept. of Health and Human
Services; U.S. Dept. of Agriculture. http://purl.access.gpo.gov/
GPO/LPS57108.

Published jointly every five years by the Department of Health and
Human Services, Office of Disease Prevention and Health Promotion, the
Department of Agriculture, Center for Nutrition Policy and Promotion,
and the Agricultural Research Service.

First five editions, 1980–2000, had title *Nutrition and your health:
Dietary guidelines for Americans.* Print equivalents for these editions pub-
lished in *Home and garden bulletin* (U.S. Dept. of Agriculture) no. 232.
Current and earlier online editions linked from http://www.health.gov/
DietaryGuidelines/.

Description based on the 2005 Web edition.

Contents: ch. 1, "Background and purpose of the dietary guidelines
for Americans"; ch. 2, "Adequate nutrients within calorie needs"; ch. 3,
"Weight management"; ch. 4, "Physical activity"; ch. 5, "Food groups
to encourage"; ch. 6, "Fats"; ch. 7, "Carbohydrates"; ch. 8, "Sodium and
potassium"; ch. 9, "Alcoholic beverages"; ch. 10, "Food safety"; Appendix
A, "Eating patterns"; Appendix B, "Food sources and selected nutrients."
These guidelines provide authoritative advice for people two years old and
older about how good dietary habits can promote health and reduce risk
for major chronic diseases. Additional information and access to related
documents and resources can be found at http://www.healthierus.gov/
dietaryguidelines/.

A related title, *A healthier you: Based on the dietary guidelines for Americans*, provides practical information about healthy food choices, healthy
eating habits, and physical activity.

703 Genetics home reference. Lister Hill National Center for
Biomedical Communications, National Library of Medicine,
National Institutes of Health, Department of Health and Human
Services. 2003–. Bethesda, Md.: National Library of Medicine.
http://purl.access.gpo.gov/GPO/LPS74916.

Aims to make genetics and its relationship to disease accessible to the
general public. Information is presented in a question and answer format,
with explanation on how a disease is inherited, the symptoms, and what
treatments are available. Provides general information on genes, gene

maps, genetic markers, chromosomes, DNA, and details on the specific genes related to a particular disease. Includes a "help me understand genetics page," a glossary of genetics terms, links to clinical trials, etc. Updated as new information becomes available. A detailed description at http://www.nlm.nih.gov/pubs/factsheets/ghr.html.

704 **Health care almanac: Every person's guide to the thoughtful and practical sides of medicine.** 2nd ed. Lorri A. Zipperer, American Medical Association. xiv, 546 p. Chicago: American Medical Association, 1998. ISBN: 0899709001.
362.1097303   R104.H43

1st ed. (1993) had title: *The healthcare resource and reference guide*; rev. 1995 ed. had title: *Health care almanac: A resource guide to the medical field.*
   Addresses common queries by physicians and patients, including health and medical practice-related issues. In three sections: (1) Dictionary-style directory arranged alphabetically by subject, with the names of organizations that may be able to provide information on specific subjects; (2) Outlines major administrative units of the American Medical Association (AMA), with an historical overview since 1846; (3) Tools to help navigate the almanac: listing of sources and index which is also intended to serve cross-referencing needs. Includes "Principles of Medical Ethics," "The Hippocratic Oath," and "Patient Bill of Rights." Provides information and glossaries on managed care, tort reform, Medicare, background on terminal care and advanced directives and end-of-life issues, patient safety, home health care, etc. This print resource can be supplemented with web-based, possibly more up-to-date information found on the AMA website (American Medical Association [homepage] [451]) with its professional resources section, including online ethics resources; DoctorFinder (209); and other links.

705 **Health care resources on the Internet: A guide for librarians and health care consumers.** M. Sandra Wood. xxi, 205 p. New York: Haworth Information Press, 2000. ISBN: 0789006324.
025.0661   R119.9.H39

Contents: ch. 1, Use of the Internet at the reference desk (Nancy Calabretta); ch. 2, Natural language and beyond: tips for search services (Eric P. Delozier); ch. 3, Megasites for health care information (Cindy A. Gruwell, Scott Marsalis); ch. 4, MEDLINE on the Internet (Helen-Ann Brown, Valerie G. Rankow); ch. 5, Searching the Internet for diseases (Alexa Mayo, Cynthia R. Phyillaier); ch. 6, Consumer health information on the Internet (Janet M. Coggan); ch. 7, Alternative medicine on the Net (Suzanne M.

Shultz, Nancy I. Henry, Esther Y. Dell); ch. 8, Government resources on the Net (Nancy J. Allee); ch. 9, Health-related statistical information on the Net (Dawn M. Littleton, Kathryn Robbins); ch. 10, Electronic journals on the Internet (Virginia A. Lingle); ch. 11, Searching international medical resources on the World Wide Web (Jeri Ann Risin). Provides a list of selected websites and also general information on developing skills and techniques for Internet searching for health-related information, including evidence-based medicine. Includes a "Comparative Chart of MED-LINE Searching Systems." A practical resource, useful for librarians, health care professionals, and general readers.

Finding and using health and medical information on the Internet (London: Aslib-IMI, 2001) by Sue Welsh et al. and Sydney S. Chellen's *Essential guide to the Internet for health professionals* (London; New York: Routledge, 2003) are other guides on how to locate biomedical information effectively. Even though some of the content in these three resources needs updating, they nevertheless remain useful guides.

706   **Healthfinder.gov.** Office of Disease Prevention and Health
        Promotion (U.S.). 1997–. Washington: U.S. Department of Health
        and Human Services. http://purl.access.gpo.gov/GPO/LPS45861.
                                                                    Z6673

Healthfinder® is a project coordinated by the Office of Disease Prevention and Health Promotion (ODPHP) and its National Health Information Center.

Gateway and search engine to help locate health-related information from federal and state government agencies, clearinghouses, nonprofit organizations, and universities. Provides links to selected resources on diseases, conditions, and injuries. Tabs for an A–Z "health library" and "consumer guides" (e.g., medical errors, patient privacy, Medicare, Medicaid), with links to online publications, databases, medical dictionaries. For consumers and health professionals. Selected by the Medical Library Association (MLA) as one of its "'Top Ten' Most Useful Websites" (http://www.mlanet.org/resources/medspeak/topten.html).

707   **Health reference series (Omnigraphics, Inc.).** Karen Bellenir.
        Detroit: Omnigraphics, Inc., 1990–.

Online access to a list of titles and a link to a detailed "Contents Guide" (http://www.omnigraphics.com/category_view.php?ID=3). New editions and new and forthcoming titles in 2007 include sourcebooks on adolescent health, alcoholism, allergies, autism and developmental disorders, cancer, congenital disorders, cosmetic and reconstructive surgery, death and dying, ear, nose, and throat disorders, eating disorders, endocrine and metabolic disorders, fitness and exercise, podiatry, sports injuries, and stress-related disorders. Volumes in this series provide information on a wide variety of medical topics, including diseases, treatments, and related topics. Individual volumes contain information issued by different government agencies, professional associations, research centers, journals, and other sources. Another series appropriate for consumer health collections by the same publisher is *Teen health series.*

708 **International travel and health.** World Health Organization. 2005–. Geneva, Switzerland: World Health Organization. http://www.who.int/ith/en/.

RA638.I58

Description based on the 2007 ed., a "collaboration of travel medicine experts and end-users of *International travel and health* who have provided advice and information."—*Acknowledgments.* Also available as a print edition.

Contents: ch. 1, "Health risks and precautions: General considerations"; ch. 2, "Mode of travel: Health considerations"; ch. 3, "Environmental health risks"; ch. 4, "Injuries and violence"; ch. 5, "Infectious diseases of potential risk for travellers"; ch. 6, "Vaccine-preventable diseases and vaccines"; ch. 7, "Malaria; Country lists: Yellow fever vaccination requirements, recommendations and malaria situation."

Provides information on the main health risks for travelers at specific destinations with different modes of travel. Website also provides related links on, e.g., disease outbreaks (e.g., avian influenza, drug-resistant tuberculosis, etc.), International Health Regulations (2005) (926), and Global Health Atlas (http://www.who.int/globalatlas/). Intended for medical professionals; also useful to consumers.

Health Information for International Travel (633) is another resource for travel information.

709 **Interpretation of diagnostic tests.** 8th ed. Jacques B. Wallach. Philadelphia: Wolters Kluwer Health/Lippincott, Williams & Wilkins, 2007. ISBN: 9780781730.

616.0756 RB38.2.W35

1st ed., 1970; 7th ed., 2000. Also available online via Ovid.

Information about tests and diseases, also new technologies and techniques used in testing (e.g., genetic testing, DNA probes, and monoclonal antibodies). Includes sections on normal values, specific laboratory examinations, diseases of organ systems, and drugs and laboratory test values; also on bioterrorism. Appendixes include a list of abbreviations and acronyms, and a table of conversion factors. Subject index. Designed for clinicians, but also useful for health consumers. Available online via Books@Ovid.

Similar print titles include *Laboratory tests and diagnostic procedures* (318), *Mosby's manual of diagnostic and laboratory tests* (325), and *Tietz clinical guide to laboratory tests* (334); a web-based resource is *Lab tests online: a public resource on clinical lab testing from the laboratory professionals who do the testing* (Washington: American Association for Clinical Chemistry, 2001–).

710   **MayoClinic.com.** Mayo Foundation for Medical Education and Research, Mayo Clinic. 1998–. [Rochester, Minn.]: Mayo Foundation for Medical Education and Research. http://www.mayoclinic.com/.

RA776.5

Formerly had title: Mayo Health Oasis.

Searchable website. Separate pages for diseases and conditions A–Z and first aid, drugs (prescription and over-the-counter drug information from Micromedex [1084]) and supplements (with information from Natural Standard [1277]), treatment decisions, healthy living (i.e., collection of information and tools to provide help to stay healthy). "Ask a specialist" (i.e., Mayo Clinic specialists answer select questions from readers).

In addition to MedlinePlus (463) and this website, there are many other sites that receive excellent reviews and are frequently used by consumers. Some prominent examples include Familydoctor.org (http://familydoctor.org/), Hardin MD (457), NetWellness (http://www.netwellness.org/), NOAH: New York Online Access to Health (http://www.noahhealth.org/), and WebMD (http://www.webmd.com/).

711   **The Medical Library Association consumer health reference service handbook.** Donald A. Barclay, Deborah D. Halsted, Medical Library Association. xxv, 197 p., ill. New York: Neal-Schuman Publ., 2001. ISBN: 1555704182.

025.0661   RA776.B234

Contents: pt. 1, Consumer health essentials for librarians; pt. 2, Consumer health resources for librarians; pt. 3, Consumer health services for libraries. Information for librarians providing consumer health services. Includes standard sources for answering questions, selected consumer health websites, and also methods that can be used to establish consumer health information services. CD-ROM includes templates for developing a consumer health website. Includes bibliographical references and index.

712   **The Medical Library Association encyclopedic guide to searching and finding health information on the Web.** P. F. Anderson, Nancy J. Allee. 3 v. New York: Neal-Schuman Publ., 2004. ISBN: 1555704948.

025.0661   R859.7.I58M436

Contents: v. 1, Search strategies/quick reference guide; v. 2, Diseases and disorders/mental health and mental disorders; v. 3, Health and wellness/life stages and reproduction, and cumulative index. A comprehensive guide written by experienced health sciences librarians. Recommends search terms, search strategies, and search engines for checking the Internet for answers to health-related questions. Useful for both health care consumers and librarians involved in teaching health information literacy. Companion website at http://www-personal.umich.edu/~pfa/mlaguide/indextest.html. Also available on CD-ROM, with search capability and links to over 11,000 websites.

713   **The Medical Library Association guide to cancer information: Authoritative, patient-friendly print and electronic resources.** Ruti Malis Volk, Medical Library Association. New York: Neal-Schuman, 2007. ISBN: 9781555705855.

616.9940025   RC262.M427

Contents: pt. I: Key resources for finding cancer information; pt. II, Key resources for finding information on specific types of cancer. A guide for medical, academic, and public libraries to help in the provision of reliable cancer information for patients, caregivers, and other healthcare consumers. May also prove to be helpful for building consumer health collections. Includes "concepts and terminology followed by in-depth descriptions of twenty-five specific types of adult cancer and ten childhood cancers" (*Publ. notes*) and cancer-related topics (e.g., chemotherapy, radiation, nutrition, fertility, cancer prevention, cancer quality-of-life issues and supportive care), with a detailed list of authoritative resources in various formats (print, audiovisuals, electronic) and for different users. Index.

714   **MedlinePlus.** U.S. National Library of Medicine. 1998–. Bethesda,
       Md.: U.S. Dept. of Health and Human Services, National Library
       of Medicine. http://medlineplus.gov/.

025.04; 651.504261; 613   RA776.5

MedlinePlus®

   A consumer health reference database with information from the
National Library of Medicine (NLM) (427), the National Institutes of
Health (NIH) (470), other government agencies, and various health-
related organizations. A continually expanding and updated resource.
Information on over 700 diseases and conditions, as well as drug information (prescription, nonprescription), herbs and supplements, an illustrated medical encyclopedia and dictionary, interactive patient tutorials,
lists of hospitals, physicians, and dentists, and health news. Provides preformulated MEDLINE (425)/PubMed® (432) searches for recent articles.
Includes *NIH MedlinePlus Magazine*, a new quarterly guide for patients
and their families, providing authoritative medical and healthcare information. "MedlinePlus en español" toggles between English and Spanish.
Provides links to browse selected health information in multiple languages
other than English and Spanish at http://www.nlm.nih.gov/medlineplus/
languages/languages.html. "Go Local" links users to relevant health information in their own city, county, and state. Detailed descriptive information is available at http://www.nlm.nih.gov/pubs/factsheets/medlineplus.
html.

715   **National guideline clearinghouse.** Agency for Healthcare Research
       and Quality, American Medical Association, American Association
       of Health Plans. 1998–. [Rockville, Md.]: Agency for Healthcare
       Research and Quality. http://www.guideline.gov/.

                                                                       R723.7

Originally created by Agency for Healthcare Research and Quality (AHQR)
(733), American Medical Association (AMA) (451), and American Association of Health Plans (now America's Health Insurance Plans [AHIP]).

   Contains evidence-based clinical practice guidelines, protocols, and
related documents, with searching and browsing options. Searchable by
keyword, disease/condition, treatment/intervention, guideline category,
organization and organization type, intended user, clinical specialty,
methods to assess and analyze evidence, etc. Related resources (http://
www.guideline.gov/resources/resources.aspx) include annotated bibliographies, bioterrorism resources, a glossary, guideline archive (lists withdrawn or superseded guidelines), guideline index (complete listing of

the guideline summaries available on the website), National Library of Medicine (NLM) and National Center for Biotechnology Information (NCBI) links (PubMed [432], Health Services Technology Assessment Texts [HSTAT], part of the NCBI Bookshelf http://www.ncbi.nlm.nih.gov/entrez/query.fcgi?db=Books&itool=toolbar), patient resources links, and others.

Other related sites include National Quality Measures Clearinghouse (NQMC) (889) and Quality Tools (892).

716 **National Library of Medicine guide to finding health information.** National Library of Medicine. 2001–. Bethesda, Md.: National Institutes of Health. http://www.nlm.nih.gov/services/guide.html.

Contents: How Can the National Library of Medicine Help Me with My Research?; Why Should I Go to a Public Library, and What Can I Find There?; What Other Resources Can I Find at a Medical Library, and How Do I Find One That Is Open to Me?; How Can I Get Information From Other Government or Health-Related Organizations?; How Do I Search for Other Medical Information on the Web?; How Do I Evaluate the Information I Find?

Overview and starting points for researchers concerning services provided by the National Library of Medicine, other government agencies, and health-related organizations. Provides links to consumer health information resources and professional health literature resources.

717 **NORD guide to rare disorders.** National Organization for Rare Disorders. lxiv, 895 p., [16] p. of plates, ill. (some color). Philadelphia: Lippincott, Williams & Wilkins, 2003. ISBN: 0781730635.

616   RC48.8.N385

NORD (National Organization for Rare Disorders) is "a non-profit voluntary health agency dedicated to the identification, treatment, and cure of all orphan diseases."—*Pref.*

Contents: ch. 1, Autoimmune & connective tissue disorders; ch. 2, Cardiovascular disorders; ch. 3, Chromosomal disorders; ch. 4, Dermatologic disorders; ch. 5, Dysmorphic disorders; ch. 6, Emerging/infectious diseases; ch. 7, Endocrine disorders; ch. 8, Gastroenterologic disorders; ch. 9, Hematologic/oncologic disorders; ch. 10, Inborn errors of metabolism; ch. 11, Neurologic disorders; ch. 12, Neuromuscular disorders; ch. 13, Ophthalmologic disorders; ch. 14, Pulmonary disorders; ch. 15, Renal disorders; ch. 16, Skeletal disorders.

At what point a disease is considered rare differs among countries. In the U.S., a disease is considered a rare or an "orphan" disease if it is a low-incidence disease that affects fewer than 200,000 people. This resource "covers about 800 of the estimated 6,000 rare diseases [and] presents many of the signs and symptoms that can be an aid in the diagnosis and differentiation of rare diseases in addition to possible treatment."—*Foreword.* Lists resources which provide help to patients and families affected by a rare disorder. Includes a "List of Orphan Products Approved for Marketing." Index. For physicians and other health professionals, patients, and students. Other resources in this area can be located via National Organization for Rare Disorders, Inc. (428) and NIH's Office of Rare Diseases (476).

718 **Nutrition.gov.** Food and Nutrition Information Center. Beltsville, Md.: National Agricultural Library. http://www.nutrition.gov.

RA784

Maintained by Food and Nutrition Information Center (FNIC).

Access to information from across the federal government on food, food safety, nutrition, healthy eating, dietary supplements, and physical fitness. Includes specialized nutrition information for infants, children, teens, adult women and men, and seniors, as well as the latest nutrition-related news. Provides search capabilities and resource lists for different audiences, e.g., caregivers, consumers, health care workers, kids and teens, parents, researchers, and teachers.

Healthier US (http://www.healthierus.gov) provides access to consumer resources concerning nutrition, physical fitness, and disease.

719 **Quackwatch.** Stephen Barrett. [1996]–. [Allentown, Pa.]: Stephen Barrett, MD http://www.quackwatch.org.

615.8   R730

Founded in 1969 as the Lehigh Valley Committee Against Health Fraud, incorporated in 1970. Assumed its current name in 1997. Maintained by Dr. S. Barrett and a network of volunteers and expert advisors. Affiliated with the National Council Against Health Fraud (http://www.ncahf.com/) and Bioethics Watch (http://www.bioethicswatch.org/).

"Nonprofit corporation whose purpose is to combat health-related frauds, myths, fads, fallacies, and misconduct. Its primary focus is on quackery-related information that is difficult or impossible to get elsewhere. Activities include: Investigating questionable claims; Answering inquiries about products and services; Advising quackery victims; Distributing reliable publications; Debunking pseudoscientific claims; Reporting illegal marketing; Assisting or generating consumer-protection lawsuits; Improving the quality of health information on the Internet; Attacking misleading advertising on the Internet."—*Website*

In addition, includes a list of websites that provide access to 21 special areas—autism, chiropractic, dentistry, diet and nutrition, mental health, and other topics of interest to consumers. Its "Internet Health Pilot" site provides links to many other reliable health sites; its "Casewatch" site contains legal matters and regulatory issues. The contents of all sites can be searched simultaneously or individually (http://www.quackwatch.org/wgsearch.html).

720   The rights of patients: The authoritative ACLU guide to the rights of patients. 3rd ed. George J. Annas. xxi, 387 p. Carbondale, Ill.: Southern Illinois University Press, 2004. ISBN: 0809325152.
344.7303211   KF3823.A96

Title varies: 1st ed., 1975, had title: *The rights of hospital patients: The basic ACLU guide to a hospital patient's rights*; 2nd ed., 1989, had title: *The rights of patients: The basic ACLU guide to patient rights.*

American Civil Liberties Union (ACLU).

(ACLU handbook series).

Contents: (I) Patient rights; (II) The patient rights advocate; (III) Reforming American medicine; (IV) Hospitals; (V) Emergency medicine; (VI) Informed choice; (VII) Choices about surgery and children's care; (VIII) Reproductive health; (IX) Research; (X) Medical records; (XI) Privacy and confidentiality; (XII) Care of the dying; (XIII) Suffering, pain, and suicide; (XIV) Death, organ donation, and autopsy; (XV) Patient safety and medical malpractice. Appendixes: (A) Internet resources; (B) Convention on human rights and biomedicine; (C) Childbearing patient bill of rights. Index.

"Offers fully documented exposition and explanation of the rights of patients from birth to death. A resource not only for patients and their families but also for physicians, hospital administrators, medical and nursing students, and other health care workers."—*Publ. notes.* Emphasizes the importance of having a patient rights advocate, with a section "tips for advocates" in most chapters.

721   What your patients need to know about psychiatric medications. Robert E. Hales, Stuart C. Yudofsky, Robert H. Chew. xvii, 356 p. Washington: American Psychiatric Publishing, 2005. ISBN: 1585622036.
615.788   RM315.H328

Contents: "Medications in pregnancy"; "Antianxiety medication"; "Medications for treatment of insomnia"; "Antidepressants: Selective serotonin reuptake inhibitors and mixed-action antidepressants"; "Tricyclic antidepressants"; "Monoamine oxidase inhibitors"; "Mood stabilizers"; "First-generation antipsychotics"; "Second-generation antipsychotics"; "Treatment of attention-deficit/hyperactivity disorder in adults"; "Stimulants"; "Cognitive enhancers for treatment of Alzheimer's disease and other forms of dementia"; index.

Provides relevant and easy-to-understand information about commonly asked questions about psychiatric medications. Information about each medication presented in a standard format: brand name; generic name; available strengths; available in generic; medication class; general information; dosing information; common side effects; adverse reactions and precautions; use in pregnancy and breastfeeding; possible drug interactions; overdose; special considerations. Accompanied by CD-ROM that contains PDF files of the pages as they appear in the book. Also available as part of Psychiatry Online (1294).

Handbooks

722   **Handbook of non-prescription drugs.** American Pharmaceutical Association. ill. Washington: American Pharmaceutical Association, 1967–. ISSN: 0889-7816.

615.105   RS250.N66

Title varies: *Handbook of nonprescription drugs: An interactive approach to self-care.* Description based on 15th ed., 2006.

Contents: sec. 1, "The practitioner's role in self-care"; sec. 2, "Pain and fever disorders"; sec. 3, "Reproductive and genital disorders"; sec. 4, "Respiratory disorders"; sec. 5, "Gastrointestinal disorders"; sec. 6, "Nutrition and nutritional supplementation"; sec. 7, "Ophthalmic, otic, and oral disorders"; sec. 8, "Dermatologic disorders"; sec. 9, "Other medical disorders"; sec. 10, "Home medical equipment"; sec. 11, "Complementary and alternative medicine"; appendix 1, "Pregnancy and lactation risk categories for selected nonprescription medications and nutritional supplements"; appendix 2, "Botanical medicines to avoid in pregnancy and lactation."

A compilation of facts on home remedies in 55 chapters with broad headings, such as asthma, diabetes mellitus, headache, musculoskeletal injuries and disorders, sexually transmitted infections, etc. Each chapter includes a case study in outline format and discusses the etiology of the condition; the anatomy, physiology, and pathophysiology of the affected systems; the signs and symptoms; the treatment and adjunctive measures; an evaluation of ingredients in over-the-counter products; and important patient and product considerations. Bibliographic references at the end of each chapter. Subject index. Useful for pharmacists, other health professionals, and consumers. E-book download available with 15th edition.

723   Medicare handbook. Center for Medicare Advocacy. New York: Aspen Publishers, c2000–. ISSN: 1530-8979.

368   KF3608.A4M436

Description based on 2007 ed. Contents: (1) An introduction to Medicare coverage and appeals; (2) Hospital coverage; (3) Skilled nursing facility coverage; (4) Home health coverage; (5) Hospice coverage; (6) Medicare Part B: supplemental medical insurance; (7) Medicare-Advantage: coordinated care plans, private fee-for-service, and other delivery of services options; (8) Medigap services; (9) Medicare's relationship with private insurance; (10) Dual eligibility: issues for Medicare beneficiaries also eligible for Medicaid; (11) Prescription drug coverage. Resource to help understand Medicare's rules and regulations. Further helpful, detailed information can also be found on the Medicare website (Medicare: the official U.S. government site for people with medicare at http://www.medicare.gov), part of the Centers for Medicare & Medicaid Services (742).

724   The Merck manuals. Merck and Co. 1995–. Whitehouse Station, N.J.: Merck and Co. http://www.merck.com/pubs/.

"A trusted source for medical information." —*Website*

Overview of the various titles and editions of the Merck manuals, organized in categories by user group, with information about online availability, online in other languages, as printed book or PDA download, and appropriate links. Under "patients and caregivers" lists the *Merck manual of medical information—home edition* (Whitehouse Station, N.J.: Merck Research Laboratories, 2003) (available online, online in other languages, and also as printed book) and the *Merck manual of health and aging* (available online and as printed book). Under "healthcare professionals" lists the *Merck manual of diagnosis and therapy* (Rahway, N.J.: Merck, 1950–) (available online, online in other languages, as PDA download, and as printed book); *Merck manual of geriatrics* (available online, online in other languages, and as printed book). The listing also includes under "chemists" the *Merck index* (Whitehouse Station, N.J.: Merck, 2006) (available online and available as printed book) and the *Merck veterinary manual* (Rahway, N.J.: Merck and Co., 1955–) (available online, as PDA download, and as printed book).

MerckSource (http://www.mercksource.com/pp/us/cns/cns_home. jsp) is a related website intended for healthcare consumers as a good starting point, together with MedlinePlus [463]. It provides information concerning medical conditions, health news, searches topics in Spanish. Its "resource library" and "health tool" tabs provide additional useful information.

725 **The nutrition desk reference.** 3rd ed. Robert H. Garrison, Elizabeth Somer. xxii, 663 p., ill. New Canaan, Conn.: Keats, 1995. ISBN: 0879836652.

613.2 QP141.G33

1st ed., 1985; 2nd ed., 1990. Description based on 3rd online ed., also available online since 2000 via netLibrary.

Contents: pt. 1, "Dietary factors"; pt. 2, "Nutrition and cancer"; pt. 3, "Nutrition and cardiovascular disease"; pt. 4, "Nutrition and disease"; pt. 5, "Dietary recommendations."

Presents basic nutrition information, biochemical explanations, and important nutrition-related topics in concise format and readable style. For health professionals and general readers. Figures, tables, glossary, and index. Also available via netLibrary. Information found in this desk reference can be updated with online publications, for example, via PubMed (432) and Nutrition (MedlinePlus) (763) and other nutrition-related pages in MedlinePlus (463).

726 **Patients' rights in the age of managed health care.** Lisa Yount. 280 p. New York: Facts On File, 2001. ISBN: 0816042586.

344.73041 KF3823.Y68

Provides overview of the issues in health care delivery, patients' rights and applicable laws, a chronology of significant events, and also a guide to further research in patients' rights issues. Glossary, index, and annotated bibliography. *The rights of patients: The authoritative ACLU guide to the rights of patients* (600) provides further information.

727 **USP DI.** United States Pharmacopeial Convention. Greenwood Village, Colo.: Thomson Micromedex, 1982–. ISSN: 0740-6916.

615.1 RM300.U83

1980–81 ed. had title: *United States pharmacopeia dispensing information: USP DI.* Since 1982, *USP DI®* (United States Pharmacopeial Convention Drug Information), issued in three volumes. Subtitle varies. Publ. varies: since 1998 publ. by Thomson Micromedex.

Description based on 27th ed., 2007, 3 v.: v. 1, *Drug information for the health care professional*; v. 2, *Advice for the patient®: Drug information in lay language*; v. 3, *Approved drug products and legal requirements.* Vol. 1 and 2 are also available online via Micromedex® Healthcare Series (1084). However, title of v. 2 of the online edition was changed in 2007 to *Detailed drug information for the consumer™.*

"The drug information in the *USP DI* represents the evidence-based conclusions of 35 expert advisory panels who have meticulously reviewed all material to ensure its accuracy and currency."—*Pref.* Vol. 1 lists DI monographs in alphabetic order by chemical name, with information on use, pharmacology, precautions, side effects, dosage information, etc. The index includes established names, cross-references by brand names (U.S. and Canadian), and older nonproprietary names. Vol. 2 is written for consumers in "patient-friendly language" and printed in large type. Includes numerous appendixes, including "precaution listings" (e.g., pregnancy, pediatrics, geriatrics, dental, athletes). Vol. 3 answers legal and regulatory questions, and questions about discontinued drugs. Also addresses generic substitution for brand names and provides extensive information from the FDA, including its Electronic Orange Book: Approved Drug Products with Therapeutic Equivalence Evaluations (1158).

Indexes; Abstract journals; Databases

728   Dietary supplements labels database. National Library of Medicine (U.S.). 2007–. Bethesda, Md.: National Library of Medicine. http://dietarysupplements.nlm.nih.gov/dietary/.

Produced by National Library of Medicine (NLM) (427), Specialized Information Services (SIS); based on Dietary Supplements On-Line Database.

Offers information on the ingredients of more than 2,000 selected brands of dietary supplements in the United States. Searchable by brand name, uses noted on the product, specific active ingredient, and manufacturer. Intended for researchers and consumers. Answers many questions users of dietary supplements might have concerning ingredients shown on labels of specific brands, chemical ingredients, animal products, proven medical benefits, toxicity of specific ingredients, etc. Ingredients of dietary supplements are linked to other NLM databases, e.g., MedlinePlus (463) and PubMed (432). Helpful FAQ section.

729 **Drug information portal.** National Library of Medicine (U.S.). 2008–. Bethesda, Md.: National Library of Medicine. http://druginfo.nlm.nih.gov/.

"Gateway to selected drug information from the National Library of Medicine (427) and other key government agencies [with] access to over 12,000 selected drugs."—*About This Portal.* Can be searched by a drug's trade or generic name. Provides a summary of the information about the drug, and links to further related information, such as MedlinePlus (463), AIDSinfo (447), MEDLINE (425)/PubMed® (432), LactMed (1572), HSDB (1569), Dietary Supplements Labels Database (728), TOXLINE (1578), DailyMed (626), ClinicalTrials.gov (191), PubChem (444), ChemIDplus (1563), Drugs@FDA (1283), and others. For the public, health care professionals, and researchers.

730 **NLM gateway.** National Library of Medicine (U.S.). 2000–. Bethesda, Md.: National Library of Medicine. http://gateway.nlm. nih.gov/.

RA11

Allows simultaneous searching of information resources at the National Library of Medicine (NLM). Databases include MEDLINE (425)/PubMed (432) and the NLM Catalog (482) as well as other resources, including information on current clinical trials and consumer health information (MedlinePlus [463]). Currently provides access to 21 databases and other information resources (for a complete list of databases and other details, see http://www.nlm.nih.gov/pubs/factsheets/gateway.html). An overview of the search results is presented in several categories (bibliographic resources, consumer health resources, and other information), with a listing of the individual databases and the number of results within these categories.

731 **PubMed.** U.S. National Center for Biotechnology Information, National Library of Medicine, National Institutes of Health. 1996–. Bethesda, Md.: U.S. National Center for Biotechnology Information. http://www.ncbi.nlm.nih.gov/sites/entrez/.

PubMed®, developed and maintained by the National Center for Biotechnology Information (NCBI) at the National Library of Medicine®

(NLM) (427). It is available via the NCBI Entrez (3) retrieval system. PubMed also provides access to the other Entrez molecular biology resources (*PubMed Overview*). Starting May 23, 2007, NCBI is changing to a new version of Entrez in a phased implementation (cf. Nahin AM. New and Improved PubMed®/Entrez and New URL *NLM tech. bull.*, 2007 May–Jun.; [356]: http://www.nlm.nih.gov/pubs/techbull/mj07/mj07_issue_cover.html).

Provides a search interface for more than 16 million bibliographic citations and abstracts in the fields of medicine, nursing, dentistry, veterinary medicine, health care systems, and preclinical sciences. It provides access to articles indexed for MEDLINE® (425) and for selected life sciences journals. PubMed subsets found under the "Limits" tab are: MEDLINE and PubMed Central®, several journal groups (i.e., core clinical journals, dental journals, and nursing journals), and topical subsets (AIDS, bioethics, cancer, complementary medicine, history of medicine, space life sciences, systematic reviews, and toxicology). "Linkout" provides access to full-text articles.

For detailed information see the PubMed fact sheet at http://www.nlm.nih.gov/pubs/factsheets/pubmed.html. For a brief overview of searching PubMed, see the PubMed Quick Start at http://www.ncbi.nlm.nih.gov/books/bv.fcgi?rid=helppubmed.section.pubmedhelp.PubMed_Quick_Start. For details on the now completed OLDMEDLINE retrospective conversion projects, see http://www.nlm.nih.gov/pubs/techbull/so06/so06_oldmedline_status.html.

732 **State cancer legislative database program (SCLD).** National Cancer Institute. Bethesda, Md.: National Cancer Institute, National Institutes of Health. http://www.scld-nci.net/index.cfml.

Database providing summaries of state laws and resolutions on the major cancers and cancer-related topics. Kept up-to-date via *SCLD update.* A site map (http://www.scld-nci.net/sitemap.cfml) provides easy access to the various information products associated with the SCLD program. Considered a resource for a variety of audiences, including universities and research centers, professional organizations, and the public.

Internet Resources

733 **Agency for Healthcare Research and Quality (AHRQ).** Agency for Healthcare Research and Quality (U.S.). 1990s–. Rockville, Md.: Agency for Healthcare Research and Quality. http://www.ahrq.gov.

"The Agency for Healthcare Research and Quality (AHRQ) is the lead Federal agency charged with improving the quality, safety, efficiency, and effectiveness of health care for all Americans. As one of 12 agencies within the Department of Health and Human Services, AHRQ supports health services research that will improve the quality of health care and promote evidence-based decision making."—*AHRQ at a glance (http://www.ahrq. gov/about/ataglance.htm)*

Searchable website ("search AHRQ" and "A–Z Quick Menu") provides access to a variety of resources, with links to clinical and consumer health information, research findings, funding opportunities, data and surveys, quality assessment, specific populations (minorities, women, elderly, and others), and public health preparedness (bioterrorism and response). Links to a large number of full-text documents, including links to the tools, literature, and news in patient safety (e.g., *AHRQ patient safety network*) and tips on how to prevent medical errors.

734 **AIDSinfo.** U.S. Department of Health and Human Services, National Institutes of Health (U.S.), AIDS Clinical Trials Information Service. Bethesda, Md.: National Institutes of Health. http://www.aidsinfo.nih.gov.

RA643.8

Result of merging two previous U.S. Dept. of Health and Human Services (DHHS) projects. Supersedes the AIDS Clinical Trials Information Service (ACTIS) and the HIV/AIDS Treatment Information Service (ATIS).

Resource for current information on federally and privately funded clinical trials for AIDS patients and HIV-infected persons, federally approved HIV treatment and prevention guidelines, and medical practice guidelines. Provides access to a searchable HIV/AIDS drugs database (via "Drugs" tab) that includes approved and investigational anti-HIV medications, including side effects, dosages, and interactions with other drugs or food; also access to brochures, fact sheets, and other Web resources on HIV/AIDS, current and archived versions of DHHS guidelines, and a searchable HIV glossary (English and Spanish). For HIV/AIDS patients, the general public, health care providers, and researchers.

Additional major HIV/AIDS resources can be accessed via the following sites: Fact sheet, AIDS Information Resources (http://www.nlm. nih.gov/pubs/factsheets/aidsinfs.html), Specialized Information Services: HIV/AIDS Information (http://sis.nlm.nih.gov/hiv.html), CDC National

Prevention Information Network (NPIN) (http://www.cdcnpin.org/scripts/hiv/index.asp), UNAIDS: Joint United National Programming on HIV/AIDS (http://www.unaids.org/en/), and AIDS Treatment Data Network (http://www.atdn.org/).

735   American Academy of Family Physicians [homepage]. American Academy of Family Physicians. 1998–. Leawood, Kan.: American Academy of Family Physicians. http://www.aafp.org/online/en/home.html.

616.007; 610.9206   R130.3

Searchable website with resources for AAFP (American Academy of Family Physicians) members, residents, students, patients, and the general public. Contains information, software, photographs, graphics, and other materials, providing access to information on a variety of clinical and research resources for medical and healthcare topics. Examples are "Familydoctor.org" (http://familydoctor.org/online/famdocen/home.html), an online "Dictionary of common Medical Terms," health trackers, health calculators, how to find a family doctor (http://familydoctor.org/cgi-bin/memdir.pl), and "Conditions A to Z" (http://familydoctor.org/online/famdocen/home/common.html), also available as (*AAFP conditions A to Z* via STAT!Ref). Also provides public health resources on various topics (http://www.aafp.org/online/en/home/clinical/publichealth.html) e.g., cultural proficiency, health disparities/minority health, disease prevention, etc.

736   American Academy of Pediatrics. American Academy of Pediatrics. 1995–. Elk Grove Village, Ill.: American Academy of Pediatrics. http://www.aap.org/.

610.9206; 618.92

American Academy of Pediatrics (AAP) official website.

   This searchable website provides information for health consumers on various topics of concern to parents relating to the health and safety of children (e.g., finding a pediatrician, various diseases and conditions, immunization, behavioral and mental health topics, car safety seats, Internet safety, toy safety resources, and many others). Also provides information for AAP members and other medical professionals, such as links to AAP policy statements and clinical practice guidelines, and access to Red Book® Online which includes the latest clinically tested guidelines of approx. 200 conditions. Also provides information on professional education, research, clinical and technical reports by or endorsed by the AAP, other AAP publications, etc.

737   American Cancer Society [homepage]. American Cancer Society. 1990s–. Atlanta: American Cancer Society. http://www.cancer.org.
RC261

Cancer information presented for health professionals, patients, and other health consumers. Includes the full text of *Cancer facts and figures* (515) and other statistics, providing incidence and trends of the major types of cancer survival rates and distribution of cancer by race and ethnicity. Also includes support programs and services, resources for healthy living, clinical trials, treatment decisions, tools to understand treatment options (including alternative treatments, and possible side effects), and an online glossary of cancer-related terms. Information in English and Spanish. Also contains Asian-language cancer education materials.

738   American Dental Association. American Dental Association. 1995–. Chicago: American Dental Association. http://www.ada.org/.

Official website of the American Dental Association (ADA), founded in 1859.

Provides information for dental professionals concerning education and testing, practice management, and patient care. Includes a list of dental schools (http://www.ada.org/prof/ed/programs/search_ddsdmd_us.asp), accreditation, and licensure, and links to national dental organizations. Resources for consumers include, for example, "Oral Health Topics A–Z" (http://www.ada.org/public/topics/alpha.asp), "Find a dentist" (http://www.ada.org/public/disclaimer.asp), and a "Glossary of dental terms" (http://www.ada.org/public/resources/glossary.asp). Includes a "History of Medicine" timeline (Ancient Origins, Middle Ages–Renaissance, 18th century, 19th century, 20th century) (http://www.ada.org/public/resources/history/index.asp), and a selected bibliography of history of dentistry books found in the ADA Library. Some of the resources are restricted to ADA members.

739   Association of Cancer Online Resources (ACOR). Association of Cancer Online Resources (ACOR). 1995–. New York: Association of Cancer Online Resources, Inc. http://acor.org/.

Contents: Mailing lists; Support & resources; Types of cancer; Treatment options; Clinical trials; Publications; Partnerships; Help ACOR.

"ACOR is a unique collection of online communities designed to provide timely and accurate information in a supportive environment" (*Website*), developing and hosting Internet-based knowledge systems to make it possible to find and use relevant cancer information and oncology resources. ACOR publications include a bibliography of cancer books, a series of cancer fact sheets, and the latest scientific abstracts relating to cancer. Contains links to the National Cancer Institute (166).

740 Biodefense and bioterrorism (MedlinePlus). National Library of Medicine (U.S.), National Institutes of Health (U.S.). 2000–. Washington: U.S. National Library of Medicine, National Institutes of Health, Dept. of Health and Human Services. http://www.nlm. nih.gov/medlineplus/biodefenseandbioterrorism.html.

A Health Topic within MedlinePlus (463). Contents: Overviews; Treatment; Prevention/Screening; Alternative medicine; Coping; Specific conditions; Related issues; Pictures and photographs; Research; Journal articles; Dictionaries/Glossaries; Directories; Organizations; Law and policy; Children.

Collection of links from a variety of government agencies, professional associations, and organizations, with representative bioterrorism resources selections from the Centers for Disease Control and Prevention (CDC) (940), National Institute of Allergy and Infectious Diseases, American Medical Association, American Academy of Family Physicians, American Psychiatric Association, Dept. of Homeland Security, and others. Listing and map for identifying local biodefense and bioterrorism services (via "Go Local" http://www.nlm.nih.gov/medlineplus/golocal/index.html). Related information also at Disaster preparation and recovery (MedlinePlus) (746), Emergency preparedness and response (CDC) (1485), and the World Health Organization's "Bioterrorism" page (http://www.who. int/topics/bioterrorism/en/) provides additional resources and links.

741 Cancer.gov. National Cancer Institute. 1990s–. Bethesda, Md.: National Cancer Institute. http://www.cancer.gov/.

A metasite for cancer information for health care professionals as well as patients. Provides extensive information on all aspects of cancer as a disease and current cancer treatment, including, for example, complementary and alternative medicine, screening, prevention, and genetics. Links for searching the PubMed (432) cancer literature subset and PDQ Query at http://www.cancer.gov/cancertopics/pdq/cancerdatabase.

742   **Centers for Medicare and Medicaid services (U.S.).** Centers for
Medicare and Medicaid Services (U.S.), U.S. Health Care Financing
Administration. 2001–. Baltimore, Md.: Centers for Medicare
and Medicaid Services, U.S. Dept. of Health and Human Services.
http://cms.hhs.gov/.

Centers for Medicare and Medicaid Services (CMS), formerly Health Care
Financing Administration.

Detailed information on Medicare, the federal health insurance
program for people 65 years and older and for younger people with
certain disabilities, providing details on enrollment, benefits, and other
data; Medicaid, a joint federal and state program (state programs vary
from state to state) that helps with medical costs for people with low
income and limited means; SCHIP (State Children's Health Insurance
Program); regulation and guidance manuals and Health Insurance Portability and Accountability Act (HIPAA), research, statistics, data and
systems. Also provides various tools and resources helpful in navigating
this website (http://www.cms.hhs.gov/home/tools.asp), for example a
"participating physician directory," a "glossary tool" and an "acronym
lookup tool."

743   **Dental health (MedlinePlus).** National Library of Medicine
(U.S.), National Institutes of Health (U.S.). 200?–. Bethesda, Md.:
U.S. National Library of Medicine, National Institutes of Health,
Dept. of Health and Human Services. http://www.nlm.nih.gov/
medlineplus/dentalhealth.html.

A Health Topic within MedlinePlus (463). Collection of links to information from government agencies and professional associations and
organizations, with access to selected oral health resources. Provides
basic information, research findings, a "reference shelf" with dental dic-
tionaries/glossaries, directories, organizations, statistics, etc. "Go Local"
link helps to identify services and providers for dental health in the U.S.
Website also provides links to related MedlinePlus topics, e.g., child dental
health, cosmetic dentistry, orthodontia, and others.

744   **DermAtlas.** Bernard A. Cohen, Christoph U. Lehmann, Johns
Hopkins University. 2000–. Baltimore: Johns Hopkins University.
http://www.dermatlas.org.

International collaborative project providing access to a growing collection of dermatology images. As of Mar. 2010, contains more than 11,550

images by more than 500 contributors. Searchable by keywords, diagnosis, category of disease, body site, and pigmentation. Also provides links to other dermatology websites. For health care professionals, patients, and other health care consumers.

DermIS (http://www.dermis.net/dermisroot/en/home/index.htm) is another example of an online collection of dermatology images and links to related information from various academic institutions worldwide.

745 Directories (MedlinePlus). National Library of Medicine (U.S.),
National Institutes of Health (U.S.). 200?–. Bethesda, Md.: U.S.
National Library of Medicine, National Institutes of Health,
Dept. of Health and Human Services. http://www.nlm.nih.gov/
medlineplus/directories.html.

RC48

Pt. of MedlinePlus (463).

Contents: Doctors and dentists—general; Hospital and clinics—general; Doctors and dentists—specialists; Other healthcare providers; Hospitals and clinics—specialized; Other healthcare facilities and services; Libraries.

Links to directories to help find health professionals, services, and facilities. Includes, for example, access to the American Medical Association's DoctorFinder (209), how to find a dentist, a Medicare participants physicians directory, and many others.

746 Disaster preparation and recovery (MedlinePlus). National
Library of Medicine (U.S.), National Institutes of Health (U.S.).
2000–. Washington: National Library of Medicine. http://www.
nlm.nih.gov/medlineplus/disasterpreparationandrecovery.html.

Disaster preparation and recovery guides for the public from various organizations including the Dept. of Homeland Security, Federal Emergency Management Agency, American Red Cross, and Centers for Disease Control and Prevention (940). Listing of MedlinePlus (463) "related topics" pages and links, e.g., Biodefense and Bioterrorism (MedlinePlus) (740), coping with disasters, posttraumatic stress disorder, safety issues, and others.

747 Drug abuse (MedlinePlus). National Library of Medicine (U.S.).
2000?–. Bethesda, Md.: National Library of Medicine. http://www.
nlm.nih.gov/medlineplus/drugabuse.html.

A Health Topic in MedlinePlus (463).

Contents: Overviews; Latest News; Diagnosis/Symptoms; Treatment; Prevention/Screening; Specific Conditions; Related Issues; Pictures and Photographs; Games; Clinical Trials; Research; Journal Articles; Dictionaries/Glossaries; Directories; Organizations; Newsletters/Print Publications; Law and Policy; Statistics; Children; Teenagers; Men; Women; Seniors; Other Languages.

Collection of links on substance abuse from a variety of government agencies, professional associations, and organizations, such as the National Institute on Drug Abuse (1505), the Office of National Drug Control, Substance Abuse and Mental Health Services Administration (SAMHSA) (769), National Library of Medicine (427), American Medical Association (451), American Academy of Family Physicians (448), and others. Also links to related MedlinePlus topics, e.g., alcoholism, prescription drug abuse, and substance abuse, to name a few.

748   Drug information portal. National Library of Medicine (U.S.). 2008–. Bethesda, Md.: National Library of Medicine. http://druginfo.nlm.nih.gov/.

"Gateway to selected drug information from the National Library of Medicine (427) and other key government agencies. [with] access to over 12,000 selected drugs."—*About This Portal.* Can be searched by a drug's trade or generic name. Provides a summary of the information about the drug, and links to further related information, such as MedlinePlus (463), AIDSinfo (447), MEDLINE (425)/PubMed® (432), LactMed (1572), HSDB (1569), Dietary Supplements Labels Database (728), TOXLINE (1578), DailyMed (626), ClinicalTrials.gov (191), PubChem (444), ChemIDplus (1563), Drugs@FDA (1283), and others. For the public, health care professionals, and researchers.

749   Drugs, supplements, and herbal information (MedlinePlus). National Library of Medicine (U.S.). 2003?–. Bethesda, Md.: National Library of Medicine, National Institutes of Health, U.S. Dept. of Health and Human Services. http://www.nlm.nih.gov/medlineplus/druginformation.html.

Pt. of MedlinePlus® (463).

Generic or brand name drugs, arranged A–Z, with prescription and over-the-counter medication information from MedMaster™ (American Society of Health-System Pharmacists [ASHP]). For additional drug information, see the MedlinePlus Drug Therapy topic pages (http://

www.nlm.nih.gov/medlineplus/drugtherapy.html). Also provides access to information on herbs and supplements from Natural Standard© (1277). Additional herb and supplement information can be found via MedlinePlus Complementary and Alternative Therapies topics (http://www.nlm. nih.gov/medlineplus/complementaryandalternativetherapie s.html).

750   Genetics home reference. Lister Hill National Center for
        Biomedical Communications, National Library of Medicine,
        National Institutes of Health, Department of Health and Human
        Services. 2003–. Bethesda, Md.: National Library of Medicine.
        http://purl.access.gpo.gov/GPO/LPS74916.

Aims to make genetics and its relationship to disease accessible to the general public. Information is presented in a question and answer format, with explanation on how a disease is inherited, the symptoms, and what treatments are available. Provides general information on genes, gene maps, genetic markers, chromosomes, DNA, and details on the specific genes related to a particular disease. Includes a "help me understand genetics page," a glossary of genetics terms, links to clinical trials, etc. Updated as new information becomes available. A detailed description at http://www.nlm.nih.gov/pubs/factsheets/ghr.html.

751   Health fraud (MedlinePlus). National Library of Medicine
        (U.S.). 2000?–. Bethesda, Md.: U.S. National Library of Medicine,
        National Institutes of Health, Dept. of Health & Human Services.
        http://www.nlm.nih.gov/medlineplus/healthfraud.html.

A Health Topic in MedlinePlus (463).

    Contents: Overviews; Related issues; Journal articles; Organizations; Law and policy; Seniors.

    Collection of links on health scams and quackery, how to detect health fraud, how to report unlawful sales of medical products, etc. Quackwatch (622) provides additional information in this area.

752   Health system (MedlinePlus). National Library of Medicine
        (U.S.). 200?–. Bethesda, Md.: U.S. National Library of Medicine,
        National Institutes of Health, Dept. of Health and Human
        Services. http://www.nlm.nih.gov/medlineplus/healthsystem.html.

List of links to a wide variety of healthcare-related topics, with each link leading to a separate page within MedlinePlus (463). Provides extensive reference information on the particular topic. Examples include assisted

CONSUMER HEALTH

333

living, health occupations, caregivers, personal medical records, home care services, emergency medical services, health facilities, health insurance, managed care, home care services, hospice care, nursing homes, patients rights, patient safety, veterans and military health, and many others.

753   **Lab tests online.** American Association for Clinical Chemistry. 2001–. Washington: American Association for Clinical Chemistry. http://www.labtestsonline.org.

Produced and maintained by the American Association for Clinical Chemistry, in collaboration with several other professional societies.

Provides patients and other health consumers with reliable information on clinical laboratory tests that are commonly used to diagnose various diseases and conditions and their interpretation. Also provides links to additional resources and websites.

Print titles containing information about lab tests include *Interpretation of diagnostic tests* (315), *Laboratory tests and diagnostic procedures* (318), *Mosby's manual of diagnostic and laboratory tests* (325), and *Tietz clinical guide to laboratory tests* (334).

754   **MedlinePlus.** U.S. National Library of Medicine. 1998–. Bethesda, Md.: U.S. Dept. of Health and Human Services, National Library of Medicine. http://medlineplus.gov/.

025.04; 651.504261; 613   RA776.5

MedlinePlus®

A consumer health reference database with information from the National Library of Medicine (NLM) (427), the National Institutes of Health (NIH) (470), other government agencies, and various health-related organizations. A continually expanding and updated resource. Information on over 700 diseases and conditions, as well as drug information (prescription, nonprescription), herbs and supplements, an illustrated medical encyclopedia and dictionary, interactive patient tutorials, lists of hospitals, physicians, and dentists, and health news. Provides preformulated MEDLINE (425)/PubMed® (432) searches for recent articles. Includes *NIH MedlinePlus Magazine*, a new quarterly guide for patients and their families, providing authoritative medical and health-care information. "MedlinePlus en español" toggles between English and Spanish. Provides links to browse selected health information in multiple languages other than English and Spanish at http://www.nlm.nih.gov/medlineplus/languages/languages.html. "Go Local" links users to relevant health information in their own city, county, and state. Detailed descriptive information is available at http://www.nlm.nih.gov/pubs/factsheets/medlineplus.html.

755 **MedlinePlus go local.** National Library of Medicine (U.S.), National Institutes of Health (U.S.). 200?–. Bethesda, Md.: National Library of Medicine. http://www.nlm.nih.gov/medlineplus/golocal/index.html.

A joint project of the National Library of Medicine (NLM) (427) and National Institutes of Health with libraries and library consortia throughout the U.S. Starting in 2010, NLM and its partners are phasing out the MedlinePlus Go Local project.

   Provides links to health services in geographic areas to assist in finding local services and resources. Each MedlinePlus (463) health topic links to services related to that particular topic in the area selected by the user, with a standardized format for each state: services by location; services by providers, facilities, and services; services for diseases and health issues; all services; health information.

756 **Men's health (MedlinePlus).** National Library of Medicine (U.S.). 200?–. Bethesda, Md.: National Library of Medicine, National Institutes of Health, Dept. of Health and Human Services. http://www.nlm.nih.gov/medlineplus/menshealth.html.

RA777.8

A MedlinePlus® (463) Health Topic. Collection of links for a variety of resources on men's health (e.g., specific conditions, treatments, prevention/screening, etc.) and also related issues and topics.

757 **National Cancer Institute.** National Cancer Institute. Bethesda, Md.: National Cancer Institute. http://www.cancer.gov/.

Website created by the National Cancer Institute (NCI), a division of the National Institutes of Health (NIH).

   Contents: NCI Home, Cancer Topics, Clinical Trials, Cancer Statistics, Research and Funding, News, About NCI.

   Links to cancer-related information for health professionals, medical students, and patients. Provides guidance to searching the cancer literature in PubMed (432) by searching the "cancer subset" and access to already prepared searches on more than 100 different topics. Non-PubMed citations previously found in CANCERLIT, a database no longer being maintained,

CONSUMER HEALTH

consist primarily of meeting abstracts from the annual meetings of the American Society of Clinical Oncology (ASCO) and the American Association for Cancer Research (AACR). ASCO abstracts for recent years are available via http://www.asco.org, AACR abstracts at http://aacrmeeting-abstracts.org/. Also provides access to PDQ: Physician Data Query (http://www.cancer.gov/cancertopics/pdq), a database with the latest information about cancer treatment, screening, prevention, genetics, etc.

The NCI website includes descriptions of various types of cancer (A–Z List of Cancers: http://www.cancer.gov/cancertopics/alphalist/) and related topics, with links to diagnosis and treatment information and supportive care, information on clinical trials, cancer prevention, cancer statistics (e.g., SEER Cancer Statistics Review [547]), cancer statistics tools, cancer mortality maps and graphs, and related NCI websites. Links to the Dictionary of Cancer Terms (143) and various cancer vocabulary resources (e.g., NCI Thesaurus, NCI Metathesaurus, and NCI Terminology Browser), NCI Drug Dictionary, NCI publications, etc. Available both in English and Spanish.

758   **National Institute of Nursing Research.** National Institute of Nursing Research. 1997–. Bethesda, Md.: National Institute of Nursing Research. http://www.ninr.nih.gov/.

RT81.5

The mission of the National Institute of Nursing Research (NINR) is "to promote and improve the health of individuals, families, communities, and populations. This mission is accomplished through support of research in a number of science areas. Among those areas of research are chronic and acute diseases, health promotion and maintenance, symptom management, health disparities, caregiving, self-management, and the end of life."—*Main page.* Links to NINR publications and meeting reports; information on nursing, minority/ethnic nurses, regional nursing research, and professional nurses and practice organizations; federal government links, links to search engines; and other resources. Also contains "health links for the public" to several federal government sites.

759   **National Organization for Rare Disorders, Inc.** National Organization for Rare Disorders. 1999–. Danbury, Conn.: National Organization for Rare Disorders. http://www.rarediseases.org/.

RC48

The National Organization for Rare Disorders (NORD) provides alphabetical Index of Rare Diseases and several searchable databases—namely, Rare

Disease Database, Index of Organizations (list of organizations), and Organizational Database (patient organizations)—as well as advice on how to interpret search results. Other resources in this area can be located via *NORD guide to rare disorders* (428) and NIH's Office of Rare Diseases (476).

760   **National Patient Safety Foundation (NPFS).** National Patient
       Safety Foundation. North Adams, Mass.: National Patient Safety
       Foundation. http://www.npsf.org.

Independent, not-for-profit organization, with the mission to "measurably improve patient safety."—*Main page.* Searchable website, with links to online patient safety resources and organizations. Information is presented in different categories (e.g., health care quality and safety, medication safety, surgical safety, cancer treatment safety, and others) for different user groups, such as health professionals, patients and families, and researchers.

761   **National Women's Health Information Center.** National Women's
       Health Information Center. 1990s–. Fairfax, Va.: U.S. Department
       of Health and Human Services. http://www.4woman.gov/.
613.04240285; 615.507; 305.40285

National Women's Health Information Center (NWHIC) is a federal government resource for women's health information. Presents reliable information on women's health concerns and issues for health professionals and health consumers. Links to organizations concerned with women's health, health tools, health topics, publications of interest and concern to women of all ages, and statistics via Quick Health Data Online (http://www.4woman.gov/quickhealthdata/). Link to girlshealth.gov with health information for young girls and educators.

   Other examples of Internet resources with valuable information for health consumers, health professionals, and researchers include Women's Health (MedlinePlus) (http://www.nlm.nih.gov/medlineplus/womenshealth.html); Women's Health (General), National Institutes of Health (http://health.nih.gov/result.asp/729); and Women's Health (NIH) (http://health.nih.gov/search.asp/28).

762   **Nursing home compare.** Centers for Medicare and Medicaid
       Services, U.S. Dept. of Health and Human Services. 1990s–.
       Baltimore: Centers for Medicare and Medicaid Services. http://
       www.medicare.gov/nhcompare/home.asp.

CONSUMER HEALTH

337

Produced by Centers for Medicare and Medicaid Services (U.S.) (742)

Includes nursing homes that are Medicare or Medicaid certified and provide a full range of skilled nursing care, but also other types of facilities with different levels of care and possibly licensed only at the state level. Searchable by geography (state, county), by proximity (city, zip code), or by name. Part of the Medicare website at http://www.medicare.gov/, which also provides access to additional search tools to compare, for example, prescription drug plans, health plans, and hospitals; information on finding a physician; and answers to other health care questions.

763 Nutrition (MedlinePlus). National Library of Medicine (U.S.). 2000?–. Bethesda, Md.: U.S. National Library of Medicine, National Institutes of Health, Dept. of Health and Human Services. http://www.nlm.nih.gov/medlineplus/nutrition.html.

A Health Topic within MedlinePlus® (463).

Contents: Overviews; Latest news; Related issues; Health check tools; Tutorials; Clinical trials; Research; Journal articles; Directories; Organizations; Law and policy; Teenagers; Women.

Selected links to a wide range of nutrition-related information provided by government agencies, societies, professional associations, organizations, and foundations. Also provides links to related topics with separate pages in MedlinePlus, e.g., breast feeding, child nutrition, dietary fats, fiber, and protein, eating disorders, food safety, infant and toddler nutrition, obesity, vegetarian diets, and others. "Go Local" link helps to identify nutrition services and providers in the U.S.

764 The nutrition source. Harvard School of Public Health. 2002–. Boston: Harvard School of Public Health. http://www.hsph.harvard.edu/nutritionsource/.

Contents: Interpreting News on Diet; Frequently Asked Questions; Ask the Expert; Food Pyramids; Fats and Cholesterol; Carbohydrates; Protein; Fiber; Fruits and Vegetables; Calcium and Milk; Alcohol; Vitamins; Healthy Weight; Exercise; Type 2 Diabetes; Food Service and Healthy Eating; More Information.

"The aim of the Harvard School of Public Health Nutrition Source is to provide timely information on diet and nutrition for clinicians, allied health professionals, and the public. The contents of this Web site are not intended to offer personal medical advice."—*Main page*

765 **Office of Dietary Supplements.** National Institutes of Health Office of Dietary Supplements. 1999–. Bethesda, Md.: National Institutes of Health Office of Dietary Supplements. http://dietary-supplements.info.nih.gov/index.aspx.

National Institutes of Health (NIH) Office of Dietary Supplements (ODS); U.S. Dept. of Agriculture (USDA).

ODS homepage includes extensive health information on dietary supplement use and safety and nutrient recommendations. Provides access to NIH and USDA databases and research resources, such as the International Bibliographic Information on Dietary Supplements (IBIDS) database (1145), Computer Access to Research on Dietary Supplements (CARDS), Annual Bibliography of Significant Advances in Dietary Supplement Research (1097), USDA's National nutrient database for standard reference, and others made available via the USDA Nutrient Data Laboratory (1139). For health professionals, researchers, students, and health consumers.

766 **Office of Rare Diseases.** National Institutes of Health (U.S.). 2002–. Bethesda, Md: National Institutes of Health. http://rarediseases.info.nih.gov.

Answers questions about rare diseases for patients and other health consumers, healthcare providers, researchers, educators, students, and others interested in rare diseases. Links to definitions, causes, treatments, and publications about rare diseases, provides resources on genetic information, genetic research, genetic testing laboratories and clinics, genetic counseling services, and patient support groups. Also includes information on rare diseases research and research resources. Other reference sources in this area include, for example, National Organization for Rare Disorders, Inc. (428) and *NORD guide to rare disorders* (329).

767 **OncoLink.** Abramson Cancer Center of the University of Pennsylvania. 1994–. Philadelphia: University of Pennsylvania. http://cancer.med.upenn.edu/.
615.507; 616.992; 616.994

Contents: Types of cancer; Cancer treatment information; Coping with cancer; Cancer resources and news; Ask the cancer expert; OncoLink Library.

Designed for educational purposes to help cancer patients, families, health care professionals, and the general public to get accurate cancer-related information. Provides comprehensive information about specific types of cancer, updates on cancer treatment, and news about research advances, with information provided at various levels, from introductory to in-depth.

768   PDRhealth. Thomson Healthcare. 2008–. Montvale, N.J.: Thomson Healthcare. http://www.pdrhealth.com/home/home. aspx.

Launched as PDRhealth.com in Nov. 2007, now called PDRhealth, which is a revised Thomson website, previously also called PDRhealth or PDR Health.

Provides prescription drug and supplement information (based on information found in *Physicians' desk reference: PDR* [1250], including drug interactions [e.g., "interaction checker"], side effects, dosages, alternative therapies for brand-name and generic prescription drugs, over-the-counter drugs, herbals, and supplements. Also provides information on diseases and conditions, treatment options, online health tools [e.g., HDL and LDL cholesterol level risk factor analyzer], clinical trials, and surgery.

769   Substance Abuse and Mental Health Services Administration (SAMHSA). Substance Abuse and Mental Health Services Administration. Rockville, Md.: Substance Abuse and Mental Health Services Administration. http://www.samhsa.gov.

Substance Abuse and Mental Health Services Administration (SAMHSA), part of U.S. Dept. of Health and Human Services (HHS) (769).

SAMHSA has as its mission "building resilience and facilitating recovery for people with or at risk for mental or substance use disorders. gearing all of its resources. toward that outcome."—*About Us.* Searchable website. Provides resources for prevention, treatment, and rehabilitation services for patients with various forms of mental illness and addictions. Includes three centers: SAMHSA's Center for Mental Health Services (CMHS), Center for Substance Abuse Prevention (CSAP), and Center for Substance Abuse Treatment (CSAT). Examples of SAMHSA resources include Mental Health Services Locator (http://mentalhealth.samhsa.gov/databases/) and Substance Abuse Treatment Facility Locator (http://dasis3.samhsa.gov/), both with clickable maps to locate different programs throughout the United States; Prevention Online (PREVLINE; http://ncadi.samhsa.gov/); a list of hotline numbers (http://mentalhealth.samhsa.gov/hotlines/); and related links (e.g., Mental Health on the Internet; http://mentalhealth. samhsa.gov/links/). SAMHSA's Office of Applied Statistics (http://www.

oas.samhsa.gov/) provides the latest data on alcohol, tobacco, and illegal drugs as well as other statistical data and resources.

770   U.S. Food and Drug Administration [home page]. Food and Drug Administration. Washington: Food and Drug Administration. http://www.fda.gov.

The Food and Drug Administration (FDA) regulates foods, drugs, medical devices, biologics (vaccines, blood products, etc.), and radiation-emitting products (e.g., cell phones, lasers, microwaves, etc.). Searchable website (http://www.fda.gov/search.html), with FDA A–Z index that provides links to a large number of online resources. This search engine will not, however, find information that is in the numerous databases on the FDA site. A collection of databases can be found at http://www.fda.gov/search/databases.html and can be accessed separately.

Major FDA centers include the Center for Drug Evaluation (CDER) ("consumer watchdog in America's healthcare system"; http://www.fda.gov/cder/index.html), which evaluates drugs before they can be sold and provides resources such as Drugs@FDA (1283), Electronic Orange Book (1158), and National Drug Code Directory (1183). Another FDA center is the Center for Food Safety and Applied Nutrition (CFSAN) (http://www.cfsan.fda.gov/~dms/foia.html), with resources on foods and food safety, such as the GRAS (Generally Recognized as Safe) list of substances (http://www.cfsan.fda.gov/~dms/grasguid.html), the "bad bug book," and publications on food-borne illness, FDA food code, allergens, dietary supplements, etc. Additional FDA centers provide information on biologics, cosmetics, medical devices, radiological health, toxicological research, and veterinary medicine.

Other examples of resources provided at the FDA site include access to the "blue book" (i.e., *Requirements of laws and regulations enforced by the U.S. Food and Drug Administration*), oncology tools, patient safety portal, special health issues, and information on bioterrorism, trans fats, vaccines, xenotransplantation, and many other subjects and topics relating to human and animal drugs and biologics, foods, and medical devices. Information is tailored to the needs of different user groups, with separate pages for consumers, patients, health professionals, state/local officials, industry, press, women, and children. Frequently requested FDA documents can be accessed via an "electronic reading room" (http://www.fda.gov/foi/electrr.htm). Milestones in U.S. Food and Drug Law History 1820–2005 is available at http://www.fda.gov/opacom/backgrounders/miles.html.

771   **Videos of surgical procedures (MedlinePlus).** National Library of Medicine (U.S.). 2004?–. Bethesda, Md.: National Library of Medicine, National Institutes of Health, U.S. Dept. of Health and Human Services. http://www.nlm.nih.gov/medlineplus/ surgeryvideos.html.

Pt. of MedlinePlus® (463). Provides links to prerecorded webcasts of surgical procedures, that is, actual operations performed at medical centers in the U.S. since Jan. 2004. Intended for educational purposes.

4 > DENTISTRY

772   **Academy of General Dentistry.** 1996–. Chicago: Academy of General Dentistry. http://www.agd.org/.

Academy of General Dentistry (AGD), a nonprofit organization of more than 35,000 general dentists, founded in 1952.

   In addition to professional resources for dentists, website also provides consumer-oriented oral health resources—e.g., help with finding a dentist (http://www.agd.org/findadentist/default.asp); A–Z list of oral health resources, including an oral health glossary (http://www.agd.org/public/ oralhealth/).

773   **FDI World Dental Federation [homepage].** FDI World Dental Federation. Ferney-Voltaire, France: FDI World Dental Federation. http://www.fdiworldental.org/home/home.html.

FDI (Fédération Dentaire Internationale); FDI World Dental Federation. Collaborates with the World Health Organization (WHO) Oral Health Unit (http://www.who.int/oral_health/en/) and other WHO departments.

   FDI's mission is to promote oral and general health and "the art, science, and practice of dentistry" [and plays the role of] "the authoritative, worldwide voice of dentistry."—*Website.* Offers a variety of resources to dentistry and oral health, such as facts and figures, publications, a two-digit notation system to identify teeth with a number, list of dental schools (*World directory of dental schools* [792]), and others. In collaboration with WHO addresses global oral health issues and other public health issues related to oral health.

Bibliography

774   **Dental bibliography: Literature of dental science and art as found in the libraries of the New York Academy of Medicine and Bernhard Wolf Weinberger.** 2nd ed. Bernhard Wolf Weinberger, First District Dental Society of the State of New York. 2 v. in 1. [New York]: First District Dental Society, State of New York, [1929]–1932.

Z6668.N53

1st ed., 1916.

Repr. 1998, 1929, 2 v. in 1 (Mansfield Centre, Conn.: Martino Fine Books).

Contents: [pt. I], A reference index; pt. II, A subject index, with additional reference index.

"Though far from a complete dental bibliography, it contains every important dental publication that has been published, thereby enabling those who are interested in dental research and study to fulfill their needs."—*Pref.* Subject index covers only dental books, not dental periodicals. Includes sections on "Medical classics containing dental citations" (p. 178–83) and "Earliest dental books published, 1530–1810" (p. 220–22). Pt. 2 updates the previous volume.

Biography

775   **African American firsts in science and technology.** Raymond B. Webster. xiii, 461 p., ill. Detroit: Gale Group, 1999. ISBN: 0787638765.

508.996073   Q141.W43

Chronology of firsts in various fields: Agriculture and Everyday Life, Dentistry and Nursing, Life Science, Math and Engineering, Medicine, Physical Science, and Transportation. Includes bibliography, index by year, occupational index, general index, and citations for first achievements. Over 1,200 entries, 100 illustrations.

Classification

776   **Application of the international classification of diseases to dentistry and stomatology: ICD-DA.** 3rd ed. World Health Organization. 238 p. Geneva, [Switzerland]: World Health Organization, 1995. ISBN: 9241544678.

617.5220012   RK51.5.W67

1st ed. (WHO), 1973 (companion to the *International classification of disease* [ICD], 8th rev.); 2nd ed., 1978 (companion to the ICD 9th rev.). Derived from the 1992–94 print version of the ICD-10 (*International statistical classification of diseases and related health problems* [84]) and prepared as a companion volume to the ICD-10.

Contents: "The International Classification of Diseases—ICD-DA"; "Recommended use of ICD-DA"; "ICD-DA tabular list"; "Extract from numerical index of morphology of neoplasms (ICD-O)"; "Annex 1. Histological typing of odontogenic tumours"; "Annex 2. Histological typing of salivary gland tumors."

Provides "a comprehensive and consistent classification of oral diseases and oral manifestations of other diseases, standard recording system for all oral diseases and conditions, [and] by means of the recording system, to make possible the collection of data that will allow the prevalence of oral diseases and conditions to be compared at an international level."—*Introd.*

Includes a tabular section and a comprehensive alphabetical index. Neoplasm section includes both malignant and benign tumors. Use of ICD-DA is recommended "at the national, regional, institutional, or individual practice level." Includes bibliographical references and index. Related publications are *International classification of diseases for oncology: ICD-O* (81), *Histological typing of odontogenic tumours*, and *Histological typing of salivary gland tumours.*

Dictionaries

777   **Academy of General Dentistry.** 1996–. Chicago: Academy of
      General Dentistry. http://www.agd.org/.

Academy of General Dentistry (AGD), a nonprofit organization of more than 35,000 general dentists, founded in 1952.

In addition to professional resources for dentists, website also provides consumer-oriented oral health resources—e.g., help with finding a dentist (http://www.agd.org/findadentist/default.asp); A–Z list of oral health resources, including an oral health glossary (http://www.agd.org/public/oralhealth/).

778   **American Dental Association.** American Dental Association.
      1995–. Chicago: American Dental Association. http://www.ada.org/.

Official website of the American Dental Association (ADA), founded in 1859.

Provides information for dental professionals concerning education and testing, practice management, and patient care. Includes a list of dental schools (http://www.ada.org/prof/ed/programs/search_ddsdmd_us.asp), accreditation, and licensure, and links to national dental organizations. Resources for consumers include, for example, "Oral Health Topics A–Z" (http://www.ada.org/public/topics/alpha.asp), "Find a dentist" (http://www.ada.org/public/disclaimer.asp), and a "Glossary of dental terms" (http://www.ada.org/public/resources/glossary.asp). Includes a "History of Medicine" timeline (Ancient Origins, Middle Ages–Renaissance, 18th century, 19th century, 20th century) (http://www.ada.org/public/resources/history/index.asp), and a selected bibliography of history of dentistry books found in the ADA Library. Some of the resources are restricted to ADA members.

779 **CDT: Current dental terminology.** American Dental Association. Chicago: American Dental Association, 1991–.

RK28

American Dental Association (ADA). Description based on 2007–08 ed. (publ. 2006).

Consists of the ADA's Code on Dental Procedures and Nomenclature, instructions for the use of the code, and tooth numbering systems. Described as a "standardized coding system to document and to communicate accurate information about dental treatment procedures and services to agencies involved in adjucating insurance claims."—*Website.* Available in print, CD-ROM, and e-book format (http://www.ada.org/ada/prod/catalog/index.asp).

780 **Dictionary of dentistry English-Spanish, Spanish-English = Diccionario de odontologia Ingles-Espanol, Espanol-Ingles.** Ana Veronica Franscini-Paiva. 421 p. Barcelona, Spain: Editorial Quintessence, 2005. ISBN: 8489873364.

RK27.F73

Dental terms and biomedical terms associated with dentistry, with translations in both English and Spanish.

781 **Drug dictionary for dentistry.** J. G. Meechan, R. A. Seymour. 434 p. Oxford; New York: Oxford University Press, 2002. ISBN: 0192632744.

617.606103   RK701.M44

Includes drugs prescribed by dentists and drugs that a dental patient may already be taking, describing use, dosage, drug-drug interactions, and reasons why they shouldn't be used. Drugs are listed by their approved name. An appendix lists trade names and cross-references to the approved name of the drug. Written for dental practitioners and students. Available online via netLibrary.

782   Harty's dental dictionary. 3rd ed. Peter A. Heasman, Giles McCracken, F. J. Harty. Edinburgh; New York: Churchill Livingstone, 2007. ISBN: 9780443102.

617.6003   RK27.H37

1st ed., 1987 and 2nd ed., 1994 had title: *Concise illustrated dental dictionary*. Updated edition.

Offers brief definitions for a comprehensive range of dental terminology, including both common and more exotic terms. Includes cross-references and line drawings illustrating anatomical features and dental instruments. Appendixes include a chronological table of the development and eruption of the teeth and information about dental schools and dental organizations. Useful to dental practitioners and dental students, however "directed primarily towards health care professionals outside of the United States."—*Publ. notes*

783   Heinemann dental dictionary. 4th ed. Jenifer E. H. Fairpo, C. Gavin Fairpo. xvi, 347 p. Oxford; Boston: Butterworth Heinemann, 1997. ISBN: 0750622083.

617.6/003   RK27.F35

1st ed., 1962, had title: *Heinemann modern dictionary for dental students*; 3rd ed., 1987. A major revision.

Provides brief definitions of terms, including many obsolete terms from the early dental literature. Cross-references from the older terminology to the preferred term. American terms are included, although the clinical terminology is based on British and ISO standard vocabulary (cf. *Pref.*). Anatomical charts of the head and neck show arteries, veins, muscles, and nerves; an appendix lists dental periodicals, with country of origin and frequency of publication. List of commonly used abbreviations for dental institutions, degrees, etc.

784   Mosby's dental dictionary. 2nd ed. Charles A. Babbush, Margaret J. Fehrenback, Mary Emmons. St. Louis; London: Mosby, Inc., 2007. ISBN: 9780323049634.

1st ed., 1998, ed. by Thomas J. Zwemer; also a 2004 ed., by Scott Stocking and Jyothimai Gubili (ed. consultants: Thomas Zwemer, Margaret J. Fehrenbach, Mary Emmons, and Mary Ann Tiedemann).

Includes approx. 9,500 terms related to dentistry and related sciences, dental office management, and medical terms in common use. Ill. with diagrams, photographs, and line drawings. Contains several appendixes; e.g., American Dental Association dental codes, an overview of the Health Insurance Portability and Accountability Act, symbols and abbreviations used in dentistry, tooth numbering systems. Online access to the 2004 ed. via Credo Reference (London; Boston: Credo Reference).

785   Mosby's dental drug reference. 8th ed. Arthur H. Jeske. 1415 p. St. Louis: Mosby, Inc., an affiliate of Elsevier, Inc., 2007. ISBN: 9780323052665.

RK701

1st ed., 1994; 7th ed., 2005.

Alphabetical arrangement of drugs that dental patients may be taking, listed by generic name and indexed by brand name, with drug monograph information presented in a consistent format. Provides information on side effects, precautions, contraindications, and drug interactions. Also includes alternative therapies. Therapeutic and pharmacologic index. Accompanied by CD-ROM that contains color images of conditions resulting from drugs patients are taking, and also customizable patient handouts. Intended for dental professionals, but also useful for health consumers.

DENTISTRY

347

786   Stedman's medical dictionary for the dental professions: Illustrated. Lippincott, Williams and Wilkins. xxix, 568, 80 p., 16 p. of plates, ill. (some color), 1 CD-ROM. Philadelphia: Lippincott, Williams and Wilkins, 2007. ISBN: 0781768659.

617.603   RK27.S744

Title varies: also called *Medical dictionary for the dental professions.*

A to Z listing, with 13,000 terms, approx. 500 color and black-and-white images and illustrations. Icons are used to identify images, common medical prefixes, suffixes, and combining forms. Contains tooth numbering systems, dental imaging errors, guidelines for infection control, weights and measures, and information about the different dental professions and professional organizations. Also indicates the Mendelian Inheritance in Man number (OMIM: Online Mendelian Inheritance in Man [330]) and

Terminologia Anatomica Latin term. Accompanying CD-ROM includes all of the terms of the print edition and provides search capabilities and audio pronunciations for approx. 8,500 terms and all of the images from the dictionary.

Directories

787 **ADEA official guide to dental schools.** American Dental Education Association. Washington: American Dental Education Association, 2001–. ISSN: 2152-5196.

617.6007117   RK91.A582a; Q617.6A

Continues: *Admission requirements of American dental schools,* 1963–74 (published in cooperation with the Council on Dental Education) and *Admission requirements of U.S. and Canadian dental schools,* [10th]–38th ed., 1974/75–2001 (published by American Association of Dental Schools). 2001–. published by the American Dental Education Association (ADEA).

Description based on 2009 ed. "for students entering in Fall 2010."

Contents: pt. 1, "Becoming a dentist"; pt. 2, "Learning about dental schools".

Provides an extensive range of information for each school: general information, description of programs, admission requirements, application processes and timetables, costs, financing options and scholarships for dental education, etc. Information is based on data collected from ADEA, ADA, and data provided by the dental schools. Familiarizes the reader with the dental profession. Additional information about dental education and the ADEA at http://www.adea.org/.

788 **American dental directory.** American Dental Association. ill. Chicago: American Dental Association, 1947–2001. ISSN: 0065-8073.

617.6002573   RK37.A25

American dentists are listed by state and city, with an alphabetical index of names. Gives address and indicates specialization and dental school, with year of graduation. Additional sections on affiliate members of the American Dental Association (ADA), i.e., foreign dental graduates who are practicing in a country other than the U.S., and associate and honorary members. Also includes national dental organizations and dental organizations outside the U.S. Since 2001, no longer publ. in print format.

Continued by an online directory, ADA Member Directory (American Dental Association, [2002?]–).

789 Barron's guide to medical and dental schools. 11th ed. Saul Witschnitzer, Edith Wischnitzer. Hauppauge, N.Y.: Barron's, 2006. ISBN: 9780764133.

610.71173   R690.W558

1st ed., 1982 (based on *Barron's guide to medical, dental, and allied health science careers* [1974], and its updated versions, published in 1975 and 1977); 10th ed., 2003.

Contents: pt.1. Medicine; pt. 2. Dentistry.

Intended as a guidance manual for pre-professional students. Presents basic data and detailed information for accredited medical, dental, and osteopathic schools in the U.S. and Canada, such as admissions requirements, curriculum, grading and promotion policies, facilities and special features of an institution, etc. Includes a full-length model Medical College Admission Test (MCAT) with answers, and selected questions from recent Dental College Admission Tests (DAT), sample essays for medical student applications, and other advice for students considering a medical or dental career. Separate chapter on opportunities for women and minorities.

790 Directories (MedlinePlus). National Library of Medicine (U.S.), National Institutes of Health (U.S.). 200?–. Bethesda, Md.: U.S. National Library of Medicine, National Institutes of Health, Dept. of Health and Human Services. http://www.nlm.nih.gov/medlineplus/directories.html.

RC48

Pt. of MedlinePlus (463).

Contents: Doctors and dentists—general; Hospital and clinics—general; Doctors and dentists—specialists; Other healthcare providers; Hospitals and clinics—specialized; Other healthcare facilities and services; Libraries.

Links to directories to help find health professionals, services, and facilities. Includes, for example, access to the American Medical Association's DoctorFinder (209), how to find a dentist, a Medicare participants physicians directory, and many others.

DENTISTRY

791   **DIRLINE.** National Institutes of Health (U.S.). [1983?–.] Bethesda, Md.: U.S. National Institutes of Health, Dept. of Health and Human Services. http://dirline.nlm.nih.gov/.

DIRLINE® (Directory of Information Resources Online), maintained by the National Library of Medicine (NLM) (427).

Online annotated directory of organizations, research resources, projects, databases, and other information resources concerned with health and biomedicine from a variety of sources, including federal, state, and local government agencies, academic and research institutions, and also consumer health-related resources such as self-help groups and health hotlines. Resources are mostly from the U.S. but also include some international resources. Currently contains over 8,000 entries, with topics on most diseases and conditions and health services research and technology assessment. Can be searched using MeSH® (Medical Subject Headings) (575), keywords, or by name and location of a resource. Detailed information on DIRLINE can be found via a fact sheet prepared by NLM: http://www.nlm.nih.gov/pubs/factsheets/dirlinfs.html.

792   **World directory of dental schools.** FDI World Dental Federation. 1993–. Ferney-Voltaire, France: FDI World Dental Federation. http://www.fdiworldental.org/resources/assets/dentalschoolsdirectory.pdf.

FDI (Fédération Dentaire Internationale); FDI World Dental Federation (773).

Listing of dental schools worldwide by country, with contact and other information provided by the individual dental schools. Latest version dated Dec. 2004. Also accessible via Dental Schools Directory (http://www.fdiworldental.org/resources/6_0schools.html).

Encyclopedias

793   **Encyclopedia of biomaterials and biomedical engineering.** Gary E. Wnek, Gary L. Bowlin. 2 v., ill. New York: Marcel Dekker, 2004. ISBN: 0824755626.

610.2803   R857.M3E53

Describes applications "utilizing traditional engineering approaches to analyze and solve problems in life sciences in medicine" (*Pref.*), such as biosensors, implants, orthopedic devices, and tissue engineering. Intended to be multidisciplinary and comprehensive. Contains more than 175 articles averaging about ten pages in length. Articles are signed. Contributors (more than 400, largely from the U.S.) are predominantly from academia, but some are from industry. Arranged alphabetically. Includes brief contents (inside front cover), table of contents, cross-references, article references, and index.

2nd ed. (New York: Informa Healthcare USA, 2008) will be published in 2008 in both print and online formats.

Guides

794   **A consumer's guide to dentistry.** 2nd ed. Gordon J. Christensen. x, 214 p., color ill. St. Louis: Mosby, 2002. ISBN: 0323014836.

617.6   RK61.C57

1st ed., 1994.

Contents: Ch. 1 "How to use this book," finding solutions to your oral problems; ch. 2 "Divisions in dentistry," types of dentists; ch. 3 "Finding the right dentist," what to consider in your choice of dentists; ch. 4 "Managed care," managed care programs in dentistry; ch. 5 "Pain control," controlling pain in dentistry; ch. 6 "Infection control," infection control in the dental office; ch. 7 "Endodontics," root canals, dead teeth, inside of teeth; ch. 8 "Esthetic dentistry," cosmetic dentistry, improving your smile; ch. 9 "Geriatric dentistry," dentistry for mature people; ch. 10 "Implant dentistry," substitutes for tooth roots placed into your jaw; ch. 11 "Occlusion," your bite, the way your teeth come together, temporomandibular joints, temporomandibular dysfunction; ch. 12 "Oral and maxillofacial surgery," oral pathology, oral medicine diseases, and surgery related to the oral and facial areas; ch. 13 "Orthodontics," straightening teeth; ch. 14 "Pediatric dentistry," dentistry for children; ch. 15 "Periodontics," gums and bone surrounding teeth, ch. 16 "Prosthodontics," fixed crowns or bridges cemented onto teeth; ch. 17 "Prosthodontics," removable dentures replacing all or some teeth; ch. 18 "Restorative or operative dentistry," fillings for teeth; ch. 19 "Preventing the need for dental treatment"; ch. 20 "Additional sources of information."

Written for the dental patient, provides information about dental health and various treatment options for dental problems. Illustrations.

Handbooks

795   **ADA/PDR guide to dental therapeutics.** 4th ed. American Dental Association. 1008 p. Chicago: American Dental Association, 2006. ISBN: 1563636042.

RK701.A33

1st (1998)–3rd (2003) ed. had title: *ADA guide to dental therapeutics.*

This edition produced by the American Dental Association (ADA) in partnership with the Physicians' Desk Reference. Authoritative guide to dental therapeutics, covering approx. 2,500 brand names and generic drugs. Contains section on oral manifestations of systemic agents. Appendix includes U.S. controlled substances, smoking cessation, and related products. Other PDR-related titles include *Physicians' desk reference: PDR* (1250), *PDR drug guide for mental health professionals* (1242), *PDR guide to drug interactions, side effects, and indications* (1247), *PDR for herbal medicines* (1244), *PDR for nonprescription drugs, dietary supplements, and herbs* (1245), *PDR for nutritional supplements* (1246), *PDR nurse's drug handbook* (1064), *Physicians' desk reference for ophthalmic medicines* (1249), *PDR guide to biological and chemical warfare response, PDR guide to terrorism response,* and other titles. PDR and its major companion volumes are also found in the PDR® Electronic Library (1243).

796   CDT: Current dental terminology. American Dental Association. Chicago: American Dental Association, 1991–.

RK28

American Dental Association (ADA). Description based on 2007–08 ed. (publ. 2006).

Consists of the ADA's Code on Dental Procedures and Nomenclature, instructions for the use of the code, and tooth numbering systems. Described as a "standardized coding system to document and to communicate accurate information about dental treatment procedures and services to agencies involved in adjucating insurance claims."—*Website.* Available in print, CD-ROM, and e-book format (http://www.ada.org/ada/prod/catalog/index.asp).

797   Dental anatomy: Its relevance to dentistry. 6th ed. Julian B. Woelfel, Rickne C. Scheid. viii, 422 p., ill. Philadelphia: Lippincott, Williams and Wilkins, 2002. ISBN: 0781727979.

611.314   QM311.W64

Title varies: 1st ed., 1974: *An outline for dental anatomy,* Dorothy Permar; 2nd ed., 1979: *Permar's outline for dental anatomy*; 3rd ed., 1984: *Dental anatomy and its correlation with dental health service,* Julian B. Woelfel and Dorothy Permar; 5th ed., 1997.

There is a newer edition (Philadelphia: Lippincott, Williams & Wilkins, c2007) of this work in *Guide to reference.* While intended as a study guide for dental students, it can also serve as a reference book for dental anatomy and dental terminology. Includes an overview of teeth, description of each adult tooth, roots, root morphology, normal oral structures, and also dental anomalies. Illustrated with drawings, photographs, and charts. Includes techniques to draw, sketch, and carve teeth. Index.

798   Dental materials: Properties and manipulation. 9th ed. John M. Powers, John C. Wataha. x, 373 p., ill. St. Louis: Mosby/Elsevier, 2008. ISBN: 9780323049.

617.695   RK652.5.C7

1st ed., 1975; 8th ed., 2004.

Contents: (1) "Introduction to restorative dental materials," (2) "Properties of materials," (3) "Preventive dental materials," (4) "Direct esthetic restorative materials," (5) "Dental amalgam," (6) "Finishing, polishing, and cleansing materials," (7) "Cements," (8) "Impression materials," (9) "Model and die materials," (10) "Waxes," (11) "Casing alloys, wrought alloys, and solders," (12) "Casting of dental alloys," (13) "Polymers in prosthodontics," (14) "Dental ceramics," (15) "Dental implants."

This rev. ed. describes materials commonly used by dentists, dental hygienists, and dental assistants. Contains photographs, drawings, tables, and glossary. Associated website, intended for students and instructors, provides instructional video clips and various other aids useful in teaching and learning. Intended as an introductory text but also useful as a reference tool.

799   Dental terminology. 2nd ed. Charline M. Dofka. 370 p. Clifton Park, N.Y.: Thomson Delmar Learning, 2007. ISBN: 1418015229.

617.60014   RK28.D64

1st ed., 2000.

Contents: ch. 1, "Introduction to dental terminology"; ch. 2, "Anatomy and oral structures"; ch. 3, "Tooth origin and formation"; ch. 4, "Practice and facility setups"; ch. 5, "Infection control"; ch. 6, "Emergency care"; ch. 7, "Examination and prevention"; ch. 8, "Pain management/pharmacology"; ch. 9, "Radiography"; ch. 10, "Tooth restorations"; ch. 11, "Cosmetic dentistry"; ch. 12, "Prosthodontics"; ch. 13, "Endodontics"; ch. 14, "Oral and maxillofacial surgery"; ch. 15, "Orthodontics"; ch. 16, "Periodontics"; ch. 17, "Pediatric dentistry"; ch. 18, "Dental laboratory procedures"; ch. 19, "Business procedures." Full contents at http://www.loc.gov/catdir/toc/ecip072/2006032040.html.

This rev. ed. contains common dental terms used in dental practice and in the various dental specialties. Includes audio CD with pronunciations.

800 **Drug information handbook.** North American ed. Charles Lacy, Laura Armstrong, Morton Goldman, Leonard Lance, Lexi-Comp, Inc., American Pharmaceutical Association. Hudson, Ohio; Washington: Lexi-Comp; American Pharmaceutical Association, 1994–. ISSN: 1533-4511.

615   RM301.12.D783

Publ. in cooperation with the Amer. Pharmacists Assoc. (APhA).

1st ed., 1993/94. Available in North Amer. and internat. editions. Description based on 15th ed., 2007.

(Lexi-Comp's clinical reference library).

Concise, comprehensive, and user-friendly drug reference. Alphabetical listing of 1,400 drug monographs, with new drugs and updates to monographs since the last edition. Includes detailed information in consistent format (33 fields), such as dosage, drug interactions, adverse reactions (by occurrence, overdose, and toxicology), etc., with warnings highlighted. Appendix. Pharmacologic category index. For clinicians and healthcare professionals.

Several other comprehensive print pharmacology handbooks, also publ. by Lexi-Comp and frequently updated, include *Anesthesiology and critical care drug handbook* (1999–. ; 7th ed., 2006); *Drug information handbook for advanced practice nursing* (1990–. ; 8th ed., 2007); *Drug information handbook for dentistry* (1996– ; 12th ed., 2007); *Drug information handbook for oncology* (2000– ; 6th ed., 2007); *Drug information handbook for psychiatry: A comprehensive reference of psychotropic, nonpsychotropic, and herbal agents* (1999– ; 6th ed., 2006); *Drug information handbook for the allied health professional* (1995– ; 12th ed., 2005); *Geriatric dosage handbook* (1993– ; 11th ed., 2006); *Infectious diseases handbook: Including antimicrobial therapy & diagnostic test/procedures* (1994– ; 6th ed., 2006); *Natural therapeutics pocket guide* (2000– ; 2nd ed., 2003); *Pediatric dosage handbook* (1992– ; 13th ed., 2006); and *Pharmacogenomics handbook* (2003– ; 2nd ed., 2006). Also available online as pt. of Lexi-Comp Online™ (http://webstore.lexi.com/Store/ONLINE) and Lexi-Comp ONLINE for Dentistry (http://webstore.lexi.com/Store/ONLINE/Lexi-Comp-ONLINE-for-Dentistry).

801 **Law and risk management in dental practice.** Burton R. Pollack. xii, 284 p. Chicago: Quintessence Publ. Co., 2002. ISBN: 0867154160.

617.60068   RK58.P65

Contents: (1) Introduction to the judicial system of the United States; (2) The regulation of dental practice; (3) The dentist-patient relationship: contract law; (4) Is it negligence, malpractice, or breach of contract?; (5) Statute of limitations and statute of repose: how long the patient has to sue; (6) Experts and the standards of care; (7) Vicarious liability and respondeat superior; (8) Does the dentist have to treat?; (9) Consent, informed consent, and informed refusal; (10) Abandonment and dismissal of a patient; (11) Taking the medical-dental history; (12) Patient records; (13) Trial of a suit in malpractice: res ipsa loquitur, hearsay evidence, and contributory negligence; (14) What to do and what not to do if you are sued; (15) Dentist as witness; (16) Reports on jury trials and disciplinary proceedings; (17) Risk management in dental practice; (18) Office audit risk assessment for the general dentist; (19) Insuring a dental practice; Appendix: Legal terms with dental applications.

Information on the U.S. judicial system and basic legal information for dental professionals. Another legal resource, *Law, liability, and ethics for medical office professionals* (595) provides additional information.

Histories

802 **American Dental Association.** American Dental Association. 1995–. Chicago: American Dental Association. http://www.ada. org/.

Official website of the American Dental Association (ADA), founded in 1859.

Provides information for dental professionals concerning education and testing, practice management, and patient care. Includes a list of dental schools (http://www.ada.org/prof/ed/programs/search_ddsdmd_us.asp), accreditation, and licensure, and links to national dental organizations. Resources for consumers include, for example, "Oral Health Topics A–Z" (http://www.ada.org/public/topics/alpha.asp), "Find a dentist" (http://www.ada.org/public/disclaimer.asp), and a "Glossary of dental terms" (http://www.ada.org/public/resources/glossary.asp). Includes a "History of Medicine" timeline (Ancient Origins, Middle Ages–Renaissance,

18th century, 19th century, 20th century) (http://www.ada.org/public/ resources/history/index.asp), and a selected bibliography of history of dentistry books found in the ADA Library. Some of the resources are restricted to ADA members.

803 The American dentist: A pictorial history with a presentation of early dental photography in America. Richard A. Glenner, Audrey B. Davis, Stanley B. Burns. viii, 194 p., ill. Missoula, Mont.: Pictorial Histories Publ. Co., 1990. ISBN: 0929521056.

MLCM9301439(R)

History of American dentistry as represented by dental photography, considered an important part of the development of dentistry as a "scientifically based practice with specific educational standards. Intended to introduce the reader to major components of a dentist's career and how it grew out of American society, as well as contributing to this society over the past century and a half."—*Pref.* Twenty-one chapters, including early dental equipment, dental education in America, women becoming dentists, military dentistry in World War I and World War II, and more. Notes and index.

804 A bibliography of dentistry in America, 1790–1840. Milton B. Asbell. ix, 107, [1] p., ill. Cherry Hill, N.J.: Printed for the author by Sussex House Publ., 1973.

016.617600973   Z6668.A8

Imprint supplied from label mounted on p. [108]. Intends to list all books and articles on dentistry during the period indicated. Separate chronological list of books and articles. Locates copies of the books. List of journals searched, p. 80–84.

805 Dentistry: An illustrated history. Malvin E. Ring. 12, 319 p., ill., ports. (some color). New York; St. Louis: Abrams; C.V. Mosby, 1985. ISBN: 0810911000.

617.6009   RK29.R54

Contents: (I) The primitive world; (II) The ancient Near East; (III) The classical world; (IV) The early Middle Ages; (V) The Islamic world; (VI) The Far East; (VII) The late Middle Ages in Western Europe; (VIII) The Renaissance; (IX) The 17th century in Europe; (X) The 18th century in Europe; (XI) America: from the earliest times to the mid-19th century; (XII) The late 19th century in the U.S. and Europe; (XIII) The 20th century. Overview of the history of dentistry, from the earliest times to the

20th century. Illustrations, bibliography, and index. A brief bibliography of selected list of additional dental history books compiled by the American Dental Association (ADA) can be found as part of the ADA website (http://www.ada.org/prof/resources/library/histdent.asp).

806   A history of dentistry from the most ancient times until the end of the eighteenth century. Vincenzo Guerini, National Dental Association. x, [17]–355 p., ill., pl., ports., facsims. Philadelphia; New York: Lea & Febiger, 1909.

RK29.G8

Frequently reprinted. Published under the auspices of the National Dental Assoc. of the United States of America. A classic in this field, well documented by footnotes to sources. Includes name and subject index.

807   History of periodontology. Fermin A. Carranza, Gerald Shklar. ix, 214 p., ill. Chicago: Quintessence Publ., 2003. ISBN: 0867154241.
617.632   RK361.C373

Contents: pt. I, The prehistoric era and early civilizations; pt. II, Classical and Medieval ages; pt. III, The modern era; pt. IV, The nineteenth century; pt. V, The twentieth century. Covers the history of periodontology from prehistoric times to the present. Includes the important contributions from the basic biological and medical sciences and also from technology. Describes the accomplishments of many individuals, past and present, and their contributions to the development of the specialty of periodontics. Illustrations, index of persons, and subject index.

808   An introduction to the history of dentistry: With medical & dental chronology & bibliographic data. Bernhard Wolf Weinberger. 2 v., ill., ports., facsims. St. Louis: C.V. Mosby Co., 1948.
617.609   RK29.W39

Vol. 2 has title: *An introduction to the history of dentistry in America.* Describes the origin, evolution, and growth of knowledge of dentistry through the 19th century; presents the history of dentistry "graphically and biographically."—*Pref.* Includes bibliography of important literature in the history of dentistry; chronology of important related events in history, medicine, and dentistry. Index of personal names; subject index. Based in part on the author's earlier work, *Orthodontics: An historical review of its origin and evolution* (St. Louis: Mosby, 1926, 2 v.).

DENTISTRY

357

809 A sourcebook of dental medicine: Being a documentary history of dentistry and stomatology from the earliest times to the middle of the twentieth century. Gerald Shklar, David A. Chernin. xxi, 839 p., ill. Waban, Mass: Maro Publ., 2002. ISBN: 0971748004.

(Dental classics in perspective; 3)

   Contents: pt. I, Knowledge of dental medicine in primitive times and early ages of civilization (seven chapters); pt. II, The classical and Middle Ages—ancient and Medieval times (four chapters); pt. III, The Renaissance and its influence (seven chapters); pt. IV, The modern era (four chapters). This documentary history presents, in English translation, the major existing primary sources and original texts dealing with tooth and oral diseases. Presented in 22 chapters, starting with prehistoric times and ending with the 20th century. Each chapter begins with a introductory description of the particular era. Includes bibliographical references and indexes.

Indexes; Abstract journals; Databases

810 **Dental abstracts.** American Dental Association. ill. [Chicago]: American Dental Association, 1956–. ISSN: 0011-8486.

617.6082   RK1.A5416

Bimonthly. Imprint varies. Abstracts of state-of-the-art articles from selected English-language dental and medical journals published worldwide. Each issue currently contains approx. 50 abstracts, with developments and advances in general dentistry and dental specialties, including graphs, tables, and figures from the original articles. Author and subject indexes since 1990 in the November/December issue. Available online via Elsevier Science Direct. An earlier title, also titled *Dental abstracts*, publ. 1941–50 by Columbia University School of Dental and Oral Surgery, provides access to some of the earlier dental literature as an index of "dental progress. valuable to the research worker as a comprehensive guide to the literature."—*Pref.* of this time period.

811 **Index to dental literature.** American Dental Association; National Library of Medicine (U.S.). Chicago: American Dental Association, 1962–1999. ISSN: 00193992.

016.60016   Z6668.I45; RK51

1839/75–1936/38 (publ. 1921–39) had title: *Index of the periodical dental literature published in the English language*; 1939–61, *Index to dental periodical literature in the English language*; 1962–99 (print version discontinued).

Continued as part of MEDLINE (425)/PubMed (432). An author and subject index to dental periodical literature. Since 1962, includes periodicals in foreign languages. Contains lists of dental books, and theses and dissertations that have been accepted for degrees by schools of dentistry. Since 1965, coverage has been expanded to include articles in nondental journals. Relevant content can be found in MEDLINE/PubMed. A search in PubMed can be limited to "dental journals" subset.

812 Lexi-Comp online. Lexi-Comp, Inc. 1978–. Hudson, Ohio: Lexi-Comp, Inc. http://www.lexi.com/web/toursol.jsp.

Point-of-care drug and clinical information resource, with links to primary literature. Contains 15 clinical databases (e.g., Lexi-Drugs Online, AHFS, Lexi-Natural Products Online, Nursing Lexi-Drugs Online, Pharmacogenomics, Poisoning and Toxicology, Lab Tests and Diagnosis, and several others) and provides drug information and treatment recommendation for diseases and conditions. Also includes other features, e.g., an online interaction tool (Lexi-Interact) and medical calculator (Lexi-CALC). For pharmacists, physicians, nurses, and dentists. Detailed information available at the Lexi-Comp website "tour portal" (http://www.lexi.com/web/toursol.jsp).

813 MEDLINE. National Library of Medicine (U.S.). 1900s–. Bethesda, Md.: National Library of Medicine (U.S.). http://purl.access.gpo. gov/GPO/LPS4708.

MEDLINE®—Medical Literature Analysis and Retrieval System Online (National Library of Medicine®—NLM), primary subset of PubMed® (432) and part of the Entrez (3) databases provided by the National Center for Biotechnology Information (NCBI). Coverage extends back to 1950, with some older material (cf. http://www.nlm.nih.gov/services/oldmed. html).

Bibliographic database, providing comprehensive access to the international biomedical literature from the fields of medicine, nursing, dentistry, veterinary medicine, allied health, and the preclinical sciences. It is also a primary source of information from the international literature on biomedicine, including the following topics as they relate to biomedicine and health care: Biology, environmental science, marine biology, plant and animal science, biophysics, and chemistry. For indexing articles, NLM uses Medical Subject Headings MeSH® (575), a controlled vocabulary of biomedical terms. MEDLINE can also be searched via the NLM Gateway (429). An increasing number of MEDLINE citations contain a link to the free full-text articles.

The MEDLINE database is the electronic counterpart of *Index Medicus®* (420), *Index to dental literature* (811), and the *International nursing index* (1081).

For detailed information, see the MEDLINE fact sheet at http://www.nlm.nih.gov/pubs/factsheets/medline.html.

814   NLM gateway. National Library of Medicine (U.S.). 2000–.
Bethesda, Md.: National Library of Medicine. http://gateway.nlm.nih.gov/.

RA11

Allows simultaneous searching of information resources at the National Library of Medicine (NLM). Databases include MEDLINE (425)/PubMed (432) and the NLM Catalog (482) as well as other resources, including information on current clinical trials and consumer health information (MedlinePlus [463]). Currently provides access to 21 databases and other information resources (for a complete list of databases and other details, see http://www.nlm.nih.gov/pubs/factsheets/gateway.html). An overview of the search results is presented in several categories (bibliographic resources, consumer health resources, and other information), with a listing of the individual databases and the number of results within these categories.

815   PubMed. U.S. National Center for Biotechnology Information, National Library of Medicine, National Institutes of Health. 1996–. Bethesda, Md.: U.S. National Center for Biotechnology Information. http://www.ncbi.nlm.nih.gov/sites/entrez/.

PubMed®, developed and maintained by the National Center for Biotechnology Information (NCBI) at the National Library of Medicine® (NLM) (427). It is available via the NCBI Entrez (3) retrieval system. PubMed also provides access to the other Entrez molecular biology resources (*PubMed Overview*). Starting May 23, 2007, NCBI is changing to a new version of Entrez in a phased implementation (cf. Nahin AM. New and Improved PubMed®/Entrez and New URL *NLM tech. bull.*, 2007 May–Jun.; [356]: http://www.nlm.nih.gov/pubs/techbull/mj07/mj07_issue_cover.html).

Provides a search interface for more than 16 million bibliographic citations and abstracts in the fields of medicine, nursing, dentistry, veterinary medicine, health care systems, and preclinical sciences. It provides access to articles indexed for MEDLINE® (425) and for selected life sciences journals. PubMed subsets found under the "Limits" tab are: MEDLINE and PubMed Central®, several journal groups (i.e., core clinical journals, dental journals, and nursing journals), and topical subsets (AIDS, bioethics, cancer, complementary medicine, history of medicine, space life sciences, systematic reviews, and toxicology). "Linkout" provides access to full-text articles.

For detailed information see the PubMed fact sheet at http://www.nlm.nih.gov/pubs/factsheets/pubmed.html. For a brief overview of searching PubMed, see the PubMed Quick Start at http://www.ncbi.nlm.nih.gov/books/bv.fcgi?rid=helppubmed.section.pubmedhelp.PubMed_Quick_Start. For details on the now completed OLDMEDLINE retrospective conversion projects, see http://www.nlm.nih.gov/pubs/techbull/so06/so06_oldmedline_status.html.

Internet Resources

816   American Dental Association. American Dental Association. 1995–. Chicago: American Dental Association. http://www.ada.org/.

Official website of the American Dental Association (ADA), founded in 1859.

Provides information for dental professionals concerning education and testing, practice management, and patient care. Includes a list of dental schools (http://www.ada.org/prof/ed/programs/search_ddsdmd_us.asp), accreditation, and licensure, and links to national dental organizations. Resources for consumers include, for example, "Oral Health Topics A–Z" (http://www.ada.org/public/topics/alpha.asp), "Find a dentist" (http://www.ada.org/public/disclaimer.asp), and a "Glossary of dental terms" (http://www.ada.org/public/resources/glossary.asp). Includes a "History of Medicine" timeline (Ancient Origins, Middle Ages–Renaissance, 18th century, 19th century, 20th century) (http://www.ada.org/public/resources/history/index.asp), and a selected bibliography of history of dentistry books found in the ADA Library. Some of the resources are restricted to ADA members.

817   Dental Health (MedlinePlus). National Library of Medicine (U.S.), National Institutes of Health (U.S.). 200?–. Bethesda, Md.: U.S. National Library of Medicine, National Institutes of Health, Dept. of Health and Human Services. http://www.nlm.nih.gov/medlineplus/dentalhealth.html.

A Health Topic within MedlinePlus (463). Collection of links to information from government agencies and professional associations and organizations, with access to selected oral health resources. Provides basic information, research findings, a "reference shelf" with dental dictionaries/glossaries, directories, organizations, statistics, etc. "Go Local" link helps to identify services and providers for dental health in the U.S. Website also provides links to related MedlinePlus topics, e.g., child dental health, cosmetic dentistry, orthodontia, and others.

818   **General Dental Council.** General Dental Council. 2005?–. London: General Dental Council. http://www.gdc-uk.org/.

General Dental Council (GDC) is a regulatory body which provides patient protection and maintains statutory responsibilities for education and professional conduct and development of the dentists and dental auxiliaries in the U.K. Provides extensive web-based information and links for the public, including news, publications, and events, with an A–Z index and a list of links, including professional organizations (e.g., link to the British Dental Association [BDA] "Find a Dentist" http://www. bda-findadentist.org.uk/), dental education, U.K. regulatory bodies, various government health departments, and information for patients. Makes available, for example, "Dentists Register or Dental Care Professionals Register" database (http://www.gdc-uk.org/Search+our+registers/Home. htm) to check if a dentist, dental hygienist, or dental therapist is registered to practice in the U.K. *The dentists register* is available as a print resource, 1879 to the present.

819   **MedEdPORTAL.** Association of American Medical Colleges. 2006–. Washington: Association of American Medical Colleges. http://www.aamc.org/mededportal/.

Description based on MedEdPORTAL (version 1.4).

A project by the Association of American Medical Colleges (AAMC) that provides access to teaching resources used in medical education. Designed to help faculty publish and share educational resources. MedEdPORTAL staff review submissions for relevance and appropriateness before they are published on the site. Includes a user review feature. All approved user reviews are listed at the end of each published resource's details page. Information about copyright and copyright symbols can be found in the "Overview" section of the website.

MedEdPORTAL publications are cataloged using medical subject headings (MeSH: Medical Subject Headings [575]). Currently includes over 100 Virtual Patients (VPs), "interactive programs that simulate real-life clinical scenarios."—*Publisher's description.* To locate these and other resources, MedEdPORTAL can be browsed by discipline (list of subject areas and number of available resources within each category). Also searchable by keyword.

AAMC also participates in Health Education Assets Library (HEAL) (458), a repository of health sciences images, videos, and audio files from different collections.

5 > HEALTH CARE

820   **Dictionary of health economics and finance.** David E. Marcinko, Hope R. Hetico. 436 p. New York: Springer Publ., 2006. ISBN: 0826102549.
338.47362103   RA410.A3D53

Definitions, abbreviations and acronyms, and eponyms of medical economics and health care sector terminology. Bibliography. A similar title is *The dictionary of health economics* (149).

821   **Health care terms.** 4th ed. Vergil N. Slee, Debora A. Slee, H. Joachim Schmidt. 638 p., ill. Saint Paul, Minn.: Tringa Press, 2001. ISBN: 1889458023.
362.103   RA423.S545

1st ed., 1986; 3rd ed., 1996. Also called *Slee's health care terms.*

Provides 6,000 concise definitions for terms from a wide range of disciplines in the healthcare field, including administration, organization, finance, statistics, law, and governmental regulation. Many cross-references. Pays particular attention to acronyms. Terms used in definitions are italicized to indicate the term is defined elsewhere in the dictionary; related terms may be grouped together under one term, such as the many entries under the term "hospital." Intended for all types of healthcare consumers.

822   **Health services research and public health information programs.** National Library of Medicine (U.S.). Bethesda, Md.: National Library of Medicine, U.S. National Institutes of Health, Dept. of Health and Human Services. http://www.nlm.nih.gov/hsrph.html.

Lists resources from multiple National Library of Medicine (NLM) (427) programs, including collaborative projects (e.g., HSR information central [882]), links to several databases, e.g., HSRProj (Health Services Research Projects in Progress), HSRR (Health Services and Sciences Research Resources), Health Services/Technology Assessment Text (HSTAT), American Indian and Asian American Health, and others. Also provides pre-formulated PubMed (432) search filters and search strategies. Its outreach and training resources, with links to their full text, include "Finding and using health statistics," "Health economics: information resources," Health technology assessment 101 (HTA 101), "Public health information and data tutorial," publications, and informatics. Also provides access to various online publications, informatics resources, and links to additional information and related products.

823   **Introduction to health services.** 7th ed. Stephen J. Williams, Paul R Torrens. vii, 384 p., ill. (some color). Clifton Park, N.Y.: Thomson Delmar Learning, 2008. ISBN: 9781418012892.

362.10973   RA395.A3I495

1st ed., 1980; 6th ed., 2001.

Contents: Understanding health systems: The organization of health care in the United States; Technology in the U.S. health care system; Population and disease patterns and trends; Financing health systems; Private health insurance and managed care; Public health: joint public-private responsibility in an era of new threats; Ambulatory health care services and organizations; Hospitals and health systems; The continuum of long-term care; Mental and behavioral health services; The pharmaceutical industry; Health care professionals; Understanding health policy; The quality of health care; Ethical issues in public health and health services; The future of health services.

This revised edition "builds on a well-established format written by nationally recognized authors with updated research and statistics."— *Publ. notes.* Provides a description of the structure and function of the U.S. healthcare system, including the healthcare industry and healthcare provider organizations. Includes historical and current perspectives and recent changes in healthcare delivery.

824   **Jonas and Kovner's health care delivery in the United States.** 8th ed. Steven Jonas, Anthony R. Kovner, James Knickman. xxxi, 753 p., ill. New York: Springer, 2005. ISBN: 0826120873.

362.10973   RA395.A3J656

1st ed., *Health care delivery in the United States*, by Steven Jonas; 7th ed., 2002.

Contents: http://www.loc.gov/catdir/toc/ecip059/2005006979.html.

Examines the state of health care delivery in the U.S. and answers questions regarding health policy. This textbook helps to understand the characteristics of U.S. health care, its complexities, and its provision. Examines how changes in the healthcare system affects the health of the population, the cost of health care, access to care, and related issues. A chapter provides "a comparative analysis of health systems in wealthy nations." Includes bibliographical references and index.

Bibliography

825   American health care in transition: A guide to the literature.
Barbara A. Haley, Brian Deevey. xii, 336 p. Westport, Conn.: Greenwood Press, 1997. ISBN: 0313273235.

362.10973   RA395.A3H3426

(Bibliographies and indexes in medical studies ; no. 14). This annotated bibliography includes periodical articles and government publications, covering the literature 1979–1996. Index.

826   The health care crisis in the United States: A bibliography.
Joan Nordquist. 72 p. Santa Cruz, Calif.: Reference and Research Services, 1997. ISBN: 0937855901.

016.36210973   Z6675.E2N67; RA395.A3

(Contemporary social issues ; no. 46).

Entries are organized under broad topics and cover areas such as medical care, cost of medical care, right to health care, and delivery of health care. Provides a good starting point for further research. Includes books, journals, dissertations, congressional hearings, and other publications. HealthSTAR (Ovid) (440), MEDLINE® (425)/PubMed® (432), NLM gateway (429), and CINAHL (439), for example, could be used to update information found in this bibliography.

827   Health services research methodology core library recommendations, 2007. AcademyHealth, National Library of Medicine (U.S.). 2007. Bethesda, Md.: National Library of Medicine. http://www.nlm.nih.gov/nichsr/corelib/hsrmethods. html.

Produced by AcademyHealth; National Library of Medicine (NLM) (427); National Information Center on Health Services Research and Health Care (NICHSR).

List of books, journals, bibliographic databases, websites, and other media; useful for collection development librarians and researchers interested in health services research methods. Lists both "core" materials and "desired" materials in areas such as general health policy, health economics, health services research, public health, and several others. The NICHSR website (http://www.nlm.nih.gov/nichsr/outreach.html) lists links to several other recommended lists, including Health Economics Core Library Recommendation, Health Outcomes Core Library Recommendation, Health Policy Core Library Recommendation, and other information.

828   **Health Services Technology Assessment Texts (HSTAT).** National Library of Medicine (U.S.). 1994?–. Bethesda, Md.: National Library of Medicine (U.S.), National Institutes of Health, Dept. of Health and Human Services. http://hstat.nlm.nih.gov.

Coordinated by the National Library of Medicine's National Information Center on Health Services Research and Health Care Technology (NICHSR). Part of the "NCBI Bookshelf" (http://www.ncbi.nlm.nih.gov/sites/entrez?db=Books).

Searchable collection of full-text documents containing results of health services research, evidence reports and technology assessments, consensus conference reports, clinical practice guidelines (e.g., HIV/AIDS approved guidelines and information), reports of the Surgeon General, and other health information in support of health care decision making. Intended for health care providers, health service researchers, policy makers, payers, consumers, and information professionals. Further details in the *HSTAT fact sheet* (http://www.nlm.nih.gov/pubs/factsheets/hstat.html).

829   **The history of the health care sciences and health care, 1700–1980: A selective annotated bibliography.** Jonathon Erlen. xvi, 1028 p. New York: Garland, 1984. ISBN: 0824091663.
016.610903   Z6660.8.E74; R148

(Garland reference library of the humanities; v. 398).

Contains 5,004 entries with descriptive annotations; arranged alphabetically by topic. Includes English-language books, journal articles, government documents, unpublished masters' theses, and PhD dissertations. Index. Intended for researchers and students.

830   Introduction to health services research. National Library
of Medicine (U.S.). 2007–. Bethesda, Md.: National Library of
Medicine. http://www.nlm.nih.gov/nichsr/ihcm/index.html.

Produced by National Information Center on Health Services Research
(NICHSR) of the National Library of Medicine (NLM).

Contents: Introduction and Purpose; Course Objectives; Modules:
(1) What Is Health Services Research? (HSR); (2) Brief History of Health
Services Research and Key Projects and Milestones; (3) Selected Players
(Federal and Private); (4) Search the Literature of HSR: Databases; (5)
Quality Filtering and Evidence-Based Medicine and Health; (6) Basic
Components of a Study; (7) Librarians' Role in Health Services Research;
Selected HSR Internet Sites; Essential Concepts; Bibliography; Glossaries;
Review Sections.

Provides extensive information on health services issues, health services research, study design, bibliography of articles and books, databases,
and literature analysis.

831   Recent dissertations in the medical humanities. Jonathon Erlen,
University of Pittsburgh Health Sciences Library System. 2001–.
Pittsburgh: Health Sciences Library, University of Pittsburgh
Medical Center. http://www.hsls.pitt.edu/guides/histmed/
researchresources/dissertations/.

Provides a monthly current awareness service for selected recent medical
dissertation and theses. Arranged by topics, currently covers the following areas: AIDS (social and historical contexts); alternative medicine
(social and historical contexts); art and medicine; biomedical ethics; history of medicine prior to 1800; history of medicine and health care; history of science and technology; literature/theater and medicine; nursing
history; pharmacy/pharmacology and history; philosophy and medicine;
psychiatry/psychology and history; public health/international health;
religion and medicine; women's health and history. To view complete
citations, abstracts, and full-text of dissertations requires a subscription to Proquest Dissertations and Theses (PQDT) (Ann Arbor, Mich.:
ProQuest).

832   U.S. health law and policy, 2001: A guide to the current literature.
Donald H. Caldwell, American Health Lawyers Association. xxi,
593 p. San Francisco; Chicago: Jossey-Bass; Health Forum, 2001.
ISBN: 0787955043.

016.34473041   KF3821.A1C35

Earlier edition had title: *U.S. health law and policy 1999: A guide to the current literature*, 1998.

Contents: pt. 1, Medical facilities and organizations; pt. 2, Regulatory matters; pt. 3, Licensure, liability, and labor issues; pt. 4, Selected health care policy topics. Appendixes: (A) Health law periodicals, digests, and newsletters; (B) Reference sources and government serials; (C) Computer databases and Internet sites; (D) State-by-state synopsis of selected statutes of limitation laws; (E) Table of acronyms and abbreviations; (F) Glossary; (G) Relevant federal agencies; (H) Selected nongovernmental agencies; (I) State laws governing medical records; (J) Health Care Financing Administration regional offices. Subject, name, title indexes.

This rev. ed. is a comprehensive annotated bibliographic guide to the healthcare law and policy literature and related legal issues. Sources are books, journals, government documents, and websites. Entries provide publication information and a brief synopsis of the content of the citation. A future edition is planned.

Dictionaries

833 **The dictionary of health economics.** Anthony J. Culyer.
Northampton, Mass.: Edward Elgar, 2005. ISBN: 1843762080.
362.103   RA410.A3C85

Definitions of terms, concepts, and methods from the field of health economics and related fields, such as epidemiology, pharmacoeconomics, medical sociology, medical statistics, and others. Alphabetical arrangement. Personal names are included only when they are part of a headword. Also includes health economists' professional organizations, but no government agencies or research groups in universities (cf. *Pref.*). For health services researchers and professionals. Also available as an e-book. A similar title is *Dictionary of health economics and finance* (150).

834 **Dictionary of health insurance and managed care.** David Edward
Marcinko. New York: Springer, 2006. ISBN: 0826149944.
368.382003   RA413.D53

Up-to-date health insurance, managed care plans and programs, health care industry terminology and definitions, abbreviatons, and acronyms. Available online via netLibrary.

835 **Dictionary of medical sociology.** William C. Cockerham, Ferris
Joseph Ritchey. xxvi, 169 p. Westport, Conn.: Greenwood Press,

1997. ISBN: 0313292698.

306.46103   RA418.C655

Positioned at the intersection of arguably the softest of the soft sciences (sociology) and the hardest of the hard sciences (medicine), medical sociology has developed at a rapid pace over the last two decades to richly inform both of its parent disciplines. This dictionary from 1997 defines key terms from the newly-emerging field at that time, but also demonstrates how each discipline informs and expands the other. A useful reference tool, and also an informal guide to the newly-created field. Includes bibliographical references and index.

836   **The European multilingual thesaurus on health promotion in 12 languages.** Laura Dorst, Giancarlo Pocetta, Kerstin Karlström, Commission of the European Communities. 2001. Woerden, The Netherlands: NIGZ Netherlands Institute for Health Promotion and Disease Prevention. http://www.hpmulti.net/.

International collaborative project. Includes the key terminology of health education, health promotion, and patient education related to health behavior. Alphabetical display of terms in English (used as the source language) with 11 equivalent terms in Danish, Dutch, English, Finnish, French, German, Greek, Italian, Norwegian, Portuguese, Spanish, and Swedish. As described on the website, the thesaurus consists of the following other parts: Macrostructure (English), with systematic display of terms according to the macrostructure; Permuted index (English); Alphabetical display of the preferred and nonpreferred terms with the hierarchical and associative relationships (Danish, Dutch, English, Finnish, French, German, Greek, Italian, Norwegian, Portuguese, Spanish, and Swedish); Key index (Danish-English, Dutch-English, Finnish-English, French-English, German-English, Greek-English, Italian-English, Norwegian-English, Portuguese-English, Spanish-English, Swedish-English). Available as PDF file and text file.

837   **Health care defined: A glossary of current terms.** Bruce Goldfarb. xi, 347 p. Baltimore: Williams & Wilkins, 1997. ISBN: 0683036157.

362.103   RA423.G65

Scholarly resource. Explains the terminology used in the healthcare field, e.g., medical care, delivery of health care, and health services terminology. Contains approx. 3,000 essential terms and explains them in non-medical terminology. Includes bibliographical references (p. 313–315). Useful for insurance and legal professionals.

838 **Health services cyclopedic dictionary: A compendium of health-care and public health terminology.** 3rd ed. Thomas C. Timmreck. xii, 860 p., color ill. Sudbury, Mass.: Jones and Bartlett Publishers, 1997. ISBN: 0867205156.

362.1068   RA393.T56

1st ed. (1982) and 2nd ed. (1987) had title: *Dictionary of health services management.*

(The Jones and Bartlett series in health sciences).

This rev. and exp. ed. contains terminology and definitions from the fields of health services and medical care, health administration, health care reform, public health, environmental health, epidemiology, managed care, and other related areas.

839 **The managed health care dictionary.** 2nd ed. Richard Rognehaugh. xii, 261 p. Gaithersburg, Md.: Aspen Publ., 1998. ISBN: 0834211440.

362.10425803   RA413.R58

1st ed., 1996.

Includes over 1,000 terms with definitions, including slang, acronyms, etc., many with cross-references. Does not include medical specialties and health professions. Intended for health professionals, patients, and others. Another more recent title is *Dictionary of health insurance and managed care* (151).

840 **The progressive era's health reform movement: A historical dictionary.** Ruth C. Engs. xxii, 419 p. Westport, Conn.: Praeger, 2003. ISBN: 0275979326.

362.1097303   RA395.A3E547

Covers 1880–1925, the time period labeled the Progressive era of the United States. Entries cover individuals (biographical information/assessment of historical importance), events, crusades (e.g., exercise, vegetarian diets, alternative health care), legislation, publications, and terms. Includes entries on the health reform movement and campaigns against alcohol, tobacco, drugs, and sexuality. For scholars, students, and general readers. "Selected chronology" (p. [371]–407), bibliographical references, and index. Available online via netLibrary.

841 **Slee's health care terms.** 5th ed. Debora A. Slee, Vergil N. Slee, H. Joachim Schmidt. 700 p. Sudbury, Mass.: Jones and Bartlett Publ., 2007. ISBN: 9780763746155.

362.103   RA423.S55

1st ed., 1986; 4th ed., 2001. Also called *Health care terms.*

Provides concise definitions for terms from a wide range of disciplines in the healthcare field, including administration, organization, finance, statistics, law, and governmental regulation. Many cross-references. Pays particular attention to acronyms. Terms used in definitions are italicized to indicate the term is defined elsewhere in the dictionary; related terms may be grouped together under one term, such as the many entries under the term "hospital." Intended for all types of healthcare consumers.

Directories

842   **AHA guide to the health care field.** American Hospital
       Association. Chicago: Healthcare Infosource, Inc., 1997–.
                                                   RA977.A1A46;RA977. A44

Title varies: 1949–71, pt. 2 of Aug. issue (called "Guide issue," 1956–70) of *Hospitals*, which superseded *American hospital directory* (1945–48); 1972–73, *The AHA guide to the health care field*; 1974–96, *American Hospital Association guide to the health care field.*

"America's directory of hospitals and health care systems."—*Cover* Description based on 2006–07 ed.

"Provides basic data reflecting the delivery of health care in the United States and associated territories."—*Introd.* Four major sections, each with table of contents and explanatory information: (A) Hospitals, institutional, and associate members; (B) networks, health care systems, and alliances; (C) lists of health organizations, agencies, and providers; and (D) indexes. Current edition also available in CD-ROM format.

Statistical information concerning hospitals is published in *AHA hospital statistics* (508).

843   **DIRLINE.** National Institutes of Health (U.S.). [1983?–.] Bethesda,
       Md.: U.S. National Institutes of Health, Dept. of Health and
       Human Services. http://dirline.nlm.nih.gov/.

DIRLINE® (Directory of Information Resources Online), maintained by the National Library of Medicine (NLM) (427).

Online annotated directory of organizations, research resources, projects, databases, and other information resources concerned with health and biomedicine from a variety of sources, including federal, state, and local government agencies, academic and research institutions, and also consumer health-related resources such as self-help groups and health hotlines. Resources are mostly from the U.S. but also include some international resources. Currently contains over 8,000 entries, with topics on most diseases and conditions and health services research and technology assessment. Can be searched using MeSH® (Medical Subject Headings) (575), keywords, or by name and location of a resource. Detailed information on DIRLINE can be found via a fact sheet prepared by NLM: http://www.nlm.nih.gov/pubs/factsheets/dirlinfs.html.

844 Health care standards: Official directory. ECRI. Plymouth
Meeting, Pa.: ECRI, 1990–. ISSN: 1044-4076.
362.1021873   RA399.A3H43

Description based on 18th ed., 2006.

ECRI (http://www.ecri.org), formerly the Emergency Care Research Institute, is a nonprofit health services research agency and a Collaborating Center of the World Health Organization (WHO) (951). Provides information and technical assistance to the healthcare community to support safe and cost-effective patient care. The Agency for Healthcare Research and Quality (AHRQ) (733) has designated ECRI an Evidence-based Practice Center. ECRI is also responsible for performing the technical work of developing and maintaining AHRQ's National Guideline Clearinghouse and the National Quality Measures Clearinghouse. Contains health care standards issued by medical societies, professional associations, government agencies, and other health-related organizations, with approx. "38,000 titles of standards, practice guidelines, position papers, technical statements, technology assessments, advisories, policies, procedures, hazard reports, recommended practices, and other official documents, federal and state health-care related laws and regulations, and contact information for the issuing organizations" (cf. *Publ. notes*). Arranged under keywords; abbreviations; organizations and their standards; law, legislation, and regulation (federal and state); and names and addresses (federal and state). Intended for use in clinical and legal settings by researchers, educators, and legal professionals. Also available as HCS Online, providing daily updates and enhanced search results. Further details for both the print and online editions are provided at https://www.ecri.org/Products/Pages/healthcare_standards_directory.asp x.

845 Who's who in medicine and healthcare. New Providence, N.J.:
Marquis Who's Who, c1996–. ISSN: 0000-1708.
R153.W43

Description based on 6th ed. (2006–07). Compilation of biographical information on medical professionals, including administrators, educators, researchers, clinicians, and other medical and healthcare personnel. Listings include full name, occupation, date/place of birth, family background, education summary, writings, and association memberships and awards. Includes a section on "Ten who made a difference." Also available online on Who's Who on the Web (http://www.marquiswhoswho.com).

Encyclopedias

846   Encyclopedia of cancer and society. Graham A. Colditz. 3 v., ill. (some color). Thousand Oaks, Calif.: Sage, 2007. ISBN: 9781412949.
616.994003   RC254.5.E48

Addresses the issues surrounding cancer and its effects on society. Describes the different types of cancer; possible causes; suspected carcinogens; cancer treatments, including alternative treatments and diets; and controversies in treatment and research. Contains information on the relationship between race and ethnicity and cancer risk, socioeconomic factors, cancer researchers, cancer associations, hospitals and treatment centers, health and medical policy issues, cancer incidence rates for other countries, and many other related topics. Includes a chronology of cancer from 3000 BCE to the present as well as an "Atlas of cancer" (p. A1–A16). Intended for students, practitioners, and researchers.

847   Encyclopedia of health care management. Michael J. Stahl. xxxvii, 621 p., ill. Thousand Oaks, Calif.: Sage, 2004. ISBN: 0761926747.
362.1068   RA971.E52

Alphabetical list of entries at the beginning of the book provides an overview of the terminology and variety of subject areas covered in this resource including business and economics, statistics, law, clinical research, informatics, and others. A reader's guide with the following major headings is provided: Accounting and activity-based costing, Economics, Finance, Health policy, Human resources, Information technology, Institutions and organizations, International health care issues, Legal and regulatory issues, Managed care, Marketing and customer value, Operations and decision making, Pharmaceuticals and clinical trials, Quality, Statistics and data mining, and Strategy. The main section, consisting of approx. 650 entries, is alphabetically arranged. Each entry contains the term's definition, background, and other relevant information. Includes tables on health care acronyms, medical degrees, medical legislation, and others. Cross-references, list of further readings, and websites. Index. Also available online from Sage eReference (http://www.sage-ereference.com/public/browse.php).

848 **Health care policy and politics A to Z.** 2nd ed. Julie Rovner. xii, 282 p., ill. Washington: CQ Press, 2003. ISBN: 1568028520.

362.1042   RA395.A3R685

1st ed., 2000.

Concise entries and definitions important in understanding health care, health policy, and related areas and issues. Includes health policy timeline, a list of key health care policy acronyms, suggested readings, sources for further information, and index.

Guides

849 **The Blackwell companion to medical sociology.** William C. Cockerham. xiii, 528 p., ill. Oxford; Malden, Mass.: Blackwell, 2001; repr. 2005. ISBN: 0631217037.

306.461   RA418.B5736

Global and comprehensive survey of the emerging field of medical sociology. Twenty-six signed chapters draw out topics in Western medicine to show how sociological theory and analysis enrich the clinical understanding of each area. A second section covers countries in every corner of the globe: Canada, Mexico, Brazil, countries in both Western and Eastern Europe, Africa, the Arab world, Israel, Australia, Japan, and China. Cultural constructs from the discipline of sociology inform medical practice and understanding. A thoroughly useful textbook for understanding the field. Includes bibliographical references and index.

850 **Health care almanac: Every person's guide to the thoughtful and practical sides of medicine.** 2nd ed. Lorri A. Zipperer. American Medical Association. xiv, 546 p. Chicago: American Medical Association, 1998. ISBN: 0899709001.

362.1097303   R104.H43

1st ed. (1993) had title: *The healthcare resource and reference guide*; rev. 1995 ed. had title: *Health care almanac: A resource guide to the medical field*.

Addresses common queries by physicians and patients, including health and medical practice-related issues. In three sections: (1) Dictionary-style directory arranged alphabetically by subject, with the names of organizations that may be able to provide information on specific subjects; (2)

Outlines major administrative units of the American Medical Association (AMA), with an historical overview since 1846; (3) Tools to help navigate the almanac: listing of sources and index which is also intended to serve cross-referencing needs. Includes "Principles of Medical Ethics," "The Hippocratic Oath," and "Patient Bill of Rights." Provides information and glossaries on managed care, tort reform, Medicare, background on terminal care and advanced directives and end-of-life issues, patient safety, home health care, etc. This print resource can be supplemented with web-based, possibly more up-to-date information found on the AMA website (American Medical Association [homepage] [451]) with its professional resources section, including online ethics resources; DoctorFinder (209); and other links.

851 **Health care resources on the Internet: A guide for librarians and health care consumers.** M. Sandra Wood. xxi, 205 p. New York: Haworth Information Press, 2000. ISBN: 0789006324.

025.0661   R119.9.H39

Contents: ch. 1, Use of the Internet at the reference desk (Nancy Calabretta); ch. 2, Natural language and beyond: tips for search services (Eric P. Delozier); ch. 3, Megasites for health care information (Cindy A. Gruwell, Scott Marsalis); ch. 4, MEDLINE on the Internet (Helen-Ann Brown, Valerie G. Rankow); ch. 5, Searching the Internet for diseases (Alexa Mayo, Cynthia R. Phyillaier); ch. 6, Consumer health information on the Internet (Janet M. Coggan); ch. 7, Alternative medicine on the Net (Suzanne M. Shultz, Nancy I. Henry, Esther Y. Dell); ch. 8, Government resources on the Net (Nancy J. Allee); ch. 9, Health-related statistical information on the Net (Dawn M. Littleton, Kathryn Robbins); ch. 10, Electronic journals on the Internet (Virginia A. Lingle); ch. 11, Searching international medical resources on the World Wide Web (Jeri Ann Risin). Provides a list of selected websites and also general information on developing skills and techniques for Internet searching for health-related information, including evidence-based medicine. Includes a "Comparative Chart of MEDLINE Searching Systems." A practical resource, useful for librarians, health care professionals, and general readers.

Finding and using health and medical information on the Internet (London: Aslib-IMI, 2001) by Sue Welsh et al. and Sydney S. Chellen's *Essential guide to the Internet for health professionals* (London; New York: Routledge, 2003) are other guides on how to locate biomedical information effectively. Even though some of the content in these three resources needs updating, they nevertheless remain useful guides.

HEALTH CARE

375

Handbooks

852 **Contemporary issues in healthcare law and ethics.** 3rd ed. Dean M. Harris. 377 p. Chicago; Washington: Health Administration Press; AUPHA Press, 2007. ISBN: 9781567932.

344.730321   KF3825.Z9.H3

1st ed., 1999, had title *Healthcare law and ethics: Issues for the age of managed care*; 2nd ed., 2003.

Contents: (1) "The role of law in the U.S. healthcare system"; (2) "Managing and regulating the healthcare system"; (3) "Patient care issues"; (4) "Legal and ethical issues in health insurance and managed care"; table of cases; table of statutes; table of regulations; index.

This revised and updated edition presents essential information and examines legal and ethical issues in health care. Includes, for example, the U.S. Supreme Court's decisions on physician-assisted suicide, partial-birth abortion, issues in emergency contraception, HIPAA Privacy Rule, medical malpractice, reporting of medical errors, and other topics. Also available as e-book via netLibrary.

853 **CPT handbook for psychiatrists.** 3rd ed. Chester W. Schmidt, Rebecca Yowell, Ellen Jaffe. xiii, 140 p., ill. Washington: American Psychiatric Publishing, 2004. ISBN: 1585621579.

616.890012   RC465.6.S36

1st ed., 1993; 2nd ed., 1999.

CPT (Current Procedural Terminology).

Contents: ch. 1, "Basics of CPT"; ch. 2, "Introduction to documentation"; ch. 3, "Codes and documentation for psychiatric services"; ch. 4, "Codes and documentation for other mental health services"; ch. 5, "Codes and documentation for evaluation and management services"; ch. 6, "Medicare"; ch. 7, "Health insurance issues"; ch. 8, "Putting it all together for accurate coding." Appendixes: A, "The CPT coding system"; B, "Modifiers"; C, "ECT information, consent form, and record template"; D, "Vignettes for evaluation and management codes"; E, "Documentation templates"; F, "Examples of relative value units (RVUs)(2004)"; G, "National distribution of evaluation and management code selection by psychiatrists"; H, "American Psychiatric Association CPT Coding Service and additional resources"; I, "Center for Medicare and Medicaid services (CMS) regional offices"; J, "Medicare pt. B carriers"; K, "Health Insurance Portability and Accountability Act (HIPAA)"; L, "CPT psychiatric code matrix."

Explains the structure and function of CPT, how to use the psychiatric therapeutic procedure codes, and how CPT affects the practice of psychiatry. This edition includes "changes mandated by the Health Insurance Portability and Accountability Act and other changes in the way psychiatry is currently practiced."—*Pref.*

854   Delivering health care in America: A systems approach. 4th ed. Leiyu Shi, Douglas A. Singh. 649 p. Sudbury, Mass.: Jones and Bartlett, 2008. ISBN: 9780763745127.

362.10973   RA395.A3S485

1st ed., 1998; 3rd ed., 2004.

Contents: ch. 1, A distinctive system of health care delivery; ch. 2, Beliefs, values, and health; ch. 3, The evolution of health services in the United States; ch. 4, Health services professionals; ch. 5, Medical technology; ch. 6, Health services financing; ch. 7, Outpatient and primary care services; ch. 8, Inpatient facilities and services; ch. 9, Managed care and integrated organizations; ch. 10, Long-term care; ch. 11, Health services for special populations; ch. 12, Cost, access, and quality; ch. 13, Health policy; ch. 14, The future of health services delivery.

Provides a basic introduction and overview of the U.S. healthcare system, with coverage of all aspects of healthcare delivery including quality, cost, and health and medical policy. Includes bibliographical references and index. The 3rd ed. (2004) is available online via netLibrary.

855   Essentials of managed health care. 5th ed. Peter R. Kongstvedt. xxi, 841 p., ill. Sudbury, Mass.: Jones and Bartlett, 2007. ISBN: 9780763739836.

362.104258   RA413.E87

1st ed., 1989; 4th ed., 2001 had title *The managed health care handbook.* 5th ed., 2007 is the rev. ed. of two different titles by the same author: *The managed health care handbook,* 4th ed., 2001, and rev. ed. of *Essentials of managed health care,* 4th ed., 2001.

Contents: section 1: Introduction to managed health care (ch. 1–4); section 2: The health care delivery system (ch. 5–8); section 3: Medical management (ch. 9–16); section 4: Operational management and marketing (ch. 17–25); section 5: Special markets (ch. 26–29); section 6: Legal and regulatory issues (ch. 30–33); glossary; index. Intended as a guide and a resource to the managed health care system, with information on types of managed care plans and integrated healthcare delivery systems, physician networks in managed health care, prescription drug benefits in managed health care, etc.

856   **Handbook of research on informatics in healthcare and biomedicine.** Athina A. Lazakidou. xxx, 437, 11 p., ill. Hershey, Pa.: Idea Group Reference, 2006. ISBN: 1591409829.

610.285   R853.D37H36

Contents: section 1, Medical data and health information systems; section 2, Standardization and classification systems in medicine; section 3, Virtual reality applications in medicine; section 4, Virtual learning environments in healthcare and biomedicine; section 5, Computer assisted diagnosis; section 6, Data mining and medical decision making; section 7, Current aspects of knowledge management in medicine; section 8, Telemedicine and e-health services; section 9, Image processing and archiving systems; section 10, Signal processing techniques; section 11, Use of new technologies in biomedicine; section 12, Ergonomic and safety issues in computerized medical equipment; section 13, Health economics and health services research. Provides information on new trends, computer applications, and advanced technologies in health care and biomedicine. Key terms and their definitions; cross-referencing of key terms; index. Available online via netLibrary.

857   **Health care reform around the world.** Andrew C. Twaddle. xiii, 419 p., ill. Westport, Conn.: Auburn House, 2002. ISBN: 0865692882.

362.1   RA394.H4145

Describes health care reform efforts and trends in different countries, with roughly comparable information for the countries included. Ch. 1 is an international comparison of health care system reforms—United Kingdom, Eastern and Western Europe, United States, the Middle East, Latin America, Asia, and Oceania. Online edition available via Greenwood Digital Collection (ebooks.greenwood.com/browse/index.jsp) and netLibrary.

858   **Health care systems around the world: Characteristics, issues, reforms.** Marie L. Lassey, William R. Lassey, Martin J. Jinks. xiii, 370 p., ill., maps. Upper Saddle River, N.J.: Prentice Hall, 1997. ISBN: 0131042335.

362.1   RA393.L328

Contents: Introduction, basic issues and concepts; The countries and their characteristics; The United States, high-technology and limited access; Canada, challenges to public payment for universal care; Japan, preventive health care as cultural norm; Germany, a tradition of universal health care; France, centrally controlled and locally managed; The Netherlands, gradual adaptation; Sweden, decentralized comprehensive care; The United Kingdom, the economy model; The Czech Republic, a new mixture of public and private services; Hungary, creating a remodeled system; Russia, transition to market and consumer orientation; China, privatizing socialist health care; Mexico, modernizing structure and expanded rural services; Organization variations and reforms; Economic organization of health care, comparative perspectives; Expectations for reform, a glimpse at the future. Description and analysis of health care systems in different countries, addressing demographic, social, and economic characteristics, also health promotion, prevention of disease, and health care. Includes bibliographical references and index.

859 **Health care systems of the developed world: How the United States' system remains an outlier.** Duane A. Matcha. x, 198 p., ill. Westport, Conn.: Praeger, 2003. ISBN: 027597992X.

362.10973   RA441.M38

Contents: ch. 1, Introduction; ch. 2, The United States; ch. 3, Canada; ch. 4, United Kingdom; ch. 5, Germany; ch. 6, Sweden; ch. 7, Japan; ch. 8, Conclusion. Provides an introduction to selected major healthcare systems, with consideration of their historical and political basis. Provides a framework for analysis and comparison of the different systems. Various tables and figures related to health insurance, personal health care expenditures, self-rated health status, future concerns, and others. Includes bibliographical references and index. *World health systems: Challenges and perspectives* (Chicago: Health Administration Pr., 2002) presents profiles of health systems in 28 countries. A 1997 publication, *Health care systems around the world: Characteristics, issues, reforms* (Upper Saddle River, N.J.: Prentice Hall, 1997), provides additional information in this area. Milton I. Roemer's *National health systems of the world*, publ. 1991–93, remains an important title. It consists of a comprehensive study and analysis of national health systems in 68 industrialized, middle-income, and very poor countries, with a cross-national analysis of the major health care issues within different systems.

860 **The law and the public's health.** 7th ed. Kenneth R. Wing, Benjamin Gilbert. xiii, 391 p. Chicago: Health Administration Press, 2007.

344.7304   KF3775.W5

Contents: ch. 1, "The law and the legal system"; ch. 2, "The power of the state governments in matters affecting health care"; ch. 3, "Government power and the right to privacy"; ch. 4, "The constitutional discretion of the state and federal governments to limit or condition social welfare benefits"; ch. 5, "Government regulation of health care providers and payers"; ch. 6, "The scope of discretion of administrative agencies in matters affecting health and health care"; ch. 7, "The fraud and abuse laws"; ch. 8, "The antitrust laws: Government enforcement of competition"; ch. 9, "Malpractice: Liability for negligence in the delivery and financing of health care"; ch. 10, "Health care business law: Legal considerations in the structuring of health care entities and their transactions."

Intended as an introductory text for schools of public health and law-related courses, this book can also serve as a reference book in the health care field. Provides an introduction to the law, the legal system, and principles applicable to the delivery and financing of health care but is not considered a treatise on health law. Includes bibliographical references and index.

Also available as an e-book via netLibrary.

861 Medical records and the law. 4th ed. William H. Roach, American Health Information Management Association. xix, 591 p. Sudbury, Mass.: Jones and Bartlett Publ., 2006. ISBN: 0763734454.

344.73041   KF3827.R4R63

1st ed., 1985; 3rd ed., 1998.

Contents: ch. 1, Introduction to the American legal system; ch. 2, Medical records and managed care; ch. 3, Medical record requirements; ch. 4, Medical records entries; ch. 5, Documenting consent to treatment; ch. 6, Access to health information; ch. 7, Reporting and disclosure requirements; ch. 8, Documentation and disclosure: special areas of concern; ch. 9, HIV/AIDS: mandatory reporting and confidentiality; ch. 10, Discovery and admissibility of medical records; ch. 11, Legal theories in improper disclosure cases; ch. 12, Risk management and quality management; ch. 13, Electronic health records; ch. 14, Health information in medical research; Index. Provides information on the growth of electronic health record systems and electronic data networks. Addresses the issues related to medical research involving human subjects and how patient information can be used.

862 Medicare handbook. Center for Medicare Advocacy. New York: Aspen Publishers, c2000–. ISSN: 1530-8979.

368   KF3608.A4M436

Description based on 2007 ed. Contents: (1) An introduction to Medicare coverage and appeals; (2) Hospital coverage; (3) Skilled nursing facility coverage; (4) Home health coverage; (5) Hospice coverage; (6) Medicare Part B: supplemental medical insurance; (7) Medicare-Advantage: coordinated care plans, private fee-for-service, and other delivery of services options; (8) Medigap services; (9) Medicare's relationship with private insurance; (10) Dual eligibility: issues for Medicare beneficiaries also eligible for Medicaid; (11) Prescription drug coverage. Resource to help understand Medicare's rules and regulations. Further helpful, detailed information can also be found on the Medicare website (Medicare: the official U.S. government site for people with medicare at http://www.medicare.gov), part of the Centers for Medicare & Medicaid Services (742).

863   Patients' rights in the age of managed health care. Lisa Yount. 280
        p. New York: Facts On File, 2001. ISBN: 0816042586.
344.73041   KF3823.Y68

Provides overview of the issues in health care delivery, patients' rights and applicable laws, a chronology of significant events, and also a guide to further research in patients' rights issues. Glossary, index, and annotated bibliography. *The rights of patients: The authoritative ACLU guide to the rights of patients* (600) provides further information.

864   The U.S. health care delivery system: Fundamental facts,
        definitions, and statistics. Kim M. Garber, American Hospital
        Association. xi, 86 p., ill. Chicago: Health Forum: AHA Pr., 2006.
        ISBN: 1556483309.
362.10973   RA445.U85

Contents: ch. 1, Patient care; ch. 2, Caregivers; ch. 3, Facilities; ch. 4, Money; ch. 5, Government and other types of oversight. "Organized for quick answers and easy understanding."—*Publ. notes.* Overview of the U.S. health-care system, the practice of healthcare management, and delivery of health care. Contains industry data and research findings. Glossary and index.

865   World health systems: Challenges and perspectives. Bruce Fried,
        Laura M. Gaydos. xii, 563 p., ill. Chicago: Health Administration
        Pr., 2002. ISBN: 0585426422.
362.1   RA441.W676

Contents: pt. I, Current issues facing global health systems; pt. II, Profiled countries: the wealthy countries (ch. 4–15); The transitional countries (ch. 16–28); The very poor countries (ch. 29–31); glossary of terms; index. Presents profiles of health systems in 28 countries. Organized in three categories by the wealth of each nation: wealthy, transitional, and very poor. Addresses the various challenges health services face, how they are organized, and how they are financed. Each chapter includes disease patterns and health system financing, also the "history, present status and future challenges of their health systems."—*Pref.* Available online via netLibrary.

Indexes; Abstract journals; Databases

866   AgeLine. AARP (American Association of Retired People). 2004–. Ipswich, Mass.: EBSCO. http://www.ebscohost.com/thisTopic. php?marketID=1&topicID=23.

HQ1061

AgeLine is a comprehensive index, with abstracts. Provides coverage of the scholarly and professional literature on aging and age-related matters, including the delivery of health care to the older population and its costs, and various public policy issues. Covers 1978 to the present, with selected coverage from 1966–77. Materials include books, chapters from books, journal articles, dissertations, videos, and a surprisingly broad range of gray literature. Does not include book reviews, editorials, newspapers, individual conference papers, and statistical data.

Full text is linked when available, and ordering information is provided for priced publications. Publications indexed in this database use *Thesaurus of aging terminology*, a controlled vocabulary of subject terms, currently in its 8th ed.

Formerly a free database provided by the American Association of Retired People (AARP), AgeLine is now only available via subscription through EBSCOhost. Website provides clear user information for the database and excellent guidance for those of any age or academic level, writing about aging matters. Also of note is AARP's companion Internet Resources on Aging at http://www.aarp.org/internetresources/.

Appropriate for school, general, and research collections.

867   CINAHL. Cinahl Information Systems, EBSCO. 1982–. Ipswich, Mass.: EBSCO. http://www.ebscohost.com/cinahl/.

CINAHL® [database]. Title varies. Online version: 1984–1992 (with coverage 1982–.), publ. by Cinahl Information Systems; 1993–., publ. jointly by EBSCO and Cinahl Information Systems. Also available in different enhanced versions: CINAHL® with Full Text, CINAHL® Plus™, and CINAHL® Plus with Full Text. Comparisons of the different versions at http://www.ebscohost.com/uploads/thisTopic-dbTopic-592.pdf.

Print version: 1956–76 entitled: *Cumulative index to nursing and allied health literature*; 1977–. *Cumulative index to nursing and allied health literature®* (continues to be published in print).

Authoritative database for the professional literature of nursing and allied health. Provides references to journal articles, books, book chapters, pamphlets, audiovisual materials, dissertations, educational software, selected conference proceedings, standards of professional practice, and more. Some full-text material is included. Currently indexes a large number of journals, as well as publications from the American Nurses' Association and the National League for Nursing. Allows for application of specific interest category filter, e.g., evidence-based practice, informatics, patient safety, public health, women's health, and others. Subject access is provided by *CINAHL subject heading list: Alphabetic list, tree structures, permuted list* (1093). Complements *International nursing index* (1081), publ. 1966–2000.

868 **The Cochrane Library.** Cochrane Collaboration. 1996–.
Hoboken, N.J.: Wiley Interscience. ISSN: 1465-1858. http://www3.
interscience.wiley.com/cgi-bin/mrwhome/106568753/HOME.

R723.7

Acronyms: Evidence-based medicine (EBM); Evidence-based Health Care (EBHC).

Imprint varies: 1996–2003, Update Software Ltd., Oxford, U.K.; publ. by Wiley Interscience 2004–. Produced by contributors to the Cochrane Collaboration (founded in 1993 and named after the British epidemiologist, Archie Cochrane) and consists of a group of experts in the various clinical specialties who apply EBM criteria to the review and selection of studies, perform meta-analyses, and then write detailed topical reviews.

The Cochrane Library consists of several online databases that provide systematic reviews, meta-analyses of the literature, and randomized clinical trials: Cochrane Database of Systematic Reviews (CDSR)—Cochrane Reviews and protocols; Database of Abstracts of Reviews of Effectiveness (DARE)—Other Reviews; Cochrane Central Register of Controlled Trials (CENTRAL)—Clinical Trials; Cochrane Methodology Register (CMR)—Methods Studies; Health Technology Assessment Database (HT)—Health Technology; and NHS Economic Evaluation Database (NHSEED). Further

HEALTH CARE

383

detailed descriptions can be found at http://www3.interscience.wiley.com/cgi-bin/mrwhome/106568753/ProductDescriptions.html. Also available via Ovid and EBSCO.

The major product of the Cochrane Collaboration is the Cochrane Database of Systematic Reviews, prepared mostly by healthcare professionals who work as volunteers in one of the many Cochrane Review Groups. Editorial teams oversee the preparation and updating of the reviews and applying quality standards. Provides access to full-text review articles reviewing the effects of health care.

Other examples of EBM and EBHC resources include ACP Journal Club and ACP PIER (American College of Physicians), Clinical Evidence (BMJ), DynaMed (EBSCO), InfoRetriever/InfoPOEMS (http://www.Info-POEMS.com), Evidence Matters, PubMed (432)/PubMed Clinical Queries (systematic reviews and meta-analyses [http://www.ncbi.nlm.nih.gov/entrez/query/static/clinical.shtml]), Turning Research Into Practice [TRIP] database, Health Services Technology Assessment Text [HSTAT] [419], NLM gateway [429], searching across several government information systems [e.g., PubMed [432], ClinicalTrials.gov [191], HSRProj, etc.], National Guideline Clearinghouse [715], and others.

Many websites from various organizations and universities provide EBM and EBHC-related subject guides, e.g., EBM Resource Center, New York Academy of Medicine [http://www.ebmny.org/], "Evidence-Based Practice" subject guide [Hardin Library for the Health Sciences, The University of Iowa http://www.lib.uiowa.edu/hardin/eb.html], "Evidence Based Medicine" [Welch Medical Library, Johns Hopkins University http://www.welch.jhu.edu/internet/ebr.html], and many others.

Print EBM/EBHC resources are, for example, Sharon E. Strauss and R. Brian Haynes' *Evidence-based medicine: How to practice and teach EBM* [3rd ed., 2005; author varies: 1st and 2nd ed. by David L. Sackett] and *Clinical epidemiology: How to do clinical practice research* [3rd ed., 2006], by R. Brian Haynes.

869 HealthSTAR (Ovid). National Library of Medicine (U.S.). 2000–. Sandy, Utah: Ovid Technologies. http://www.ovid.com/site/products/ovidguide/hstrdb.htm.

Ovid HealthSTAR (HSTR); HealthSTAR (Health Services Technology, Administration, and Research).

"Comprised of data from the National Library of Medicine's (NLM) MEDLINE and former HealthSTAR databases. contains citations to the published literature on health services, technology, administration, and research. It focuses on both the clinical and non-clinical aspects of health care delivery. Offered by Ovid as a continuation of NLM's now-defunct HealthSTAR database. Retains all existing backfile citations and is updated with new journal citations culled from MEDLINE. Contains citations and abstracts (when available) to journal articles, monographs, technical reports, meeting abstracts and papers, book chapters, government documents, and newspaper articles from 1975 to the present."—*Publ. notes.* A list of NLM's retired databases, including the original HealthSTAR database, can be found at http://www.nlm.nih.gov/services/pastdatabases. html.

Relevant content on health services research, health technology, health administration, health policy, health economics, etc., can also be found in MEDLINE® (425)/PubMed® (432), NLM® Gateway (429), and also CINAHL® (439).

870 **Hospital and health administration index.** American Hospital Association, Resource Center., National Library of Medicine (U.S.). Chicago: American Hospital Association, 1995–1999. ISSN: 1077-1719.

016.36211   Z6675.H75H67; RA963

1945–54, *Index of current hospital literature*; 1955–57, *Hospital periodical literature index*; 1957–94, *Hospital literature index*, cumulated at five-year intervals for the 1945–77 volumes as *Cumulative index of hospital literature.* Discontinued; last published in 1999. Described as a "primary guide to literature on hospital and other health care facility administration, including multi-institutional systems, health policy and planning, and the administrative aspects of health care delivery. Special emphasis is given to the theory of health care systems in general; health care in industrialized countries, primarily in the United States; and provision of health care both inside and outside of health care facilities."—*Introd.* A separate online database, HealthSTAR (Health Services Technology, Administration, and Research) for this literature, previously maintained by NLM, is no longer available (cf. list of NLM's retired databases at http://www.nlm.nih.gov/services/pastdatabases.html). Relevant content is available via MEDLINE (425)/PubMed (432) or HealthSTAR (Ovid) (440), and also CINAHL (439).

871 **PubMed.** U.S. National Center for Biotechnology Information, National Library of Medicine, National Institutes of Health. 1996–. Bethesda, Md.: U.S. National Center for Biotechnology Information. http://www.ncbi.nlm.nih.gov/sites/entrez/.

PubMed®, developed and maintained by the National Center for Biotechnology Information (NCBI) at the National Library of Medicine® (NLM) (427). It is available via the NCBI Entrez (3) retrieval system. PubMed also provides access to the other Entrez molecular biology resources (*PubMed Overview*). Starting May 23, 2007, NCBI is changing to a new version of Entrez in a phased implementation (cf. Nahin AM. New and Improved PubMed®/Entrez and New URL *NLM tech. bull.*, 2007 May–Jun.; [356]: http://www.nlm.nih.gov/pubs/techbull/mj07/mj07_issue_cover.html).

Provides a search interface for more than 16 million bibliographic citations and abstracts in the fields of medicine, nursing, dentistry, veterinary medicine, health care systems, and preclinical sciences. It provides access to articles indexed for MEDLINE® (425) and for selected life sciences journals. PubMed subsets found under the "Limits" tab are: MEDLINE and PubMed Central®, several journal groups (i.e., core clinical journals, dental journals, and nursing journals), and topical subsets (AIDS, bioethics, cancer, complementary medicine, history of medicine, space life sciences, systematic reviews, and toxicology). "Linkout" provides access to full-text articles.

For detailed information see the PubMed fact sheet at http://www.nlm.nih.gov/pubs/factsheets/pubmed.html. For a brief overview of searching PubMed, see the PubMed Quick Start at http://www.ncbi.nlm.nih.gov/books/bv.fcgi?rid=helppubmed.section.pubmedhelp.PubMed_Quick_Start. For details on the now completed OLDMEDLINE retrospective conversion projects, see http://www.nlm.nih.gov/pubs/techbull/so06/so06_oldmedline_status.html.

Internet Resources

872 **Agency for Healthcare Research and Quality (AHRQ).** Agency for Healthcare Research and Quality (U.S.). 1990s–. Rockville, Md.: Agency for Healthcare Research and Quality. http://www.ahrq.gov.

"The Agency for Healthcare Research and Quality (AHRQ) is the lead Federal agency charged with improving the quality, safety, efficiency, and effectiveness of health care for all Americans. As one of 12 agencies within the Department of Health and Human Services, AHRQ supports health services research that will improve the quality of health care and promote evidence-based decision making."—*AHRQ at a glance* (*http://www.ahrq.gov/about/ataglance.htm*)

Searchable website ("search AHRQ" and "A–Z Quick Menu") provides access to a variety of resources, with links to clinical and consumer health information, research findings, funding opportunities, data and surveys, quality assessment, specific populations (minorities, women, elderly, and others), and public health preparedness (bioterrorism and response). Links to a large number of full-text documents, including links to the tools, literature, and news in patient safety (e.g., *AHRQ patient safety network*) and tips on how to prevent medical errors.

873   American Hospital Association. American Hospital Association. Chicago: American Hospital Association. http://www.aha.org/aha_app/index.jsp.

Founded in 1898, the association represents hospitals, health care networks, and their consumers. The website provides "Fast Facts on U.S. Hospitals," reports and studies, trends, testimony, regulations, and a section for members only. Some information is only available for a fee.

874   Centers for Medicare and Medicaid services (U.S.). Centers for Medicare and Medicaid Services (U.S.), U.S. Health Care Financing Administration. 2001–. Baltimore, Md.: Centers for Medicare and Medicaid Services, U.S. Dept. of Health and Human Services. http://cms.hhs.gov/.

Centers for Medicare and Medicaid Services (CMS), formerly Health Care Financing Administration.

Detailed information on Medicare, the federal health insurance program for people 65 years and older and for younger people with certain disabilities, providing details on enrollment, benefits, and other data; Medicaid, a joint federal and state program (state programs vary from state to state) that helps with medical costs for people with low income and limited means; SCHIP (State Children's Health Insurance Program); regulation and guidance manuals and Health Insurance Portability and Accountability Act (HIPAA), research, statistics, data and systems. Also provides various tools and resources helpful in navigating this website (http://www.cms.hhs.gov/home/tools.asp), for example a "participating physician directory," a "glossary tool" and an "acronym lookup tool."

875   The Dartmouth atlas of health care. Dartmouth Institute for Health Policy and Clinical Practice, Dartmouth Medical School, American Hospital Association. Lebanon, N.H.: Dartmouth

Institute for Health Policy and Clinical Practice. http://www.
dartmouthatlas.org/atlases.shtm.

The Dartmouth Atlas Project started as a series of books and is now accessible via a web-based resource, providing access to the *Dartmouth atlas of health care* series (national editions, specialty-specific editions, state editions, and regional editions). Describes and illustrates quality, cost, and delivery of healthcare services in the U.S. and geographic variations in practice patterns, with description of the physician workforce and distribution of resources. Written for health policy analysts and other health professionals. The home page at http://www.dartmouthatlas.org/index.shtm provides additional information.

876   **Healthcare Cost and Utilization Project (HCUP).** Agency for
       Healthcare Research and Quality (AHRQ). Rockville, Md.: Agency
       for Healthcare Research and Quality, U.S. Dept. of Health and
       Human Services. http://www.hcup-us.ahrq.gov/home.jsp.

"Family of health care databases and related software tools and products made possible by a Federal-State-Industry partnership sponsored by the Agency for Healthcare Research and Quality (AHRQ) (733)."—*Website*

Website designed to answer HCUP-related questions. Provides information on HCUP databases (e.g., Nationwide Inpatient Sample, State Inpatient Databases, State Ambulatory Surgery Databases, and others), tools and software products (e.g., HCUPnet, an interactive tool for identifying, tracking, analyzing, and comparing statistics on hospital care; Clinical Classifications Software, and others), and offers technical assistance to HCUP users.

877   **Health Resources and Services Administration (HRSA).** Health
       Resources and Services Administration. 1999–. Washington:
       Department of Health and Human Services. http://www.hrsa.gov/.

Health Resources and Services Administration (HRSA), pt. of U.S. Dept. of Health and Human Services (HHS) (877).

HRSA provides leadership and direction for various major national programs, such as organ donation and transplantation, HIV/AIDS, drug pricing, programs related to rural health, health information technology, telehealth, emergency preparedness, and bioterrorism. Also provides information and data on the health professions, a "geospatial data warehouse," health workforce analysis and other reports, and a variety of other topics and links to related sites both within the HRSA and other agencies and programs.

878   **Health services research methodology core library recommendations, 2007.** AcademyHealth, National Library of Medicine (U.S.). 2007. Bethesda, Md.: National Library of Medicine. http://www.nlm.nih.gov/nichsr/corelib/hsrmethods. html.

Produced by AcademyHealth; National Library of Medicine (NLM) (427); National Information Center on Health Services Research and Health Care (NICHSR).

List of books, journals, bibliographic databases, websites, and other media; useful for collection development librarians and researchers interested in health services research methods. Lists both "core" materials and "desired" materials in areas such as general health policy, health economics, health services research, public health, and several others. The NICHSR website (http://www.nlm.nih.gov/nichsr/outreach.html) lists links to several other recommended lists, including Health Economics Core Library Recommendation, Health Outcomes Core Library Recommendation, Health Policy Core Library Recommendation, and other information.

879   **Health system (MedlinePlus).** National Library of Medicine (U.S.). 200?–. Bethesda, Md.: U.S. National Library of Medicine, National Institutes of Health, Dept. of Health and Human Services. http://www.nlm.nih.gov/medlineplus/healthsystem.html.

List of links to a wide variety of healthcare-related topics, with each link leading to a separate page within MedlinePlus (463). Provides extensive reference information on the particular topic. Examples include assisted living, health occupations, caregivers, personal medical records, home care services, emergency medical services, health facilities, health insurance, managed care, home care services, hospice care, nursing homes, patients rights, patient safety, veterans and military health, and many others.

880   **Healthy People 2010.** National Center for Health Statistics (NCHS). Hyattsville, Md.: Centers for Disease Control (U.S.), National Center for Health Statistics. http://www.cdc.gov/nchs/ hphome.htm.

RA395.A3

Contents: Healthy people 2010: Understanding and improving health; Healthy people 2010: Objectives for improving health; Appendixes; Tracking healthy people 2010.

Described as a "national initiative of the U.S. Dept. of Health and Human Services [HHS] that brings together national, state, and local

HEALTH CARE

389

organizations, businesses, communities, and individuals to improve the health of all Americans, eliminate disparities in health, and improve years and quality of life. Since its inception in 1979, it has been coordinated by the Office of Disease Prevention and Health Promotion."—*Website.* Represents the third time that HHS has developed ten-year health objectives for the nation. Previous reports include *Healthy people 2000* (http://purl. access.gpo.gov/GPO/LPS3745) and *Healthy people: The Surgeon General's report on health promotion and disease prevention: Background papers: Report to the Surgeon General on health promotion and disease prevention* (Washington, D.C.: Institute of Medicine, 1979). "Healthy People DATA 2010," an interactive database system accessible via CDC WONDER (1399) provides various reports and data. A search interface providing searches for published literature related to the Healthy People 2010 was added to the "special queries" section of PubMed (432).

Also available in print format: *Tracking healthy people 2010: Healthy people 2010* (Washington, D.C.: U.S. Dept. of Health and Human Services, 2000 [Nov. 2000 version]), which supersedes the conference edition, entitled *Healthy people 2010* (Washington, D.C.: U.S. Dept. of Health and Human Services, 2000 [Jan. 2000]).

881   Healthy women. Centers for Disease Control and Prevention
(U.S.); National Center for Health Statistics (U.S.). 2004.
Hyattsville, Md.: National Center for Health Statistics, Centers for
Disease Control and Prevention, U.S. Dept. of Health and Human
Services. http://www.cdc.gov/nchs/datawh/statab/chartbook.htm.
RA408.W65

Title varies: Suggested title for website: Healthy Women: State Trends in Health and Mortality; suggested citation for print version, publ. in 2004 as *Women's health and mortality chartbook* by K. M. Brett and Suzanne G. Hayes.

Provides access to the PDF version of *Women's health and mortality chartbook*, developed by NCHS with support from the Office on Women's Health. It describes the health of people in each state in the U.S. by sex, race, and age by reporting current data on critical issues of relevance to women. Because of the large file size, this report has been broken into four accessible PDF files. Users may also download the entire report. Website provides help for using tables.

Other publications in this area include *Women's health data book: A profile of women's health in the United States,* ed. by D. Misra, a collaborative publication by the Jacobs Institute of Women's Health and the Henry

J. Kaiser Family Foundation (Kaiser Family Foundation [884]) since 1992, complemented by *State profiles on women's health: Women's health issues,* publ. since 1998.

882 HSR information central. 1993–. Bethesda, Md.: National Library of Medicine (U.S.), National Institutes of Health, Dept. of Health and Human Services. http://www.nlm.nih.gov/hsrinfo/.

Contents: Literature and guidelines; Data tools and statistics; Grants and funding; Legislation; Training and education; Meetings and conferences; Discussion and e-mail lists; Alphabetic list (all websites in alphabetic order); Subject list (websites arranged by categories: federal agencies; associations; data sets and data sources; epidemiology and health statistics; evidence based medicine and health technology assessment; Funding; Health policy and health economics; informatics; public health; rural health; state resources; disparities).

Developed by the National Library of Medicine (427) to serve the information needs of the health services research community, in partnership with other government agencies and institutes (e.g., Agency for Healthcare Research and Quality [AHRQ] [733], National Cancer Institute [166], the Cecil C. Sheps Center for Health Services Research, and the Health Services Research and Development Service [HSR&D] at the Veterans Administration, and others).

883 Introduction to health services research. National Library of Medicine (U.S.). 2007–. Bethesda, Md.: National Library of Medicine. http://www.nlm.nih.gov/nichsr/ihcm/index.html.

Produced by National Information Center on Health Services Research (NICHSR) of the National Library of Medicine (NLM).

Contents: Introduction and Purpose; Course Objectives; Modules: (1) What Is Health Services Research? (HSR); (2) Brief History of Health Services Research and Key Projects and Milestones; (3) Selected Players (Federal and Private); (4) Search the Literature of HSR: Databases; (5) Quality Filtering and Evidence-Based Medicine and Health; (6) Basic Components of a Study; (7) Librarians' Role in Health Services Research; Selected HSR Internet Sites; Essential Concepts; Bibliography; Glossaries; Review Sections.

Provides extensive information on health services issues, health services research, study design, bibliography of articles and books, databases, and literature analysis.

884   **Kaiser Family Foundation.** Henry J. Kaiser Family Foundation.
2000–. Menlo Park, Calif.: Henry J. Kaiser Family Foundation.
http://www.kff.org/.

362.1; 361.7

The Henry J. Kaiser Family Foundation is an independent philanthropy
focusing on major health care issues. Website contains statistics on Medicare, Medicaid, the uninsured in each state of the United States, minority
health, etc. Links to resources on health policy covering such topics as
women's health policy, HIV/AIDS, and media programs. A wide variety
of resources are accessible via the following tabs found on the website:
(1) KaiserNetwork.org (http://www.kaisernetwork.org/): search for recent
daily reports and webcasts; (2) StateHealthFacts (http://www.statehealth-
facts.org/): source for state health data; (3) Kaiseredu.org (http://www.
kaiseredu.org/): provides easy access to the latest data, research, analysis,
and developments in health policy and includes narrated slide tutorials, background reference libraries, and issue modules on current topics
and policy debates; (4) GlobalHealthReporting.org (http://www.global-
healthreporting.org/): global data on HIV/AIDS, tuberculosis, malaria
and more; (5) GlobalHealthFacts.org (http://www.globalhealthfacts.org/):
companion site to globalhealthreporting; (6) Health08.org (http://www.
health08.org/): election news, analysis, and events.

885   **Lister Hill National Center for Biomedical Communications
[homepage].** Lister Hill National Center for Biomedical
Communications; National Library of Medicine (U.S.). Bethesda,
Md.: U.S. National Library of Medicine. http://www.lhncbc.nlm.
nih.gov.

A research and development division of the National Library of Medicine
(NLM), "seeking to improve access to high-quality biomedical information for individuals around the world" in support of NLM's mission.
Prominent examples resulting from its medical informatics research (as
listed in the Center's fact sheet [http://www.nlm.nih.gov/pubs/factsheets/
lister_hill.html]) include ClinicalTrials.gov [191], The Visible Human
Project® [502], Unified Medical Language System® [89], Profiles in Sci-
ence® [48], Genetics home reference [703], NLM® Gateway [429], and
others.

886   **MEPS Medical Expenditure Panel Survey.** U.S. Agency for
Healthcare Research and Quality. 1996–. Bethesda, Md.: Agency

for Healthcare Research and Quality. http://www.meps.ahrq.gov/mepsweb/.

RA408.5

Produced by Agency for Health Care Research and Quality (AHRQ) (733).

"Set of large-scale surveys of families and individuals, their medical providers (doctors, hospitals, pharmacies, etc.), and employers across the United States. MEPS collects data on the specific health services that Americans use, how frequently they use them, the cost of these services, and how they are paid for, as well as data on the cost, scope, and breadth of health insurance held by and available to U.S. workers."—*Website.* Provides information on health expenditures, utilization of health services, health insurance, and nursing homes, and reimbursement mechanisms. MEPS topics include access to health care, children's health, children's insurance coverage, health care disparities, mental health, minority health, the uninsured, and other topics. Further details concerning the survey background, data overview, and frequently asked questions are provided at the website. Provides full-text access to MEPS publications: highlights, research findings, statistical briefs, etc.

887   National Information Center on Health Services Research and Health Care Technology (NICHSR). National Library of Medicine (U.S.). 2002–. Bethesda, Md.: National Library of Medicine, National Institutes of Health, U.S. Dept. of Health and Human Services. http://www.nlm.nih.gov/nichsr/.

Health Services Research (HSR); NICHSR; National Library of Medicine® (NLM®) (427).

NICHSR coordinates NLM's HSR information programs, with links to databases and retrieval services, HSR Information Central (882), presentations, publications, and other information. An alphabetic list (http://www.nlm.nih.gov/hsrinfo/alphahsre.html) and a subject list (http://www.nlm.nih.gov/hsrinfo/hsrsites.html) of related websites, providing a large number of HSR-related links: federal agencies; associations; data sets and data sources; epidemiology and health statistics; evidence-based medicine and health technology assessment; funding; health policy and health economics; informatics; public health; rural health; state resources; disparities, and others.

A related page is NLM's Health Services Research & Public Health Information Programs (822), a website that lists resources from multiple NLM programs.

HEALTH CARE

393

888   National Patient Safety Foundation (NPFS). National Patient Safety Foundation. North Adams, Mass.: National Patient Safety Foundation. http://www.npsf.org.

Independent, not-for-profit organization, with the mission to "measurably improve patient safety."—*Main page.* Searchable website, with links to online patient safety resources and organizations. Information is presented in different categories (e.g., health care quality and safety, medication safety, surgical safety, cancer treatment safety, and others) for different user groups, such as health professionals, patients and families, and researchers.

889   National Quality Measures Clearinghouse (NQMC). National Quality Measures Clearinghouse (U.S.). 2002–. Rockville, Md.: U.S. Agency for Healthcare Research and Quality. http://www. qualitymeasures.ahrq.gov/.

"The National Quality Measures Clearinghouse™ (NQMC) is a public repository for evidence-based quality measures and measure set."—*Website.* Sponsored by the Agency for Healthcare Research and Quality (AHRQ) (133).

Provides detailed information on quality measures, with summaries of the measures and their development, links to their full-text when available, and ordering information for the measure. Allows for comparison of measures. Can be browsed by disease/condition, treatment/intervention, and by several other categories. Also contains a measure archive (complete list of measures that have been withdrawn from the NQMC website), a measure index (complete list of measure summaries available through the NQMC website), and a list of measures most viewed.

Other related sites are National Guideline Clearinghouse™ (NGC) (326) and Quality Tools (892).

890   NLM gateway. National Library of Medicine (U.S.). 2000–. Bethesda, Md.: National Library of Medicine. http://gateway.nlm. nih.gov/.

RA11

Allows simultaneous searching of information resources at the National Library of Medicine (NLM). Databases include MEDLINE (425)/PubMed (432) and the NLM Catalog (482) as well as other resources, including information on current clinical trials and consumer health information (MedlinePlus [463]). Currently provides access to 21 databases and other information resources (for a complete list of databases and other details, see http://www.nlm.nih.gov/pubs/factsheets/gateway.html). An overview of the search results is presented in several categories (bibliographic resources, consumer health resources, and other information), with a listing of the individual databases and the number of results within these categories.

891   Partners in information access for the public health workforce.
U.S. National Library of Medicine. 2003–. Bethesda, Md.: U.S. National Library of Medicine, National Institutes of Health, Dept. of Health and Human Services. http://phpartners.org/.

"Collaboration of U.S. government agencies, public health organizations, and health sciences libraries which provides timely, convenient access to selected public health resources on the Internet [with the mission of] helping the public health workforce find and use information effectively to improve and protect the public's health."—*Website*

Provides links to the individual partner websites, such as Agency for Healthcare Research and Quality (AHRQ) (733), American Public Health Association (APHA), Association of Schools of Public Health (ASPH), Association of State and Territorial Health Officials (ASTHO), Centers for Disease Control and Prevention (CDC) (940), Medical Library Association (MLANET) (465), National Library of Medicine (427), and several other organizations. Provides extensive information on several public health topics (currently to bioterrorism, environmental health, and HIV/ AIDS). For additional information and links see the Partners in Information Access for the Public Health Workforce fact sheet at http://www.nlm.nih.gov/nno/partners.html.

892   QualityTools. Agency for Healthcare Research and Quality (AHRQ). Rockville, Md.: Agency for Healthcare Research and Quality. http://www.qualitytools.ahrq.gov/.

Clearinghouse for practical tools for measuring and possibly improving the quality of health care. Each entry contains several elements as appropriate, such as summary, tool availability, URL, description, tool category, audience, key features, target population, target population age, association with vulnerable populations, and other elements. The "Tool Index" (http://www.qualitytools.ahrq.gov/whatsnew/whatsnew_docindex.aspx) provides a complete list of all tools, listed alphabetically by developer of the tool(s).

Information is also presented for several specific user groups: (1) Providers: guideline-related tools; patient/medication safety tools; benchmarking and comparative data; disease/condition tools; prevention and wellness tools; (2) Policymakers: guideline-related tools; benchmarking and comparative data; disease/condition tools; prevention and wellness tools; quality improvement strategies; (3) Patients and consumers, to help individuals to make informed healthcare decisions: medication and safety tools; disease/condition tools; prevention and wellness tools; healthcare information services; (4) Payers and Purchasers: guideline-related tools; patient/medication safety tools; benchmarking and comparative data; disease/condition tools; prevention and wellness tools; quality improvement strategies.

Related sites are Agency for Healthcare Research and Quality (AHRQ) (733), National Guideline Clearinghouse™ (NGC) (326), and National Quality Measures Clearinghouse™ (NQMC) (889).

893 State snapshots. Agency for Healthcare Research and Quality. 2007–. Rockville, Md.: Agency for Healthcare Research and Quality. http://statesnapshots.ahrq.gov/statesnapshots/index.jsp.

Based on data collected from the *National healthcare quality report* (http://purl.access.gpo.gov/GPO/LPS62498). Also called *NHRQ state snapshots*. Linked Agency for Healthcare Research and Quality (733) website.

Provides "state-specific health care quality information including strengths, weaknesses, and opportunity for improvement [to] better understand healthcare quality and disparities."—*Website*. A "state selection map" (http://statesnapshots.ahrq.gov/statesnapshots/map.jsp?menuID=2&state=) allows users to choose a particular state and compare it to other states in terms of healthcare quality, types of care (preventive, acute, and chronic), settings of care (hospitals, ambulatory care, nursing home, and home health), several specific conditions, and clinical preventive services. Provides help with interpretation of results and a methods section.

The Kaiser Family Foundation (884) makes a comparable website available: "State Health Facts" (http://www.statehealthfacts.org). Provides statistical data and health policy information on various health topics, with a standardized menu for information about each state ("individual state profiles" tab) and to find out how it compares to the U.S. overall ("50 state comparisons" tab). Categories include demography and the economy, health status, health coverage and the uninsured, Medicaid and SCHIP, health costs and budgets, Medicare, managed care and health insurance, providers and service use, minority health, women's health, and HIV/AIDS.

894 U.S. Dept. of Health and Human Services (HHS). U.S. Dept. of Health and Human Services (HHS). 1997–. Washington: U.S. Dept. of Health and Human Services. http://www.os.dhhs.gov/.

HHS has the mission "to enhance the health and well-being of Americans by providing for effective health and human services and by fostering strong, sustained advances in the sciences underlying medicine, public health, and social services."—*Website*

Overview and links to all HHS offices: Office for Civil Rights; Office of Global Health Affairs; Surgeon General, and many others. Also provides overview and links to the HHS agencies: Administration for Children and Families; Administration on Aging; Agency for Healthcare Research and Quality (AHRQ) (733); Agency for Toxic Substances and Disease Registry (1397); Centers for Disease Control and Prevention (CDC) (940); Centers for Medicare and Medicaid Services (742); Food and Drug Administration (630); Health Resources and Services Administration (877); Indian Health Service (IHS) (1401); National Institutes of Health (NIH) (470); Substance Abuse and Mental Health Services Administration (769). "HHS Acronyms and Abbreviations" at http://www.hhs.gov/acronyms.html. Includes a "Reference Collections" page (http://www.hhs.gov/reference/index.html) which provides an extensive collection of resources, including dictionaries and glossaries, encyclopedias, databases, indexes, and various other reference resources, publications, reports, and statistics. Provides policy information (e.g., science policy issues; Surgeon General priorities; legal information; HHS-related publications and reports).

Statistics

895 AHA hospital statistics. American Hospital Association. Chicago: Health Forum, 2005–. ISSN: 0090-6662.

RA981.A2A6234

Title varies: Prior to 1971 issued as part 1 of the annual guide issue of *Hospitals*; 1971–90, *Hospital statistics*; 1991–97, *American Hospital Association hospital statistics*; 1998–2004, *Hospital statistics*. Editions starting in 1998 draw data from the 1996– *AHA annual survey of hospitals*. Statistical complement to the *AHA guide to the health care field* (199). Description based on 2006 ed. Subtitle: *The comprehensive reference source for analysis and comparison of hospital trends.* Reference source for analysis and comparison of hospital trends. Recent additions include community health indicators, utilization, personnel, and finance by all metropolitan statistical areas (MSAs), five-year trend data, breakdowns between inpatient and outpatient care, facilities and services information. Includes "Historical trends in utilization, personnel, and finances for selected years from 1946-2004." A glossary (p. 199–210) explains specific terms used in the tables and text of this volume. Hospitals included are not necessarily identical to those included in the *AHA guide to the health care field* (199).

896   **American health: Demographics and spending of health care consumers.** New Strategist Publications, Inc. xvi, 504 p., ill. Ithaca, N.Y.: New Strategist Publications, 2005–. ISBN: 1885070748.

614.4273   RA445.A442

Publ. 1998–2000 as *Best of health: Demographics of health care consumers.* (American consumer series).

Description based on 1st, 2005 ed.; 2nd ed., 2007.

Contents: ch. 1, Addictions; ch. 2, Aging; ch. 3, Alternative medicine; ch. 4, Attitudes towards health care; ch. 5, Births; ch. 6, Health care coverage and cost; ch. 7, Deaths; ch. 8, Disability; ch. 9, Diseases and conditions; ch. 10, Health care visits; ch. 11, Hospital care; ch. 12, Mental health; ch. 13, Sexual attitudes and behavior; ch. 14, Weight and exercise. Detailed table of contents: http://www.loc.gov/catdir/toc/fy0606/2005284141.html.

Data on health care consumers from many different sources, including information from the federal government (e.g., National Center for Health Statistics [539], incl. *Health, United States* [529], Consumer Expenditure Survey [http://www.bls.gov/cex/], MEPS Medical Expenditure Panel Survey [886], to name a few). Contains 300 tables, graphs, a glossary, bibliographical references (p. 493–495) and index. Available online via netLibrary.

897   **DHHS Data Council gateway to data and statistics.** U.S. Department of Health and Human Services. 200?–. Washington: U.S. Department of Health and Human Services. http://www.hhs-stat.net/about.htm.

RA407.3

Provides access to key health and human services data and statistics. Covers information sponsored by federal, state, and local governments. Complements other government resources such as FirstGov (http://www.usa.

gov/) and FedStats (519). Links to health and human services surveys and data systems sponsored by Federal agencies. Datafinder leads to websites that contain statistics and data. The MetaDirectory is a comprehensive list and description of the statistical and surveillance systems supported by HHS agencies. Other key resources links lead to additional information.

898   Faststats A to Z. National Center for Health Statistics (NCHS). Hyattsville, Md.: U.S. Dept. of Health and Human Services, Centers for Disease Control and Prevention, National Center for Health Statistics. http://www.cdc.gov/nchs/fastats/Default.htm.

Provides topic-appropriate public health statistics (e.g., birth data, morbidity and mortality statistics, and health care use) and relevant links to further information and publications. Includes state and territorial data, with clickable map for individual state data. Also includes data derived from the "Behavioral Risk Factor Surveillance System (BRFSS)," which compiles data for 16 negative behaviors.

899   Health and healthcare in the United States: County and metro area data. NationsHealth Corporation. 2 v., maps. Lanham, Md.: Bernan Press, c1999–c2001. ISSN: 1526-1573.

362   RA407.3.H415

1st ed., 1999–2nd ed., 2000; 2nd ed. technical consultant, Russell G. Bruce.
Compendium of health-related statistics and reference maps for each of the 3,000 counties and the 80 metropolitan areas in the U.S.—demographics, vital statistics, healthcare resources, and Medicare data. Based on information from the National Center for Health Statistics (539) and the U.S. Bureau of the Census. Accompanying CD-ROMs make it possible to manipulate the data.

900   Health care state rankings. Morgan Quitno Corporation. Lawrence, Kans.: Morgan Quitno Corp, c1993–. ISSN: 1065-1403.

362.10973   RA407.3.H423

Description based on 15th ed., 2007. Subtitle: *Health care in the 50 United States*. Contains data relating to medical care, delivery of health care, and health status indicators, which are derived from federal and state government sources, and from professional and private organizations. Presented in tabular form, with tables arranged in seven categories: Birth and reproductive health; Deaths; Facilities (hospitals, nursing homes, etc.); Finance; Incidence of disease; Personnel; Physical fitness. Appendix (with 2005 and 2006 charts), sources, and index. Another title, *Health care state perspectives,* includes state-specific reports for each of the 50 states.

901   Health data for all ages (HDAA). National Center for Health Statistics. 200?–. Atlanta: National Center for Health Statistics. http://www.cdc.gov/nchs/health_data_for_all_ages.htm.

Searchable website presents tables that provide Centers for Disease Control and Prevention (CDC) (940) health statistics for infants, children, adolescents, adults, and older adults. Table topics include pregnancy and birth, health conditions/risk factors, health care access and use, mortality, and others, and topics can be customized with characteristics such as age, gender, race/ethnicity, and geographic location.

902   Health, United States. National Center for Health Statistics. 1975–. Rockville, Md.: National Center for Health Statistics. http://purl. access.gpo.gov/GPO/LPS2649.

Description based on the 2006 ed. (30th annual report).

Subtitle of this edition: With Vhartbook on Trends in the Health of Americans with Special Feature on Pain.

"An annual report on trends in health statistics. The report consists of two main sections: a chartbook containing text and figures that illustrates major trends in the health of Americans; and a trend tables section that contains 147 detailed data tables. The two main components are supplemented by an executive summary, a highlights section, an extensive appendix and reference section, and an index."—*NCHS website.* Hyperlinks to tables and graphs. Also provides easy access to other online resources provided by NCHS, for example, Faststats A–Z (518), Healthy People 2010 (530), and other websites.

903   Healthy People 2010. National Center for Health Statistics (NCHS). Hyattsville, Md.: Centers for Disease Control (U.S.), National Center for Health Statistics. http://www.cdc.gov/nchs/ hphome.htm.

RA395.A3

Contents: Healthy people 2010: Understanding and improving health; Healthy people 2010: Objectives for improving health; Appendixes; Tracking healthy people 2010.

Described as a "national initiative of the U.S. Dept. of Health and Human Services [HHS] that brings together national, state, and local organizations, businesses, communities, and individuals to improve the health of all Americans, eliminate disparities in health, and improve years and quality of life. Since its inception in 1979, it has been coordinated by the Office of Disease Prevention and Health Promotion."—*Website*. Represents the third time that HHS has developed ten-year health objectives for the nation. Previous reports include *Healthy people 2000* (http://purl. access.gpo.gov/GPO/LPS3745) and *Healthy people: The Surgeon General's report on health promotion and disease prevention: Background papers: Report to the Surgeon General on health promotion and disease prevention* (Washington, D.C.: Institute of Medicine, 1979). "Healthy People DATA 2010," an interactive database system accessible via CDC WONDER (1399) provides various reports and data. A search interface providing searches for published literature related to the Healthy People 2010 was added to the "special queries" section of PubMed (432).

Also available in print format: *Tracking healthy people 2010: Healthy people 2010* (Washington, D.C.: U.S. Dept. of Health and Human Services, 2000 [Nov. 2000 version]), which supersedes the conference edition, entitled *Healthy people 2010* (Washington, D.C.: U.S. Dept. of Health and Human Services, 2000 [Jan. 2000]).

904 **Healthy women.** Centers for Disease Control and Prevention (U.S.); National Center for Health Statistics (U.S.). 2004. Hyattsville, Md.: National Center for Health Statistics, Centers for Disease Control and Prevention, U.S. Dept. of Health and Human Services. http://www.cdc.gov/nchs/datawh/statab/chartbook.htm.

RA408.W65

Title varies: Suggested title for website: Healthy Women: State Trends in Health and Mortality; suggested citation for print version, publ. in 2004 as *Women's health and mortality chartbook* by K. M. Brett and Suzanne G. Hayes.

Provides access to the PDF version of *Women's health and mortality chartbook*, developed by NCHS with support from the Office on Women's Health. It describes the health of people in each state in the U.S. by sex, race, and age by reporting current data on critical issues of relevance to women. Because of the large file size, this report has been broken into four accessible PDF files. Users may also download the entire report. Website provides help for using tables.

Other publications in this area include *Women's health data book: A profile of women's health in the United States*, ed. by D. Misra, a collaborative publication by the Jacobs Institute of Women's Health and the Henry J. Kaiser Family Foundation (Kaiser Family Foundation [884]) since 1992, complemented by *State profiles on women's health: Women's health issues,* publ. since 1998.

905   **Mental health, United States.** National Institute of Mental Health (U.S.). Rockville, Md.: U.S. Dept. of Health and Human Services, Public Health Service, Alcohol, Drug Abuse, and Mental Health Administration, National Institute of Mental Health, Div. of Biometry and Epidemiology, 1983–. ISSN: 0892-0664.

362.20973   RA790.6.M463

Description based on the 2000 ed.

Contains statistical reports and data on trends in mental health services, derived to a large extent from national surveys conducted by SAMSHA (Substance Abuse and Mental Health Services Administration) Center for Mental Health Services in collaboration with various major national, state, and professional associations. Three new sections in this edition: Section 1 contains an editorial on likely future directions and an overview of the mental health field over the past 100 years; Section 2 reports on the current status of mental health statistics; and Section 3 on the current status of mental health services. Section 4, as in previous editions, provides current mental health statistics. Electronic full-text of some volumes (1998 [executive summary only], 2000, and 2002) also available from the SAMSHA National Mental Health Information Center website http://purl.access.gpo.gov/GPO/LPS24728.

906   **MEPS Medical Expenditure Panel Survey.** U.S. Agency for Healthcare Research and Quality. 1996–. Bethesda, Md.: Agency for Healthcare Research and Quality. http://www.meps.ahrq.gov/mepsweb/.

RA408.5

Produced by Agency for Health Care Research and Quality (AHRQ) (733).

"Set of large-scale surveys of families and individuals, their medical providers (doctors, hospitals, pharmacies, etc.), and employers across the United States. MEPS collects data on the specific health services that Americans use, how frequently they use them, the cost of these services, and how they are paid for, as well as data on the cost, scope, and breadth of health insurance held by and available to U.S. workers."—*Website.* Provides information on health expenditures, utilization of health services, health insurance, and nursing homes, and reimbursement mechanisms.

MEPS topics include access to health care, children's health, children's insurance coverage, health care disparities, mental health, minority health, the uninsured, and other topics. Further details concerning the survey background, data overview, and frequently asked questions are provided at the website. Provides full-text access to MEPS publications: highlights, research findings, statistical briefs, etc.

907   OECD health data. Organisation for Economic Co-operation and Development. Paris: Organisation for Economic Co-operation and Development. http://www.oecd.org/health/healthdata.

Title varies: SourceOECD Health Data.

Part of SourceOECD (Organisation for Economic Co-operation and Development, [Paris, France]: OECD), which contains publications (monographs, periodicals, and statistical databases) issued by the OECD.

Interactive database and source of statistics on health and health care systems of the OECD member states. Allows cross-country comparisons of national health care systems. Includes, for example, health status, health care resources, health care utilization, expenditure on health, and health care financing. Available in online and CD-ROM formats.

908   Physician compensation and production survey. Medical Group Management Association. Englewood, Colo.: Center for Research in Ambulatory Health Care Administration, 1992–. ISSN: 1064-4563.

331   R728.5.P48152

Description based on 2007 report, with data from 2006 survey.

Contents: section 1, Key findings and demographics; section 2, Physician compensation and benefits; section 3, Physician productivity; section 4, Physician time worked; section 5, Summary tables; section 6, Nonphysician providers; section 7, Physician placement starting salaries.

"Data on compensation for healthcare professionals and on medical group practices and financial operations will assist in evaluating the ranges of compensation and productivity for both physicians and nonphysician providers."—*Publ. notes.* The Bureau of Labor Statistics website "Sector 62—Health Care and Social Assistance" (http://www.bls.gov/oes/current/oessrci.htm#62) also provides extensive information in this area as part of its occupational employment and wage estimates.

Physician socioeconomic statistics (formed by the union of *Physician marketplace statistics* and *Socioeconomic characteristics of medical practice*), publ. by the American Medical Association, was discontinued in 2003.

909 Portrait of health in the United States. Daniel Melnick, Beatrice A. Rouse. xxi, 376 p., ill. Lanham, Md.: Bernan, 2001. ISBN: 089059189X.

614.4273   RA410.53.P675

"Major statistical trends & guide to resources" (*Cover*).

"Presents a picture of American health using a variety of measures ranging from self-perceived health status and reported acute and chronic health conditions to more objective measures such as life expectancy, medical diagnosis, hospitalization, and death rates. Data not found easily elsewhere are included."—*Pref.* Compiled from results reported by federal and public health agencies. Includes, for example, societal trends, health outcomes, leading chronic and acute health conditions and causes of death, incidence, mortality and survival rates of various illnesses, access to care, insurance and costs, life expectancy, quality of life issues, and other relevant information. Also available online via netLibrary.

910 Publications from the National Center for Health Statistics for the period 1898–2004 on DVD. Centers for Disease Control and Prevention (U.S.), National Center for Health Statistics (U.S.). 2 DVD-ROMs, color [Rockville, Md.]: U.S. Dept. of Health and Human Services, Centers for Disease Control, National Center for Health Statistics, 2004.

RA407.3

National Center for Health Statistics (NCHS) (1403); National Office of Vital Statistics; U.S. Census Bureau. Compilation of most of the NCHS publications and selected data products. Disk 1 includes Advance data reports; Vital and health statistics series reports; Monthly vital statistics report summaries and supplements; Health, United States; and other miscellaneous reports. Disk 2 includes Vital statistics of the United States and Life tables published by NCHS, the National Office of Vital Statistics, and the U.S. Census Bureau.

911 Secondary data sources for public health: A practical guide. Sarah Boslaugh. x, 152 p. Cambridge, [England, U.K.]; New York: Cambridge University Press, 2007. ISBN: 052169023.

362.10727   RA409.B66

Part of Practical Guides to Biostatistics and Epidemiology.

Contents: ch. 1, "An introduction to secondary analysis"; ch. 2, "Health services utilization data"; ch. 3, "Health behaviors and risk factors data";

ch. 4, "Data on multiple health topics"; ch. 5, "Fertility and mortality data"; ch. 6, "Medicare and Medicaid data"; ch. 7, "Other sources of data"; appendixes: I, "Acronyms"; II, "Summary of data sets and years available"; III, "Data import and transfer".

This guide lists the major sources of secondary data for health-related subjects that are important in epidemiology and public health research. They are often stored in different locations and not necessarily easily accessible. Examples include the National Hospital Discharge Survey, the Healthcare Cost Utilization Project, the Behavioral Risk Factor Surveillance System, the National Health and Nutrition Survey, Medicare Public Use Files, Web portals to statistical data, etc. Description of each resource includes title, focus, core section, data collection, and information on accessing data and ancillary materials. Includes bibliography and index.

912   Statistical abstract of the United States. U.S. Dept. of the Treasury, Bureau of Statistics, U.S. Dept. of Commerce and Labor, U.S. Bureau of Foreign and Domestic Commerce, U.S. Bureau of the Census, ill. Washington: U.S. G.P.O., 1878–. ISSN: 0081-4741.
317.3   HA202

A single-volume work presenting quantitative summary statistics on the political, social, and economic organization of the United States. Statistics given in the tables cover a period of several years. Indispensable in any library: it serves not only as a first source for statistics of national importance but also as a guide to further information, as references are given to the sources of all tables. Includes a table of contents arranged by broad subject areas and a detailed alphabetical index. Also available online from the Census Bureau at http://www.census.gov/compendia/statab/.

Supplement: *County and city data book* (Washington: U.S. Dept. of Commerce, Bureau of the Census, 1949–).

913   Statistical methods for health care research. 5th ed. Barbara Hazard Munro. xiii, 494 p., ill. Philadelphia: Lippincott, Williams & Wilkins, 2005. ISBN: 0781748402.
610.727   RT81.5.M86

1st ed., 1986; 4th ed., 2000.

Contents: http://www.loc.gov/catdir/toc/ecip0416/2004007098.html. Explains statistical methods frequently used in the health care literature. Includes charts, graphs, and examples from the literature. New material on regression diagnostics has been added. Associated website.

914 **The U.S. health care delivery system: Fundamental facts, definitions, and statistics.** Kim M. Garber, American Hospital Association. xi, 86 p., ill. Chicago: Health Forum: AHA Pr., 2006. ISBN: 1556483309.

362.10973   RA445.U85

Contents: ch. 1, Patient care; ch. 2, Caregivers; ch. 3, Facilities; ch. 4, Money; ch. 5, Government and other types of oversight. "Organized for quick answers and easy understanding."—*Publ. notes.* Overview of the U.S. healthcare system, the practice of healthcare management, and delivery of health care. Contains industry data and research findings. Glossary and index.

915 **Women's health USA.** U.S. Dept. of Health and Human Services, Maternal and Child Health Bureau. 2002–. Rockville, Md.: U.S. Dept. of Health and Human Services, Maternal and Child Health Bureau. http://purl.access.gpo.gov/GPO/LPS21379.

Part of Health Resources and Services Administration (HRSA) (877), within the U.S. Dept. of Health and Human Services (HHS) (894).

Description based on 5th online ed., 2006.

Contents: Population Characteristics; Health Status; Health Services Utilization; Indicators in Previous Editions; Site Map.

Collection of current and historical data on health challenges facing women, with information on life expectancy and addressing topics such as postpartum depression, smoking, alcohol, illicit drug use, etc. Brings together the latest available information from various government agencies (HHS, U.S. Dept. of Agriculture, U.S. Dept. of Labor, U.S. Dept. of Justice).

National Women's Health Information Center, Womenshealth.gov (http://www.womenshealth.gov/), provides extensive further information.

6 > INTERNATIONAL AND GLOBAL HEALTH

916 **Health information for international travel.** Phyllis E. Kozarsky, Paul M. Arguin, Ava W. Navin, U.S. Centers for Disease Control and Prevention. 1974–. Atlanta: U.S. Dept. of Health and Human Services, Centers for Disease Control and Prevention. http://purl.access.gpo.gov/GPO/LPS3580.

Part of the Centers for Disease Control (CDC) (940) Travelers' Health website (http://wwwn.cdc.gov/travel/default.aspx). Also called "Yellow book" or "CDC yellow book." Description based on the 2008 ed., also issued in print with title *CDC health information for international travel 2008* (Philadelphia, Pa.: Elsevier Mosby, 2007). Previous print eds. issued since 1989 as a serial, *International travel health guide*.

Contents: ch. 1, "Introduction"; ch. 2, "Pre- and posttravel general health recommendations"; ch. 3, "Geographic distribution of potential health hazards to travelers"; ch. 4, "Prevention of specific infectious diseases"; ch. 5, "Yellow fever vaccine requirements and information on malaria risk and prophylaxis, by country"; ch. 6, "Noninfectious risks during travel"; ch. 7, "Conveyance and transportation issues"; ch. 8, "International travel with infants and young children"; ch. 9, "Advising travelers with specific needs."

Provides comprehensive information on vaccination requirements and recommendations for international travelers concerning health risks.

The World Health Organization's website, International Travel and Health (1451), also offers extensive travel information.

Dictionaries

917   **Historical dictionary of the World Health Organization.** Kelley Lee. xliv, 333 p., ill. Lanham, Md.: Scarecrow Press, 1998. ISBN: 0810833719.

353.6211   RA8.L44

(Historical dictionaries of international organizations series; no. 15).

Provides information on the history of the World Health Organization (WHO) and its contributions to international health cooperation. Includes an extensive bibliography on WHO documents and writings about WHO and a chronology of selected major events in the history of international health organizations. Several appendixes, for example, constitution of WHO, chronological list of member states, and WHO directors. Additional related information available on the World Health Organization (WHO) home page (951).

Directories

918   **DIRLINE.** National Institutes of Health (U.S.). [1983?–.] Bethesda, Md: U.S. National Institutes of Health, Dept. of Health and Human Services. http://dirline.nlm.nih.gov/.

DIRLINE® (Directory of Information Resources Online), maintained by the National Library of Medicine (NLM) (427).

Online annotated directory of organizations, research resources, projects, databases, and other information resources concerned with health and biomedicine from a variety of sources, including federal, state, and local government agencies, academic and research institutions, and also consumer health-related resources such as self-help groups and health hotlines. Resources are mostly from the U.S. but also include some international resources. Currently contains over 8,000 entries, with topics on most diseases and conditions and health services research and technology assessment. Can be searched using MeSH® (Medical Subject Headings) (575), keywords, or by name and location of a resource. Detailed information on DIRLINE can be found via a fact sheet prepared by NLM: http://www.nlm.nih.gov/pubs/factsheets/dirlinfs.html.

Encyclopedias

919   Encyclopedia of global health. Yawei Zhang. 4 v. (xli, 1938, 1–64 p.), ill. Los Angeles: Sage, 2008. ISBN: 9781412941.
362.103   RA441.E53

Major headings listed in "Reader's guide": children's health; countries: Africa, Americas, Asia, Europe, Pacific; diseases, cancers; diseases, localized; diseases, systemic; drugs and drug companies; health sciences; men's health; mental health; organizations and associations; procedures and therapies; research; society and health; women's health.

Interdisciplinary reference to physical and mental health topics and current health status for countries worldwide. A–Z arrangement. Includes entries on national health policies, biographies of physicians, researchers, medical institutes and other organizations, drugs, surgical operations, etc. Chronology of major medical advances (8000 BCE–2007 CE), a glossary of health-related definitions, cross-references, and bibliographic citations. For both health professionals and general readers. Available online via Sage eReference.

920   Encyclopedia of health care management. Michael J. Stahl. xxxvii, 621 p., ill. Thousand Oaks, Calif.: Sage, 2004. ISBN: 0761926747.
362.1068   RA971.E52

Alphabetical list of entries at the beginning of the book provides an overview of the terminology and variety of subject areas covered in this resource including business and economics, statistics, law, clinical research, informatics, and others. A reader's guide with the following major headings is provided: Accounting and activity-based costing, Economics, Finance, Health policy, Human resources, Information technology, Institutions and organizations, International health care issues, Legal and regulatory issues, Managed care, Marketing and customer value, Operations and decision making, Pharmaceuticals and clinical trials, Quality, Statistics and data mining, and Strategy. The main section, consisting of approx. 650 entries, is alphabetically arranged. Each entry contains the term's definition, background, and other relevant information. Includes tables on health care acronyms, medical degrees, medical legislation, and others. Cross-references, list of further readings, and websites. Index. Also available online from Sage eReference (http://www.sage-ereference.com/public/browse.php).

Handbooks

921 **The Blackwell companion to medical sociology.** William C. Cockerham. xiii, 528 p., ill. Oxford; Malden, Mass.: Blackwell, 2001; repr. 2005. ISBN: 0631217037.

306.461   RA418.B5736

Global and comprehensive survey of the emerging field of medical sociology. Twenty-six signed chapters draw out topics in Western medicine to show how sociological theory and analysis enrich the clinical understanding of each area. A second section covers countries in every corner of the globe: Canada, Mexico, Brazil, countries in both Western and Eastern Europe, Africa, the Arab world, Israel, Australia, Japan, and China. Cultural constructs from the discipline of sociology inform medical practice and understanding. A thoroughly useful textbook for understanding the field. Includes bibliographical references and index.

922 **Health care reform around the world.** Andrew C. Twaddle. xiii, 419 p., ill. Westport, Conn.: Auburn House, 2002. ISBN: 0865692882.

362.1   RA394.H4145

Describes health care reform efforts and trends in different countries, with roughly comparable information for the countries included. Ch. 1 is an international comparison of health care system reforms—United Kingdom, Eastern and Western Europe, United States, the Middle East, Latin

America, Asia, and Oceania. Online edition available via Greenwood Digital Collection (ebooks.greenwood.com/browse/index.jsp) and netLibrary.

923 **Health care systems around the world: Characteristics, issues, reforms.** Marie L. Lassey, William R. Lassey, Martin J. Jinks. xiii, 370 p., ill., maps. Upper Saddle River, N.J.: Prentice Hall, 1997. ISBN: 0131042335.

362.1   RA393.L328

Contents: Introduction, basic issues and concepts; The countries and their characteristics; The United States, high-technology and limited access; Canada, challenges to public payment for universal care; Japan, preventive health care as cultural norm; Germany, a tradition of universal health care; France, centrally controlled and locally managed; The Netherlands, gradual adaptation; Sweden, decentralized comprehensive care; The United Kingdom, the economy model; The Czech Republic, a new mixture of public and private services; Hungary, creating a remodeled system; Russia, transition to market and consumer orientation; China, privatizing socialist health care; Mexico, modernizing structure and expanded rural services; Organization variations and reforms; Economic organization of health care, comparative perspectives; Expectations for reform, a glimpse at the future. Description and analysis of health care systems in different countries, addressing demographic, social, and economic characteristics, also health promotion, prevention of disease, and health care. Includes bibliographical references and index.

924 **Health care systems of the developed world: How the United States' system remains an outlier.** Duane A. Matcha. x, 198 p., ill. Westport, Conn.: Praeger, 2003. ISBN: 027597992X.

362.10973   RA441.M38

Contents: ch. 1, Introduction; ch. 2, The United States; ch. 3, Canada; ch. 4, United Kingdom; ch. 5, Germany; ch. 6, Sweden; ch. 7, Japan; ch. 8, Conclusion. Provides an introduction to selected major healthcare systems, with consideration of their historical and political basis. Provides a framework for analysis and comparison of the different systems. Various tables and figures related to health insurance, personal health care expenditures, self-rated health status, future concerns, and others. Includes bibliographical references and index. *World health systems: Challenges and perspectives* (Chicago: Health Administration Pr., 2002) presents profiles of health systems in 28 countries. A 1997 publication, *Health care systems around the world: Characteristics, issues, reforms* (Upper Saddle River, N.J.:

Prentice Hall, 1997), provides additional information in this area. Milton I. Roemer's *National health systems of the world*, publ. 1991–93, remains an important title. It consists of a comprehensive study and analysis of national health systems in 68 industrialized, middle-income, and very poor countries, with a cross-national analysis of the major health care issues within different systems.

925   International guidelines on HIV/AIDS and human rights. Office of the United Nations High Commissioner for Human Rights (OHCHR); UNAIDS Joint United Nations Programme on HIV/AIDS. 2006. Geneva, [Switzerland]: United Nations OHCHR. http://www.ohchr.org/english/issues/hiv/guidelines.htm.

Organized jointly by the Office of the United Nations High Commissioner for Human Rights (OHCHR) and the UNAIDS Joint United Nations Programme on HIV/AIDS.

2006 consolidated version of the Second (Geneva, 23–25 Sep. 1996) and Third (Geneva, 25–26 July 2002) International Consultation on HIV/AIDS and Human Rights.

Contents: (I) Guidelines for state action: (A) Institutional responsibilities and processes; (B) Law review, reform and support services; (C) Promotion of a supportive and enabling environment; (II) Recommendations for dissemination and implementation of the guidelines on HIV/AIDS and human rights: (A) States; (B) United Nationals system and regional intergovernmental bodies; (C) Nongovernmental organizations; (III) International human rights obligations and HIV: (A) Human rights standards and the nature of State obligations; (B) Restrictions and limitations; (C) The application of specific human rights in the context of the HIV epidemic; Annex 1, History of the recognition of the importance of human rights in the context of HIV; Annex 2, List of participants at the Second International Consultation on HIV/AIDS and Human Rights; Annex 3, List of participants at the Third International Consultation on HIV/AIDS and Human Rights.

"A tool for States in designing, co-ordinating and implementing effective national HIV/AIDS policies and strategies. Human rights standards apply in the context of HIV/AIDS and translating them into practical measures that should be undertaken at the national level, based on three broad approaches: improvement of government capacity for multi-sectoral coordination and accountability; reform of laws and legal support services, with a focus on anti-discrimination, protection of public health, and improvement of the status of women, children and marginalized groups; and support and increased private sector and community participation to respond ethically and effectively to HIV/AIDS.

OHCHR encourages governments, national human rights institutions, non-governmental organizations and people living with HIV and AIDS to use the Guidelines for training, policy formulation, advocacy, and the development of legislation on HIV/AIDS-related human rights."—*Website*

926 **International health regulations (2005).** World Health Organization. 2007 Geneva, Switzerland: World Health Organization. http://www.who.int/csr/ihr/en/.

Rev. ed., with the new regulations in force on June 15, 2007. Also publ. as print edition, with 2005 also available as an e-book. Supersedes *International health regulations* (1969), publ. in several different print editions. Title varies: previously called *International sanitary regulations*.

Part of WHO's Epidemic and Pandemic Alert and Response (EPR) (http://www.who.int/csr/en/).

Considered a code of practices and procedures for the prevention of the spread of disease, "in consideration of the increases in international travel and trade, and emergence and re-emergence of new international disease threats" (*Publ. notes*), with the goal of preventing and protecting against the international spread of disease.

Frequently asked questions about this resource can be found at http://www.who.int/csr/ihr/howtheywork/faq/en/index.html.

A History of WHO and International Cooperation in Public Health timeline (prepared by the WHO Centre for Health Development–WHO Kobe Centre [WKC]) is located at http://www.who.or.jp/GENERAL/history_wkc.html.

927 **A practical guide to global health service.** Edward O'Neil, American Medical Association. xxxv, 402 p. Chicago: American Medical Association, 2006. ISBN: 1579476732.

610.737   RA390.U5O54

OMNI Med ("loosely translated from the Latin meaning 'health care for all'" [*Pref.*]) is a nongovernmental organization founded by the author in 1998.

Contents: ch. 1, Overcoming obstacles: cultural and practical guidelines; ch. 2, Travel, health, and safety guidelines; ch. 3, The Omni Med database of international health service opportunities; ch. 4, Cross-referencing guide to the database; ch. 5, Other relevant organizations; Appendix A, Useful web sites; Appendix B, About Omni Med.

"A health providers guide to the practical aspects of serving internationally, including data on more than 300 organizations that send health providers overseas."—*Publ. notes.* Organization profiles include concise descriptions, contact information, and practical information about length of service terms, personnel sought, areas served, and availability of funding, training, room and board, and other essential information (e.g., trip planning, travel and safety guidelines, commonly encountered illnesses, information about the culture of a particular country, etc.). Written for persons interested in medical volunteering. Glossary; bibliography.

928 **World health and disease.** 3rd ed. Alastair Gray, P. R. Payne. 352 p., ill. (some color). Buckingham, [England, U.K.]; Philadelphia: Open University Press, 2001. ISBN: 033520838X.

614.42   RA651.G65

1st ed., 1985, had title *Health of nations*; [2nd] rev. ed., 1993. Vol. 3 of *Health and disease* series.

Contents: ch. 1, "Introduction"; ch. 2, "World patterns of mortality"; ch. 3, "Mortality and morbidity: causes and determinants"; ch. 4, "Livelihood and survival: A case study of Bangladesh"; ch. 5, "The world transformed: Population and the rise of industrial society"; ch. 6, "The decline of infectious diseases: The case of England"; ch. 7, "Health in a world of wealth and poverty"; ch. 8, "Population and development prospects"; ch. 9, "Contemporary patterns of disease in the United Kingdom"; ch. 10, "Explaining inequalities in health in the United Kingdom"; ch. 11, "Food, health and disease: A case study."

Presents a global view of human health. "Examines contemporary and historical patterns of health and disease in the U.K. and the rest of the world. The book draws on the disciplines of demography, epidemiology, history, the social sciences and biology."—*Pref.* Index and annotated guide to further reading and to selected Internet resources. Intended for students, health professionals, and others.

929 **World health systems: Challenges and perspectives.** Bruce Fried, Laura M. Gaydos. xii, 563 p., ill. Chicago: Health Administration Pr., 2002. ISBN: 0585426422.

362.1   RA441.W676

INTERNATIONAL AND GLOBAL HEALTH

413

Contents: pt. I, Current issues facing global health systems; pt. II, Profiled countries: the wealthy countries (ch. 4–15); The transitional countries (ch. 16–28); The very poor countries (ch. 29–31); glossary of terms; index. Presents profiles of health systems in 28 countries. Organized in three categories by the wealth of each nation: wealthy, transitional, and very poor. Addresses the various challenges health services face, how they are organized, and how they are financed. Each chapter includes disease patterns and health system financing, also the "history, present status and future challenges of their health systems."—*Pref.* Available online via netLibrary.

Histories

930   Historical dictionary of the World Health Organization. Kelley Lee. xliv, 333 p., ill. Lanham, Md.: Scarecrow Press, 1998. ISBN: 0810833719.

353.6211   RA8.L44

(Historical dictionaries of international organizations series; no. 15).

Provides information on the history of the World Health Organization (WHO) and its contributions to international health cooperation. Includes an extensive bibliography on WHO documents and writings about WHO and a chronology of selected major events in the history of international health organizations. Several appendixes, for example, constitution of WHO, chronological list of member states, and WHO directors. Additional related information available on the World Health Organization (WHO) home page (951).

931   The value of health: A history of the Pan American Health Organization. Marcos Cueto. 239 p. Washington: Pan American Health Organization, 2007. ISBN: 9781580462631.

362.1   RA10.C8413

(Scientific and technical publication; 600) Pan American Health Organization (PAHO) (950).

Contents: ch. 1, The origins of international public health in the Americas; ch. 2, The birth of a new organization; ch. 3, The consolidation of an identity; ch. 4, For a continent free of disease; ch. 5, Health, development, and community participation; v. 6, Validity and renewal.

History of PAHO, contributions of individuals in PAHO, and also contemporary issues. Endnotes, bibliography, and index.

932 **WHO historical collection.** World Health Organization. 2000s–. Geneva, Switzerland: World Health Organization. http://www.who. int/library/collections/historical/en/print.html.

Produced by World Health Organization (WHO) (951); part of WHO Library and Information Networks for Knowledge (LNK).

Covers conferences before the founding of the WHO, WHO official records, International Sanitary Conventions (since 1851), and official records, reports, and other published materials from the Office International d'Hygiène Publique (OIHP), the health organization of the League of Nations (UNRRA). Includes materials on plague, cholera, and yellow fever, and also more recent epidemics; international classifications and nomenclatures of diseases; and public health and medicine monographs on public health in different countries and languages. Related links are, for example, WHOLIS: World Health Organization Library Database (484) and WHO Archives (http://www.who.int/archives/en/index.html). The distinctions between the WHO library, the WHO archives, and WHO records are described at http://www.who.int/archives/fonds_collections/ partners/en/index.html.

Indexes; Abstract journals; Databases

933 **Food Safety Research Information Office at the National Agricultural Library.** National Agricultural Library (U.S.). 2002–. Beltsville, Md.: National Agricultural Library, Food Safety Research Information Office. http://fsrio.nal.usda.gov/index.php.

TX537

Produced by National Agricultural Library (NAL); Food Service Research Information Office (FSRIO).

A major component of this searchable website is its "Research Projects Database" for locating information on food safety and related research. Categories currently in use in this database include food and food products, food composition and characteristics, food quality characteristics, food handling and processing, on-farm food safety, diseases and poisonings, sanitation and pathogen control, contaminants and contamination, government policy and regulations, methodology and quality standards, human health and epidemiology, education and training, facilities and sites, and pathogen biology.

Complements information found, for example, in *Food safety handbook* (1128), *Food safety: A reference handbook* by Nina E. Redman (2nd ed., 2007), *Foodborne disease handbook*, ed. by Y. H. Hui (2nd ed., 2001), *Foodborne diseases*, ed. by Dean O. Cliver and Hans Rieman (2nd ed., 2002), and Shabir Simjee's *Foodborne diseases* (2007).

934   **Global health.** C.A.B. International. 1973–. [Wallingford, Oxfordshire, U.K.]: CABI. http://www.cabi.org/datapage. asp?iDocID=169.

RA441

Formerly known as *CAB health.*

Global health, 1973–. (Derived from *CAB abstracts* [1143] and *Public health and tropical medicine databases*; *Global health archive*, 1910–83 [derived from six former print abstracting sources]). Includes records from the Bureau of Hygiene and Tropical Diseases to 1983.

Online databases available through CAB Direct, Ovid, EBSCO, and Dialog. Indexes journals, books, book chapters, conference proceedings, and other resources, mostly English-language publications, but also in other languages. Useful databases for searching the international health and public health literature, in addition to searching MEDLINE [425] and EMBASE [414]. For researchers, health professionals, policy makers, and students.

935   **International clinical trials registry platform search portal (ICTRP).** World Health Organization. 200?–. Geneva, [Switzerland]: World Health Organization. http://www.who.int/ trialsearch/.

Produced by World Health Organization (WHO) (951).

Database to locate information about clinical trials. Described by Tim Evans (WHO) as a "collaborative international initiative led by WHO that facilitates the identification of all clinical trials, regardless of whether or not they have been published." For health care researchers.

936   **International digest of health legislation = Recueil international de législation sanitaire.** World Health Organization. 2000–. [Geneva, Switzerland]: World Health Organization. http://www. who.int/idhl-rils/index.cfm.

K3569.2

International Digest of Health Legislation (IDHL) online database, available in English and French (Recueil international de législation sanitaire). Continues print version, publ. 1948–99; 1909–46(?) had title: *Bulletin mensuel de l'Office international d'Hygiène publique.*

Selection of national and international health legislation. Titles and summaries of texts of legislation, with links to the full texts of the legislation whenever available. The database can be searched by country, subject, volume, issue, or keyword. Includes the following subject categories, with detailed scope notes (http://www.who.int/idhl-rils/frame.cfm?language=english): General provisions, health manpower, health care facilities and services, disease control and medical care, oral health, family health, human reproduction and population policies, care of the elderly and rehabilitation, mental health, control of smoking, alcoholism, and drug abuse, ethical issues and professional responsibility, death and related issues, nutrition and food, consumer protection, pharmaceuticals and medical devices, poisons and other hazardous substances, occupational health and safety, environmental protection, radiation protection, accident prevention, sports and recreation, and health information and statistics.

937   **POPLINE.** Johns Hopkins University Bloomberg School of Public Health. Baltimore: Johns Hopkins University Bloomberg School of Public Health. http://db.jhuccp.org/ics-wpd/popweb/.

HQ766

POPLINE (Population Information Online) is a database on reproductive health with international coverage. Provides bibliographic citations with abstracts to English-language published and unpublished biomedical and social science literature on population research, demography, family planning, and related health issues. Includes links to full-text documents, RSS feeds for topical searches, and other special features. Detailed list of subjects covered internationally and in reference to developing countries at http://db.jhuccp.org/ics-wpd/popweb/aboutpl.html.

938   **PubMed.** U.S. National Center for Biotechnology Information, National Library of Medicine, National Institutes of Health. 1996–. Bethesda, Md.: U.S. National Center for Biotechnology Information. http://www.ncbi.nlm.nih.gov/sites/entrez/.

PubMed®, developed and maintained by the National Center for Biotechnology Information (NCBI) at the National Library of Medicine® (NLM) (427). It is available via the NCBI Entrez (3) retrieval system. PubMed also provides access to the other Entrez molecular biology resources (*PubMed Overview*). Starting May 23, 2007, NCBI is changing to a new version of Entrez in a phased implementation (cf. Nahin AM. New and Improved

PubMed®/Entrez and New URL *NLM tech. bull.*, 2007 May–Jun.; [356]: http://www.nlm.nih.gov/pubs/techbull/mj07/mj07_issue_cover.html).

Provides a search interface for more than 16 million bibliographic citations and abstracts in the fields of medicine, nursing, dentistry, veterinary medicine, health care systems, and preclinical sciences. It provides access to articles indexed for MEDLINE® (425) and for selected life sciences journals. PubMed subsets found under the "Limits" tab are: MEDLINE and PubMed Central®, several journal groups (i.e., core clinical journals, dental journals, and nursing journals), and topical subsets (AIDS, bioethics, cancer, complementary medicine, history of medicine, space life sciences, systematic reviews, and toxicology). "Linkout" provides access to full-text articles.

For detailed information see the PubMed fact sheet at http://www.nlm.nih.gov/pubs/factsheets/pubmed.html. For a brief overview of searching PubMed, see the PubMed Quick Start at http://www.ncbi.nlm.nih.gov/books/bv.fcgi?rid=helppubmed.section.pubmedhelp.PubMed_Quick_Start. For details on the now completed OLDMEDLINE retrospective conversion projects, see http://www.nlm.nih.gov/pubs/techbull/so06/so06_oldmedline_status.html.

Internet Resources

939   **amfAR.** American Foundation for AIDS Research. 1999–. New York; Washington: American Foundation for AIDS Research. http://www.amfar.org.

"amfAR™, the Foundation for AIDS Research, is one of the world's leading nonprofit organizations dedicated to the support of AIDS research, HIV prevention, treatment education, and the advocacy of sound AIDS-related public policy."—*Website*

Provides basic HIV/AIDS facts and statistics, HIV testing, information about various therapies (approved or under development), young people and HIV/AIDS, women and HIV/AIDS, global initiatives, and many other related topics and links.

"amfAR global links," formerly know as *HIV/AIDS treatment directory*, and "HIV/AIDS treatment insider," available 2000-5, have ceased publication. *The AmFAR AIDS handbook: The complete guide to understanding HIV and AIDS*, a comprehensive guide to help readers understand HIV/AIDS, treatment options, and how treatment decisions are made, has not been updated since 1999.

940   **Centers for Disease Control and Prevention (U.S.).** Centers for
       Disease Control and Prevention (U.S.). 1998–. Atlanta: Centers for
       Disease Control and Prevention, U.S. Dept. of Health and Human
       Services. http://www.cdc.gov/.

The Centers for Disease Control and Prevention (CDC), part of the Dept.
of Health and Human Services (HHS), is considered "the principal agency
in the United States government for protecting the health and safety of
all Americans and for providing essential human services."—*Website.* It is
involved in public health efforts to monitor health, to prevent and control
infectious and chronic diseases, injury, workplace hazards, disability, and
environmental health threats. The CDC works with partners in the U.S.
(http://www.cdc.gov/partners/) and worldwide, such as the World Health
Organization (951).

The CDC site map (http://www.cdc.gov/about/sitemap.htm) provides
a listing of the many different centers, institutes, and offices associated
with the CDC, linking each to its own website containing a variety of
information resources. Examples include the National Center for Health
Statistics [NCHS] (539), National Center for Environmental Health
(NCEH) (http://www.cdc.gov/nceh/), National Center for Injury Prevention and Control (NCIPC) "Injury Center" (http://www.cdc.gov/ncipc/),
National Office of Public Health Genomics (1506), Coordinating Office
for Global Health (http://www.cdc.gov/cogh/index.htm), Coordinating
Office for Emergency Preparedness and Response (http://www.bt.cdc.
gov/), to name a few. An A–Z index (http://www.cdc.gov/az.do/) provides
extensive information on many diseases and various other health topics
found on the CDC website, with new topics being added frequently. CDC
WONDER (1399) provides a search interface to a variety of health-related
topics and statistics. For health professionals and general users.

941   **Global health atlas.** World Health Organization. 2003–. Geneva,
       [Switzerland]: World Health Organization. http://www.who.int/
       globalatlas/.

Title varies: WHO's Communicable Disease Global Atlas; Global Atlas
of Infectious Disease; Global Atlas of Infectious Diseases: an Interactive
Information and Mapping System.

World Health Organization (951) Internet resource "bringing together
for analysis and comparison standardized data and statistics for infectious
diseases at country, regional, and global levels. The analysis and interpretation of data are further supported through information on demography, socioeconomic conditions, and environmental factors."—*Website.*

Searchable database which allows users to create reports, charts, and maps (e.g., geographic areas can be selected to create maps of diseases). Links to related sites.

942 Globalhealth.gov. U.S. Dept. of Health and Human Services. 1990s–. Washington: U.S. Dept. of Health and Human Services. http://globalhealth.gov/index.html.

Produced by HHS Office of Global Health Affairs (OGHA). Title varies: Global Health.gov; GlobalHealth.

Provides access to information about major global health topics, such as avian influenza, HIV/AIDS, malaria, etc. and links to partner organizations (e.g., WHO [951], PAHO [950], and others) and information on international travel, health regulation, refugee health, and related areas. CDC's (940) Coordinating Office for Global Health (http://www.cdc.gov/cogh/) provides additional information and resources.

943 Global health library. World Health Organization. 2005–. Geneva, Switzerland: World Health Organization. http://www.who.int/ghl/en/index.html.

Produced by Global Health Library (GHL); World Health Organization (WHO) (951); the Knowledge Management and Sharing Department of WHO (WHO/KMS).

A WHO collaborative project with many partners worldwide, such as U.N. bodies, national libraries of medicine, various public health institutes, academic and special libraries, and others. Points to reliable health information from various providers and in various formats. Provides access to the international scientific and technical literature and links to further information and access to global and regional indexes and international agencies (e.g., PAHO [950], WHOLIS [484]), various directories, and other information via its Global Health Library Virtual Platform [http://www.globalhealthlibrary.net/php/index.php]. Designed for different users and user groups, including health professionals, patients, their families, and the general public.

944 HealthMap. Clark Freifeld, John Brownstein, Children's Hospital [Boston] Informatics Program, Harvard-MIT Division of Health Sciences and Technology. [2006–.] [New Haven, Conn.]: Clark Freifeld and John Brownstein. http://www.healthmap.org/.

Title varies: HEALTHmap: Global Disease Alert Mapping System.

"Brings together disparate data sources to achieve a unified and comprehensive view of the current global state of infectious diseases and their effect on human and animal health. Integrates outbreak data of varying reliability, ranging from news sources (such as Google News [Mountain View, Calif.: Google, [200?]]) to curated personal accounts (such as ProMED) to validated official alerts (such as World Health Organization [951]). Through an automated text processing system, the data is aggregated by disease and displayed by location for user-friendly access to the original alert. provides a jumping-off point for real-time information on emerging infectious diseases and has particular interest for public health officials and international travelers."—*Website.* Official alerts from WHO are available via *Disease outbreak news,* which is part of WHO's "Epidemic and Pandemic Alert and Response (EPR)" website (http://www.who.int/csr/don/en/). EuroSurveillance (http://www.euro-surveillance.org/), a program of the European Centre for Disease Prevention and Control (http://www.ecdc.europa.eu), is another data source. Uses marker icons (square-shaped: country-level marker; round: state, province, and local) and low or high "heat index," with further explanation at http://www.healthmap.org/about.php. Provides links for information on particular diseases to Wikipedia (San Francisco: Wikimedia Foundation, 2001–), the World Health Organization (WHO) (951), the Centers for Disease Control and Prevention (CDC) (940), PubMed (432), and Google Trends. Available in different views, i.e., as map, satellite, or hybrid map.

945   **International health data reference guide.** National Center for Health Statistics (U.S.). ill. Hyattsville, Md.: U.S. Dept. of Health and Human Services, Public Health Service, National Center for Health Statistics, [1984?]–.

362.1021   RA407.A58

Description based on 11th ed., 2003.

"Provides information collected in 2003 on the availability of selected national vital, hospital, health personnel resources, and population-based health survey statistics. Information for 40 nations. Main purpose is to provide information not readily available in published form. It is not designed to provide information on the availability of measures such as crude birth and death rates or life expectancy at birth."—*Pref.* Biennial. Also available online on the National Center for Health Statistics (NCHS) (539) website at http://purl.access.gpo.gov/GPO/LPS24629.

946   **International health (MedlinePlus).** National Library of Medicine (U.S.). 2000?–. Bethesda, Md.: National Library of Medicine. http://www.nlm.nih.gov/medlineplus/internationalhealth.html.

A Health Topic within MedlinePlus (463). Provides extensive global health information, with access to various online reference resources, links to major organizations (e.g., Centers for Disease Control, World Health Organization), foundations (e.g., Henry J. Kaiser Family Foundation), research, journal articles, law and policy information (e.g., International Health Regulations [2005] [926]), WHO and UNICEF statistics, etc. Links to related MedlinePlus topics, such as Traveler's Health and Health System (MedlinePlus) (463). Go Local link and map help to identify services and providers in the United States.

947   **Kaiser Family Foundation.** Henry J. Kaiser Family Foundation. 2000–. Menlo Park, Calif.: Henry J. Kaiser Family Foundation. http://www.kff.org/.
362.1; 361.7

The Henry J. Kaiser Family Foundation is an independent philanthropy focusing on major health care issues. Website contains statistics on Medicare, Medicaid, the uninsured in each state of the United States, minority health, etc. Links to resources on health policy covering such topics as women's health policy, HIV/AIDS, and media programs. A wide variety of resources are accessible via the following tabs found on the website: (1) KaiserNetwork.org (http://www.kaisernetwork.org/): search for recent daily reports and webcasts; (2) StateHealthFacts (http://www.statehealthfacts.org/): source for state health data; (3) Kaiseredu.org (http://www.kaiseredu.org/): provides easy access to the latest data, research, analysis, and developments in health policy and includes narrated slide tutorials, background reference libraries, and issue modules on current topics and policy debates; (4) GlobalHealthReporting.org (http://www.globalhealthreporting.org/): global data on HIV/AIDS, tuberculosis, malaria and more; (5) GlobalHealthFacts.org (http://www.globalhealthfacts.org/): companion site to globalhealthreporting; (6) Health08.org (http://www.health08.org/): election news, analysis, and events.

948   **Malaria atlas project (MAP).** Malaria Public Health and Epidemiology Group, Centre for Geographic Medicine, Kenya. 2006–. Nairobi, Kenya; Oxford, England, [U.K.]: Centre for Geographic Medicine, Kenya; University of Oxford. http://www.map.ox.ac.uk/MAP_overview.html.

"MAP is a joint project between the Malaria Public Health & Epidemiology Group, Centre for Geographic Medicine, Kenya and the Spatial Ecology & Epidemiology Group, University of Oxford, UK with collaborating nodes in America and Asia Pacific region."—*Overview*. Funded by the Wellcome Trust, United Kingdom.

Provides an overview of the MAP project and enables viewers to browse worldwide malaria and malaria-control data and also allows the submission of new data. Offers health links (e.g., malaria, general health, and food security and health), global and regional links, and links to malaria-related organizations. Also provides research-related links, including libraries, a listing of online resources, databases for literature searching, tutorials, and information about various software tools. Further details about this project and its future plans can be found on the MAP website.

949 NLM gateway. National Library of Medicine (U.S.). 2000–. Bethesda, Md.: National Library of Medicine. http://gateway.nlm.nih.gov/.

RA11

Allows simultaneous searching of information resources at the National Library of Medicine (NLM). Databases include MEDLINE (425)/PubMed (432) and the NLM Catalog (482) as well as other resources, including information on current clinical trials and consumer health information (MedlinePlus [463]). Currently provides access to 21 databases and other information resources (for a complete list of databases and other details, see http://www.nlm.nih.gov/pubs/factsheets/gateway.html). An overview of the search results is presented in several categories (bibliographic resources, consumer health resources, and other information), with a listing of the individual databases and the number of results within these categories.

950 Pan American Health Organization (PAHO). Pan American Health Organization. 1990s–. Washington: Pan American Health Organization. http://www.paho.org/.

RA438.A45

Published by World Health Organization (WHO); United Nations.

PAHO is WHO's regional office for the Americas, an international public health agency with the mission to improve health and living standards of the countries of the Americas.

Searchable website, with detailed information about PAHO's governance and mission, links to basic health indicators, core health data, country health profiles, trends and situation analysis, information products, and other related information. Includes, for example, Regional Core Health Data Initiative (http://www.paho.org/english/dd/ais/coredata. htm), including access to PAHO's Basic Country Health Profiles for the Americas (http://www.paho.org/English/DD/AIS/cp_index.htm), which provides mortality statistics for the Americas and health profiles for all countries in North and South America.

Provides access to PAHO electronic books (English and Spanish) at http://www.paho.org/Project.asp?SEL=PR&LNG=ENG&ID=360.

A related title is *Health in the Americas* (959).

951   **World Health Organization (WHO).** World Health Organization (WHO). 1995–. Geneva, [Switzerland]: World Health Organization. http://www.who.int/en/.

"The World Health Organization is the United Nations specialized agency for health. It was established on 7 April 1948. WHO's objective, as set out in its Constitution, is the attainment by all peoples of the highest possible level of health. Health is defined in WHO's Constitution as a state of complete physical, mental and social well-being and not merely the absence of disease or infirmity."—*WHO website.* WHO is governed by 193 Member States through the World Health Assembly, composed of representatives from WHO's Member States.

Searchable website on international health. Contains news concerning current international health issues and disease outbreaks; general WHO information and governance; country list of member states with health information; online access to "Basic Documents" (http://www.who.int/gb/ bd/E/index.html) and other WHO publications (http://www.who.int/publications/en/); health topics (http://www.who.int/topics/en/); drug topics, with publications (e.g., International pharmacopoeia [1181] and information on policy and quality and safety standards, essential drugs, and traditional medicine ["Medicines Home" http://www.who.int/medicines/en/]), International travel and health [708], and vaccination requirements; bioethics topics [Ethics and health [611]]; epidemiological and statistical information ["Guide to Statistical Information at WHO," http://www.who.int/ whosis/en], law-related publications (e.g., International health regulations [2005] [926] and International digest of health legislation [936]); research tools such as WHO's library database WHOLIS [484], WHOSIS [WHO statistical information system] [556], Burden of Disease statistics[http:// www.who.int/topics/global_burden_of_disease/en/]; mortality data; statistics by disease or condition; the WHO family of international classifications [90], and many other important internal and external links. Information available in English, French, or Spanish.

952   **World Medical Association Ethics Unit.** World Medical
Association. 2003–. Ferney-Voltaire, France: World Medical
Association. http://www.wma.net/e/ethicsunit/.

Produced by World Medical Association (WMA).

Coordinates the WMA's ethics policies with the goal "to establish
and promote the highest possible standards of ethical behavior and care
by physicians."—*About* (http://www.wma.net/e/ethicsunit/index.htm).
Serves as a clearinghouse of ethics information resources for national
medical associations and physicians, develops new resources, and collaborates with other international organizations involved in medical ethics
and health and human rights. Makes accessible the online version of John
R. Williams's *Medical ethics manual* (http://www.wma.net/e/ethicsunit/
resources.htm), a list of codes and declarations of adopted ethics policies
and declarations in order of their date of first adoption and amendments,
including the International Code of Medical Ethics and Declaration of
Helsinki: Ethical Principles for Medical Research Involving Human Subjects, as well as many others. Also provides a list of health and human
rights organizations and resources.

Statistics

953   **European health for all database (HFA-DB).** World Health
Organization Regional Office for Europe. 2000s–. Copenhagen,
Denmark: World Health Organization Regional Office for Europe.
http://data.euro.who.int/hfadb/.

Description based on Jan. 2007 version.

Provides basic health statistics and health trends for the member states
of the WHO European Region, with approx. 600 health indicators, including basic demographic and socioeconomic indicators; some lifestyle- and
environment-related indicators; mortality, morbidity, and disability; hospital discharges; and health care resources, utilization, and expenditures.
Can be used as a tool for international comparison and for assessing the
health situation and trends in any European country.

954   **Finding and using health statistics.** National Information Center
on Health Services Research and Health Care Technology, National
Library of Medicine (U.S.). 2008–. Bethesda, Md.: National Library
of Medicine. http://www.nlm.nih.gov/nichsr/usestats/.

Contents: "Introduction"; "About health statistics" ("Importance"; "Uses";
"Sources"; "Health statistics enterprise"); "Finding health statistics"

("Challenges"; "Natural structure"; "Strategies"; "Internet strategies"); "Supporting material" (including a glossary, exercises, and examples).

"This course describes the range of available health statistics, identifies their sources and helps you understand how to use information about their structure as you search."—*Main page*

Reviews various approaches to finding health statistics and provides help with developing search strategies. Links to numerous relevant examples of statistical web resources and portals from federal and state governments, universities, and private organizations. Provides a good introduction and overviews for health professionals, students, and reference librarians.

955   **The global burden of disease: A comprehensive assessment of mortality and disability from diseases, injuries, and risk factors in 1990 and projected to 2020.** Christopher J. L. Murray, Alan D. Lopez, Harvard School of Public Health. xxxii, 990 p. Cambridge, Mass.: Publ. by the Harvard School of Public Health on behalf of the World Health Organization and the World Bank, 1996. ISBN: 0674354486.

614.42   RA441.G56

(Global burden of disease and injury series; v. 1) "The Global Burden of Disease Series provides, on a global and regional level, a detailed and internally consistent approach to meeting. information needs. concerning epidemiological conditions and disease burden."—*Foreword.* GDB is considered to have set new standards for measuring population health. It also attempts to provide a comparative index of the burden of each disease or injury, i.e., the number of disability-adjusted life years lost as a result of either premature death or years lived with disability. The findings attempt to provide a comprehensive assessment of the health of populations. Results are only approximate, with the reliability of data considered poor for some regions of the world; with estimates of causes of death, incidence and prevalence of disease, injury, and disability, measures and projections of disease burden, and measures of risk factors. Other titles in this series include, e.g., Global health statistics: A compendium of incidence, prevalence, and mortality estimates for over 200 conditions (524), *Health dimensions of sex and reproduction: The global burden of sexually transmitted diseases, HIV, maternal conditions, perinatal disorders, and congenital anomalies,* and *The global epidemiology of infectious diseases.* Another related title is *Global burden of disease and risk factors* (522) and the World Health Organization's "Global burden of disease estimates" website (http://www.who.int/healthinfo/bod-estimates/en/index.html), with recent results and links.

956 **Global burden of disease and risk factors.** Alan D. Lopez, Disease Control Priorities Project. xxix, 475 p., ill. [New York]: Washington: Oxford University Press; World Bank, 2006. ISBN: 9780821362.

362.1   RA441.G5613

Disease Control Priorities Project is a partnership of the Fogarty International Center (U.S. National Institutes of Health), the World Bank, The World Health Organization, and the Population Reference Bureau.

Contents: ch. 1, Measuring the Global Burden of Disease and risk factors, 1990–2001; ch. 2, Demographic and epidemiological characteristics of major regions, 1990–2001; ch. 3, The burden of disease and mortality by condition: data, methods, and results for 2001; ch. 4, Comparative quantification of mortality and burden of disease attributable to selected risk factors; ch. 5, Sensitivity and uncertainty analyses for burden of disease and risk factor estimates; ch. 6, Incorporating deaths near the time of birth into estimates of the Global Burden of Disease.

Presents the results of the "Global Burden of Disease Study" (quantification of the impact of diseases, injuries, and risk factors on population health) and the CEA (Cost-Effectiveness Analysis) Study and a description of the global epidemiology of diseases, injuries, and risk factors. Resource for researchers interested in the development of methods to measure disease burden and in global and regional health policy.

Related titles are, e.g., *The global burden of disease: A comprehensive assessment of mortality and disability from diseases, injuries, and risk factors* (955), *Global health statistics: A compendium of incidence, prevalence, and mortality estimates for over 200 conditions* (524), and the World Health Organization's "Global burden of disease estimates" website (http://www.who. int/healthinfo/bodestimates/en/index.html), with recent results and links.

Available online at http://bibpurl.oclc.org/web/13502.

957 **Global health atlas.** World Health Organization. 2003–. Geneva, [Switzerland]: World Health Organization. http://www.who.int/ globalatlas/.

Title varies: *WHO's Communicable Disease Global Atlas; Global Atlas of Infectious Disease; Global Atlas of Infectious Diseases: An Interactive Information and Mapping System.*

World Health Organization (951) Internet resource "bringing together for analysis and comparison standardized data and statistics for infectious diseases at country, regional, and global levels. The analysis and interpretation of data are further supported through information on demography, socioeconomic conditions, and environmental factors."—*Website.*

Searchable database which allows users to create reports, charts, and maps (e.g., geographic areas can be selected to create maps of diseases). Links to related sites.

958   **Global health statistics: A compendium of incidence, prevalence, and mortality estimates for over 200 conditions.** Christopher J. L. Murray, Alan D. Lopez, World Health Organization. vii, 906 p. Boston; Cambridge, Mass: Publ. by The Harvard School of Public Health on behalf of the World Health Organization and the World Bank. Distributed by Harvard University Press, 1996. ISBN: 0674354494.

614.42   RA407.M87

(Global burden of disease and injury series; 2)

Provides information on the underlying epidemiological statistics for over 200 conditions and several chapters with detailed data for each condition.

Part of the Global burden of disease series which "provides, on a global and regional level, a detailed and internally consistent approach to meeting information needs concerning epidemiological conditions and disease burden. Volumes summarize epidemiological knowledge about all major conditions and most risk factors."—*Foreword*

Other titles in this series include, for example, *The global burden of disease: A comprehensive assessment of mortality and disability from diseases, injuries, and risk factors in 1990 and projected to 2020* (955), *Health dimensions of sex and reproduction: The global burden of sexually transmitted diseases, HIV, maternal conditions, perinatal disorders, and congenital anomalies,* and *The global epidemiology of infectious diseases.* Other related titles are *Global burden of disease and risk factors* (522)and the World Health Organization's "Global burden of disease estimates" website (http://www.who.int/healthinfo/bodestimates/en/index.html), with recent results and links.

959   **Health in the Americas.** Pan American Sanitary Bureau. ill. Washington: Pan American Health Organization, Pan American Sanitary Bureau, Regional Office of the World Health Organization, 1998–.

610.8s; 362.1091812   RA10.P252

Published by Pan American Health Organization (PAHO) (950); "Salud en las Américas."

Title varies: Previously had title *Summary of reports on the health conditions in the Americas* and *Health conditions in the Americas*. Description based on 2007 ed. (2 v.): v. 1, Regional analysis; v. 2, Country-by-country assessment.

Health data, facts, health trends, and related information for Central and South America, with emphasis on health disparities. Provides a vision for the future of health and health challenges in the Americas. Also available online through netLibrary; both print and online versions in English or Spanish.

A complement to this publication is *Health statistics from the Americas*, publ. in print format 1991–98, and now online (2003 ed. http://www.paho.org/english/dd/pub/SP_591.htm and 2006 ed. http://www.paho.org/English/DD/AIS/HSA2006.htm).

960 Health statistics (MedlinePlus). National Library of Medicine (U.S.). 2000–. Bethesda, Md.: National Library of Medicine. http://www.nlm.nih.gov/medlineplus/healthstatistics.html.

Part of MedlinePlus (463); National Library of Medicine (NLM) (427).

Contents: Overviews; Latest News; Related Issues; Research; Journal Articles; Directories; Organizations; Newsletters/Print Publications; Law and Policy; Children; Teenagers; Men; Women; Seniors.

Provides helpful links to various types of health and vital statistics for consumers and health professionals. FAQ Statistics (http://www.nlm.nih.gov/services/statistics.html) is another website made available by NLM that answers questions on how to find statistics for U.S. and global health and medicine topics.

961 International health data reference guide. National Center for Health Statistics (U.S.), ill. Hyattsville, Md.: U.S. Dept. of Health and Human Services, Public Health Service, National Center for Health Statistics, [1984?]–.

362.1021   RA407.A58

Description based on 11th ed., 2003.

"Provides information collected in 2003 on the availability of selected national vital, hospital, health personnel resources, and population-based health survey statistics. Information for 40 nations. Main purpose is to provide information not readily available in published form. It is not designed to provide information on the availability of measures such as crude birth and death rates or life expectancy at birth."—*Pref.* Biennial. Also available online on the National Center for

Health Statistics (NCHS) (539) website at http://purl.access.gpo.gov/ GPO/LPS24629.

962   OECD health data. Organisation for Economic Co-operation and Development. Paris: Organisation for Economic Co-operation and Development. http://www.oecd.org/health/healthdata.

Title varies: SourceOECD Health Data.

Part of SourceOECD (Organisation for Economic Co-operation and Development, [Paris, France]: OECD), which contains publications (monographs, periodicals, and statistical databases) issued by the OECD.

Interactive database and source of statistics on health and health care systems of the OECD member states. Allows cross-country comparisons of national health care systems. Includes, for example, health status, health care resources, health care utilization, expenditure on health, and health care financing. Available in online and CD-ROM formats.

963   WHO global infobase. World Health Organization. 2000s?–. Geneva, Switzerland: World Health Organization. http://www.who. int/infobase.

Produced by World Health Organization (WHO) (951).

Title varies: also called WHO Global InfoBase Online.

"Data warehouse that collects, stores and displays information on chronic diseases and their risk factors for all WHO member states."—*Main page.* Provides information on health topics, e.g., alcohol and its relationship to disease and injury, blood pressure, cholesterol, diet, overweight and obesity, physical activity, tobacco, diabetes, oral health, visual impairment, and other topics, such as mortality estimates. Information comes from various national surveys, and WHO collaborates with its regional offices to keep information up to date. Provides individual country pages, allows comparison of countries, and displays comparable risk factor data. Extensive help pages include glossary, FAQ page, definitions of terms used, etc.

964   WHOSIS. World Health Organization. [1994]–. Geneva, [Switzerland]: World Health Organization. http://www.who.int/ whosis/.

Published by World Health Organization (WHO).

Provides description and online access to statistical and epidemiological information, data, and tools available from WHO and other sites: mortality and health status, disease statistics, health systems statistics, risk factors and health services, and inequities in health. Provides links to several databases: WHOSIS database, with the latest "core health indicators" from WHO sources (including *The world health report* [559] and *World health statistics* [560]), which make it possible to construct tables for any combination of countries, indicators and years, Causes of Death database, WHO Global InfoBase Online, Global Health Atlas, and Reproductive Health Indicators database.

965 The world health report. World Health Organization. 1995–.
Geneva, [Switzerland]: World Health Organization. ISSN: 1020-3311. http://www.who.int/whr/.

614.405   RA8.A265

Pt. of WHOSIS (WHO Statistical Information System) a guide to statistical information (556). Description based on the 2006 online ed., has subtitle: "working together for health." Also available in print format. 2007 ed. ("promoting international health security") due Aug. 2007.

"Every year. takes a new and expert look at global health, focusing on a specific theme, while assessing the current global situation. Using the latest data gathered and validated by WHO, each report paints a picture of the changing world."—*Website.* Website also provides links to the full-text reports 1995–2005, each with focus on a special theme: 1995, "bridging the gaps"; 1996, "fighting disease, fostering development"; 1997 "conquering suffering, enriching humanity"; 1998, "life in the 21st century: a vision for all"; 1999, "making a difference"; 2000, "health systems: improving performance"; 2001, "mental health: new understanding, new hope"; 2002, "reducing risks, promoting healthy life"; 2003, "shaping the future"; 2004, "changing history"; 2005, "make every mother and child count;" 2006, "working together for health."

966 World health statistics. World Health Organization. 2005–.
Geneva, Switzerland: World Health Organization. http://www.who.int/healthinfo/statistics/en/.

1939/46–96 publ. as *World health statistics annual = Annuaire de statistiques sanitaires mondiales* (print version).

Part of WHOSIS: WHO Statistical Information System (556).

Description based on online 3rd ed., 2007 ed. (http://www.who.int/whosis/whostat2007.pdf).

Contents: pt. 1, "Ten statistical highlights in global public health." Pt. 2, "World health statistics": "Health status: Mortality"; "Health status: Morbidity"; "Health services coverage"; "Risk factors"; "Health systems"; "Inequities in health"; "Demographic and socioeconomic statistics."

"Presents the most recent health statistics for WHO's 193 Member States. collated from publications and databases produced by WHO's technical programmes and regional offices. Selected on the basis of their relevance to global health, the availability and quality of the data, and the accuracy and comparability of estimates. The statistics for the indicators are derived from an interactive process of data collection, compilation, quality assessment and estimation occurring among WHO's technical programmes and its Member States."—*Introd.* Print version also available.

7 > MEDICAL JURISPRUDENCE

967 **Clinical manual of psychiatry and law.** Robert I. Simon, Daniel W. Shuman. Washington: American Psychiatric Publ., 2007.

614.15   RA1151.S56

Contents: (1) Psychiatry and the law; (2) The doctor-patient relationship; (3) Confidentiality and testimonial privilege; (4) Informed consent and the right to refuse treatment; (5) Psychiatric treatment: tort liability; (6) Seclusion and restraint; (7) Involuntary hospitalization; (8) The suicidal patient; (9) Psychiatric responsibility and the violent patient; (10) Maintaining treatment boundaries: clinical and legal issues. Appendix A: Suggested readings; Appendix B: Glossary of legal terms; Index.

Covers a variety of topics concerning the requirements and legal regulations of psychiatric practice, including treatment issues that may lead to liability and malpractice lawsuits.

Clinical handbook of psychiatry and law (Philadelphia: Lippincott, Williams and Wilkins, 2007) covers topics such as confidentiality and privilege, legal issues in emergency psychiatry and inpatient psychiatry, forensic evaluations, the clinician in court, and others.

Bibliography

968 **U.S. health law and policy, 2001: A guide to the current literature.** Donald H. Caldwell, American Health Lawyers Association. xxi,

593 p. San Francisco; Chicago: Jossey-Bass; Health Forum, 2001. ISBN: 0787955043.

016.34473041 KF3821.A1C35

Earlier edition had title: *U.S. health law and policy 1999: A guide to the current literature*, 1998.

Contents: pt. 1, Medical facilities and organizations; pt. 2, Regulatory matters; pt. 3, Licensure, liability, and labor issues; pt. 4, Selected health care policy topics. Appendixes: (A) Health law periodicals, digests, and newsletters; (B) Reference sources and government serials; (C) Computer databases and Internet sites; (D) State-by-state synopsis of selected statutes of limitation laws; (E) Table of acronyms and abbreviations; (F) Glossary; (G) Relevant federal agencies; (H) Selected nongovernmental agencies; (I) State laws governing medical records; (J) Health Care Financing Administration regional offices. Subject, name, title indexes.

This rev. ed. is a comprehensive annotated bibliographic guide to the healthcare law and policy literature and related legal issues. Sources are books, journals, government documents, and websites. Entries provide publication information and a brief synopsis of the content of the citation. A future edition is planned.

Dictionaries

969 **Attorney's illustrated medical dictionary.** Ida Dox. 1 (various pagings), ill. (some color). St. Paul, Minn.: West Group, 2002.

KF8933.A44

1st ed., 1997. At head of title: American jurisprudence proof of facts, 3rd series. Includes index of illustrations. "Replaces Am. Jur. Proof of Facts Taber's Cyclopedic Medical Dictionary" (*insert from West Group*). Kept up-to-date with supplements. Concise definitions of approx. 30,000 terms, synonyms, pronunciations, 3,500 illustrations, index of illustrations, and references to further information. Other dictionaries are J. E. Schmidt's *Attorneys' dictionary of medicine* or Schmidt's *Attorneys' dictionary of medicine illustrated*, a loose-leaf publication also referred to as *Attorney's dictionary of medicine and word finder*.

970 **The concise dictionary of medical-legal terms: A general guide to interpretation and usage.** Joseph A. Bailey. 148 p., ill. New York: Parthenon Publ., 1998. ISBN: 1850706808.

614.103 RA1017.B35

As used in this dictionary, medical-legal covers the regulation and utilization of medicine by the legal profession (cf. *Foreword*). Designed as a guide to common words and phrases used in medicine and law, it is "particularly designed to help those just entering the medical-legal field. For more detailed specific knowledge the reader should consult more comprehensive references that are specific to his or her legal system."—*Pref.* Illustrations, tables, and diagrams.

971   **Dictionary of ethical and legal terms and issues: The essential guide for mental health professionals.** Len Sperry. xi, 277 p. New York: Routledge, 2007. ISBN: 0415953219.

174.2   RC455.2.E8.S655

Contents: pt. 1, "Dictionary of ethical and legal terms"; pt. 2, "Ethical issues and considerations"; pt. 3, "Legal issues and considerations"; appendix: "Key legal cases and legislation impacting mental health practice"; index.

Concise guide to the key ethical and legal issues and considerations; codes and statutes; and key legal opinions, legislation, and regulations relevant to everyday mental health practice in the United States. Pt. 2 and 3 present particular topics in some detail, with definitions of key terms. Intended for graduate and undergraduate students and as a ready-reference source for mental health practitioners. Also available as an e-book.

972   **Health care defined: A glossary of current terms.** Bruce Goldfarb. xi, 347 p. Baltimore: Williams & Wilkins, 1997. ISBN: 0683036157.

362.103   RA423.G65

Scholarly resource. Explains the terminology used in the healthcare field, e.g., medical care, delivery of health care, and health services terminology. Contains approx. 3,000 essential terms and explains them in non-medical terminology. Includes bibliographical references (p. 313–315). Useful for insurance and legal professionals.

973   **Health services cyclopedic dictionary: A compendium of health-care and public health terminology.** 3rd ed. Thomas C. Timmreck. xii, 860 p., color ill. Sudbury, Mass.: Jones and Bartlett Publishers, 1997. ISBN: 0867205156.

362.1068   RA393.T56

1st ed. (1982) and 2nd ed. (1987) had title: *Dictionary of health services management.*

(The Jones and Bartlett series in health sciences).

This rev. and exp. ed. contains terminology and definitions from the fields of health services and medical care, health administration, health care reform, public health, environmental health, epidemiology, managed care, and other related areas.

Directories

974   **DIRLINE.** National Institutes of Health (U.S.). [1983?–]. Bethesda, Md.: U.S. National Institutes of Health, Dept. of Health and Human Services. http://dirline.nlm.nih.gov/.

DIRLINE® (Directory of Information Resources Online), maintained by the National Library of Medicine (NLM) (208).

Online annotated directory of organizations, research resources, projects, databases, and other information resources concerned with health and biomedicine from a variety of sources, including federal, state, and local government agencies, academic and research institutions, and also consumer health-related resources such as self-help groups and health hotlines. Resources are mostly from the U.S. but also include some international resources. Currently contains over 8,000 entries, with topics on most diseases and conditions and health services research and technology assessment. Can be searched using MeSH® (Medical Subject Headings) (575), keywords, or by name and location of a resource. Detailed information on DIRLINE can be found via a fact sheet prepared by NLM: http://www.nlm.nih.gov/pubs/factsheets/dirlinfs.html.

975   **Health care standards: Official directory.** ECRI. Plymouth Meeting, Pa.: ECRI, 1990–. ISSN: 1044-4076.

362.1021873   RA399.A3H43

Description based on 18th ed., 2006.

ECRI (http://www.ecri.org), formerly the Emergency Care Research Institute, is a nonprofit health services research agency and a Collaborating Center of the World Health Organization (WHO) (951). Provides information and technical assistance to the healthcare community to support safe and cost-effective patient care. The Agency for Healthcare Research and Quality (AHRQ) (733) has designated ECRI an Evidence-based Practice Center. ECRI is also responsible for performing the technical work of developing and maintaining AHRQ's National Guideline Clearinghouse and the National Quality Measures Clearinghouse. Contains health care standards issued by medical societies, professional associations, government agencies, and other health-related organizations, with approx. "38,000 titles of standards, practice guidelines, position papers, technical statements, technology assessments, advisories, policies, procedures, hazard reports, recommended practices, and other official documents, federal and state health-care related laws and regulations, and contact information for the issuing organizations" (cf. *Publ. notes*). Arranged under keywords; abbreviations; organizations and their standards; law, legislation, and regulation (federal and state); and names and addresses (federal and state). Intended for use in clinical and legal settings by researchers, educators, and legal professionals. Also available as HCS Online, providing daily updates and enhanced search results. Further details for both the print and online editions are provided at https://www.ecri.org/Products/Pages/healthcare_standards_directory.asp x.

Encyclopedias

976 **Encyclopedia of forensic and legal medicine.** Jason Payne-James. 4 v., ill., ports. Amsterdam, [The Netherlands]; Boston: Elsevier Academic Press, 2005. ISBN: 0125479700.

614.103   RA1017.E53

Contents: v. 1, A–Co; v. 2, Cr–H; v. 3, I–Ri; v. 4, Ro–Z, index.

Comprehensive overview of forensic and legal medicine and related specialties and issues. Detailed table of contents, glossary, cross-references, further reading, and index. Includes diagrams, tables, and color images. Online edition available from Elsevier Science Direct.

977 **Encyclopedia of forensic sciences.** Jay A. Siegel, Pekka J. Saukko, Geoffrey C. Knupfer. 3 v. (xxxviii, 1440, lxv, lvii p.), ill. (some color). San Diego, Calif.: Academic Press, 2000. ISBN: 0122272153.

363.2503   HV8073.E517

Considers basic principles of forensic science and a wide range of topics, including theories, methods, and techniques used by forensic scientists. Covers, for example, accident investigation, crime scene investigation, clinical forensic medicine (e.g., overview, defense wounds, self-inflicted injury, child abuse, sexual assault, gunshot wounds, etc.), autopsy, "psychological autopsies," medicolegal causes of death, DNA data banks, alcohol and drug analysis, ethical aspects, etc. Also available online via Elsevier Science Direct.

978 **Lawyers' medical cyclopedia of personal injuries and allied specialties.** 5th ed. Richard M. Patterson. 1A–B, 3A–B, 4A–B,

5A–B, ill. Newark, N.J: LexisNexis, c2002–c2005. ISBN: 1558340378.

RA1022.U6L38

1st ed., 1958–62; 4th ed., 1977–99 (10 v.). Publication of the current (5th) ed. in progress.

"Authoritative reference for attorneys involved in personal injury, medical malpractice, workers' compensation, social security, disability income, and health insurance cases. Offers in-depth information and case-law on hundreds of medical and surgical specialties. Written by physicians skilled at translating complex anatomy, physiology, and medical treatment into clear language."—*Publ. notes.* Kept up-to-date by pocket parts and revised volumes. Includes bibliographical references and indexes.

Guides

979 **The Blackwell guide to medical ethics.** Rosamond Rhodes, Leslie Francis, Anita Silvers. 435 p. Malden, Mass.: Blackwell Publ., 2007. ISBN: 9781405125833.

174.2   R724.B515

(Blackwell philosophy guides; 21.)

Contents: part I, Individual decisions about clinical issues: (1) Patient decisions; (2) Individual decisions of physicians and other health care professionals; part II, Legislative and judicial decisions about social policy: (1) Liberty; (2) Justice.

"Helpful tool for navigating the complex literature and diverse views on the key issues in medical ethics. Employing crucial distinctions between the personal decisions of patients, the professional decisions of individual health care providers, and political decisions about public policy, the chapters in the volume address the most central and controversial topics in medical ethics."—*Publ. notes.* Includes bibliographical references and index.

Handbooks

980 **BioLaw: A legal and ethical reporter on medicine, health care, and bioengineering.** James F. Childress. (loose-leaf). Frederick, Md.: University Publications of America, 1986–.

1983–1985 had title: *Bioethics reporter.*

Editors: 1986–. James F. Childress et al.

Loose-leaf; updated between editions. Has supplement: Biolaw. micro-fiche supplement.

Each annual consists of 2 v.: v. 1, Resource manual, contains essays on biological, medical, and health care issues with ethical and legal implications; v. 2, includes updates on many previously published topics and special sections on laws, regulations, court cases, etc. Each update comes with a cumulative subject index covering both volumes and a cumulative index to court cases.

981 **Clinical handbook of psychiatry and the law.** 4th ed. Paul S. Appelbaum, Thomas G. Gutheil. 322 p. Philadelphia: Lippincott, Williams and Wilkins, 2007. ISBN: 0781778913.

344.73041   KF2910.P75G87

1st ed., 1982; 3rd ed., 2000.

Contents: ch. 1, "Confidentiality and privilege"; ch. 2, "Legal issues in emergency psychiatry"; ch. 3, "Legal issues in inpatient psychiatry"; ch. 4, "Malpractice and other forms of liability"; ch. 5, "Competence and substitute decision making"; ch. 6, "Forensic evaluations"; ch. 7, "Clinicians and lawyers"; ch. 8, "The clinician in court"; index.

Provides up-to-date information for clinicians on "how law affects practice, and how psychiatry can contribute to the law" (*Pref.*) and discussion of its interrelated clinical and legal aspects. Each chapter has the following seven sections: Case examples, legal issues, clinical issues, pitfalls, case example epilogues, action guide, and suggested readings.

982 **Contemporary issues in healthcare law and ethics.** 3rd ed. Dean M Harris. 377 p. Chicago; Washington: Health Administration Press; AUPHA Press, 2007. ISBN: 9781567932.

344.730321   KF3825.Z9.H3

1st ed., 1999, had title *Healthcare law and ethics: Issues for the age of managed care*; 2nd ed., 2003.

Contents: (1) "The role of law in the U.S. healthcare system"; (2) "Managing and regulating the healthcare system"; (3) "Patient care issues"; (4) "Legal and ethical issues in health insurance and managed care"; table of cases; table of statutes; table of regulations; index.

This revised and updated edition presents essential information and examines legal and ethical issues in health care. Includes, for example, the U.S. Supreme Court's decisions on physician-assisted suicide, partial-birth abortion, issues in emergency contraception, HIPAA Privacy Rule, medical malpractice, reporting of medical errors, and other topics. Also available as e-book via netLibrary.

983 **Health and human rights: Basic international documents.** 2nd ed. Stephen P. Marks, Francois-Xavier Bagnoud Center for Health and Human Rights. xiii, 392 p. Cambridge, Mass.: Francois-Xavier Bagnoud Center for Health and Human Rights, 2006. ISBN: 0674023773.

RA418.H3872

1st ed., c2004.

(Harvard series on health and human rights).

"Updated and expanded from the previous edition to provide the practitioner, scholar, and advocate with access to the most basic instruments of international law and policy that express the values of human rights for advancing health. The topics covered include professional ethics; research and experimentation; treatment of prisoners and detainees; patients' rights; right to health; right to life; freedom from torture, war crimes, crimes against humanity, and genocide; the right to an adequate standard of living; women and reproductive health; children; persons with disabilities; rights of older persons; infectious diseases; business, trade, and intellectual property; occupational health and safety; biotechnology; and protection of the environment."—*Publ. notes.* Sample documents include a selection of previously published documents: Universal declaration of human rights, Declaration of Geneva (Geneva Convention), Nuremberg code, Convention on the elimination of all forms of discrimination against women, Convention on the rights of the child, and others.

984 **International guidelines on HIV/AIDS and human rights.** Office of the United Nations High Commissioner for Human Rights (OHCHR); UNAIDS Joint United Nations Programme on HIV/AIDS. 2006 Geneva, [Switzerland]: United Nations OHCHR. http://www.ohchr.org/english/issues/hiv/guidelines.htm.

Organized jointly by the Office of the United Nations High Commissioner for Human Rights (OHCHR) and the UNAIDS Joint United Nations Programme on HIV/AIDS.

2006 consolidated version of the Second (Geneva, 23–25 Sep. 1996) and Third (Geneva, 25–26 July 2002) International Consultation on HIV/AIDS and Human Rights.

Contents: (I) Guidelines for state action: (A) Institutional responsibilities and processes; (B) Law review, reform and support services; (C) Promotion of a supportive and enabling environment; (II) Recommendations for dissemination and implementation of the guidelines on HIV/

AIDS and human rights: (A) States; (B) United Nationals system and regional intergovernmental bodies; (C) Nongovernmental organizations; (III) International human rights obligations and HIV: (A) Human rights standards and the nature of State obligations; (B) Restrictions and limitations; (C) The application of specific human rights in the context of the HIV epidemic; Annex 1, History of the recognition of the importance of human rights in the context of HIV; Annex 2, List of participants at the Second International Consultation on HIV/AIDS and Human Right; Annex 3, List of participants at the Third International Consultation on HIV/AIDS and Human Rights.

"A tool for States in designing, co-ordinating and implementing effective national HIV/AIDS policies and strategies. Human rights standards apply in the context of HIV/AIDS and translating them into practical measures that should be undertaken at the national level, based on three broad approaches: improvement of government capacity for multi-sectoral coordination and accountability; reform of laws and legal support services, with a focus on anti-discrimination, protection of public health, and improvement of the status of women, children and marginalized groups; and support and increased private sector and community participation to respond ethically and effectively to HIV/ AIDS.

OHCHR encourages governments, national human rights institutions, non-governmental organizations and people living with HIV and AIDS to use the Guidelines for training, policy formulation, advocacy, and the development of legislation on HIV/AIDS-related human rights."—*Website*

985   International health regulations (2005). World Health
Organization. 2007. Geneva, Switzerland: World Health
Organization. http://www.who.int/csr/ihr/en/.

Rev. ed., with the new regulations in force on June 15, 2007. Also publ. as print edition, with 2005 also available as an e-book. Supersedes *International health regulations* (1969), publ. in several different print editions. Title varies: previously called *International sanitary regulations.*

Part of WHO's Epidemic and Pandemic Alert and Response (EPR) (http://www.who.int/csr/en/).

Considered a code of practices and procedures for the prevention of the spread of disease, "in consideration of the increases in international travel and trade, and emergence and re-emergence of new international disease threats" (*Publ. notes*), with the goal of preventing and protecting against the international spread of disease.

Frequently asked questions about this resource can be found at http://www.who.int/csr/ihr/howtheywork/faq/en/index.html.

A History of WHO and International Cooperation in Public Health timeline (prepared by the WHO Centre for Health Development–WHO Kobe Centre [WKC]) is located at http://www.who.or.jp/GENERAL/history_wkc.html.

986 Law and risk management in dental practice. Burton R. Pollack. xii, 284 p. Chicago: Quintessence Publ. Co., 2002. ISBN: 0867154160.

617.60068   RK58.P65

Contents: (1) Introduction to the judicial system of the United States; (2) The regulation of dental practice; (3) The dentist-patient relationship: contract law; (4) Is it negligence, malpractice, or breach of contract?; (5) Statute of limitations and statute of repose: how long the patient has to sue; (6) Experts and the standards of care; (7) Vicarious liability and respondeat superior; (8) Does the dentist have to treat?; (9) Consent, informed consent, and informed refusal; (10) Abandonment and dismissal of a patient; (11) Taking the medical-dental history; (12) Patient records; (13) Trial of a suit in malpractice: res ipsa loquitur, hearsay evidence, and contributory negligence; (14) What to do and what not to do if you are sued; (15) Dentist as witness; (16) Reports on jury trials and disciplinary proceedings; (17) Risk management in dental practice; (18) Office audit risk assessment for the general dentist; (19) Insuring a dental practice; Appendix: Legal terms with dental applications.

Information on the U.S. judicial system and basic legal information for dental professionals. Another legal resource, *Law, liability, and ethics for medical office professionals* (595) provides additional information.

987 The law and the public's health. 7th ed. Kenneth R. Wing, Benjamin Gilbert. xiii, 391 p. Chicago: Health Administration Press, 2007.

344.7304   KF3775.W5

Contents: ch. 1, "The law and the legal system"; ch. 2, "The power of the state governments in matters affecting health care"; ch. 3, "Government power and the right to privacy"; ch. 4, "The constitutional discretion of the state and federal governments to limit or condition social welfare benefits"; ch. 5, "Government regulation of health care providers and payers"; ch. 6, "The scope of discretion of administrative agencies in matters affecting health and health care"; ch. 7, "The fraud and abuse laws"; ch. 8, "The antitrust laws: Government enforcement of competition";

ch. 9, "Malpractice: Liability for negligence in the delivery and financing of health care"; ch. 10, "Health care business law: Legal considerations in the structuring of health care entities and their transactions."

Intended as an introductory text for schools of public health and law-related courses, this book can also serve as a reference book in the health care field. Provides an introduction to the law, the legal system, and principles applicable to the delivery and financing of health care but is not considered a treatise on health law. Includes bibliographical references and index.

Also available as an e-book via netLibrary.

988 **Law, liability, and ethics for medical office professionals.** 4th ed. Myrtle Flight. x, 350 p. Clifton Park, N.Y.: Thomson/Delmar Learning, 2004. ISBN: 1401840337.

344.730411   KF2905.F58

1st ed., 1988; 3rd ed., 1998.

Contents: ch. 1, From examining room to courtroom; ch. 2, Functioning within the legal system; ch. 3, Intent makes the difference; ch. 4, Your words may form a contract; ch. 5, Anatomy of a medical malpractice case; ch. 6, Health care is big business; ch. 7, The medical record: the medical assistant's responsibility; ch. 8, Introduction to ethics; ch. 9, Privacy, confidentiality, privileged communication: the nexus of law and ethics; ch. 10, Birth and the beginning of life; ch. 11, Professional ethics and the living; ch. 12, Ethics: death and dying; Appendixes: (A) The civil and criminal case processes; (B) Answers to cases for discussion; Glossary; Bibliography; Index.

Provides basic information in medical law and ethics for medical professionals and helps with understanding their rights and the rights of the patients.

Another legal resource, designed for dental professionals, is *Law and risk management in dental practice* (986).

989 **Legal and ethical issues for health professionals.** George D. Pozgar. xii, 378 p. Boston: Jones and Bartlett Publ., 2005. ISBN: 0763726338.

174.2   KF3821.P68

Contents: ch. 1, Introduction to ethics; ch. 2, Contemporary ethical dilemmas; ch. 3, Health Care Ethics Committee; ch. 4, End-of-life dilemmas; ch. 5, Development of law; ch. 6, Introduction to law; ch. 7,

Government, ethics, and the law; ch. 8, Organizational ethics and the law; ch. 9, Health care professionals' ethical and legal issues; ch. 10, Physicians' ethical and legal issues; ch. 11, Employee rights and responsibilities; ch. 12, Patient consent; ch. 13, Patient abuse; ch. 14, Patient rights and responsibilities.

Overview of the ethical and legal issues and their interrelationship in the health care field. Guide to additional resources. Includes glossary, bibliographical references, and index.

990   **Legal medicine.** 7th ed. American College of Legal Medicine. xv, 748 p., ill. Philadelphia; London: Elsevier Mosby, 2007. ISBN: 9780323037532.

344.73041   KF3821.L44

1st edition, 1988, had title *Legal medicine: Legal dynamics of medical encounters*; 6th ed., 2004.

Contents: pt. 1, "Medical licensure, credentialing and privileging, profiling, and impairment"; pt. 2, "Business aspects of medical practice"; pt. 3, "Medicolegal and ethical encounters"; pt. 4, "Professional medical liability"; pt. 5, "Care of special patients"; pt. 6, "Forensic science and medicine"; pt. 7, "Legal aspects of public health"; pt. 8, "International contributions"; glossary: "Selected health care and legal terminology"; case index; subject index.

This updated and expanded edition explores the legal issues and problems of medical practice and provides answers to health care–related legal questions. Contains new chapters on patient safety, medication errors, apology to patients, medical malpractice overview, liability of pharmacists, and no-fault liability. Useful as a reference for health professionals.

991   **Medical records and the law.** 4th ed. William H. Roach, American Health Information Management Association. xix, 591 p. Sudbury, Mass.: Jones and Bartlett Publ., 2006. ISBN: 0763734454.

344.73041   KF3827.R4R63

1st ed., 1985; 3rd ed., 1998.

Contents: ch. 1, Introduction to the American legal system; ch. 2, Medical records and managed care; ch. 3, Medical record requirements; ch. 4, Medical records entries; ch. 5, Documenting consent to treatment; ch. 6, Access to health information; ch. 7, Reporting and disclosure requirements; ch. 8, Documentation and disclosure: special areas of concern; ch.

9, HIV/AIDS: mandatory reporting and confidentiality; ch. 10, Discovery and admissibility of medical records; ch. 11, Legal theories in improper disclosure cases; ch. 12, Risk management and quality management; ch. 13, Electronic health records; ch. 14, Health information in medical research; Index. Provides information on the growth of electronic health record systems and electronic data networks. Addresses the issues related to medical research involving human subjects and how patient information can be used.

992 Medicare handbook. Center for Medicare Advocacy. New York: Aspen Publishers, c2000–. ISSN: 1530-8979.

368   KF3608.A4M436

Description based on 2007 ed. Contents: (1) An introduction to Medicare coverage and appeals; (2) Hospital coverage; (3) Skilled nursing facility coverage; (4) Home health coverage; (5) Hospice coverage; (6) Medicare Part B: supplemental medical insurance; (7) Medicare-Advantage: coordinated care plans, private fee-for-service, and other delivery of services options; (8) Medigap services; (9) Medicare's relationship with private insurance; (10) Dual eligibility: issues for Medicare beneficiaries also eligible for Medicaid; (11) Prescription drug coverage. Resource to help understand Medicare's rules and regulations. Further helpful, detailed information can also be found on the Medicare website (Medicare: the official U.S. government site for people with medicare at http://www.medicare.gov), part of the Centers for Medicare & Medicaid Services (742).

993 Nurse practitioner's legal reference. Springhouse Corp. xii, 361 p., ill. Springhouse, Pa.: Springhouse Corp., 2001. ISBN: 1582550972.

344.730414   RT82.8.N8646

Contents: ch. 1, Nurse practitioner practice and the law; ch. 2, Legal risks and responsibilities on the job; ch. 3, Legal issues on the job; ch. 4, Legal risks while off duty; ch. 5, Malpractice liability; ch. 6, Legal aspects of documentation; ch. 7, Ethical decision making; ch. 8, Ethical conflicts in clinical practice; ch. 9, Ethical conflicts in professional practice; ch. 10, Patients' rights; ch. 11, NPs in a changing health care marketplace.

Provides coverage of legal issues affecting nurses and the nursing profession, including issues currently facing legislative and judicial review. Contains several appendixes: "Understanding the Judicial Process," "Interpreting Legal Citations," and "Types of Law." Court case citation index and a general index.

994   Patients' rights in the age of managed health care. Lisa Yount. 280
p. New York: Facts On File, 2001. ISBN: 0816042586.

344.73041   KF3823.Y68

Provides overview of the issues in health care delivery, patients' rights and
applicable laws, a chronology of significant events, and also a guide to
further research in patients' rights issues. Glossary, index, and annotated
bibliography. *The rights of patients: The authoritative ACLU guide to the
rights of patients* (600) provides further information.

995   The public health law manual. 3rd ed. Frank P. Grad, American
Public Health Association. Washington: American Public Health
Association, 2005. ISBN: 0875530427.

1st ed., 1965, had title *Public health manual: A handbook on the legal aspects
of public health administration and enforcement*; 2nd ed., 1990, had title
*Public health law manual: A handbook on the legal aspects of public health
administration and enforcement.*

   "The purpose of this manual: Achieving the most effective use of legal
powers; recognition of legal problems and their management; effective use
of available legal assistance; improving communication between the public
health and legal professions; continuing dialogue."—*Foreword.* Intended
for use by health care professionals and public health administrators in
planning, developing, and implementing public health programs. Deals
with basic legal procedures in public health enforcement—restrictions
of persons; permits, licenses, and registration; searches and inspections;
embargo, seizure, etc.—and with legal administrative techniques of public
health administration. This edition emphasizes issues in environmental
health law, legal aspects of personal health services, right to privacy, "right
to die" issues, and discussion of various related issues. Provides an overview of public health policies and public health law and a summary of
international responses to SARS, bioterrorism, global warming, etc.

**996   The rights of patients: The authoritative ACLU guide to the
rights of patients.** 3rd ed. George J. Annas. xxi, 387 p. Carbondale,
Ill.: Southern Illinois University Press, 2004. ISBN: 0809325152.

344.7303211   KF3823.A96

Title varies: 1st ed., 1975, had title: *The rights of hospital patients: The basic
ACLU guide to a hospital patient's rights*; 2nd ed., 1989, had title: *The rights
of patients: The basic ACLU guide to patient rights.*
   American Civil Liberties Union (ACLU).

(ACLU handbook series).

Contents: (I) Patient rights; (II) The patient rights advocate; (III) Reforming American medicine; (IV) Hospitals; (V) Emergency medicine; (VI) Informed choice; (VII) Choices about surgery and children's care; (VIII) Reproductive health; (IX) Research; (X) Medical records; (XI) Privacy and confidentiality; (XII) Care of the dying; (XIII) Suffering, pain, and suicide; (XIV) Death, organ donation, and autopsy; (XV) Patient safety and medical malpractice. Appendixes: (A) Internet resources; (B) Convention on human rights and biomedicine; (C) Childbearing patient bill of rights. Index.

"Offers fully documented exposition and explanation of the rights of patients from birth to death. A resource not only for patients and their families but also for physicians, hospital administrators, medical and nursing students, and other health care workers."—*Publ. notes.* Emphasizes the importance of having a patient rights advocate, with a section "tips for advocates" in most chapters.

997   **Source book in bioethics.** Albert R. Jonsen, Robert M. Veatch, LeRoy Walters. ix, 510 p. Washington: Georgetown University Press, 1998. ISBN: 0878406832.

174.209   R724.S599

Contents: Ethics of research with human subjects; A short history; Ethics of death and dying; Changing attitudes toward death and medicine; Ethical issues in human genetics; Issues in genetics; Ethical issues arising from human reproductive technologies and arrangements; Readings on human reproduction; Ethical issues in the changing health care system; The changing health care scene. Collection of significant documents in bioethics and social ethics, covering the time period from 1947–95, with original text reprinted either in full or abridged format, presenting a historical survey of bioethics and major ethical issues in healthcare and key bioethical decisions. Includes legislative documents and reports by various organizations and governments. Bibliographical references and index.

Indexes; Abstract journals; Databases

998   **International digest of health legislation = Recueil international de législation sanitaire.** World Health Organization. 2000–. [Geneva, Switzerland]: World Health Organization. http://www. who.int/idhl-rils/index.cfm.

K3569.2

International Digest of Health Legislation (IDHL) online database, available in English and French (Recueil international de législation sanitaire). Continues print version, publ. 1948–99; 1909–46(?) had title: *Bulletin mensuel de l'Office international d'Hygiène publique.*

Selection of national and international health legislation. Titles and summaries of texts of legislation, with links to the full texts of the legislation whenever available. The database can be searched by country, subject, volume, issue, or keyword. Includes the following subject categories, with detailed scope notes (http://www.who.int/idhl-rils/frame.cfm?language=english): General provisions, health manpower, health care facilities and services, disease control and medical care, oral health, family health, human reproduction and population policies, care of the elderly and rehabilitation, mental health, control of smoking, alcoholism, and drug abuse, ethical issues and professional responsibility, death and related issues, nutrition and food, consumer protection, pharmaceuticals and medical devices, poisons and other hazardous substances, occupational health and safety, environmental protection, radiation protection, accident prevention, sports and recreation, and health information and statistics.

999 LexisNexis congressional. Congressional Information Service. 1998–. Bethesda, Md.: LexisNexis. http://www.lexisnexis.com/academic/1univ/cong/.

348.731   JK1108

Indexes congressional bills, hearings, reports, prints, debates, and public laws, with more recent materials accessible in full text. Also includes indexes to the *U.S. code* and regulations enacted by the executive branch and hot policy topics. Members of Congress and their committee assignments are indexed 1989–present. Legislative histories of public laws are searchable 1969–present.

LexisNexis Congressional includes all material covered in the CD-ROM index Congressional Masterfile 2 (Bethesda, Md.: CIS, 1970–), as well as the print index *CIS index annual* (Washington: Congressional Information Service, 1970–2000). Additional modules are online versions of Congressional Masterfile 1 (Bethesda, Md.: Congressional Information Service, 1995), *CIS index to unpublished US House committee hearings* (1833–1936 [Bethesda, Md.: Congressional Information Service, 1988], 1937–46 [Bethesda, Md.: Congressional Information Service, 1990], 1947–54 [Bethesda, Md.: Congressional Information Service, 1992], 1955–58 [Bethesda, Md.: Congressional Information Service, 1994], 1959–64 [Bethesda, Md.: Congressional Information Service, 1997], and 1965–68 with 1947–64 supplement [Bethesda, Md.: Congressional Information Service, 1999]), *CIS index to unpublished US Senate committee hearings* (1823–1964 [Bethesda, Md.: Congressional Information Service, 1986], 1965–68 [Bethesda, Md.: Congressional Information Service, 1989], 1969–72 with 1913–68 supplement [Bethesda, Md.: Congressional Information Service, 1995], 1973–76 [Bethesda, Md.: Congressional Information Service, 1998]), *CIS Senate executive documents and reports* (Washington, D.C.: Congressional Information Service, 1987), *CIS U.S. congressional committee hearings index* (Bethesda, Md.: Congressional Information Service, 1981–1985), *CIS U.S. congressional committee prints index* (Washington: Congressional Information Service, 1980), and *CIS U.S. serial set index* (Washington: Congressional Information Service, c1975–c1998).

1000 POPLINE. Johns Hopkins University Bloomberg School of Public Health. Baltimore: Johns Hopkins University Bloomberg School of Public Health. http://db.jhuccp.org/ics-wpd/popweb/.

HQ766

POPLINE (Population Information Online) is a database on reproductive health with international coverage. Provides bibliographic citations with abstracts to English-language published and unpublished biomedical and social science literature on population research, demography, family planning, and related health issues. Includes links to full-text documents, RSS feeds for topical searches, and other special features. Detailed list of subjects covered internationally and in reference to developing countries at http://db.jhuccp.org/ics-wpd/popweb/aboutpl.html.

1001 PubMed. U.S. National Center for Biotechnology Information, National Library of Medicine, National Institutes of Health. 1996–. Bethesda, Md.: U.S. National Center for Biotechnology Information. http://www.ncbi.nlm.nih.gov/sites/entrez/.

PubMed®, developed and maintained by the National Center for Biotechnology Information (NCBI) at the National Library of Medicine® (NLM) (427). It is available via the NCBI Entrez (3) retrieval system. PubMed also provides access to the other Entrez molecular biology resources (*PubMed Overview*). Starting May 23, 2007, NCBI is changing to a new version of Entrez in a phased implementation (cf. Nahin AM. New and Improved PubMed®/Entrez and New URL *NLM tech. bull.*, 2007 May–Jun; [356]: http://www.nlm.nih.gov/pubs/techbull/mj07/mj07_issue_cover.html).

Provides a search interface for more than 16 million bibliographic citations and abstracts in the fields of medicine, nursing, dentistry, veterinary medicine, health care systems, and preclinical sciences. It provides access to articles indexed for MEDLINE® (425) and for selected life sciences journals. PubMed subsets found under the "Limits" tab are: MEDLINE and PubMed Central®, several journal groups (i.e., core clinical journals, dental journals, and nursing journals), and topical subsets (AIDS, bioethics, cancer, complementary medicine, history of medicine, space life sciences, systematic reviews, and toxicology). "Linkout" provides access to full-text articles.

For detailed information see the PubMed fact sheet at http://www.nlm.nih.gov/pubs/factsheets/pubmed.html. For a brief overview of searching PubMed, see the PubMed Quick Start at http://www.ncbi.nlm.nih.gov/books/bv.fcgi?rid=helppubmed.section.pubmedhelp.PubMed_Quick_Start. For details on the now completed OLDMEDLINE retrospective conversion projects, see http://www.nlm.nih.gov/pubs/techbull/so06/so06_oldmedline_status.html.

1002 State cancer legislative database program (SCLD). National Cancer Institute. Bethesda, Md.: National Cancer Institute, National Institutes of Health. http://www.scld-nci.net/index.cfml.

Database providing summaries of state laws and resolutions on the major cancers and cancer-related topics. Kept up-to-date via *SCLD update*. A site map (http://www.scld-nci.net/sitemap.cfml) provides easy access to the various information products associated with the SCLD program. Considered a resource for a variety of audiences, including universities and research centers, professional organizations, and the public.

1003 THOMAS. Edward F. Willett, Library of Congress. [1995–.] [Washington, D.C.]: Library of Congress. http://thomas.loc.gov.
025.06   KF49.T56

Search for bills by keyword, status, bill number, or sponsor for the current Congress. Search bills from multiple congresses for the 101st Congress (1989) forward; separate search interfaces are provided for Public Laws, Congressional Record, presidential nominations, committee reports, roll call votes, and treaties. Table of appropriations bills available for FY 1998 forward. Links to current activity in Congress, educational materials, and to a detailed explanation of the legislative process.

Internet Resources

1004 American Health Lawyers Association (AHLA). American Health Lawyers Association. Washington: American Health Lawyers Association. http://www.healthlawyers.org/.

"Educational organization devoted to legal issues in the healthcare field."—*Website.* Provides a list of suggested websites as a starting point for conducting research, links to government agencies and original materials, healthcare and health law websites, documents, and other law-related materials. Access to full-text documents may be restricted to members.

Another website, the Health Law section of the American Bar Association (ABA)(http://www.abanet.org/health/), also provides a variety of links.

1005 American Medical Association. American Medical Association. 1995–. Chicago: American Medical Association. http://www.ama-assn.org/.

This searchable website provides a variety of professional resources and standards for AMA members, including, for example, information sources on medical ethics, public health (e.g., eliminating health disparities, health preparedness, disaster response, obesity), medical science, legal issues, and AMA history (with timeline and highlights of AMA history). Also provides information on medical education and licensure as well as online resources and other links for medical school students and residents. Includes a section for patients, with access to patient education resources.

Other useful AMA-related links include, for example, DoctorFinder (209) and PolicyFinder (http://www.ama-assn.org/ama/noindex/category/11760.html), *Code of medical ethics, current opinions with annotations* (Chicago: American Medical Association), *Current procedural terminology: CPT* (573), FREIDA (212), *Graduate medical education directory* (213), *Health professions career and education directory* (214), and *State medical licensure requirements and statistics* (548). Many of these resources have general reference value in academic and public libraries.

1006 Bioethics resources on the web. National Institutes of Health (U.S.). 2000–. [Bethesda, Md.]: National Institutes of Health (NIH), Office of Extramural Research (OER), Inter-Institute Bioethics Groups (BIG). http://purl.access.gpo.gov/GPO/LPS55764.

Web page sponsored by the NIH Office of Science Policy (OSP) and the NIH Inter-Institute Bioethics Interest Group in cooperation with the NIH Office of Extramural Research (OER).

Annotated list of resources and web links that provide access to NIH and other federal resources, relevant organizations, documents, background information, and various positions on bioethical issues, with emphasis on research ethics, genetics, and medicine and healthcare topics. A link to "Health Law Resources" is provided at http://bioethics.od.nih. gov/legal.html.

1007 Drug abuse (MedlinePlus). National Library of Medicine (U.S.). 2000?–. Bethesda, Md.: National Library of Medicine. http://www. nlm.nih.gov/medlineplus/drugabuse.html.

A Health Topic in MedlinePlus (463).

Contents: Overviews; Latest News; Diagnosis/Symptoms; Treatment; Prevention/Screening; Specific Conditions; Related Issues; Pictures and Photographs; Games; Clinical Trials; Research; Journal Articles; Dictionaries/Glossaries; Directories; Organizations; Newsletters/Print Publications; Law and Policy; Statistics; Children; Teenagers; Men; Women; Seniors; Other Languages.

Collection of links on substance abuse from a variety of government agencies, professional associations, and organizations, such as the National Institute on Drug Abuse (1505), the Office of National Drug Control, Substance Abuse and Mental Health Services Administration (SAMHSA) (769), National Library of Medicine (427), American Medical Association (451), American Academy of Family Physicians (448), and others. Also links to related MedlinePlus topics, e.g., alcoholism, prescription drug abuse, and substance abuse, to name a few.

1008 Ethics and health [Internet resource]. World Health Organization (WHO). 2002–. Geneva, [Switzerland]: World Health Organization. http://www.who.int/ethics/en/.

World Health Organization (WHO) Dept. of Ethics, Trade, Human Rights and Health Law (ETH); WHO Dept. Sustainable Development and Environmental Health (SDE); WHO Research Ethics Review Committee; U.N. Inter-Agency Committee on Bioethics; National Bioethics Commissions.

"This site has been created as an aid to persons, both inside and outside WHO, seeking information about bioethics, including the ethical aspects of healthcare delivery and planning as well as the ethics of clinical care, research, and biotechnology, [with] information about a range of topics in ethics."—*Website.* Reflects various collaborative projects within WHO and also other agencies and provides links to various bioethics topics, full text of ethics publications, ethical considerations and guidelines for research and good clinical practice.

1009 Genomic Resource Centre. World Health Organization, Human Genetics Programme. 2003–. Geneva, [Switzerland]: World Health Organization. http://www.who.int/genomics/en/.

Genomic Resource Centre (GRC), developed by the World Health Organization (WHO) (951), addresses the ethical, legal, and social implications (ELSI) of human genomics.

"The GRC serves as a platform to highlight the latest scientific research as well as practical health care applications of human genomics and its ethical, social and legal implications."—*Website.* Addresses areas of medical genetics, such as genetic counselling, presymptomatic diagnosis, population genetics, and ethics and genomics. "ELSI genetics resource directory" (http://www.who.int/genomics/elsi/regulatory_data/en/index. html) provides online resources on ELSI of human genetics, ethics organizations, guidelines, codes, declarations, legislations, etc. For health professionals, policy makers, patients and their families, and the general public.

1010 Health fraud (MedlinePlus). National Library of Medicine (U.S.). 2000?–. Bethesda, Md.: U.S. National Library of Medicine, National Institutes of Health, Dept. of Health & Human Services. http://www.nlm.nih.gov/medlineplus/healthfraud.html.

A Health Topic in MedlinePlus (463).

Contents: Overviews; Related issues; Journal articles; Organizations; Law and policy; Seniors.

Collection of links on health scams and quackery, how to detect health fraud, how to report unlawful sales of medical products, etc. Quackwatch (622) provides additional information in this area.

1011 International health (MedlinePlus). National Library of Medicine (U.S.). 2000?–. Bethesda, Md.: National Library of Medicine. http://www.nlm.nih.gov/medlineplus/internationalhealth.html.

A Health Topic within MedlinePlus (463). Provides extensive global health information, with access to various online reference resources, links to major organizations (e.g., Centers for Disease Control, World Health Organization), foundations (e.g., Henry J. Kaiser Family Foundation), research, journal articles, law and policy information (e.g., International Health Regulations [2005] [926]), WHO and UNICEF statistics, etc. Links to related MedlinePlus topics, such as Traveler's Health and Health System (MedlinePlus) (463). Go Local link and map help to identify services and providers in the United States.

1012 **National Human Genome Research Institute (U.S.).** National Human Genome Research Institute. 1995–. Bethesda, Md.: National Human Genome Research Institute, National Institutes of Health, U.S. Dept. of Health and Human Services. http://genome.gov/.

QH445.2

National Human Genome Research Institute (NHGRI), previously known as National Center for Human Genome Research (NCHGR), which was established in 1989 because of the Human Genome Project (HGP), since 1990 is a collaborative project of the U.S. Dept. of Energy (DOE) and National Institutes of Health (NIH) to map the human genome; and since HGP's completion in 1993, to apply genome technologies to the study of specific diseases. In 1996, the Center for Inherited Disease Research (CIDR) was also established (cofunded by eight NIH institutes and centers) to study the genetic components of complex disorders. A timeline, 1988 to the present, provides further details about HPG, its completion in 2003, associated events, research, and relevant publications at http://genome.gov/10001763.

Provides access to information, databases, and links to other resources concerning research, grants, health, policy and ethics, educational resources, etc. Some examples include the NHGRI Policy and Legislation Database http://genome.gov/PolicyEthics/LegDatabase/pubsearch.cfm, Online Bioethics Resources (620), the Ethical, Legal and Social Implications (ELSI) Research Program, and Initiatives and Resources for Minority and Special Populations (http://genome.gov/10001192), information on current research projects (e.g., the ENCODE Project [ENCyclopedia Of DNA Elements], a pilot project for testing and comparing new methods to identify functional sequences in DNA), model organisms, creation of Centers of Excellence in Genomic Science, the Genetics Variation Program, the Haplotype Map, gene discovery and technology development, establishment of the Center for Inherited Disease Research, and much more.

1013 **NLM gateway.** National Library of Medicine (U.S.). 2000–. Bethesda, Md.: National Library of Medicine. http://gateway.nlm. nih.gov/.

RA11

Allows simultaneous searching of information resources at the National Library of Medicine (NLM). Databases include MEDLINE (425)/PubMed (432) and the NLM Catalog (482) as well as other resources, including information on current clinical trials and consumer health information (MedlinePlus [463]). Currently provides access to 21 databases and other information resources (for a complete list of databases and other details, see http://www.nlm.nih.gov/pubs/factsheets/gateway.html). An overview of the search results is presented in several categories (bibliographic resources, consumer health resources, and other information), with a listing of the individual databases and the number of results within these categories.

1014 **Online bioethics resources.** National Human Genome Research Institute (U.S.). 2000s–. Bethesda, Md.: National Institutes of Health. http://genome.gov/10001744.

Produced by National Human Genome Research Institute (NHGRI), which includes the Ethical, Legal and Social Issues (ELSI) Program.

Provides information about the ELSI research program (http://genome. gov/10001618) and an extensive collection of selected online bioethics resources, including ELSI websites, programs, and reports from NHGRI, National Institutes of Health (NIH) (470), U.S. Dept. of Health and Human Services (HHS), Bioethics resources on the web (609), U.S. Dept. of Energy (DOE), and other resources.

Also provides access to the "NHGRI Policy and Legislation Database," which contains federal and state laws/statutes; federal legislative materials; and federal administrative and executive materials, including regulations, institutional policies, and executive orders, with focus on subject areas such as privacy of genetic information and confidentiality, informed consent, insurance and employment discrimination, genetic testing and counseling, and commercialization and patenting.

1015 **Public health law materials.** Centers for Disease Control and Prevention (U.S.), Dept. of Health and Human Services. 200?–. Atlanta: Centers for Disease Control and Prevention, Dept. of Health and Human Services. http://www2a.cdc.gov/phlp/lawmat. asp.

Provides access to public health topics, including general public health law and international public health law. Includes emergency preparedness topics (e.g., bioterrorism, disease outbreaks and incidents, natural disasters, and general emergency preparedness). Pt. of the Public Health Law Program (CDC) (940) website (http://www2a.cdc.gov/phlp/) which also provides an A–Z topics list with information on a variety of areas and subjects related to public health law and legal issues, including a list of state public health departments.

1016 Quackwatch. Stephen Barrett. [1996]–. [Allentown, Pa.]: Stephen Barrett, MD http://www.quackwatch.org.

615.8 R730

Founded in 1969 as the Lehigh Valley Committee Against Health Fraud, incorporated in 1970. Assumed its current name in 1997. Maintained by Dr. S. Barrett and a network of volunteers and expert advisors. Affiliated with the National Council Against Health Fraud (http://www.ncahf.com/) and Bioethics Watch (http://www.bioethicswatch.org/).

"Nonprofit corporation whose purpose is to combat health-related frauds, myths, fads, fallacies, and misconduct. Its primary focus is on quackery-related information that is difficult or impossible to get elsewhere. Activities include: Investigating questionable claims; Answering inquiries about products and services; Advising quackery victims; Distributing reliable publications; Debunking pseudoscientific claims; Reporting illegal marketing; Assisting or generating consumer-protection lawsuits; Improving the quality of health information on the Internet; Attacking misleading advertising on the Internet."—*Website*

In addition, includes a list of websites that provide access to 21 special areas—autism, chiropractic, dentistry, diet and nutrition, mental health, and other topics of interest to consumers. Its "Internet Health Pilot" site provides links to many other reliable health sites; its "Casewatch" site contains legal matters and regulatory issues. The contents of all sites can be searched simultaneously or individually (http://www.quackwatch.org/wgsearch.html).

1017 U.S. Dept. of Health and Human Services (HHS). U.S. Dept. of Health and Human Services (HHS). 1997–. Washington: U.S. Dept. of Health and Human Services. http://www.os.dhhs.gov/.

HHS has the mission "to enhance the health and well-being of Americans by providing for effective health and human services and by fostering strong, sustained advances in the sciences underlying medicine, public health, and social services."—*Website*

Overview and links to all HHS offices: Office for Civil Rights; Office of Global Health Affairs; Surgeon General, and many others. Also provides overview and links to the HHS agencies: Administration for Children and Families; Administration on Aging; Agency for Healthcare Research and Quality (AHRQ) (733); Agency for Toxic Substances and Disease Registry (1397); Centers for Disease Control and Prevention (CDC) (940); Centers for Medicare and Medicaid Services (742); Food and Drug Administration (630); Health Resources and Services Administration (877); Indian Health Service (IHS) (1401); National Institutes of Health (NIH) (470); Substance Abuse and Mental Health Services Administration (769). "HHS Acronyms and Abbreviations" at http://www.hhs.gov/acronyms.html. Includes a "Reference Collections" page (http://www.hhs.gov/reference/index.html) which provides an extensive collection of resources, including dictionaries and glossaries, encyclopedias, databases, indexes, and various other reference resources, publications, reports, and statistics. Provides policy information (e.g., science policy issues; Surgeon General priorities; legal information; HHS-related publications and reports).

Statistics

1018 State medical licensure requirements and statistics. American Medical Association. Chicago: American Medical Association, 1999–. ISSN: 1549-4055.

362.172   RA396.A3U2

1999/2000–. (publ. 2000)–

1982–98: *U.S. medical licensure statistics and licensure requirements* (title varies). Description based on 2007 ed.

Contents: Licensure policies and regulations of state medical/osteopathic boards; Statistics of state medical licensing boards; Medical licensing examinations and organizations; Information for international medical graduates; Federal and national programs and activities; Other organizations and programs; Appendixes (including a "Glossary of Medical Licensure Terms").

"Presents current information and statistics on licensure in the United States and possessions. Data were obtained from a number of sources, including state boards of medical examiners, the Federation of State Medical Boards, National Board of Medical Examiners, Educational Commission for Foreign Graduates, and the United States Medical Licensing

Examination."—*Foreword.* Includes 54 allopathic and 14 osteopathic boards of medical examiners.

A related Internet resource on medical licensure is found at http://www.ama-assn.org/go/licensure.

8 > NURSING

1019 **Encyclopedia of nursing research.** 2nd ed. Joyce J. Fitzpatrick, Meredith Wallace. xxxvi, 795 p. New York: Springer Publ., 2006. ISBN: 0826198120.

610.73072   RT81.5.E53

1st ed., 1998.

Key terms and concepts in nursing research. A "comprehensive, yet concise and authoritative guide to existing nursing research literature since 1983."—*Pref.* Nursing care; services; education; specialties; historical, philosophical, and cultural issues, etc. New entries in this updated ed. include, for example, cancer survivorship, disparities in minority mental health, and formal nursing languages. Cross-references. Written for nursing researchers and graduate students in nursing. Subject index. Available as an e-book via netLibrary. A companion volume is *Dictionary of nursing theory and research* (1033).

Bibliography

1020 **A bibliography of nursing literature 1859–1960: With an historical introduction.** Alice M. C. Thompson, Royal College of Nursing; National Council of Nurses of the United Kingdom, King Edward's Hospital Fund for London. xx, 132 p. London: Library Association for the Royal College of Nursing; National Council of Nurses of the United Kingdom; in association with King Edward's Hospital Fund for London, 1968. ISBN: 0853654700.

016.61073   Z6675.N7T45; RT41

Contents: v. 1, 1859–1960; v. 2, 1961–70; v. 3, 1971–76, ed. by Frances Walsh.

A guide to the first 125 years of nursing literature, covering periodical and monographic literature from English-speaking countries. In five main sections: (1) History of nursing; (2) Biography; (3) Nursing as a profession; (4) Specialties of knowledge and practice; and (5) Hospitals. No index.

1021 Celebrating nursing history. Margaret Allen, Medical Library Association. 1994–. Chicago: Medical Library Association. http://nahrs.library.kent.edu/resource/reports/weeding.html.

Produced by Medical Library Association (MLA), Nursing and Allied Health Resources Section (NAHRS). Reprint of article originally publ. in *NAHRS newsletter*, Apr. 1994, updated Oct. 2005.

Contents: What to Keep; Significant Nursing Books to Find and Keep; Periodicals to Keep; Sources Used for Some of These Comments and Selections; Reprints; Films and Videos; How and Where to Search; Other Sources for Historical Research; Why Go to Historical Sources?; Other Articles of Interest.

Provides an annotated bibliography of nursing books, reports, landmark studies, periodicals, films, videos, and other resources for historical research in nursing and related allied health literature. Chronological arrangement under the different headings. Intended to answer questions on archives, weeding, and other collection management issues posed by nursing librarians and others interested in the history of nursing.

1022 Essential nursing resources. Susan Kaplan Jacobs, Ysabel Bertolucci, Interagency Council on Information Resources for Nursing (ICIRN). 2007. New York: Interagency Council on Information Resources for Nursing. http://nln.allenpress.com/pdfserv/i1536-5026-028-05-0276.pdf.

Produced by Interagency Council on Information Resources in Nursing (ICIRN); National League for Nursing (NLN).

Description based on "24th ed." in PDF format. Originally publ. in *Nursing education perspectives* 28(5):300–09 (2007). Open access PDF version provided by Allen Press. Also accessible online in HTML format on the NLN website at http://www.nln.org/nlnjournal/nursingreferences.htm. Previous editions had title: *Essential nursing references.*

Contents: Meta-sites for nursing information; Alerting services/blogs/RSS feeds; Archives; Audiovisuals; Bibliographies/book lists; Bioethics; Complementary/alternative medicine; Consumer health/patient information; Databases and indexes; Evidence-based practice databases/indexes/resources; Dictionaries; Drugs, toxicology, environmental, occupational health; Education/career information; Grants resources; History of nursing; Informatics; Patient safety; Public health/disaster preparedness; Statistics; Writers' manuals and guides.

"Presented as a resource for locating nursing information and for collection development. Includes print, multimedia, and electronic sources to support nursing practice, education, administration, and research activities."—*Introd.* This edition includes new sections on alerting services, blogs, RSS feeds, consumer health/patient education, informatics, public health/disaster preparedness, and patient safety.

1023 **Nursing history resources.** American Association for the History of Nursing. 2005?–. Wheat Ridge, Colo.: American Association for the History of Nursing. http://www.aahn.org/resource.html.

Produced by American Association for the History of Nursing (AAHN; http://www.aahn.org/).

Contents: Archives and History Centers; Conferences, Exhibits and Celebrations; Funding; Internet Resources; Journals; New Books and Publications; Organizations; Videos.

Listing of selected available nursing resources, including Internet resources, for the history of nursing. Provides links to other nursing history organizations, nursing education, and related government websites. Includes, for example, a link to nursing history centers, museums, and archives (http://www.aahn.org/centers.html) and a page entitled Black Nurses in History: A Bibliography and Guide to Web Resources (http://www4.umdnj.edu/camlbweb/blacknurses.html), prepared by the University of Medicine and Dentistry of New Jersey.

1024 **Recent dissertations in the medical humanities.** Jonathon Erlen, University of Pittsburgh Health Sciences Library System. 2001–. Pittsburgh: Health Sciences Library, University of Pittsburgh Medical Center. http://www.hsls.pitt.edu/guides/histmed/researchresources/dissertations/.

Provides a monthly current awareness service for selected recent medical dissertation and theses. Arranged by topics, currently covers the following areas: AIDS (social and historical contexts); alternative medicine (social and historical contexts); art and medicine; biomedical ethics; history of medicine prior to 1800; history of medicine and health care; history of science and technology; literature/theater and medicine; nursing history; pharmacy/pharmacology and history; philosophy and medicine; psychiatry/psychology and history; public health/international health; religion and medicine; women's health and history. To view complete citations, abstracts, and full-text of dissertations requires a subscription to Proquest Dissertations and Theses (PQDT) (Ann Arbor, Mich.: ProQuest).

Biography

1025 African American firsts in science and technology. Raymond B. Webster. xiii, 461 p., ill. Detroit: Gale Group, 1999. ISBN: 0787638765.

508.996073   Q141.W43

Chronology of firsts in various fields: Agriculture and Everyday Life, Dentistry and Nursing, Life Science, Math and Engineering, Medicine, Physical Science, and Transportation. Includes bibliography, index by year, occupational index, general index, and citations for first achievements. Over 1,200 entries, 100 illustrations.

1026 American nursing: A biographical dictionary. Vern L. Bullough, Olga Maranjian Church, Alice P. Stein, Lilli Sentz. 3 v., ill. New York: Garland, 1988–2000. ISBN: 082408540X.

610.730922B   RT34.A44

Vol. 2 ed. by Vern L. Bullough, Lilli Sentz, and Alice P. Stein; v. 3 ed. by Vern L. Bullough and Lilli Sentz, and publ. by Springer.

Contains long entries for those who "made a significant contributions to nursing."—*Introd.* Vol. 1 contains entries for those who were born prior to 1890 or deceased, v. 2 includes those born before 1915 or deceased, v. 3 includes notable women in American and Canadian nursing in the 20th century. Entries include bibliographies. Vols. 1 and 2 are indexed separately by decade of birth, first nursing school attended, area of special interest or accomplishment, and state and country of birth. Covers much of the same ground as *Dictionary of American nursing biography* (1027). Of the individuals in these sources, 109 appear in both, but each provides unique information.

1027 Dictionary of American nursing biography. Martin Kaufman, Joellen Watson Hawkins, Loretta P. Higgins, Alice Howell Friedman. x, 462 p. New York: Greenwood Press, 1988. ISBN: 0313245207.

610.730922B   RT34.D53

Companion to *Dictionary of American medical biography* (74).

Contains "196 biographical sketches of persons who were important in the history of American nursing" (*Pref.*) and who died prior to Jan. 31, 1987. For each individual, includes biographical data, summary of contributions to nursing, and a list of writings and references. Appendixes list persons by place of birth, state where prominent, and specialty or occupation. Indexed by personal name, organization, place, and special subject.

Covers much of the same ground as *American nursing: A biographical dictionary* (New York: Garland, 1988–2000), but each provides unique information.

1028 **Doctors, nurses, and medical practitioners: A bio-bibliographical sourcebook.** Lois N. Magner. xiii, 371 p. Westport, Conn.: Greenwood Press, 1997. ISBN: 0313294526.
610.922B   R153.D63

Biographical information on 56 "significant but lesser known individuals outside their own country, extraordinary, yet unsung" (*Introd.*), covering the time period 1710–1924, with essays focusing on the life and career. Bibliographic references include archival materials and works written by and about the particular individual. Appendixes: (A), Listing by occupations and special interests; (B), Listing by date of birth; (C), Listing by place of birth; (D), Listing of women practitioners. Intended for students and scholars.

Dictionaries

1029 **Black's medical dictionary.** 41st ed. Harvey Marcovitch. viii, 814 p., 16 p. of plates, ill. London: A. and C. Black, 2005.
610.3

1st ed., 1906. 40th ed., 2002.

A standard dictionary of British terminology, with clear explanation of medical terms. Frequently updated. The 41st ed. includes 5,000 medical terms, including new terms and concepts (e.g., new diagnostic imaging techniques, minimally invasive surgery, gene therapy) and revisions. Many cross-references. Several appendixes provide information on subjects such as first aid, travel and health, health economics, Great Britain's National Health Service, and international organizations. Intended for nurses, healthcare professionals, students, and consumers. Available online via Credo Reference (London; Boston: Credo Reference).

1030 Churchill Livingstone's dictionary of nursing. 19th ed. Christine Brooker. x, 293 p., ill. Edinburgh, U.K.: Churchill Livingstone, 2006. ISBN: 0443101752.

610.7303   RT21.C487

A–Z entries, covering a variety of nursing topics. Appendixes have been completely updated with many new words and illustrations. Supplemented by Elsevier's Evolve website (https://evolve.elsevier.com/productPages/s_894. html) with approx. 7,500 selected dictionary entries, nursing abbreviations, and a spellchecker. An icon indicates the availability of additional material on the website. Primarily intended for health professionals and students "outside of the U.S."—*Publ. notes.* Online edition available via Credo Reference (London; Boston: Credo Reference).

1031 Concise dictionary of modern medicine. Joseph C. Segen. xix, 765 p. New York: McGraw-Hill, 2006. ISBN: 0838515355.

R121.S42

A revision of J.C. Segen's 1995 ed. of *Current med talk: A dictionary of medical terms, slang, and jargon.*

Illustrated dictionary, with 20,000 current medical terms, covering clinical and basic science aspects, also jargon and casual speech not necessarily found in other reference sources. Intended to supplement standard medical dictionaries. Also available in a 2002 ed. with the same title and as *Dictionary of modern medicine,* published in 2002, which contains 40,000 entries.

1032 Dictionary of nursing. 5th ed. E. A. Martin, Tanya A. McFerran. 584 p. Oxford; New York: Oxford University Press, 2008. ISBN: 9780199211784.

610.7303; 610.3   RT21

1st ed., 1990; 4th ed., 2003. Description based on 5th ed., 2008. Also called *Oxford dictionary of nursing.*

Vocabulary of the nursing profession and related terminology. Concise definitions of approx. 10,000 terms, pronunciation guide, some black-and-white illustrations and tables. Appendixes include, for example, reference values of biochemical and hematologic data, standard values for body weight, immunization schedule, nutritional guidelines, the nursing code of conduct, and healthcare website addresses. Many entries in the fields of medicine, surgery, anatomy, physiology, psychiatry, nutrition, and pharmacology have been adapted from the *Concise medical dictionary,* first publ. in

1980; 7th ed., 2007. Available in electronic format as part of Oxford Reference Online (Oxford; New York: Oxford University Press, 2002–).

1033 Dictionary of nursing theory and research. 3rd ed. Bethel Ann Powers, Thomas R. Knapp. xi, 210 p. New York: Springer, 2006. ISBN: 0826117740.

610.7303   RT81.5.P69

1st ed., 1990; 2nd ed., 1995.

Terminology and definitions, with notes, comments, and examples commonly found in the nursing literature. This rev. ed. includes new entries for evidence-based practice, Internet research, terms relating to epidemiological research, and others, also updated examples and references (cf. *Pref.*). Includes bibliographical references (p. 193–210). Also available as an e-book.

Considered a companion volume to *Encyclopedia of nursing research* (1019).

1034 Dorland's illustrated medical dictionary. 31st ed. W. A. Newman Dorland. xxvii, 2175 p., ill. (some color). Philadelphia: W.B. Saunders, 2007. ISBN: 9781416023647.

R121.D73

1st–22nd ed., 1900–51 had title: *The American illustrated medical dictionary*; 30th ed., c2003.

Designed to satisfy the conventional use of a dictionary; that is, to discover spelling, meaning, and derivation of specific terms and to assist in the creation of words by defining prefixes, suffixes, and stems. Includes a section on "Fundamentals of medical etymology." Reflects standard and current terminology, with official nomenclatures from various fields, for example, NLM's MeSH: Medical Subject Headings (575), Terminologia Anatomica (1998), and several others. Also includes eponyms, acronyms, abbreviations, pronunciation, cross-references, etc. Illustrated throughout. In this ed., several appendixes have been updated and reorganized (for example, the tables of weights and measures and conversion tables) and a new appendix provides a list of phobias. For health professionals and students in medicine, nursing, and allied health. CD-ROM includes *Dorland's pocket medical dictionary* for PDA and download access to *Dorland's electronic medical speller*. Internet access for subscribers at http://www.dorlands.com/wsearch.jsp. Also available online via Credo Reference (London; Boston: Credo Reference).

1035 Encyclopedia and dictionary of medicine, nursing, and allied health. 7th ed. Benjamin Frank Miller. xxxi, 2262 p., [40] p. of plates, ill. (chiefly color). Philadelphia: Saunders, 2003. ISBN: 0721697917.

610.3   R121.M65

1st ed. (1972) had title *Encyclopedia and dictionary of medicine and nursing*; 6th ed. (1997) had title *Miller-Keane encyclopedia and dictionary of medicine, nursing, and allied health.*

A concise work intended for students and workers in the nursing and allied health fields. Clear definitions and and explanations of the current multidisciplinary terminology. This edition has 3,900 new terms, including the "latest changes for diagnosis-related groups, nursing diagnoses, and key nursing taxonomies."—*Foreword*; for example, definitions are provided for the complete vocabulary of the Unified Nursing Language System. Pronunciation guides; a list of stems, prefixes, and suffixes; and 32 page color atlas of human anatomy.

The print resource is supplemented by a CD-ROM that contains spellchecker software, derived from *Dorland's medical speller* 3.0, and also by a website where updates relating to major changes in health professional vocabularies are posted (http://evolve.elsevier.com/millerkeane/)—cf. *Foreword.*

1036 Medical dictionary (MedlinePlus). National Library of Medicine (U.S.). 2002–. Bethesda, Md.: National Library of Medicine. http://www.nlm.nih.gov/medlineplus/mplusdictionary.html.

R121

Part of MedlinePlus (463). This online dictionary, based on *Merriam-Webster's medical dictionary*, can be searched from the MedlinePlus home page (via "Dictionary" tab). Contains definitions for words and phrases used by health care professionals, a pronunciation guide, and brief biographies of individuals (after whom particular diseases are named). Most MedlinePlus Health Topics pages contain a link or links to additional online dictionaries and/or glossaries from various sources.

Numerous online medical dictionaries and glossaries are also available from many other sources. They include titles made available from various government agencies, organizations, and commercial publishers. Some examples include online medical dictionaries accessible via Credo Reference (currently 24 titles) [London; Boston: Credo Reference], Deciphering Medspeak [http://www.mlanet.org/resources/medspeak/;

MLANET [465]], Diabetes Dictionary [http://diabetes.niddk.nih.gov/dm/
pubs/dictionary/index.htm; National Institute of Diabetes and Digestive
and Kidney Diseases], Dictionary of Cancer Terms [National Cancer Insti-
tute] [143], mediLexicon [http://www.medilexicon.com; MedicineNet],
On-line Medical Dictionary [http://cancerweb.ncl.ac.uk/omd/index.html;
by Dr. Graham Clark], Talking Glossary of Genetics Terms [http://www.
nhgri.nih.gov/glossary.cfm; National Human Genome Research Institute],
and many others.

1037 Melloni's illustrated dictionary of medical abbreviations. Biagio
John Melloni, June L. Melloni. 485 p., ill. New York: Parthenon
Publ. Group, 1998. ISBN: 1850707081.

610.148 R121.M539

Abbreviations compiled from recent medical texts and journals. Approx.
15,000 entries and 150 ill. A–Z arrangement.

1038 Melloni's illustrated dictionary of obstetrics and gynecology.
June L. Melloni, Ida Dox, Harrison H. Sheld. 401 p., ill.
(some color). New York: Parthenon Publ. Group, 2000. ISBN:
1850707103.

618.03 RG45.M45

Contains over 15,000 concise definitions, including terms from other
disciplines that are related to female health. Includes 280 ill., with color
correlation of a defined term and its illustration. Cross-references, pronunciation guide, and relevant abbreviations. For health professionals and
students.

1039 Mosby's dictionary of medicine, nursing and health professions.
7th ed. Mosby, Inc. xiv, 43, 2247 p., color ill. St. Louis: Mosby
Elsevier, 2006. ISBN: 0323035620.

610.3 R121.M89

1st ed., 1982, and 2nd ed., 1986, had title: *Mosby's medical and nursing
dictionary*; 3rd ed., 1990, and 4th ed., 2002, had title: *Mosby's medical, nursing, and allied health dictionary*; 5th ed., 1998, and 6th ed., 2001, had title:
Mosby's medical, nursing, and allied health dictionary.

This updated edition reflects recent developments in medical and
healthcare terminology. Encyclopedic-style definitions and approx. 2,450
color illustrations, photographs, and a "color atlas of human anatomy,"
organized by organ system. Appendixes include, e.g., reference information

such as normal laboratory values for children and adults, units of measurement, dietary guide and U.S. dietary reference intakes, complementary and alternative medicine, herbs and natural supplements, American Sign Language guidelines, and three major nursing classifications. A website is provided for purchasers on Mosby's Electronic Resource Links and Information Network (MERLIN), with links to medical, nursing, and allied health organizations (cf. *Foreword*).

Available online via Credo Reference (London; Boston: Credo Reference).

1040 Say it in Spanish: A guide for health care professionals. 3rd ed.
Esperanza Villanueva Joyce, Maria Elena Villanueva. xiii, 440 p., ill. St. Louis: Saunders, 2004. ISBN: 0721604242.
468.242102461   R121.J69
1st ed., 1996; [2nd ed.], 1999.

Contains commonly used English words and phrases in health-care settings, with their Spanish translation and pronunciation. Includes information on Hispanic culture and popular health beliefs. For health-care workers who communicate with Spanish-speaking patients. Alphabetical word index; phrase and sentence index. Includes audio CD.

1041 Stedman's medical abbreviations, acronyms and symbols. 4th ed.
Thomas Lathrop Stedman. xxviii, 875, 214 p. Baltimore: Wolters Kluwer Health/Lippincott Williams & Wilkins, 2008. ISBN: 9780781772.
610.148   R123.S69

Title varies: 1st ed., 1992, had title *Stedman's abbreviation: Abbreviations, acronyms and symbols*; 2nd ed., 1999, *Stedman's abbreviations, acronyms, and symbols*; 3rd ed., 2003, *Stedman's abbrev.: Abbreviations, acronyms and symbols.*

This updated edition contains approx. 75,000 abbreviations, acronyms, and symbols for medical, health, and nursing professionals, medical transcriptionists, medical editors and copy editors, and others. Abbreviations in boldface; multiple meanings listed alphabetically, with explanatory material in parentheses. Includes "do not use" abbreviations. Fourteen appendixes. Also available as a CD-ROM and a downloadable file.

Recent editions of other Stedman's dictionaries include *Stedman's medical dictionary* (Baltimore: Lippincott, Williams & Wilkins, 2006) (28th ed., 2006), *Stedman's medical dictionary for the health professions and nursing* (6th ed., 2008) (108), and *The American Heritage medical dictionary* (2007 ed.) (91), formerly titled *The American Heritage Stedman's medical dictionary.*

1042 **Stedman's medical dictionary for the health professions and nursing: Illustrated.** 6th ed. Thomas Lathrop Stedman. xl, 1696, 589 p., ill. (some color), 1 CD-ROM. Philadelphia: Wolters Kluwer Health/Lippincott, Williams and Wilkins, 2008. ISBN: 9780781776189.

610.3   R121.S8

Title varies. 1st ed., 1986, had title *Stedman's pocket medical dictionary*; 2nd ed., 1994, *Stedman's concise medical dictionary*; 3rd ed., 1997, *Stedman's concise medical dictionary: Illustrated*; 4th ed., 2001, *Stedman's concise medical dictionary for the health professions*; 5th ed., 2005, *Stedman's medical dictionary for the health professions and nursing.*

This revised edition provides concise definitions with pronunciation keys. Contains 54,000 entries, 68 appendixes with extensive information (e.g., nursing classifications), and many color and black-and-white illustrations. Accompanying CD-ROM contains the full text of the print edition, with audio-pronunciation, anatomy animations, various images, and medical/pharmaceutical spellchecker.

Recent editions of other Stedman's dictionaries include, for example, *Stedman's medical dictionary* (Baltimore: Lippincott, Williams & Wilkins, 2006) (28th ed., 2006); *The American Heritage medical dictionary* (2007 ed.) (91), formerly titled *The American Heritage Stedman's medical dictionary*; and *Stedman's medical abbreviations, acronyms and symbols* (4th ed., 2008) (117).

Directories

1043 **DIRLINE.** National Institutes of Health (U.S.). [1983?–.] Bethesda, Md.: U.S. National Institutes of Health, Dept. of Health and Human Services. http://dirline.nlm.nih.gov/.

DIRLINE® (Directory of Information Resources Online), maintained by the National Library of Medicine (NLM) (427).

Online annotated directory of organizations, research resources, projects, databases, and other information resources concerned with health and biomedicine from a variety of sources, including federal, state, and local government agencies, academic and research institutions, and also consumer health-related resources such as self-help groups and health hotlines. Resources are mostly from the U.S. but also include some international resources. Currently contains over 8,000 entries, with topics on most diseases and conditions and health services research and technology assessment. Can be searched using MeSH® (Medical Subject Headings) (575), keywords, or by name and location of a resource. Detailed information on DIRLINE can be found via a fact sheet prepared by NLM: http://www.nlm.nih.gov/pubs/factsheets/dirlinfs.html.

1044 **Official guide to graduate nursing programs.** National League for Nursing. Sudbury, Mass.: Jones and Bartlett, 2004–.

RT75.O345

1st ed. (2000) had title: *Official guide to graduate nursing schools.*

(Guide to graduate nursing programs).

Comprehensive directory of graduate nursing programs (master's and doctoral), with reliable data collected by the NLN. Provides help in retrieving information about each school and comparing different programs, with basic information and facts on every school and program presented in a consistent format. In three main parts: (1) Introductory section; (2) School profiles; (3) Expanded school profiles, with information provided directly by the different schools. Includes two indexes: listing of schools by graduate specialty programs, and an alphabetical listing of schools.

Other directories related to nursing programs published by the NLN include the *Official guide to undergraduate and graduate nursing programs* (1045), *Guide to state-approved schools of nursing, LPN/LVN*, and *Guide to state-approved schools of nursing, RN.*

1045 **Official guide to undergraduate and graduate nursing programs.** 2nd ed. National League for Nursing. v, 1268 p. Sudbury, Mass.: Jones and Bartlett Publ., 2004. ISBN: 0763718076.

610.73071173 RT73.O34

1st ed., 2000 has title: *Official guide to undergraduate and graduate nursing schools.*

(Guide to undergraduate and graduate nursing programs).

Provides information on accredited undergraduate and graduate nursing schools and nursing programs. In three parts: (1) Introductory section; (2) School profiles; (3) Expanded school profiles. Includes two indexes: listing of schools by graduate specialty programs, and an alphabetical listing of schools.

Other directories related to nursing programs published by the NLN include *Official guide to graduate nursing programs* (1044), *Guide to state-approved schools of nursing, LPN/LVN,* and *Guide to state-approved schools of nursing, RN.*

1046 Peterson's nursing programs. 10th ed. Peterson's (Firm); American Association of Colleges of Nursing. Lawrenceville, N.J.: Thomson/Peterson's, 2005–.

Publ. in cooperation with the American Association of Colleges of Nursing.

1994–2002 had title: *Peterson's guide to nursing programs*; 2003–04: *Nursing programs.* Description based on 13th ed., 2007 ("Nursing programs 2008").

Profiles 3,600 undergraduate, graduate, and postdoctoral nursing programs in the U.S. and Canada, degree programs, and full-time, part-time, and distance learning options, also continuing education programs. Companion websites with limited entries at http://iiswinprd03.petersons.com/nursing/ and at http://www.petersons.com/nursing/announcements/nurse.asp?.

Encyclopedias

1047 Encyclopedia of aging. 4th ed. Richard Schulz. 2 v., 720 p. New York: Springer, 2006. ISBN: 0826148433.

305.2603   HQ1061.E53

From the 1st ed. in 1987, this encyclopedia has provided a thorough presentation of a wide range of items, issues, and facts dealing with aging. Now in its 4th ed., it documents in thoughtful essays many aspects of the lives of older persons, as well as issues and services for the elderly. Made up of some 600 essays, including 200 that are entirely new, with others significantly updated. Multidisciplinary, covering relevant materials from biology, physiology, genetics, medicine, psychology, nursing, social services, sociology, economics, technology, and political science. Extensive listing of further resources, cross-references, and thorough index. Definitive work on gerontology and geriatrics. A must-have reference title for general and research collections. Available as an e-book.

1048 The encyclopedia of elder care: The comprehensive resource on geriatric and social care. 2nd ed. Liz Capezuti, Eugenia L. Siegler, Mathy Doval Mezey. xxxvii, 860 p. New York: Springer, 2008. ISBN: 9780826102.

362.19897003   RC954.E53

1st ed., 2001.

"Designed to encapsulate all aspects of care for an aging population: a comprehensive, multidisciplinary compilation of topics that reflects the breadth and depth of issues of concerns to those who care for older individuals—from individual to society, from patient to professional, from symptom to treatment."—*Pref.* Entries address elder care in the areas of society, community, caregiving, and the individual. Intended for professionals from a variety of health professions and for students. Organized alphabetically by topic, with listing of Internet resources and bibliographic references. Electronic edition available from netLibrary.

1049 The Gale encyclopedia of nursing and allied health. 2nd ed.
Jacqueline L. Longe. 5 v. Detroit: Thomson Gale, 2006. ISBN: 1414403747.

610.7303   RT21.G353

1st ed., 2002.

Contents: v. 1, A-C; v. 2, D-H; v. 3, I-O; v. 4, P-S; v. 5, T-Z, organizations, glossary, general index.

Articles on various aspects of nursing and allied health, with lists of resources. Alphabetically-arranged entries are written in a standardized format, with definitions, descriptions, key terms, print and nonprint resources, and information specific to the subject treated. Covered, for example, are various diseases and disorders, treatments, tests and procedures, equipment/tools, current health issues, human biology/body systems, education, training, work settings for the different health professions, etc. Cross-references, color illustrations, and sketches. "Appendix of nursing and allied health organizations." Comprehensive general index. Also available online through Gale Virtual Reference Library (Farmington Hills, Mich.: Gale Cengage Learning, 2002–).

1050 Historical encyclopedia of nursing. Mary Ellen Snodgrass. xvii, 354 p., ill. Santa Barbara, Calif.: ABC-CLIO, 1999.

610.7309   RT31.S66

Covers the history of nursing and healing from ancient times to the present. Includes key nursing concepts and individuals, medical topics, organizations, wars, etc. Articles list sources, including websites. Black-and-white illustrations and "see also" references. "Timeline of landmarks in nursing" (p. 297–310), "Works by and about healers" (p. 311–13), bibliographical references (p. 315–33), and index.

Handbooks

1051 Clinical Care Classification (CCC) system manual: A guide to nursing documentation. Virginia K. Saba. New York: Springer, 2006. ISBN: 0826102689.

651.504261   RT50.S23

Clinical Care Classification (CCC); Clinical Care Classification System (CCCS), formerly known as Home Health Care Classification System; Clinical Care Costing Methods (CCCM).

Contents: pt. 1, "Overview"; pt. 2, "Research, integration, and evaluation"; pt. 3, "Terminology uses; appendixes".

The CCCS consists of two interrelated terminologies—the CCCS of nursing diagnoses and outcomes, and the CCCS of nursing interventions, both of which are classified by 21 care components. "The Clinical Care Classification (CCC) System. is the only standard coded nursing terminology that is based on sound research using the nursing process model framework and that meets the Patient Medical Record Information (PMRI) comparability requirement. The CCC System allows patient care data generated by nurses to be incorporated into the PMRI database, and enables nurses' contributions to patient outcomes to be studied and acknowledged."—*Foreword*

Includes bibliography of major CCCS articles published 1991–2006 and a chapter on the CCC framework and terminology tables.

Other nursing terminologies (and links to information about them) include, for example, Nursing Diagnoses, Definitions, and Classification International (NANDA-I; http://www.nanda.org), Nursing Interventions Classification System (NIC; http://www.ncvhs.hhs.gov/970416w4.htm), Nursing Outcomes Classification (NOC; http://www.ncvhs.hhs.gov/970416w5.htm), Omaha System (http://www.omahasystem.org), and others. Several of these and additional nursing terminologies are also included in the Unified Medical Language System (UMLS) (89) metathesaurus and are mapped partly or completely to SNOMED International: Systematized Nomenclature of Medicine (Copenhagen, Denmark: International Health Terminology Standards Development Organisation, 2002–).

1052 Drug information handbook. North American ed. Charles Lacy, Laura Armstrong, Morton Goldman, Leonard Lance, Lexi-Comp, Inc., American Pharmaceutical Association. Hudson, Ohio;

Washington: Lexi-Comp; American Pharmaceutical Association, 1994–. ISSN: 1533-4511.

615   RM301.12.D783

Publ. in cooperation with the Amer. Pharmacists Assoc. (APhA).

1st ed., 1993/94. Available in North Amer. and internat. editions. Description based on 15th ed., 2007.

(Lexi-Comp's clinical reference library).

Concise, comprehensive, and user-friendly drug reference. Alphabetical listing of 1,400 drug monographs, with new drugs and updates to monographs since the last edition. Includes detailed information in consistent format (33 fields), such as dosage, drug interactions, adverse reactions (by occurrence, overdose, and toxicology), etc., with warnings highlighted. Appendix. Pharmacologic category index. For clinicians and healthcare professionals.

Several other comprehensive print pharmacology handbooks, also publ. by Lexi-Comp and frequently updated, include *Anesthesiology and critical care drug handbook* (1999–. ; 7th ed., 2006); *Drug information handbook for advanced practice nursing* (1990–. ; 8th ed., 2007); *Drug information handbook for dentistry* (1996– ; 12th ed., 2007); *Drug information handbook for oncology* (2000– ; 6th ed., 2007); *Drug information handbook for psychiatry: A comprehensive reference of psychotropic, nonpsychotropic, and herbal agents* (1999– ; 6th ed., 2006); *Drug information handbook for the allied health professional* (1995– ; 12th ed., 2005); *Geriatric dosage handbook* (1993– ; 11th ed., 2006); *Infectious diseases handbook: Including antimicrobial therapy & diagnostic test/procedures* (1994– ; 6th ed., 2006); *Natural therapeutics pocket guide* (2000– ; 2nd ed., 2003); *Pediatric dosage handbook* (1992– ; 13th ed., 2006); and *Pharmacogenomics handbook* (2003– ; 2nd ed., 2006). Also available online as pt. of Lexi-Comp Online™ (http://webstore.lexi.com/Store/ONLINE) and Lexi-Comp ONLINE for Dentistry (http://webstore.lexi.com/Store/ONLINE/Lexi-Comp-ONLINE-for-Dentistry).

1053 The family practice desk reference. 4th ed. Charles E. Driscoll, Edward T. Bope. xi, 1035 p., ill. Chicago: AMA Press, 2003. ISBN: 1579471900.

610   RC55.F22

1st ed., 1986 had title: *Handbook of family practice*; 3rd ed., 1996.

Includes aspects of health and illness management for common conditions and diseases encountered by family physicians. Organized by "life-cycle approach" (*Pref.*), e.g., care of children, maternity care, women's health, men's health, and by body system (e.g., cardiovascular, respiratory, gastrointestinal, etc.). Entries in standardized format, each with a table of contents and list of references, and organized by conditions. Each chapter presents symptoms using differential diagnosis tables, laboratory values, and diagnostics.

1054 Guide to the code of ethics for nurses: Interpretation and application. Marsha Diane Mary Fowler, American Nurses Association. 176 p. Silver Spring, Md.: American Nurses Association, 2008. ISBN: 9781558102.

174.2   RT85.G85

Produced by American Nurses Association (ANA).

Intended as a guide to the *Code of ethics for nurses with interpretive statements* (Washington, D.C.: American Nurses Association, 2001) on how to apply ethical standards and values in nursing practice. Each chapter discusses a single code provision and provides the text of the code of ethics, the history, purpose, theory, application, case studies, and examples. Includes bibliographical references and index.

1055 Health professionals style manual. Shirley H. Fondiller, Barbara J. Nerone. New York: Springer, 2006. ISBN: 0826102077.

808.06661   R119.F66

Rev. ed. of *Health professionals stylebook*, 1993.

Contents: ch. 1, "Style and substance: The dynamic duo"; ch. 2, "From principles to practice: The art of effective writing"; ch. 3, "Understanding usage: An alphabetical guide to specific writing tips and pitfalls"; ch. 4, "Be clear and direct: How to avoid redundancies, euphemisms, and cliches"; ch. 5, "Harness the potential of computers and the Internet." Appendixes: A, "Common abbreviations and acronyms in health care"; B, "Commonly misspelled words"; C, "Using prefixes and suffixes"; D, "Common proofreader's marks"; E, "Electronic resources"; F, "Referencing." Includes references for further reading and index.

Provides guidelines about writing clearly and effectively, covering American usage only. Addresses style, style errors, English grammar, composition techniques, and other areas of technical writing. Can be used as a supplement to other style manuals. For researchers and students in the various health professions.

1056 Interpreting the medical literature. 5th ed. Stephen H. Gehlbach.
   x, 293 p., ill. New York: McGraw-Hill, 2006. ISBN: 0071437894.
610.7222   R118.6.G43

First edition, 1982; 4th ed., 2002.

Contents: ch. 1, "Tasting an article"; ch. 2, "Study design: General considerations"; ch. 3, "Study design: The case-control approach"; ch. 4, "Study design: The cross-sectional and follow-up approaches"; ch. 5, "Study design: The experimental approach"; ch. 6, "Study design: Variations"; ch. 7, "Making measurements"; ch. 8, "Analysis: Statistical significance"; ch. 9, "Analysis: Some statistical tests"; ch. 10, "Interpretation: Sensitivity, specificity, and predictive value"; ch. 11, "Interpretation: Risk"; ch. 12, "Interpretation: Causes"; ch. 13, "Cases series, editorials, and reviews"; ch. 14, "A final word"; Index.

Assists with understanding and utilizing the information presented in medical studies and reports and also with the critical reading and interpretation of conflicting studies. Provides clinical examples from the published medical and public health literature.

1057 Legal, ethical, and political issues in nursing. 2nd ed. Tonia D.
   Aiken. xxii, 458 p., ill., map. Philadelphia: F.A. Davis, 2004.
362.17321   RT86.5.A37

Contents: pt. 1, "Nursing practice"; pt. 2, "Nursing and the law"; pt. 3, "Nursing ethics"; pt. 4, "Liability in professional practice"; pt. 5, "Professional issues."

Provides an overview of the responsibilities of nurses, with focus on legal and ethical issues and considerations a nurse may encounter in clinical practice. List of resources at the end of each chapter. For nursing educators and students. Available online via netLibrary.

1058 The Lippincott manual of nursing practice. 8th ed. Lippincott,
   Williams & Wilkins. xvii, 1866 p., color ill. Philadelphia:
   Lippincott, Williams & Wilkins, 2006.
610.7   RT51.B78

1st ed., 1974; 7th ed., 2001.

Contents: pt. 1, "Nursing process and practice"; pt. 2, "Medical-surgical nursing"; pt. 3, "Maternity and neonatal nursing"; pt. 4, "Pediatric nursing"; pt. 5, "Psychiatric nursing."

Comprehensive reference for all types of nursing care. Gives a step-by step explanation of a total physical examination and diagnostic procedures.

Identifies normal and abnormal conditions and discusses appropriate observations, with illustrations for procedures, clinical manifestations, management, and health education. New and expanded material in this edition includes several revised chapters, with new material, for example, in patient safety, the Health Insurance Portability and Accountability Act, Healthy People 2010, and emerging infections. Five appendixes, with information on interpretation of diagnostic studies, conversion tables, pediatric laboratory values, herbal preparation, and sources for further information. Subject index. Also available in electronic format via Books@ Ovid and restricted to subscribers.

1059 Mosby's manual of diagnostic and laboratory tests. 2nd ed.
Kathleen Deska Pagana, Timothy James Pagana. xi, 1166 p., color ill. St. Louis: Mosby, 2002. ISBN: 032301609X.

616.0756   RB38.2.P34

1st ed., 1998.

Contents: "Guidelines for proper test preparation and performance"; "Blood studies"; "Electrodiagnostic tests"; "Endoscopic studies"; "Fluid analysis studies"; "Manometric studies"; "Microscopic studies"; "Nuclear scanning"; "Stool tests"; "Ultrasound studies"; "Urine studies"; "X-ray studies"; "Miscellaneous studies"; bibliography; appendixes: (A) "Alphabetical list of tests"; (B) "List of tests by body systems"; (C) "Disease and organ panels"; (D) "Abbreviations for diagnostic and laboratory tests." Index, with names of all tests and their synonyms and other terms within tests.

Provides information and explanation on clinically relevant laboratory and diagnostic tests, including procedures and patient care before, during, and after a particular test, contraindications, and potential complications. Includes bibliographical references (p. 1085–88) and index.

Similar print titles include *Interpretation of diagnostic tests* (709), *Laboratory tests and diagnostic procedures* (318), *Tietz clinical guide to laboratory tests* (334); a Web-based resource is Lab Tests Online: A Public Resource on Clinical Lab Testing from the Laboratory Professionals Who Do the Testing (319).

NURSING

475

1060 NANDA, NOC, and NIC linkages: Nursing diagnoses, outcomes, and interventions. 2nd ed. Marion Johnson, North American Nursing Diagnosis Association. 698 p. St. Louis: Mosby Elsevier, 2006. ISBN: 0323031943.

610.73   RT48.6

1st ed., 2001, had title *Nursing diagnoses, outcomes, and interventions.*

Contents: pt. 1, "Languages and applications": ch. 1, "The languages"; ch. 2, "Development of the linkages"; ch. 3, "Linkage applications"; pt. 2, "NANDA, NOC, and NIC linkages: Diagnoses linked to NOC and NIC"; "'Risk for' diagnoses linked to NOC and NIC"; appendixes: (A) "NOC outcome labels and definitions"; (B) "NIC interventions labels and definitions."

Three standardized languages recognized by the American Nurses Association: NANDA (North American Diagnosis Association) International, NOC (Nursing Outcomes Classification), NIC (Nursing Interventions Classification).

Describes the common nursing classification system languages and terminology related to nursing diagnoses, the nursing process, nursing care methods and standards, and outcome assessment and their linkages to NANDA. Mostly in tabular format. Reference to help with the development of a care plan. Companion website. A similar title is Wilkinson's *Nursing diagnosis handbook with NIC interventions and NOC outcomes.*

1061 Nurse practitioner's legal reference. Springhouse Corp. xii, 361 p., ill. Springhouse, Pa.: Springhouse Corp., 2001. ISBN: 1582550972.
344.730414   RT82.8.N8646

Contents: ch. 1, Nurse practitioner practice and the law; ch. 2, Legal risks and responsibilities on the job; ch. 3, Legal issues on the job; ch. 4, Legal risks while off duty; ch. 5, Malpractice liability; ch. 6, Legal aspects of documentation; ch. 7, Ethical decision making; ch. 8, Ethical conflicts in clinical practice; ch. 9, Ethical conflicts in professional practice; ch. 10, Patients' rights; ch. 11, NPs in a changing health care marketplace.

Provides coverage of legal issues affecting nurses and the nursing profession, including issues currently facing legislative and judicial review. Contains several appendixes: "Understanding the Judicial Process," "Interpreting Legal Citations," and "Types of Law." Court case citation index and a general index.

1062 Nursing Interventions Classification (NIC). 5th ed. Gloria M. Bulechek, Howard Karl Butcher, Joanne McCloskey Dochterman. xxxvi, 938 p., ill. St. Louis: Mosby/Elsevier, 2008. ISBN: 9780323053.
610.73012   RT42.N858

1st ed., 1992; 4th ed., 2004.

Contents: (1) "Construction and use of the classification"; (2) "Taxonomy of nursing interventions"; (3) "The classification"; (4) "Care interventions for nursing specialty areas"; (5) "Estimated time and education level necessary to perform NIC interventions"; (6) appendixes.

This updated edition provides an overview of the interventions performed by all nurses and of the NIC taxonomy, with different groupings representing the areas of nursing practice and coding guidelines. Includes 542 interventions. Interventions can be used with diagnostic classifications, e.g., NANDA (North American Nursing Diagnosis Association), ICD (International Classification of Diseases [82]), DSM (*Diagnostic and statistical manual: DSM-IV-TR* [Washington: American Psychiatric Association, 2000]), and those included in clinical information systems (e.g., SNOMED International [Copenhagen, Denmark: International Health Terminology Standards Development Organisation, 2002–]). Interventions are listed alphabetically, and each intervention has been assigned a unique number. Appendixes include new, revised, and retired interventions since the last edition, selected publications, abbreviations, and several other resources. Has associated website and companion book, *NANDA, NOC, and NIC linkages: Nursing diagnoses, outcomes, and interventions* (1060).

1063 Nursing procedures and protocols. Lippincott, Williams & Wilkins. x, 661 p., ill. Philadelphia: Lippincott, Williams & Wilkins, 2003. ISBN: 1582552371.

610.73   RT49.N88

Contents: ch. 1, "Fundamentals"; ch. 2, "Infection control"; ch. 3, "Medication administration"; ch. 4, "Intravascular therapy"; ch. 5, "Cardiovascular care"; ch. 6, "Pulmonary care"; ch. 7, "Neurologic care"; ch. 8, "Gastrointestinal care"; ch. 9, "Renal and urologic care"; ch. 10, "Musculoskeletal care"; ch. 11, "Skin care"; ch. 12, "Endocrine and hematologic care."

Presents a wide range of research-based protocols and procedures for application in clinical settings, including patient information tips. Describes various procedures and medical equipment and provides step-by-step instructions and explanations, with cross-references to related information. Includes illustrations, checklists, tables, and flowcharts and uses several logos (evidence-based logo, troubleshooting logo, alert logo) to draw attention to certain information.

1064 PDR nurse's drug handbook. Delmar Cengage Learning. ill. Clifton Park, N.Y.: Delmar Cengage Learning, 2000–. ISSN: 1535-4601.

615   RM125

Title varies: *PDR nurse's handbook*; *Physician's desk reference nurse's drug handbook*; *Nurse's drug handbook*. Description based on 2007 ed. of *PDR nurse's drug handbook*; publ. varies: now Thomson Delmar Learning; distr. by CENGAGE Learning.

Description of the major prescription drugs, with phonetic pronunciation of drug name, drug classification, drug interactions, FDA warnings, etc. Includes various aids to prevent medication errors (e.g., listing of drug names that sound alike, administration and storage of drugs, etc.). Includes a visual identification guide. For nursing students, nurses, and other health care professionals.

Related titles include *Physicians' desk reference: PDR* (1250), *ADA/PDR guide to dental therapeutics* (795), *PDR drug guide for mental health professionals* (1242), *PDR guide to drug interactions, side effects, and indications* (1247), *PDR for herbal medicines* (1244), *PDR for nonprescription drugs, dietary supplements, and herbs* (1245), *PDR for nutritional supplements* (1246), *Physicians' desk reference for ophthalmic medicines* (1249), also *PDR guide to biological and chemical warfare response*, and *PDR guide to terrorism response*, and other titles.

PDR and its major companion volumes are available online in the PDR Electronic Library (1243).

1065 Professional guide to signs and symptoms. 5th ed. Lippincott Williams & Wilkins. x, 918 p., ill. Philadelphia: Lippincott Williams & Wilkins, 2007. ISBN: 1582555109.

616.047   RC69.P77

1st ed., 1993; 4th ed., 2003.

Alphabetically organized reference tool helpful for identification and interpretation of selected signs and symptoms of various diseases, agents of bioterrorism, signs and symptoms associated with herbs, and laboratory test results. This edition also contains advice on how to conduct a patient history and a table of English-Spanish translations. Selected references and index. Also available online via Books@Ovid. A related title, *Professional guide to diseases*, has been regularly updated since 1981, with the 8th ed. published in 2005.

1066 Resources for nursing research: An annotated bibliography. 4th ed. Cynthia G. L. Clamp, Stephen Gough, Lucy Land. xi, 419 p.

London; Thousand Oaks, Calif.: Sage, 2004. ISBN: 0761949917.
016.61073   Z6675.N7.C53; RT81.5
1st ed., 1991; 3rd ed., 1999.

Contents: pt. 1, "Sources of literature"; pt. 2, "Methods of inquiry"; pt. 3, "The background to research in nursing."

Bibliography of sources for nursing research, with approx. 3,000 entries with brief annotations, including literature (papers, books, and Internet resources) published since 1998. Expanded section on electronic resources in this edition. Cross-references, several appendixes (for example, "Computer programs for design and analysis"), author and subject indexes. "Intended for all those with an interest in nursing research—students, teachers, librarians, practitioners and researchers."—*Introd.*

Also available as an e-book.

1067 Saunders nursing drug handbook 2008. Barbara B. Hodgson, Robert J. Kizior. xvi, 151, 1362 p. St. Louis: Saunders, 2007. ISBN: 9781416040.

Title varies: 1993–1997 had title *Nurse's drug handbook*; 1998–. titled *Saunders nursing drug handbook.*

Contains generic and brand names of drugs, pharmacokinetics, action, therapeutic effect, interactions, adverse reactions, toxic effects, etc. and their nursing implications. Similar specialized nursing drug references include, for example, *Mosby's nursing drug reference, Intravenous medications: A handbook for nurses and allied health professionals,* and *Mosby's pediatric drug consult.* The 2007 ed. is available as an e-book.

Histories

1068 American nursing: A history. 4th ed. Philip Arthur Kalisch, Beatrice J. Kalisch. ix, 500 p, ill. Philadelphia: Lippincott, Williams & Wilkins, 2004. ISBN: 0781739691.
362.1730973   RT4.K34
First three editions (1978–95) had title, *The advance of American nursing.*

"The purpose of this book is to place nursing's past in a broader social, cultural, and economic context. While largely a history of nursing in the United States, it explores the impact of the profession on American society; helps students appreciate the history and complexity of nursing and the U.S. health care system; develops a framework, past and present, for assessing current and emerging issues in health care."—*Pref.* Divided into 22 chapters on subjects including the founding of early schools of nursing, public health nursing, nursing during the different wars, the hospital industry, minorities in nursing, health care reform and nursing, and a look toward the future. Index.

1069 Celebrating nursing history. Margaret Allen, Medical Library Association. 1994–. Chicago: Medical Library Association. http://nahrs.library.kent.edu/resource/reports/weeding.html.

Produced by Medical Library Association (MLA), Nursing and Allied Health Resources Section (NAHRS). Reprint of article originally publ. in *NAHRS newsletter*, Apr. 1994, updated Oct. 2005.

Contents: What to Keep; Significant Nursing Books to Find and Keep; Periodicals to Keep; Sources Used for Some of These Comments and Selections; Reprints; Films and Videos; How and Where to Search; Other Sources for Historical Research; Why Go to Historical Sources?; Other Articles of Interest.

Provides an annotated bibliography of nursing books, reports, landmark studies, periodicals, films, videos, and other resources for historical research in nursing and related allied health literature. Chronological arrangement under the different headings. Intended to answer questions on archives, weeding, and other collection management issues posed by nursing librarians and others interested in the history of nursing.

1070 Doctors, nurses, and medical practitioners: A bio-bibliographical sourcebook. Lois N. Magner. xiii, 371 p. Westport, Conn.: Greenwood Press, 1997. ISBN: 0313294526.

610.922B R153.D63

Biographical information on 56 "significant but lesser known individuals outside their own country extraordinary yet unsung" (*Introd.*), covering the time period 1710–1924, with essays focusing on the life and career. Bibliographic references include archival materials and works written by and about the particular individual. Appendixes: (A), Listing by occupations and special interests; (B), Listing by date of birth; (C), Listing by place of birth; (D), Listing of women practitioners. Intended for students and scholars.

1071 Historical encyclopedia of nursing. Mary Ellen Snodgrass. xvii, 354 p., ill. Santa Barbara, Calif.: ABC-CLIO, 1999.

610.7309 RT31.S66

Covers the history of nursing and healing from ancient times to the present. Includes key nursing concepts and individuals, medical topics,

MEDICAL & HEALTH SCIENCES

organizations, wars, etc. Articles list sources, including websites. Black-and-white illustrations and "see also" references. "Timeline of landmarks in nursing" (p. 297–310), "Works by and about healers" (p. 311–13), bibliographical references (p. 315–33), and index.

1072 A history of nursing, from ancient to modern times: A world view. 5th ed. Isabel Maitland Stewart, Anne L. Austin. 516 p., ill. New York: Putnam, [1962].
610.7309 RT31.S7

1st ed., 1920, by L. L. Dock and I. M. Stewart, had title *A short history of nursing* and was based on Dock and M. Adelaide Nutting, *A history of nursing: The evolution of nursing systems from the earliest times to the foundation of the first English and American training schools for nurses.*

Intended especially for student nurses. Pt. 1 consists of eight chapters sketching the history of nursing from ancient to modern times; pt. 2, 11 chapters on nursing today in various countries throughout the world. Includes a general classified bibliography and selected bibliographies for each chapter. Subject and name index.

1073 Nurse-midwifery: The birth of a new American profession. Laura Elizabeth Ettinger. xvi, 269 p., ill. Columbus, Ohio: Ohio State University Press, 2006. ISBN: 0814210236.
618.2 RG950.E77

Contents: ch. 1, "Conception: Nurse-midwives and the professionalization of childbirth"; ch. 2, "Eastern Kentucky's frontier nursing service: Mary Breckinridge's mission, survival strategies, and race"; ch. 3, "New York City's Maternity Center Association: Educational opportunities and urban constraints"; ch. 4, "Transitions: New directions, new limitations"; ch. 5, "Traditions: Home birth in a high-tech age"; ch. 6, "Don't push: Struggling to create a political strategy and professional identity"; Epilogue, "Afterbirth: Learning from the past, looking to the future."

Historical study of the emergence and rise of nurse-midwifery as a profession and barriers experienced by nurse-midwives today. Notes, bibliography, and index.

An earlier title, *American midwives, 1860 to the present*, is a historical study of the changing role of the midwife in American society between 1860 and 1978, with explanation of the use of the terms midwifery and obstetrics, and chapters devoted to the early 20th-century midwife debate and its proponents, along with other relevant topics. Bibliography: p. [153]–91.

1074 **Nursing, a historical bibliography.** Bonnie Bullough, Vern L. Bullough, Barrett Elcano. xxiv, 408 p. New York: Garland, 1981. ISBN: 0824095111.

016.6107309   Z6675.N7.B84; RT31

Garland Reference Library of Social Science v. 66.

A bibliography of some 3,500 references collected from major sources. The cutoff date is 1978. Includes index.

1075 **Nursing history resources.** American Association for the History of Nursing. 2005?–. Wheat Ridge, Colo.: American Association for the History of Nursing. http://www.aahn.org/resource.html.

Produced by American Association for the History of Nursing (AAHN; http://www.aahn.org/).

Contents: Archives and History Centers; Conferences, Exhibits and Celebrations; Funding; Internet Resources; Journals; New Books and Publications; Organizations; Videos.

Listing of selected available nursing resources, including Internet resources, for the history of nursing. Provides links to other nursing history organizations, nursing education, and related government websites. Includes, for example, a link to nursing history centers, museums, and archives (http://www.aahn.org/centers.html) and a page entitled Black Nurses in History: A Bibliography and Guide to Web Resources (http://www4.umdnj.edu/camlbweb/blacknurses.html), prepared by the University of Medicine and Dentistry of New Jersey.

1076 **Nursing, the finest art: An illustrated history.** 2nd ed. M. Patricia Donahue. xix, 535 p., ill. (some color), color maps. St. Louis: Mosby, 1996. ISBN: 0815127278.

610.7309   RT31.D66

1st ed., 1985.

Contents: ch. 1, "The origin of nursing"; ch. 2, "Ancient civilizations"; ch. 3, "Nursing in a Christian world"; ch. 4, "Nursing in a changing world: Aristocratic and military influences"; ch. 5, "Nursing in transition: The dark period and the dawn of modern times"; ch. 6, "The development of nursing in America"; ch. 7, "Advancing toward new frontiers"; ch. 8, "Nurses in action: Wars of the twentieth century"; ch. 9, "The age of expansion"; ch. 10, "An era of change and challenge"; ch. 11, "Contact and diversity."

Chronologically-arranged chapters present a "visual and literary perspective on the evolution of nursing" (*Foreword*) that is "created and

influenced by major social, political, and historical forces in society."—
Pref. Includes 400 color and halftone illustrations and artwork. Includes
bibliographical references (p. 511–24), list of plates, and index.

1077   **The path we tread: Blacks in nursing worldwide, 1854–1994.** 3rd
ed. Mary Elizabeth Carnegie, Josephine A. Dolan. xxi, 329 p., ill.,
maps. New York: National League of Nursing Press, 1995. ISBN:
0887376401.

610.7308996073   RT83.5.C37

1st ed. (1984) had title *The path we tread: Blacks in nursing, 1854–1984*;
2nd ed. (1991) had title *The path we tread: Blacks in nursing, 1854–1990*.

Traces the history and historical evolution of the nursing profession,
the accomplishments of black nurses in leadership roles, and the "constant
struggle to gain a rightful position in the health care system for black
nurses."—*Foreword*

Indexes; Abstract journals; Databases

1078   **CINAHL.** Cinahl Information Systems, EBSCO. 1982–. Ipswich,
Mass.: EBSCO. http://www.ebscohost.com/cinahl/.

CINAHL® [database]. Title varies. Online version: 1984–1992 (with coverage 1982–.), publ. by Cinahl Information Systems; 1993–., publ. jointly
by EBSCO and Cinahl Information Systems. Also available in different
enhanced versions: CINAHL® with Full Text, CINAHL® Plus™, and
CINAHL® Plus with Full Text. Comparisons of the different versions at
http://www.ebscohost.com/uploads/thisTopic-dbTopic-592.pdf.

Print version: 1956–76 entitled: *Cumulative index to nursing and allied
health literature*; 1977–. *Cumulative index to nursing and allied health literature*® (continues to be published in print).

Authoritative database for the professional literature of nursing and
allied health. Provides references to journal articles, books, book chapters,
pamphlets, audiovisual materials, dissertations, educational software,
selected conference proceedings, standards of professional practice, and
more. Some full-text material is included. Currently indexes a large number of journals, as well as publications from the American Nurses' Association and the National League for Nursing. Allows for application of
specific interest category filter, e.g., evidence-based practice, informatics,
patient safety, public health, women's health, and others. Subject access is

provided by *CINAHL subject heading list: Alphabetic list, tree structures, permuted list* (1093). Complements *International nursing index* (1081), publ. 1966–2000.

1079 Health and wellness resource center. Gale Group. 2001–.
Farmington Hills, Mich.: Gale; Cengage Learning. http://www.gale.com/HealthRC/.

Provides access to a collection of Gale reference titles (e.g., *Gale encyclopedia of cancer* [Detroit: Thomson/Gale, 2005], *Gale encyclopedia of childhood and adolescence* [Detroit: Gale, 1998], *Gale encyclopedia of genetic disorders* [Detroit: Thomson/Gale, 2005], *Gale encyclopedia of medicine* [Detroit: Thomson; Gale Group, 2005], *Medical and health information directory* [216]), and others; access to full-text articles from the periodical literature; pamphlets; news; and other content, such as access to selected health websites. Also makes available add-on modules [e.g., Alternative Health Module with, for example, the *Gale encyclopedia of alternative medicine* [Detroit: Thomson/Gale, 2005], and the Disease Profiler Module with health statistics]. "Ever-growing electronic resource center for all levels of health research" (*Publ. notes*), particularly for nursing and allied health professionals and consumer health, public, and health science libraries.

Other Gale resources include Health Reference Center—Academic [418] and Gale Virtual Reference Library [Farmington Hills, Mich.: Gale Cengage Learning, 2002–].

1080 Health reference center—academic. Gale Group. 1999–.
Farmington Hills, Mich.: Gale; Cengage Learning. http://www.galegroup.com.

R11

Available on either InfoTrac or Powersearch platform (customer must choose).

A multisource database and integrated collection of nursing, allied health, and medicine journals; consumer health magazines; newsletters; newspaper articles; pamphlets; and reference books. Records are available in a combination of indexing, abstract, and full-text formats. Designed for nursing and allied health students as well as consumer health researchers.

Other Gale resources include a consumer health resource, Health and Wellness Resource Center (632), and Gale Virtual Reference Library (Farmington Hills, Mich.: Gale Cengage Learning, 2002–).

1081 **International nursing index.** American Journal of Nursing Company, Institute for Scientific Information, National Library of Medicine (U.S.), American Nurses' Association, National League for Nursing. New York: American Journal of Nursing Company, 1966–2000. ISSN: 0020-8124.

610.73016   Z6675.N7.I5

Print version discontinued in 2000. Currently searchable in MEDLINE (425)/PubMed (432). Relevant content can also be found in CINAHL (439).

A computer-produced index using MEDLARS (Medical Literature Analysis and Retrieval System) facilities. Because subject headings were originally chosen for a medical index, a "Nursing thesaurus," included in the annual cumulation, gives commonly used nursing terms as cross-references to the subject headings used in the index. Cross-references from MeSH: Medical Subject Headings (575) are included in each annual cumulation since 1972. Also includes brief sections listing nursing publications of organizations and agencies as well as books published by or for nurses. A list of doctoral dissertations by nurses appears in the annual cumulative volume.

1082 **Lexi-Comp online.** Lexi-Comp, Inc. 1978–. Hudson, Ohio: Lexi-Comp, Inc. http://www.lexi.com/web/toursol.jsp.

Point-of-care drug and clinical information resource, with links to primary literature. Contains 15 clinical databases (e.g., Lexi-Drugs Online, AHFS, Lexi-Natural Products Online, Nursing Lexi-Drugs Online, Pharmacogenomics, Poisoning and Toxicology, Lab Tests and Diagnosis, and several others) and provides drug information and treatment recommendation for diseases and conditions. Also includes other features, e.g., an online interaction tool (Lexi-Interact) and medical calculator (Lexi-CALC). For pharmacists, physicians, nurses, and dentists. Detailed information available at the Lexi-Comp website "tour portal" (http://www.lexi.com/web/toursol.jsp).

1083 **MEDLINE.** National Library of Medicine (U.S.). 1900s–. Bethesda, Md.: National Library of Medicine (U.S.). http://purl.access.gpo.gov/GPO/LPS4708.

MEDLINE®—Medical Literature Analysis and Retrieval System Online (National Library of Medicine®—NLM), primary subset of PubMed® (425) and part of the Entrez (3) databases provided by the National Center for Biotechnology Information (NCBI). Coverage extends back to 1950, with some older material (cf. http://www.nlm.nih.gov/services/oldmed. html).

Bibliographic database, providing comprehensive access to the international biomedical literature from the fields of medicine, nursing, dentistry, veterinary medicine, allied health, and the preclinical sciences. It is also a primary source of information from the international literature on biomedicine, including the following topics as they relate to biomedicine and health care: Biology, environmental science, marine biology, plant and animal science, biophysics, and chemistry. For indexing articles, NLM uses Medical Subject Headings MeSH® (575), a controlled vocabulary of biomedical terms. MEDLINE can also be searched via the NLM Gateway (429). An increasing number of MEDLINE citations contain a link to the free full-text articles.

The MEDLINE database is the electronic counterpart of *Index Medicus®* (420), *Index to dental literature* (811), and the *International nursing index* (1081).

For detailed information, see the MEDLINE fact sheet at http://www. nlm.nih.gov/pubs/factsheets/medline.html.

1084 Micromedex healthcare series. Thomson Micromedex. [199?–.] Greenwood Village, Colo.: Thomson Micromedex. http://www. micromedex.com/products/hcs/.

Micromedex Healthcare Series; also called Healthcare Series Online.

Intended for clinicians. Includes a variety of resources for finding information on drugs, toxicology, emergency, acute care, and disease data as well as alternative medicine information. Drug resources include DRUGDEX, DRUG-REAX, IDENTIDEX, IV Index, *Index nominum* (Medpharm Scientific, 2004), *Martindale: The complete drug reference* (1182), *Physicians' desk reference: PDR* (1250), POISINDEX, *Red book* (1255), REPRORISK, and *USP DI* (727). Emergency and disease data can be found, for example, in DISEASEDEX and alternative therapies in AltMedDex and other Thomson products. Searchable across either all databases, by specific database(s), and by groups of databases. Drugs can be searched by trade or generic drug name. Specific drug database search and drug topic search provide, for example, a drug evaluation overview, dosing information, pharmacokinetics, contraindications, precautions, adverse reactions, single and multiple drug interactions, IV compatibility, teratogenicity, therapeutic uses, and comparative efficacy.

A matrix of all Micromedex products and versions in this series, with listing of the individual titles, various format options, and indication of whether a particular title is also available in print can be found at http://www.micromedex.com/support/faqs/plat_matrix.html. Help with citing the various Micromedex versions is provided at http://www.micromedex.com/about_us/legal/cite/.

1085 **NLM gateway.** National Library of Medicine (U.S.). 2000–. Bethesda, Md.: National Library of Medicine. http://gateway.nlm.nih.gov/.

RA11

Allows simultaneous searching of information resources at the National Library of Medicine (NLM). Databases include MEDLINE (425)/PubMed (432) and the NLM Catalog (482) as well as other resources, including information on current clinical trials and consumer health information (MedlinePlus [463]). Currently provides access to 21 databases and other information resources (for a complete list of databases and other details, see http://www.nlm.nih.gov/pubs/factsheets/gateway.html). An overview of the search results is presented in several categories (bibliographic resources, consumer health resources, and other information), with a listing of the individual databases and the number of results within these categories.

1086 **Nursing studies index.** Virginia Henderson, Yale University. 4 v. New York: Garland, 1984. ISBN: 0824065158.
016.61073   Z6675.N7.N869; RT41

Contents: v. 1, 1900–29 (publ. 1972); v. 2, 1930–49 (publ. 1970); v. 3, 1950–56 (publ. 1966); v. 4, 1957–59 (publ. 1963).

Subtitle: *An annotated guide to reported studies, research in progress, research methods and historical materials, in periodicals, books, and pamphlets published in English.*

Provides retrospective coverage for a wide range of materials not treated elsewhere. The number of journals covered varies from 110 in v. 1 to 239 in v. 4, according to availability at the time of publication. Annotations note study methods used and nature and scope of the investigation, and they frequently indicate the author's qualifications and the auspices under which the work was done. Includes unpublished doctoral dissertations but not master's theses. Subject arrangement with author index.

1087 **PubMed.** U.S. National Center for Biotechnology Information, National Library of Medicine, National Institutes of Health. 1996–. Bethesda, Md.: U.S. National Center for Biotechnology Information. http://www.ncbi.nlm.nih.gov/sites/entrez/.

PubMed®, developed and maintained by the National Center for Biotechnology Information (NCBI) at the National Library of Medicine® (NLM) (427). It is available via the NCBI Entrez (3) retrieval system. PubMed also provides access to the other Entrez molecular biology resources (*PubMed Overview*). Starting May 23, 2007, NCBI is changing to a new version of Entrez in a phased implementation (cf. Nahin AM. New and Improved PubMed®/Entrez and New URL *NLM tech. bull.*, 2007 May–Jun.; [356]: http://www.nlm.nih.gov/pubs/techbull/mj07/mj07_issue_cover.html).

Provides a search interface for more than 16 million bibliographic citations and abstracts in the fields of medicine, nursing, dentistry, veterinary medicine, health care systems, and preclinical sciences. It provides access to articles indexed for MEDLINE® (425) and for selected life sciences journals. PubMed subsets found under the "Limits" tab are: MEDLINE and PubMed Central®, several journal groups (i.e., core clinical journals, dental journals, and nursing journals), and topical subsets (AIDS, bioethics, cancer, complementary medicine, history of medicine, space life sciences, systematic reviews, and toxicology). "Linkout" provides access to full-text articles.

For detailed information see the PubMed fact sheet at http://www.nlm.nih.gov/pubs/factsheets/pubmed.html. For a brief overview of searching PubMed, see the PubMed Quick Start at http://www.ncbi.nlm.nih.gov/books/bv.fcgi?rid=helppubmed.section.pubmedhelp.PubMed_Quick_Start. For details on the now completed OLDMEDLINE retrospective conversion projects, see http://www.nlm.nih.gov/pubs/techbull/so06/so06_oldmedline_status.html.

Internet Resources

1088 **National Institute of Nursing Research.** National Institute of Nursing Research. 1997–. Bethesda, Md.: National Institute of Nursing Research. http://www.ninr.nih.gov/.

RT81.5

The mission of the National Institute of Nursing Research (NINR) is "to promote and improve the health of individuals, families, communities, and populations. This mission is accomplished through support of research in a number of science areas. Among those areas of research are chronic and acute diseases, health promotion and maintenance, symptom management, health disparities, caregiving, self-management, and the end of life."—*Main page.* Links to NINR publications and meeting reports; information on nursing, minority/ethnic nurses, regional nursing research, and professional nurses and practice organizations; federal government links, links to search engines; and other resources. Also contains "health links for the public" to several federal government sites.

1089 National Patient Safety Foundation (NPFS). National Patient Safety Foundation. North Adams, Mass.: National Patient Safety Foundation. http://www.npsf.org.

Independent, not-for-profit organization, with the mission to "measurably improve patient safety."—*Main page.* Searchable website, with links to online patient safety resources and organizations. Information is presented in different categories (e.g., health care quality and safety, medication safety, surgical safety, cancer treatment safety, and others) for different user groups, such as health professionals, patients and families, and researchers.

1090 Nursing history resources. American Association for the History of Nursing. 2005?–. Wheat Ridge, Colo.: American Association for the History of Nursing. http://www.aahn.org/resource.html.

Produced by American Association for the History of Nursing (AAHN; http://www.aahn.org/).

Contents: Archives and History Centers; Conferences, Exhibits and Celebrations; Funding; Internet Resources; Journals; New Books and Publications; Organizations; Videos.

Listing of selected available nursing resources, including Internet resources, for the history of nursing. Provides links to other nursing history organizations, nursing education, and related government websites. Includes, for example, a link to nursing history centers, museums, and archives (http://www.aahn.org/centers.html) and a page entitled Black Nurses in History: A Bibliography and Guide to Web Resources (http://www4.umdnj.edu/camlbweb/blacknurses.html), prepared by the University of Medicine and Dentistry of New Jersey.

1091 OncoLink. Abramson Cancer Center of the University of Pennsylvania. 1994–. Philadelphia: University of Pennsylvania. http://cancer.med.upenn.edu/.

615.507; 616.992; 616.994

Contents: Types of cancer; Cancer treatment information; Coping with cancer; Cancer resources and news; Ask the cancer expert; OncoLink Library.

Designed for educational purposes to help cancer patients, families, health care professionals, and the general public to get accurate cancer-related information. Provides comprehensive information about specific types of cancer, updates on cancer treatment, and news about research advances, with information provided at various levels, from introductory to in-depth.

Statistics

1092 **Statistical methods for health care research.** 5th ed. Barbara Hazard Munro. xiii, 494 p., ill. Philadelphia: Lippincott, Williams & Wilkins, 2005. ISBN: 0781748402.

610.727   RT81.5.M86

1st ed., 1986; 4th ed., 2000.

Contents: http://www.loc.gov/catdir/toc/ecip0416/2004007098.html. Explains statistical methods frequently used in the health care literature. Includes charts, graphs, and examples from the literature. New material on regression diagnostics has been added. Associated website.

Thesauruses

1093 **CINAHL. subject heading list: Alphabetic list, tree structures, permuted list.** CINAHL Information Systems. Glendale, Calif.: Cinahl Information Systems, 1994–. ISSN: 1522-1156.

025.4961073   Z695.1.N8.N87

Published in 1984 as *CINAHL subject headings*; 1986–93 had title *Nursing and allied health (CINAHL). subject heading list.* Annual.

The subject thesaurus to CINAHL (1093) and its print version, *Cumulative index to nursing and allied health literature.* Includes more than 11,000 CINAHL subject headings specifically for nursing and allied health and also many from the National Library of Medicines's MeSH (575).

9 > NUTRITION

1094 **Codex alimentarius.** Joint FAO/WHO Food Standards
Programme; Codex Alimentarius Commission. [200?.] Rome;
Geneva, [Switzerland]: Food and Agriculture Organization of
the United Nations; World Health Organization. http://www.
codexalimentarius.net/web/index_en.jsp#/.

The *Codex alimentarius* (Latin for "Food Law" or Code) is a collection of
international food standards adopted by the Codex Alimentarius Commission and presented in a uniform manner. These standards include raw,
semiprocessed, and processed foods.

1095 **Dietary guidelines for Americans, 2005.** U.S. Department of
Health [2005]. Washington: U.S. Dept. of Health and Human
Services; U.S. Dept. of Agriculture. http://purl.access.gpo.gov/
GPO/LPS57108.

Published jointly every five years by the Department of Health and
Human Services, Office of Disease Prevention and Health Promotion, the
Department of Agriculture, Center for Nutrition Policy and Promotion,
and the Agricultural Research Service.

First five editions, 1980–2000, had title *Nutrition and your health:
Dietary guidelines for Americans*. Print equivalents for these editions pub-
lished in *Home and garden bulletin* (U.S. Dept. of Agriculture) no. 232.
Current and earlier online editions linked from http://www.health.gov/
DietaryGuidelines/.

Description based on the 2005 Web edition.

Contents: ch. 1, "Background and purpose of the dietary guidelines
for Americans"; ch. 2, "Adequate nutrients within calorie needs"; ch. 3,
"Weight management"; ch. 4, "Physical activity"; ch. 5, "Food groups
to encourage"; ch. 6, "Fats"; ch. 7, "Carbohydrates"; ch. 8, "Sodium and
potassium"; ch. 9, "Alcoholic beverages"; ch. 10, "Food safety"; Appendix
A, "Eating patterns"; Appendix B, "Food sources and selected nutrients."

These guidelines provide authoritative advice for people two years and
older about how good dietary habits can promote health and reduce risk
for major chronic diseases. Additional information and access to related
documents and resources can be found at http://www.healthierus.gov/
dietaryguidelines/.

A related title, *A healthier you: Based on the dietary guidelines for Americans*, provides practical information about healthy food choices, healthy eating habits, and physical activity.

1096 Food and Nutrition Information Center. Food and Nutrition Information Center. Beltsville, Md.: Food and Nutrition Information Center. http://www.nal.usda.gov/fnic/.

351; 640.73; 371.7; 612.3; 641.3   RA784

The Food and Nutrition Information Center (FNIC), located at the National Agricultural Library (NAL) of the U.S. Dept. of Agriculture (USDA), provides online global nutrition information. The FNIC website contains multiple links to reliable food and nutrition and metabolism information for consumers and nutrition professionals. The A–Z list (http://www.nal.usda.gov/fnic/topics_a-z.shtml) includes important topics (e.g., infant nutrition, childhood obesity, weight control, etc.), or browse by subject for dietary guidance, food labeling, and many other major categories. Also included are links to resource lists for specific nutrition topics (http://www.nal.usda.gov/fnic/resource_lists.shtml) and to FNIC and other nutrition-related databases (http://www.nal.usda.gov/fnic/databases.shtml).

Bibliography

1097 Annual bibliography of significant advances in dietary supplement research. National Institutes of Health Office of Dietary Supplements, Consumer Healthcare Products Association. 1999–. Bethesda, Md.: National Institutes of Health Office of Dietary Supplements. http://ods.od.nih.gov/Research/Annual_Bibliographies.aspx.

Annual bibliography presenting significant research on dietary supplements, selected each year by an international team of expert reviewers; National Institutes of Health (NIH) Office of Dietary Supplements (ODS) (765) selects the top 25 for publication in this bibliography. Useful for students, nutrition and health professionals, and others conducting nutrition-related research. The International Bibliographic Information on Dietary Supplements (IBIDS) (1145) database and several other dietary supplement–related NIH and USDA databases can be accessed from the ODS website.

Dictionaries

1098 **Bender's dictionary of nutrition and food technology.** 8th ed. David A. Bender, Arnold E. Bender. vii, 539 p. Boca Raton, Fla.; Cambridge, England, [U.K.]: CRC Press; Woodhead, 2006. ISBN: 0849376017.

1st ed., 1960; 7th ed., 1999.

Rev. ed. Designed to define the broad range of words used by individuals involved in nutrition and food technology. Includes 6,100 terms, covering a wide range of disciplines, many cross-references, nutrient composition data, and U.S.-recommended daily amounts of nutrients, for example. Bibliography. Also available online via Knovel (Norwich, N.Y.: Knovel, 2003–).

1099 **CRC desk reference for nutrition.** 2nd ed. Carolyn D. Berdanier. xiv, 518 p., ill. Boca Raton, Fla.: CRC/Taylor & Francis, 2005. ISBN: 0849338352.

613.203   QP141.B523

1st ed., 1998.

Concise encyclopedic dictionary of terms used in nutrition and related sciences, including medical, biochemical, and physiological terminology, with a few biotechnology and food technology terms. Focus is clinical. Alphabetic arrangement for entries of varying length and complexity, cross-references, figures, and tables. Includes drugs to treat nutrition-related conditions. Web addresses for food composition tables and recommendations for nutrient intakes. Appendixes provide information about meal planning and food selection as well as various metabolic maps. Some illustrations. For nutritionists, nurses, physicians, and other health professionals and students.

1100 **A dictionary of food and nutrition.** 2nd ed. David A. Bender, Arnold E. Bender. 583 p. Oxford; New York: Oxford University Press, 2005. ISBN: 0198609612.

641.303   TX349.B4115

1st ed., 1995.

Nontechnical guide to terms found on "food labels, in advertising, or in the media."—*Publ. note.* Contains 6,000 entries on various aspects of food, food groups, nutrition, and diet in relation to health. International in scope. Appendixes list food additives, vitamins, nutrients, etc. Also available in electronic format as a searchable database as part of Oxford Reference Online (Oxford; New York: Oxford University Press, 2002–).

1101 Dictionary of food ingredients. 4th ed. Robert S. Igoe, Y. H. Hui. v, 234 p. Gaithersburg, Md.: Aspen, 2001. ISBN: 0834219522.

641.03   TX551.I26

Defines more than 1,000 food ingredients: "currently used additives, including natural ingredients, FDA-approved artificial ingredients, and compounds used in food processing."—*Pref.* Contents: pt. 1, "Ingredients dictionary"; pt. 2, "Ingredient categories"; pt. 3, "Additives/substances for use in foods listed under Title 21 of the Code of Federal Regulations (Washington: National Archives and Records Administration Office of the Federal Register)"; pt. 4, "Food additives E numbers in the European Union"; and pt. 5, "Bibliography." Intended for professionals and students; also appropriate for general use.

1102 Dictionary of food science and technology. International Food Information Service. x, 413 p. Oxford, U.K.: Blackwell, 2005. ISBN: 1405125055.

The 7,852 entries contain "a large number of definitions of terms which are specific to food science and technology (covering sensory analysis, consumer research, food composition, nutrition [food-related, not clinical aspects], catering and food safety) and is augmented with definitions of terms from cognate disciplines (including chemistry, biochemistry, physics, microbiology, public health, economics, engineering and packaging)."—*Pref.* Word selection reflects the recent application of biotechnology to food science. Entries organized alphabetically letter by letter, not by whole word. Definitions are sufficiently detailed for research but most useful for students of food science and nutrition and the general public. Appendixes. Also available online via Knovel (Norwich, N.Y.: Knovel, 2003–).

1103 Dictionary of nutraceuticals and functional foods. N. A. M. Eskin, Snait Tamir. 507 p., ill. Boca Raton, Fla.: Taylor & Francis/ CRC Press, 2006. ISBN: 0849315727.

613.203   QP144.F85.E85

Functional foods and nutraceuticals series, no. 8.

Concise, science-based information on nutraceutical and functional food products and compounds, with mention of their roles in the promotion of health and the prevention of disease. Includes chemical structures and other illustrations, figures, tables, and literature references. Arranged alphabetically. Based on peer-reviewed literature. For researchers, teachers, students. Also available as an e-book through netLibrary and via FOODnetBASE, part of CRCnetBASE (Boca Raton, Fla.; London: CRC Press; Taylor and Francis).

1104 Elsevier's dictionary of nutrition and food processing: In English, German, French, and Portuguese. H. E. Philippsborn. Boston: Elsevier, 2002. ISBN: 0444510176.

613.203   QP141.P515

Includes indexes.

Brief definitions of approx. 6,000 English words or phrases translated into the three languages and identified with the discipline in which they are predominantly used, e.g, agriculture (Agr.), products and production terminology (Prod.), biochemistry (Biochem.), and medical terms (Med.). The alphabetically-arranged English words and phrases in the "Basic table" are numbered. Words in the other three languages are listed in separate sections and are keyed to the number assigned to the English term in the basic table. For researchers.

1105 Nutrients A to Z: A user's guide to foods, herbs, vitamins, minerals and supplements. 3rd rev. ed. Michael Sharon. viii, 344 p. London: Carlton Books, 2004. ISBN: 1853755265.

613.203

[1st ed.], 1998; [new ed.], 1999. Imprint varies.

Ready reference, with useful descriptions and definitions for various foods, vitamins, minerals, herbs, and supplements. Written in nontechnical language. For general readers and health professionals and useful in both public and academic libraries. Contains list for herbal associations and herb suppliers in the United States and the United Kingdom. Index lists common and alternative names.

1106 Nutrition and diet therapy reference dictionary. 5th ed. Rosalinda T. Lagua, Virginia Serraon Claudio. ix, 407 p., ill. Ames, Iowa: Blackwell, 2004. ISBN: 0813810027.

613.203   RM217.L34

1st ed., 1969; 4th ed., 1996.

Covers all aspects of nutrition. Entries include definition, suggested nutrition therapy, and dietary guidelines. Includes different diets, nutrition therapy for various disorders, and drugs and their effects on nutrition. Also includes brand names of nutritional products. The 50 appendixes cover topics including Dietary Reference Intakes, body mass index, national nutrition objectives for 2010, dietary guidelines for Americans, biochemical assessment of nutritional status, and websites for public health nutrition. For both health professionals and general readers.

Directories

1107 DIRLINE. National Institutes of Health (U.S.). [1983?–.] Bethesda, Md.: U.S. National Institutes of Health, Dept. of Health and Human Services. http://dirline.nlm.nih.gov/.

DIRLINE® (Directory of Information Resources Online), maintained by the National Library of Medicine (NLM) (208).

Online annotated directory of organizations, research resources, projects, databases, and other information resources concerned with health and biomedicine from a variety of sources, including federal, state, and local government agencies, academic and research institutions, and also consumer health-related resources such as self-help groups and health hotlines. Resources are mostly from the U.S. but also include some international resources. Currently contains over 8,000 entries, with topics on most diseases and conditions and health services research and technology assessment. Can be searched using MeSH® (Medical Subject Headings) (575), keywords, or by name and location of a resource. Detailed information on DIRLINE can be found via a fact sheet prepared by NLM: http://www.nlm.nih.gov/pubs/factsheets/dirlinfs.html.

Encyclopedias

1108 Diets and dieting: A cultural encyclopedia. Sander L. Gilman. xii, 308 p., ill. New York: Routledge, 2008. ISBN: 9780415974.
613.2503   RM214.5.G55

Cultural history of diets and dieting, covering the period from ancient Greece and Rome to the present. Background information on various diets, dieting, and weight loss. Includes biographies of historical and contemporary figures associated with dieting. Alphabetical arrangement. Each article provides a list of references and further reading. Useful as a resource for students and researchers. Also available as an e-book via netLibrary.

1109 Encyclopedia of common natural ingredients used in food, drugs, and cosmetics. 2nd ed. Albert Y. Leung, Steven Foster. xxxv, 649 p. New York: Wiley, 1996. ISBN: 0471508268.

660.63   QD415.A25L48

1st ed., 1980.

Provides data on approx. 500 natural ingredients. Updates all entries of the previous ed. and includes a new category, Health Foods/Herbal Teas. Covers the identification, processing, preparation, and use for each ingredient. Excludes prescription drugs and medicinal herbs not readily available in commerce. Arrangement is by common name. Entries give Latin name, synonyms, general description, chemical composition, pharmacology or biological activities, uses, commercial preparations, and references. Includes a new classification for Chinese medicinal herbs, published for the first time in English. Glossary of commonly encountered terms used in the botanical industry. Indexed.

1110 Encyclopedia of diet fads. Marjolijn Bijlefeld, Sharon K. Zoumbaris. xv, 242 p., ill. Westport, Conn.: Greenwood Press, 2003. ISBN: 0313322236.

613.2503   RM222.2.B535

Entries for various kinds of diets and major weight loss programs, with appropriate comments, criticisms, and suggested dietary guidelines. Additional entries and information on nutrition in health and illness, vitamins, etc. Introduction includes a brief history of dieting and fad diets. Annotated list of websites and several other appendixes. For general readers and allied health professionals.

1111 Encyclopedia of food and culture. Solomon H. Katz, William Woys Weaver. 3 v., ill. (some color). New York: Scribner, 2003. ISBN: 0684805685.

394.1203   GT2850.E53

Nimbly covers an enormous scope of no less than food and nutrition and their place in history and culture on a global basis. Some 600 signed articles in three volumes range in length from 250 to 10,000 words. As an example of coverage, the 75 entries under the letter "C" begin with Cabbage, include Julia Child, and then move on to Civilization and Food; Social Class; Climate and Food; Cocktail Party; Cocktails; Codex Alimentarius; Coffee; Food Coloring; and finish with Cucumbers, Melons and Other Cucurbits; Evolution of Cuisine; Curds; Curry; Custard and Puddings; and Cutlery. Throughout, content is enriched by 450 photos and other illustrations, recipes, menus, especially useful timelines, many bibliographic and cross-references, and a necessary navigation device: A thorough index. Available as an e-book.

1112 Encyclopedia of foods: A guide to healthy nutrition. Mayo Clinic. xi, 516 p., color ill. San Diego, Calif.: Academic Press, 2002. ISBN: 0122198034.

641.3003   TX349.E475

Contents: pt. 1, "A guide to healthy nutrition: Optimizing health"; "Nutrients and other food substances"; "Food-health connection"; "Planning meals: Selecting healthful foods, plus two weeks of menus"; "Preparing healthful meals"; pt. 2, "Encyclopedia of foods"; "Fruits"; "Vegetables"; "Grains"; "Dairy goods"; "Meat and other high-protein foods"; "Fats, oils, and sweets"; "Others."

Contains discussion of dietary guidelines and the relationship between diet and various diseases. Appendix includes reading list, selected websites, charts of dietary reference intakes, and information about nutrients in foods, vitamins, and minerals. Color photographs, diagrams, and other illustrations. Useful for public and academic libraries.

1113 Encyclopedia of food science and technology. 2nd ed. F. J. Francis. 4 v. (xxi, 2768 p.), ill. New York: Wiley, 2000. ISBN: 0471192856.

664.003   TP368.2.E62

"This encyclopedia features A-to-Z coverage of all aspects of food science, including: the properties, analysis, and processing of foods; genetic engineering of new food products; and nutrition. Contains information useful to food engineers, chemists, biologists, ingredient suppliers, and other professionals involved in the food chain."—*Publisher Description*

See   http://www.wiley.com/WileyCDA/WileyTitle/productCd-0471192856.html.

Comprehensive work with approx. 400 articles. Contains black-and-white photographs, illustrations, charts, and tables. Each article has a detailed bibliography. Vol. 1 has front section with conversion factors, abbreviations, and unit symbols; v. 4 has an extensive index. A reviewer in the *Journal of food biochemistry* (27[1]:83-89) suggests this work is most suitable for a readership with a background in food science or a related field. Available online via Knovel (Norwich, N.Y.: Knovel, 2003–).

1114 **Encyclopedia of food sciences and nutrition.** 2nd ed. Benjamin
Caballero, Luiz C. Trugo, Paul M. Finglas. 10 v., ill. Amsterdam [The
Netherlands]; New York: Academic Press, 2003. ISBN: 9999901271.

664.003   TX349.E47

1st ed., 1993, had title *Encyclopaedia of food science, food technology and
nutrition.*

Contents: v. 1, A–Bro; v. 2, Bro–Cla; v. 3, Cle–End; v. 4, Ene–Fru; v. 5,
Fru–I; v. 6, J-M; v. 7, N–Pre; v. 8, Pre–Soy; v. 9, Soy–V; v. 10, W–Z ; Index.

This revised, expanded, and updated edition contains articles covering
a wide variety of topics in food science, food technology, and nutrition.
International in scope. For food scientists and technologists, nutritionists,
public health researchers, and others. Also available online via the Elsevier
ScienceDirect platform.

1115 **Encyclopedia of human nutrition.** 2nd ed. M. J. Sadler, James
J. Strain, Benjamin Caballero. 4 v., ill. (some color). Amsterdam
[The Netherlands]; Boston: Elsevier; Academic Press, 2005. ISBN:
0121501108.

613.203   QP141.E526

Revised and expanded from 1999 1st ed.

The subject area of nutrition has widened, with extensive research and
new knowledge being generated in recent years in areas such as "the mapping of the human genome, the links between molecular bioenergetics
and lifespan, the influence of nutrients on viral mutations."—*Introd.* Topics are listed alphabetically and presented in a rigorous but concise way.
Each entry contains a contents list for the particular article in addition to
the contents list at the beginning of each volume. Many entries reflect the
recognition of the importance of diet and lifestyle as well as reduction of
risk. Synonyms, cross-references, graphs, and diagrams. Intended for general readers and also for health professionals. Available online via Elsevier
Reference Works on Science Direct http://www.info.sciencedirect.com/
content/books/ref_works/collections / humnut/.

1116 **The Gale encyclopedia of diets: A guide to health and nutrition.**
Jacqueline L. Longe, Thomson Gale (Firm). 2 v. Detroit: Thomson
Gale, 2007. ISBN: 9781414429.

613.203   RA784.G345

Addresses a wide range of diets and related health and nutrition issues,
with the intent to supplement advice given by health professionals. Signed

articles include a list of additional resources, with definitions of terms, cross-references, and "see also" references. Index. Written for health consumers and general readers. For public, academic, and health science libraries. Available electronically through Gale Virtual Reference Library (Farmington Hills, Mich.: Gale Cengage Learning, 2002–).

Other resources providing information on diets include, for example, *Encyclopedia of human nutrition* (682) and *Encyclopedia of nutrition and good health*, published in various editions since 1997.

1117 Nutrition and well-being A to Z. Delores C. S. James. 2 v., ill. Detroit: Macmillan Reference USA, 2004. ISBN: 0028657071.
613.203   RA784.N838

Contents: v. 1, A–H; v. 2, I–Z.

Provides information on the effects of nutrition and diet on diseases and on quality of life. Covers nutritional concepts, dietary habits, current nutritional research, legislation, influential persons in nutrition and medicine, and health organizations. Explores historical aspects of nutrition and well-being in different countries. Alphabetical arrangement, with definitions of major terms in sidebars, related references, and bibliography at the end of each article. Illustrations, photographs, tables, glossary, and index. For students, researchers, and health professionals. Available as an e-book.

Guides

1118 Nutrition.gov. Food and Nutrition Information Center. Beltsville, Md.: National Agricultural Library. http://www.nutrition.gov.
                                                                                     RA784

Maintained by Food and Nutrition Information Center (FNIC).

Access to information from across the federal government on food, food safety, nutrition, healthy eating, dietary supplements, and physical fitness. Includes specialized nutrition information for infants, children, teens, adult women and men, and seniors, as well as the latest nutrition-related news. Provides search capabilities and resource lists for different audiences, e.g., caregivers, consumers, health care workers, kids and teens, parents, researchers, and teachers. Healthier US (http://www.healthierus.gov) provides access to consumer resources concerning nutrition, physical fitness, and disease.

Handbooks

1119 ABC of nutrition. 4th ed. A. Stewart Truswell, Patrick G. Wall. vii, 140 p., ill. London: BMJ, 2003. ISBN: 0727916645.

613.2   QP141.T785

1st ed., 1986; 3rd ed., 1999.

Guidelines for appropriate nutrition and diet therapy for heart disease, blood pressure, various chronic diseases, and cancer. Includes nutritional recommendations for women who are pregnant or nursing, children, and adults. Also covers eating disorders and obesity and nutritional deficiencies in both developing and affluent countries. Illustrations, charts. Includes bibliographical references and index. Also available online via netLibrary.

1120 The biochemistry of human nutrition: A desk reference. 2nd ed. Sareen Annora Stepnick Gropper, Eva May Nunnelley Hamilton. xxiii, 263 p., ill. Belmont, Calif.: Wadsworth/Thomson Learning, 2000. ISBN: 0534515436.

QP141.G76

Rev. ed. of *The biochemistry of human nutrition*, 1987.

Alphabetically-arranged definitions and descriptions of nutrition-related biochemical terminology and concepts, with illustrations of structural formulas and biochemical pathways. Includes nutrition-related diseases and nutrient deficiencies.

1121 Bowes and Church's food values of portions commonly used. Anna De Planter Bowes, Charles Frederick Church, Helen Nichols Church, Jean A. Thompson Pennington. tables. Philadelphia: Lippincott, 1980–. ISBN: 0781744296.

641.10212   TX551.B64

Title varies. Earlier editions by Anna De Planter Bowes and Helen Nichols Church; 1st ed., 1937, had title *Food values of portions commonly served*; 2nd–12th ed., 1939–75, *Food values of portions commonly used*; 13th–19th ed., 1980–2010, *Bowes and Church's food values of portions commonly used*. Description based on 18th ed., 2005.

This ready reference provides data on food composition and the nutritional value of foods, listing 8,500 common foods. The main section provides tables of nutrient contents of foods; foods are arranged in

32 sections by food type. Includes brand-name products, prepared and restaurant foods, conversion tables, DRI (dietary reference intake) tables, estimated energy requirements, acceptable macronutrient distribution ranges, and heat, weight, and volume conversions. Bibliography, general index, and various other supplementary tables, including a list of scientific names for plants and animals used in food, food name synonyms, bibliography for food composition data, and index of food names. Considered a classic work. Intended for dietitians, nutritionists, and students of nutrition and dietetics.

1122 **The Cambridge world history of food.** Kenneth F. Kiple, Kriemhild Coneè Ornelas. 2 v. (xlii, 2153 p.), ill. Cambridge, England, [U.K.]; New York: Cambridge University Press, 2000. ISBN: 052140214X.

641.309   TX353.C255

Multidisciplinary scholarly work, with sections on prehistoric and historic food patterns of various peoples, major animal and vegetable staple foods and beverages, past and present diets, nutritional science to evaluate the quality of diets, and the relationship of nutrition and health. Pt. 8, "A historical dictionary of the world's plant foods," provides brief histories of fruits and vegetables and also contains synonyms. Tables, graphs, and black-and-white pictures. Subject index; Latin name index; Personal name index. Available online to subscribers through http://www.gale.com.

1123 **DRI, dietary reference intakes: The essential guide to nutrient requirements.** Jennifer J. Otten, Jennifer Pitzi Hellwig, Linda D. Meyers. xiii, 543 p., ill. Washington: National Academies Press, 2006. ISBN: 0309100917.

612.3   QP141.D75

Summarizes *Recommended dietary allowances* (U.S. National Research Council), 1943–.

Recommended Dietary Allowances (RDAs) have been renamed and are now called Dietary Reference Intakes (DRIs). Eight separate volumes of DRIs, published between 1998 and 2005 by National Academies Press, are summarized in this reference volume. Reviews function of each nutrient in the human body, food sources, usual dietary intakes, and effects of deficiencies and excessive intakes. Information provided includes estimated average requirement, recommended dietary allowance, adequate intake level, and tolerable upper intake. Provides recommendations for health maintenance and the reduction of chronic disease risk. Other related areas are also addressed, such as nutrition labeling, dietary planning, etc. Online version, available from National Academies Press at http://www.nap.edu/catalog/11537.html, contains only the references, not the full text of the printed book.

1124 Fenaroli's handbook of flavor ingredients. 5th ed. George A. Burdock, Giovanni Fenaroli. xxx, 2009 p., ill. Boca Raton, Fla.: CRC Press, 2005. ISBN: 0849330343.

664.5   TP418.B86

Standard reference for flavor ingredients, prepared for food engineers and scientists who require data about the toxicology of flavor-related chemicals and ingredients. Alphabetical entries for either chemical or common name. For each entry, the handbook lists (where appropriate) primary name, synonyms, CAS number, FEMA number, NAS number, EINECS number, EEC number, CoE number, JECFA number, description, sensory thresholds, molecular structure, empirical formula/MW, specifications, natural occurrence, synthesis, consumption, food functions, regulations/guidelines. Glossary and index. Available online via netLibrary and CRCnetBASE.

1125 Fennema's food chemistry. 4th ed. Srinivasan Damodaran, Kirk Parkin, Owen R. Fennema. 1144 p., ill. Boca Raton, Fla.: CRC Press/Taylor & Francis, 2008. ISBN: 0824723457.

664   TX541.F65

1st (1976) through 3rd (1996) editions had title *Food chemistry*. 3rd ed. also available online via netLibrary.

Contents: pt. 1, "Major food components"; pt. 2, "Minor food components"; pt. 3, "Food systems"; pt. 4, appendixes: (A) "International system of units (SI): The modernized metric system"; (B) "Conversion factors" (non-SI units to SI units); (C) "Greek alphabet"; (D) "Calculating relative polarities of compounds using the fragmental constant approach to predict log P values."

Rev. ed., with coverage of food analysis and food composition, and topics such as carbohydrates, lipids, proteins, enzymes, vitamins and minerals, colorants, flavors, food additives, nutraceuticals, toxicants, etc., and their role in human health. Contains, for example, a chapter entitled "Introduction to food chemistry" and a new chapter entitled "Impact of biotechnology on food supply and quality."

1126 Food additives data book. Jim Smith, Lily Hong-Shum. xvii, 1016
p., ill. Oxford, U.K.: Blackwell Science, 2003. ISBN: 0632063955.
664.06   TX553.A3F562

Concise data summary for nearly 350 food additives, organized by category: acidulants, antioxidants, emulsifiers, enzymes, flavor enhancers,
flour additives, gases, nutritive additives, polysaccharides, preservatives,
sequestrants, solvents, and sweeteners. Each entry includes, as appropriate,
category, food use, synonyms, formula, molecular mass, alternative forms,
properties and appearance, boiling point, melting range, flash point, ion-
ization constant, density, heat of combustion, vapor pressure, purity, water
content, heavy metal content maximum, arsenic content, ash, solubility,
function in foods, alternatives, technology of use in foods, synergists,
food safety issues, legislation, and references. Includes list of contributors.
Index. Also available as an e-book through Knovel (Norwich, N.Y.: Knovel,
2003–) and netLibrary.

1127 Food chemicals codex. 5th ed. Institute of Medicine (U.S.),
Committee on Food Chemicals Codex. 998 p. Washington:
National Academy Press, 2003. ISBN: 0309088666.
664.06021873   TP455.F66

1st ed., 1966; 2nd ed., 1972; 3rd ed., 1981; 4th ed., 1996.

This work is mandated by the U.S. Food and Drug Administration.
The 5th ed. contains 1,077 descriptions of food additives or chemicals.
The work is divided into five sections: general provisions and requirements; monograph specifications; flavor chemicals; infrared spectra;
and ten appendixes grouped under general tests and assays. Monograph
descriptions usually include a common name, a chemical name, a drawing
of chemical structure, chemical formula, formula weight, CAS number, a
short description, food function, and assay tests and requirements. Flavor
chemicals descriptions include name, formula, physical form, solubility,
refractive index, and specific gravity. Includes illustrations, charts. Index.
Also available online via Knovel (Norwich, N.Y.: Knovel, 2003–).

In the preface it is noted: "Because of its regulatory status in countries
other than the United States, and its worldwide use, the *Food Chemicals
Codex* contains some monographs for chemicals not currently allowed in
foods in the United States."

The 6th ed. will be released in spring 2008 by the United States Pharmacopeia, with an update in 2009, and a 7th ed. scheduled for 2010. See
http://www.usp.org/fcc/.

1128 Food safety handbook. Ronald H. Schmidt, Gary Eugene Rodrick. xiii, 850 p., ill. Hoboken, N.J.: Wiley-Interscience, 2003. ISBN: 0471210641.

363.192   TP373.5. F67

"The intent of this book is to define and categorize the real and perceived safety issues surrounding food, to provide scientifically non-biased perspectives on these issues, and to provide assistance to the reader in understanding these issues. While the primary professional audience for the book includes food technologists and scientists in the industry and regulatory sector, the book should provide useful information for many other audiences."—*Pref.*

Thirty-eight chapters written by specialists are divided into eight sections: characteristics of food safety and risk; biological food hazards; chemical and physical food hazards; systems for food safety surveillance and risk prevention; food safety operations in food processing, handling, and distribution; food safety in retail foods; diet, health, and food safety; and worldwide food safety issues. Chapters have bibliographies. Index.

Also available online through netLibrary and Knovel (Norwich, N.Y.: Knovel, 2003–).

1129 Food Safety Research Information Office at the National Agricultural Library. National Agricultural Library (U.S.). 2002–. Beltsville, Md.: National Agricultural Library, Food Safety Research Information Office. http://fsrio.nal.usda.gov/index.php.

TX537

Produced by National Agricultural Library (NAL); Food Service Research Information Office (FSRIO).

A major component of this searchable website is its "Research Projects Database" for locating information on food safety and related research. Categories currently in use in this database include food and food products, food composition and characteristics, food quality characteristics, food handling and processing, on-farm food safety, diseases and poisonings, sanitation and pathogen control, contaminants and contamination, government policy and regulations, methodology and quality standards, human health and epidemiology, education and training, facilities and sites, and pathogen biology.

Complements information found, for example, in *Food safety handbook* (1128), *Food safety: A reference handbook* by Nina E. Redman (2nd ed., 2007), *Foodborne disease handbook*, ed. by Y. H. Hui (2nd ed., 2001),

Foodborne diseases, ed. by Dean O. Cliver and Hans Rieman (2nd ed., 2002), and Shabir Simjee's *Foodborne diseases* (2007).

1130 Handbook of nutraceuticals and functional foods. 2nd ed. Robert E. C. Wildman. 541 p., ill. Boca Raton, Fla.: CRC Press/Taylor & Francis, 2007. ISBN: 0849364094.

613.2   QP144.F85.H36

1st ed., 2001.

Contents: http://www.loc.gov/catdir/toc/fy0709/2006045563.html.

Collection of current topics and data on nutraceutical compounds and functional foods, with new and revised chapters in this edition that reflect the scientific advances in this field. For professionals and students in food chemistry and engineering as well as in the nutritional, pharmaceutical, and biomedical sciences. Includes bibliographical figures, tables, references, and index. Available as an e-book through netLibrary.

1131 Handbook of nutrition and food. 2nd ed. Carolyn D. Berdanier, Johanna T. Dwyer, Elaine B. Feldman. 1265 p., [8] p. of plates, ill. (some color). Boca Raton, Fla.: Taylor & Francis, 2008. ISBN: 9780849392.

612.3   QP141.H345

1st ed., 2002.

Contents: pt. 1, "Food" (ch. 1–5); pt. 2, "Nutrition science" (ch. 6–12); pt. 3, "Nutrition throughout life" (ch. 13–20); pt. 4, "Nutrition assessment" (ch. 21–37); pt. 5, "Clinical nutrition" (ch. 38–75); Index.

Contains information on food composition, nutrient data, and nutrient needs throughout the human life cycle, nutritional status assessment, SI conversion factors, etc. Chapters on such topics as clinical nutrition, various diets, and sports nutrition include references and bibliographies for further reading. Much of the information is presented in tables, charts, and graphs. Tables on food additives; food contaminants; toxins and foodborne illness; edible, toxic, and medicinal plants; chemical and physical properties of vitamins and minerals; etc. Many of the large data sets found in the previous edition have been placed on the Web, resulting in many more listings of Web addresses in this edition. Web addresses to USDA food composition data are provided. In addition to human nutrition, contains a section on animal nutrition. Electronic version of 2nd ed. available via netLibrary; 1st ed. as pt. of CRCnetBASE (Boca Raton, Fla.; London: CRC Press; Taylor and Francis).

Complements B. B. Desai's *Handbook of nutrition and diet* (online version via netLibrary), which discusses the effects of nutrition and diet on the human body and the nutritional management of diseases.

1132 Handbook of vitamins. 3rd ed. Robert B. Rucker. xiii, 600 p., ill. New York: Marcel Dekker, 2001. ISBN: 058540741X.

612.399   QP771.H35

1st ed., 1984, had title *Handbook of vitamins: Nutrition, biochemical, and clinical aspects*; 2nd ed., rev. and expanded, 1991.

Intends "to provide basic and fundamental background material to aid the reader in assessing the importance of new findings regarding vitamin function. Written with a varied audience in mind: the clinician, the biochemist, the advanced nutrition student, and the dietitian."— *Pref.* Each chapter provides information on a particular vitamin, its history, chemistry, structure, nomenclature, content in food, metabolism, biochemical function, deficiency sign, nutritional requirements, safe levels of intake, etc. Bibliographic references with each chapter. Subject index. Also available as an e-book to institutions affiliated with netLibrary.

1133 The health professional's guide to popular dietary supplements.
3rd ed. Allison Sarubin-Fragakis, Cynthia Thomson, American Dietetic Association. 682 p. Chicago: American Dietetic Association, 2007. ISBN: 088091363.

613.28   RM258.5.S27

1st ed., 2000; 2nd ed., 2002.

Alphabetical guide to supplements, with comments on their safety and literature references concerning scientific evidence. Summary table for each supplement lists media and marketing claims, efficacy, drug/supplement interactions, key points, food sources, dosage and bioavailability research, and safety. Appendixes include information on government regulation of dietary supplements, dietary intake tables and intake assessment, and additional resources. Includes bibliographical references and index. Similarly, *The health professional's guide to dietary supplements* covers 120 dietary supplements, including Web resources.

Information in these books can be supplemented with resources such as MEDLINE (425), the International Bibliographic Information on Dietary Supplements (IBIDS) Database (1145), Natural Medicines Comprehensive Database (637), and Natural Standard (1277).

1134 **Krause's food and nutrition therapy.** 12th ed. L. Kathleen Mahan, Sylvia Escott-Stump. xxiv, 1352 p., ill. (some color). St. Louis: Saunders; Elsevier, 2008. ISBN: 9781416034018.

615.854   RM216

Title varies: 1st ed., 1952, had title *Nutrition and diet therapy in relation to nursing*; 2nd ed., 1957, through 7th ed., 1984, had title *Nutrition and diet therapy*; 11th ed., 2004, had title *Krause's food, nutrition and diet therapy*.

Contents: pt. 1, "Nutrition basics"; pt. 2, "Nutrition in the life cycle"; pt. 3, "Nutrition care process"; pt. 4, "Nutrition for health and fitness"; pt. 5, "Medical nutrition therapy."

This rev. ed. includes chapters on, e.g., nutrition and genomics, weight management, eating disorders, and medical nutrition therapy (e.g., new chapters on nutrition therapy for psychiatric conditions and developmental disabilities), with reference to physiologic and metabolic background and pathophysiology as it relates to nutrition care. Includes list of relevant websites at the end of each chapter and a large number of appendixes, including information on exchange lists for meal planning, glycemic index, glycemic load for different carbohydrates, and many others. Includes new guidelines on food intake and physical activity and exercise as well as the new food guide pyramid and MyPyramid (http://www.mypyramid.gov/).

1135 **Modern nutrition in health and disease.** 10th ed. Maurice E. Shils, Moshe Shike. xxv, 2069 p., ill. (some color). Philadelphia: Lippincott, Williams & Wilkins, 2006. ISBN: 0781741335.

613.2   QP141.M64

1st ed., 1955; 9th ed., 1999.

This is the "50th anniversary" edition.

Contents: pt. 1, "Historical landmarks in nutrition"; pt. 2, "Proteins and amino acids"; pt. 3, "Nutrition in integrated biologic systems"; pt. 4, "Nutrition needs and assessment during the life cycle"; pt. 5, "Prevention and management of disease"; pt. 6, "Diet and nutrition in health of populations"; pt. 7, "Adequacy, safety, and oversight in the food supply"; pt. 8, appendixes.

Major textbook and reference source, with comprehensive coverage of basic and clinical nutrition and its role in medicine, public health, dietetics, and nursing. Provides extensive information on nutrition's role in disease prevention, covers genetics as it applies to nutrition, and describes major scientific advances in nutrition research. Addresses public health concerns and international nutrition issues. Detailed table of contents, index, and appendixes (text and tables). Appendixes include, for example, information on conversion factors, weights and measures, national and international recommended dietary reference values, energy and protein needs, anthropometric data, therapeutic diets, and websites of interest to health professionals. Includes bibliographical references and index. Electronic full text available via Books@Ovid.

1136 Nutrition: A reference handbook. David A. Bender, Arnold E. Bender. xxxvii, 573 p. Oxford; New York: Oxford University Press, 1997. ISBN: 0192623680.

613.2 TX353.B45

Contents: ch. 1, "The historical development of nutritional concepts"; ch. 2, "Body composition"; ch. 3, "Growth and development"; ch. 4, "Reference intakes, dietary goals and nutrition labelling of foods"; ch. 5, "Energy balance and overview of metabolism"; ch. 6, "Physiology of feeding and digestion"; ch. 7, "Carbohydrates"; ch. 8, "Lipids: Fats and oils"; ch. 9, "Alcohol and alcoholic beverages"; ch. 10, "Protein nutrition"; ch. 11, "Overnutrition: Problems of overweight and obesity"; ch. 12, "World food supplies and protein-energy malnutrition"; ch. 13, "Vitamin A and carotenes"; ch. 14, "Vitamin D, calcium and phosphorus"; ch. 15, "Vitamin E and selenium"; ch. 16, "Vitamin K"; ch. 17, "Thiamin (vitamin B1)"; ch. 18, "Riboflavin (vitamin B2)"; ch. 19, "Niacin"; ch. 20, "Vitamin B6"; ch. 21, "Folate and vitamin B12"; ch. 22, "Vitamin C"; ch. 23, "Biotin, pantothenic acid and other organic compounds"; ch. 24, "Iron"; ch. 25, "Mineral nutrition"; ch. 26, "Food processing"; ch. 27, "Adverse reactions to foods"; ch. 28, "Systematic classification of foods"; ch. 29, "Miscellaneous tables."

Encyclopedic dictionary with tables of data, references to the original sources, cross-references, bibliography, and index. "For anyone working in the broad fields of diet and health, food and nutrition."—*Pref.*

1137 The nutrition desk reference. 3rd ed. Robert H. Garrison, Elizabeth Somer. xxii, 663 p., ill. New Canaan, Conn.: Keats, 1995. ISBN: 0879836652.

613.2 QP141.G33

1st ed., 1985; 2nd ed., 1990. Description based on 3rd online ed., also available online since 2000 via netLibrary.

Contents: pt. 1, "Dietary factors"; pt. 2, "Nutrition and cancer"; pt. 3, "Nutrition and cardiovascular disease"; pt. 4, "Nutrition and disease"; pt. 5, "Dietary recommendations."

Presents basic nutrition information, biochemical explanations, and important nutrition-related topics in concise format and readable style.

For health professionals and general readers. Figures, tables, glossary, and index. Also available via netLibrary. Information found in this desk reference can be updated with online publications, for example, via PubMed (432) and Nutrition (MedlinePlus) (763) and other nutrition-related pages in MedlinePlus (463).

1138 Nutrition diagnosis and intervention: Standardized language for the nutrition care process. American Dietetic Association. iv, 287 p., ill. Chicago: American Dietetic Association, 2007. ISBN: 0880913665.

615.854   RM216.N8373

Provides terminology and definitions of three steps of the nutrition care process, i.e., nutrition assessment, nutrition diagnosis, and nutrition intervention. A future publication will provide updates and also examine two additional steps of this process relating to nutrition monitoring and evaluation.

1139 USDA nutrient data laboratory. Nutrient Data Laboratory, U.S. Department of Agriculture. [199?]–. Beltsville, Md.: Nutrient Data Laboratory, U.S. Department of Agriculture. http://www.ars.usda. gov/ba/bhnrc/ndl.

612.3641.3

Its mission is "to develop authoritative food composition databases and state of the art methods to acquire, evaluate, compile and disseminate composition data on foods available in the United States."— *Main page.* Contains links to historical information of 115 years of USDA food composition tables (http://www.ars.usda.gov/Aboutus/docs. htm?docid=9418). Currently, the National Nutrient Data Bank contains information for approx. 130 nutrients for more than 7,000 foods. Its major database is USDA National Nutrient Database for Standard Reference (SR), release 19 (http://www.ars.usda.gov/Services/docs.htm?docid=8964; also online via Knovel [Norwich, N.Y.: Knovel, 2003–]), for determining the nutrient content of foods (published previously in print format in *Agricultural handbook* no. 8 and supplements and *Home and garden bulletin* no. 72). Also provides links to food composition information from other countries (e.g., Canada, Australia, New Zealand, and others), food consumption surveys, food labeling, general nutrition information (e.g., Nutrition.gov [718], Dietary Guidelines for Americans 2005 [Washington: U.S. Dept.of Health and Human Services; U.S. Dept. of Agriculture,

2005]), dietary supplements databases (USDA is working with the Office of Dietary Supplements and other federal agencies to develop a Dietary Supplement Ingredient Database [DSID] at http://www.ars.usda.gov/dsid), and other resources.

1140 WHO child growth standards. World Health Organization. 2006. Geneva, Switzerland: World Health Organization. http://www.who.int/childgrowth/en/index.html.

Since the late 1970s, the National Center for Health Statistics (539)/WHO (951) growth reference has been in use to chart children's growth. It was based on data from a limited sample of children from the United States and is now considered less adequate for international comparisons. In 1997, WHO, in collaboration with the United Nations University, undertook the Multicentre Growth Reference Study (MGRS), which is a community-based, multicountry project with more than 8,000 children from Brazil, Ghana, India, Norway, Oman, and the United States. The new standards are the result of this study, which had as its goal "to develop a new international standard for assessing the physical growth, nutritional status and motor development in all children from birth to age five."—*Press release.* The first new growth charts released (Apr. 2007) include weight-for-age, length/height-for-age, and weight-for-length/height growth indicators as well as a Body Mass Index (BMI) standard for children up to age 5, and standards for sitting, standing, walking, and several other key motor developments.

The title of the print version is *WHO child growth standards: Length/height-for-age, weight-for-age, weight-for-length, weight-for-height and body mass index–for–age: Methods and development.*

Indexes; Abstract journals; Databases

1141 AGRICOLA. National Agricultural Library (U.S.). [1970–.] Washington: National Agricultural Library (U.S.). http://agricola.nal.usda.gov.

025.0663   S494.5.A8

"AGRICOLA (AGRICultural OnLine Access) serves as the catalog and index to the collections of the National Agricultural Library, as well as a primary public source for world-wide access to agricultural information. The database covers materials in all formats and periods, including printed works from as far back as the 15th century. The records describe publications and resources encompassing all aspects of agriculture and allied disciplines, including animal and veterinary sciences, entomology, plant sciences, forestry, aquaculture and fisheries, farming and farming systems, agricultural economics, extension and education, food and human nutrition, and earth and environmental sciences."—*National Agricultural Library Website.* In the 1990s, AGRICOLA was the definitive index for domestic agricultural information. Unfortunately, continuous funding cuts to the NAL budget have severely diminished AGRICOLA's scope and usefulness. AGRICOLA remains a very good index for pre-2000 agricultural publications. The researcher may wish to consult CAB Abstracts (1143) for a more comprehensive review of the agricultural literature since 2000.

1142　**Annual bibliography of significant advances in dietary supplement research.** National Institutes of Health Office of Dietary Supplements, Consumer Healthcare Products Association. 1999–. Bethesda, Md.: National Institutes of Health Office of Dietary Supplements. http://ods.od.nih.gov/Research/Annual_ Bibliographies.aspx.

Annual bibliography presenting significant research on dietary supplements, selected each year by an international team of expert reviewers; National Institutes of Health (NIH) Office of Dietary Supplements (ODS) (765) selects the top 25 for publication in this bibliography. Useful for students, nutrition and health professionals, and others conducting nutrition-related research. The International Bibliographic Information on Dietary Supplements (IBIDS) (1145) database and several other dietary supplement–related NIH and USDA databases can be accessed from the ODS website.

1143　**CAB abstracts.** Commonwealth Agricultural Bureaux. [1970–.] Wallingford, Oxfordshire, U.K.: CABI. http://www.cabi.org/ datapage.asp?iDocID=165.

A major bibliographic, abstracting, and indexing database in the applied life sciences. CABI subject scope is broad and deep, including all aspects of agriculture, forestry, human nutrition, veterinary medicine, and the environment from 150 countries and more than 50 languages. The database contains more than 5.2 million records, with some 200,000 added annually, and nearly all records have an abstract. The records are indexed using the CAB thesaurus. *CAB abstracts* is available online from numerous distributors including CAB Direct, Dialog, EBSCO, ISI Web of Knowledge (422), and Ovid/SilverPlatter.

1144 Dietary supplements labels database. National Library of Medicine (U.S.). 2007–. Bethesda, Md.: National Library of Medicine. http://dietarysupplements.nlm.nih.gov/dietary/.

Produced by National Library of Medicine (NLM) (427), Specialized Information Services (SIS); based on Dietary Supplements On-Line Database. Offers information on the ingredients of more than 2,000 selected brands of dietary supplements in the United States. Searchable by brand name, uses noted on the product, specific active ingredient, and manufacturer. Intended for researchers and consumers. Answers many questions users of dietary supplements might have concerning ingredients shown on labels of specific brands, chemical ingredients, animal products, proven medical benefits, toxicity of specific ingredients, etc. Ingredients of dietary supplements are linked to other NLM databases, e.g., MedlinePlus (463) and PubMed (432). Helpful FAQ section.

1145 International bibliographic information on dietary supplements (IBIDS) database. National Institutes of Health Office of Dietary Supplements. [1999]–. Bethesda, Md.: National Institutes of Health Office of Dietary Supplements. http://ods.od.nih.gov/Health_Information/IBIDS.aspx.

615.3280160285   RM258.5

Database produced by the Office of Dietary Supplements (ODS) (765) of the National Institutes of Health and maintained by the Food and Nutrition Information Center of the National Agricultural Library, U.S. Department of Agriculture.

Title varies: IBIDS: International Bibliographic Information on Dietary Supplements; IBIDS Database; NIH Office of Dietary Supplements IBIDS Database.

Provides citations to scientific literature on dietary supplements, including vitamins, minerals, botanical and herbal supplements, and other nutritional topics. Links are provided to ODS publications in PDF format and to other links in the field of dietetics. For scientists, researchers, and the general public. The ODS homepage also provides access to other NIH and USDA databases.

ODS also issues the annual bibliography *Annual bibliography of significant advances in dietary supplement research* (1097), presenting significant dietary supplement research.

1146 **NLM gateway.** National Library of Medicine (U.S.). 2000–.
Bethesda, Md.: National Library of Medicine. http://gateway.nlm.
nih.gov/.

RA11

Allows simultaneous searching of information resources at the National
Library of Medicine (NLM). Databases include MEDLINE (425)/PubMed
(432) and the NLM Catalog (482) as well as other resources, including
information on current clinical trials and consumer health information
(MedlinePlus [463]). Currently provides access to 21 databases and other
information resources (for a complete list of databases and other details,
see http://www.nlm.nih.gov/pubs/factsheets/gateway.html). An overview
of the search results is presented in several categories (bibliographic
resources, consumer health resources, and other information), with a
listing of the individual databases and the number of results within these
categories.

1147 **Nutrition abstracts and reviews series A.** CAB International.
1990–. [Wallingford, England, U.K.]: CAB International. http://
www.cabi.org/AbstractDatabases.asp?SubjectArea=&PID=79.

Vol. 1 (Oct. 1931) through v. 46 (1976), *Nutrition abstracts and reviews*
(NARA), Commonwealth Agricultural Bureau (CAB) International
(CABI). Split into ser. A (Human and Experimental) and ser. B (Livestock
Feeds and Feeding). Since 1977, available in print. A searchable online
back file, derived from *CAB abstracts*, is available going back to 1990; also
included in the full CAB Abstracts (1143) database, available though multiple vendors.

A searchable international abstract database that includes a variety
of biomedical and agricultural subject areas, with papers relevant to all
aspects of human nutrition selected from approx. 1,000 journals, books,
reports, and conferences. Covers techniques (analytical methodologies
for carbohydrates, fiber, lipids, proteins, etc.); foods (functional foods,
food additives, supplements; beverages, food processing, food contamination, etc.); physiological and biochemical aspects (endocrinology and
nutritional immunology, fasting, vitamins, phytochemicals, minerals,
etc.); nutrition and health (diet studies, infant feeding, sports nutrition,
nutritional status, etc.); clinical nutrition (e.g., malnutrition, obesity, food
allergies, cancer, etc.); and many other subjects.

1148 **PubMed.** U.S. National Center for Biotechnology Information,
National Library of Medicine, National Institutes of Health.

1996–. Bethesda, Md.: U.S. National Center for Biotechnology Information. http://www.ncbi.nlm.nih.gov/sites/entrez/.

PubMed®, developed and maintained by the National Center for Biotechnology Information (NCBI) at the National Library of Medicine® (NLM) (427). It is available via the NCBI Entrez (3) retrieval system. PubMed also provides access to the other Entrez molecular biology resources (*PubMed Overview*). Starting May 23, 2007, NCBI is changing to a new version of Entrez in a phased implementation (cf. Nahin AM. New and Improved PubMed®/Entrez and New URL *NLM tech. bull.*, 2007 May–Jun.; [356]: e4 http://www.nlm.nih.gov/pubs/techbull/mj07/mj07_issue_cover.html).

Provides a search interface for more than 16 million bibliographic citations and abstracts in the fields of medicine, nursing, dentistry, veterinary medicine, health care systems, and preclinical sciences. It provides access to articles indexed for MEDLINE® (425) and for selected life sciences journals. PubMed subsets found under the "Limits" tab are: MEDLINE and PubMed Central®, several journal groups (i.e., core clinical journals, dental journals, and nursing journals), and topical subsets (AIDS, bioethics, cancer, complementary medicine, history of medicine, space life sciences, systematic reviews, and toxicology). "Linkout" provides access to full-text articles.

For detailed information see the PubMed fact sheet at http://www.nlm.nih.gov/pubs/factsheets/pubmed.html. For a brief overview of searching PubMed, see the PubMed Quick Start at http://www.ncbi.nlm.nih.gov/books/bv.fcgi?rid=helppubmed.section.pubmedhelp.PubMed_Quick_Start. For details on the now completed OLDMEDLINE retrospective conversion projects, see http://www.nlm.nih.gov/pubs/techbull/so06/so06_oldmedline_status.html.

1149 USDA nutrient data laboratory. Nutrient Data Laboratory, U.S. Department of Agriculture. [199?]–. Beltsville, Md.: Nutrient Data Laboratory, U.S. Department of Agriculture. http://www.ars.usda.gov/ba/bhnrc/ndl.

612.3641.3

Its mission is "to develop authoritative food composition databases and state of the art methods to acquire, evaluate, compile and disseminate composition data on foods available in the United States."—*Main page.* Contains links to historical information of 115 years of USDA food composition tables (http://www.ars.usda.gov/Aboutus/docs.htm?docid=9418). Currently, the National Nutrient Data Bank contains information for approx. 130 nutrients for more than 7,000 foods. Its major database is USDA National Nutrient Database for Standard Reference (SR), release 19 (http://www.ars.usda.gov/Services/docs.htm?docid=8964; also online via Knovel [Norwich, N.Y.: Knovel, 2003–]), for determining the nutrient content of foods (published previously in print format in *Agricultural handbook* no. 8 and supplements and *Home and garden bulletin* no. 72). Also provides links to food composition information from other countries (e.g., Canada, Australia, New Zealand, and others), food consumption surveys, food labeling, general nutrition information (e.g., Nutrition.gov [718], Dietary Guidelines for Americans 2005 [Washington: U.S. Dept.of Health and Human Services; U.S. Dept. of Agriculture, 2005]), dietary supplements databases (USDA is working with the Office of Dietary Supplements and other federal agencies to develop a Dietary Supplement Ingredient Database [DSID] at http://www.ars.usda.gov/dsid), and other resources.

Internet Resources

1150 Nutrition.gov. Food and Nutrition Information Center. Beltsville, Md.: National Agricultural Library. http://www.nutrition.gov.

RA784

Maintained by Food and Nutrition Information Center (FNIC).

Access to information from across the federal government on food, food safety, nutrition, healthy eating, dietary supplements, and physical fitness. Includes specialized nutrition information for infants, children, teens, adult women and men, and seniors, as well as the latest nutrition-related news. Provides search capabilities and resource lists for different audiences, e.g., caregivers, consumers, health care workers, kids and teens, parents, researchers, and teachers. Healthier US (http://www.healthierus.gov) provides access to consumer resources concerning nutrition, physical fitness, and disease.

1151 Nutrition (MedlinePlus). National Library of Medicine (U.S.). 2000?–. Bethesda, Md.: U.S. National Library of Medicine, National Institutes of Health, Dept. of Health and Human Services. http://www.nlm.nih.gov/medlineplus/nutrition.html.

A Health Topic within MedlinePlus® (425).

Contents: Overviews; Latest news; Related issues; Health check tools; Tutorials; Clinical trials; Research; Journal articles; Directories; Organizations; Law and policy; Teenagers; Women.

Selected links to a wide range of nutrition-related information provided by government agencies, societies, professional associations, organizations, and foundations. Also provides links to related topics with separate pages in MedlinePlus, e.g., breast feeding, child nutrition, dietary fats, fiber, and protein, eating disorders, food safety, infant and toddler nutrition, obesity, vegetarian diets, and others. "Go Local" link helps to identify nutrition services and providers in the U.S.

1152 **The nutrition source.** Harvard School of Public Health. 2002–.
  Boston: Harvard School of Public Health. http://www.hsph.
  harvard.edu/nutritionsource/.

Contents: Interpreting News on Diet; Frequently Asked Questions; Ask the Expert; Food Pyramids; Fats and Cholesterol; Carbohydrates; Protein; Fiber; Fruits and Vegetables; Calcium and Milk; Alcohol; Vitamins; Healthy Weight; Exercise; Type 2 Diabetes; Food Service and Healthy Eating; More Information.

  "The aim of the Harvard School of Public Health Nutrition Source is to provide timely information on diet and nutrition for clinicians, allied health professionals, and the public. The contents of this Web site are not intended to offer personal medical advice."—*Main page*

1153 **Office of Dietary Supplements.** National Institutes of Health
  Office of Dietary Supplements. 1999–. Bethesda, Md.: National
  Institutes of Health Office of Dietary Supplements. http://dietary-
  supplements.info.nih.gov/index.aspx.

National Institutes of Health (NIH) Office of Dietary Supplements (ODS); U.S. Dept. of Agriculture (USDA).

  ODS homepage includes extensive health information on dietary supplement use and safety and nutrient recommendations. Provides access to NIH and USDA databases and research resources, such as the International Bibliographic Information on Dietary Supplements (IBIDS) database (1145), Computer Access to Research on Dietary Supplements (CARDS), Annual Bibliography of Significant Advances in Dietary Supplement Research (1097), USDA's National nutrient database for standard reference, and others made available via the USDA Nutrient Data Laboratory (1139). For health professionals, researchers, students, and health consumers.

1154 **USDA nutrient data laboratory.** Nutrient Data Laboratory, U.S.
  Department of Agriculture. [199?]–. Beltsville, Md.: Nutrient Data
  Laboratory, U.S. Department of Agriculture. http://www.ars.usda.
  gov/ba/bhnrc/ndl.

612.3641.3

NUTRITION

517

Its mission is "to develop authoritative food composition databases and state of the art methods to acquire, evaluate, compile and disseminate composition data on foods available in the United States."— *Main page*. Contains links to historical information of 115 years of USDA food composition tables (http://www.ars.usda.gov/Aboutus/docs. htm?docid=9418). Currently, the National Nutrient Data Bank contains information for approx. 130 nutrients for more than 7,000 foods. Its major database is USDA National Nutrient Database for Standard Reference (SR), release 19 (http://www.ars.usda.gov/Services/docs.htm?docid=8964; also online via Knovel [Norwich, N.Y.: Knovel, 2003–]), for determining the nutrient content of foods (published previously in print format in *Agricultural handbook* no. 8 and supplements and *Home and garden bulletin* no. 72). Also provides links to food composition information from other countries (e.g., Canada, Australia, New Zealand, and others), food consumption surveys, food labeling, general nutrition information (e.g., Nutrition.gov [718], Dietary Guidelines for Americans 2005 [Washington: U.S. Dept.of Health and Human Services; U.S. Dept. of Agriculture, 2005]), dietary supplements databases (USDA is working with the Office of Dietary Supplements and other federal agencies to develop a Dietary Supplement Ingredient Database [DSID] at http://www.ars.usda.gov/ dsid), and other resources.

Tables

1155 USDA nutrient data laboratory. Nutrient Data Laboratory, U.S. Department of Agriculture. [199?]–. Beltsville, Md.: Nutrient Data Laboratory, U.S. Department of Agriculture. http://www.ars.usda. gov/ba/bhnrc/ndl.
612.3641.3

Its mission is "to develop authoritative food composition databases and state of the art methods to acquire, evaluate, compile and disseminate composition data on foods available in the United States."—*Main page*. Contains links to historical information of 115 years of USDA food composition tables (http://www.ars.usda.gov/Aboutus/docs.htm?docid=9418). Currently, the National Nutrient Data Bank contains information for approximately 130 nutrients for more than 7,000 foods. Its major database is USDA National Nutrient Database for Standard Reference (SR), release 19 (http://www.ars.usda.gov/Services/docs.htm?docid=8964; also online via Knovel [Norwich, N.Y.: Knovel, 2003–]), for determining the nutrient content of foods (published previously in print format in *Agricultural handbook* no. 8 and supplements and *Home and garden bulletin* no. 72). Also provides links to food composition information from other countries (e.g., Canada, Australia, New Zealand, and others), food consumption surveys, food labeling, general nutrition information (e.g., Nutrition.gov [718], Dietary Guidelines for Americans 2005 [Washington: U.S. Dept.of Health and Human Services; U.S. Dept. of Agriculture, 2005]), dietary supplements databases (USDA is working with the Office of Dietary Supplements and other federal agencies to develop a Dietary Supplement Ingredient Database [DSID] at http://www.ars.usda.gov/dsid), and other resources.

10 > PHARMACOLOGY AND PHARMACEUTICAL SCIENCES

1156 **DailyMed.** National Library of Medicine (U.S.). [2005]–. Bethesda, Md.: U.S. National Library of Medicine, National Institutes of Health, Dept. of Health and Human Services. http://dailymed.nlm.nih.gov/.

A searchable website with growing content, providing health consumers, students, and health professionals with online information on prescription medications and labeling from FDA-approved medication package inserts. Each entry gives a description of the medication, its clinical pharmacology, indications and usage, warnings and precautions, dosage and administration, adverse reactions, etc.

Additional consumer health information about U.S. drugs provided by NLM can be found in *MedlinePlus* (463) under headings such as drugs, supplements, and herbal information, drug safety, medicines, over-the-counter medicines, pain relievers, and possibly others. PubMed (432) and its MEDLINE (425) subset and TOXLINE (1578), can be searched for references to professional journal articles.

1157 **Drug abuse (MedlinePlus).** National Library of Medicine (U.S.). 2000?–. Bethesda, Md.: National Library of Medicine. http://www.nlm.nih.gov/medlineplus/drugabuse.html.

A Health Topic in MedlinePlus (463).

Contents: Overviews; Latest News; Diagnosis/Symptoms; Treatment; Prevention/Screening; Specific Conditions; Related Issues; Pictures and Photographs; Games; Clinical Trials; Research; Journal Articles; Dictionaries/Glossaries; Directories; Organizations; Newsletters/Print Publications; Law and Policy; Statistics; Children; Teenagers; Men; Women; Seniors; Other Languages.

Collection of links on substance abuse from a variety of government agencies, professional associations, and organizations, such as the National Institute on Drug Abuse (1505), the Office of National Drug Control, Substance Abuse and Mental Health Services Administration (SAMHSA) (769), National Library of Medicine (429), American Medical Association (451), American Academy of Family Physicians (448), and others. Also links to related MedlinePlus topics, e.g., alcoholism, prescription drug abuse, and substance abuse, to name a few.

1158 **Electronic orange book.** Center for Drug Evaluation and Research. 1999–. [Rockville, Md.]: U.S. Department of Health and Human Services; Food and Drug Administration. http://purl.access.gpo. gov/GPO/LPS1445.

615.10285

Title varies: Approved Drug Products with Therapeutic Equivalence Evaluation Orange Book.

"Since the 25th edition, the Annual Edition and monthly Cumulative Supplements are published in electronic Portable Document Format (PDF). The PDF annual and cumulative supplements duplicate previous paper formats. Over time, there will be an archive page of Annual Editions and each year's December Cumulative Supplement that will provide a history of approved drug products' approvals and changes."—*Publications page*

Directory of approved drug products with therapeutic equivalence evaluations. Searchable by active ingredient, proprietary name, patents, applicant holder, and application number. Identifies drugs on the market that meet safety and efficacy requirements. Provides information to states about generic drugs that are acceptable for substitution of drug products. The following site provides additional information: http://www.fda.gov/cder/ob/obfaqs.htm.

1159 **Facts and comparisons 4.0 online.** Facts and Comparisons. 2001–. Philadelphia: Wolters Kluwer Health. http://online. factsandcomparisons.com/.

Also called F & C 4.0. More product details at http://www.factsandcomparisons.com/.

Provides access to several drug information resources and the ability to search across the different publications : *A to Z drug facts* (1204), *Drug facts and comparisons* (1215), *Drug identifier*, *Drug interaction facts* (1217), *Drug interaction facts: Herbal supplements and food*, "Investigational drugs" from *Drug facts and comparisons*, *MedFacts* (patient information), *Nonprescription drug therapy*, *Review of natural products* (St. Louis: Facts and Comparisons, 1996–), and several other resources.

1160 Medicinal plants of the world: Chemical constituents, traditional and modern medicinal uses. 2nd ed. Ivan A. Ross. ill. (some color). Totowa, N.J.: Humana Press, 2003–. ISBN: 1588292819.

615.32   RS164.R676

1st ed., 1999–2001.

This rev. ed. provides information on traditional medicinal uses, chemical constituents, pharmacological activities, clinical trials, color illustrations, Latin names, botanical descriptions, and how each medicinal plant is used around the world. Cross-references common names to country and scientific name. Index includes terms, symptoms, and treatments as well as bibliographies. Available as an e-book via netLibrary.

Bibliography

1161 Basic resources for pharmacy education. Leslie Ann Bowman, Barbara Nanstiel, American Association of Colleges of Pharmacy. 2009. Alexandria, Va.: American Association of Colleges of Pharmacy. http://www.aacp.org/governance/SECTIONS/libraryeducationalresources/Documents/2009 Basic Resources.pdf.

"A guide for those developing or maintaining the library collections that serve colleges of pharmacy. The books and other works recommended in this list are suitable for all pharmacy college libraries, but all pharmacy college libraries need not purchase every title in the list."—*Main page*

A service project of the Libraries/Educational Resources Section of the American Association of Colleges of Pharmacy. This bibliography and other reference resources for pharmacy faculty, students, and librarians are accessible via the AACP website (http://www.aacp.org/).

An older edition (Oxford; New York: Oxford University Press, 2003) of this work was previously included in *Guide to reference*.

1162 **Recent dissertations in the medical humanities.** Jonathon Erlen, University of Pittsburgh Health Sciences Library System. 2001–. Pittsburgh: Health Sciences Library, University of Pittsburgh Medical Center. http://www.hsls.pitt.edu/guides/histmed/researchresources/dissertations/.

Provides a monthly current awareness service for selected recent medical dissertation and theses. Arranged by topics, currently covers the following areas: AIDS (social and historical contexts); alternative medicine (social and historical contexts); art and medicine; biomedical ethics; history of medicine prior to 1800; history of medicine and health care; history of science and technology; literature/theater and medicine; nursing history; pharmacy/pharmacology and history; philosophy and medicine; psychiatry/psychology and history; public health/international health; religion and medicine; women's health and history. To view complete citations, abstracts, and full-text of dissertations requires a subscription to Proquest Dissertations and Theses (PQDT) (Ann Arbor, Mich.: ProQuest).

Dictionaries

1163 **Concise dictionary of pharmacological agents: Properties and synonyms.** Ian Morton, Judith Hall. viii, 342 p. Boston: Kluwer Academic, 1999. ISBN: 0751404993.

615.103   RS51.M67

Based on the three-volume *Dictionary of pharmacological agents*, publ. 1997, it is "a volume encompassing material that hitherto could only be gathered from a well-stocked library."—*Introd.* Provides an A–Z listing of drug names (details on drug names, their alternative names, alternative spellings, alternative chemical forms, with cross-references) and families of pharmacologically active agents. "Appendix A: Glossary" contains approx. 3,000 terms and acronyms; Appendix B consists of tables: (1) amino acid abbreviations (common natural); (2) amino acid abbreviations (found in literature—related and unnatural), and (3) Greek and Latin prefixes. Main articles listed alphabetically in brackets under British Approved Names (BAN), with United States Adopted Name (USAN), Japanese Accepted Name (JAN), and International Nonproprietary Name (INN). Other agents also include standard names in brackets, such as American National Standards Institute (ANSI), British Standards Institution (BSI), and International Standards Organization (ISO). For pharmacologists, medicinal chemists, and graduate students in these areas of research and study and also others in related biomedical sciences. Available online via Knovel.

1164 Dictionary for clinical trials. 2nd ed. Simon Day. xii, 249 p., ill. Chichester, U.K.; Hoboken, N.J.: John Wiley & Sons, 2007. ISBN: 0470058161.
610.724   R853.C55D39
1st ed., 1999.

This rev. and expanded ed. includes definitions for terms and short phrases from a variety of fields (e.g., medicine, statistics, epidemiology, ethics, and others) and from publications related to clinical trials, such as trial protocols, regulatory guidelines, reports, etc. Cross-references, line figures, and graphs. Available online via netLibrary.

1165 A dictionary of natural products: Terms in the field of pharmacognosy relating to natural medicinal and pharmaceutical materials and the plants, animals, and minerals from which they are derived. [2nd ed.] George Macdonald Hocking. xxix, 994 p., ill. Medford, N.J.: Plexus, 1997. ISBN: 0937548316.
615.32103   QK99.H69
Revised and updated edition of *Dictionary of terms in pharmacognosy and other divisions of economic botany*.

Subtitle describes the areas covered in this resource. Provides data on chemical, physical, and biological properties of compounds, giving their systematic and common names, their structure, and connection tables. Includes bibliographic references (p. 891–970).

Available online via CRCnetBASE (Boca Raton, Fla.; London: CRC Press; Taylor and Francis).

1166 Dictionary of pharmacoepidemiology. Bernard Bégaud. x, 171 p.
Chichester, [England, U.K.]; New York: Wiley, 2000. ISBN: 0471803618.
615.103   RM302.5.B443
English translation of Bernard Bégaud's *Dictionnaire de pharmaco-épidémiologie*, 1998.

Online access available from WileyInterScience Online Books (http://www3.interscience.wiley.com/cgi-bin/bookhome/93516142) and also via netLibrary.

As defined in this dictionary, pharmacoepidemiology is the "study of interactions between drugs and populations, or more specifically, the study of the therapeutic effect(s), risk and use of drugs, usually in large populations, using epidemiology and methods of reasoning," and the work is written for "regulatory authorities, pharmaceutical physicians, lawyers, pharmacists, researchers, evaluators and students."—*Foreword*. Complements epidemiology dictionaries.

1167 A dictionary of pharmacology and allied topics. 2nd ed.
  D. R. Laurence, John Carpenter. xi, 373 p. Amsterdam, [The Netherlands]; New York: Elsevier, 1998.
615.103   RS51.L38

1st ed., 1994, had title, *A dictionary of pharmacology and clinical drug evaluation.*
    Includes currently accepted usage for pharmacological terms and relevant terminology from other disciplines (e.g., ethics, law, social policy, statistics), with etymology for most terms, as well as terms used by official regulatory authorities. Does not include individual drugs. Intended for basic and clinical pharmacologists and others involved in clinical drug evaluation.

1168 Dictionary of pharmacovigilance. Amer Alghabban. ix, 527 p.
  London; Chicago: Pharmaceutical Press, 2004. ISBN: 0853695164.
615.7042   RM302.5.A43

Compilation of the clinical, technical, and regulatory terminology related to pharmacovigilance (or drug monitoring), which can be defined as the detection, assessment, understanding, and prevention of adverse effects of medicines and efforts to minimize risks posed by drugs to patients. International in scope. Entries include drugs, regulatory bodies, and pharmaceutical legislation.

1169 Dictionary of pharmacy. Dennis B. Worthen, Julian H. Fincher.
  xiii, 528 p. New York: Pharmaceutical Products Press, 2004. ISBN: 0789023288.
615.103   RS51.D482

Comprehensive list of terms from pharmacy and also terminology relevant to pharmacy from several other disciplines. A–Z arrangement; cross-references (see, see also, contrast, and compare). In separate sections, includes abbreviations; Latin and Greek terms; weights and measures; practice standards; the code of ethics for pharmacists; and lists of professional associations, organizations, and colleges and schools of pharmacy in the United States and Canada. Resource for pharmacy students, faculty, and practicing pharmacists.

1170 Drugs: Synonyms and properties. 2nd ed. G. W. A. Milne. xxi, 1108 p. Aldershot, [England, U.K.]: Ashgate, 2002. ISBN: 0566084910.

1st ed., 2000. "An international guide to 10,000 drugs."—*Cover*

Provides basic drug information. Organized by therapeutic categories, includes drugs, drug synonyms, and trade names. Under each therapeutic category, drugs are listed alphabetically by the U.S. Adopted Names (USAN). For each drug, the following information is included: chemical name, trade name, generic name, synonyms, registry and *Merck index* (Whitehouse Station, N.J.: Merck, 2006) number, molecular formula, melting and boiling points, various physical properties, manufacturer, and supplier directory. Three indexes: Chemical Abstracts Service (CAS) registry number, European Inventory of Existing Commercial Substances (EINECS) number, and a master index of chemical and proprietary names. Similar in content to other important drug information resources, such as the *Merck index* (Whitehouse Station, N.J.: Merck, 2006), *Physicians' desk reference* (Oradell, N.J.: Thomson Healthcare, 1974–), and *Organic-chemical drugs and their synonyms* (1173), for example.

1171 Encyclopedic reference of traditional Chinese medicine: [A manual from A–Z, symptoms, therapy, and herbal remedies]. Xinrong Yang. 660 p., color ill. Berlin; New York: Springer, 2003. ISBN: 3540428461.

610.951   R601.D538

Introduction to traditional Chinese medicine with its long history. "Owing to the Traditional Chinese Medicine literatures were written in the classical literary style and the translation into English of most of their terms was not standardized and normalized, the translation of these terms remains to be discussed by specialists and linguists. Many terms of diseases in this book have to use the terms of Western Medicine in Latin. Some terms have to be transliterated into English."—*Pref.* Acupuncture terms from WHO's 1984 publication on "Standard Acupuncture Nomenclature" (1993 ed. of *Standard acupuncture nomenclature: A brief explanation of 361 classical acupuncture point names and their multilingual comparative list* is available at http://whqlibdoc.who.int/wpro/-1993/9290611057.pdf).

Provides 5,000 entries with concise annotations, listing, as appropriate for a particular entry, symptoms, pathogenesis, diseases, therapeutic principle, herbal and other drugs. Alphabetical arrangement. Color ill.

1172 **Mosby's dental drug reference.** 8th ed. Arthur H. Jeske. 1415 p. St. Louis: Mosby, Inc., an affiliate of Elsevier, Inc., 2007. ISBN: 9780323052665.

RK701

1st ed., 1994; 7th ed., 2005.

Alphabetical arrangement of drugs that dental patients may be taking, listed by generic name and indexed by brand name, with drug monograph information presented in a consistent format. Provides information on side effects, precautions, contraindications, and drug interactions. Also includes alternative therapies. Therapeutic and pharmacologic index. Accompanied by CD-ROM that contains color images of conditions resulting from drugs patients are taking, and also customizable patient handouts. Intended for dental professionals, but also useful for health consumers.

1173 **Organic-chemical drugs and their synonyms.** 9th ed. Martin Negwer, Hans-Georg Scharnow. 7 v. (xvii, 5656 p.). Weinheim, Germany: Wiley-VCH, 2007. ISBN: 3527319395.

615.19

6th ed., 1987, is the revised and enlarged ed. and first English translation of *Organisch-chemische Arzneimittel und ihre Synonyme*, 5th ed., 1978; 8th ed., 2001.

The 9th ed. is described by the publisher as a completely revised and extensively enlarged edition.

Contents: v. 1–5, organic-chemical drugs and their synonyms; v. 6, synonym index (pt. 1: A–S); v. 7, synonym index (pt. 2: T–Z); group index; CAS number index.

This edition compiles data on 20,000 drugs, with many newly developed drugs and biopharmaceuticals. Entries include CAS registry number, structural formula, references, synonyms, and use.

1174 **Pharmaceutical medicine dictionary.** Amer Alghabban. 390 p. Edinburgh, [Scotland, U.K.]; New York: Churchill Livingstone, 2001. ISBN: 044306475X.

618.103   RS192.A445

Contains terminology related to pharmaceutical medicine and the drug development and marketing process. Available online via Credo Reference (London; Boston: Credo Reference).

1175 USP dictionary of USAN and international drug names. United States Pharmacopeial Convention. Rockville, Md.: United States Pharmacopeial Convention, 1995–. ISSN: 1076-4275.

615.1014   RS55.U54

The United States Adopted Names (USAN) Council, sponsored by the American Medical Association (AMA), the United States Pharmacopeial Convention (USP), and the American Pharmacists Association (APhA), selects appropriate and unique names for drugs. Each vol. is cumulative from June 1961 to June of the year preceding publication. "FDA-recognized, cumulative source of drug USANs."—*Publ. description*

1961–93 had title: *USAN and the USP dictionary of drug names.* Description based on 42nd ed., 2006, "the authorized list of established names for drugs in the United States of America" (*t.p.*), which supersedes the 2005 ed. and all earlier editions. Supplements are published bimonthly in the "Nomenclature" section of the *Pharmacopeial forum* (PF), accessible via the USP website at http://www.usp.org/.

Comprehensive source of generic and brand drug names. Arranged alphabetically by generic, trade, or chemical name or drug code designated number. Entries give USAN, year published as USAN, pronunciation, official compendium in which title occurs, molecular formula and weight, chemical names, CAS registry number(s), international nonproprietary name (INN), pharmacologic and/or therapeutic category, brand name(s), manufacturer, drug code designations, and graphic formula. Appendixes include, e.g., listings of drugs of brand names for USAN and other nonproprietary names, categories of pharmacological activity, molecular formulas, and code designations.

Directories

1176 World list of pharmacy schools. Welsh School of Pharmacy, Cardiff University. 2001–. Cardiff, Wales: Welsh School of Pharmacy. http://www.cardiff.ac.uk/phrmy/subsites/WWW-WSP/.

Contains address and other contact information of approx. 900 schools of pharmacy worldwide, listed by country. Entries contain hyperlinks for pharmacy schools that have their own websites. Provides a separate list of pharmacy school URLs at http://www.cardiff.ac.uk/phrmy/subsites/ WWW-WSP/SoPSchoolsURLs.html.

Dispensatories and Pharmacopoeias

1177 American drug index. Norman F. Billups, Shirley M. Billups. Philadelphia: Lippincott, 1956–. ISSN: 0065-8111.

615   RS355.A48

Description based on 54th ed., 2010.

A listing of pharmaceuticals by generic, brand, and chemical name, with brief information about manufacturer, form, size, dosage, and use. This edition has 15 major sections. The main section, "Drug monographs," is arranged alphabetically, with many cross-references. Generic names are in lowercase, and all brand-name products upper/lowercase as appropriate. Other sections include, for example, common abbreviations used in chemotherapy regimens, common systems of weight and measure, official container requirements for U.S.P. drugs, and "drug names that look alike and sound alike," and discontinued drugs.

1178 British national formulary. British Medical Association. ill. (some color). London: British Medical Association; Royal Pharmaceutical Society of Great Britain, 1957–. ISSN: 0260-535X.

Joint publication of the British Medical Association and the Royal Pharmaceutical Society of Great Britain.

Prescribing, dispensing, and administering of medications generally prescribed in the United Kingdom, with mention of dosage, side effects, contraindications, etc. Drugs are listed by generic name (i.e., BAN), followed by brand name(s) available in the United Kingdom, with information on strength, dosage, and price. Index of manufacturers and general index. Available online as part of MedicinesComplete (1236).

Also available, with some restrictions, online from the publisher (http://www.bnf.org), via CD-ROM, and as an intranet version.

1179 The British pharmacopœia. General Medical Council (Great Britain). ill. London: Constable, 1864–. ISSN: 1354-6643.

615.11   RS141.3.B75

Published continuously but irregularly since 1864 in a variety of formats.

Description based on 2007 ed., 5 v. (publ. 2006), with a separate

Veterinary volume, a CD-ROM, and access to a regularly updated website available to purchasers of the print edition (http://www.pharmacopoeia. co.uk).

Contents: v. 1, "Introduction," "General notices," "Monographs: Medicinal and pharmaceutical substances (A–I)"; v. 2, "General notices," "Monographs: Medicinal and pharmaceutical substances (J–Z)"; v. 3, "General notices," "Formulated preparations," "Blood-related products," "Immunological products," "Radiopharmaceutical preparations," "Surgical materials," "Homeopathic preparations"; v. 4, "General notices," "Infrared reference spectra," appendixes, supplementary chapters, index; [v. 5], "BP (vet)"; [v. 6], Complete edition CD; [v. 7], "Chemical reference substances catalogue."

Authoritative reference source for U.K. medicinal substances and pharmaceutical products and an official collection of quality standards. Essential resource for those involved in pharmaceutical research and development, manufacturing, and testing. Further BP details at http://www.britpharm.com/about.cfm.

1180 European pharmacopoeia. Council of Europe. Sainte Ruffine
    [France]: Maisonneuve, 1969–.

615.114   RS141.28.E95

Description based on 5th ed., 2004 (2 v.), and suppl. 5.1–5.8; also available as a CD-ROM version.

Legally binding standards for medicines in the countries that are members of the European Pharmacopoeia Convention. Contains the different types of active substances used to prepare pharmaceutical products: 1,800 monographs; 268 general methods, described and illustrated by figures or chromatograms; and descriptions of 2,210 reagents. Further details at http://www.edqm.eu/site/page_582.php.

**1181 The International pharmacopoeia: Pharmacopoea
    internationalis.** 4th ed. World Health Organization. 2 v. Geneva,
    [Switzerland]: World Health Organization, 2006.

Title varies: 1st ed., 1951–59, *Pharmacopoeia internationalis*; 2nd ed., 1967, *Specifications for the quality control of pharmaceutical preparation*; 3rd ed., 1988–94, 5 v.

Contents: v. 1, general notices and monographs for pharmaceutical substances A–O; v. 2, monographs for pharmaceutical substances P–Z; dosage forms; radiopharmaceutical preparations.

Rev. ed., with consolidation of five volumes into two volumes, with new and revised monographs. Recommends specifications for quality control of pharmaceutical preparation that can serve as references in any country. Includes mainly recommendations on widely-used medicines important to WHO (951) health programs to "achieve a wide global uniformity of quality specifications for selected pharmaceutical products, excipients, and dosage forms."—*Publ. website.* Also available electronically on CD-ROM.

Further information and related links at http://www.who.int/medicines/publications/pharmacopoeia/overview/en/in dex.html, including a link to the current version of *WHO model lists of essential medicines.*

1182 Martindale: The complete drug reference. William Martindale, Kathleen Parfitt. London: Pharmaceutical Press, 1999–. ISSN: 0263-5364.

RS141.3.M4

1st ed. (1883) through 31st ed. (1996) had title *The extra pharmacopoeia: Martindale.*

First through 15th eds. (1883–1912) comp. by W. H. Martindale and W. W. Westcott. Description based on 34th ed., 2005 (ed. Sean C. Sweetman).

"The aim of Martindale is to provide healthcare professionals with unbiased evaluated information on drugs and medicines used throughout the world."—*Pref.* International in scope, covering prescription and nonprescription drugs. In three parts: (1) "Monographs on drugs and ancillary substances containing data on 5,300 drug monographs (from analgesics to vaccines)"; (2) "Supplementary drugs and other substances, containing information on new and investigational drugs and obsolete drugs still of interest"; (3) "Preparations, with brief details of official and proprietary preparations." Includes a directory of 9,500 manufacturers. General index covers drugs and diseases.

Available online as part of Micromedex Healthcare Series (1084) and MedicinesComplete (1236). Both of these resources contain several additional drug resources. A CD-ROM edition is also available.

1183 National drug code directory. Center for Drug Evaluation and Research (U.S.). 2001–. Rockville, Md.: Center for Drug Evaluation and Research. http://www.fda.gov/cder/ndc/database/default.htm.

RS353

Continues print ed., published 1969–95. Web access available since 2001.

The National Drug Code (NDC) system provides product identification for human drugs, i.e., prescription drugs and selected over-the-counter products, including foreign drug products with commercial distribution in the United States. Searchable by proprietary name, NDC number (unique 10-digit, 3-segment number), active ingredient, or firm name. Background information is provided at http://www.fda.gov/cder/ndc/index.htm, and further information about the NDC system can be found at http://www.fda.gov/cder/ndc/database/faq.htm.

1184 Pharmacopoeia of the People's Republic of China. English ed. Zhonghua Renmin Gongheguo wei sheng bu yao dian wei yuan hui. 2 v. Beijing, [China]: Chemical Industry Press, 2000. ISBN: 7502529810.

RS141.64.C5413

Rev. ed.

Also called *Chinese Pharmacopoeia 2000*, abbreviated as *Ch. P 2000*.

Contents: "Membership of the 7th Pharmacopoeia Commission of the People's Republic of China"; "Editorial Board of the Pharmacopoeia of the People's Republic of China (Engl. Edition)"; "Preface"; "History of the Pharmacopoeia of the People's Republic of China; Additions"; "Omissions, General Notices; Monographs, pt. 1: Chinese materia medica, oils, fats, etc."; pt. 2: "Traditional Chinese patent medicine and simple preparations"; appendixes; index.

Official compendium on drugs, covering traditional Chinese medicines and most of the Western medicines. Contains 2,691 new and revised monographs (962 in v. 1 and 1,699 in v. 2) and a number of new and revised appendixes. Entries provide a description of the drug or substance, identification, information on reference standards and testing methods for purity, dosage, precaution, storage, and strength for each drug.

1185 Pharmacopoeias and related literature in Britain and America, 1618–1847. David L. Cowen. viii, 296 p., ill., maps. Aldershot, [England,U.K.]; Burlington, Vt.: Ashgate/Variorum, 2001. ISBN: 0860788423.

615.114109   RS141.3.C675

Bibliographic and historical studies, previously scattered in a variety of publications, giving "evidence of the tremendous influence that British pharmacopoeial literature exerted on the Continent, on America, and on far reaches of the Empire."—*Pref.*

1186 The United States pharmacopeia. 20th rev. ed. United States
Pharmacopeial Convention. ill. Rockville, Md.: United States
Pharmacopeial Convention, 1979–. ISSN: 0195-7996.

615.1173   RS141.2.P5

Supersedes *The pharmacopoeia of the United States of America* and *The
national formulary*. Merger of *Pharmacopoeia of the United States* and
American Pharmaceutical Association national formulary. The combination of the two compendia in one volume (beginning with the 30th ed.
[2007] in 3 v.) is entitled *The United States pharmacopeia–national formulary (USP-NF)*.

United States Pharmacopeial Convention (USPC); United States
Pharmacopeia (USP); National Formulary (NF).

Kept up to date between revisions by supplements. Available in print,
CD, and Internet versions. Also available in a Spanish-language edition
(print only): *Farmacopea de los Estados Unidos de América. Formulario
nacional*.

Description based on the three-volume *USP31-NF26* 2008 print ed.,
with subtitle *The official compendia of standards*.

Contents: v. 1, table of contents; front matter; USP general notices;
general chapters TOC; general chapters; reagents; reference tables;
dietary supplements; NF general notices; NF monographs; complete
index; v. 2, table of contents; general chapters TOC; USP general notices;
USP monographs A–L; complete index; v. 3, table of contents; general
chapters TOC; USP general notices; USP monographs M–Z; complete
index.

An official compendium of drug information of the USPC, which is
responsible for setting standards, test procedures, and specifications for
drugs, biologics, dietary supplements, medical devices, and other health
care products. The NF includes standards for excipients (inactive ingredients), botanicals, and other ingredients used in drug preparations. The
USP (U.S. Pharmacopeia) (1188) website and Frequently Asked Questions
about USP-NF (http://www.usp.org/USPNF/faq.html?USP_Print) provide further information.

A related product is *USP dictionary of USAN and international drug
names* (1175).

1187 USP DI. United States Pharmacopeial Convention. Greenwood
Village, Colo.: Thomson Micromedex, 1982–. ISSN: 0740-6916.

615.1   RM300.U83

1980–81 ed. had title: *United States pharmacopeia dispensing information: USP DI*. Since 1982, *USP DI®* (United States Pharmacopeial Convention Drug Information), issued in three volumes. Subtitle varies. Publ. varies: since 1998 publ. by Thomson Micromedex.

Description based on 27th ed., 2007, 3 v.: v. 1, *Drug information for the health care professional*; v. 2, *Advice for the patient®: Drug information in lay language*; v. 3, *Approved drug products and legal requirements*. Vol. 1 and 2 are also available online via Micromedex® Healthcare Series (1084). However, title of v. 2 of the online edition was changed in 2007 to *Detailed drug information for the consumer™*.

"The drug information in the *USP DI* represents the evidence-based conclusions of 35 expert advisory panels who have meticulously reviewed all material to ensure its accuracy and currency."—*Pref*. Vol. 1 lists DI monographs in alphabetic order by chemical name, with information on use, pharmacology, precautions, side effects, dosage information, etc. The index includes established names, cross-references by brand names (U.S. and Canadian), and older nonproprietary names. Vol. 2 is written for consumers in "patient-friendly language" and printed in large type. Includes numerous appendixes, including "precaution listings" (e.g., pregnancy, pediatrics, geriatrics, dental, athletes). Vol. 3 answers legal and regulatory questions, and questions about discontinued drugs. Also addresses generic substitution for brand names and provides extensive information from the FDA, including its Electronic Orange Book: Approved Drug Products with Therapeutic Equivalence Evaluations (1158).

1188 USP (U.S. Pharmacopeia). United States Pharmacopeial Convention. 1997–. Rockville, Md.: United States Pharmacopeial Convention. http://www.usp.org/.

Contents: About USP; USP-NF; Food Chemicals Codex (1127); Pending and Non-U.S. standards; Reference standards; USP Verified; Education; Healthcare Quality and Information; Worldwide Activities; Meeting; Products.

The United States Pharmacopeial Convention (USP) sets standards for medications sold in the United States. This website provides an overview of USP and its history (timeline 1820–2002; http://www.usp.org/aboutUSP/history.html), the USP-NF online (http://www.usp.org/USPNF/; see also related record for the United States Pharmacopeia [1186]), and other publications; reference standards, patient safety programs; development of health care information; and other activities. Extensive FAQ section for the USP-NF online (http://www.usp.org/USPNF/faq.html) provides information about available formats, special features of the online edition, differences between the editions, its legal status, many other related topics. Information is presented for several different categories of users, including consumers, pharmacists, veterinary medicine professionals, manufacturers, and others.

Encyclopedias

1189 The encyclopedia of addictive drugs. Richard Lawrence Miller. 491 p. Westport, Conn.: Greenwood Press, 2002. ISBN: 0313318077.

615.78   RM316.M555

Contents: Introduction; Drug types; Alphabetical listing of drugs; Sources for more information; Drug name index; Subject index. Provides non-technical description of approx. 130 addictive drugs, including both pharmaceutical and natural products and aspects of drug abuse. Alphabetical listing of substances, with pronunciation, alternative names (including street names), legal status (federal schedule status; discussion of schedules and scheduling), historical and present uses and misuses, abuse factors, interactions with other drugs, and findings of cancer risks and birth defects. Also includes a section on drug types in general categories. List of print and electronic sources with further information. For general readers.
Available online via netLibrary.

1190 Encyclopedia of biopharmaceutical statistics. 2nd ed., rev. and expanded. Shein-Chung Chow. viii, 1055 p., ill. New York: Marcel Dekker, 2003. ISBN: 0824742613.

615.190727   RM301.25.E53

Provides a summary of regulatory requirements and statistical methods in biopharmaceutical research and development. Includes 72 alphabetically-arranged entries on the drug review and approval process in biopharmaceutical research and development, and current standards and best practices in the clinical, laboratory, manufacturing fields, statistical design, investigation, and analysis. Also available as an e-book.

1191 Encyclopedia of clinical pharmacy. Joseph T. DiPiro, American College of Clinical Pharmacy. x, 933 p., ill., port. New York: M. Dekker, 2003. ISBN: 0824707524.

RS51.E48

Collaboration of the American College of Clinical Pharmacy (ACCP) and the American Society of Health-System Pharmacists (ASHP).

Contains procedures, consensus statements; practice guidelines; regulatory standards for pharmaceutical care; health service delivery models; ethical and legal issues and controversies related to clinical pharmacy; and information on electronic prescription, educational and training programs, and other relevant topics relating to clinical pharmaceutical practice. Each article contains references. Also available in an online version.

For pharmacists, other health professionals, and students. Appropriate for academic libraries and drug information centers. Also available as an e-book.

1192 **Encyclopedia of clinical toxicology: A comprehensive guide and reference to the toxicology of prescription and OTC drugs, chemicals, herbals, plants, fungi, marine life, reptiles and insect venoms, food ingredients, clothing, and environmental toxins.** Irving S. Rossoff. xiv, 1507 p. Boca Raton, Fla.: Parthenon, 2002. ISBN: 1842141015.

615.9003   RA1193.R67

Approx. 6,000 alphabetically-arranged entries on toxic substances that adversely affect or destroy health or cause death. Mainly human data, with data on animals where insufficient data on human toxicity are available. Entries mention synonyms and use, toxic effects, and treatment, where appropriate. An appendix, "Alternative nomenclature," functions as an index.

1193 **Encyclopedia of common natural ingredients used in food, drugs, and cosmetics.** 2nd ed. Albert Y. Leung, Steven Foster. xxxv, 649 p. New York: Wiley, 1996. ISBN: 0471508268.

660.63   QD415.A25L48

1st ed., 1980.

Provides data on approx. 500 natural ingredients. Updates all entries of the previous ed. and includes a new category, Health Foods/Herbal Teas. Covers the identification, processing, preparation, and use for each ingredient. Excludes prescription drugs and medicinal herbs not readily available in commerce.

Arrangement is by common name. Entries give Latin name, synonyms, general description, chemical composition, pharmacology or biological activities, uses, commercial preparations, and references.

Includes a new classification for Chinese medicinal herbs, published for the first time in English. Glossary of commonly encountered terms used in the botanical industry. Indexed.

1194 Encyclopedia of dietary supplements. Paul M. Coates. xviii, 819 p., ill. New York: Marcel Dekker, 2005. ISBN: 0824755049.

613.2 RM258.5.E53

"The goal is to provide readers with comprehensive yet accessible, information on the current state of science for individual supplement ingredients and extracts."—*Pref.* Includes commonly used supplements, including vitamins, minerals, and other ingredients found in foods, and also natural products, such as herb extracts. Alphabetically-arranged entries include basic information about each substance and its regulatory status. References to the scientific literature or evidence to support claims of benefit are provided. For clinicians, researchers, health care professionals, and consumers. Available both in print and online, with updates at the publisher's website. Other titles, for example, *Guide to understanding dietary supplements* (New York: Haworth Press, 2003), *Mosby's handbook of herbs and natural supplements* (St. Louis: Mosby, 2004), and *PDR for nutritional supplements* (1246), may also be useful to health professionals and consumers.

1195 Encyclopedic reference of molecular pharmacology. Stefan Offermanns, Walter Rosenthal. xxii, 1115 p., ill. (some color). Berlin; New York: Springer, 2004. ISBN: 3540428437.

615.703 RM301.65.E53

With continually expanding knowledge of the molecular basis of drug actions, pharmacogenomics, and pharmacogenetics, this reference book provides up-to-date information on the molecular mechanisms of drug action. Alphabetically-arranged entries, with essays describing groups of drugs and drug targets, cellular processes, and pathological conditions and how they can be influenced by drugs. Complemented by 1,600 keywords, tables, color figures, and cross-references. Drugs are listed in an appendix, not in the entries. Also listed in the appendix are, for example, tables listing proteins (such as receptors and transporters) and ion channels. Accompanied by a CD-ROM that provides the full text and facilitates searching. Written for scientists, advanced students, and informed laypeople. Available online via Springer eReference.

1196 Meyler's side effects of drugs: The international encyclopedia of adverse drug reactions and interactions. M. N. G. Dukes. ill. Amsterdam, [The Netherlands]; New York: Elsevier Science B.V., 1975–. ISSN: 0376-7396.

RM302.5.S52

Description based on 15th ed., 2006. 6 v. Ed. Jeffrey K. Aronson. Includes most of the content of *Side effects of drugs annual*, 23rd to 27th ed. Referred to as SED *(Meyler's side effects of drugs)* and SEDA *(Side effects of drugs annual)*.

Includes approx. 1,500 articles on drugs. Drug monographs in alphabetical order, with information within each monograph in the following sections: general information, organs and systems, long-term effects, second-generation effects, susceptibility factors (patient specific), drug administration, drug interactions, interference with diagnostic tests, diagnosis of adverse drug reactions, and managements of adverse drug reactions. Classification of adverse drug reactions according to the DoTS system (based on "dose" at which adverse reactions occur relative to the beneficial dose, the "time-course" of the reaction, and individual "susceptibility" factors (*Pref.*); drug names: recommended or proposed international nonproprietary names (rINN or pINN) when available (when not available, chemical names or brand names are used); cross-references; index of drugs, with listing of all references to a drug for which adverse effects and drug interactions have been reported. Also an index of drugs that are covered in the individual monographs. Bibliographic references. Available online via ScienceDirect at http://www.sciencedirect.com/science/referenceworks/9780444510051.

1197 Remington: The science and practice of pharmacy. Joseph P. Remington. ill. [Philadelphia, Pa.]: Lippincott, Williams and Wilkins, 1995–. ISSN: 1558-2922.

615 13   RS91.R4

1st–6th ed. had title: *The practice of pharmacy*; 7th-12th ed., *Remington's practice of pharmacy*; 13th-18th ed., *Remington's pharmaceutical sciences*. Qinquennial.

Description based on 21st ed., 2005. Eight parts include 133 chapters: pt. 1, "Orientation"; pt. 2, "Pharmaceutics"; pt. 3, "Pharmaceutical chemistry"; pt. 4, "Pharmaceutical testing, analysis, and control"; pt. 5, "Industrial pharmacy"; pt. 6, "Pharmacodynamics"; pt. 7, "Pharmaceutical and medicinal agents"; pt. 8, "Pharmacy practice": pt. 8A, "Fundamentals of pharmacy practice"; pt. 8B, "Social, behavioral, economic, and administrative sciences"; Index.

New chapters on pharmacogenomics, application of ethical principles to practice dilemmas, medication errors, re-engineering pharmacy practice, specialization in pharmacy practice, emergency patient care, and others. Includes CD-ROM.

Guides

1198 Drug information: A guide for pharmacists. 3rd ed. Patrick M. Malone, Karen L. Kier, John E. Stanovich. xxvi, 877 p., ill. New York: McGraw-Hill, 2006. ISBN: 0071437916.

615.1   RS56.2.D78

1st ed., 1996; 2nd ed., 2001.

Contents: ch. 1, "Introduction to the concept of medication information"; ch. 2, "Modified systematic approach to answering questions"; ch. 3, "Formulating effective responses"; ch. 4, "Drug information resources"; ch. 5, "Electronic information management"; ch. 6, "Literature evaluation I: Controlled clinical trials"; ch. 7, "Literature evaluation II: Beyond the basics"; ch. 8, "Pharmacoeconomics"; ch. 9, "Evidence-based clinical practice guidelines"; ch. 10, "Clinical application of statistical analysis"; ch. 11, "Professional writing"; ch. 12, "Legal aspects of drug information practice"; ch. 13, "Ethical aspects of drug information practice"; ch. 14, "Pharmacy and therapeutics committee"; ch. 15, "Drug monographs"; ch. 16, "Quality improvement and the medication use process"; ch. 17, "Medication misadventures: Adverse drug reactions and medication errors"; ch. 18, "Investigational drugs."

This informatics resource, intended for pharmacists and pharmacy students, is a guide to researching, interpreting, organizing, and using drug information.

1199 Drug information: Guide to current resources. 3rd ed. Bonnie Snow, Medical Library Association. xvii, 546 p., ill. New York: Neal-Schuman, 2008. ISBN: 9781555706166.

016.6151   Z6675.P5S64; RS91

1st ed., 1989; 2nd ed., 1999.

Provides an introduction to a wide selection of relevant print and online pharmacology and therapeutics reference sources and discusses common problems in the provision of information concerning drugs. Contains background information on pharmacological terminology, legal and regulatory issues, and marketing and business data. Chapters on industrial pharmacy and market research and competitive intelligence resources. Also included are a detailed contents listing, a keyword index, a glossary that defines pharmaceutical and information science terminology used in the text, practicum exercises, and other useful appendixes.

An older edition (Oxford; New York: Oxford University Press, 2003) of this work was previously included in *Guide to reference.*

1200 Herbal medicines: A guide for healthcare professionals.
  3rd ed. Joanne Barnes, Linda Anderson, J. Phillipson. 710 p. London; Chicago: Pharmaceutical Press, 2007. ISBN: 0853696233.
615.321   RM666.H33
1st ed., 1996; 2nd ed., 2002.

This revised and rewritten edition includes 152 herbal monographs. Describes phytochemical, pharmacological, and clinical aspects of each herb. Each monograph provides species, family, synonym(s), part(s) used, pharmacopeial and other monograph references, etc. Includes chemical structure drawings, color photographs, and a directory of product names and suppliers. Quality, safety, and legal requirements are addressed. Includes an overview of U.K. and European legislation concerning herbal products. Appendixes group herbs by their specific actions. Bibliographical references and index. Also available as a book and CD-ROM package and online as part of MedicinesComplete (1236).

1201 Using the pharmaceutical literature. Sharon Srodin. xiv, 323 p., ill. New York: Taylor & Francis, 2006. ISBN: 0824729668.
615.19   RS56.U85

Contents: ch. 1, "Introduction: The drug discovery and development process"; ch. 2, "Chemistry"; ch. 3, "Genomics, proteomics, and bioinformatics"; ch. 4, "Toxicology"; ch. 5, "Pharmacology"; ch. 6, "Drug regulation"; ch. 7, "Sales and marketing"; ch. 8, "Competitive intelligence"; ch. 9, "Pharmacoeconomics"; ch. 10, "Intellectual property"; ch. 11, "Medical devices and combination products."

"The chapters in this book correspond to a key stage or components of the drug development process and cover the types of information typically required at each point."—*Pref.* Intended as a guide and collection development tool for pharmaceutical and medical information professionals. Provides an overview of key resources such as databases, online directories, websites, reports, and periodicals. Special attention is given to devices and drug delivery systems. Includes definitions of industry terminology. Also available as an e-book via netLibrary.

Handbooks

1202 The ABC clinical guide to herbs. Mark Blumenthal, Josef Brinckmann, Bernd Wollschlaeger. xxx, 480 p., ill. Austin, Tex.: American Botanical Council, 2003. ISBN: 1588901572.

615.321   RM666.H33.A175

Comprehensive information on 29 popular drugs available in the United States. Each monograph contains primary (supported by clinical trials) and potential uses, dosage, duration of use, pregnancy and lactation guidelines, adverse effects, etc. Also provides background information on herbal medicine, with a brief history of medicinal herbs in North America, legal and regulatory status of herbs and phytomedicines, consumer use, herb safety, etc. Includes bibliographical references and index. Resource for clinicians, researchers, educators, and general readers.

1203 ADA/PDR guide to dental therapeutics. 4th ed. American Dental Association. 1008 p. Chicago: American Dental Association, 2006. ISBN: 1563636042.

RK701.A33

1st (1998)–3rd (2003) ed. had title: *ADA guide to dental therapeutics.*

This edition produced by the American Dental Association (ADA) in partnership with the Physicians' Desk Reference. Authoritative guide to dental therapeutics, covering approx. 2,500 brand names and generic drugs. Contains section on oral manifestations of systemic agents. Appendix includes U.S. controlled substances, smoking cessation, and related products. Other PDR-related titles include *Physicians' desk reference: PDR* (1250), *PDR drug guide for mental health professionals* (1242), *PDR guide to drug interactions, side effects, and indications* (1247), *PDR for herbal medicines* (1244), *PDR for nonprescription drugs, dietary supplements, and herbs* (1245), *PDR for nutritional supplements* (1246), *PDR nurse's drug handbook* (1064), *Physicians' desk reference for ophthalmic medicines* (1249), *PDR guide to biological and chemical warfare response, PDR guide to terrorism response*, and other titles. PDR and its major companion volumes are also found in the PDR® Electronic Library (1243).

1204 A to Z drug facts. St. Louis: Facts and Comparisons, 1999–.

RM301.12.A2

8th ed., 2007.

Alphabetically organized drug reference. Drug monographs with pharmacological and patient care information. Includes action of the drug, indications, dosage, adverse reactions, interactions, side effects, laboratory test interference, etc. Available online as part of Facts and Comparisons 4.0 Online (1159).

1205 Botanical medicines: The desk reference for major herbal supplements. 2nd ed. Dennis J. McKenna, Kenneth Jones, Kerry Hughes, Sheila Humphrey. xx, 1138 p., ill. New York: Haworth Herbal Press, 2002. ISBN: 0789012650.

615.32   RM258.5.M38

Rev. ed. of *Natural dietary supplements*, 1998.

Comprehensive coverage of 34 commonly used herbal products. Each herb monograph covers scientific name, family name, common name, historical perspective, traditional uses, therapeutic applications, clinical studies, recommended doses, safety concerns, contraindications, drug interactions, and pregnancy and lactation. Two appendixes review the quality of herbal supplements and the key provisions of the Dietary Supplement Health and Education Act (DSHEA). Index. Written for health care professionals and also useful to consumers.

1206 Burger's medicinal chemistry and drug discovery. 6th ed. Alfred Burger, Donald J. Abraham. 6 v., ill. (some color). Hoboken, N.J.: Wiley, 2003. ISBN: 0471370320.

615.19   RS403.B8

1st ed., 1951, to 4th ed., 1980–1, had title *Medicinal chemistry*. 5th ed., 1995–7.

Contents: v. 1, "Drug discovery"; v. 2, "Drug discovery and drug development"; v. 3, "Cardiovascular agents and endocrines"; v. 4, "Autocoids, diagnostics, and drugs from new biology"; v. 5, "Chemotherapeutic agents"; v. 6, "Nervous system agents."

Updated and expanded ed. Comprehensive resource for information on drug studies and drug research, with the latest developments in medicinal drug research and drug development. Includes high priority areas and subjects, such as molecular modeling in drug design, virtual screening, bioinformatics, chemical information computing systems in drug discovery, structural biology of drug action, etc. Includes bibliographical references and index. For medical and science libraries. Also available in electronic format.

1207 **Catalog of teratogenic agents.** 12th ed. Thomas H. Shepard, Ronald J. Lemire. 545 p. Baltimore: Johns Hopkins University Press, 2007. ISBN: 0801887429.

QM

1st ed., [1973]; 11th ed., 2004.

Title varies. Also referred to as *Shepard's catalog of teratogenic agents*; *Shepard's catalog.*

Teratology can be defined as the study of the adverse effects of drugs on the fetus. This scholarly and professional resource covers information on chemicals, food additives, household products, environmental pollutants, pharmaceuticals, and viruses as well as fetal exposure to these various agents. Also includes gene mutations that can cause congenital defects. Alphabetically arranged by chemical name, lists synonyms and CAS registry numbers. Author index; agent index. Available online as part of Thomson Micromedex (*Micromedex healthcare series* [1084]) REPRO-RISK system, with further information about this and related databases described at http://www.micromedex.com/support/faqs/plat_matrix.html.

1208 **Clarke's analysis of drugs and poisons: In pharmaceuticals, body fluids and postmortem material.** 3rd ed. Anthony C. Moffat, M. David Osselton, B. Widdop, E. G. C. Clarke. 2 v. (xii, 3–564, viii, 567–1935, llxxxiv p.), ill. London: Pharmaceutical Press, 2004. ISBN: 0853694737.

1st ed., 1969–75, and 2nd ed., 1986, had title *Clarke's isolation and identification of drugs in pharmaceuticals, body fluids, and post-mortem material.*

Contents: v. 1, analytical toxicology; methodology and analytical techniques; v. 2, drug and poison monographs (1,737); indexes of analytical and toxicological data.

This revised and expanded edition provides analytical procedures used in analytical toxicology and data for drugs and poisons as well as applications of these techniques in areas such as forensic toxicology, workplace drug testing, drug abuse in sports, pesticide poisoning, and others. Drug and poison monographs provide physical properties, analytical methods, pharmacokinetic data, and toxicity data. Mass spectra are included within the monographs. Indexes of analytical data include CAS numbers, molecular formulas, therapeutic classes, color tests, molecular weights, melting points, thin-layer chromatographic data, gas chromatographic (GC) data, high-performance liquid chromatographic (HPLC) data, ultraviolet absorption maxima, infrared peaks, mass spectral data of drugs and pesticides, reagents, E numbers (i.e., for food additives approved in the European Union), and a medical glossary. Subject index covering both volumes at the end of v. 1 as well as v. 2. Intended for use primarily by forensic toxicologists, pathologists, and other scientists and students in these areas of study. Available online as part of MedicinesComplete (1236).

1209 Clinical pharmacology. Gold Standard. 199?–. [Tampa, Fla.]: Gold Standard. http://www.clinicalpharmacology.com/.

Produced by Gold Standard (http://www.goldstandard.com/index.htm).

Provides concise drug monographs for U.S. prescription drugs, herbal and nutritional supplements, over-the-counter products, and new and investigational drugs; overviews of various drug classes; and various search capabilities (e.g., by generic name, indication, contraindication, and therapeutic classification). Allows for the creation of a variety of customized reports. Includes patient handouts written by pharmacists. Available in a variety of formats (see http://www.clinicalpharmacology.com/marketing/about_cp.html). Considered a helpful tool for pharmacists, physicians, and other health professionals.

1210 The complete German Commission E monographs. Mark Blumenthal, Werner R. Busse, Bundesinstitut für Arzneimittel und Medizinprodukte (Germany). xxii, 685 p. Austin, Tex.; Boston: American Botanical Council; Integrative Medicine Communications, 1998. ISBN: 096555550X.

615.321   RM666.H33.C67

Commissioned by the American Botanical Council (ABC), English translation of the monographs from the original German monographs of the Commission E, a German government special expert committee established in 1978 to evaluate the safety and efficacy of herbs and herbal products on the market in Germany.

Contents: pt. 1, "Introduction"; pt. 2, "Monographs"; pt. 3, "Therapeutic indexes"; pt. 4, "Chemical and taxonomic indexes"; pt. 5, "European regulatory literature"; pt. 6, appendix.

Contains a lists of monographs by approval status, approved and unapproved herbs and herbal combinations. A typical entry contains the name, composition, and actions of the drug and its uses, contraindications, side effects, interactions with other drugs, dosage, and mode of administration. Chemical glossary and index; taxonomic cross-reference by English common name, botanical name, and pharmacopoeial name; excerpts for the German and European pharmacopoeias; and the European Economic Community (EEC) standards for quality of of herbal remedies. Appendix includes, for example, abbreviations and symbols, weights and measures, publication dates of Commission E monographs, list of European Scientific Cooperative on Phytotherapy (ESCOP) monographs, and list of World Health Organization (WHO) monographs. For use by pharmacists, physicians, and other health professionals; researchers; and health consumers. A related title, also edited by Mark Blumenthal, is *Herbal medicine: Expanded Commission E monographs*, published in 1999.

1211 The complete guide to medical writing. Mark Stuart. 491 p.
London; Chicago: Pharmaceutical Press, 2007. ISBN: 0853696675.
808.06661   R119

Contents: sec. 1, "Medical writing essentials"; sec. 2, "Reviews and reports"; sec. 3, "Medical journalism and mass media"; sec. 4, "Medical writing in education"; sec. 5, "Medical writing for medical professionals"; sec. 6, "Medical publishing"; appendixes: (1) "Common medical abbreviations"; (2) "Measurements"; (3) "Normal values for common laboratory tests"; (4) "Proof correction marks"; (5) "A to Z of medical terms in plain English."

Covers aspects of scientific and medical writing, medical journalism, and medical publishing. Resource for medical professionals and students to provide help with writing, communicating, and presenting scientific and medical information clearly and accurately, with examples from the pharmaceutical sciences. Covers copyright and patient confidentiality. For authors and editors.

1212 Comprehensive medicinal chemistry II. David J. Triggle, John Taylor. 8 v., ill. (some color), ports. (some color). Amsterdam [The Netherlands]: Elsevier, 2006. ISBN: 0080445136.

1st ed., 1990.

Description based on rev. and expanded edition.

Contents: v. 1, *Global perspective* (P. Kennewell); v. 2, *Research and development* (W.H. Moos); v. 3, *Technologies* (H. Kubinyi); v. 4, *Computer-assisted drug design* (J.S. Mason); v. 5, *ADME-Tox approaches* (B. Testa and H. van de Waterbeemd); v. 6, *Therapeutic areas I* (M. Williams); v. 7, *Therapeutic areas II* (J. Plattner and M.C. Desai); v. 8, *Case histories and cumulative subject index* (J.B. Taylor and D.J. Triggle).

Comprehensive reference resource on medicinal chemistry and drug research. Includes recent changes in genomics, proteomics, bioinformatics, combinatorial chemistry, high-throughput technologies, computer-assisted design, and other areas of high current interest. Intended mainly for scientists in the pharmaceutical sciences and biotechnology and for science and medical libraries. Also available online via ScienceDirect at http://www.sciencedirect.com/science/referenceworks/9780080450445.

1213 Desk reference to nature's medicine. Steven Foster, Rebecca
L. Johnson. 416 p., color ill. Washington: National Geographic
Society, 2006. ISBN: 0792236661.
615.321   RS164.F698

A–Z listing of 150 medicinal plants, arranged by common standard name, with Latin name also provided. Information about each plant includes a detailed description, its habitat, distribution, current and traditional uses, history, folklore, toxicity, etc. Includes color photographs, botanical drawings, range maps. Includes essays on the medicinal plants of Africa, Australia and New Zealand, Central and South America, China, Europe, India, North America, the Middle East, and Oceania. Glossary, Latin name index, and subject index. Intended for general readers. Complements information found, for example, in *The complete German Commission E monographs* (1210), *Herbal medicine: Expanded Commission E monographs* (1229), and *PDR for herbal medicines* (1244).

1214 Dietary supplements. 3rd ed. Pamela Mason. 387 p. London;
Chicago: Pharmaceutical Press, 2007. ISBN: 0853696535.
613.28

Title and imprint varies: 1st ed., 1995, had title *Handbook of dietary supplements: Vitamins and other supplements*; 2nd ed., 2001.

This comprehensive resource covers the most commonly used vitamins, minerals, and dietary supplements in the United States, the United Kindgom, and Europe. Includes information on interactions with drugs. For pharmacists and other health professionals. Includes bibliographical references and index.

1215 Drug facts and comparisons. Facts and Comparisons. St. Louis:
Facts and Comparisons, 1982–. ISSN: 0277-9714.
615.1   RM300.F33

Volumes in 1953–81 had title *Facts and comparisons. Drug Facts and comparisons* adapted from Facts and Comparisons loose-leaf drug information service. Description based on 61st ed., 2007.

Comprehensive drug information, intended as a reference source for health professionals. This edition incorporates 27 new drugs. Organized by therapeutic drug classes, with each entry (monograph) giving detailed information. A typical entry includes indications, administration and dosage, actions, contraindications, warnings and precautions, drug interactions, adverse reactions, overdosage treatment, and essential patient information. A "color locator" aids in identifying tablets and capsules. Drugs are arranged by dosage form, color, size, and shape. A "Keeping up" section provides information on new developments concerning orphan drugs and investigational drugs. Index (generic names, brand names, group names, also synonyms, pharmacological actions, and therapeutic uses); manufacturer/distributors index; Canadian trade name index.

Available in electronic format as part of a Web-based version entitled Facts and Comparisons 4.0 Online (1159), which also makes available several additional drug information resources.

1216 **Drug information handbook.** North American ed. Charles Lacy, Laura Armstrong, Morton Goldman, Leonard Lance, Lexi-Comp, Inc., American Pharmaceutical Association. Hudson, Ohio; Washington: Lexi-Comp; American Pharmaceutical Association, 1994–. ISSN: 1533-4511.

615   RM301.12.D783

Publ. in cooperation with the Amer. Pharmacists Assoc. (APhA).

1st ed., 1993/94. Available in North Amer. and internat. editions. Description based on 15th ed., 2007.

(Lexi-Comp's clinical reference library).

Concise, comprehensive, and user-friendly drug reference. Alphabetical listing of 1,400 drug monographs, with new drugs and updates to monographs since the last edition. Includes detailed information in consistent format (33 fields), such as dosage, drug interactions, adverse reactions (by occurrence, overdose, and toxicology), etc., with warnings highlighted. Appendix. Pharmacologic category index. For clinicians and healthcare professionals.

Several other comprehensive print pharmacology handbooks, also publ. by Lexi-Comp and frequently updated, include *Anesthesiology and critical care drug handbook* (1999–. ; 7th ed., 2006); *Drug information handbook for advanced practice nursing* (1990–. ; 8th ed., 2007); *Drug information handbook for dentistry* (1996– ; 12th ed., 2007); *Drug information handbook for oncology* (2000– ; 6th ed., 2007); *Drug information handbook for psychiatry: A comprehensive reference of psychotropic, nonpsychotropic, and herbal agents* (1999– ; 6th ed., 2006); *Drug information handbook for the allied health professional* (1995– ; 12th ed., 2005); *Geriatric dosage handbook* (1993– ; 11th ed., 2006); *Infectious diseases handbook: including antimicrobial therapy & diagnostic test/procedures* (1994– ; 6th ed., 2006); *Natural therapeutics pocket guide* (2000– ; 2nd ed., 2003); *Pediatric dosage handbook* (1992– ; 13th ed., 2006); and *Pharmacogenomics handbook* (2003– ; 2nd ed., 2006). Also available online as pt. of Lexi-Comp Online™ (http://webstore.lexi.com/Store/ONLINE) and Lexi-Comp ONLINE for Dentistry (http://webstore.lexi.com/Store/ONLINE/Lexi-Comp-ONLINE-for-Dentistry).

1217 Drug interaction facts. David S. Tatro, Facts and Comparisons. St. Louis: Facts and Comparisons, 1988–. ISSN: 0899-4951.

615.7045   RM302.D76

Publ. varies. Previously published by J. B. Lippincott, now by Facts and Comparisons™ (Wolters Kluwer Health).

Since 1983 available in a monthly loose-leaf format, since 1988 in bound format. Description based on 2007 ed., ed. by David S. Tatro.

Presents drug–drug and drug–food interactions. Drug interaction monographs are arranged alphabetically according to the principal drug affected. Each monograph has the following sections: interacting drugs (including generic and trade names), clinical significance, effects, mechanisms and management, and discussion, with primary literature references. Indexed by generic, class, and trade names. Clinically significant interactions are identified in the index. Intended for health care professionals and pharmacists. Also available electronically through Facts and Comparisons 4.0 Online (1159).

Drug interaction facts: Herbal supplements and food (St. Louis: Facts and Comparisons, 2002–) is a companion volume; since 2005 also available in electronic format via Facts and Comparisons 4.0 Online (1159).

A similar resource by the same publisher, published in loose-leaf and bound formats for many years, is Hansten and Horn's *Drug interactions: Analysis and management* (1218). Several other Facts and Comparisons bound products include *A to Z drug facts* (1204), *American drug index* (1177), *ImmunoFacts* (St. Louis: Facts and Comparisons, 2002–), *Ophthalmic drug facts* (1241), *The review of natural products* (1256), and others.

1218 Drug interactions: Analysis and management. Philip D. Hansten, John R. Horn. xviii, 1531 p. St. Louis: Wolters Kluwer Health; Facts & Comparisons, 2006. ISBN: 1574392603.

615.7045   RM302.H352

Also referred to as DIAM. Adapted from Hansten and Horn's *Drug interactions analysis and management* loose-leaf information service through the Jan. 2006 update.

Provides an analysis of the clinical importance of drug interactions and consideration of potential harm (with assigned "significance" numbers: 1 = avoid combination, 2 = usually avoid combination, 3 = minimize risk, 4 = no action needed, and 5 = no interaction). Includes prescription and nonprescription drugs as well as herbal medicines, with management options for each interaction. Not included are drugs of abuse and drugs used in anesthesiology. Bibliographical references and index, with generic drug names, class names, and trade names.

1219 Drugs in pregnancy and lactation. Gerald G. Briggs. Baltimore: Williams and Wilkins, 1983–. ISSN: 0897-6112.

618.32071   RG627.6.D79D798

Triennial. Description based on 8th ed., 2008.

This updated edition summarizes data on specific drugs. Arranged in alphabetical order, each drug monograph provides the U.S. generic name, pharmacologic class, risk factor, fetal risk summary, breast feeding summary, and references where available. An appendix arranges the drugs by pharmacologic category, allowing comparison of drugs within the same pharmacologic class to determine different risk factors. Written for clinicians caring for pregnant women. Another print resource is *Drugs for pregnant and lactating women* (Philadelphia: Saunders/Elsevier, 2009) by Carl P. Weiner and Catalin Buhimschi. An online resource, LactMed (part of TOXNET [1580]), is a web-based peer-reviewed database with information on drugs and lactation.

1220 Encyclopedic reference of traditional Chinese medicine: [A manual from A–Z, symptoms, therapy, and herbal remedies]. Xinrong Yang. 660 p., color ill. Berlin; New York: Springer, 2003. ISBN: 3540428461.

610.951   R601.D538

Introduction to traditional Chinese medicine with its long history. "Owing to the Traditional Chinese Medicine literatures were written in the classical literary style and the translation into English of most of their terms was not standardized and normalized, the translation of these terms remains to be discussed by specialists and linguists. Many terms of diseases in this book have to use the terms of Western Medicine in Latin. Some terms have to be transliterated into English."—*Pref.* Acupuncture terms from WHO's 1984 publication on "Standard Acupuncture Nomenclature" (1993 ed. of *Standard acupuncture nomenclature: A brief explanation of 361 classical acupuncture point names and their multilingual comparative list* is available at http://whqlibdoc.who.int/wpro/-1993/9290611057.pdf).

Provides 5,000 entries with concise annotations, listing, as appropriate for a particular entry, symptoms, pathogenesis, diseases, therapeutic principle, herbal and other drugs. Alphabetical arrangement. Color ill.

1221 The 5-minute herb and dietary supplement consult. Adriane Fugh-Berman. xv, 475 p. Philadelphia: Lippincott, Williams & Wilkins, 2003. ISBN: 0683302736.

615.321   RM666.H33.F835

Ready-reference resource, arranged alphabetically by botanical or dietary supplement, with Latin and biological names. Entries include concise description, appropriate dosage, pharmacokinetics, drug interactions, risks, etc. For academic medical, and public libraries.

1222 Guide to popular natural products. 3rd ed. Facts and Comparisons. xi, 367 p., color ill. St. Louis: Facts and Comparisons, 2003.

615.321   RM666.H33.G85

1st ed., 1999; 2nd ed., 2001.

Abridged from *The review of natural products* (1256). Includes "more than 125 of the most commonly used herbs and natural products, each fully referenced and peer-reviewed."—*Publ. notes.* Alphabetical listing of products, with common names, patient information, references, and brief sections on botany, history, pharmacology, and toxicology. Color photographs, charts, and sources of natural product information. Index.

1223 Handbook of contemporary neuropharmacology. David Robert Sibley, Israel Hanin, Michael Kuhar. 3 v. Hoboken, N.J.: John Wiley & Sons, 2007. ISBN: 9780471660.

615.78   RM315.H3434

Contents: (1) "Basic neuropharmacology"; (2) "Mood disorders"; (3) "Anxiety and stress disorders"; (4) "Schizophrenia and psychosis"; (5) "Substance abuse and addictive disorders"; (6) "Pain"; (7) "Sleep and arousal"; (8) "Development and developmental disorders"; (9) "Neurodegenerative and seizure disorders"; (10) "Neuroimmunology"; (11) "Eating and metabolic disorders."

Reference for nervous system neuropharmacology, with recent advances in neuropharmacology, drug development and therapy, and treatment of various diseases and conditions. Reference for graduate students, physicians and other health professionals, and researchers. A useful resource for academic and special libraries. Also available online via Wiley InterScience (http://www.interscience.wiley.com/reference/hcn). Includes index.

1224 Handbook of medicinal herbs. 2nd ed. James A. Duke, Mary Jo Bogenschutz-Godwin, Judi duCellier. 870 p., ill. (some color). Boca Raton, Fla.: CRC Press, 2002. ISBN: 0849312841.

615.321   QK99.A1.D83

Publ. in 1985 under the title *CRC handbook of medicinal herbs.*

Provides well-documented information for 800 plant species having medicinal or folk medicinal uses. All entries include the species' scientific name and authority, the scientific name of the plant family, and one or two colloquial or common names. Most entries have four sections giving uses, folk medicinal applications, chemistry, and toxicity. Most plants are illustrated. Extensive tables, bibliography, and index. Available online via netLibrary.

1225 Handbook of non-prescription drugs. American Pharmaceutical Association. ill. Washington: American Pharmaceutical Association, 1967–. ISSN: 0889-7816.

615.105   RS250.N66

Title varies: *Handbook of nonprescription drugs: An interactive approach to self-care.* Description based on 15th ed., 2006.

Contents: sec. 1, "The practitioner's role in self-care"; sec. 2, "Pain and fever disorders"; sec. 3, "Reproductive and genital disorders"; sec. 4, "Respiratory disorders"; sec. 5, "Gastrointestinal disorders"; sec. 6, "Nutrition and nutritional supplementation"; sec. 7, "Ophthalmic, otic, and oral disorders"; sec. 8, "Dermatologic disorders"; sec. 9, "Other medical disorders"; sec. 10, "Home medical equipment"; sec. 11, "Complementary and alternative medicine"; appendix 1, "Pregnancy and lactation risk categories for selected nonprescription medications and nutritional supplements"; appendix 2, "Botanical medicines to avoid in pregnancy and lactation."

A compilation of facts on home remedies in 55 chapters with broad headings, such as asthma, diabetes mellitus, headache, musculoskeletal injuries and disorders, sexually transmitted infections, etc. Each chapter includes a case study in outline format and discusses the etiology of the condition; the anatomy, physiology, and pathophysiology of the affected systems; the signs and symptoms; the treatment and adjunctive measures; an evaluation of ingredients in over-the-counter products; and important patient and product considerations. Bibliographic references at the end of each chapter. Subject index. Useful for pharmacists, other health professionals, and consumers. E-book download available with 15th edition.

1226 **Handbook of pharmaceutical excipients.** 5th ed. Raymond
C. Rowe, Paul J. Sheskey, Siân C. Owen, American Pharmacists Association. xxi, 918 p., ill. London; Greyslake, Ill.; Washington: Pharmaceutical Press; American Pharmacists Association, 2006. ISBN: 1582120587.

615.19   RS201.E87.H36

1st ed., 1986; 4th ed., 2003.

Contents: http://www.loc.gov/catdir/toc/ecip061/2005028523.html.

Comprehensive guide to the physical and chemical properties, uses, and safety of pharmaceutical excipients. Cross-references and index, with listings of excipients by chemical, nonproprietary, or trade name. Includes comments by contributors.

Also available as CD-ROM and online as part of MedicinesComplete (online version has title Pharmaceutical Excipients) (1236).

1227 **Handbook on injectable drugs.** Lawrence A. Trissel, American Society of Hospital Pharmacists. Bethesda, Md.: American Society of Hospital Pharmacists, 1977–. ISSN: 1544-1059.

615.13   RM143.H36

Available in print and CD versions. Description based on print version of the 14th ed., 2007.

Intended for use as a professional reference and guide to the literature on the clinical pharmaceutics of parenteral medications. Provides information on "accurate and appropriate" *(Publ. note)* uses of drug therapy and important safety considerations. Includes 379 drug monographs, listed alphabetically by generic name; cross-reference monographs include *AHFS drug information*® (Bethesda, Md.: American Society of Hospital Pharmacists, 1989–), administration, stability, brand names, and four compatibility tables for each drug. Available online via MedicinesComplete (1236).

1228 Herbal drugs and phytopharmaceuticals: A handbook for practice on a scientific basis. 3rd ed. Max Wichtl, Josef A. Brinckmann, Michael P. Lindenmaier. xliii, 704 p., ill. (some color). Stuttgart, [Germany]; Boca Raton, Fla.: Medpharm; CRC Press, 2004. ISBN: 3887631005.

RM666.H33.T43813

1st ed., 1994; 2nd ed., 2001. Third edition edited and translated from the 2nd German ed. by Norman Grainger Bisset; German edition edited by Max Wichtl.

Translation of the revised and expanded 4th ed. of Max Wichtl's *Teedrogen und phytopharmaka.*

Describes various aspects of herbal drugs used in tea preparation and phytopharmaceuticals. Includes 212 herbal drugs. Monographs have uniform structure. Each monograph contains Latin and English names, the pharmacopoeia to which a drug officially belongs, illustration, description, pharmacological names, plant source, synonyms, origin, constitutents, storage, and references. Includes British, Canadian, and U.S. regulation for herbal products. Several indexes. For pharmacists, physicians, food scientists, and students.

1229 Herbal medicine: Expanded Commission E monographs. Mark Blumenthal, Alicia Goldberg, Joseph Brinckmann. 519 p. Newton, Mass.: Integrative Medicine Communications, 2000. ISBN: 0967077214.

RM666.H33

Based on *The complete German Commission E monographs* (1210), this edition contains expanded monographs, color photographs, and more information about chemistry, pharmacology, dosage, administration, etc. Contains a comparison chart of leading herbal brands.

1230 Herbal medicines: A guide for healthcare professionals. 3rd ed. Joanne Barnes, Linda Anderson, J. Phillipson. 710 p. London; Chicago: Pharmaceutical Press, 2007. ISBN: 0853696233.

615.321   RM666.H33

1st ed., 1996; 2nd ed., 2002.

This revised and rewritten edition includes 152 herbal monographs. Describes phytochemical, pharmacological, and clinical aspects of each herb. Each monograph provides species, family, synonym(s), part(s) used, pharmacopeial and other monograph references, etc. Includes chemical structure drawings, color photographs, and a directory of product names and suppliers. Quality, safety, and legal requirements are addressed. Includes an overview of U.K. and European legislation concerning herbal products. Appendixes group herbs by their specific actions. Bibliographical references and index. Also available as a book and CD-ROM package and online as part of MedicinesComplete (1236).

1231 An illustrated Chinese materia medica. Jing-Nuan Wu. 706 p., color ill. New York: Oxford University Press, 2005. ISBN: 0195140176.

615.320951   RS180.C5.W785

Contents: introduction (including a history and theory of traditional Chinese medicine and modern research on Chinese medicinal herbs); illustrated materia medica (p. 31–669); appendix; selected bibliography; glossary; Latin (pharmaceutical) name index; English name index.

Alphabetical listing of medicinal materials (herbs, plants, and animal parts). Each entry includes a color illustration and follows the same outline format, providing a description under the following subheadings: Latin (pharmaceutical) name; English name; part used; flavor, property, and channel tropism; functions; clinical use and major combinations; dosage and administration; and precautions. Also available online via netLibrary.

1232 Illustrated manual of nursing practice. 3rd ed. Lippincott, Williams & Wilkins. xiii, 1490 p., ill. Philadelphia: Lippincott, Williams & Wilkins, 2002. ISBN: 1582550824.

610.73   RT41.I44

1st ed., 1991; 2nd ed., 1994.

Updated and rev. edition.

Overview of all areas of nursing practice, clinical assessments, and intervention. Presents information according to the nursing process and body systems. Includes ethical and legal issues as well as complementary or alternative therapies. Appendixes on infection control, normal laboratory test values, common antibiotics, dangerous drug interactions, and therapeutic drug-monitoring guidelines. Index.

1233 **Index nominum, international drug directory = Internationales Arzneistoff- und Arzneimittelverzeichnis = Repertoire international des substances médicamenteuses et spécialités pharmaceutiques.** 18th ed. Schweizerischer Apotheker-Verein. ill. Medpharm Scientific, 2004. ISBN: 3887631013.

Title varies. Publ. in loose-leaf format since 1957, in bound version since 1971; 17th ed., 2000. Description based on 18th rev. ed., 2004.

Contains 4,500 human drug monographs of 102 different countries (complete) and additional partial information for 39 countries. Monographs include International Non-Proprietary Names (INNs); chemical names, structures, and formulas; brand names; manufacturers; and various other codes and formulas used in drug nomenclature. Alphabetical index of trade names. Available online as part of Micromedex Healthcare Series (1084), described as an "international guide to drugs and derivatives from 133 countries."—*Website* (http://www.micromedex.com/products/indexnominum/).

1234 **Litt's drug eruption reference manual including drug interactions.** 10th ed. Jerome Z. Litt. color ill. London; New York: Taylor & Francis, 2004.

RL803.D78

Editions from 1990s to 2003 had title *Drug eruption reference manual.* Description based on 13th ed., 2007, updated and enlarged edition.

Information on drug eruptions and interactions to assist with diagnosis of skin eruptions caused by medications. In alphabetical order by medication name (1,100 generic and approx. 6,000 trade name drugs), lists more than 1,000 adverse reactions (skin, hair, nails, eyes, and other). Describes common reaction patterns to certain drugs, drug-drug interactions, etc. Cross-references by drug and trade names. References. Accompanied by CD-ROM containing color illustrations and access to drug profiles listed in the manual.

Available online as Litt's Drug Eruption Global Database (http://www.drugeruptiondata.com). It is regularly updated with new drugs, references, drug interactions, and reaction patterns and is searchable by drug names, drug reactions, drug categories, drug interactions, and drug combinations.

1235 **Medicinal plants of the world: An illustrated scientific guide to important medicinal plants and their uses.** Ben-Erik Van Wyk,

Michael Wink. 480 p., ill. (some color). Portland, Ore.: Timber Press, 2004. ISBN: 0881926027.

615.321   RS164.V295

Contents: "Medicine systems of the world"; "Plant parts used"; "Dosage forms"; "Use of medicinal plant products"; "Active ingredients"; "Quality control and safety"; "Efficacy of medicinal plant products"; "Regulation of herbal remedies and phytomedicines"; "The plants in alphabetical order"; "Health disorders and medicinal plants"; "Overview of secondary metabolites and their effects"; "Quick guide to commercialized medicinal plants."

Guide to 320 plants with color photos, alphabetically arranged by scientific name, with mention of common names in several different languages. Contains a "quick guide" chart with 900 plants, providing species, family, and common names, place of origin, plant parts used, related medicinal systems (African, Ayurvedic, Chinese, or European), and main indications. Chapter cross-references indications to their main botanical therapies. Medicinal use by governmental bodies in pharmacopoeias is mentioned. Glossary, list for further reading, and general index. Written for general readers. A comparable title is *Herbal drugs and phytopharmaceuticals: A handbook for practice on a scientific basis* (1228).

1236 MedicinesComplete. Royal Pharmaceutical Society of Great Britain. 2000–. London: Pharmaceutical Press. http://www.medicinescomplete.com.

Provides online access to the following drug information sources published by Pharmaceutical Press: *AHFS drug information* (Bethesda, Md.: American Society of Hospital Pharmacists, 1989–); *BNF for children*; *British national formulary* (1178); *Clarke's analysis of drugs and poisons* (1208); *Dietary supplements*; *Herbal medicines* (London; Chicago: Pharmaceutical Press, 2007); *Martindale: The complete drug reference* (1182); *MeReC bulletin*; *Pharmaceutical excipients* (print ed. has title *Handbook of pharmaceutical excipients* [1226]), *Stockley's drug interactions* (1257), and *Stockley's interaction alerts*.

1237 The Merck index: An encyclopedia of chemicals, drugs, and biologicals. 14th ed. Maryadele J. O'Neil. 2564 p.; 1 CD-ROM, ill. Whitehouse Station, N.J.: Merck, 2006. ISBN: 091191000X.

1st ed., 1989; 13th ed., 2001. Subtitle varies.

Concise descriptions of more than 10,000 organic and inorganic chemicals, drugs, and biological substances, chosen for inclusion on the basis of their importance. Entries give formulas, alternate names, physical properties, uses, toxicity, and journal and patent references. A separate table gives CAS Registry Numbers. Miscellaneous tables include radioactive isotopes, standard solutions, conversion factors, prescription notation, and over 450 organic name reactions. Formula index. Detailed cross-index of alternate names. Index by therapeutic category (both medical and veterinary) and biological activity. Accompanying CD provides added searchability features.

"This new edition has been extensively revised and provides enhanced coverage of traditional medicines, neutraceuticals, and cosmeceuticals. An expanded therapeutic category index covers more than forty new categories and cross-references."—*Publ. description*

Available online; details at http://www.merckbooks.com/mindex/online.html.

1238 Mosby's drug consult. Mosby. St. Louis: Mosby, 2002–.
615.1   RS55.2.P48; RM301.45

Editions in 1991–2 had title *Physicians' generix*; 1993–7, *Physicians' genRx*; 8th ed. (1998) through 11th ed. (2001), *Mosby's genRx*.

Description based on 17th ed., which is the last scheduled print edition. Online versions were discontinued as of Dec. 31, 2006. Future plans for this title are unknown as of Aug. 2007.

Contents: sec. 1, "Keyword index"; "International brands index"; sec. 2, "Drug information"; sec. 3, "Herbal information"; appendix A, "Comparative drug tables"; appendix B, "Additional information and tables"; appendix C, "Supplier profiles."

Drug monographs include drug class; generic, U.S. brand, and international brand names; off-label uses; cost of therapy; and detailed prescribing information. Alphabetical arrangement by generic drug name. Includes companion CD-ROM that contains the text of the print edition, Drug Master Plus with drug interactions, Patient Drug Consult with customizable patient handouts, images of pills, and commonly used herbs and supplements. Intended as a professional drug reference.

Other drug-related resources by the same publisher include *Mosby's dental drug reference* (645), *Mosby's medical drug reference* (a portable reference with information on the most commonly prescribed drugs, their side effects, interactions, and cost of therapy), *Mosby's handbook of herbs and natural supplements*, *Mosby's handbook of herbs and supplements and their therapeutic uses, Mosby's handbook of drug-herb and drug-supplement interactions,* and *Mosby's ocular drug consult.*

1239 Natural medicines comprehensive database. Jeff M. Jellin, Therapeutic Research Faculty. 1999–. Stockton, Calif.: Therapeutic Research Faculty. http://www.naturaldatabase.com/.

RM258.5

Available in a professional and a consumer version. Publication varies.

Compilation of natural medicines distributed in the U.S. Contains up-to-date clinical and research information for natural (i.e., herbal and and nonherbal) medicines and dietary supplements distributed in the U.S. Products can be found by most commonly used name, brand name (with editor's comments as appropriate or necessary), ingredient names, scientific names (botanical names), or popular names, with search features to find the safe use (with safety ratings based on evidence: likely safe; possibly safe; possibly unsafe; likely unsafe; unsafe), adverse effects (between natural and pharmaceutical products), interactions ("natural product/drug interaction checker"); also a "natural product effectiveness checker" for each natural medicine. Suitable for pharmacists, physicians, and students in the healthcare field, all types of medical libraries, and also for consumers. Also available in print version since 1999 (11th ed., 2009). Everything in the book is also contained in the web version, which has important added features, such as daily updates, additional search capabilities, patient education handouts, and hyperlinked references, to name a few.

1240 Nutraceuticals: A guide for healthcare professionals. 2nd ed. Brian Lockwood, Lisa Rapport. 426 p. London; Chicago: Pharmaceutical Press, 2007. ISBN: 0853696594.

615.854   QP144.F85

1st ed., 2002.

Contents: (1) "Introduction"; (2) "Monographs"; (3) "Source, manufacture and analysis of major nutraceuticals"; (4) "Metabolism, bioavailability and pharmacokinetics of nutraceuticals"; (5) "Joint health"; (6) "Cardiovascular health"; (7) "Eye health"; (8) "Mental health"; (9) "Sleep enhancement"; (10) "Cancer prevention"; (11) "Bone health"; (12) "Respiratory health"; (13) "Women's health"; (14) "Weight management"; (15) "Skin health"; (16) "Oral health"; (17) "Sporting performance/enhancement"; (18) "Animal health"; (19) "Meta-analyses/systemic reviews"; (20)

"Synergism, beneficial interactions and combination products"; (21) "Emerging nutraceuticals"; (22) "Adverse effects"; (23) "Quality"; (24) "Conclusions."

Examines the medical and scientific evidence for the use of nutraceuticals for prevention or treating various diseases. Presents new research, new products, and new therapeutic applications. Index.

1241 Ophthalmic drug facts: ODF. J.B. Lippincott. St. Louis: Facts and Comparisons Division, J.B. Lippincott, 1989–. ISSN: 1043-1780.

617.7061   RE994.O64

Publ. varies. Description based on *Ophthalmic drug facts 2007*, publ. 2006.

Contents: ch. 1, "Dosage forms and routes of administration"; ch. 2, "Ophthalmic dyes"; ch. 3, "Local anesthetics"; ch. 4, "Mydriatics and cycloplegics"; ch. 5, "Antiallergy and decongestant agents"; ch. 6, "Anti-inflammatory agents"; ch. 7, "Artificial tear solutions and ocular lubricants"; ch. 8, "Anti-infective agents"; ch. 9, "Ocular hypotensive agents"; ch. 10, "Hyperosmotic agents"; ch. 11, "Surgical adjuncts"; ch. 12, "Agents for retinal disease"; ch. 13, "Contact lens care"; ch. 14, "Miscellaneous products"; ch. 15, "Extemporaneous preparations"; ch. 16, "Systemic drugs affecting the eye"; ch. 17, "Systemic medications used for ocular conditions."

Current drug monographs for eye care professionals and students. Twelve chapters organized according to therapeutic use, group comparable drugs to provide comparative information. Additional chapters treat dosage forms, routes of administration, systemic drugs, and investigational drugs with information presented in a standardized format. Includes both prescription and over-the-counter products. Also includes charts, tables, and illustrations. Appendix includes orphan drugs, manufacturer index, and chapter summary tables. Index lists generic, brand, and therapeutic group names and many synonyms. Also available as an online product from the publisher and through Ovid.

1242 PDR drug guide for mental health professionals. Thomson Medical Economics. Montvale, N.J.: Thomson Medical Economics, 2002–. ISSN: 1546-3443.

615   RM315.P387

Description based on 3rd ed., 2007.

Written in nontechnical language, profiles psychotropic drugs commonly used in psychiatry, with recommended dosage, approved uses, physical and psychological side effects, food and drug interactions, etc. Also includes psychotropic herbs and supplements. Includes street drug profiles and a glossary of street drug names and color photos of psycho-tropic tablets and capsules. Indexed by generic and trade name and clinical disorder/symptom or drug class. Reference for health professionals taking care of psychiatric patients.

Related titles include *Physicians' desk reference: PDR* (1250), *ADA/PDR guide to dental therapeutics* (795), *PDR guide to drug interactions, side effects, and indications, PDR for herbal medicines (1244), PDR for nonpre-scription drugs, dietary supplements, and herbs* (1245), *PDR for nutritional supplements* (1246), *PDR nurse's drug handbook* (1064), *Physicians' desk reference for ophthalmic medicines* (1249), *PDR guide to biological and chemical warfare response, PDR guide to terrorism response*, and other titles.

PDR and its major companion volumes are also found in the PDR Electronic Library (1243).

1243 PDR electronic library. Thomson Micromedex. 1998–. Greenwood Village, Colo.: Thomson Micromedex. http://www. micromedex.com/products/pdrlibrary/.

Publisher varies.

Provides access to FDA-approved package insert information con-tained in the *Physicians' desk reference: PDR* (1250), the *PDR for nonpre-scription drugs, dietary supplements, and herbs: The definitive guide to OTC medications* (1245), and the *PDR for ophthalmic medicines* (Montvale, N.J.: Thomson Healthcare, 2000–), as well as *PDR for herbal medicines* (1244) and the online version of *Stedman's medical dictionary* (Baltimore: Lip-pincott, Williams & Wilkins, 2006). Allows search and retrieval of data by brand and generic names of drugs, by manufacturers, and by prescribing categories, drug interactions, side effects, dosages, uses, contraindications, etc. Includes photos, charts, tables, and chemical structures. Intended users include pharmacists, drug information specialists, health care pro-fessionals, and consumers.

Also available on CD-ROM that contains the text of the print *Physi-cians' desk reference: PDR* (1250).

1244 PDR for herbal medicines. Thomson Healthcare. color ill. Montvale, N.J.: Thomson, 1998–. ISSN: 1099-9566.
615   RS164.P375; RS75.P554
Description based on 4th ed., 2007.

Contents: alphabetical index; therapeutic category index; indications index; homeopathic indications index; Asian indications index; side effects

index; drug/herb interactions guide; safety guide; common herbal terminology; herb identification guide; herbal monographs; nutritional supplement monographs.

Comprehensive resource on herbal medicines, with scientific data and
findings concerning safety and interactions. Each monograph contains
information on effects, contraindications, precautions, adverse reactions,
and dosage.

Related titles include *Physicians' desk reference: PDR* (1250), *ADA/
PDR guide to dental therapeutics* (795), *PDR drug guide for mental health
professionals* (1242), *{record}PDR guide to drug interactions, side effects, and
indications, PDR for nonprescription drugs, dietary supplements, and herbs*
(1245), *PDR for nutritional supplements* (1246), *PDR nurse's drug handbook* (1064), *Physicians' desk reference for ophthalmic medicines* (1249),
*PDR guide to biological and chemical warfare response, PDR guide to terror-
ism response*, and other titles.

PDR and its major companion volumes are also found in the PDR
Electronic Library (1243).

**1245 PDR for nonprescription drugs, dietary supplements, and herbs:
The definitive guide to OTC medications.** Thomson PDR. ill.
Montvale, N.J.: Thomson PDR, 2005–.
615.704   RM671.A1.P48; RS250.P5

Title varies. Editions in 1980–98 had title *Physicians' desk reference for nonprescription drugs*; 1999–2005: *Physicians' desk reference for nonprescription
drugs and dietary supplements*.

Description based on 28th ed., 2007, *PDR for nonprescription drugs,
dietary supplements, and herbs*.

Makes available essential information on nonprescription drugs. Contains therapeutic class overviews, drug comparison charts, and product
information on over-the-counter medications. Arranged alphabetically
by body system or condition, then by indication. Contains sections on
supplements, vitamins, and herbal remedies.

Related titles include *Physicians' desk reference: PDR* (1250), *ADA/
PDR guide to dental therapeutics* (795), *PDR drug guide for mental health
professionals* (1242), *PDR guide to drug interactions, side effects, and indications* (1247), *PDR for herbal medicines* (1244), *PDR for nutritional supplements* (1246), *PDR nurse's drug handbook* (1064), *Physicians' desk reference
for ophthalmic medicines, PDR guide to biological and chemical warfare
response, PDR guide to terrorism response*, and others.

PDR and its major companion volumes are also found in the PDR Electronic Library (1243).

1246 PDR for nutritional supplements. Medical Economics Company. ill. Montvale, N.J.: Thomson Healthcare, 2001–. ISSN: 1534-3642. 613   RM258.5.P37

Covers nonherbal nutritional supplements and provides FDA-approved descriptions and information on vitamins, minerals, sports nutrition products, probiotics, hormones, enzymes, cartilage products, and others, with detailed descriptions of the supplements, side effects, and potential interactions with prescription and nonprescription drugs. Contains summary information on published studies. Includes "Companion drug index," which lists common diseases, the prescription drugs to treat these diseases, their side effects, and the over-the-counter products to provide relief.

Related titles include *Physicians' desk reference: PDR* (1250), *ADA/PDR guide to dental therapeutics* (795), *PDR drug guide for mental health professionals* (1242), *PDR guide to drug interactions, side effects, and indications* (1247), *PDR for herbal medicines* (1244), *PDR for nonprescription drugs, dietary supplements, and herbs* (1245), *PDR nurse's drug handbook* (1064), *Physicians' desk reference for ophthalmic medicines* (1249), *PDR guide to biological and chemical warfare response, PDR guide to terrorism response,* and others.

PDR and its major companion volumes are also found in the PDR Electronic Library (1243).

1247 PDR guide to drug interactions, side effects, and indications. Montvale, N.J.: Thomson PDR, 2006–. ISSN: 1933-706X. 615   RS75.P37

Formerly had title *PDR companion guide.*

This guide is based on eight clinical indexes: drug interactions index, side effects index, indications index, imprint identification guide, food interactions cross-reference, contraindications index, international drug name index, and generic availability guide. Serves as a complement to the (*Physicians desk reference: PDR* [Oradell, N.J.: Thomson Healthcare, 1974–]), *PDR for nonprescription drugs, dietary supplements, and herbs* (1245), and *Physicians' desk reference for ophthalmic medicines* (1249).

Related titles include *ADA/PDR guide to dental therapeutics* (795), *PDR drug guide for mental health professionals* (1242), *PDR for herbal medicines* (1246), *PDR for nutritional supplements* (1244), *PDR nurse's drug handbook* (1064), *PDR guide to biological and chemical warfare response,* *PDR guide to terrorism response,* and others.

PDR and its major companion volumes are available online in the PDR Electronic Library (1243).

1248 PDR nurse's drug handbook. Delmar Cengage Learning. ill. Clifton Park, N.Y.: Delmar Cengage Learning, 2000–. ISSN: 1535-4601.

615   RM125

Title varies: *PDR nurse's handbook; Physician's desk reference nurse's drug handbook; Nurse's drug handbook.* Description based on 2007 ed. of *PDR nurse's drug handbook;* publ. varies: now Thomson Delmar Learning; distr. by CENGAGE Learning.

Description of the major prescription drugs, with phonetic pronunciation of drug name, drug classification, drug interactions, FDA warnings, etc. Includes various aids to prevent medication errors (e.g., listing of drug names that sound alike, administration and storage of drugs, etc.). Includes a visual identification guide. For nursing students, nurses, and other health care professionals.

Related titles include *Physicians' desk reference: PDR* (1250), *ADA/PDR guide to dental therapeutics* (795), *PDR drug guide for mental health professionals* (1242), *PDR guide to drug interactions, side effects, and indications* (1247), *PDR for herbal medicines* (1244), *PDR for nonprescription drugs, dietary supplements, and herbs* (1245), *PDR for nutritional supplements* (1246), *Physicians' desk reference for ophthalmic medicines* (1249), also *PDR guide to biological and chemical warfare response,* and *PDR guide to terrorism response,* and other titles.

PDR and its major companion volumes are available online in the PDR Electronic Library (1243).

1249 Physicians' desk reference for ophthalmic medicines. Medical Economics Company. Montvale, N.J.: Thomson Healthcare, 2000–. ISSN: 1535-461X.

RE994.P57

Also called *PDR for ophthalmic medicines.* Annual.

Description based on 35th ed., 2007, by Douglas J. Rhee et al. Publisher varies; now publ. by Thomson PDR.

Contents: sec. 1, "Indices"; sec. 2, "Pharmaceuticals in ophthalmology"; sec. 3, "Suture materials"; sec. 4, "Ophthalmic lenses"; sec. 5, "Vision standards and low-vision aids"; sec. 6, "Product identification guide"; sec. 7, "Product information on pharmaceuticals and equipment."

Provides information and references on ophthalmic drugs and agents and instrumentation, equipment, supplies, lenses, vision standards, etc. used in ophthalmology and optometry, with detailed description prepared by the manufacturers. Indexed by manufacturer, product name, product category, and active ingredients. Color product identification section. Intended for eye care professionals. May also be useful to health consumers.

Related titles include *Physicians' desk reference: PDR* (1250), *ADA/PDR guide to dental therapeutics* (795), *PDR drug guide for mental health professionals* (1242), *PDR guide to drug interactions, side effects, and indications* (1247), *PDR for herbal medicines* (1244), *PDR for nonprescription drugs, dietary supplements, and herbs* (1245), *PDR for nutritional supplements* (1246), *PDR nurse's drug handbook* (1064), *PDR guide to biological and chemical warfare response, PDR guide to terrorism response*, and other titles.

PDR and its major companion volumes are available online in the PDR Electronic Library (1243).

1250 Physicians' desk reference: PDR. Medical Economics Company. ill. Oradell, N.J.: Thomson Healthcare, 1974–. ISSN: 0093-4461.

615.1   RS75.P5

Title varies: editions in 1947–73 entitled *Physicians' desk reference to pharmaceutical specialties and biologicals.* Description based on 61st ed., 2007. Imprint varies; now publ. by Thomson PDR, in cooperation with participating manufacturers. Available in print, on CD-ROM, and via the Internet (http://www.PDR.net). PDR and its major companion volumes are also found in the PDR Electronic Library (1243) on CD-ROM and as a Web-based resource. Also available as part of Micromedex Healthcare Series (1084).

"Contains Food and Drug Administration (FDA)-approved labeling for drugs as well as prescription information provided by manufacturers for grandfathered drugs and other drugs marketed without FDA approval under current FDA policies. Some dietary supplements and other products are also included."—*Foreword*

Principal sections: (1) manufacturers' index, an alphabetical index by manufacturer's name; (2) brand and generic name index; (3) product category index; (4) product identification guide, showing tablets and capsules in color and actual size; (5) product information, the main section of the book, listing approx. 4,000 pharmaceuticals by manufacturer, giving full descriptions of composition, action, use, dosage, side effects, etc.; and (6) diagnostic products information section, arranged alphabetically by manufacturer. Product descriptions have been provided and approved by the manufacturers. Includes a national directory of drug information centers, alphabetically arranged by state and city, FDA use-in-pregnancy ratings list, state AIDS drug assistance programs, patient assistance programs, and also several other special drug-related lists and instructions.

Other PDR titles include *ADA/PDR guide to dental therapeutics* (795), *PDR drug guide for mental health professionals* (1242), *PDR guide to drug interactions, side effects, and indications* (1247), *PDR for herbal medicines* (1244), *PDR for nonprescription drugs, dietary supplements, and herbs* (1245), *PDR for nutritional supplements* (1246), *PDR nurse's drug handbook* (1064), *Physicians' desk reference for ophthalmic medicines* (1249), *PDR guide to biological and chemical warfare response*, *PDR guide to terrorism response*, and other titles.

Other clinical information PDR products include the *PDR monthly prescribing guide* (drug reference designed specifically for use at the point of care), mobilePDR (software that allows retrieval of concise drug summaries), PDR.net (online source for FDA-approved and other manufacturer-supplied labeling information), and *PDR pharmacopoeia pocket dosing guide*.

1251 Phytochemical dictionary: A handbook of bioactive compounds from plants. 2nd ed. J. B. Harborne, Herbert Baxter, Gerard P. Moss. x, 976 p., ill. London; Philadelphia: Taylor and Francis, 1999. ISBN: 0748406204.

572.2   QK898.B54P48

Covering more than 3,000 organic compounds occurring in plants, this dictionary is potentially useful to food scientists, nutritionists, plant biochemists, and biologists. Emphasizes economically important or biologically active substances, such as flavorings, scents, and antimicrobial compounds. Entries are arranged in five major bioenergetic categories of chemical compounds: carbohydrates and lipids, nitrogen-containing compounds, alkaloids, phenolics, and terpenoids. Compounds are grouped according to chemical class and subclass; chemical structures appear in nearly all entries, along with common name and synonyms, molecular weight and formula, Chemical Abstracts Service registry number, and brief description of use by humans or biological activity. References to the literature appear with the introduction to each section. Subject and species indexes are provided.

1252 **Poisoning and toxicology handbook.** 4th ed. Jerrold B. Leikin, Frank P. Paloucek. xlv, 1331 p., ill. Boca Raton, Fla.: CRC Press/ Taylor & Francis Group, 2008. ISBN: 9781420044.

615.9   RA1215.P65

1st ed., 1998; 3rd ed., 2002.

Contents: sec. 1, "Medicinal agents"; sec. 2, "Nonmedicinal agents"; sec. 3, "Biological agents"; sec. 4, "Herbal agents"; sec. 5, "Antidotes and drugs used in toxicology"; sec. 6, "Diagnostic tests/procedures"; appendix; index.

Provides detailed information on approx. 900 drugs and poisons, including environmental toxins, and related special topics and resources. Includes listings of U.S. poison control centers and organizations that offer toxicology and teratology information services.

1253 **Psychodynamic diagnostic manual (PDM).** American Psychoanalytic Association. Silver Spring, Md.: Alliance of Psychoanalytic Organizations, 2006. ISBN: 0976775824.

Intended as a complement to the DSM (*Diagnostic and statistical manual of mental disorders: DSM-IV-TR* [80]) and ICD (*ICD-10 classification of mental and behavioural disorders* [Geneva, Switzerland: World Health Organization, 1992]) classifications, it is described as "a diagnostic framework that attempts to characterize an individual's range of functionality—the depth as well as the surface of emotional, cognitive, and social patterns. based on current neuroscience, treatment outcome research, and other empirical investigations."—*Introd.*

1254 **Rational phytotherapy: A reference guide for physicians and pharmacists.** 5th ed. Volker Schulz, Rudolf Hänsel, Mark Blumenthal. 417 p. Berlin; New York: Springer, 2004. ISBN: 3540408320.

615.321   RM666.H33.S3813

1st ed., 1983, had title *Therapie mit Phytopharmaka*; 4th ed., 2001, *Rational phytotherapy: A physician's guide to herbal medicine.*

Contents: (1) "Medicinal plants, phytomedicine, and phytotherapy"; (2) "Central nervous system"; (3) "Cardiovascular system"; (4) "Respiratory system"; (5) "Digestive system"; (6) "Urinary tract"; (7) "Gynecologic indications for herbal remedies"; (8) "Skin, trauma, rheumatism, and pain"; (9) "Agents that increase resistance to disease."

Rev. and exp. ed.

Practice-oriented introduction to phytotherapy. Includes selected herbal remedies considered by the authors to have pharmacological and clinical effectiveness, with information on dosage and form of application. "The authors are highly experienced in the field of postgraduate medical education and, with this work, present an indispensable reference book for the medical practice."—*Publisher's website*

1255 Red book. Thomson Healthcare. ill. Montvale, N.J.: Thomson Healthcare, 2004–. ISSN: 1556-3391.

338   HD9666.1.D75

Volumes in 1941/42–1943/44 had title *Drug topics price book* (continues the "Red book price list section" of the *Druggists' circular*, issues semiannually 1897–1940); 1944–92 had title *Drug topics red book*; 1993–94, *Red book*; 1995–2003, *Drug topics red book.*

Red book description based on 2006 ed.

Product, pricing, and clinical and pharmaceutical reference information for prescription and over-the-counter (OTC) drugs, many with full-color photographs. Provides nationally recognized average wholesale prices and direct and federal upper-limit prices for prescription drugs. Also includes prices for reimbursable medical supplies and, for example, a vitamin comparison table of popular multivitamin products, a guide to herbal/alternative medicines, a list of FDA-approved new drugs, generics, and OTC products, and also a list of "Web sites worth watching." Includes poison control centers and manufacturers, pharmaceutical wholesalers, and third-party administrator directories. Intended for pharmacists and other health care professionals. For electronic delivery options, see http://www.micromedex.com/products/redbook.

1256 The review of natural products. Ara DerMarderosian, John A. Beutler, Facts and Comparisons. St. Louis: Facts and Comparisons, 1996–. ISSN: 1541-1435.

615   QK99.A1.R47

Volumes from 1898 to 1995 had title *Lawrence review of natural products.*

Alphabetically arranged monographs with Latin scientific names, common names, synonyms, historical names, botanical and other related information, and historical uses of products in folk medicine. Monograph entries also provide chemical and pharmacological information, interactions with drugs and other natural products, toxicology, patient information, use during pregnancy and lactation, and literature references.

"Clinical overview" box at the beginning of each monograph. Primary index; therapeutic index. Intended for pharmacists and health care professionals.

Guide to popular natural products (1222) is an abridged edition of this title. Available as an e-book in Facts and Comparisons 4.0 Online (1159).

1257 Stockley's drug interactions: A source book of interactions, their mechanisms, clinical importance and management. 7th ed. Ivan H. Stockley, Karen Baxter. 1208 p. London; Chicago: Pharmaceutical Press, 2006. ISBN: 0853696640.

RM302.S76

1st ed. (1981) through 5th ed. (1999) had title *Drug interactions: A source book of interactions, their mechanism, clinical importance and management*; 8th ed. due Nov. 2007. Description based on 7th ed., 2006.

Comprehensive source of international drug interaction information, based on published clinical papers and reports, with British and American drug names. Covers drug-drug, drug-food, and drug-herb interactions. This edition contains approx. 2,800 drug interaction monographs, with more than 14,000 drug interactions (*publ. notes*) and revision of previous text. Each monograph contains a summary, with details of the particular interaction, its clinical importance, and how to manage it. Interaction monographs are presented alphabetically in 34 chapters, grouped by therapeutic use or pharmacological activity.

Available online as part of MedicinesComplete (1236) and searchable by drug name (up to 12 drugs at once), synonyms and codes, international proprietary names, and drug groups.

1258 Tyler's honest herbal: A sensible guide to the use of herbs and related remedies. 4th ed. Steven Foster, Varro E. Tyler. xxi, 442 p. New York: Haworth Herbal Press, 1999. ISBN: 0789007053.

615.321   RM666.H33T94

Title varies: 1st ed. (1981) had title *The honest herbal*; 2nd ed. (1987), *The new honest herbal*; 3rd ed., 1993. Provides references and peer-reviewed scientific data on the uses of herbs and herbal remedies. Includes approx. 100 herbs. Arranged in alphabetical order by common name, each entry describes the plant with the appropriate nomenclature, botanical information, the chemistry and pharmacology of its active ingredients, its traditional uses, positive and negative features when used for therapeutic purposes, folklore, and other facts. An evaluation by the author based on available evidence follows for each herb. Mentions possible safety concerns. Includes a chapter on laws and regulations. References to the literature. For general readers and as a starting point for scientists; index. *Tyler's herbs of choice* (re-issued in 1999 as *Tyler's herbs of choice: The therapeutic use of phytomedicinals*) provides related information.

1259 **What your patients need to know about psychiatric medications.** Robert E. Hales, Stuart C. Yudofsky, Robert H. Chew. xvii, 356 p. Washington: American Psychiatric Publishing, 2005. ISBN: 1585622036.

615.788   RM315.H328

Contents: "Medications in pregnancy"; "Antianxiety medication"; "Medications for treatment of insomnia"; "Antidepressants: Selective serotonin reuptake inhibitors and mixed-action antidepressants"; "Tricyclic antidepressants"; "Monoamine oxidase inhibitors"; "Mood stabilizers"; "First-generation antipsychotics"; "Second-generation antipsychotics"; "Treatment of attention-deficit/hyperactivity disorder in adults"; "Stimulants"; "Cognitive enhancers for treatment of Alzheimer's disease and other forms of dementia"; index.

Provides relevant and easy-to-understand information about commonly asked questions about psychiatric medications. Information about each medication presented in a standard format: brand name; generic name; available strengths; available in generic; medication class; general information; dosing information; common side effects; adverse reactions and precautions; use in pregnancy and breastfeeding; possible drug interactions; overdose; special considerations. Accompanied by CD-ROM that contains PDF files of the pages as they appear in the book. Also available as part of Psychiatry Online (1294).

1260 **Wiley handbook of current and emerging drug therapies.** Wiley. 8 v., ill. Hoboken, N.J.: Wiley-Interscience, 2007–. ISBN: 9780470040.

615.58   RM301.12.W55

Contents: pt. 1, "Introduction"; pt. 2, "Oncology"; pt. 3, "Immune system"; pt. 4, "Metabolic diseases"; pt. 5, "Infectious diseases"; pt. 6, "Emerging technologies and business opportunities"; pt. 7, "Global markets and national policy"; pt. 8, "New opportunities in drug discovery and pipeline development."

"Comprehensive reference to established and future drug treatments for more than 60 important diseases and indications in every major therapeutic area."—*Publ. notes.* Current information and resource for biomedical and pharmaceutical research and drug discovery, including emerging technologies, markets, and information on the status of trials. Also available in a regularly updated version from Wiley (http://www. interscience.wiley.com/mrw/cedt).

Histories

1261 150 years of caring: A pictorial history of the American Pharmaceutical Association. George B. Griffenhagen. viii, 305 p., ill. Washington: American Pharmaceutical Association, 2002. ISBN: 1582120404.

615.106073   RS67.U6G754

"This book is primarily about the men and women who provided the leadership of the national professional society of pharmacists in the U.S.A. and professionals who are responsible for the appropriate use of medication to achieve optimal therapeutic outcomes."—*Pref.* More than 300 illustrations. Chapters on the practitioners of pharmacy, pharmaceutical scientists, pharmaceutical educators, law enforcement officials, drug manufacturers, pharmaceutical distributors, women, minorities, students, and the military. Changes in terminology "to define a qualified practitioner of pharmacy" are described in ch. 41. Ch. 1 includes a list of articles published in the *Journal of the American Pharmaceutical Association* commemorating the APhA Sesquicentennial. Appendixes: (A) "APhA annual meetings 1852–2002"; (B) "APhA past president trivia"; (C) "Biographies of APhA presidents 1852–2002"; (D) "The leadership of APhA 1852–2002"; (E) "Sources of information" (includes APhA code of ethics); (F) "Index of persons" (with indication of portrait and/or biographical sketch).

1262 Chronicles of pharmacy. A. C. Wootton. 2 v., ill. London: Macmillan, 1910.

615.109   RS61.W7

Repr.: Boston: Milford House, [1971] (2 v. in 1); Tuckahoe, N.Y.: USV Pharmaceutical Corp., 1972.

In narrative form; describes the discovery and use of various drugs, medicines, and nostrums from ancient times through the 19th century. Includes some biographical material of famous apothecaries. Indexed.

1263 **Dictionary of protopharmacology: Therapeutic practices, 1700–1850.** J. Worth Estes. xvii, 215, [13] p., ill. Canton, Mass.: Science History, 1990. ISBN: 0881350680.

615.109033   RM36.E88

Provides definitions of drugs commonly prescribed by English-speaking physicians between approx. 1700 and 1850. Some 3,000 entries, including botanical drugs, chemicals, and mixtures and patent medicines. Many synonyms and cross-references.

1264 **Drug discovery: A history.** Walter Sneader. viii, 468 p., ill. Hoboken, N.J.: Wiley, 2005. ISBN: 0471899798.

615.1909   RS61.S637

Contents: pt. 1, "Legacy of the past"; pt. 2, "Drugs from naturally occurring prototypes: (I) Phytochemicals; (II) Biochemicals; (III) Drugs from microorganisms"; pt. 3, "Synthetic drugs."

Presents an overview and review of the discovery of therapeutic compounds, from prehistoric times to the present. Chapters on plant products, hormones, antibiotics, and fungi and medicinal compounds developed from them as well as on the origins and discoveries of synthetic compounds. Includes chemical structures, bibliographical references, and index. Available as an e-book from netLibrary.

1265 **A guide to pharmacy museums and historical collections in the United States and Canada.** George B. Griffenhagen, Ernst Walter Stieb, Beth D. Fisher, American Institute of the History of Pharmacy. xii, 143 p., ill. Madison, Wisc.: American Institute of the History of Pharmacy, 1999. ISBN: 0931292344.

615.107473   RS123.U6G75

Title varies: 1956, *Pharmacy museums*, by George Griffenhagen; 1972, *Pharmacy museums and historical collections on public view, U.S.A.*, by Sami K. Hamarneh; 1981, *Pharmacy museums and historical collections on public view in the United States and Canada*, by Sami K. Hamarneh and Ernst Stieb; 1988, *Pharmacy museums and historical collections in the United States and Canada* (Publication American Institute of the History of Pharmacy, n.s.; no. 11). (Publication American Institute of the History of Pharmacy; n.s.; no. 18). Museums are described and listed in alphabetical order by state or province and city. Includes sites of historical pharmacy markers. Name index.

1266 An historical account of pharmacology to the 20th century.
Chauncey Depew Leake. xi, 210 p. Springfield, Ill.: Thomas, [1975].
ISBN: 0398032777.
615.109   RM41.L4

American Lecture Series no. 970.

Contents: ch. 1, "An historical account of pharmacology"; ch. 2, "Protopharmacology: Prehistoric empirical drug lore"; ch. 3, "Protopharmacology: Codified empirical drug use"; ch. 4, "Graeco-Roman medicine"; ch. 5, "The Muslim drug innovations"; ch. 6, "Drugs in medieval Europe"; ch. 7, "Drug development in the Renaissance"; ch. 8, "Drugs in the 17th and 18th centuries"; ch. 9, "The first part of the 19th century"; ch. 10, "Pharmacology in the second half of the 19th century"; ch. 11, "Progress and promise: Transition of pharmacology from the 19th century into the 20th."

Overview of the history of pharmacology. Name index; subject index. For historians of medicine and science and also general readers.

1267 The history of pharmacy: A selected annotated bibliography.
Gregory Higby, Elaine Condouris Stroud, David L. Cowen. xi, 321 p., ill. New York: Garland, 1995. ISBN: 0824097688.
615.109   Z6675.P5.H53; RS61

Contents: pt. 1, "Bibliographies and general studies": (1a) "Bibliographies, encyclopedias, dictionaries"; (1b) "General historical literature and historiography"; (1c) "National studies"; (1d) "Company histories"; (1e) "Biographies"; pt. 2, "Special subjects": (2a) "Practice of pharmacy"; (2b) "Basic pharmaceutical disciplines"; (2c) "Materia medica (drugs) and drug therapy: General, pre-1600, post-1600"; (2d) "Laws and regulations"; (2e) "Professional pharmaceutical literature: Classics, historical studies"; (2f) "Professional and social aspects"; (2g) "Economic and business aspects"; (2h) "Education"; (2i) "Manufacturing (not including company histories)"; (2j) "Equipment and museology"; (2k) "Patent medicines and quackery"; pt. 3, "Pharmacy in the arts": (3a) "Architecture and interior design"; (3b) "Painting, sculpture, graphic arts, and photography"; (3c) "Creative literature"; (3d) "Music."

"Broad overview of the literature that emphasizes the most important and essential works" (*Introd.*), i.e., a selective guide to the secondary literature. Designed for graduate students and teachers. Author index.

1268 Kremers and Urdang's history of pharmacy. 4th ed. Edward
Kremers, George Urdang, Glenn Sonnedecker. xv, 571 p., ill.
Philadelphia: Lippincott, 1976. ISBN: 0397520743.

615.409   RS61.K73

1st ed., 1940, had title *History of pharmacy: A guide and a survey*; 3rd ed.,
1963.

   Contents: pt. 1, "Pharmacy's early antecedents": (1) "Ancient prelude";
(2) "The Arabs and the European Middle Ages"; pt. 2, "The rise of professional pharmacy in representative countries of Europe": (3) "Changing
medicaments and the modern pharmacists"; (4) "The development in
Italy"; (5) "The development in France"; (6) "The development in Germany"; (7) "The development in Britain"; (8) "Some international trends";
pt. 3, "Pharmacy in the United States": (9) "The North American colo-
nies"; (10) "The Revolutionary War"; (11) "Young republic and pioneer
expansion"; (12) "The growth of associations"; (13) "The rise of legislative
standards"; (14) "The development of education"; (15) "The establishment of a literature"; (16) "Economic and structural development"; pt. 4:
(17) "The American pharmacist in public service"; (18) "Contributions by
pharmacists to science and industry."

   A survey of the history of pharmaceutical science and a "sociohistori-
cal view of pharmacy evolving as a profession in the Western world showing the international character of pharmacy and its development."—*Pref.*
Several appendixes (e.g., "Representative drugs of the American Indians,"
"Founding of state pharmaceutical associations," "Pharmaceutical literature: Some bibliographic historical notes," and others). Glossary, notes,
references, and index.

**1269 Pharmacopoeias and related literature in Britain and America,
1618–1847.** David L. Cowen. viii, 296 p., ill., maps. Aldershot,
[England, U.K.]; Burlington, Vt.: Ashgate/Variorum, 2001. ISBN:
0860788423.

615.114109   RS141.3.C675

Bibliographic and historical studies, previously scattered in a variety of
publications, giving "evidence of the tremendous influence that British
pharmacopoeial literature exerted on the Continent, on America, and on
far reaches of the Empire."—*Pref.*

1270 Pharmacy in history. George Edward Trease. vii, 265 p., ill., ports.
London: Baillière, Tindall and Cox, [1964].

615.109   RS61.T7

Contents: pt. 1: "Our inheritance from ancient civilizations": ch. 1, "From folk medicine to Galen"; ch. 2, "From Galen to the Middle Ages"; ch. 3, "Early technology"; ch. 4, "Early alchemy"; pt. 2: "The chronological development of English pharmacy": ch. 5, "Introduction"; ch. 6, "The Roman occupation and the Dark Ages"; ch. 7, "From the Norman Conquest to King John"; ch. 8, "The thirteenth century, 1216–1307"; ch. 9, "The fourteenth century, 1307–1399"; ch 10, "The fifteenth century, 1400–1485"; ch. 11, "The early Tudors, 1485–1558"; ch. 12, "The reign of Elizabeth I, 1558–1603"; ch. 13, "The early Stuarts and the Commonwealth, 1603–1660"; ch. 14, "From Charles II to Queen Anne, 1660–1714"; ch. 15, "George I and George II, 1714–1760"; ch. 16," George III, 1760–1820"; ch. 17, "1820–1870"; ch. 18, "From 1870 to 1901"; ch. 19, "Pharmaceutical preparations of the 19th century"; ch. 20, "The twentieth century." Index.

Introductory historical survey of British pharmaceutical history. Contains quotations from the literature of the different periods of the development of pharmacy, and selected illustrations.

1271 U.S. Food and Drug Administration [home page]. Food and Drug Administration. Washington: Food and Drug Administration. http://www.fda.gov.

The Food and Drug Administration (FDA) regulates foods, drugs, medical devices, biologics (vaccines, blood products, etc.), and radiation-emitting products (e.g., cell phones, lasers, microwaves, etc.). Searchable website (http://www.fda.gov/search.html), with FDA A–Z index that provides links to a large number of online resources. This search engine will not, however, find information that is in the numerous databases on the FDA site. A collection of databases can be found at http://www.fda.gov/search/databases.html and can be accessed separately.

Major FDA centers include the Center for Drug Evaluation (CDER) ("consumer watchdog in America's healthcare system"; http://www.fda.gov/cder/index.html), which evaluates drugs before they can be sold and provides resources such as Drugs@FDA (1283), Electronic Orange Book (1158), and National Drug Code Directory (1183). Another FDA center is the Center for Food Safety and Applied Nutrition (CFSAN) (http://www.cfsan.fda.gov/~dms/foia.html), with resources on foods and food safety, such as the GRAS (Generally Recognized as Safe) list of substances (http://www.cfsan.fda.gov/~dms/grasguid.html), the "bad bug book," and publications on food-borne illness, FDA food code, allergens, dietary supplements, etc. Additional FDA centers provide information on biologics, cosmetics, medical devices, radiological health, toxicological research, and veterinary medicine.

Other examples of resources provided at the FDA site include access to the "blue book" (i.e., *Requirements of laws and regulations enforced by the U.S. Food and Drug Administration*), oncology tools, patient safety portal, special health issues, and information on bioterrorism, trans fats, vaccines, xenotransplantation, and many other subjects and topics relating to human and animal drugs and biologics, foods, and medical devices. Information is tailored to the needs of different user groups, with separate pages for consumers, patients, health professionals, state/local officials, industry, press, women, and children. Frequently requested FDA documents can be accessed via an "electronic reading room" (http://www.fda.gov/foi/electrr. htm). Milestones in U.S. Food and Drug Law History 1820–2005 is available at http://www.fda.gov/opacom/backgrounders/miles.html.

Indexes; Abstract journals; Databases

1272 **Dietary supplements labels database.** National Library of Medicine (U.S.). 2007–. Bethesda, Md.: National Library of Medicine. http://dietarysupplements.nlm.nih.gov/dietary/.

Produced by National Library of Medicine (NLM) (427), Specialized Information Services (SIS); based on Dietary Supplements On-Line Database.

Offers information on the ingredients of more than 2,000 selected brands of dietary supplements in the United States. Searchable by brand name, uses noted on the product, specific active ingredient, and manufacturer. Intended for researchers and consumers. Answers many questions users of dietary supplements might have concerning ingredients shown on labels of specific brands, chemical ingredients, animal products, proven medical benefits, toxicity of specific ingredients, etc. Ingredients of dietary supplements are linked to other NLM databases, e.g., MedlinePlus (463) and PubMed (432). Helpful FAQ section.

1273 **Drug information portal.** National Library of Medicine (U.S.). 2008–. Bethesda, Md.: National Library of Medicine. http:// druginfo.nlm.nih.gov/.

"Gateway to selected drug information from the National Library of Medicine (427) and other key government agencies. [with] access to over 12,000 selected drugs."—*About This Portal.* Can be searched by a drug's trade or generic name. Provides a summary of the information about the drug, and links to further related information, such as MedlinePlus (463), AIDSinfo (447), MEDLINE (425)/PubMed® (432), LactMed (1572), HSDB (1569), Dietary Supplements Labels Database (728), TOXLINE (1578), DailyMed (626), ClinicalTrials.gov (191), PubChem (444), ChemIDplus (1563), Drugs@FDA (1283), and others. For the public, health care professionals, and researchers.

1274 International pharmaceutical abstracts. Thomson Scientific. 199?–. Philadelphia: Thomson Scientific. http://scientific.thomson. com/products/ipa/.

615   RS1

Also called IPA. Published in print since 1964. Launched and distributed electronically in 1970, with coverage back to 1964. The Thomson Corporation, already involved in the production of the IPA database since 2001, assumed ownership of IPA in 2005 from the American Society of Health-System Pharmacists (ASHP), its previous publisher. Currently available in print (semimonthly) and in a variety of electronic formats from several vendors.

Indexes the international literature in applied pharmacology, including state pharmacy journals, abstracts of presentations at major pharmacy meetings, related health and medical journals, and journals of alternative and herbal medicine. Approx. 18,000 records annually. Each IPA record includes an English-language abstract. Intended for pharmacists and life science researchers.

1275 Lexi-Comp online. Lexi-Comp, Inc. 1978–. Hudson, Ohio: Lexi-Comp, Inc. http://www.lexi.com/web/toursol.jsp.

Point-of-care drug and clinical information resource, with links to primary literature. Contains 15 clinical databases (e.g., Lexi-Drugs Online, AHFS, Lexi-Natural Products Online, Nursing Lexi-Drugs Online, Pharmacogenomics, Poisoning and Toxicology, Lab Tests and Diagnosis, and several others) and provides drug information and treatment recommendation for diseases and conditions. Also includes other features, e.g., an online interaction tool (Lexi-Interact) and medical calculator (Lexi-CALC). For pharmacists, physicians, nurses, and dentists. Detailed information available at the Lexi-Comp website "tour portal" (http://www.lexi.com/web/toursol.jsp).

1276 Micromedex healthcare series. Thomson Micromedex. [199?–.] Greenwood Village, Colo.: Thomson Micromedex. http://www.micromedex.com/products/hcs/.

Micromedex Healthcare Series; also called Healthcare Series Online.

Intended for clinicians. Includes a variety of resources for finding information on drugs, toxicology, emergency, acute care, and disease data as well as alternative medicine information. Drug resources include DRUGDEX, DRUG-REAX, IDENTIDEX, IV Index, *Index nominum* (Medpharm Scientific, 2004), *Martindale: The complete drug reference* (1182), *Physicians' desk reference: PDR* (1248), POISINDEX, *Red book* (1255), REPRORISK, and *USP DI* (727). Emergency and disease data can be found, for example, in DISEASEDEX and alternative therapies in AltMedDex and other Thomson products. Searchable across either all databases, by specific database(s), and by groups of databases. Drugs can be searched by trade or generic drug name. Specific drug database search and drug topic search provide, for example, a drug evaluation overview, dosing information, pharmacokinetics, contraindications, precautions, adverse reactions, single and multiple drug interactions, IV compatibility, teratogenicity, therapeutic uses, and comparative efficacy.

A matrix of all Micromedex products and versions in this series, with listing of the individual titles, various format options, and indication of whether a particular title is also available in print can be found at http://www.micromedex.com/support/faqs/plat_matrix.html. Help with citing the various Micromedex versions is provided at http://www.micromedex.com/about_us/legal/cite/.

1277 **Natural standard.** Natural Standard. 2003–. Cambridge, Mass.: Natural Standard. http://www.naturalstandard.com.

R733

International collaboration, with contributors from academic institutions. Provides evidence-based information and expert opinions about complementary and alternative therapies. Individual monographs provide information in support of clinical decision making. Contains several databases: Herbs and Supplements, Condition Center, Health and Wellness, Dictionary, Interactions, and Brand Names. Individual entries provide an overview of clinically oriented research and historical background of various herbal products. A typical entry, such as that for peppermint oil, includes related terms, essential-oil constituents, leaf constituents, selected brand names (e.g., Ben-Gay), combination products, and a note on a different species of mint with similar appearances. Also provides detailed background information on its medicinal use, including historical information dating back to ancient Egypt, Greece, and Rome. Furthermore, includes information about use for different medical conditions and illnesses, contraindications, safety rating, tradition/theory (i.e., proposed uses that have not been tested in humans and for which safety and effectiveness may not have been scientifically proven), dosing (recommendations for adults and children), safety (allergies, side effects and warnings, pregnancy and breast feeding), interactions (with drugs, herbs, and supplements), author information, and bibliographical references and links to PubMed (432) abstracts.

Information on herbs and supplements in MedlinePlus (463) is taken from Natural Standard.

1278 NLM gateway. National Library of Medicine (U.S.). 2000–. Bethesda, Md.: National Library of Medicine. http://gateway.nlm. nih.gov/.

RA11

Allows simultaneous searching of information resources at the National Library of Medicine (NLM). Databases include MEDLINE (425)/PubMed (432) and the NLM Catalog (427) as well as other resources, including information on current clinical trials and consumer health information (MedlinePlus [463]). Currently provides access to 21 databases and other information resources (for a complete list of databases and other details, see http://www.nlm.nih.gov/pubs/factsheets/gateway.html). An overview of the search results is presented in several categories (bibliographic resources, consumer health resources, and other information), with a listing of the individual databases and the number of results within these categories.

1279 PubMed. U.S. National Center for Biotechnology Information, National Library of Medicine, National Institutes of Health. 1996–. Bethesda, Md.: U.S. National Center for Biotechnology Information. http://www.ncbi.nlm.nih.gov/sites/entrez/.

PubMed®, developed and maintained by the National Center for Biotechnology Information (NCBI) at the National Library of Medicine® (NLM) (427). It is available via the NCBI Entrez (3) retrieval system. PubMed also provides access to the other Entrez molecular biology resources (*PubMed Overview*). Starting May 23, 2007, NCBI is changing to a new version of Entrez in a phased implementation (cf. Nahin AM. New and Improved PubMed®/Entrez and New URL *NLM tech. bull.*, 2007 May–Jun.; [356]: http://www.nlm.nih.gov/pubs/techbull/mj07/mj07_issue_cover.html).

Provides a search interface for more than 16 million bibliographic citations and abstracts in the fields of medicine, nursing, dentistry, veterinary medicine, health care systems, and preclinical sciences. It provides access to articles indexed for MEDLINE® (425) and for selected life sciences journals. PubMed subsets found under the "Limits" tab are: MEDLINE and PubMed Central®, several journal groups (i.e., core clinical journals, dental journals, and nursing journals), and topical subsets (AIDS, bioethics, cancer, complementary medicine, history of medicine, space life sciences, systematic reviews, and toxicology). "Linkout" provides access to full-text articles.

For detailed information see the PubMed fact sheet at http://www.nlm.nih.gov/pubs/factsheets/pubmed.html. For a brief overview of searching PubMed, see the PubMed Quick Start at http://www.ncbi.nlm.nih.gov/books/bv.fcgi?rid=helppubmed.section.pubmedhelp.PubMed_Quick_Start. For details on the now completed OLDMEDLINE retrospective conversion projects, see http://www.nlm.nih.gov/pubs/techbull/so06/so06_oldmedline_status.html.

1280 **U.S. Food and Drug Administration [home page].** Food and Drug Administration. Washington: Food and Drug Administration. http://www.fda.gov.

The Food and Drug Administration (FDA) regulates foods, drugs, medical devices, biologics (vaccines, blood products, etc.), and radiation-emitting products (e.g., cell phones, lasers, microwaves, etc.). Searchable website (http://www.fda.gov/search.html), with FDA A–Z index that provides links to a large number of online resources. This search engine will not, however, find information that is in the numerous databases on the FDA site. A collection of databases can be found at http://www.fda.gov/search/databases.html and can be accessed separately.

Major FDA centers include the Center for Drug Evaluation (CDER) ("consumer watchdog in America's healthcare system"; http://www.fda.gov/cder/index.html), which evaluates drugs before they can be sold and provides resources such as Drugs@FDA (1283), Electronic Orange Book (1158), and National Drug Code Directory (1183). Another FDA center is the Center for Food Safety and Applied Nutrition (CFSAN) (http://www.cfsan.fda.gov/~dms/foia.html), with resources on foods and food safety, such as the GRAS (Generally Recognized as Safe) list of substances (http://www.cfsan.fda.gov/~dms/grasguid.html), the "bad bug book," and publications on food-borne illness, FDA food code, allergens, dietary supplements, etc. Additional FDA centers provide information on biologics, cosmetics, medical devices, radiological health, toxicological research, and veterinary medicine.

Other examples of resources provided at the FDA site include access to the "blue book" (i.e., *Requirements of laws and regulations enforced by the U.S. Food and Drug Administration*), oncology tools, patient safety portal, special health issues, and information on bioterrorism, trans fats, vaccines, xenotransplantation, and many other subjects and topics relating to human and animal drugs and biologics, foods, and medical devices. Information is tailored to the needs of different user groups, with separate pages for consumers, patients, health professionals, state/local officials, industry, press, women, and children. Frequently requested FDA documents can be accessed via an "electronic reading room" (http://www. fda.gov/foi/electrr.htm). Milestones in U.S. Food and Drug Law History 1820–2005 is available at http://www.fda.gov/opacom/backgrounders/ miles.html.

1281 **WISER (Wireless Information System for Emergency Responders).** National Library of Medicine (U.S.). 2004–. Besthesda, Md.: National Library of Medicine. http://wiser.nlm. nih.gov.

PDA application designed to assist first responders in hazardous materials incidents, including substance identification support, physical character-istics, human health information, and advice on containment and sup-pression. Content from TOXNET (1586)'s HSDB (Hazardous Substance Data Bank) (1569). Further information about PDA and desktop/laptop versions available at the website.

Internet Resources

1282 **Drug information portal.** National Library of Medicine (U.S.). 2008–. Bethesda, Md.: National Library of Medicine. http:// druginfo.nlm.nih.gov/.

"Gateway to selected drug information from the National Library of Medi-cine (427) and other key government agencies. [with] access to over 12,000 selected drugs."—*About This Portal.* Can be searched by a drug's trade or generic name. Provides a summary of the information about the drug, and links to further related information, such as MedlinePlus (463), AIDSinfo (447), MEDLINE (425)/PubMed® (432), LactMed (1572), HSDB (1569), Dietary Supplements Labels Database (728), TOXLINE (1578), DailyMed (626), ClinicalTrials.gov (191), PubChem (444), ChemIDplus (1563),

Drugs@FDA (1283), and others. For the public, health care professionals, and researchers.

1283 **Drugs@FDA.** U.S. Food and Drug Administration, Center for Drug and Evaluation Research. Washington: U.S. Food and Drug Administration, Center for Drug and Evaluation Research. http://www.accessdata.fda.gov/scripts/cder/drugsatfda.

RM300

Includes FDA-approved brand-name and generic drug products. Searchable by drug name, active ingredient, new drug application number (NDA), abbreviated new drug application (ANDA), and biologics license application (BLA). Provides a drug's FDA history and helps with finding labels for approved drug products. Also provides monthly drug approval reports. Further information and answers to questions relating to this website can be found at http://www.fda.gov/Drugs/InformationOnDrugs/ucm075234.htm.

1284 **Drugs, supplements, and herbal information (MedlinePlus).** National Library of Medicine (U.S.). 2003?–. Bethesda, Md.: National Library of Medicine, National Institutes of Health, U.S. Dept. of Health and Human Services. http://www.nlm.nih.gov/medlineplus/druginformation.html.

Pt. of MedlinePlus® (463).

Generic or brand name drugs, arranged A–Z, with prescription and over-the-counter medication information from MedMaster™ (American Society of Health-System Pharmacists [ASHP]). For additional drug information, see the MedlinePlus Drug Therapy topic pages (http://www.nlm.nih.gov/medlineplus/drugtherapy.html). Also provides access to information on herbs and supplements from Natural Standard (1277). Additional herb and supplement information can be found via MedlinePlus Complementary and Alternative Therapies topics (http://www.nlm.nih.gov/medlineplus/complementaryandalternativetherapie s.html).

1285 **FAQ.** National Library of Medicine (U.S.). 1999–. Bethesda, Md.: National Library of Medicine. http://www.nlm.nih.gov/services/drug.html.

In addition to suggestions such as asking a doctor or pharmacist, answers questions about where to find information about U.S. drugs. Provides a listing of Internet links to online information about drugs, supplements, and herbal information, and additional suggestions where to find this type of information. Also provides a link to information about international (non-U.S.) drugs: International drug information FAQ (1286).

1286 FAQ international drug information. National Library of
Medicine (U.S.). 2000–. Bethesda, Md.: National Library of
Medicine. http://www.nlm.nih.gov/services/drug_intl.html.

Produced by the National Library of Medicine (NLM) (427).

In addition to making suggestions such as to ask a doctor or pharmacist, answers questions about where to find information about international (non-U.S.) drugs. Provides a list of NLM resources and links to specific country/regional resources (e.g., Australia, Canada, European Union, South Africa, United Kingdom, and several others). A listing for U.S. drug information FAQs is also available, i.e., U.S. Drug Information FAQ (1285).

1287 Traditional medicine (WHO). World Health Organization. 200?–.
Geneva, Switzerland: World Health Organization. http://www.who.
int/topics/traditional_medicine/en/.

Defines traditional medicine according to MeSH (MeSH: Medical Subject Headings [575]) as "systems of medicine based on cultural beliefs and practices handed down from generation to generation. The concept includes mystical and magical rituals, herbal therapy, and other treatments which may not be explained by modern medicine."—*Main page.* The site "provides links to descriptions of activities, reports, news and events, as well as contacts and cooperating partners in the various WHO programmes and offices working on this topics."—*Main page.* World Health Organization (WHO) (951) publications answer questions related to standardization and regulation.

1288 U.S. Food and Drug Administration [home page]. Food and Drug
Administration. Washington: Food and Drug Administration.
http://www.fda.gov.

The Food and Drug Administration (FDA) regulates foods, drugs, medical devices, biologics (vaccines, blood products, etc.), and radiation-emitting products (e.g., cell phones, lasers, microwaves, etc.). Searchable website (http://www.fda.gov/search.html), with FDA A–Z index that provides links to a large number of online resources. This search engine will not, however, find information that is in the numerous databases on the FDA site. A collection of databases can be found at http://www.fda.gov/search/databases.html and can be accessed separately.

Major FDA centers include the Center for Drug Evaluation (CDER) ("consumer watchdog in America's healthcare system"; http://www.fda.gov/cder/index.html), which evaluates drugs before they can be sold and provides resources such as Drugs@FDA (1283), Electronic Orange Book (1158), and National Drug Code Directory (1183). Another FDA center is the Center for Food Safety and Applied Nutrition (CFSAN) (http://www.cfsan.fda.gov/~dms/foia.html), with resources on foods and food safety, such as the GRAS (Generally Recognized as Safe) list of substances (http://www.cfsan.fda.gov/~dms/grasguid.html), the "bad bug book," and publications on food-borne illness, FDA food code, allergens, dietary supplements, etc. Additional FDA centers provide information on biologics, cosmetics, medical devices, radiological health, toxicological research, and veterinary medicine.

Other examples of resources provided at the FDA site include access to the "blue book" (i.e., *Requirements of laws and regulations enforced by the U.S. Food and Drug Administration*), oncology tools, patient safety portal, special health issues, and information on bioterrorism, trans fats, vaccines, xenotransplantation, and many other subjects and topics relating to human and animal drugs and biologics, foods, and medical devices. Information is tailored to the needs of different user groups, with separate pages for consumers, patients, health professionals, state/local officials, industry, press, women, and children. Frequently requested FDA documents can be accessed via an "electronic reading room" (http://www.fda.gov/foi/electrr.htm). Milestones in U.S. Food and Drug Law History 1820–2005 is available at http://www.fda.gov/opacom/backgrounders/miles.html.

1289 **WHO drug information.** World Health Organization. Geneva, Switzerland: World Health Organization. ISSN: 1010-9609. http://www.who.int/druginformation.

RS189.W47

Quarterly journal, available since 1987 in print and also online since 1996.

Provides an overview of topics relating to drug development and regulation that are of current relevance, with the latest international news, prescribing and access of medicines worldwide. Also introduces newly-released guidance documents. Includes lists of proposed and recommended International Nonproprietary Names for Pharmaceutical Substances (INN). For health professionals and policy makers. Further information and links to INNs, the current 16th ed. (Mar. 2009 and Mar. 2010 update) of the *WHO model list of essential medicines*, and other related WHO publications can be found at http://www.who.int/medicines/publications/en/.

1290 WISER (Wireless Information System for Emergency Responders). National Library of Medicine (U.S.). 2004–. Bethesda, Md.: National Library of Medicine. http://wiser.nlm.nih.gov.

PDA application designed to assist first responders in hazardous materials incidents, including substance identification support, physical characteristics, human health information, and advice on containment and suppression. Content from TOXNET (1580)'s HSDB (Hazardous Substance Data Bank) (1569). Further information about PDA and desktop/laptop versions available at the website.

Thesauruses

1291 EMTREE thesaurus. Excerpta Medica (Firm). Amsterdam; New York: Excerpta Medica, 1991–. ISSN: 09293299.

Z699.5.M39E49

Developed from 1974–90, *Master list of medical indexing terms (MALIMET)*; EMTAGS (discont. in 1998) and EMCLAS (i.e., the original subject classification system for EMBASE [414]) integration into EMTREE (1988–91). Annual updates.

Description based on 2006 ed.

Cover title: *EMTREE: The life science thesaurus.* Contents: v. 1, Alphabetical index; v. 2, Tree structure; v. 3, Permuted term index.

Hierarchically structured drug and disease controlled vocabulary used for subject indexing and for searching the biomedical literature (e.g., EMBASE, with "preferred terms" [i.e., drug and medical terms]), synonyms, and MeSH®: Medical Subject Headings (575). Contains a list of EMBASE section headings which, with a few exceptions, correspond to the titles of the Excerpta Medica abstract journals, published since 1947, and searchable in EMBASE since 1974. Also available online.

11 > PSYCHIATRY

1292 **Health and psychosocial instruments (HaPI).** Ovid Technologies, Inc., Behavioral Measurement Database Services. New York: Ovid Technologies. http://www.ovid.com/site/catalog/DataBase/866.jsp?t op=2&mid=3&bottom=7&subsection=10.

Comprehensive bibliographic coverage of a wide variety of evaluation and measurement tools for health and psychosocial studies for practitioners, educators, researchers, and students.

1293 **PEP archive.** Psychoanalytic Electronic Publishing. London: Psychoanalytic Electronic Publishing. http://www.p-e-p.org/.

The PEP Archive is a full-text, indexed, and hyperlinked collection of more than 20 premier journals on psychoanalysis since 1920, the full text of the *Standard edition of the complete psychological works of Sigmund Freud*, the complete correspondence of Sigmund Freud with other leading physicians and psychoanalysts of his time, and more than 20 other classic books by noted psychoanalytic authors. Also available in CD-ROM format.

1294 **PsychiatryOnline.** American Psychiatric Publishing. 2005–. Arlington, Va.: American Psychiatric Publishing. http://www. psychiatryonline.com.

RC435

Also called American Psychiatry Online Library (APOL).

Online system providing access to several psychiatry journals and reference texts in psychiatry and psychopharmacology, self-assessment tools, citation linking, and "see also" links. Examples include *American journal of psychiatry*; the *DSM-IV-TR* (Washington: American Psychiatric Association, 2000) and the *American Psychiatric Association practice guidelines for the treatment of psychiatric disorders* (1338); *American Psychiatric Publishing textbook of clinical psychiatry*; and *What your patients need to know about psychiatric medications* (721).

Bibliography

1295 **Core readings in psychiatry: An annotated guide to the literature.** 2nd ed. Michael H. Sacks, William H. Sledge, Catherine

Warren. xxv, 944 p. Washington: American Psychiatric Press, 1995.
ISBN: 0880485590.

616.89   RC454.C655

1st ed., 1984 (ed. Michael H. Sachs, William H. Sledge, and Phyllis Rubinton).

Contents: pt. 1, "Basic sciences: Biological, psychological, and social" (ch. 1–10); pt. 2, "Psychopathology" (ch. 11–30); pt. 3, "Assessment" (ch. 31–35); pt. 4, "Treatment" (ch. 36–51); pt. 5, "Normality and development" (ch. 52–66).

"Designed to be an introduction and guide to the entire psychiatric literature."—*Introd.* Broad survey, presenting 66 topical chapters by mental health specialists, with selected annotated literature citations. New areas of study since the previous edition include AIDS, neurospychiatry, models of psychoanalytic thoughts, child development, and medical economics. Resource for clinicians, educators, and students.

Classification

1296 Diagnostic and statistical manual of mental disorders: DSM-IV-TR. 4th ed. American Psychiatric Association. xxxvii, 943 p. Washington: American Psychiatric Association, 2000. ISBN: 0890420246.

616.89075   RC455.2.C4.D536

Prepared by the Task Force on DSM-IV and other committees and work groups of the American Psychiatric Association. 1st ed., 1952; 4th ed., 1994, has title *Diagnostic and statistical manual of mental disorders: DSM-IV.*

Essential resource for mental health professionals, viewed by researchers and clinicians as the accepted classification system for psychiatric disorders. Contains all diagnostic criteria plus systematic description of disorders, using a numerical code system. Includes an explanation of the code system and instructions for its use, description of disorders, glossary, classification history, alphabetic and numeric listing of diagnoses, and indexes of symptoms, diagnoses, and codes. Several appendixes, including, for example, a glossary of technical terms, annotated listing of changes in DSM-IV, and "Outline for cultural formulation and glossary of culture-bound syndromes."

In addition to correcting factual errors, updating codes, and making other improvements in the DSM-IV text in this edition, changes were made to reflect new information since the DSM-IV literature reviews were completed in 1992. Organization of the manual: instructions for use are followed by the diagnostic criteria for each of the DSM-IV disorders, along with descriptive text (p. 39–743). Eleven appendixes. Available online at http://psychiatryonline.com/.

Publication of the 5th ed., *Diagnostic and statistical manual of mental disorders: DSM-5*, is scheduled for May 2013. Details of the DSM-5 development process are available at http://www.DSM5.org/.

1297 The ICD-10 classification of mental and behavioural disorders: Clinical descriptions and diagnostic guidelines. World Health Organization. xii, 362 p. Geneva, [Switzerland]: World Health Organization, 1992. ISBN: 9241544228.

616.890012   RC455.2.C4I34

Adopted by the World Health Organization, Jan. 1993. A related title is *The ICD-10 classification of mental and behavioural disorders: Diagnostic criteria for research*, published by WHO in 2003.

Developed from ch. 5 of the *International statistical classification of diseases and related health problems* (84). An internationally agreed-upon psychiatric classification system, with descriptions of clinical features for each disorder, diagnostic guidelines, and codes for mental and behavioral disorders.Includes index. Full text available online at http://www.who.int/classifications/icd/en/bluebook.pdf. A companion volume is *Lexicon of psychiatric and mental terms* (Geneva, Switzerland: World Health Organization, 1994).

Another major title in the area of classification of mental disorders is *Diagnostic and statistical manual of mental disorders: DSM-IV-TR* (1296).

1298 Intellectual disability: Definition, classification, and systems of supports. 11th ed. American Association on Intellectual and Developmental Disabilities. xvi, 259 p., ill. Washington: American Association on Intellectual and Developmental Disabilities, 2010. ISBN: 9781935304043.

616.8588   RC570.C515

1st ed. (1921)–10th ed. (2002) had title: *Mental retardation: Definition, classification, and systems of support*.

AAIDD (American Association on Intellectual and Developmental Disabilities).

Written by the AAIDD Ad Hoc Committee on Terminology and Classification, consisting of 18 experts in disability, medicine, policy, special education, law, and other fields.

Contents: Pt. I, "Understanding intellectual disability and its assessment"; pt. II, "Diagnosis and classification of intellectual disability"; pt. III, "Systems of support"; pt. IV, "Implications."

In the 11th ed., the AAIDD presents its first official definition of the term "intellectual disability" (formerly mental retardation) and diagnostic system of intellectual disability based on three criteria: significant limitations in both intellectual functioning and adaptive behavior expressed in conceptual, social, and practical adaptive skills and age of onset before the age of 18.

Contains current and authoritative information on defining, classifying, and diagnosing intellectual disability and systems of support for people living with intellectual disability. Disability is being considered within the context of an individual's personal and environmental factors, and what support might be appropriate to improve a person's functioning and quality of life. Discusses various dimensions of support areas in a person's life, i.e., resources or strategies that promote the development, education, interests, and well-being of a person. Includes tables, figures, a glossary, references, and index, also historical definitions of mental retardation as formulated by the American Association on Mental Retardation (AAMR) and the American Psychiatric Association (APA). Intended for professionals in developmental disability, clinical psychologists, physicians, psychiatrists, students, and others.

An older edition (Oxford; New York: Oxford University Press, 2003) of this work was previously included in *Guide to reference*.

1299 Psychodynamic diagnostic manual (PDM). American Psychoanalytic Association. Silver Spring, Md.: Alliance of Psychoanalytic Organizations, 2006. ISBN: 0976775824.

Intended as a complement to the DSM (*Diagnostic and statistical manual of mental disorders: DSM-IV-TR* [1296]) and ICD (*ICD-10 classification of mental and behavioural disorders* [Geneva, Switzerland: World Health Organization, 1992]) classifications, it is described as "a diagnostic framework that attempts to characterize an individual's range of functionality—the depth as well as the surface of emotional, cognitive, and social patterns. based on current neuroscience, treatment outcome research, and other empirical investigations."—*Introd.*

Dictionaries

1300 American psychiatric glossary. 8th ed. Narriman C. Shahrokh, Robert E. Hales. ix, 255 p. Washington: American Psychiatric Publishing, 2003. ISBN: 1585620939.

616.89003   RC437.S76

First five editions, 1957–80, had title *A psychiatric glossary: The meaning of words most frequently used in psychiatry*. Seventh edition, 1994.

Includes "Outline of schools of psychiatry." Concise compendium of psychiatric terminology, with brief definitions. Incorporates the nomenclature of the *Diagnostic and statistical manual of mental disorders: DSM-IV-TR* (1296) of the American Psychiatric Association. More than 500 new terms in this edition. Includes abbreviations, tables of psychiatric medications and commonly abused drugs, legal terms, psychological tests, research terms, and list of mental health resources, with pertinent websites. Considered a standard reference, intended for professionals and also laypersons.

1301 APA dictionary of psychology. Gary R. VandenBos, American
Psychological Association. Washington: American Psychological
Association, 2006. ISBN: 9781591473800.

150.3   BF31.V295

Over 25,000 terms and definitions encompassing such areas of research and application as personality, development, interpersonal relations, memory, motivation, perception, cognition, language, and communication, among others. Provides coverage of psychological concepts, processes, and therapies across all the major subdisciplines of psychology—including clinical, experimental, social, developmental, personality, school and educational, industrial and organizational, and health. Amply cross-referenced, directing the user to synonyms and antonyms, acronyms and abbreviations, related terms and concepts. Four appendixes, each gathering entries thematically into one synoptic listing, covering biographies; institutions, associations, and organizations; psychological therapies and interventions; and psychological tests and assessment instruments.

1302 The Blackwell dictionary of neuropsychology. J. Graham
Beaumont, Pamela M. Kenealy, Marcus Rogers. xix, 788 p., ill.
Cambridge, Mass.: Blackwell Publishers, 1996. ISBN: 0631178961.

612.803   QP360.B577

Extended entries by international contributors provide a broad perspective on the study of neuropsychology. Entries cover key topics. Alphabetical organization and cross-referencing provide immediate access to the complex vocabulary of this field. Enhanced by illustrations and tables.

1303 Campbell's psychiatric dictionary. 9th ed. Robert Jean Campbell.
xx, 1051 p. Oxford; New York: Oxford University Press, 2009.
ISBN: 9780195341591.

616.89003   RC437.H5

1st ed., 1940; 8th ed., 2003. Early editions had title *Psychiatric dictionary*.

A standard dictionary in the field of psychiatry and allied professions, this expanded edition contains the extensive terminology of psychiatry, neuroscience, cognitive and clinical psychology, and related fields, with many new words and encyclopedic treatment of many terms. Also contains brief biographical entries. Useful for specialists as well as for non-specialists.

An older edition (Oxford; New York: Oxford University Press, 2003) of this work was previously included in *Guide to reference*.

1304 Comprehensive glossary of psychiatry and psychology. Harold
I. Kaplan, Benjamin J. Sadock, Robert Cancro. xi, 215 p., color ill.
Baltimore: Williams & Wilkins, 1991. ISBN: 068304527X.
616.89003   RC437.K36

Concise definitions of terms from the behavioral sciences, psychiatry, psychology, and social work, neurochemistry, neuroimmunology, and neurophysiology.

**1305 Dictionary of cognitive science: Neuroscience, psychology,
artificial intelligence, linguistics, and philosophy.** Olivier Houdé,
Daniel Kayser, Vivian Waltz, Christian Cav. xxxv, 428 p. New York:
Psychology Press, 2004. ISBN: 1579582516.
153.03   BF311.V56713

Translation of *Vocabulaire de sciences cognitives* (1998), a collaborative effort of 60 (mostly French) scholars. Presents 130 terms drawn from five major disciplines of cognitive science: neuroscience, psychology, artificial intelligence, linguistics, and philosophy. Instead of merely defining those terms, the editors divide them into sections corresponding to the five areas and explain them within the context of the applicable disciplines. Concluding each entry is a bibliography of selected sources, updated from the original French version. Not as broad and in-depth as its nearest competitor, *The MIT encyclopedia of the cognitive sciences* (1336), still a good resource for definitions of basic concepts in cognitive science, making it suitable for students. Available as an e-book.

**1306 Dictionary of ethical and legal terms and issues: The essential
guide for mental health professionals.** Len Sperry. xi, 277 p. New
York: Routledge, 2007. ISBN: 0415953219.
174.2   RC455.2.E8.S655

Contents: pt. 1, "Dictionary of ethical and legal terms"; pt. 2, "Ethical issues and considerations"; pt. 3, "Legal issues and considerations"; appendix: "Key legal cases and legislation impacting mental health practice"; index.

Concise guide to the key ethical and legal issues and considerations; codes and statutes; and key legal opinions, legislation, and regulations relevant to everyday mental health practice in the United States. Pt. 2 and 3 present particular topics in some detail, with definitions of key terms. Intended for graduate and undergraduate students and as a ready-reference source for mental health practitioners. Also available as an e-book.

1307 Dictionary of existential psychotherapy and counselling. Emmy Van Deurzen, Raymond Kenward. 228 p. London; Thousand Oaks, Calif.: SAGE, 2005. ISBN: 0761970940.

616.891403   RC489.E93.V357

Includes existential terminology and concepts; biographies of major philosophers (this dictionary is "considered generally philosophical" [*Introd.*] by the authors), psychotherapists, and theorists ("non-existential writers considered to have contributed to existential thinking."—*Introd.*); and related subjects not exclusively existential (e.g., humanistic psychology). Alphabetically arranged, with cross-references and many quotations. Includes bibliographical references (p. 222–228). For both general readers and professionals.

1308 A dictionary of psychology. 2nd ed. Andrew M. Colman. xii, 861 p., ill. Oxford; New York: Oxford University Press, 2006. ISBN: 9780192806321.

150.3   BF31.C65

Over 11,000 entries covering all branches of psychology. Clear, concise descriptions offer extensive coverage of key areas, including cognition, sensation and perception, emotion and motivation, learning and skills, language, mental disorders, and research methods. Entries extend to related disciplines, including psychoanalysis, psychiatry, the neurosciences, and statistics, and are extensively cross-referenced for ease of use, covering word origins and derivations as well as definitions. Also includes appendixes covering over 800 commonly used abbreviations and symbols as well as a list of phobias and phobic stimuli, with definitions. Available as part of Oxford Reference Online (Oxford; New York: Oxford University Press, 2002–).

1309 The dictionary of psychology. Raymond J. Corsini. xv, 1156 p., ill. Philadelphia: Brunner/Mazel, 1999. ISBN: 158391028X.

150.3   BF31.C72

More than 13,000 entries as well as nine appendixes on such topics as terms used by the DSM-IV manual of mental disorders, prescription terms, measuring instruments, and brief biographies of noted psychologists through history.

1310 Dictionary of psychology and psychiatry: English–German/ German–English/Englisch–deutsch/deutsch–Englisch. 2nd ed. R. Haas. Seattle, Wash.: Hogrefe and Huber, 2003. ISBN: 0889373027.

This two-volume English–German/German–English dictionary is generally regarded as the most exhaustive bilingual compilation of psychological terms.

1311 A historical dictionary of psychiatry. Edward Shorter. ix, 338 p. New York: Oxford University Press, 2005. ISBN: 0195176685.

616.89003   RC438.S53

Contains key terms and concepts for psychiatry and the neurosciences, trends in psychiatry, pharmacological developments, and social themes. Includes important individuals, places, institutions, and dates in the development of psychiatry, with emphasis on the mid-19th century to the present. Bibliographical references and index. For clinicians, scientists, and general readers. Available as an e-book via netLibrary and ebrary.

1312 International dictionary of psychoanalysis = Dictionnaire international de la psychanalyse. A de Mijolla. 3 v. Detroit: Macmillan Reference USA, 2005. ISBN: 0028659244.

616.891703   RC501.4.D4313

Translation of French *Dictionnaire international de la psychanalyse*, ed. Alain de Mijolla, 2002.

Contents: v. 1, A–F; v. 2, G–Pr; v. 3, Ps–Z.

Considers the history and modern practice of psychoanalysis and its subfields, including the relationship between psychoanalysis and other disciplines. International resource, with 1,569 entries. The American edition contains more than 200 new articles, which include discussion of concepts, the history of psychoanalysis in different countries, and biographies of major deceased psychoanalysts and their major works. Multilingual glossary (from English into French, German, Italian, Portuguese, and Spanish). Includes 19th- and 20th-century chronology. Also available online via Gale Virtual Reference Library (Farmington Hills, Mich.: Gale Cengage Learning, 2002–).

1313 Lexicon of psychiatric and mental health terms. 2nd ed. World Health Organization. 108 p. Geneva, [Switzerland]: World Health Organization, 1994. ISBN: 924154466X.

616.890014   RC436.5.L49

1st ed., 1989.

"The second edition is designed as a companion volume to the *ICD-10 classification of mental and behavioural disorders* (Geneva, Switzerland: World Health Organization, 1992). Contains some 700 terms that appear in the text of the ICD-10 and that, in the judgment of experts, require definitions. Some of these, common to both ICD-9 and ICD-10, have been reproduced, with minor modifications" (*Introd.*, p. 2) from the 1st ed. Included are names of psychiatric diseases and conditions, names of signs and symptoms, and related psychopathological terms, terminology used in psychiatric classification, and also some mental health terms.

1314 Lexicon of psychiatry, neurology, and the neurosciences. 2nd ed. Frank J. Ayd. vii, 1104 p. Philadelphia: Lippincott, Williams & Wilkins, 2000.

616.803   RC334.A96

1st ed., 1995.

This enlarged edition provides brief descriptions of psychiatric and neurological diseases and disorders and related terminology, with journal and book references cited within entries. Also includes concise information about psychiatric drugs, with comments on adverse reactions and interactions with other drugs. Subject index.

1315 Wiley's English-Spanish and Spanish-English dictionary of psychology and psychiatry = Diccionario de psicología y psiquiatría inglés-español español-inglés Wiley. Steven M. Kaplan. viii, 593 p. New York: Wiley, 1995. ISBN: 0471014605.

150.3   BF31.K36

The only book of its kind provides concise, comprehensive, and current bilingual coverage of virtually every word or phrase used in the study and practice of psychiatry and psychology. Contains more than 62,000 entries—30,000+ in each language—covering all disciplines and sub-disciplines, both research and clinical. Gender-neutral equivalents are provided, and in cases where the gender-specific term is the norm, both are given. For idiomatic expressions, conceptual equivalents are provided rather than literal translations.

Directories

1316 **DIRLINE.** National Institutes of Health (U.S.). [1983?–.] Bethesda, Md.: U.S. National Institutes of Health, Dept. of Health and Human Services. http://dirline.nlm.nih.gov/.

DIRLINE® (Directory of Information Resources Online), maintained by the National Library of Medicine (NLM) (427).

Online annotated directory of organizations, research resources, projects, databases, and other information resources concerned with health and biomedicine from a variety of sources, including federal, state, and local government agencies, academic and research institutions, and also consumer health-related resources such as self-help groups and health hotlines. Resources are mostly from the U.S. but also include some international resources. Currently contains over 8,000 entries, with topics on most diseases and conditions and health services research and technology assessment. Can be searched using MeSH® (Medical Subject Headings) (575), keywords, or by name and location of a resource. Detailed information on DIRLINE can be found via a fact sheet prepared by NLM: http://www.nlm.nih.gov/pubs/factsheets/dirlinfs.html.

1317 **General residency training and subspecialties in psychiatry.** American Psychiatric Association. 2006–. Arlington, Va.: American Psychiatric Association. http://www.psych.org/edu/res_fellows/rf/trainingsub.cfm.

Part of the American Psychiatric Institute for Research and Education (APIRE), affiliated with the American Psychiatric Association (APA).

Gateway for psychiatry residents and fellows, providing online information on the various subspecialties in psychiatry (e.g., child and adolescent, geriatric, addiction, forensic, psychosomatic psychiatry, and others) and their training requirements (http://www.psych.org/edu/res_fellows/rf/trainingsub.cfm). Website also provides various resource links. Information on the individual programs are provided via FREIDA online (212), AMA's fellowship and residency electronic interactive database.

Directory of psychiatry residency training programs, a print resource published by APA 1982–97, has been discontinued.

1318 Substance Abuse and Mental Health Services Administration (SAMHSA). Substance Abuse and Mental Health Services Administration. Rockville, Md.: Substance Abuse and Mental Health Services Administration. http://www.samhsa.gov.

Substance Abuse and Mental Health Services Administration (SAMHSA), part of U.S. Dept. of Health and Human Services (HHS) (769).

SAMHSA has as its mission "building resilience and facilitating recovery for people with or at risk for mental or substance use disorders. gearing all of its resources toward that outcome."—*About Us*. Searchable website. Provides resources for prevention, treatment, and rehabilitation services for patients with various forms of mental illness and addictions. Includes three centers: SAMHSA's Center for Mental Health Services (CMHS), Center for Substance Abuse Prevention (CSAP), and Center for Substance Abuse Treatment (CSAT). Examples of SAMHSA resources include Mental Health Services Locator (http://mentalhealth.samhsa.gov/databases/) and Substance Abuse Treatment Facility Locator (http://dasis3.samhsa.gov/), both with clickable maps to locate different programs throughout the United States; Prevention Online (PREVLINE; http://ncadi.samhsa.gov/); a list of hotline numbers (http://mentalhealth.samhsa.gov/hotlines/); and related links (e.g., Mental Health on the Internet; http://mentalhealth.samhsa.gov/links/). SAMHSA's Office of Applied Statistics (http://www.oas.samhsa.gov/) provides the latest data on alcohol, tobacco, and illegal drugs as well as other statistical data and resources.

Encyclopedias

1319 Comprehensive clinical psychology. Alan S. Bellack, Michel Hersen. 11 v., ill. Amsterdam, [The Netherlands]; New York: Pergamon, 1998. ISBN: 0080427073.

616.89   RC467.C597

Contents: v. 1, *Foundations*, ed. Eugene Walker; v. 2, *Professional issues*, ed. Arthur N. Wiens; v. 3, *Research methods*, ed. Nina R. Schooler; v. 4, *Assessment*, ed. Cecil R. Reynolds; v. 5, *Children and adolescents*, ed. Thomas Ollendick; v. 6, *Adults*, ed. Paul Salkovskis; v. 7, *Clinical geropsychology*, ed. Barry Edelstein; v. 8, *Health psychology*, ed. Derek W. Johnston and Marie

Johnston; v. 9, *Applications in diverse populations*, ed. Nirbhay N. Singh; v. 10, *Sociocultural and individual differences*, ed. Cynthia D. Belar; v. 11, *Indexes.*

Review of the field of clinical psychology, including its historical, theoretical, and scientific foundations. Scholarly reviews of clinical topics and professional issues. Bibliographical references. Also available online via Elsevier Science Direct.

1320 Encyclopedia of behavior modification and cognitive behavior therapy. Michel Hersen, Johan Rosqvist. 3 v., xx, 1637 p., ill. Thousand Oaks, Calif.: Sage, 2005. ISBN: 0761927476.
616.89142003   RC489.B4E485

Broader in scope than the *Encyclopedia of cognitive behavior therapy*, this set brings together the expertise of both researchers and practitioners. Includes a volume each on adult and child clinical applications. A third volume on educational applications is particularly valuable for classroom and school contexts. Five anchor articles in each volume summarize current trends and treatment directions. Each volume includes an alphabetical list of its entries, an extensive general bibliography, and a comprehensive index. Each entry contains brief background, description of the treatment strategy, discussion of potential complications, a case illustration, a brief list of recent publications, and, if appropriate, a summary of research. Entries for prominent contributors to the field chronicle their professional careers.

1321 Encyclopedia of cognitive science. Lynn Nadel. 4 v., ill. Hoboken, N.J.: John Wiley, 2005. ISBN: 0470016191.

BF311.E53

A massive encyclopedia which aims to capture current thinking about the relatively new field of cognitive science. An excellent overview article, "What is cognitive science?" is followed by more than 400 topical entries written by experts in their field. Essays are clearly laid out and well illustrated, suggesting further readings. Extensive subject index provides easy access to related materials. Glossary. Available as an online database.

1322   Encyclopedia of forensic sciences. Jay A. Siegel, Pekka J. Saukko, Geoffrey C. Knupfer. 3 v. (xxxviii, 1440, lxv, lvii p.), ill. (some color). San Diego, Calif.: Academic Press, 2000. ISBN: 0122272153.
363.2503   HV8073.E517

Considers basic principles of forensic science and a wide range of topics, including theories, methods, and techniques used by forensic scientists.

Covers, for example, accident investigation, crime scene investigation, clinical forensic medicine (e.g., overview, defense wounds, self-inflicted injury, child abuse, sexual assault, gunshot wounds, etc.), autopsy, "psychological autopsies," medicolegal causes of death, DNA data banks, alcohol and drug analysis, ethical aspects, etc. Also available online via Elsevier Science Direct.

1323 Encyclopedia of mental health. Howard S. Friedman. 3 v., ill. San Diego, Calif.: Academic Press, 1998. ISBN: 0122266757.
616.89003   RA790.5.E53

Contents: v. 1, A–Di; v. 2, Do–N; v. 3, O–Z, index. "Taking into account new knowledge about the genetic, biological, developmental, social, societal and cultural nature of human beings, bring[s] together emerging trends of mental health validity (or invalidity) of psychiatric diagnosis (and DSM IV), including standards for psychotherapy, models of normality, and psychiatric epidemiology."—*Pref.* Each article contains an outline, a glossary, cross-references, and a bibliography. Aimed at a wide range of users, including students, researchers, and allied health professionals. Another encyclopedia with the same title by Ada P. Kahn is part of the Facts On File Library of health and living series (678), a collection of titles on medical subjects for general readers which is also available online via Health Reference Center (Facts On File, Inc.) (689).

1324 Encyclopedia of obesity and eating disorders. 3rd ed. Dana K. Cassell, David H. Gleaves. 362 p. New York: Facts On File, 2006. ISBN: 0816061971.
616.8526003   RC552.E18.C37

1st ed., 1994; 2nd ed., 2000.

Provides concise entries on the causes, symptoms, and treatments, including pharmacotherapy, of obesity and the various eating disorders (e.g., anorexia nervosa, bulimia, etc.). Lists sources of information, websites, audiovisuals, and other resources. Bibliography and index. For general readers and health professionals.

Part of *Facts On File library of health and living* (678) series. Available online via Health Reference Center (689).

1325 Encyclopedia of psychology. Alan E. Kazdin. 8 v., 29 cm. Washington; Oxford; New York: American Psychological Association; Oxford University Press, 2000. ISBN: 1557986509.
150.3   BF31.E52

Covers methods, findings, advances, and applications in the broad field of psychology from historical topics to new areas of development. Extensive cross-references guide users to related topics among the eight volumes. Each signed entry includes alternate spellings and synonyms, as well as bibliographies and further references.

1326 Encyclopedia of psychotherapy. Michel Hersen, William H. Sledge. 2 v., ill. Amsterdam, [The Netherlands]; Boston: Academic Press, 2002. ISBN: 0123430100.

616.891403   RC475.7.E55

Vol. 1, A–H; v. 2, I–Z.

Broad coverage of the field, with detailed information on the major psychotherapies currently practiced and also the classical treatments previously in use. The 233 alphabetically-arranged topics address "clinical, theoretical, cultural, historical, and administrative and policy issues" (*Pref.*), including contemporary schools, approaches and techniques, and measurement of outcomes. Most articles follow a similar format: description of treatment, theoretical basis, applications and exclusions, empirical studies, case illustration, and summary. Each article also contains an outline, a glossary of relevant terms, cross-references, and a list of further readings. Each volume has separate pagination. Index includes subjects but no names. For an academic audience. Also available online as part of Elsevier's Reference Works on Science Direct (http://www.info.sciencedirect.com/content/books/ref_works/collections/).

1327 Encyclopedia of statistics in behavioral science. Brian S. Everitt, David C. Howell. 4 v., 2208 p., ill. Hoboken, N.J.: John Wiley & Sons, 2005. ISBN: 0470860804.

150.15195   BF39.E498

Essential reference work for researchers, educators, and students in the fields of applied psychology, sociology, market research, consumer behavior, management science, decision making, and human resource management and a valuable addition to both the psychological and statistical literature. Contains over 600 articles; contributions from eminent psychologists and statisticians worldwide. Emphasizes practical, nontechnical methods with wide-ranging applications. Extensively cross-referenced. Available in print and online.

1328 Encyclopedia of stress. 2nd ed. George Fink. Boston: Elsevier, 2007. ISBN: 0120885034.

1st ed., 2000.

"Comprehensive reference source on stressors, the biological mechanisms involved in the stress response, the effects of activating the stress response mechanisms, and the disorders that may arise as a consequence of acute or chronic stress. Includes a wide range of related topics such as neuroimmune interactions, cytokines, enzymatic disorders, effects on the cardiovascular system, immunity and inflammation, and physical illnesses. It also goes beyond the biological aspects of stress to cover topics such as stress and behavior, psychiatric and psychosomatic disorders, workplace stress, post-traumatic stress, stress-reduction techniques, and current therapies."—*Publ. notes.* For researchers, clinicians, professionals, and students. Available online via Elsevier ScienceDirect.

Ada P. Kahn's *The encyclopedia of stress and stress-related diseases,* part of the Facts On File Library of health and living series (678) and available online via Health Reference Center (Facts On File, Inc.) (689), provides accessible content on stress and stress-related diseases for all types of readers and libraries.

1329 Encyclopedia of the neurological sciences. Michael J. Aminoff, Robert B. Daroff. 4 v., ill. (some color). Amsterdam, [The Netherlands]; Boston: Academic Press, 2003. ISBN: 0122268709.
612.803   RC334.E535
v. 1, A–De; v. 2, Di–L; v. 3, M–Ph; v. 4, Pi–Z, index.

Approx. 1,000 concise entries in 32 subject areas deal with basic science aspects and clinical issues of the neurological sciences, including neurology, neuroanatomy, neurobiology, neurosurgery, psychiatry, and other related areas. Alphabetical sequence by title, with groupings according to specific discipline. Suggestions for further reading at the end of each entry. Includes biographies of famous neuroscientists. Some graphics. Outline of contents in v. 4. Extensive cross-references. Subject index. Written for readers from other disciplines, not necessarily for the specialist. Also available online via ScienceDirect.

1330 The Freud encyclopedia: Theory, therapy, and culture. Edward Erwin. xxvii, 641 p. New York: Routledge, 2002. ISBN: 0415936772.
150.1952092   BF173.F6176

More than 250 signed entries reflect much of the recent international scholarship on Freud's largely unproven theories, which continue to provide insights and exert tremendous influence. Each entry contains a list of references, and ample cross-references are provided. Available as an e-book.

1331 Gabbard's treatments of psychiatric disorders. 4th ed. Glen
O. Gabbard. xxvi, 960 p., ill. Washington: American Psychiatric
Publishing, 2007. ISBN: 9781585622.

616.891   RC480.T69

1st ed., 1989, had title *Treatments of psychiatric disorders: A task force report
of the American Psychiatric Association*, 4 v.; 2nd ed., 1995 (2 v.), and 3rd
ed., 2001 (2 v.), had title *Treatments of psychiatric disorders.*

Contents: pt. 1, "Disorders usually first diagnosed in infancy, childhood, or adolescence" (ed. E.B. Weller and J.F. McDermott); pt. 2,
"Delirium, dementia, and amnestic and other cognitive disorders" (ed.
S.C. Yudofsky and R.E. Hales); pt. 3, "Substance-related disorders" (ed.
H. D. Kleber and M. Galanter); pt. 4, "Schizophrenia and other psychotic
disorders" (ed. R. L. Munich and C.A. Tamminga); pt. 5, "Mood disorders"
(ed. A. J. Rush); pt. 6, "Anxiety disorders, dissociative disorders, and adjustment disorders" (ed. F. R. Schneier, L.A. Mellman, and D. Spiegel); pt. 7,
"Somatoform and factitious disorders" (ed. K.A. Phillips); pt. 8, "Sexual
and gender identity disorders" (ed. S. B. Levine and R. T. Segraves); pt. 9,
"Eating disorders" (ed. A. S. Kaplan and K. A Halmi); pt. 10, "Personality
disorders" (ed. J.G. Gunderson); pt. 11, "Sleep disorders" (ed. K. Doghramji and Anna Ivanenko); pt. 12, "Disorders of impulse control" (ed.
Susan L. McElroy).

Current approaches, treatments, and therapies for common psychiatric disorders and mental illnesses. Provides comprehensive descriptions of
the disorders and covers multiple approaches, including pharmacologic,
psychodynamic, behavioral, cognitive, family, individual, and group treatments, recognizing evolving knowledge and preferred treatments as well
as acceptable alternatives. Includes data from new and controlled studies.
Includes bibliographical references and index. Useful for graduate research
and health professionals.

PSYCHIATRY

599

1332 The Gale encyclopedia of childhood and adolescence. Jerome
Kagan, Susan B. Gall. xiii, 752 p., ill. Detroit: Gale, 1998. ISBN:
0810398842.

305.23103   HQ772.G27

More than 700 signed essays by experts in the field cover key theories and
issues in child development and offer suggestions for further reading. Provides detailed name and subject indexes. Available online as part of Health
and Wellness Resource Center (632).

1333 **The Gale encyclopedia of mental health.** 2nd ed. Laurie J.
Fundukian, Jeffrey Wilson. 2 v., color ill. Detroit: Thomson Gale,
2008. ISBN: 9781414429878.

616.89003   RC437.G35

1st ed., 2003, had title *The Gale encyclopedia of mental disorders.*

Provides an overview of mental health and illness, diagnostic procedures, psychotherapy, and various other treatments, including drugs,
herbal preparations, and alternative therapies. Includes mostly disorders
recognized by the American Psychiatric Association, but also mentions
some not formally recognized as distinct disorders. Disease and medication entries are in a standardized format. Diseases include definition,
description, causes and symptoms, demographics, diagnosis, treatment,
prognosis, prevention, and resources. Medications include definition, purpose, description, recommended dosage, precautions, side effects, interactions, and resources.

Available electronically through Gale Virtual Reference Library (Farmington Hills, Mich.: Gale Cengage Learning, 2002–).

1334 **The Gale encyclopedia of psychology.** 2nd ed. Bonnie B.
Strickland. xiii, 701 p., ill. Detroit: Gale Group, 2001. ISBN:
0787647861.

150.3   BF31.G35

Covers the entire spectrum of psychological terms, theories, personalities,
and experiments. Designed to be of use to both students and the general
public, with signed entries ranging from 25 to 1,000 words. Provides suggestions for further reading and a subject index. Available as an e-book.

1335 **Mental disorders of the new millennium.** Thomas G. Plante. 3 v.
Westport, Conn.: Praeger, 2006. ISBN: 0275987817.

616.89   RC454.M462

Praeger Perspectives series.

Contents: v. 1, *Behavioral issues*; v. 2, *Public and social problems*; v. 3,
Biology and function.

Provides an overview of mental disorders. Vol. 1 includes articles
on behavioral issues such as narcissism, anger disorders, pathological
gambling, kleptomania, mood disorders in children and adolescents,
adult depression, suicide, self-injurious behavior, etc. Vol. 2 includes, for
example, articles discussing post-traumatic stress disorder among U.S. veterans, family violence, homicide-suicide, social and developmental issues
of youth gangs, adolescent substance abuse, workaholism, psychopathology in culture, etc. Vol. 3 includes aspects of psychobiology, with articles

on postpartum depression, mental retardation, autism, attention deficit/ hyperactivity disorder, obsessive-compulsive disorder, eating disorders, body dysmorphic disorder, gender identity disorders, etc. Bibliographical references and index. For health professionals, graduate students, and general readers. Available as an e-book via Greenwood Digital Collection (http://ebooks.greenwood.com/).

1336 The MIT encyclopedia of the cognitive sciences. Robert W. Wilson, Frank C. Keil. cxxxvii, 964 p. Cambridge, Mass.: MIT Press, 1999. ISBN: 0262232006.

MITECS represents the methodological and theoretical diversity of this changing field. With 471 concise entries written by leading researchers in the field, providing accessible introductions to important concepts in the cognitive sciences, as well as references or further readings. Six extended essays collectively serve as a road map to the articles and provide overviews of six major areas: philosophy; psychology; neurosciences; computational intelligence; linguistics and language; and culture, cognition, and evolution. Available online via MIT CogNet (Cambridge, Mass.: MIT Press, 2000?–) as an e-book at http://cognet.mit.edu/library/erefs/mitecs/.

1337 The Oxford companion to the mind. 2nd ed. R. L. Gregory. xx, 1004 p., ill. Oxford; New York: Oxford University Press, 2004. ISBN: 0198662246.

128.2   BF31.O94

Part dictionary and part encyclopedia, features entries ranging from a few sentences to several pages. Its purpose is to teach a wide range of users about the mind, and topics covered include brain imaging, children's drawings of human figures, hypnosis, delirium, free association, and illusions. Biographical entries are also included, along with many helpful ill. The signed entries include *see* and *see also* references, and most of the longer articles provide brief bibliographies. List of contributors, glossary, and index. Available electronically from Oxford Reference Online (Oxford; New York: Oxford University Press, 2002–) and NetLibrary.

Guides

1338 American Psychiatric Association practice guidelines for the treatment of psychiatric disorders. American Psychiatric Association. xii, 1600 p. Arlington, Va.: American Psychiatric Association, 2006. ISBN: 0890423830.

616.89   RC480.A528

The American Psychiatric Association (APA) has published recommendations about the practice of psychiatry since 1851. Since 1991, the APA has been involved in the practice guideline development process to ensure the development of reliable and valid guidelines consistent with the recommendations of the American Medical Association and the Institute of Medicine. Practice guidelines provide recommendations to help make treatment decisions supported by the best available evidence from current research and expert consensus. In addition to providing recommendations that may improve patient care, the guidelines may also be used for education by medical students and residents and psychiatrists seeking recertification, other mental health professionals, and the general public. Further information on APA practice guidelines, the APA guideline development process, and electronic access to a few guidelines is available at http://www.psych.org/psych_pract/treatg/pg/prac_guide.cfm?pf=y.

Handbooks

1339 **Assessment scales in old age psychiatry.** 2nd ed. Alistair Burns, Brian Lawlor, Sarah Craig. 383 p. London; New York: Martin Dunitz, 2004. ISBN: 1841841684.

618.97689   RC473.P78

1st ed., 1999.

Contents: (1) "Depression"; (2) "Dementia" ("Cognitive assessment"; "Neuropsychiatric assessments"; "Activities of daily living"; "Global assessments/quality of life"); (3) "Global mental health assessments"; (4) "Physical examination"; (5) "Delirium"; (6) "Caregiver assessments"; (7) "Memory functioning"; (8) "Other scales."

Collection of psychiatric rating scales that support the valid measurement and diagnosis of signs and symptoms of mental disorders in older people. Includes approx. 200 scales, i.e., all scales from the previous edition and also additional scales, with commentaries. Includes a section covering neuropsychological tests. Available online via netLibrary.

1340 **Cambridge handbook of psychology, health, and medicine.** 2nd ed. Susan Ayers. Cambridge, [England, U.K.]; New York: Cambridge University Press, 2007. ISBN: 9780521605.

616.0019   R726.5.C354

Description based on 1st ed., 1997.

Interdisciplinary encyclopedic handbook, intended primarily as a reference text for psychologists and health professionals. Addresses areas of psychology relevant to medicine and behavioral factors in relation to medical conditions. Chapters are arranged alphabetically, with many cross-references. Includes bibliographical references and index.

1341 Clinical handbook of psychiatry and the law. 4th ed. Paul S. Appelbaum, Thomas G. Gutheil. 322 p. Philadelphia: Lippincott, Williams and Wilkins, 2007. ISBN: 0781778913.

344.73041   KF2910.P75G87

1st ed., 1982; 3rd ed., 2000.

Contents: ch. 1, "Confidentiality and privilege"; ch. 2, "Legal issues in emergency psychiatry"; ch. 3, "Legal issues in inpatient psychiatry"; ch. 4, "Malpractice and other forms of liability"; ch. 5, "Competence and substitute decision making"; ch. 6, "Forensic evaluations"; ch. 7, "Clinicians and lawyers"; ch. 8, "The clinician in court"; index.

Provides up-to-date information for clinicians on "how law affects practice, and how psychiatry can contribute to the law" (*Pref.*) and discussion of its interrelated clinical and legal aspects. Each chapter has the following seven sections: Case examples, legal issues, clinical issues, pitfalls, case example epilogues, action guide, and suggested readings.

1342 Clinical manual of psychiatry and law. Robert I. Simon, Daniel W. Shuman. p. Washington: American Psychiatric Publishing, 2007.

614.15   RA1151.S56

Contents: (1) Psychiatry and the law; (2) The doctor-patient relationship; (3) Confidentiality and testimonial privilege; (4) Informed consent and the right to refuse treatment; (5) Psychiatric treatment: tort liability; (6) Seclusion and restraint; (7) Involuntary hospitalization; (8) The suicidal patient; (9) Psychiatric responsibility and the violent patient; (10) Maintaining treatment boundaries: clinical and legal issues. Appendix A: Suggested readings; Appendix B: Glossary of legal terms; Index.

Covers a variety of topics concerning the requirements and legal regulations of psychiatric practice, including treatment issues that may lead to liability and malpractice lawsuits.

Clinical handbook of psychiatry and law (Philadelphia: Lippincott, Williams and Wilkins, 2007) covers topics such as confidentiality and privilege, legal issues in emergency psychiatry and inpatient psychiatry, forensic evaluations, the clinician in court, and others.

1343 **Companion to psychiatric studies.** 7th ed. Eve C. Johnstone. 836 p. Edinburgh, [Scotland]; New York: Churchill Livingstone, 2004. ISBN: 0443072639.

1st ed., 1973; 6th ed., 1998.

Comprehensive resource and guide, covering basic sciences and psychiatric practice, an "overview of the psychiatric 'terrain' as it is currently perceived by a wide range of specialists."—*Pref.* Evidence-based principles and Web links are introduced in this edition. Includes bibliographical references and index.

1344 **The complete writing guide to NIH behavioral science grants.** Lawrence M. Scheier, William L. Dewey. 506 p. New York: Oxford University Press, 2007. ISBN: 9780195320275.

362.1079   RA11.D6C65

Contents: ch. 1, Peer review at the National Institutes of Health; ch. 2, Drug abuse research collaboration in the 21st century; ch. 3, A brief guide to the essentials of grant writing; ch. 4, Sample size, detectable difference, and power; ch. 5, Exploratory/developmental and small grant award mechanisms; ch. 6, Funding your future: What you need to know to develop a pre- or postdoctoral training application; ch. 7, Unique funding opportunities for underrepresented minorities and international researchers; ch. 8, R01 grants: The investigator-initiated cornerstone of biomedical research; ch. 9, P50 research center grants; ch. 10, P20 and P30 center grants: Developmental mechanisms; ch. 11, The K award: an important part of the NIH funding alphabet soup; ch. 12, T32 grants at the NIH: Tips for success; ch. 13, SBIR funding: A unique opportunity for the entrepreneurial researchers; ch. 14, Federal grants and contracts outside of NIH; ch. 15, The financing and cost accounting of science: Budgets and budget administration; ch. 16, Documenting human subjects protections and procedures; ch. 17, Navigating the maze: Electronic submission; ch. 18, Revisions and resubmissions; ch. 19, Concluding remarks: The bottom line. Appendix 1: The NIH Web sites; Appendix 2: NIH institutes, centers, and their websites.

Presents important considerations in developing research proposals and funding mechanisms for both junior and established researchers. Provides practical information on how to construct and write successful grants, electronic grant submission, revising research proposals, etc. Useful to researchers, clinicians, and educators in a wide variety of subject areas who are interested in submitting grants to the NIH.

1345 Comprehensive handbook of personality and psychopathology. Michel Hersen, Jay C. Thomas. 3 v., ill. Hoboken, N.J.: John Wiley & Sons, 2006. ISBN: 0471479454.

618.9289   RC456.C66

Presents an overview of the foundations of major theories of personality, covering such broad topics as personality and everyday functioning, adult psychopathology, and child psychopathology. Each section compiled by experts in their fields. Available as an e-book.

1346 Comprehensive handbook of psychopathology. 3rd ed. Patricia B. Sutker, Henry E. Adams. xviii, 970 p., ill. New York: Kluwer Academic/Plenum, 2001. ISBN: 030646490X.

616.89   RC454.C636

1st ed., 1984; 2nd ed., 1993.

"Resource textbook that covers both general and specific topics in psychopathology. Useful to researchers, practitioners, and graduate and other advanced students in the mental health professions."—*Pref.* In six main parts: (1) "Issues in psychopathology"; (2) "Neurotic and psychotic disorders"; (3) "Personality disorders"; (4) "Disorders associated with social and situational problems"; (5) "Disorders associated with physical trauma and medical illness"; (6) "Disorders arising in specific life stages." Chapters by specialists focus on overviews of clinical description, research, and theories, with extensive references. Indexed. Available as an e-book.

1347 Comprehensive handbook of psychotherapy. Florence Whiteman Kaslow, Jeffrey J. Magnavita, Terence Patterson, Robert F. Massey, Sharon Davis Massey, Jay Lebow. 4 v., ill. New York: Wiley, 2002. ISBN: 0471018481.

616.8914   RC480.C593

Contents: v. 1, *Psychodynamic/object relations* (ed. Florence W. Kaslow); v. 2, *Cognitive-behavioral approaches*; v. 3, *Interpersonal/humanistic/existential*; v. 4, *Integrative/eclectic*.

Intends to present the state of the art of psychotherapy, including history, theory, major schools, practice trends and research, reflecting the globalization of the field. Written from a biopsychosocial perspective. Author and subject index in each volume. For graduate students, faculty, clinicians, and researchers. Some volumes available as e-books.

1348 Concise rules of APA style. American Psychological Association. ix, 212 p., ill. Washington: American Psychological Association, 2005. ISBN: 1591472520.

808.06615   BF76.7.C66

Compiled from the 5th ed. of the *Publication manual of the American Psychological Association* (1372), this handy work covers topics such as concise and bias-free writing, punctuation, spelling, and capitalization, italicizing and abbreviating, the use of numbers, metrication and statistics, tables and figures, footnotes and appendixes, and quotations. Provides very helpful reference examples, including those from electronic and audiovisual media, a cross-reference to the publication manual, and a checklist for manuscript submission.

1349 CPT handbook for psychiatrists. 3rd ed. Chester W. Schmidt, Rebecca Yowell, Ellen Jaffe. xiii, 140 p., ill. Washington: American Psychiatric, 2004. ISBN: 1585621579.

616.890012   RC465.6.S36

1st ed., 1993; 2nd ed., 1999.

CPT (Current Procedural Terminology).

Contents: ch. 1, "Basics of CPT"; ch. 2, "Introduction to documentation"; ch. 3, "Codes and documentation for psychiatric services"; ch. 4, "Codes and documentation for other mental health services"; ch. 5, "Codes and documentation for evaluation and management services"; ch. 6, "Medicare"; ch. 7, "Health insurance issues"; ch. 8, "Putting it all together for accurate coding." Appendixes: A, "The CPT coding system"; B, "Modifiers"; C, "ECT information, consent form, and record template"; D, "Vignettes for evaluation and management codes"; E, "Documentation templates"; F, "Examples of relative value units (RVUs)(2004)"; G, "National distribution of evaluation and management code selection by psychiatrists"; H, "American Psychiatric Association CPT Coding Service and additional resources"; I, "Center for Medicare and Medicaid services (CMS) regional offices"; J, "Medicare pt. B carriers"; K, "Health Insurance Portability and Accountability Act (HIPAA)"; L, "CPT psychiatric code matrix."

Explains the structure and function of CPT, how to use the psychiatric therapeutic procedure codes, and how CPT affects the practice of psychiatry. This edition includes "changes mandated by the Health Insurance Portability and Accountability Act and other changes in the way psychiatry is currently practiced."—*Pref.*

1350 Current psychiatric therapy II. David L. Dunner. xxx, 657 p. Philadelphia: W.B. Saunders, 1997. ISBN: 0721659896.

616.891   RC480.C86

1st ed., 1993.

This updated edition is based on DSM-IV nomenclature. Summarizes available knowledge on treatment and pharmacological approaches and indicates potential changes in treatment for the future. Includes clinical characteristics, diagnostic criteria, and epidemiology of various conditions. Intended for psychiatrists, family physicians, internists, psychologists, social workers, and individuals in training in the mental health field. Each chapter reviews a particular condition and provides general guidelines for treatment and the particular author's treatment preferences.

1351 Diagnostic and statistical manual of mental disorders: DSM-IV-TR. 4th ed. American Psychiatric Association. xxxvii, 943 p. Washington: American Psychiatric Association, 2000. ISBN: 0890420246.

616.89075   RC455.2.C4.D536

Prepared by the Task Force on DSM-IV and other committees and work groups of the American Psychiatric Association. 1st ed., 1952; 4th ed., 1994, has title *Diagnostic and statistical manual of mental disorders: DSM-IV.*

Essential resource for mental health professionals, viewed by researchers and clinicians as the accepted classification system for psychiatric disorders. Contains all diagnostic criteria plus systematic description of disorders, using a numerical code system. Includes an explanation of the code system and instructions for its use, description of disorders, glossary, classification history, alphabetic and numeric listing of diagnoses, and indexes of symptoms, diagnoses, and codes. Several appendixes, including, for example, a glossary of technical terms, annotated listing of changes in DSM-IV, and "Outline for cultural formulation and glossary of culture-bound syndromes."

In addition to correcting factual errors, updating codes, and making other improvements in the DSM-IV text in this edition, changes were made to reflect new information since the DSM-IV literature reviews were completed in 1992. Organization of the manual: instructions for use are followed by the diagnostic criteria for each of the DSM-IV disorders, along with descriptive text (p. 39–743). Eleven appendixes. Available online at http://psychiatryonline.com/.

PSYCHIATRY

Publication of the 5th ed., *Diagnostic and statistical manual of mental disorders: DSM-5*, is scheduled for May 2013. Details of the DSM-5 development process are available at http://www.DSM5.org/.

1352 Drug information handbook. North American ed. Charles Lacy, Laura Armstrong, Morton Goldman, Leonard Lance, Lexi-Comp, Inc., American Pharmaceutical Association. Hudson, Ohio; Washington: Lexi-Comp; American Pharmaceutical Association, 1994–. ISSN: 1533-4511.

615   RM301.12.D783

Publ. in cooperation with the Amer. Pharmacists Assoc. (APhA).

1st ed., 1993/94. Available in North Amer. and internat. editions. Description based on 15th ed., 2007.

(Lexi-Comp's clinical reference library).

Concise, comprehensive, and user-friendly drug reference. Alphabetical listing of 1,400 drug monographs, with new drugs and updates to monographs since the last edition. Includes detailed information in consistent format (33 fields), such as dosage, drug interactions, adverse reactions (by occurrence, overdose, and toxicology), etc., with warnings highlighted. Appendix. Pharmacologic category index. For clinicians and healthcare professionals.

Several other comprehensive print pharmacology handbooks, also publ. by Lexi-Comp and frequently updated, include *Anesthesiology and critical care drug handbook* (1999–. ; 7th ed., 2006); *Drug information handbook for advanced practice nursing* (1990–. ; 8th ed., 2007); *Drug information handbook for dentistry* (1996– ; 12th ed., 2007); *Drug information handbook for oncology* (2000– ; 6th ed., 2007); *Drug information handbook for psychiatry: A comprehensive reference of psychotropic, non-psychotropic, and herbal agents* (1999– ; 6th ed., 2006); *Drug information handbook for the allied health professional* (1995- ; 12th ed., 2005); *Geriatric dosage handbook* (1993– ; 11th ed., 2006); *Infectious diseases handbook: Including antimicrobial therapy & diagnostic test/procedures* (1994– ; 6th ed., 2006); *Natural therapeutics pocket guide* (2000– ; 2nd ed., 2003); *Pediatric dosage handbook* (1992– ; 13th ed., 2006); and *Pharmacogenomics handbook* (2003– ; 2nd ed., 2006). Also available online as pt. of Lexi-Comp Online™ (http://webstore.lexi.com/Store/ONLINE) and Lexi-Comp ONLINE for Dentistry (http://webstore.lexi.com/Store/ONLINE/Lexi-Comp-ONLINE-for-Dentistry).

1353 Ethics. American Psychiatric Association. Arlington, Va.: American Psychiatric Association. http://www.psych.org/psych_pract/ethics/ethics.cfm.

Produced by the American Psychiatric Association (APA) (1390).

Provides online access to APA's ethics-related publications, originally published in print version in 2001: *Opinions of the Ethics Committee on the principles of medical ethics: With annotations especially applicable to psychiatry*, which includes the APA's procedures for handling complaints of unethical conduct, and *Ethics primer of the American Psychiatric Association*.

1354 Gabbard's treatments of psychiatric disorders. 4th ed. Glen O. Gabbard. xxvi, 960 p., ill. Washington: American Psychiatric, 2007. ISBN: 9781585622.

616.891   RC480.T69

1st ed., 1989, had title *Treatments of psychiatric disorders: A task force report of the American Psychiatric Association*, 4 v.; 2nd ed., 1995 (2 v.), and 3rd ed., 2001 (2 v.), had title *Treatments of psychiatric disorders*.

Contents: pt. 1, "Disorders usually first diagnosed in infancy, childhood, or adolescence" (ed. E.B. Weller and J.F. McDermott); pt. 2, "Delirium, dementia, and amnestic and other cognitive disorders" (ed. S.C. Yudofsky and R.E. Hales); pt. 3, "Substance-related disorders" (ed. H. D. Kleber and M. Galanter); pt. 4, "Schizophrenia and other psychotic disorders" (ed. R. L. Munich and C.A. Tamminga); pt. 5, "Mood disorders" (ed. A. J. Rush); pt. 6, "Anxiety disorders, dissociative disorders, and adjustment disorders" (ed. F. R. Schneier, L.A. Mellman, and D. Spiegel); pt. 7, "Somatoform and factitious disorders" (ed. K.A. Phillips); pt. 8, "Sexual and gender identity disorders" (ed. S. B. Levine and R. T. Segraves); pt. 9, "Eating disorders" (ed. A. S. Kaplan and K. A Halmi); pt. 10, "Personality disorders" (ed. J.G. Gunderson); pt. 11, "Sleep disorders" (ed. K. Doghramji and Anna Ivanenko); pt. 12, "Disorders of impulse control" (ed. Susan L. McElroy).

Current approaches, treatments, and therapies for common psychiatric disorders and mental illnesses. Provides comprehensive descriptions of the disorders and covers multiple approaches, including pharmacologic, psychodynamic, behavioral, cognitive, family, individual, and group treatments, recognizing evolving knowledge and preferred treatments as well as acceptable alternatives. Includes data from new and controlled studies. Includes bibliographical references and index. Useful for graduate research and health professionals.

1355 Handbook of clinical child psychology. 3rd ed. C. Eugene Walker, Michael C. Roberts. xx, 1177 p., ill. New York: Wiley, 2001. ISBN: 0471244066.

618.9289   RJ503.3.H36

1st ed., 1983; 2nd ed., 1992.

Contents: sec. 1, "Child development"; sec. 2, "Diagnostic assessment of children"; sec. 3, "Problems of early life"; sec. 4, "Problems of childhood"; sec. 5, "Problems of adolescence"; sec. 6, "Intervention strategies"; sec. 7, "Special topics."

This edition reflects the growth of the field of child psychology in recent years, providing background information in child development and "consideration of more specific disorders of childhood in the context of human development."—*Pref.* Includes bibliographical references and indexes. Intended as a reference work for graduate students, researchers, and clinicians. Available online via netLibrary.

1356 Handbook of clinical health psychology. Susan P. Llewelyn, Paul Kennedy. xvii, 605 p., ill. Chichester, West Sussex, U.K.; Hoboken, N.J.: J. Wiley, 2003. ISBN: 0471485446.

616.0019   R726.7.H3542

Comprehensive overview of the practice of clinical health psychology. Provides authoritative summaries of research evidence in health care and demonstrates how findings are put into practice. Useful detailed and integrated reference work for clinical and health psychologists in academic, practice, and training settings. Available as an e-book.

1357 Handbook of clinical health psychology. Thomas J. Boll, Suzanne Bennett Johnson, Nathan W. Perry. v. 1–3. Washington: American Psychological Association, c2002–2004. ISBN: 1557989095.

616.89   R726.7.H354

Vol. 1, *Medical disorders and behavioral applications* (ed. Suzanne Bennett Johnson, Nathan W. Perry, Jr., and Ronald H. Rozensky); v. 2, *Disorders of behavior and health* (ed. James M. Raczynski, Laura C. Leviton); v. 3, *Models and perspectives in health psychology* (ed. Robert G. Frank, Andrew Baum, and Jan L. Wallander).

Explores the role of behavior and psychology in the development, progression, intervention, and treatment of a wide range of medical conditions related to disorders of behavior and health. Emphasizes health-related behavior changes. For researchers and practitioners in clinical psychology. Includes bibliographical references and index.

1358 Handbook of contemporary neuropharmacology. David Robert Sibley, Israel Hanin, Michael Kuhar. 3 v. Hoboken, N.J.: John Wiley & Sons, 2007. ISBN: 9780471660.

615.78   RM315.H3434

Contents: (1) "Basic neuropharmacology"; (2) "Mood disorders"; (3) "Anxiety and stress disorders"; (4) "Schizophrenia and psychosis"; (5) "Substance abuse and addictive disorders"; (6) "Pain"; (7) "Sleep and arousal"; (8) "Development and developmental disorders"; (9) "Neurodegenerative and seizure disorders"; (10) "Neuroimmunology"; (11) "Eating and metabolic disorders."

Reference for nervous system neuropharmacology, with recent advances in neuropharmacology, drug development and therapy, and treatment of various diseases and conditions. Reference for graduate students, physicians and other health professionals, and researchers. A useful resource for academic and special libraries. Also available online via Wiley InterScience (http://www.interscience.wiley.com/reference/hcn). Includes index.

1359 Handbook of eating disorders. 2nd ed. Janet Treasure, Ulrike Schmidt, Eric van Furth. xvi, 479 p., ill. Chichester, [England, U.K.]; Hoboken, N.J.: Wiley, 2003. ISBN: 0471497681.

616.8526   RC552.E18.H36

1st ed., 1993, had title *Handbook of eating disorders: Theory, treatment, and research.*

Overview of the developing field of eating disorders, including obesity, with many advances in knowledge and understanding since the previous edition. For researchers and clinicians. Also available in a condensed version entitled *The essential handbook of eating disorders.* Also available as an e-book.

1360 Handbook of neurologic rating scales. 2nd ed. Robert M. Herndon. xiv, 441 p. New York: Demos Medical Publ., 2006. ISBN: 1888799927.

616.80475   RC348.H296

1st ed., 1997.

Contents: ch. 1, Introduction to clinical neurologic scales (Robert M. Herndon and Gary Cutter); ch. 2, Generic and general use scales (Robert M. Herndon); ch. 3, Pediatric developmental scales (Roger A. Brumback); ch. 4, Pediatric neurologic and rehabilitation rating scales (Raphael Corcoran Sneed, Edward L. Manning, and Cathy F. Hansen); ch. 5, Amyotrophic lateral sclerosis clinimetric scales: Guidelines for administration and scoring (Benjamin Rix Brooks); ch. 6, Scales for the assessment of movement disorders (Stephen T. Gancher); ch. 7, Multiple sclerosis and demyelinating diseases (Robert M. Herndon and Jeffrey I. Greenstein); ch. 8, Assessment of the elderly with dementia (Richard Camicioli and Katherine Wild); ch. 9, Clinical stroke scales (Wayne M. Clark and J. Maurice

Hourihane); ch. 10, Peripheral neuropathy and pain scales (Robert M. Herndon); ch. 11, Diagnostic headache criteria and instruments (Elcio J. Piovesan and Stephen D. Silberstein); ch. 12, Scales for assessment of ataxia (Robert M. Herndon); ch. 13, Assessment of traumatic brain injury (Risa Nakase-Richardson, Frances Spinosa, Charles F. Swearingen, and Domenic Esposito); ch. 14, Health-related quality-of-life scales for epilepsy (James J. Cereghino); ch. 15, Rehabilitation outcome measures (Samuel T. Gontkovsky and Risa Nakase-Richardson); ch. 16, Human immunodeficiency virus-associated cognitive impairment (Giovanni Schifitto and Michelle D. Gaugh); ch. 17, Summary and conclusions (Robert M. Herndon).

Reference source on methods of measurement and rating scales used in neurology to assess neurologic disease. Useful in the design of clinical trials and for interpreting the literature of clinical trials in neurology.

1361 Handbook of psychiatric education. Jerald Kay, Edward K. Silberman, Linda Pessar. xiv, 379 p., ill. Washington: American Psychiatric, 2005. ISBN: 1585621897.

616.890071173   RC459.5.U6.H36

Contents: (1) "Preclinical undergraduate curricula"; (2) "Psychiatric clerkships"; (3) "Undergraduate electives"; (4) "Evaluation of students"; (5) "Administration of the residency program"; (6) "What and how to teach in the residency program"; (7) "New teaching technologies and approaches for medical students and residents"; (8) "Teaching psychiatric residents to become effective educators"; (9) "The accreditation process: Challenges and benefits"; (10) "Evaluation of residents"; (11) "Special problems and challenges in the residency program"; (12) "Special events in the residency program"; (13) "Recruitment of residents"; (14) "Major issues in psychiatric education."

Reference guide for academic psychiatric educators with focus on undergraduate and graduate medical education issues and recent changes in medical education. Describes the role of technology in psychiatric education. Includes, for example, sections on electronic reference sources, new teaching technologies, online continuing education sources, and finding medical information on the Internet. Includes bibliographical references and index. Also includes a brief version of *Handbook of psychiatric education and faculty development*, publ. 1999, which includes information on careers in academic psychiatry, psychiatric residency, psychiatric administration, etc.

1362 Handbook of psychiatric measures. 2nd ed. A. John Rush, Michael B. First, Deborah Blacker, American Psychiatric

Association. 828 p., 1 CD-ROM. Washington: American Psychiatric Association, 2008. ISBN: 9781585622.

616.89075   RC473.P78.A46

1st ed., 2000.

Contents: sec. 1, "Introduction to the handbook"; sec. 2, "General measures (non-disorder specific)"; sec. 3, "Measures related to DSM-IV diagnostic categories"; appendix A, "DSM-IV-TR classification"; appendix B, "List of measures included on the CD-ROM"; appendix C, "Index of measures"; appendix D, "Index of abbreviations for measures." General index.

Revised edition. Compendium on rating scales, tests, and measures that may be useful in caring for patients with mental illness and in understanding and using clinical measures. Overview text for each chapter and a text section for each measure. Test sections for each measure include goals, description, practical issues, psychometric properties, clinical utility, and references to suggested readings. Accompanying CD-ROM includes complete copies of measures that are in the public domain, or for which copyright was granted, and also the text of the *Handbook of psychiatric measures* in searchable form.

Another widely used reference is E. J. Mill's *Nursing procedures*, available both in print and online as part of Books@Ovid.

PSYCHIATRY

1363 Handbook of psychology. Irving B. Weiner, Donald K. Freedheim, John A. Schinka. 12 v., ill. (some color). New York: Wiley, 2003. ISBN: 0471176699.

150   BF121.H1955

The first two volumes cover history and research methods; each of the next ten, a particular area of psychology: biological, experimental, personality and social, developmental, educational, clinical, health, assessment, forensic, and industrial and organizational. Leading national and international scholars collaborated to produce each volume, with chapters ranging from established theories to the most modern research and developments. Each of the 12 volumes contains its own author and subject indexes. Available as e-books.

1364 Handbook of research methods in clinical psychology. Michael C. Roberts, Stephen S. Ilardi. xi, 455 p., ill. Malden, Mass.: Blackwell, 2003. ISBN: 0631226737.

616.890072   RC467.8.H36

Title varies: also called *Blackwell handbook of research methods in clinical psychology*.

Contents: pt. 1, "Clinical psychology research"; pt. 2, "Research designs"; pt. 3, "Topics of research."

Treatment of research methodologies used in clinical psychology (e.g., experimental design, statistical analysis, validity, ethics in research, cultural diversity, and the scientific process of publishing) and applications of research to the fields of child and adult psychopathology. Scholarly resource for researchers and students. For academic libraries. Includes bibliographical references and index. Full text available online via Credo Reference (London; Boston: Credo Reference) and netLibrary.

Another resource, publ. in 1999, also entitled *Handbook of research methods in clinical psychology*, by Kendall, covers similar ground.

1365 **Handbook of the psychology of aging.** 6th ed. James E. Birren, K. Warner Schaie, Ronald P. Abeles, Margaret Gatz, Timothy A. Salthouse. xxi, 564 p., ill. Amsterdam, [The Netherlands]; Boston: Elsevier Academic Press, 2006. ISBN: 0121012646.

155.67   BF724.55.A35H36

Twenty signed essays delve into the psychology of aging from a variety of perspectives. Beginning with questions raised by theoretical issues in aging, articles discuss cognitive neuroscience, lifespan theory, how reading and language relate to aging, as well as what can be learned from problem solving, motivation, and even attitudes toward aging. Volume concludes with consideration of wisdom, memory, and religion in later life. Readable essays that present some weighty material in comprehensible form. A useful volume for both general and research collections.

1366 **The Harvard guide to psychiatry.** 3rd ed. Armand M. Nicholi. xiv, 856 p., ill. Cambridge, Mass.: Belknap Press, 1999. ISBN: 067437570X.

616.89   RC454.N47

1st ed., 1978, had title *The Harvard guide to modern psychiatry*; 2nd ed., 1988, had title *The new Harvard guide to psychiatry*.

Contents: pt. 1, "Examination and evaluation"; pt. 2, "Brain and behavior"; pt. 3, "Psychopathology"; pt. 4, "Principles of treatment and management"; pt. 5, "Special populations"; pt. 6, "Psychiatry and society."

This edition considers advances since 1988, which includes the release of DSM-IV (*Diagnostic and statistical manual of mental disorders:*

DSM-IV-TR [1296]), neurobiology of mental disorders, neuroimaging, psychopharmacology, increased use of psychoactive drugs, advances in molecular biology, etc. The "Psychiatry and society" section has chapters on race and cultures in psychiatry, ethical issues, psychiatry and managed care, and psychiatry and the law. Bibliographical references and index. For mental health professionals, general readers, and academic and public libraries.

1367 Measuring health: A guide to rating scales and questionnaires.
3rd ed. Ian McDowell. xvi, 748 p., ill. Oxford; New York: Oxford University Press, 2006. ISBN: 9780195165.

614.42   RA408.5.M38

1st ed., 1987; 2nd ed., 1996.

Overview of the field of health measurement, with in-depth information on selected commonly-used instruments (e.g., measurement of pain, general health status, quality of life, mental status, etc.) with the purpose of measuring health status in research studies. Provides description of methods, comparisons, and critical reviews of health measurement instruments or scales and their quality, indicating purpose, conceptual basis, reliability, validity, etc. This edition includes 104 scales. For health care researchers, epidemiologists, and social scientists. Index. Available as an e-book via netLibrary.

1368 Mental health in America: A reference handbook. Donna R.
Kemp. xiv, 315 p. Santa Barbara, Calif.: ABC-CLIO, 2007. ISBN: 1851097899.

362.2   RA790.6.K45

Part of Contemporary World Issues series.

Contents: (1) "Background and history"; (2) "The twenty-first century: Problems, controversies, and solutions"; (3) "Worldwide perspective"; (4) "Chronology"; (5) "Biographies"; (6) "Facts and statistics"; (7) "Documents, reports, and nongovernmental organizations"; (8) "Legislation and court costs"; (9) "Organization"; (10) "Selected print and non-print resources."

Explores mental health policy and attitudes toward mental illness from the 19th century to the present; changing definitions and explanations of mental illness; and the various treatments of mental illness. Includes chronology of approaches to mental illness, statistics, legislative information, a glossary, and annotated bibliography of current literature, including websites. Index. Useful for health professionals, researchers, and students. Available as an e-book via netLibrary.

1369 The mental measurements yearbook. Oscar Krisen Buros, Buros Institute of Mental Measurements. Highland Park, N.J.: The Mental Measurements Yearbook, 1941–. ISSN: 0076-6461.
016.1512; 016.159928   Z5814.P8B932

A monumental collection of standardized measurements, now in its 17th ed. Each edition follows much the same pattern and is intended to supplement rather than supersede earlier volumes. References are numbered consecutively and each has cross-references to reviews, excerpts, and bibliographic references in earlier volumes. Information for each test includes title, intended population, author and publishers, scoring, availability of forms, parts, levels, and computer-assisted scoring, cost, time to administer, and a statement concerning validity and reliability. Tests cover English-language materials. Often referred to by the name of its founder, Buros.

1370 PDR drug guide for mental health professionals. Thomson Medical Economics. Montvale, N.J.: Thomson Medical Economics, 2002–. ISSN: 1546-3443.
615   RM315.P387

Description based on 3rd ed., 2007.

Written in nontechnical language, profiles psychotropic drugs commonly used in psychiatry, with recommended dosage, approved uses, physical and psychological side effects, food and drug interactions, etc. Also includes psychotropic herbs and supplements. Includes street drug profiles and a glossary of street drug names and color photos of psychotropic tablets and capsules. Indexed by generic and trade name and clinical disorder/symptom or drug class. Reference for health professionals taking care of psychiatric patients.

Related titles include *Physicians' desk reference: PDR* (1250), *ADA/ PDR guide to dental therapeutics* (795), *PDR guide to drug interactions, side effects, and indications, PDR for herbal medicines (1247), PDR for nonprescription drugs, dietary supplements, and herbs* (1245), *PDR for nutritional supplements* (1246), *PDR nurse's drug handbook* (1064), *Physicians' desk reference for ophthalmic medicines (1249), PDR guide to biological and chemical warfare response, PDR guide to terrorism response,* and other titles.

PDR and its major companion volumes are also found in the PDR Electronic Library (1243).

1371 **Psychologists' desk reference.** 2nd ed. Gerald P. Koocher, John C. Norcross, Sam S. Hill. xxiii, 735 p. Oxford; New York: Oxford University Press, 2005. ISBN: 019516606X.

616.89   RC467.2.P78

1st ed., 1998.

Contents: pt. 1, "Assessment and diagnosis"; pt. 2, "Psychological testing"; pt. 3, "Individual psychotherapy and treatment"; pt. 4, "Couples, family, and group treatment"; pt. 5, "Child and adolescent treatment"; pt. 6, "Biology and pharmacotherapy"; pt. 7, "Self-help resources"; pt. 8, "Ethical and legal issues"; pt. 9, "Forensic matters"; pt. 10, "Practice management"; pt. 11, "Professional resources."

Clinical psychology handbook, with a companion website containing a variety of resources. Detailed table of contents for 140 chapters, cross-references, and index. For mental health professionals. Also available online via netLibrary.

1372 **Publication manual of the American Psychological Association.** 5th ed. American Psychological Association. xxviii, 439 p., ill. Washington: American Psychological Association, 2001. ISBN: 1557988102.

808.06615   BF76.7.P83

Begun in 1952, this manual provides detailed information on writing for publication, with special reference to the use of electronic and legal resources. Covers the content and organization of a manuscript in preparation for publication, with appendixes that include a checklist for manuscript submission. Sections on data sharing and statistics have been significantly updated since the 4th ed. An electronic companion to this manual also is available under a different title, APA-Style Helper (http://www.apastyle.org/stylehelper/). At the end of 2007, the APA published a supplementary *APA style guide to electronic references*, available digitally in HTML or PDF formats (ISBN: 1-4338-0309-7; ISBN 13: 978-1-4338-0309-3).

1373 **The SAGE handbook of health psychology.** Stephen Sutton, Andrew Baum, Marie Johnston. xiii, 432 p., ill. Thousand Oaks, Calif.: SAGE Publ., 2004. ISBN: 0761968490.

616.0019   R726.7.S24

Contents: ch. 1, Context and perspectives in health psychology; ch. 2, Epidemiology of health and illness: A socio-psycho-physiological perspective; ch. 3, Biological mechanisms of health and disease; ch. 4, Determinants of health-related behaviours: Theoretical and methodological issues; ch. 5, Health-related cognitions; ch. 6, Individual differences, health and illness: The role of emotional traits and generalized expectancies; ch. 7, Stress, health and illness; ch. 8, Living with chronic illness: A contextualized, self-regulation approach; ch. 9, Lifespan, gender and cross-cultural perspectives in health psychology; ch. 10, Communicating about health threats and treatments; ch. 11, Applications in health psychology: How effective are interventions?; ch. 12, Research methods in health psychology; ch. 13, Assessment and measurement in health psychology; ch. 14, Professional issues in health psychology.

Comprehensive interdisciplinary handbook reflecting international health psychology research and issues. For advanced students, researchers, and practitioners. Includes bibliographical references and index.

1374 What your patients need to know about psychiatric medications.
Robert E. Hales, Stuart C. Yudofsky, Robert H. Chew. xvii, 356 p. Washington: American Psychiatric Publishing, 2005. ISBN: 1585622036.

615.788   RM315.H328

Contents: "Medications in pregnancy"; "Antianxiety medication"; "Medications for treatment of insomnia"; "Antidepressants: Selective serotonin reuptake inhibitors and mixed-action antidepressants"; "Tricyclic antidepressants"; "Monoamine oxidase inhibitors"; "Mood stabilizers"; "First-generation antipsychotics"; "Second-generation antipsychotics"; "Treatment of attention-deficit/hyperactivity disorder in adults"; "Stimulants"; "Cognitive enhancers for treatment of Alzheimer's disease and other forms of dementia"; index.

Provides relevant and easy-to-understand information about commonly asked questions about psychiatric medications. Information about each medication presented in a standard format: brand name; generic name; available strengths; available in generic; medication class; general information; dosing information; common side effects; adverse reactions and precautions; use in pregnancy and breastfeeding; possible drug interactions; overdose; special considerations. Accompanied by CD-ROM that contains PDF files of the pages as they appear in the book. Also available as part of Psychiatry Online (1294).

Histories

1375 A century of psychiatry. Hugh L. Freeman, Servier Research Group. 2 v., ill., ports. London: Mosby-Wolfe Medical Communications, 1999. ISBN: 0723431744.

616.89009   RC438.C457x

Collection of historical essays and biographies of mostly American and European psychiatry and psychiatrists, with one chapter on "non-Western psychiatry." Organized by decade, with ten chapters and subsections covering various topics and themes on the "innovations [and] dark periods in the history of psychiatry."—*Foreword*. For example, chapters on convulsive therapy, emergence of psychoanalysis, history of the *Diagnostic and statistical manual of mental disorders*, psychoneuroendocrinology, psychopharmacology ("Psychopharmacology 2000"), and others. Includes a list of significant events in psychiatry. Illustrated with photographs. List of further readings. Written for general readers.

1376 Fragments of neurological history. John Pearce. xvii, 633 p., ill., ports. London: Imperial College Press, 2003.

616.809   RC338.P436

A collection of articles in the history of neurology and medicine. Includes, for example, biographical reviews (e.g., Galen and Vesalius), chapter entitled "Illness of the famous, and some medical truants," and chapters on anatomical and neurophysiological phenomena, dementias, headaches, cranial nerve and various other neurological disorders, and the origins of insulin and aspirin. For neurologists, neuroscientists, physicians, and general readers. Includes bibliographical references and index.

1377 The genesis of neuroscience. A. Walker, Edward Laws, George Udvarhelyi, American Association of Neurological Surgeons. [Park Ridge, Ill.]: American Association of Neurological Surgeons, 1998. ISBN: 1879284626.

616.8009   QP353

Contents: ch. 1, Origins of neuroscience; ch. 2, From Galen through the 18th century: An overview; ch. 3, The evolution of encephalization; ch. 4, The spinal cord; ch. 5, The peripheral nerves; ch. 6, Clinical and pathological examination of patients with neurological disorders; ch. 7, Manifestation of cerebral disorders: Headache, epilepsy, sleep disorders, and cerebrovascular disease; ch. 8, Congenital anomalies of the nervous system; ch. 9, Infections and inflammatory involvement of the central nervous system; ch. 10, The evolution of neurosurgery; ch. 11, Neuroscience comes of age. Appendixes (A) The arts in the evolution of neuroscience; (B) Medical fees throughout the ages; (C) Historical glossary of neurological syndromes; (D) Bibliography of writings by A. Earl Walker; Index.

Describes the origins of neurology and neurosurgery from prehistoric times until the 19th century. Includes portraits of many neurologists and neurosurgeons. Other titles in this area include *Fragments of neurological history* (391) and *History of neurology* (400).

1378 **The history and influence of the American Psychiatric Association.** Walter E. Barton, American Psychiatric Association. xvi, 400 p., [16] p. of plates, ill., ports. Washington: American Psychiatric Press, 1987. ISBN: 0880482311.

616.89006073   RC443.B35

Follows "the development of psychiatry in America through the founding and growth of the American Psychiatric Association."—*Pref.*

1379 **History of neurology.** Fielding H. Garrison, Lawrence C. McHenry. xv, 552 p., ill., facsims., ports. Springfield, Ill.: Thomas, [1969].

616.809   RC338.G36

Contents: ch. 1, Ancient origins; ch. 2, "The Middle Ages and the Renaissance"; ch. 3, "The seventeenth century"; ch. 4, "The eighteenth century"; ch. 5, "The nineteenth century: Neuroanatomy"; ch. 6, "The nineteenth century: Neurophysiology"; ch. 7, "The nineteenth century: Neurochemistry"; ch. 8, "The nineteenth century: Neuropathology"; ch. 9, "Clinical neurology"; ch. 10, "The neurological examination"; ch. 11, "Neurological diseases."

A re-publication of Garrison's *History of neurology*, previously published in 1925 as a historical chapter in Charles L. Dana's *Textbook of nervous diseases*.

Presents a broad survey of neurology from antiquity to the beginning of the 20th century. Other more recent titles in the history of neurology are, for example, *A short history of neurology: The British contribution* (404), *The genesis of neuroscience* (392), and *Fragments of neurological history* (391), to name a few.

1380 **The history of psychiatry: An evaluation of psychiatric thought and practice from prehistoric times to the present.** Franz Alexander, Sheldon T. Selesnick. xvi, 471 p., illus., ports. New York: Harper & Row, [1966].

616.89009   RC438.A39

In four parts: "The age of psychiatry," "From the ancients through the modern era," "The Freudian age," "Recent developments." A comprehensive history of psychiatry, with chapter notes and extensive bibliography. Index.

1381 **A history of psychiatry: From the era of the asylum to the age of Prozac.** Edward Shorter. xii, 436 p., ill. New York: John Wiley & Sons, 1997. ISBN: 047115749X.

616.89009   RC438.S54

Contents: ch. 1, "The birth of psychiatry"; ch. 2, "The asylum era"; ch. 3, "The first biological psychiatry"; ch. 4, "Nerves"; ch. 5, "The psychoanalytic hiatus"; ch. 6, "Alternatives"; ch. 7, "The second biological psychiatry"; ch. 8, "From Freud to Prozac."

Presents the history of psychiatry and psychiatric thinking from the late 18th century to the present, with its major scientific and cultural developments and its major personalities. Available as an e-book from netLibrary.

The title *150 years of British psychiatry*, ed. Hugh Freeman and German E. Berrios, covers important developments in Great Britain, and *One hundred years of psychiatry*, by Emil Kraepelin and translated by Wade Baskin, presents a general review of 19th-century psychiatry in Germany.

1382 One hundred years of American psychiatry. American Psychiatric Association. xxiv, 649 p., illus., ports., facsims., tables (part fold.). New York: Columbia University Press, 1944.

RC435.A6

Contents: "Presenting the volume," by Gregory Zilboorg; "Introduction," by J. K. Hall; "The beginnings: From colonial days to the foundation of the American Psychiatric Association," by R. H. Shryock; "Psychiatry in Europe at the middle of the nineteenth century," by H. E. Sigerist; "The founding and the founders of the association," by Winfred Overholser; "The history of American mental hospitals," by S. W. Hamilton; "A century of psychiatric research in America," by J. C. Whitehorn; "American psychiatric literature during the past one hundred years," by H. A. Bunder; "The history of psychiatric therapies," by William Malamud; "The history of mental hygiene," by Albert Deutsch; "Military psychiatry: The Civil War, 1861–1865," by Albert Deutsch; "Military psychiatry: World War I, 1917–1918," by E. A. Strecker; "Military psychiatry: World War II, 1941–1943," by Albert Deutsch; "A century of psychology in its relationship to American psychiatry," by T. V. Moore; "American psychiatry as a specialty," by H. A. Bunker; "Legal aspects of psychiatry," by Gregory Zilboorg; "The influence of psychiatry on anthropology in America during the past one hundred years," by Clyde Kluckhohn.

"Intended to be a historical synthesis of a century of American psychiatric evolution, of the birth and development of a medical specialty. Intended to represent a survey of psychiatry as a growing cultural force."— *Introd.* Commemorates the 100th birthday of the American Psychiatric Association. Includes a selection of early psychiatric books (p. 226–69) and periodicals (p. 269–71). Illustrations.

1383 **Resources on the history of psychiatry.** Emily Martin, Lorna A. Rhodes, National Library of Medicine (U.S.). [2004.] Bethesda, Md.: National Library of Medicine. http://www.nlm.nih.gov/hmd/pdf/historypsychiatry.pdf.

Contents: (1) "Overview"; (2) "Prehistory of psychiatry"; (3) "History of asylums"; (4) "History of psychotropic drugs"; (5) "Race in psychiatry"; (6) "Women, children, and the history of psychiatry"; (7) "Psychiatry, war, and violence"; (8) "Forensic psychiatry"; (9) "Radical cures: Psychosurgery and ECT"; (10) "Miscellaneous notable resources."

Bibliography of selected historical materials from the HMD and NLM collection, including publications ("scientific monographs, federal or state reports, personal accounts, conference proceedings, legal briefs, armed service publications, mass market publications, teaching materials, monographs on psychiatric ethics, treatment, or social effects, manuscripts, audiovisual materials, ephemera, and so on."—*Overview.* from the 19th century to the 1970s. For scholars interested in the history of psychiatry.

1384 **A short history of neurology: The British contribution, 1660–1910.** F. Clifford Rose. ix, 282 p., ill. Oxford; Boston: Butterworth-Heinemann, 1999. ISBN: 0750641657.

616.80941   RC339.G7R68

Concise history of British neurology, with contributions from neurologists, neuroscientists, neurosurgeons, and medical historians. Includes chapters on Thomas Willis (1621–75) and other famous neuroscientists, the evolution of British neurology in comparison to other countries, neurological texts, and other important areas in the development of neurology. Includes bibliographical references and index.

1385 **Three hundred years of psychiatry, 1535–1860: A history presented in selected English texts.** Richard Alfred Hunter, Ida Macalpine. xxvi, 1107 p., ill. Hartsdale, N.Y.: Carlisle, 1982, c1963. ISBN: 0910177007.

616.8900941   RC438.T48

Corrected reprint.

Not a systematic treatise but an attempt "to present original sources and through them trace clinical and pathological observations, nosologies, theories, [and] social and legal attitudes to mental illness. It is intended to serve the dual purpose of a sourcebook of psychiatric history aiming at biographical and bibliographical accuracy."—*Introd.* Arranged by century, the book is built on extracts from original sources, which are introduced by explanatory notes discussing the topic historically and clinically and relating it to later developments. Extracts are arranged chronologically, each headed by the author's name, dates of birth and death, qualifications, and main offices. Includes indexes.

1386 **World history of psychiatry.** John G. Howells. xxv, 770 p., ill. New York: Brunner/Mazel, [1974, c1975]. ISBN: 0876300824.

616.89009   RC438.H67

Follows the development of psychiatry, exploring different eras, stages (primitive, rational, religious, somatic, harmonization) and regions, in the context of "cultural, economic, geographical, political and ecological factors."—*Introd.*

Indexes; Abstract journals; Databases

1387 **NLM gateway.** National Library of Medicine (U.S.). 2000–. Bethesda, Md.: National Library of Medicine. http://gateway.nlm. nih.gov/.

RA11

Allows simultaneous searching of information resources at the National Library of Medicine (NLM). Databases include MEDLINE (427)/PubMed (432) and the NLM Catalog (482) as well as other resources, including information on current clinical trials and consumer health information (MedlinePlus [463]). Currently provides access to 21 databases and other information resources (for a complete list of databases and other details, see http://www.nlm.nih.gov/pubs/factsheets/gateway.html). An overview of the search results is presented in several categories (bibliographic resources, consumer health resources, and other information), with a listing of the individual databases and the number of results within these categories.

1388 **PsycINFO.** American Psychological Association. [n.d.] Washington: American Psychological Association. ISSN: 0033-2887. http://www.apa.org/psycinfo/.

150.5   BF1.P65

The most comprehensive index to the literature of psychology, indexing more than 1,200 English-language journals and reports and providing descriptive, nonevaluative abstracts. Formerly published in print as *Psychological abstracts* (ceased with 2006). Coverage has varied widely over the history of this title, extending back to 1872 in part. Abstracts are arranged by subject categories following the *Thesaurus of psychological index terms* (Washington: American Psychological Association, 2005). Coverage of books and dissertations, dropped in 1980, was resumed in 1992. Coverage of foreign-language materials was dropped in 1988. The database replaces associated indexes such as *Cumulative author index to Psychological abstracts* (Washington: American Psychological Association, 1965–1984) (1959/63–1981/83) and *Author index to Psychological index, 1894–1935,* and *Psychological abstracts, 1927–1958* (Boston: G.K. Hall, 1960–).

1389 PubMed. U.S. National Center for Biotechnology Information, National Library of Medicine, National Institutes of Health. 1996–. Bethesda, Md.: U.S. National Center for Biotechnology Information. http://www.ncbi.nlm.nih.gov/sites/entrez/.

PubMed®, developed and maintained by the National Center for Biotechnology Information (NCBI) at the National Library of Medicine® (NLM) (427). It is available via the NCBI Entrez (3) retrieval system. PubMed also provides access to the other Entrez molecular biology resources (*PubMed Overview*). Starting May 23, 2007, NCBI is changing to a new version of Entrez in a phased implementation (cf. Nahin AM. New and Improved PubMed®/Entrez and New URL *NLM tech. bull.,* 2007 May–Jun.; [356]: http://www.nlm.nih.gov/pubs/techbull/mj07/mj07_issue_cover.html).

Provides a search interface for more than 16 million bibliographic citations and abstracts in the fields of medicine, nursing, dentistry, veterinary medicine, health care systems, and preclinical sciences. It provides access to articles indexed for MEDLINE® (425) and for selected life sciences journals. PubMed subsets found under the "Limits" tab are: MEDLINE and PubMed Central®, several journal groups (i.e., core clinical journals, dental journals, and nursing journals), and topical subsets (AIDS, bioethics, cancer, complementary medicine, history of medicine, space life sciences, systematic reviews, and toxicology). "Linkout" provides access to full-text articles.

For detailed information see the PubMed fact sheet at http://www.nlm.nih.gov/pubs/factsheets/pubmed.html. For a brief overview of searching PubMed, see the PubMed Quick Start at http://www.ncbi.nlm.nih.gov/books/bv.fcgi?rid=helppubmed.section.pubmedhelp.PubMed_Quick_Start. For details on the now completed OLDMEDLINE retrospective conversion projects, see http://www.nlm.nih.gov/pubs/techbull/so06/so06_oldmedline_status.html.

Internet Resources

1390 **American Psychiatric Association.** American Psychiatric Association. 1996–?. Arlington, Va.: American Psychiatric Association. http://www.psych.org.

American Psychiatric Association (APA). International specialty society "representing 38,000 physician leaders in mental health."—*Main page*

Provides links to psychiatric education organizations, an overview of research at the APA, including DSM-IV (*Diagnostic and statistical manual of mental disorders: DSM-IV-TR* [1296]), practice guidelines (*American Psychiatric Association practice guidelines for the treatment of psychiatric disorders* [1338]), links to international psychiatric websites, psychiatric organizations by country, clinical issues, practice management, APA statements on ethics (Ethics [588]), and links to additional "outside" resources.

1391 **Drug abuse (MedlinePlus).** National Library of Medicine (U.S.). 2000?–. Bethesda, Md.: National Library of Medicine. http://www.nlm.nih.gov/medlineplus/drugabuse.html.

A Health Topic in MedlinePlus (463).

Contents: Overviews; Latest News; Diagnosis/Symptoms; Treatment; Prevention/Screening; Specific Conditions; Related Issues; Pictures and Photographs; Games; Clinical Trials; Research; Journal Articles; Dictionaries/Glossaries; Directories; Organizations; Newsletters/Print Publications; Law and Policy; Statistics; Children; Teenagers; Men; Women; Seniors; Other Languages.

Collection of links on substance abuse from a variety of government agencies, professional associations, and organizations, such as the National Institute on Drug Abuse (1505), the Office of National Drug Control, Substance Abuse and Mental Health Services Administration (SAMHSA) (769), National Library of Medicine (427), American Medical Association (451), American Academy of Family Physicians (448), and others. Also links to related MedlinePlus topics, e.g., alcoholism, prescription drug abuse, and substance abuse, to name a few.

1392 **Institute of Medicine (IOM).** Institute of Medicine. 1998–. Washington: National Academy of Sciences. http://www.iom.edu/.

The Institute of Medicine (IOM), one of the U.S. National Academies, has the mission to "serve as adviser to the nation to improve health" and "provides independent, objective, evidence-based advice to policymakers, health professionals, the private sector, and the public."—*Main page.*

Offers a list of all publications by the IOM since 1970 (http://www.iom.edu/CMS/2955.aspx), which cover a broad range of topics, including aging, child health, a variety of diseases, global health, health care quality, minority health, nutrition, public health, public policy, preventive medicine, women's health, and many other areas. The National Academies Press (http://www.nap.edu) provides online access to the publications of the four National Academies, i.e., National Academy of Sciences, National Academy of Engineering, IOM, and National Research Council.

1393 National Institute of Mental Health. National Institute of Mental Health (U.S.). 1995?–. Bethesda, Md.: National Institutes of Health. http://www.nimh.nih.gov/.

616.89   RA790.A1

Part of National Institutes of Health (NIH) (470).

Provides funding for research on mind, brain, behavior, and behavioral disorders; for research on the causes, occurrence, and treatment of mental illness; and for mental health services, including major projects such as the Human Brain Project and neuroinformatics research in support of this project. Contains topics useful for the public concerning adult and pediatric psychopathology. Provides extensive information on a variety of mental health topics (http://www.nimh.nih.gov/health/topics/index.shtml), links to NIMH publications and other resources, to other websites (e.g., Getting Help: Locate Services; http://www.nimh.nih.gov/health/topics/getting-help-locate-services/ind ex.shtml), and to mental health information available via MedlinePlus (http://www.nlm.nih.gov/medlineplus/mentalhealth.html) (463). Site index.

1394 Substance Abuse and Mental Health Services Administration (SAMHSA). Substance Abuse and Mental Health Services Administration. Rockville, Md.: Substance Abuse and Mental Health Services Administration. http://www.samhsa.gov.

Substance Abuse and Mental Health Services Administration (SAMHSA), part of U.S. Dept. of Health and Human Services (HHS) (769).

SAMHSA has as its mission "building resilience and facilitating recovery for people with or at risk for mental or substance use disorders. gearing all of its resources toward that outcome."—*About Us.* Searchable website. Provides resources for prevention, treatment, and rehabilitation services for patients with various forms of mental illness and addictions. Includes three centers: SAMHSA's Center for Mental Health Services (CMHS), Center for Substance Abuse Prevention (CSAP), and Center for Substance

Abuse Treatment (CSAT). Examples of SAMHSA resources include Mental Health Services Locator (http://mentalhealth.samhsa.gov/databases/) and Substance Abuse Treatment Facility Locator (http://dasis3.samhsa.gov/), both with clickable maps to locate different programs throughout the United States; Prevention Online (PREVLINE; http://ncadi.samhsa.gov/); a list of hotline numbers (http://mentalhealth.samhsa.gov/hotlines/); and related links (e.g., Mental Health on the Internet; http://mentalhealth.samhsa.gov/links/). SAMHSA's Office of Applied Statistics (http://www.oas.samhsa.gov/) provides the latest data on alcohol, tobacco, and illegal drugs as well as other statistical data and resources.

Statistics

1395 **Mental health, United States.** National Institute of Mental Health (U.S.). Rockville, Md.: U.S. Dept. of Health and Human Services, Public Health Service, Alcohol, Drug Abuse, and Mental Health Administration, National Institute of Mental Health, Div. of Biometry and Epidemiology, 1983–. ISSN: 0892-0664.

362.20973   RA790.6.M463

Description based on the 2000 ed.

Contains statistical reports and data on trends in mental health services, derived to a large extent from national surveys conducted by SAMSHA (Substance Abuse and Mental Health Services Administration) Center for Mental Health Services in collaboration with various major national, state, and professional associations. Three new sections in this edition: Section 1 contains an editorial on likely future directions and an overview of the mental health field over the past 100 years; Section 2 reports on the current status of mental health statistics; and Section 3 on the current status of mental health services. Section 4, as in previous editions, provides current mental health statistics. Electronic full-text of some volumes (1998 [executive summary only], 2000, and 2002) also available from the SAMSHA National Mental Health Information Center website http://purl.access.gpo.gov/GPO/LPS24728.

Treatises

1396 **Kaplan and Sadock's comprehensive textbook of psychiatry.** 8th ed. Benjamin J. Sadock, Virginia A. Sadock, Harold I. Kaplan. 2 v., ill. Philadelphia: Lippincott, Williams & Wilkins, 2004. ISBN: 0781734347.

616.89   RC454.C637

1st ed., 1967; 6th ed., 1995, had title *Comprehensive textbook of psychiatry*; 7th ed., 2000.

Encyclopedic textbook of clinical psychiatry, with close integration between the basic and clinical sciences and with both established and new approaches to psychotherapy. Rewritten and revised, with 50 new chapters in this edition, on topics including genetics and neural sciences, clinical psychiatry, and psychopharmacology. Charts, tables, diagrams, and illustrations, including color plates of major psychiatric drugs.

Also available in an electronic version, searchable by keyword, topic, chapter or image, with cross-references and links to PubMed (432). A condensed edition, *Kaplan and Sadock's synopsis of psychiatry*, 10th ed., 2007, is also available.

12 > PUBLIC HEALTH

1397 Agency for Toxic Substances and Disease Registry (ATSDR).
Agency for Toxic Substances and Disease Registry, U.S.
Department of Health and Human Services. 1999–. Atlanta:
Agency for Toxic Substances and Disease Registry. http://
www.atsdr.cdc.gov/.

Agency for Toxic Substances and Disease Registry (ATSDR), part of U.S. Dept. of Health and Human Services (HHS) (894).

Provides health information and takes public health actions to prevent harmful exposures and diseases related to toxic substances (e.g., recent examples: childhood lead poisoning prevention, drinking water concerns, anticipating the health concerns of climate change, etc.). Includes A–Z index by main topic (http://www.atsdr.cdc.gov/az/a.html), information about toxic substances, various data resources (e.g., access to the Hazardous Substance Release/Health Effects [HazDat] database, National Exposure Registry, and others), emergency response information, hazardous waste sites, a toxic substances portal (http://www.atsdr. cdc.gov/substances/index.html), and many other information sources.

1398 American Public Health Association (APHA). American Public
Health Association. 1998–. Washington: American Public Health
Association. http://www.apha.org/.

RA421

Searchable website of the American Public Health Association (APHA), an organization representing public health professionals, with the mission to protect Americans and their communities from health threats. Provides links to 24 sections (http://www.apha.org/membergroups/sections/aphasections/) representing major public health disciplines or public health programs and selected links to a wide variety of public health topics and resources (e.g., A–Z Health Topics at http://www.apha.org/advocacy/health/ and Public Health Links at http://www.apha.org/about/Public+Health+Links/). Includes a Health Disparities Projects and Interventions database, sponsored by APHA (http://www.apha.org/programs/disparitiesdb/). APHA participates in Partners in Information Access for the Public Health Workforce (891), a collaborative project to provide public health professionals with access to information resources to help them improve the health of the American public.

1399 CDC WONDER. Centers for Disease Control and Prevention (U.S.). 1998–. [Atlanta]: Centers for Disease Control and Prevention. http://purl.access.gpo.gov/GPO/LPS18322.

RA643

CDC WONDER (Wide-ranging Online Data for Epidemiologic Research), developed by the Centers for Disease Control and Prevention (CDC) (940), provides a search interface and access to a variety of reports, bibliographies on health-related topics, recommendations, and guidelines, and public-use data sets about mortality, cancer, HIV/AIDS, and others topics. Additional information and answers to a variety of questions can be found at http://wonder.cdc.gov/wonder/help/faq.html. For public health professionals and the general public.

1400 Health services research and public health information programs. National Library of Medicine (U.S.). Bethesda, Md.: National Library of Medicine, U.S. National Institutes of Health, Dept. of Health and Human Services. http://www.nlm.nih.gov/hsrph.html.

Lists resources from multiple National Library of Medicine (NLM) (427) programs, including collaborative projects (e.g., HSR information central [882]), links to several databases, e.g., HSRProj (Health Services Research Projects in Progress), HSRR (Health Services and Sciences Research Resources), Health Services/Technology Assessment Text (HSTAT), American Indian and Asian American Health, and others. Also provides preformulated PubMed (432) search filters and search strategies. Its outreach and training resources, with links to their full text, include "Finding and using health statistics," "Health economics: information resources," Health technology assessment 101 (HTA 101), "Public health information and data tutorial," publications, and informatics. Also provides access to various online publications, informatics resources, and links to additional information and related products.

1401 Indian Health Service (IHS). U.S. Department of Health and Human Services. Rockville, Md.: U.S. Department of Health and Human Services. http://www.ihs.gov/.

Part of U.S. Department of Health and Human Services (HHS) (894).

Searchable website. IHS's site map (http://www.ihs.gov/GeneralWeb/SiteMap/index.asp) provides detailed information to many IHS resources and links to American Indian sites, nationwide programs, information about IHS headquarters and area offices, press releases, reports, fact sheets, health care delivery to members of federally recognized tribes, and other information. Access to the Native Health History Database and Native Health Research Database.

1402 Injury data and resources. National Center for Health Statistics. Atlanta: National Center for Health Statistics. http://www.cdc.gov/nchs/injury.htm.

"The purpose of this Web site is to provide an overview of injury morbidity and mortality data and statistics available from the National Center for Health Statistics (NCHS) (539) and other sources and to provide details on injury surveillance methodology and tools to assist in data analysis."—*Main page.* Provides links to a variety of resources, including the International Collaborative Effort (ICE) on Injury Statistics (http://www.cdc.gov/nchs/advice.htm), relevant coding schemes, and additional resources (e.g., WISQARS: Web-based Injury Statistics Query and Reporting System [1404], CDC WONDER [1399], Faststats [518], and others).

1403 National Center for Health Statistics (NCHS). National Center for Health Statistics (U.S.). 1990s–. Hyattsville, Md.: Centers for Disease Control and Prevention. http://www.cdc.gov/nchs/.

RA409

NCHS is the primary agency for compiling and making available American health and vital statistics and data sets. Searchable website, with topically arranged site index. Its home page provides links to various resources in several categories, including What's New; Health E-stats; Information Showcase; Top 10 Links; surveys and data collection systems (data collected through personal interviews and systems based on records, with data from vital and medical records); and microdata access (including links to NCHS public-use data files and documentation and state data). Surveys and data collection systems include the National Health and Nutrition Examination Survey (NHANES), National Health Care Survey (NCHS), National Health Interview Survey (NHIS), National Immunization Survey (NIS), Longitudinal Studies of Aging (LSOAs), National Vital Statistics System (NSS), and Injury Statistics Query and Reporting System. Examples of linked resources include *Faststats A to Z* (518) and Health, United States (529). Details on NCHS publications and information products are provided at http://www.cdc.gov/nchs/products.htm.

NCHS serves as the World Health Organization's (WHO's) Collaborating Center for the Family of International Classifications for North America (North American Collaborating Center [NACC] established in 1976) and is responsible for coordinating all official disease classification activities in the United States, in close cooperation with the Canadian Institute for Health Information (CIHI), Statistics Canada, and the Pan American Health Organization. A portal to the disease classifications in North America (e.g., International Classification of Diseases, Ninth Revision, Clinical Modification: ICD-9-CM [82] and International Classification of Functioning, Disability, and Health [ICF] [83]) is provided at http://www.cdc.gov/nchs/icd9.htm.

PUBLIC HEALTH

1404 WISQARS. National Center for Injury Prevention and Control. 2000–. Atlanta: National Center for Injury Prevention and Control. http://www.cdc.gov/ncipc/wisqars.

HB1323.A2

WISQARS (Web-Based Injury Statistics Query and Reporting System), National Center for Injury Prevention and Control of the U.S. Centers for Disease Control and Prevention (940); CDC Injury Center.

Described as "an interactive database system that provides customized reports of injury-related data."—*Main page.* Injury statistics presented in two categories, i.e., fatal U.S. injury statistics and national estimates of nonfatal injuries treated in U.S. hospital emergency departments, each with links to tables, charts, tutorial, help, and FAQs. CDC's Injury Center (http://www.cdc.gov/ncipc/cmprfact.htm) provides links to a variety of injury related topics, fact sheets, Injury Fact Book (http://www.cdc.gov/ncipc/fact_book/factbook.htm), and overviews on injury response, violence prevention, and prevention of unintentional injuries.

The National Center for Health Statistics (NCHS) (1403) also makes a variety of injury data and resources available at http://www.cdc.gov/nchs/injury.htm.

Bibliography

1405 American health care in transition: A guide to the literature.
Barbara A. Haley, Brian Deevey. xii, 336 p. Westport, Conn.: Greenwood Press, 1997. ISBN: 0313273235.
362.10973   RA395.A3H3426

(Bibliographies and indexes in medical studies ; no. 14). This annotated bibliography includes periodical articles and government publications, covering the literature 1979–1996. Index.

1406 Grey literature report. New York Academy of Medicine
Library. [1999]–. [New York, N.Y.]: New York Academy of Medicine. ISSN: 1931-7050. http://www.nyam.org/library/pages/grey_literature_report.
362.1

A publication of the New York Academy of Medicine Library (http://www.nyam.org/library/).

Grey literature is defined as "that which is produced on all levels of government, academics, business and industry in print and electronic formats, but which is not controlled by commercial publishers" (cf. *Website*, New York Academy of Medicine "What is Grey Literature?" http://www.nyam.org/library/pages/what_is_grey_literature).

Considered an alerting service to new grey literature in health services research and various public health topics, assisting researchers and librarians with the identification of this literature for both reference and collection development purposes. The Academy's entire Grey Literature Collection can be searched by keyword(s). The Academy's collection policy for grey literature is found at http://www.nyam.org/library/pages/grey_literature_collection_developme nt_policy#conditions. Also included on the website is an A–Z list of grey literature producing organizations, including nonprofit and government agencies (http://www.nyam.org/library/pages/grey_literature_producing_organizations). The publications are cataloged in the New York Academy of Medicine Library Online Catalog (475).

The New York Academy of Medicine Library website provides links to its online library catalog (New York Academy of Medicine Library Online Catalog [475]), and its historical and other collections.

1407 Health of black Americans from post reconstruction to integration, 1871–1960: An annotated bibliography of contemporary sources. Mitchell F. Rice, Woodrow Jones. xxiii, 206 p. New York: Greenwood Press, 1990. ISBN: 0313263140.
016.362108996073   RA448.5.N4.R52

No. 26 of *Bibliographies and indexes in Afro-American and African studies* series.

A comprehensive annotated bibliography of the literature on "the condition of blacks [including] patterns of mortality, morbidity and utilization behaviors of blacks from slavery to the mid-20th century" that aims to provide "a fuller understanding of the history of health care inequities in the U.S."—*Introd.* In three chapters: 1871–1919, 1920–50, 1951–60. Entries give full bibliographic information. Subject and author indexes.

A companion volume by the same compilers, *Black American health: An annotated bibliography*, treats the literature of the 1970s and 1980s.

1408 Health services research methodology core library recommendations, 2007. AcademyHealth, National Library of Medicine (U.S.). 2007. Bethesda, Md.: National Library of Medicine. http://www.nlm.nih.gov/nichsr/corelib/hsrmethods. html.

Produced by AcademyHealth; National Library of Medicine (NLM) (427); National Information Center on Health Services Research and Health Care (NICHSR).

List of books, journals, bibliographic databases, websites, and other media; useful for collection development librarians and researchers interested in health services research methods. Lists both "core" materials and "desired" materials in areas such as general health policy, health economics, health services research, public health, and several others. The NICHSR website (http://www.nlm.nih.gov/nichsr/outreach.html) lists links to several other recommended lists, including Health Economics Core Library Recommendation, Health Outcomes Core Library Recommendation, Health Policy Core Library Recommendation, and other information.

1409 Healthy work: An annotated bibliography. Namir Khan, Nina Nakajima, Willem H. Vanderburg. xiv, 359 p. Lanham, Md.: Scarecrow Press, 2005. ISBN: 0810852853.
016.61362   Z6675.I5.K48; RC967

"The purpose of this annotated bibliography is to bring together diverse bodies of literature related to human work in a manner that supports preventive approaches to work design and organization. An overview of relevant literature for occupational health and safety specialists, industrial hygienists. so that they and other professionals can understand why our workplaces have become primary sources of physical and mental illness."—*Pref.* Includes bibliographical references and indexes. Author index and keyword index.

1410 Medicine, health, and bioethics: Essential primary sources.
K. Lee Lerner, Brenda Wilmoth Lerner. lvii, 513 p., ill. Detroit: Thomson/Gale, 2006. ISBN: 1414406231.

174.2   R724.M313

(Series: Social issues primary sources collection.)

Contains complete primary sources or excerpts of documents and publications published 1823–2006, illustrating major biomedical issues. Each entry includes the complete text or an excerpt with complete original citation, subject area, historical context, significance. For students, health professionals, and also general readers. Also available as an e-book.

Dictionaries

1411 Dictionary of environmental and occupational medicine: Wörterbuch Umwelt- und Arbeitsmedizin. Karl-Heinz Ohrbach. 551 p. Weinheim, [Germany]; New York: Wiley-VCH, 2001. ISBN: 3527303537.

616.9800321;616.98003   RC963.A3.O37

Includes approx. 15,000 terms and phrases (English/German and German/ English) describing environmental factors and their impact on human health, safety, and preventive medicine, with focus on the workplace. For physicians, scientists, and translators.

1412 Dictionary of environmental health. David Worthington. New York: Spon Press, 2002. ISBN: 0415267242.

616.9803   RA566.W68

(Clay's library of health and the environment)

"Provides a one-stop reference to over 3,000 common and not so common terms, concepts, abbreviations, acronyms, and a wealth of supporting data. suitable for. environmental and public health practitioners and students." —*Publ. description* Appendix I: Units and measurements;

Appendix II: Abbreviations and acronyms. Cross-references, bibliographical references, and index. Available as an e-book.

1413 A dictionary of epidemiology. 4th ed. John M. Last, Robert A.
Spasoff, International Epidemiological Association. xx, 196 p., ill.
New York: Oxford University Press, 2001. ISBN: 0195141687.
614.403   RA651.D553

1st ed., 1983; 3rd ed., 1995.

"With many new entries, updates, and other refinements" (*Pref.*), this edition provides a broad range of covered topics, including biostatistics, bioethics, community and public health, demography, and microbiology.

Definitions range from one word to short essays that incorporate tables, graphs, charts, mathematical formulas, and diagrams. The more common terms are defined, with cross-references from their synonyms.

1414 Dictionary of pharmacoepidemiology. Bernard Bégaud. x, 171
p. Chichester, [England, U.K.]; New York: Wiley, 2000. ISBN:
0471803618.
615.103   RM302.5.B443

English translation of Bernard Bégaud's *Dictionnaire de pharmaco-épidémiologie*, 1998.

Online access available from WileyInterScience Online Books (http://www3.interscience.wiley.com/cgi-bin/bookhome/93516142) and also via netLibrary.

As defined in this dictionary, pharmacoepidemiology is the "study of interactions between drugs and populations, or more specifically, the study of the therapeutic effect(s), risk and use of drugs, usually in large populations, using epidemiology and methods of reasoning," and the work is written for "regulatory authorities, pharmaceutical physicians, lawyers, pharmacists, researchers, evaluators and students."—*Foreword.* Complements epidemiology dictionaries.

1415 A dictionary of public health. John Last. New York: Oxford
University Press, 2006. ISBN: 9780195160.
362.1003   RA423.L37

Provides approx. 5,000 definitions of varying length (some include explanation and discussion as well as pointing to further information online) for many specialized terms found in the public health vocabulary. Also included are brief biographical entries for "historically significant people who have contributed to the advance of public health."—*Pref.* Bibliography and references. Electronic version via Oxford Reference Online (Oxford; New York: Oxford University Press, 2002–).

1416 Dictionary of public health promotion and education: Terms and concepts. 2nd ed. Naomi N. Modeste, Teri S. Tamayose, Helen Hopp Marshak. xii, 177 p. San Francisco: Jossey-Bass, 2004. ISBN: 0787969192.

613.03   RA440.5.M634

1st ed., 1996.

This expanded edition, intended for public health professionals and students, provides definitions for frequently used terms in public health education and promotion and related public health disciplines. Emphasizes "terms relevant to the four settings of health promotion and education—community, workplace, primary care, and school."—*Foreword*

Includes a list of health and professional organizations, references, and recommended reading. An online version is available via netLibrary.

1417 The European multilingual thesaurus on health promotion in 12 languages. Laura Dorst, Giancarlo Pocetta, Kerstin Karlström, Commission of the European Communities. 2001. Woerden, The Netherlands: NIGZ Netherlands Institute for Health Promotion and Disease Prevention. http://www.hpmulti.net/.

International collaborative project. Includes the key terminology of health education, health promotion, and patient education related to health behavior. Alphabetical display of terms in English (used as the source language) with 11 equivalent terms in Danish, Dutch, English, Finnish, French, German, Greek, Italian, Norwegian, Portuguese, Spanish, and Swedish. As described on the website, the thesaurus consists of the following other parts: Macrostructure (English), with systematic display of terms according to the macrostructure; Permuted index (English); Alphabetical display of the preferred and nonpreferred terms with the hierarchical and associative relationships (Danish, Dutch, English, Finnish, French, German, Greek, Italian, Norwegian, Portuguese, Spanish, and Swedish); Key index (Danish-English, Dutch-English, Finnish-English, French-English, German-English, Greek-English, Italian-English, Norwegian-English, Portuguese-English, Spanish-English, Swedish-English). Available as PDF file and text file.

1418 Health services cyclopedic dictionary: A compendium of health-care and public health terminology. 3rd ed. Thomas C.

Timmreck. xii, 860 p., color ill. Sudbury, Mass.: Jones and Bartlett Publishers, 1997. ISBN: 0867205156.

362.1068   RA393.T56

1st ed. (1982) and 2nd ed. (1987) had title: *Dictionary of health services management.*
(The Jones and Bartlett series in health sciences).
This rev. and exp. ed. contains terminology and definitions from the fields of health services and medical care, health administration, health care reform, public health, environmental health, epidemiology, managed care, and other related areas.

1419 Illustrated dictionary and resource directory of environmental and occupational health. 2nd ed. Herman Koren. 701 p., ill. Boca Raton, Fla.: CRC Press, 2005. ISBN: 1566705908.

616.98003   RA566.K59

1st ed., 1996, had title *Illustrated dictionary of environmental health and occupational safety.*
Interdisciplinary resource covering a variety of fields (for example, epidemiology, microbiology, toxicology, and computer science) relevant to environmental and occupational health and safety, with approx. 16,000 terms and cross-references for synonyms, abbreviations, and acronyms. The resource directory lists professional and government organizations. For professionals, students, and general readers. Also available online via netLibrary.

1420 Lewis' dictionary of occupational and environmental safety and health. Jeffrey W. Vincoli. 1093 p., ill. Boca Raton, Fla.: Lewis, 2000. ISBN: 1566703999.

363.1103   T55.L468

Comprehensive resource for the terminology of the interdisciplinary area of industrial safety and environmental health. Includes approx. 25,000 definitions.
Available online via CRCnetBASE (Boca Raton, Fla.; London: CRC Press; Taylor and Francis).

1421 Medical statistics from A to Z. 2nd ed. Brian Everitt. vi, 248 p., ill. Cambridge; New York: Cambridge University Press, 2006. ISBN: 0521867630.

610.727   RA407.E943

1st ed., 2003.

Contains approx. 1,500 terms with definitions and references for further reading. Written in non-technical language. For health professionals and students.

1422 Slee's health care terms. 5th ed. Debora A. Slee, Vergil N. Slee, H. Joachim Schmidt. 700 p. Sudbury, Mass.: Jones and Bartlett Publ., 2007. ISBN: 9780763746155.

362.103   RA423.S55

1st ed., 1986; 4th ed., 2001. Also called *Health care terms.*

Provides concise definitions for terms from a wide range of disciplines in the healthcare field, including administration, organization, finance, statistics, law, and governmental regulation. Many cross-references. Pays particular attention to acronyms. Terms used in definitions are italicized to indicate the term is defined elsewhere in the dictionary; related terms may be grouped together under one term, such as the many entries under the term "hospital." Intended for all types of healthcare consumers.

Directories

1423 Directory of health and human services data resources.
Department of Health and Human Services (U.S.). [1999]–.
Washington: Department of Health and Human Services. http://aspe.os.dhhs.gov/datacncl/datadir/.

Updates and expands the 1995 *HHS directory of minority health and human resources data resources.* Title varies; also called *Directory of minority health and human services data.*

Compilation of information about major data collection systems of the U.S. Department of Health and Human Services (HHS). Provides information about each data system, including links to relevant websites. Intended for policy makers, administrators, researchers, and the public as a reference document on data and statistical resources within HHS.

1424 DIRLINE. National Institutes of Health (U.S.). [1983?–.] Bethesda, Md: U.S. National Institutes of Health, Dept. of Health and Human Services. http://dirline.nlm.nih.gov/.

DIRLINE® (Directory of Information Resources Online), maintained by the National Library of Medicine (NLM) (427).

Online annotated directory of organizations, research resources, projects, databases, and other information resources concerned with health and biomedicine from a variety of sources, including federal, state, and local government agencies, academic and research institutions, and also consumer health-related resources such as self-help groups and health hotlines. Resources are mostly from the U.S. but also include some international resources. Currently contains over 8,000 entries, with topics on most diseases and conditions and health services research and technology assessment. Can be searched using MeSH® (Medical Subject Headings) (575), keywords, or by name and location of a resource. Detailed information on DIRLINE can be found via a fact sheet prepared by NLM: http://www.nlm.nih.gov/pubs/factsheets/dirlinfs.html.

1425 **A practical guide to global health service.** Edward O'Neil, American Medical Association. xxxv, 402 p. Chicago: American Medical Association, 2006. ISBN: 1579476732.

610.737   RA390.U5O54

OMNI Med ("loosely translated from the Latin meaning 'health care for all'" [*Pref.*]) is a nongovernmental organization founded by the author in 1998.

Contents: ch. 1, Overcoming obstacles: cultural and practical guidelines; ch. 2, Travel, health, and safety guidelines; ch. 3, The Omni Med database of international health service opportunities; ch. 4, Cross-referencing guide to the database; ch. 5, Other relevant organizations; Appendix A, Useful web sites; Appendix B, About Omni Med.

"A health providers guide to the practical aspects of serving internationally, including data on more than 300 organizations that send health providers overseas."—*Publ. notes.* Organization profiles include concise descriptions, contact information, and practical information about length of service terms, personnel sought, areas served, and availability of funding, training, room and board, and other essential information (e.g., trip planning, travel and safety guidelines, commonly encountered illnesses, information about the culture of a particular country, etc.). Written for persons interested in medical volunteering. Glossary; bibliography.

1426 **www.health.gov.** Office of Disease Prevention and Health Promotion. Washington: U.S. Department of Health and Human Services. http://www.health.gov/.

Coordinated by the Office of Disease Prevention and Health Promotion, Office of Public Health Service, U.S. Dept. of Health and Human Services (HHS).

"Portal to the Web sites of a number of multi-agency health initiatives and activities of the U.S. Department of Health and Human Services (HHS)

PUBLIC HEALTH

639

and other Federal departments and agencies."—*Main page*. Provides links to general health information (e.g., Healthfinder [706], National Health Information Center [http://www.health.gov/nhic/], MedlinePlus [463], and others), special initiatives (e.g., Healthy People 2010 [530], Dietary Guidelines for Americans 2005 [Washington: U.S. Dept.of Health and Human Services; U.S. Dept. of Agriculture, 2005], and others), health news, the major federal agencies (U.S. Dept. of Health and Human Services [894] and its agencies, Office of Public Health and Science [http://www.osophs.dhhs.gov/ophs/], Office of the Surgeon General [http://www.surgeongeneral.gov/]), and other key government agencies with "direct health responsibilities" (e.g., Dept. of Defense [DoD], Environmental Protection Agency [EPA], Dept. of Veterans Affairs [VA], Occupational Safety and Health Administration [OSHA], and others).

Encyclopedias

1427 **Encyclopaedia of occupational health and safety.** 4th ed. Jeanne Mager Stellman, International Labour Organization. v. 2–4, ill. Geneva, [Switzerland]: International Labour Organization, 1998. ISBN: 9221092038.

616.980303   RC963.A3.E53

Prepared under the auspices of the International Labour Organization.

1st ed., 1930, had title *Occupation and health*; 2nd ed., 1971; 3rd ed., 1983. Sometimes cited as *ILO encyclopedia of occupational health and safety*.

Contents: v. 1, *The body*; v. 2, *Hazards*; v. 3, *Chemicals, industries and occupations*; v. 4, *Guides, indexes (index by subject, index to chemicals, and guide to units and abbreviations), directory of experts.*

Consists of a collection of signed articles on the basic information available in the field by international specialists, with recent bibliographic references. In 105 chapters, entries cover various aspects of toxicology, occupational illnesses and injuries, diseases of migrant workers, and institutions active in the field of occupational health. Preventive safety measures are stressed, and technical and social solutions to problems are offered. Intends to provide "theoretical and ethical underpinnings to the ongoing work of achieving the goal of social justice in a global economy."—*Pref.*

Table of contents with search interface to access words and phrases in the text (http://www.ilocis.org/en/contilo.html).

1428 Encyclopedia of aging and public health. Sana Loue, Martha Sajatovic. 843 p. New York: Springer, 2007. ISBN: 0387337539.

Interdisciplinary resource for professionals in the fields of public health and geriatrics. Contains entries on health and diseases of adults as they age, and quality and accessibility of care for an aging population. Includes biological, psychosocial, historical, ethical, and legal aspects. Entries include references and resource lists. Available as an e-book as part of Springer eReference.

1429 Encyclopedia of biostatistics. 2nd ed. P. Armitage, Theodore Colton. 8 v. Chichester, [England, U.K.]; West Sussex, [England, U.K.]: John Wiley, 2005. ISBN: 047084907X.

610.21   RA409.E53

1st ed., 1998 (6 v.). Description based on rev. and enl. ed., 2005 (8 v.).

Contents: v. 1, A–Chap; v. 2, Char–Dos; v. 3, Dou–Gre; v. 4, Gro–Mar; v. 5, Mas–Nui; v. 6, Nul–Ran; v. 7, Rao–Str; v. 8, Stu–Z, index.

Biostatistics can be defined as the application of statistical methods to the life sciences, medicine, and the health sciences. Clinical epidemiology, clinical trials, disease modeling, epidemiology, statistical computing, and vital and health statistics are some examples of the areas covered. This edition contains more than 1,300 articles, with approx. 300 revised and 182 new entries. New topics include, for example, applications of biostatistics to bioinformatics, study of the human genome, and outbreaks of infectious-disease epidemics. Bibliographies, many cross-references, author index, and a selected list of review articles. Available both in print and online through http://www.interscience.wiley.com.

1430 Encyclopedia of bioterrorism defense. Richard F. Pilch, Raymond A. Zilinskas. xiii, 555 p., ill. Hoboken, N.J.: Wiley-LISS, 2005. ISBN: 0471467170.

363.32   HV6433.3.E53

Single volume containing 136 entries written by 99 expert contributors on topics related to bioterrorism in fields of social, natural, and physical sciences; engineering; policy; and government. Articles explore interdependent issues surrounding science, legislation, international government relations, and social response related to the existence and potential use of biological warfare. Entries provide references, further reading suggestions, and websites. Most articles provide background in their main subjects, and some specifically address historical topics, such as the Palestinian Islamic Jihad and Weather Underground groups. Thorough index with cross-references. Recommended for public and academic libraries. Available as an e-book.

1431 Encyclopedia of epidemiology. Sarah Boslaugh. 2 v., ill. Los Angeles: Sage, 2008. ISBN: 9781412928.

614.403   RA652.E533

Reader's guide topics: "Behavioral and social science"; "Branches of epidemiology"; "Data"; "Diseases and conditions"; "Epidemiological concepts"; "Ethics"; "Genetics"; "Health care economics and management"; "History and biography"; "Infrastructure"; "Medical care and research"; "Specific populations"; "Statistics and research methods"; "Women's health issues."

Approx. 650 articles of varying length on basic epidemiologic concepts. Covers research methods, statistical information relating to diseases, biographical information, etc. Each article includes bibliography and "see also" references. Useful as a supplementary resource for health professionals and general readers. Available electronically through Sage eReference and also via Gale Virtual Reference Library (Farmington Hills, Mich.: Gale Cengage Learning, 2002–).

1432 Encyclopedia of health and behavior. Norman B. Anderson. 2 v. Thousand Oaks, Calif.: Sage, 2004. ISBN: 0761923608.

610.3   R726.5.E53

Contents: v. 1, A–G; v. 2, H–W.

Health and behavior as an area of study can be defined as an interdisciplinary field of health science, health care, and public health that focuses on the interaction of behavioral, psychological, emotional, social, cultural, and biological factors with physical health outcomes. Approx. 200 entries such as stress and health, pain management, social support, health, smoking, health promotion and disease prevention, and HIV/AIDS. Includes policy and organizational issues, including health care costs. Cross-references. Appendix with online resources and an annotated listing of organizations. Author and subject indexes. For scholars, health professionals, and also general readers. Available online through http://www.gale.com.

1433 Encyclopedia of infectious diseases: Modern methodologies. Michel Tibayrenc. 747 p., [24] p. of plates, ill. (some color), maps (some color). Hoboken, N.J.: Wiley-Liss, 2007. ISBN: 0471657328.

362.1969003   RA643.E53

Provides coverage of modern multidisciplinary approaches and applications of newly developed technologies to the study of infectious diseases and their surveillance and control. Emphasis is on medical applications. Articles on AIDS, malaria, SARS and influenza, evolution of pathogens and the relationship between human genetic diversity and the spread of infectious diseases, uses of various technologies, and various specialized topics (e.g., bioterrorism, antibiotics, using a geographic information system to spatially investigate infectious disease, representation of infectious diseases in art, and others). Includes list of web resources. For an academic audience. Available online via NetLibrary.

Carol Turkington and Bonnie Lee Ashby's *Encyclopedia of infectious diseases*, 3rd ed., 2007 (part of the Facts On File library of health and living series [678]), is also a useful resource, intended for health professionals, general readers, and public libraries.

1434 Encyclopedia of obesity. Kathleen Keller. 2 v., ill., port. Los
Angeles: Sage, 2008. ISBN: 9781412952385.

362.196398003   RC628.E53

"Reader's guide" topics: biological or genetic contributions to obesity; children and obesity; dietary interventions to treat obesity; disordered eating and obesity; environmental contributions to obesity; health implications of obesity; medical treatments for obesity; new research frontiers on obesity; obesity and ethnicity/race; obesity and the brain or obesity and behavior; obesity as a public health crisis; psychological influences and outcomes of obesity; societal influences and outcomes of obesity; women and obesity; worldwide prevalence of obesity.

This interdisciplinary resource explores a variety of topics on obesity, health conditions, and issues related to obesity. Written in nontechnical language and intended as a starting point for different audiences, from scholars to the general public. References at the end of each entry. Glossary and index in both volumes. Available online via Sage eReference.

1435 Encyclopedia of primary prevention and health promotion.
Thomas Gullotta, Martin Bloom, Child and Family Agency of
Southeastern Connecticut. xi, 1179 p., ill. New York: Kluwer
Academic/Plenum, 2003. ISBN: 0306472961.

613.03   RA427.8.E53

A sponsored publication of the Child and Family Agency of Southeastern Connecticut.

Pt. 1, "Foundation topics in primary prevention and health promotion," includes, for example, sections on definitions and the history of health promotion, and ethical considerations. Pt. 2, "Primary prevention and human health promotion topics," covers a wide range of interdisciplinary topics, such as aggressive behavior, environmental health, creativity, suicide, and violence, to name a few. Included are strategies that work or are promising, as well as those that do not work. International resource, written in a standard format that allows cross-comparison.

1436 Encyclopedia of public health. Lester Breslow. 4 v., ill., map. New York: Macmillan Reference USA; Gale Group, 2002. ISBN: 0028653548.

362.103   RA423.E53

Approx. 900 alphabetically-arranged entries with brief bibliographies in the key areas of public health, with topics such as epidemiology, environmental health, drug abuse, bioterrorism, etc. Includes overviews, definitions, and biographical entries. Each entry begins with an outline of the article. Glossary entries explain key terms. Extensive use of cross-references. Appendix includes text of core documents and publications of historical importance in the field of public health. A broad outline is found at the back of v. 4. Index. For general readers, students, and health professionals. Available as an e-book from Gale and NetLibrary.

1437 Encyclopedia of women's health. Sana Loue, Martha Sajatovic, Keith B. Armitage. vii, 710 p. New York: Kluwer Academic/Plenum, 2004. ISBN: 0306480735.

613.04244   RA778.E5825

Covers the history of women's health as well as current topics and issues. Interdisciplinary resource, including topics from medicine, psychology, law, and other areas and perspectives. Also includes alternative and complementary health topics. Suggested readings. Written for both general readers and health professionals. Available online via Springer eReference.

1438 Essentials of medical geology: Impacts of the natural environment on public health. O. Selinus, B. J. Alloway. xiv, 812 p., ill. (some color). Amsterdam, [The Netherlands]; Boston: Elsevier Academic Press, 2005. ISBN: 0126363412.

614.42   RA566.E87

Contents: sec. 1, "Medical geology: Perspectives and prospects"; sec. 2, "Pathways and exposures"; sec. 3, "Environmental toxicology, pathology, and medical geology"; sec. 4, "Techniques and tools"; appendixes: (A) international reference values; (B) Web links; (C) glossary.

Medical geology, considered an emerging discipline, is defined by the International Working Group on Medical Geology as the science dealing with the relationship between natural geological factors and health in man and animals. Chapters address such topics as natural distribution and abundance of elements, uptake of elements from a chemical or biological point of view, geological impacts on nutrition, volcanic emissions and health, radon in air and water, arsenic in groundwater and the environment, fluoride in natural waters, water hardness and health effects, GIS in human health studies, and histochemical and microprobe analysis in medical geology. Reference tables, graphics, and maps. Index. Available online via Knovel (Norwich, N.Y.: Knovel, 2003–) and netLibrary.

Guides

1439 **Bioterrorism and public health: An Internet resource guide.** John G. Bartlett, eMedguides.com. xi, 305 p. Princeton, N.J.; Montvale, N.J.: eMedguides.com; Thomson/Physicians' Desk Reference, 2002. ISBN: 1563634279.

025.063633497   RC88.9.T47.B566

Also available online as part of Thomson's PDR eMedguides (http://www.emedguides.com/index.jsp).

Contents: http://www.loc.gov/catdir/toc/fy036/2002523094.html.

Provides brief descriptions and ratings of websites from government, public health agencies, educational institutions, and research centers. Addresses bioterrorism concerns raised by Sep. 11. Covers bioterrorism public health advisories and guidelines, clinical resources on bioterrorism, health and safety guidelines, and hazardous materials. Also addresses psychosocial issues. For electronic browsing of this book, see http://www.emedguides.com/topics.jsp?guide_id=63 (last updated July 2002; access code found on the title page of the printed guide). Can be supplemented with other, more up-to-date online resources, such as Biodefense and Bioterrorism (MedlinePlus) (463) and the website of the Institute for Biosecurity, Saint Louis University School of Public Health (http://www.bioterrorism.slu.edu/bt.htm), which links to ready-reference material and a variety of government, academic, and professional

Internet resources. For medical and academic libraries as well as public libraries.

1440 Bioterrorism: Guidelines for medical and public health management. Donald A. Henderson, Thomas V. Inglesby, Tara Jeanne O'Toole. xvii, 244 p., ill. (some color). Chicago: American Medical Association, 2002. ISBN: 157947280X.

363.32   RC88.9.T47.H46

Provides guidelines for emergency and public health personnel and other health professionals following a bioterrorist attack: how to recognize and diagnose infections (e.g., anthrax, smallpox, plague, etc.) and how to manage survivors of such an attack. Includes a chapter entitled "Bioterrorism preparedness and response: Clinician and public health agencies as essential partners."

Includes bibliographical references and index.

1441 The Blackwell companion to medical sociology. William C. Cockerham. xiii, 528 p., ill. Oxford; Malden, Mass.: Blackwell, 2001; repr. 2005. ISBN: 0631217037.

306.461   RA418.B5736

Global and comprehensive survey of the emerging field of medical sociology. Twenty-six signed chapters draw out topics in Western medicine to show how sociological theory and analysis enrich the clinical understanding of each area. A second section covers countries in every corner of the globe: Canada, Mexico, Brazil, countries in both Western and Eastern Europe, Africa, the Arab world, Israel, Australia, Japan, and China. Cultural constructs from the discipline of sociology inform medical practice and understanding. A thoroughly useful textbook for understanding the field. Includes bibliographical references and index.

1442 A practical guide to global health service. Edward O'Neil, American Medical Association. xxxv, 402 p. Chicago: American Medical Association, 2006. ISBN: 1579476732.

610.737   RA390.U5O54

OMNI Med ("loosely translated from the Latin meaning 'health care for all'" [*Pref.*]) is a nongovernmental organization founded by the author in 1998.

Contents: ch. 1, Overcoming obstacles: cultural and practical guidelines; ch. 2, Travel, health, and safety guidelines; ch. 3, The Omni Med database of international health service opportunities; ch. 4, Cross-referencing

MEDICAL & HEALTH SCIENCES

guide to the database; ch. 5, Other relevant organizations; Appendix A, Useful web sites; Appendix B, About Omni Med.

"A health providers guide to the practical aspects of serving internationally, including data on more than 300 organizations that send health providers overseas."—*Publ. notes.* Organization profiles include concise descriptions, contact information, and practical information about length of service terms, personnel sought, areas served, and availability of funding, training, room and board, and other essential information (e.g., trip planning, travel and safety guidelines, commonly encountered illnesses, information about the culture of a particular country, etc.). Written for persons interested in medical volunteering. Glossary; bibliography.

1443 **Secondary data sources for public health: A practical guide.**
Sarah Boslaugh. x, 152 p. Cambridge, [England, U.K.]; New York: Cambridge University Press, 2007. ISBN: 052169023.
362.10727   RA409.B66

Part of Practical Guides to Biostatistics and Epidemiology.

Contents: ch. 1, "An introduction to secondary analysis"; ch. 2, "Health services utilization data"; ch. 3, "Health behaviors and risk factors data"; ch. 4, "Data on multiple health topics"; ch. 5, "Fertility and mortality data"; ch. 6, "Medicare and Medicaid data"; ch. 7, "Other sources of data"; appendixes: I, "Acronyms"; II, "Summary of data sets and years available"; III, "Data import and transfer".

This guide lists the major sources of secondary data for health-related subjects that are important in epidemiology and public health research. They are often stored in different locations and not necessarily easily accessible. Examples include the National Hospital Discharge Survey, the Healthcare Cost Utilization Project, the Behavioral Risk Factor Surveillance System, the National Health and Nutrition Survey, Medicare Public Use Files, Web portals to statistical data, etc. Description of each resource includes title, focus, core section, data collection, and information on accessing data and ancillary materials. Includes bibliography and index.

Handbooks

1444 **The bioterrorism sourcebook.** Michael R. Grey, Kenneth R. Spaeth. xxxiii, 549 p., ill. New York: McGraw-Hill Medical Publ. Div., 2006. ISBN: 0071440860.
303.625   RC88.9.T47; G746

Contents: section I, Clinical principles and practices (ch. 1–9); section II, Infectious agents (ch. 10–16); section III, Biotoxins and category B and C agents (ch. 17–20); section IV, Chemical weapons (ch. 21–26); section V, Nuclear and radiation syndromes (ch. 27–30).

Clinical and public health guidance preparing for and responding to immediate and long-term bioterrorism-related conditions. Provides concise and essential information on the various aspects and agents of a bioterrorist attack and the expected consequences, with synopses, illustrations, tables, charts, and practical tips. Selected bibliography; index. Available online via McGraw-Hill's AccessMedicine.

The CDC's (940) "Emergency Preparedness and Response" site, "intended to increase the nation's ability to prepare for and respond to public health emergencies" (http://www.bt.cdc.gov/) provides extensive information resources for bioterrorism, chemical, and radiation emergencies, natural disasters, and other threats.

AHRQ's (Agency for Healthcare Research and Quality) (733) "Public Health Preparedness" (http://www.ahrq.gov/prep/) provides a wide variety of tools, resources, and resource links.

Additional resources in this area include, for example, *Bioterrorism and public health* (2002), available in print and also online via Thomson's eMedguides (http://www.eMedguides.com/bioterrorism), *Bioterrorism preparedness* (2006), also available in print and online, and others.

1445 Food safety handbook. Ronald H. Schmidt, Gary Eugene Rodrick. xiii, 850 p., ill. Hoboken, N.J.: Wiley-Interscience, 2003. ISBN: 0471210641.

363.192   TP373.5. F67

"The intent of this book is to define and categorize the real and perceived safety issues surrounding food, to provide scientifically non-biased perspectives on these issues, and to provide assistance to the reader in understanding these issues. While the primary professional audience for the book includes food technologists and scientists in the industry and regulatory sector, the book should provide useful information for many other audiences."—*Pref.*

Thirty-eight chapters written by specialists are divided into eight sections: characteristics of food safety and risk; biological food hazards; chemical and physical food hazards; systems for food safety surveillance and risk prevention; food safety operations in food processing, handling, and distribution; food safety in retail foods; diet, health, and food safety; and worldwide food safety issues. Chapters have bibliographies. Index.

Also available online through netLibrary and Knovel (Norwich, N.Y.: Knovel, 2003–).

1446 Food Safety Research Information Office at the National Agricultural Library. National Agricultural Library (U.S.). 2002–. Beltsville, Md.: National Agricultural Library, Food Safety Research Information Office. http://fsrio.nal.usda.gov/index.php.

TX537

Produced by National Agricultural Library (NAL); Food Service Research Information Office (FSRIO).

A major component of this searchable website is its "Research Projects Database" for locating information on food safety and related research. Categories currently in use in this database include food and food products, food composition and characteristics, food quality characteristics, food handling and processing, on-farm food safety, diseases and poisonings, sanitation and pathogen control, contaminants and contamination, government policy and regulations, methodology and quality standards, human health and epidemiology, education and training, facilities and sites, and pathogen biology.

Complements information found, for example, in *Food safety handbook* (1128), *Food safety: A reference handbook* by Nina E. Redman (2nd ed., 2007), *Foodborne disease handbook*, ed. by Y. H. Hui (2nd ed., 2001), *Foodborne diseases*, ed. by Dean O. Cliver and Hans Rieman (2nd ed., 2002), and Shabir Simjee's *Foodborne diseases* (2007).

1447 Handbook of environmental health. 4th ed. Herman Koren, Michael S. Bisesi. 2 v., ill. Boca Raton, Fla.: Lewis Publ., 2003. ISBN: 1566705363.

363.7   RA565.K67

1st ed., 1980; 3rd ed., 1996.

Contents: v. 1, Biological, chemical, and physical agents of environmental related disease; v. 2, Pollutant interactions in air, water, and soil.

Includes various environmental health topics, issues, and hazards such as emerging infectious diseases and microorganisms, air quality and its effect on ecosystems, toxicology, and effects of the environment on humans. Describes interactions between humans and the environment and how they affect health and welfare of individuals. Comprehensive bibliography (v. 1, p. 647–702) and indexes. Available online via netLibrary.

1448 Handbook of epidemiology. Wolfgang Ahrens. New York: Springer, 2005. ISBN: 3540005668.

Contents: sec. 1, "Concepts and methodological approaches in epidemiology"; sec. 2, "Statistical methods in epidemiology"; sec. 3, "Applications of epidemiology"; sec. 4, "Research areas in epidemiology."

Comprehensive overview of the field of epidemiology, reviewing "key issues, methodological approaches, and statistical concepts."—*Pref.* Includes areas such as molecular epidemiology, health systems research, ethical aspects, and good epidemiological practice, to name a few. Each chapter presents basic concepts, standard procedures, methods, and recent advances in the field. Intended as a reference source for health professionals involved in health-related research. Detailed table of contents and list of contributors. No index. Also available as an e-book.

1449 Health information for international travel. Phyllis E. Kozarsky, Paul M. Arguin, Ava W. Navin, U.S. Centers for Disease Control and Prevention. 1974–. Atlanta: U.S. Dept. of Health and Human Services, Centers for Disease Control and Prevention. http://purl.access.gpo.gov/GPO/LPS3580.

Part of the Centers for Disease Control (CDC) (940) Travelers' Health website (http://wwwn.cdc.gov/travel/default.aspx). Also called "Yellow book" or "CDC yellow book." Description based on the 2008 ed., also issued in print with title *CDC health information for international travel 2008* (Philadelphia, Pa.: Elsevier Mosby, 2007). Previous print eds. issued since 1989 as a serial, *International travel health guide.*

Contents: ch. 1, "Introduction"; ch. 2, "Pre- and posttravel general health recommendations"; ch. 3, "Geographic distribution of potential health hazards to travelers"; ch. 4, "Prevention of specific infectious diseases"; ch. 5, "Yellow fever vaccine requirements and information on malaria risk and prophylaxis, by country"; ch. 6, "Noninfectious risks during travel"; ch. 7, "Conveyance and transportation issues"; ch. 8, "International travel with infants and young children"; ch. 9, "Advising travelers with specific needs."

Provides comprehensive information on vaccination requirements and recommendations for international travelers concerning health risks.

The World Health Organization's website, International Travel and Health (708), also offers extensive travel information.

1450 International health regulations (2005). World Health
Organization. 2007. Geneva, Switzerland: World Health
Organization. http://www.who.int/csr/ihr/en/.

Rev. ed., with the new regulations in force on June 15, 2007. Also publ. as
print edition, with 2005 also available as an e-book. Supersedes *International
health regulations* (1969), publ. in several different print editions.
Title varies: previously called *International sanitary regulations.*

Part of WHO's Epidemic and Pandemic Alert and Response (EPR)
(http://www.who.int/csr/en/).

Considered a code of practices and procedures for the prevention of
the spread of disease, "in consideration of the increases in international
travel and trade, and emergence and re-emergence of new international
disease threats" (*Publ. notes*), with the goal of preventing and protecting
against the international spread of disease.

Frequently asked questions about this resource can be found at
http://www.who.int/csr/ihr/howtheywork/faq/en/index.html.

A History of WHO and International Cooperation in Public Health
timeline (prepared by the WHO Centre for Health Development–WHO
Kobe Centre [WKC]) is located at http://www.who.or.jp/GENERAL/
history_wkc.html.

1451 International travel and health. World Health Organization.
2005–. Geneva, Switzerland: World Health Organization. http://
www.who.int/ith/en/.

RA638.I58

Description based on the 2007 ed., a "collaboration of travel medicine
experts and end-users of *International travel and health* who have provided
advice and information."—*Acknowledgments.* Also available as a print
edition.

Contents: ch. 1, "Health risks and precautions: General considerations"; ch. 2, "Mode of travel: Health considerations"; ch. 3, "Environmental health risks"; ch. 4, "Injuries and violence"; ch. 5, "Infectious
diseases of potential risk for travellers"; ch. 6, "Vaccine-preventable diseases and vaccines"; ch. 7, "Malaria; Country lists: Yellow fever vaccination
requirements, recommendations and malaria situation."

Provides information on the main health risks for travelers at specific destinations with different modes of travel. Website also provides
related links on, e.g., disease outbreaks (e.g., avian influenza, drug-
resistant tuberculosis, etc.), *International health regulations* (2005) (926),

and Global Health Atlas (http://www.who.int/globalatlas/). Intended for medical professionals; also useful to consumers.

Health Information for International Travel (633) is another resource for travel information.

1452 The law and the public's health. 7th ed. Kenneth R. Wing, Benjamin Gilbert. xiii, 391 p. Chicago: Health Administration Press, 2007.

344.7304   KF3775.W5

Contents: ch. 1, "The law and the legal system"; ch. 2, "The power of the state governments in matters affecting health care"; ch. 3, "Government power and the right to privacy"; ch. 4, "The constitutional discretion of the state and federal governments to limit or condition social welfare benefits"; ch. 5, "Government regulation of health care providers and payers"; ch. 6, "The scope of discretion of administrative agencies in matters affecting health and health care"; ch. 7, "The fraud and abuse laws"; ch. 8, "The antitrust laws: Government enforcement of competition"; ch. 9, "Malpractice: Liability for negligence in the delivery and financing of health care"; ch. 10, "Health care business law: Legal considerations in the structuring of health care entities and their transactions."

Intended as an introductory text for schools of public health and law-related courses, this book can also serve as a reference book in the health care field. Provides an introduction to the law, the legal system, and principles applicable to the delivery and financing of health care but is not considered a treatise on health law. Includes bibliographical references and index.

Also available as an e-book via netLibrary.

1453 Measuring health: A guide to rating scales and questionnaires. 3rd ed. Ian McDowell. xvi, 748 p., ill. Oxford; New York: Oxford University Press, 2006. ISBN: 9780195165.

614.42   RA408.5.M38

1st ed., 1987; 2nd ed., 1996.

Overview of the field of health measurement, with in-depth information on selected commonly-used instruments (e.g., measurement of pain, general health status, quality of life, mental status, etc.) with the purpose of measuring health status in research studies. Provides description of methods, comparisons, and critical reviews of health measurement instruments or scales and their quality, indicating purpose, conceptual basis, reliability, validity, etc. This edition includes 104 scales. For health care researchers, epidemiologists, and social scientists. Index. Available as an e-book via netLibrary.

1454 Medical response to terrorism: Preparedness and clinical practice. Daniel C. Keyes, Jonathan L. Burstein, Richard B. Schwartz. xiii, 449 p., ill. Philadelphia: Lippincott, Williams & Wilkins, 2005. ISBN: 0781749867.

362.18   RC88.9.T47.M43

Contents: pt. 1, "Agents of terrorism and medical management"; pt. 2, "All-hazards preparedness for terrorism."

    Describes various biological agents (anthrax, plague, smallpox, etc.) and threats, including chemical, biochemical, and nuclear terrorism. Provides guidance with the preparedness for emergency situations and with the diagnosis and management of exposure. Includes practice drills and disaster simulations. Bibliographic references and index. Available online via Books@Ovid.

1455 Mental health in America: A reference handbook. Donna R. Kemp. xiv, 315 p. Santa Barbara, Calif.: ABC-CLIO, 2007. ISBN: 1851097899.

362.2   RA790.6.K45

Part of Contemporary World Issues series.

    Contents: (1) "Background and history"; (2) "The twenty-first century: Problems, controversies, and solutions"; (3) "Worldwide perspective"; (4) "Chronology"; (5) "Biographies"; (6) "Facts and statistics"; (7) "Documents, reports, and nongovernmental organizations"; (8) "Legislation and court costs"; (9) "Organization"; (10) "Selected print and non-print resources."

    Explores mental health policy and attitudes toward mental illness from the 19th century to the present; changing definitions and explanations of mental illness; and the various treatments of mental illness. Includes chronology of approaches to mental illness, statistics, legislative information, a glossary, and annotated bibliography of current literature, including websites. Index. Useful for health professionals, researchers, and students. Available as an e-book via netLibrary.

1456 National Center for Environmental Health. National Center for Environmental Health (U.S.). Atlanta: Centers for Disease Control and Prevention. http://www.cdc.gov/nceh/.

The National Center for Environmental Health (NCEH) has the mission to maintain, improve, and promote a healthy environment. Its searchable data resources page (http://www.cdc.gov/nceh/data.htm) and its A–Z index (http://www.cdc.gov/nceh/topics.htm) provide links to a variety of public environmental data sources, health topics, query engines, and other key resources. Highlights the major data systems with a national scope where public health and environmental data can be downloaded from the Internet. For health professionals and students.

1457 Praeger handbook of black American health: Policies and issues behind disparities in health. 2nd ed. Ivor Lensworth Livingston. 2 v. (xlvii, 911 p.), ill., maps. Westport, Conn: Praeger, 2004. ISBN: 0313324778.

362.108996073   RA448.5.N4H364

1st ed., 1994.

Contents: v. 1 (pt. I), Cardiovascular and related chronic conditions (ch. 1–6); v. 1 (pt. II), General chronic conditions ch. 7–13; v. 1 (pt. III), Lifestyle, social, and mental outcomes (ch. 14–26); v. 2 (pt. IV), Sociopolitical, environmental, and structural challenges (ch. 27–38); v. 2 (pt. V), Ethics, research, technology, and social policy issues (ch. 39–47).

This rev. and exp. ed. addresses crucial issues in disparities in health status and access to health care for African Americans, with identification of preventive strategies, interventions, and possible solutions (e.g., ch. 47, "Eliminating racial and ethnic disparities in health: A framework for action"). Index. For professionals and students in public health, medicine, health psychology, health policy, medical sociology, nursing, and possibly other areas of research, education, and study. Also available as an e-book.

Craig Haynes' *Ethnic minority: A selected annotated bibliography*, publ. in 1997, remains a good bibliography to start research in health disparities, complemented by "A selected, annotated list of materials that support the development of policies designed to reduce racial and ethnic health disparities," by Joan E. Donatiello, Peter Droese, and Soo H. Kim (*Journal of the Medical Library Association* 92[2]: 257–65, Apr. 2004, available online via http://www.pubmedcentral.nih.gov/articlerender.fcgi?artid=385308.

Healthy People 2010 [530], National Institutes of Health [NIH] [470], and the Centers for Disease Control and Prevention [CDC] [940] have as a goal to support research that advances the elimination of health disparities among ethnic groups and among the various vulnerable and at-risk populations. Other resources exploring and documenting minority health and health disparities with the goal of promoting racial parity include, for example, "National Library of Medicine Strategic Plan for Addressing Health Disparities 2004–2008" (http://www.nlm.nih.gov/pubs/plan/ nlm_health_disp_2004_2008.html), "National Healthcare Disparities Report" (http://www.ahrq.gov/qual/nhdr06/nhdr06.htm), "Native-American Health" via MedlinePlus [463], NLM's "Native Outreach Activities," (http://www.nlm.nih.gov/medlineplus/nativeamericanhealth.html), "Hispanic outreach activities" (http://sis.nlm.nih.gov/outreach/hispanicamerican.html), "Minority Health—Specific Populations Groups" (http://sis. nlm.nih.gov/outreach/minorityhealth.html), and other websites.

1458 Proctor and Hughes' chemical hazards of the workplace. 5th ed.
Nick H. Proctor, James P. Hughes, Gloria J. Hathaway. xi, 785 p.
Hoboken, N.J.: Wiley-Interscience, 2004.

615.902   RA1229.P76

1st ed., 1978; 4th ed., 1996.

Contents: (1) "Introduction: Toxicological concepts"; (2) "The chemical hazards"; (3) "CAS number index"; (4) "Index of compounds and synonyms." Detailed contents at http://www.loc.gov/catdir/toc/ ecip0410/2003024018.html.

Covers the effects on human health of chemicals likely to be encountered in various places of work. Each monograph includes chemical formula, CAS number, Threshold Limit Value, synonyms for the chemical, physical properties, uses, routes of exposure, toxicological information, carcinogenicity, mutagenicity, fetotoxicity, clinical effects of overexposure and treatment, and significant odor characteristics. For health professionals and students. Available online from Wiley (http://www3.interscience. wiley.com/cgi-bin/bookhome/109871799).

Other titles in this area include, for example, *Sittig's handbook of toxic and hazardous chemicals and carcinogens* (Norwich, N.Y., U.S.A: Noyes Publications, 2002) and *Sax's dangerous properties of industrial materials* (1559).

1459 The public health law manual. 3rd ed. Frank P. Grad, American Public Health Association. Washington: American Public Health Association, 2005. ISBN: 0875530427.

1st ed., 1965, had title *Public health manual: A handbook on the legal aspects of public health administration and enforcement*; 2nd ed., 1990, had title

Public health law manual: A handbook on the legal aspects of public health administration and enforcement.

"The purpose of this manual: Achieving the most effective use of legal powers; recognition of legal problems and their management; effective use of available legal assistance; improving communication between the public health and legal professions; continuing dialogue."—*Foreword*. Intended for use by health care professionals and public health administrators in planning, developing, and implementing public health programs. Deals with basic legal procedures in public health enforcement—restrictions of persons; permits, licenses, and registration; searches and inspections; embargo, seizure, etc.—and with legal administrative techniques of public health administration. This edition emphasizes issues in environmental health law, legal aspects of personal health services, right to privacy, "right to die" issues, and discussion of various related issues. Provides an overview of public health policies and public health law and a summary of international responses to SARS, bioterrorism, global warming, etc.

1460 Statistical handbook on infectious diseases. Sarah Watstein, John Jovanovic. xxiii, 321 p., ill., maps. Westport, Conn.: Greenwood Press, 2003. ISBN: 1573563757.

614.0727   RA643.W33

Contents: (A) Nationally notifiable diseases; (B) Human Immunoficiency Virus (HIV) and Acquired Immunodeficiency Syndrome (AIDS); (C) Malaria; (D) Sexually transmitted diseases; (E) Tuberculosis; (F) Foodborne diseases; (G) Waterborne diseases; (H) Infectious disease worldwide: present issues, emerging concerns; (I) Vaccine-preventable diseases; (J) Infectious disease elimination and eradication; (K) Bioterrorism and biological warfare; Appendix: World Health Organization (WHO) regions. Glossary.

"Comprehensive statistical overview of the status of infectious disease worldwide. often hard to find, or difficult to interpret. A carefully selected array of tables and charts of authoritative statistical information, placing valuable statistics into context with introductory text."—*Publ. notes*. Selection from a variety of print and web-based sources. Includes bibliographical references (p. [315]–318) and index. For general readers and students as a good starting point for research. Available online via the Greenwood Digital Collection (http://ebooks.greenwood.com/).

MEDICAL & HEALTH SCIENCES

1461 Wallace/Maxcy-Rosenau-Last public health and preventive medicine. 15th ed. Robert B. Wallace. xxxiii, 1367 p. New York: McGraw-Hill, 2007. ISBN: 9780071441.

614.44   RA425.M382

Title varies: 1st–7th eds. had title *Preventive medicine and hygiene*; 14th ed., 1998, had title *Maxcy-Rosenau-Last public health and preventive medicine.*

Contents: sec. 1, "Public health principles and methods"; sec. 2, "Communicable diseases"; sec. 3, "Environmental health"; sec. 4, "Behavioral factors affecting health"; sec. 5, "Noncommunicable and chronic disabling conditions"; sec. 6, "Health care—planning, organization, and evaluation"; sec. 7, "Injury and violence."

This revised and updated edition includes 82 chapters, providing essential information on the delivery of public health services, coverage of new diseases and policy issues, a new chapter on bioterrorism and emergency preparedness, and inclusion of more Web-based resources for further reading. Includes bibliographical references and index. Also available online through STAT!Ref.

1462 WHO child growth standards. World Health Organization. 2006. Geneva, Switzerland: World Health Organization. http://www.who.int/childgrowth/en/index.html.

Since the late 1970s, the National Center for Health Statistics (539)/WHO (951) growth reference has been in use to chart children's growth. It was based on data from a limited sample of children from the United States and is now considered less adequate for international comparisons. In 1997, WHO, in collaboration with the United Nations University, undertook the Multicentre Growth Reference Study (MGRS), which is a community-based, multicountry project with more than 8,000 children from Brazil, Ghana, India, Norway, Oman, and the United States. The new standards are the result of this study, which had as its goal "to develop a new international standard for assessing the physical growth, nutritional status and motor development in all children from birth to age five."—*Press release.* The first new growth charts released (Apr. 2007) include weight-for-age, length/height-for-age, and weight-for-length/height growth indicators as well as a Body Mass Index (BMI) standard for children up to age 5, and standards for sitting, standing, walking, and several other key motor developments.

The title of the print version is *WHO child growth standards: Length/ height-for-age, weight-for-age, weight-for-length, weight-for-height and body mass index–for–age: Methods and development.*

1463 Women's health USA. U.S. Dept. of Health and Human Services, Maternal and Child Health Bureau. 2002–. Rockville, Md.: U.S. Dept. of Health and Human Services, Maternal and Child Health Bureau. http://purl.access.gpo.gov/GPO/LPS21379.

Part of Health Resources and Services Administration (HRSA) (877), within the U.S. Dept. of Health and Human Services (HHS) (894).

Description based on 5th online ed., 2006.

Contents: Population Characteristics; Health Status; Health Services Utilization; Indicators in Previous Editions; Site Map.

Collection of current and historical data on health challenges facing women, with information on life expectancy and addressing topics such as postpartum depression, smoking, alcohol, illicit drug use, etc. Brings together the latest available information from various government agencies (HHS, U.S. Dept. of Agriculture, U.S. Dept. of Labor, U.S. Dept. of Justice).

National Women's Health Information Center, Womenshealth.gov (http://www.womenshealth.gov/), provides extensive further information.

1464 World health and disease. 3rd ed. Alastair Gray, P. R. Payne. 352 p., ill. (some color). Buckingham, [England, U.K.]; Philadelphia: Open University Press, 2001. ISBN: 033520838X.

614.42   RA651.G65

1st ed., 1985, had title *Health of nations*; [2nd] rev. ed., 1993. Vol. 3 of *Health and disease* series.

Contents: ch. 1, "Introduction"; ch. 2, "World patterns of mortality"; ch. 3, "Mortality and morbidity: causes and determinants"; ch. 4, "Livelihood and survival: A case study of Bangladesh"; ch. 5, "The world transformed: Population and the rise of industrial society"; ch. 6, "The decline of infectious diseases: The case of England"; ch. 7, "Health in a world of wealth and poverty"; ch. 8, "Population and development prospects"; ch. 9, "Contemporary patterns of disease in the United Kingdom"; ch. 10, "Explaining inequalities in health in the United Kingdom"; ch. 11, "Food, health and disease: A case study."

Presents a global view of human health. "Examines contemporary and historical patterns of health and disease in the U.K. and the rest of the world. The book draws on the disciplines of demography, epidemiology, history, the social sciences and biology."—*Pref.* Index and annotated guide to further reading and to selected Internet resources. Intended for students, health professionals, and others.

Histories

1465 Health and British magazines in the nineteenth century. E. M. Palmegiano. ix, 282 p. Lanham, Md.: Scarecrow Press, 1998. ISBN: 0810834863.

016.6   Z6673.P288; RA776.5

Bibliography of 2,604 entries based on headlines and captions in major British Victorian serials (selected mainly from the *Wellesley index to Victorian periodicals 1824–1900* [Ann Arbor, Mich.: ProQuest Information and Learning Company]), providing a synopsis of health issues during this period that demonstrates "the evolution of popular thinking about the practice of human health and outlines major concepts and investigates the formation of essential categories still in use, such as ideas of wellness and unwellness, the meaning of care and care-givers, and the productive status of being healthy."—*Publ. notes.* Indexed by author and subject.

1466 Historical dictionary of the World Health Organization. Kelley Lee. xliv, 333 p., ill. Lanham, Md.: Scarecrow Press, 1998. ISBN: 0810833719.

353.6211   RA8.L44

(Historical dictionaries of international organizations series; no. 15).

Provides information on the history of the World Health Organization (WHO) and its contributions to international health cooperation. Includes an extensive bibliography on WHO documents and writings about WHO and a chronology of selected major events in the history of international health organizations. Several appendixes, for example, constitution of WHO, chronological list of member states, and WHO directors. Additional related information available on the World Health Organization (WHO) home page (951).

1467 A history of public health. Expanded ed. George Rosen, Elizabeth Fee, Edward T. Morman. xci, 535 p. Baltimore: Johns Hopkins University Press, 1993. ISBN: 0801846455.

614.4   RA424.R65.R68

1st ed., 1958.

An eight-part history of public health from earliest times to the present. Includes bibliography; list of memorable figures with brief biographical sketches; list of public health periodicals, arranged by country; list of worldwide public health societies and schools. Bibliographical references (p. 473–506). Subject and author indexes.

1468 **Plagues and politics: The story of the United States Public Health Service.** Fitzhugh Mullan. 223 p., ill. New York: Basic Books, 1989. ISBN: 0465057799.

353.00841   RA445.M75

Contents: ch. 1, 1798–1889, "Sailors, sinecures and reform"; ch. 2, 1890–1911, "Science, immigrants, and the public health movement"; ch. 3, 1912–20, "Public health warriors"; ch. 4, 1921–35, "Public health within limits"; ch. 5, 1936–48, "Calamity, necessity, and opportunity"; ch. 6, 1949–60, "The coming of HEW"; ch. 7, 1961–68, "Public health at the new frontier"; ch. 8, 1969–80, "Care, cost, and prevention"; ch. 9, 1981–89, "New politics, new plagues."

An illustrated history of the Public Health Service from 1798 to 1989, dealing with infectious diseases (e.g., malaria, yellow fever, typhus, etc.) and also with diseases such as AIDS, cancer, and others. Includes list of Surgeons General of the United States Public Health Service (active between 1871 and 1989) and Assistant Secretaries for Health (Dept. of Health and Human Services/Health Education and Welfare). Bibliography; index. For general readers. Available as an e-book.

1469 **Public health image library (PHIL).** Centers for Disease Control and Prevention. [1998]–. Atlanta: Centers for Disease Control and Prevention. http://phil.cdc.gov/Phil/.

Public Health Image Library (PHIL), created by a working group at the Centers for Disease Control and Prevention (CDC) (940); National Library of Medicine (NLM) (427).

Collection of a variety of single images, image sets, multimedia files, etc., with current and historical content about people, places, scientific subjects, etc. FAQ section (http://phil.cdc.gov/Phil/faq.asp) provides detailed information. Useful for public health professionals, scientists, librarians, teachers, and students.

This website also provides links to other CDC and NLM image libraries (e.g., Images from the History of Medicine [352] and Visible Human [502]). Complements other medical image collections such as Health Education Assets Library (HEAL) (458) and ImagesMD (http://www.images.md).

1470   **The value of health: A history of the Pan American Health Organization.** Marcos Cueto. 239 p. Washington: Pan American Health Organization, 2007. ISBN: 9781580462631.

362.1   RA10.C8413

(Scientific and technical publication; 600) Pan American Health Organization (PAHO) (950).

Contents: ch. 1, The origins of international public health in the Americas; ch. 2, The birth of a new organization; ch. 3, The consolidation of an identity; ch. 4, For a continent free of disease; ch. 5, Health, development, and community participation; v. 6, Validity and renewal.

History of PAHO, contributions of individuals in PAHO, and also contemporary issues. Endnotes, bibliography, and index.

1471   **WHO historical collection.** World Health Organization. 2000s–. Geneva, Switzerland: World Health Organization. http://www.who. int/library/collections/historical/en/print.html.

Produced by World Health Organization (WHO) (951); part of WHO Library and Information Networks for Knowledge (LNK).

Covers conferences before the founding of the WHO, WHO official records, International Sanitary Conventions (since 1851), and official records, reports, and other published materials from the Office International d'Hygiène Publique (OIHP), the health organization of the League of Nations (UNRRA). Includes materials on plague, cholera, and yellow fever, and also more recent epidemics; international classifications and nomenclatures of diseases; and public health and medicine monographs on public health in different countries and languages. Related links are, for example, WHOLIS: World Health Organization Library Database (484) and WHO Archives (http://www.who.int/archives/en/index.html). The distinctions between the WHO library, the WHO archives, and WHO records are described at http://www.who.int/archives/fonds_collections/partners/en/index.html.

Indexes; Abstract journals; Databases

1472   **Food Safety Research Information Office at the National Agricultural Library.** National Agricultural Library (U.S.). 2002–. Beltsville, Md.: National Agricultural Library, Food Safety Research Information Office. http://fsrio.nal.usda.gov/index.php.

                                                                TX537

Produced by National Agricultural Library (NAL); Food Service Research Information Office (FSRIO).

A major component of this searchable website is its "Research Projects Database" for locating information on food safety and related research. Categories currently in use in this database include food and food products, food composition and characteristics, food quality characteristics, food handling and processing, on-farm food safety, diseases and poisonings, sanitation and pathogen control, contaminants and contamination, government policy and regulations, methodology and quality standards, human health and epidemiology, education and training, facilities and sites, and pathogen biology.

Complements information found, for example, in *Food safety handbook* (1128), *Food safety: A reference handbook* by Nina E. Redman (2nd ed., 2007), *Foodborne disease handbook*, ed. by Y. H. Hui (2nd ed., 2001), *Foodborne diseases*, ed. by Dean O. Cliver and Hans Rieman (2nd ed., 2002), and Shabir Simjee's *Foodborne diseases* (2007).

1473 Global health. C.A.B. International. 1973–. [Wallingford, Oxfordshire, U.K.]: CABI. http://www.cabi.org/datapage. asp?iDocID=169.

RA441

Formerly known as *CAB health*.

Global health, 1973–. (Derived from *CAB abstracts* [1143] and *Public health and tropical medicine databases*; *Global health archive*, 1910–83 [derived from six former print abstracting sources]). Includes records from the Bureau of Hygiene and Tropical Diseases to 1983.

Online databases available through CAB Direct, Ovid, EBSCO, and Dialog. Indexes journals, books, book chapters, conference proceedings, and other resources, mostly English-language publications, but also in other languages. Useful databases for searching the international health and public health literature, in addition to searching MEDLINE [425] and EMBASE [414]. For researchers, health professionals, policy makers, and students.

1474 Global Index Medicus. World Health Organization. 2005?–. Geneva, Switzerland: World Health Organization. http://www.who. int/ghl/medicus/en/.

Produced by World Health Organization (WHO) (951); publ. under the auspices of WHO Regional Offices.

Intended to complement the internationally known biomedical bibliographic indexes. Although most of the significant medical periodicals published in the developed countries are indexed in MEDLINE (425) and other databases, there is still a considerable amount of important and highly relevant medical and health documentation from developing countries that is not included.

1475 HealthSTAR (Ovid). National Library of Medicine (U.S.). 2000–. Sandy, Utah: Ovid Technologies. http://www.ovid.com/site/ products/ovidguide/hstrdb.htm.

Ovid HealthSTAR (HSTR); HealthSTAR (Health Services Technology, Administration, and Research).

"Comprised of data from the National Library of Medicine's (NLM) MEDLINE and former HealthSTAR databases. contains citations to the published literature on health services, technology, administration, and research. It focuses on both the clinical and non-clinical aspects of health care delivery. Offered by Ovid as a continuation of NLM's now-defunct HealthSTAR database. Retains all existing backfile citations and is updated with new journal citations culled from MEDLINE. Contains citations and abstracts (when available) to journal articles, monographs, technical reports, meeting abstracts and papers, book chapters, government documents, and newspaper articles from 1975 to the present."—*Publ. notes.* A list of NLM's retired databases, including the original HealthSTAR database, can be found at http://www.nlm.nih.gov/services/pastdatabases. html.

Relevant content on health services research, health technology, health administration, health policy, health economics, etc., can also be found in MEDLINE® (425)/PubMed® (432), NLM® Gateway (429), and also CINAHL® (439).

1476 International digest of health legislation = Recueil international de législation sanitaire. World Health Organization. 2000–. [Geneva, Switzerland]: World Health Organization. http://www. who.int/idhl-rils/index.cfm.

K3569.2

International Digest of Health Legislation (IDHL) online database, available in English and French (Recueil international de législation sanitaire). Continues print version, publ. 1948–99; 1909–46(?) had title: *Bulletin mensuel de l'Office international d'Hygiène publique.*

Selection of national and international health legislation. Titles and summaries of texts of legislation, with links to the full texts of the legislation whenever available. The database can be searched by country, subject, volume, issue, or keyword. Includes the following subject categories, with detailed scope notes (http://www.who.int/idhl-rils/frame.cfm?language=english): General provisions, health manpower, health care facilities and services, disease control and medical care, oral health, family health, human reproduction and population policies, care of the elderly and rehabilitation, mental health, control of smoking, alcoholism, and drug abuse, ethical issues and professional responsibility, death and related issues, nutrition and food, consumer protection, pharmaceuticals and medical devices, poisons and other hazardous substances, occupational health and safety, environmental protection, radiation protection, accident prevention, sports and recreation, and health information and statistics.

1477 **NLM gateway.** National Library of Medicine (U.S.). 2000–. Bethesda, Md.: National Library of Medicine. http://gateway.nlm.nih.gov/.

RA11

Allows simultaneous searching of information resources at the National Library of Medicine (NLM). Databases include MEDLINE (425)/PubMed (432) and the NLM Catalog (482) as well as other resources, including information on current clinical trials and consumer health information (MedlinePlus [463]). Currently provides access to 21 databases and other information resources (for a complete list of databases and other details, see http://www.nlm.nih.gov/pubs/factsheets/gateway.html). An overview of the search results is presented in several categories (bibliographic resources, consumer health resources, and other information), with a listing of the individual databases and the number of results within these categories.

1478 **POPLINE.** Johns Hopkins University Bloomberg School of Public Health. Baltimore: Johns Hopkins University Bloomberg School of Public Health. http://db.jhuccp.org/ics-wpd/popweb/.

HQ766

POPLINE (Population Information Online) is a database on reproductive health with international coverage. Provides bibliographic citations with abstracts to English-language published and unpublished biomedical and social science literature on population research, demography, family planning, and related health issues. Includes links to full-text documents, RSS feeds for topical searches, and other special features. Detailed list of subjects covered internationally and in reference to developing countries at http://db.jhuccp.org/ics-wpd/popweb/aboutpl.html.

1479 PubMed. U.S. National Center for Biotechnology Information, National Library of Medicine, National Institutes of Health. 1996–. Bethesda, Md.: U.S. National Center for Biotechnology Information. http://www.ncbi.nlm.nih.gov/sites/entrez/.

PubMed®, developed and maintained by the National Center for Biotechnology Information (NCBI) at the National Library of Medicine® (NLM) (427). It is available via the NCBI Entrez (3) retrieval system. PubMed also provides access to the other Entrez molecular biology resources (*PubMed Overview*). Starting May 23, 2007, NCBI is changing to a new version of Entrez in a phased implementation (cf. Nahin AM. New and Improved PubMed®/Entrez and New URL *NLM tech. bull.*, 2007 May–Jun.; [356]: http://www.nlm.nih.gov/pubs/techbull/mj07/mj07_issue_cover.html).

Provides a search interface for more than 16 million bibliographic citations and abstracts in the fields of medicine, nursing, dentistry, veterinary medicine, health care systems, and preclinical sciences. It provides access to articles indexed for MEDLINE® (425) and for selected life sciences journals. PubMed subsets found under the "Limits" tab are: MEDLINE and PubMed Central®, several journal groups (i.e., core clinical journals, dental journals, and nursing journals), and topical subsets (AIDS, bioethics, cancer, complementary medicine, history of medicine, space life sciences, systematic reviews, and toxicology). "Linkout" provides access to full-text articles.

For detailed information see the PubMed fact sheet at http://www.nlm.nih.gov/pubs/factsheets/pubmed.html. For a brief overview of searching PubMed, see the PubMed Quick Start at http://www.ncbi.nlm.nih.gov/books/bv.fcgi?rid=helppubmed.section.pubmedhelp.PubMed_Quick_Start. For details on the now completed OLDMEDLINE retrospective conversion projects, see http://www.nlm.nih.gov/pubs/techbull/so06/so06_oldmedline_status.html.

1480 State cancer legislative database program (SCLD). National Cancer Institute. Bethesda, Md.: National Cancer Institute, National Institutes of Health. http://www.scld-nci.net/index.cfml.

Database providing summaries of state laws and resolutions on the major cancers and cancer-related topics. Kept up-to-date via *SCLD update*. A site map (http://www.scld-nci.net/sitemap.cfml) provides easy access to the various information products associated with the SCLD program. Considered a resource for a variety of audiences, including universities and research centers, professional organizations, and the public.

Internet Resources

1481 Agency for Healthcare Research and Quality (AHRQ). Agency for Healthcare Research and Quality (U.S.). 1990s–. Rockville, Md.: Agency for Healthcare Research and Quality. http://www.ahrq.gov.

"The Agency for Healthcare Research and Quality (AHRQ) is the lead Federal agency charged with improving the quality, safety, efficiency, and effectiveness of health care for all Americans. As one of 12 agencies within the Department of Health and Human Services, AHRQ supports health services research that will improve the quality of health care and promote evidence-based decision making."—*AHRQ at a glance (http://www.ahrq. gov/about/ataglance.htm)*

Searchable website ("search AHRQ" and "A–Z Quick Menu") provides access to a variety of resources, with links to clinical and consumer health information, research findings, funding opportunities, data and surveys, quality assessment, specific populations (minorities, women, elderly, and others), and public health preparedness (bioterrorism and response). Links to a large number of full-text documents, including links to the tools, literature, and news in patient safety (e.g., *AHRQ patient safety network*) and tips on how to prevent medical errors.

1482 American Academy of Family Physicians [homepage]. American Academy of Family Physicians. 1998– Leawood, Kans.: American Academy of Family Physicians. http://www.aafp.org/online/en/ home.html.

616.007; 610.9206   R130.3

Searchable website with resources for AAFP (American Academy of Family Physicians) members, residents, students, patients, and the general public. Contains information, software, photographs, graphics, and other materials, providing access to information on a variety of clinical and research resources for medical and healthcare topics. Examples are "Familydoctor.org" (http://familydoctor.org/online/famdocen/home.html), an online "Dictionary of common Medical Terms," health trackers, health calculators, how to find a family doctor (http://familydoctor.org/cgi-bin/memdir.pl),

and "Conditions A to Z" (http://familydoctor.org/online/famdocen/home/
common.html), also available as (*AAFP conditions A to Z* via STAT!Ref).
Also provides public health resources on various topics (http://www.aafp.
org/online/en/home/clinical/publichealth.html) e.g., cultural proficiency,
health disparities/minority health, disease prevention, etc.

1483 amfAR. American Foundation for AIDS Research. 1999–. New
York; Washington: American Foundation for AIDS Research.
http://www.amfar.org.

"amfAR™, the Foundation for AIDS Research, is one of the world's leading
nonprofit organizations dedicated to the support of AIDS research, HIV
prevention, treatment education, and the advocacy of sound AIDS-related
public policy."—*Website*

   Provides basic HIV/AIDS facts and statistics, HIV testing, information
about various therapies (approved or under development), young people
and HIV/AIDS, women and HIV/AIDS, global initiatives, and many other
related topics and links.

   "amfAR global links," formerly know as *HIV/AIDS treatment directory*,
and "HIV/AIDS treatment insider," available 2000-5, have ceased publication. *The AmFAR AIDS handbook: The complete guide to understanding
HIV and AIDS*, a comprehensive guide to help readers understand HIV/
AIDS, treatment options, and how treatment decisions are made, has not
been updated since 1999.

1484 Biodefense and bioterrorism (MedlinePlus). National Library
of Medicine (U.S.), National Institutes of Health (U.S.). 2000–.
Washington: U.S. National Library of Medicine, National Institutes
of Health, Dept. of Health and Human Services. http://www.nlm.
nih.gov/medlineplus/biodefenseandbioterrorism.html.

A Health Topic within MedlinePlus (463). Contents: Overviews; Treatment; Prevention/Screening; Alternative medicine; Coping; Specific conditions; Related issues; Pictures and photographs; Research; Journal
articles; Dictionaries/Glossaries; Directories; Organizations; Law and
policy; Children.

   Collection of links from a variety of government agencies, professional associations, and organizations, with representative bioterrorism
resources selections from the Centers for Disease Control and Prevention (CDC) (940), National Institute of Allergy and Infectious Diseases,
American Medical Association, American Academy of Family Physicians,

American Psychiatric Association, Dept. of Homeland Security, and others. Listing and map for identifying local biodefense and bioterrorism services (via "Go Local" http://www.nlm.nih.gov/medlineplus/golocal/index.html). Related information also at Disaster preparation and recovery (MedlinePlus) (463), Emergency preparedness and response (CDC) (1485), and the World Health Organization's "Bioterrorism" page (http://www.who.int/topics/bioterrorism/en/) provides additional resources and links.

1485 CDC: Emergency preparedness and response. Centers for Disease Control and Prevention (U.S.). 200?–. Atlanta: Centers for Disease Control and Prevention. http://www.bt.cdc.gov/.

Emergency preparedness resources for professionals and the public on bioterrorism, chemical agents, radiation emergencies, recent outbreaks and incidents (e.g., salmonella, bridge collapse, etc.) and more. "A–Z index of all agents, diseases, and other threats" and additional related topics and resources. Related sites include, for example, Biodefense and Bioterrorism (MedlinePlus) (740) and Disaster Preparation and Recovery (MedlinePlus) (746).

1486 Centers for Disease Control and Prevention (U.S.). Centers for Disease Control and Prevention (U.S.). 1998–. Atlanta: Centers for Disease Control and Prevention, U.S. Dept. of Health and Human Services. http://www.cdc.gov/.

The Centers for Disease Control and Prevention (CDC), part of the Dept. of Health and Human Services (HHS), is considered "the principal agency in the United States government for protecting the health and safety of all Americans and for providing essential human services."—*Website.* It is involved in public health efforts to monitor health, to prevent and control infectious and chronic diseases, injury, workplace hazards, disability, and environmental health threats. The CDC works with partners in the U.S. (http://www.cdc.gov/partners/) and worldwide, such as the World Health Organization (951).

The CDC site map (http://www.cdc.gov/about/sitemap.htm) provides a listing of the many different centers, institutes, and offices associated with the CDC, linking each to its own website containing a variety of information resources. Examples include the National Center for Health Statistics [NCHS] (539), National Center for Environmental Health (NCEH) (http://www.cdc.gov/nceh/), National Center for Injury

Prevention and Control (NCIPC) "Injury Center" (http://www.cdc.gov/ncipc/), National Office of Public Health Genomics (1506), Coordinating Office for Global Health (http://www.cdc.gov/cogh/index.htm), Coordinating Office for Emergency Preparedness and Response (http://www.bt.cdc.gov/), to name a few. An A–Z index (http://www.cdc.gov/az.do/) provides extensive information on many diseases and various other health topics found on the CDC website, with new topics being added frequently. CDC WONDER (1399) provides a search interface to a variety of health-related topics and statistics. For health professionals and general users.

1487   Disaster preparation and recovery (MedlinePlus). National Library of Medicine (U.S.), National Institutes of Health (U.S.). 2000–. Washington: National Library of Medicine. http://www.nlm.nih.gov/medlineplus/disasterpreparationandrecovery.html.

Disaster preparation and recovery guides for the public from various organizations including the Dept. of Homeland Security, Federal Emergency Management Agency, American Red Cross, and Centers for Disease Control and Prevention (940). Listing of MedlinePlus (463) "related topics" pages and links, e.g., Biodefense and Bioterrorism (MedlinePlus) (740), coping with disasters, posttraumatic stress disorder, safety issues, and others.

1488   Drug abuse (MedlinePlus). National Library of Medicine (U.S.). 2000?–. Bethesda, Md.: National Library of Medicine. http://www.nlm.nih.gov/medlineplus/drugabuse.html.

A Health Topic in MedlinePlus (463).

Contents: Overviews; Latest News; Diagnosis/Symptoms; Treatment; Prevention/Screening; Specific Conditions; Related Issues; Pictures and Photographs; Games; Clinical Trials; Research; Journal Articles; Dictionaries/Glossaries; Directories; Organizations; Newsletters/Print Publications; Law and Policy; Statistics; Children; Teenagers; Men; Women; Seniors; Other Languages.

Collection of links on substance abuse from a variety of government agencies, professional associations, and organizations, such as the National Institute on Drug Abuse (1505), the Office of National Drug Control, Substance Abuse and Mental Health Services Administration (SAMHSA) (769), National Library of Medicine (427), American Medical Association (451), American Academy of Family Physicians (448), and others. Also links to related MedlinePlus topics, e.g., alcoholism, prescription drug abuse, and substance abuse, to name a few.

1489 Enviro-health links. National Library of Medicine (U.S.). 2005–. Bethesda, Md.: National Library of Medicine. http://sis.nlm.nih. gov/enviro/envirohealthlinks.html.

Part of National Library of Medicine's Specialized Information Services (SIS) Environmental Health and Toxicology program.

Contents: American Indian Health; Arctic Health; Arsenic and Human Health; Asian American Health; Biological Warfare; California Wildfires; Chemical Warfare; Children's Environmental Health Information Resources; Dietary Supplements; EdCoTox; Environmental Justice; Health Effects of the Collapse of the World Trade Center; Hurricanes; Indoor Air Pollution; Keeping the Artist Safe: Hazards of Arts and Crafts Materials; Lead and Human Health; Multi-cultural Resources for Health Information; Outdoor Air Pollution; Pesticide Exposure; Special Populations: Emergency and Disaster Preparedness (Bethesda, Md.: National Library of Medicine, 2008–); Tox Web Links; Toxicogenomics; West Nile Virus: Pesticides Used for Mosquito Control.

Provides selected links to Internet resources on toxicology and environmental health topics and issues. Includes both NLM and outside resources. Guidelines for the selection of resources outside of NLM are spelled out at http://sis.nlm.nih.gov/enviro/envirohealthlinkscriteria.html.

1490 Global health atlas. World Health Organization. 2003–. Geneva, [Switzerland]: World Health Organization. http://www.who.int/ globalatlas/.

Title varies: *WHO's Communicable Disease Global Atlas; Global Atlas of Infectious Disease; Global Atlas of Infectious Diseases: an Interactive Information and Mapping System.*

World Health Organization (951) Internet resource "bringing together for analysis and comparison standardized data and statistics for infectious diseases at country, regional, and global levels. The analysis and interpretation of data are further supported through information on demography, socioeconomic conditions, and environmental factors."—*Website.* Searchable database which allows users to create reports, charts, and maps (e.g., geographic areas can be selected to create maps of diseases). Links to related sites.

1491 Globalhealth.gov. U.S. Dept. of Health and Human Services. 1990s–. Washington: U.S. Dept. of Health and Human Services. http://globalhealth.gov/index.html.

Produced by HHS Office of Global Health Affairs (OGHA). Title varies: Global Health.gov; GlobalHealth.

Provides access to information about major global health topics, such as avian influenza, HIV/AIDS, malaria, etc. and links to partner organizations (e.g., WHO [951], PAHO [950], and others) and information on international travel, health regulation, refugee health, and related areas. CDC's (940) Coordinating Office for Global Health (http://www.cdc.gov/cogh/) provides additional information and resources.

1492 Global health library. World Health Organization. 2005–. Geneva, Switzerland: World Health Organization. http://www.who.int/ghl/en/index.html.

Produced by Global Health Library (GHL); World Health Organization (WHO) (951); the Knowledge Management and Sharing Department of WHO (WHO/KMS).

A WHO collaborative project with many partners worldwide, such as U.N. bodies, national libraries of medicine, various public health institutes, academic and special libraries, and others. Points to reliable health information from various providers and in various formats. Provides access to the international scientific and technical literature and links to further information and access to global and regional indexes and international agencies (e.g., PAHO [950], WHOLIS [484], various directories, and other information via its Global Health Library Virtual Platform [http://www.globalhealthlibrary.net/php/index.php]. Designed for different users and user groups, including health professionals, patients, their families, and the general public.

1493 HealthMap. Clark Freifeld, John Brownstein, Children's Hospital [Boston] Informatics Program, Harvard-MIT Division of Health Sciences and Technology. [2006–.] [New Haven, Conn.]: Clark Freifeld and John Brownstein. http://www.healthmap.org/.

Title varies: HEALTHmap: Global Disease Alert Mapping System.

"Brings together disparate data sources to achieve a unified and comprehensive view of the current global state of infectious diseases and their effect on human and animal health. Integrates outbreak data of varying reliability, ranging from news sources (such as Google News [Mountain View, Calif.: Google, [200?]]) to curated personal accounts (such as ProMED) to validated official alerts (such as World Health Organization [951]). Through an automated text processing system, the data is aggregated by disease and displayed by location for user-friendly access to the original alert. provides a jumping-off point for real-time information on emerging infectious diseases and has particular interest for public health officials and international travelers."—*Website.* Official alerts from WHO are available via *Disease outbreak news,* which is part of WHO's "Epidemic and Pandemic Alert and Response (EPR)" website (http://www.who.int/ csr/don/en/). EuroSurveillance (http://www.eurosurveillance.org/), a program of the European Centre for Disease Prevention and Control (http:// www.ecdc.europa.eu), is another data source. Uses marker icons (square-shaped: country-level marker; round: state, province, and local) and low or high "heat index," with further explanation at http://www.healthmap. org/about.php. Provides links for information on particular diseases to Wikipedia (San Francisco: Wikimedia Foundation, 2001–), the World Health Organization (WHO) (951), the Centers for Disease Control and Prevention (CDC) (940), PubMed (432), and Google Trends. Available in different views, i.e., as map, satellite, or hybrid map.

1494 **Health Resources and Services Administration (HRSA).** Health Resources and Services Administration. 1999–. Washington: Department of Health and Human Services. http://www.hrsa.gov/.

Health Resources and Services Administration (HSRA), pt. of U.S. Dept. of Health and Human Services (HHS) (894).

HRSA provides leadership and direction for various major national programs, such as organ donation and transplantation, HIV/AIDS, drug pricing, programs related to rural health, health information technology, telehealth, emergency preparedness, and bioterrorism. Also provides information and data on the health professions, a "geospatial data warehouse," health workforce analysis and other reports, and a variety of other topics and links to related sites both within the HRSA and other agencies and programs.

1495 **Health services research methodology core library recommendations, 2007.** AcademyHealth, National Library of Medicine (U.S.). 2007. Bethesda, Md.: National Library of Medicine. http://www.nlm.nih.gov/nichsr/corelib/hsrmethods. html.

Produced by AcademyHealth; National Library of Medicine (NLM) (427); National Information Center on Health Services Research and Health Care (NICHSR).

List of books, journals, bibliographic databases, websites, and other media; useful for collection development librarians and researchers interested in health services research methods. Lists both "core" materials and "desired" materials in areas such as general health policy, health economics, health services research, public health, and several others. The NICHSR website (http://www.nlm.nih.gov/nichsr/outreach.html) lists links to several other recommended lists, including Health Economics Core Library Recommendation, Health Outcomes Core Library Recommendation, Health Policy Core Library Recommendation, and other information.

1496 Healthy People 2010. National Center for Health Statistics (NCHS). Hyattsville, Md.: Centers for Disease Control (U.S.), National Center for Health Statistics. http://www.cdc.gov/nchs/ hphome.htm.

RA395.A3

Contents: Healthy people 2010: Understanding and improving health; Healthy people 2010: Objectives for improving health; Appendixes; Tracking healthy people 2010.

Described as a "national initiative of the U.S. Dept. of Health and Human Services [HHS] that brings together national, state, and local organizations, businesses, communities, and individuals to improve the health of all Americans, eliminate disparities in health, and improve years and quality of life. Since its inception in 1979, it has been coordinated by the Office of Disease Prevention and Health Promotion."— *Website.* Represents the third time that HHS has developed ten-year health objectives for the nation. Previous reports include *Healthy people 2000* (http://purl.access.gpo.gov/GPO/LPS3745) and *Healthy people: The Surgeon General's report on health promotion and disease prevention: Background papers: Report to the Surgeon General on health promotion and disease prevention* (Washington, D.C.: Institute of Medicine, 1979). "Healthy People DATA 2010," an interactive database system accessible via CDC WONDER (1399) provides various reports and data. A search interface providing searches for published literature related to the Healthy People 2010 was added to the "special queries" section of PubMed (432).

Also available in print format: *Tracking healthy people 2010: Healthy people 2010* (Washington, D.C.: U.S. Dept. of Health and Human Services, 2000 [Nov. 2000 version]), which supersedes the conference edition, entitled *Healthy people 2010* (Washington, D.C.: U.S. Dept. of Health and Human Services, 2000 [Jan. 2000]).

1497 HIV InSite knowledge base. Laurence Peiperl, Paul Volberding,
P. T. Cohen, University of California, San Francisco. 1996(?)–. San
Francisco: University of California. http://hivinsite.ucsf.edu/InSite.
jsp?page=KB.

025.174; 616.9792; 362.1969792; 616.979201

Online adaptation of *The AIDS knowledge base* (AKB), which appeared in
several print editions (1st ed., 1990; 2nd ed., 1994; 3rd ed., 1999).

Contents: Epidemiology of HIV; Natural Science of HIV; Diagnosis
and Clinical Management of HIV; Clinical Manifestations of HIV; Infections Associated with HIV; Malignancies Associated with HIV; Transmission and Prevention of HIV; HIV Policy.

Continually updated online resource covering HIV/AIDS clinical topics and also access to selected related materials (e.g., guidelines, fact sheets,
journal articles, etc.), including both links within the HIV InSite and outside resources. For academic libraries.

1498 HSR information central. 1993–. Bethesda, Md.: National Library
of Medicine (U.S.), National Institutes of Health, Dept. of Health
and Human Services. http://www.nlm.nih.gov/hsrinfo/.

Contents: Literature and guidelines; Data tools and statistics; Grants and
funding; Legislation; Training and education; Meetings and conferences;
Discussion and e-mail lists; Alphabetic list (all websites in alphabetic
order); Subject list (websites arranged by categories: federal agencies; associations; data sets and data sources; epidemiology and health statistics; evidence based medicine and health technology assessment; Funding; Health
policy and health economics; informatics; public health; rural health; state
resources; disparities).

Developed by the National Library of Medicine (427) to serve the
information needs of the health services research community, in partnership with other government agencies and institutes (e.g., Agency for
Healthcare Research and Quality [AHRQ] [733], National Cancer Institute [166], the Cecil C. Sheps Center for Health Services Research, and
the Health Services Research and Development Service [HSR&D] at the
Veterans Administration, and others).

1499 International health (MedlinePlus). National Library of Medicine
(U.S.). 2000?–. Bethesda, Md.: National Library of Medicine.
http://www.nlm.nih.gov/medlineplus/internationalhealth.html.

A Health Topic within MedlinePlus (463). Provides extensive global health
information, with access to various online reference resources, links to

major organizations (e.g., Centers for Disease Control, World Health Organization), foundations (e.g., Henry J. Kaiser Family Foundation), research, journal articles, law and policy information (e.g., International Health Regulations [2005] [926]), WHO and UNICEF statistics, etc. Links to related MedlinePlus topics, such as Traveler's Health and Health System (MedlinePlus) (463). Go Local link and map help to identify services and providers in the United States.

1500 Kaiser Family Foundation. Henry J. Kaiser Family Foundation. 2000–. Menlo Park, Calif.: Henry J. Kaiser Family Foundation. http://www.kff.org/.
362.1; 361.7

The Henry J. Kaiser Family Foundation is an independent philanthropy focusing on major health care issues. Website contains statistics on Medicare, Medicaid, the uninsured in each state of the United States, minority health, etc. Links to resources on health policy covering such topics as women's health policy, HIV/AIDS, and media programs. A wide variety of resources are accessible via the following tabs found on the website: (1) KaiserNetwork.org (http://www.kaisernetwork.org/): search for recent daily reports and webcasts; (2) StateHealthFacts (http://www.statehealthfacts.org/): source for state health data; (3) Kaiseredu.org (http://www.kaiseredu.org/): provides easy access to the latest data, research, analysis, and developments in health policy and includes narrated slide tutorials, background reference libraries, and issue modules on current topics and policy debates; (4) GlobalHealthReporting.org (http://www.globalhealthreporting.org/): global data on HIV/AIDS, tuberculosis, malaria and more; (5) GlobalHealthFacts.org (http://www.globalhealthfacts.org/): companion site to globalhealthreporting; (6) Health08.org (http://www.health08.org/): election news, analysis, and events.

1501 Malaria atlas project (MAP). Malaria Public Health and Epidemiology Group, Centre for Geographic Medicine, Kenya. 2006–. Nairobi, Kenya; Oxford, England: Centre for Geographic Medicine, Kenya; University of Oxford. http://www.map.ox.ac.uk/MAP_overview.html.

"MAP is a joint project between the Malaria Public Health & Epidemiology Group, Centre for Geographic Medicine, Kenya and the Spatial Ecology & Epidemiology Group, University of Oxford, UK with collaborating nodes in America and Asia Pacific region."—*Overview.* Funded by the Wellcome Trust, United Kingdom.

Provides an overview of the MAP project and enables viewers to browse worldwide malaria and malaria-control data and also allows the submission of new data. Offers health links (e.g., malaria, general health, and food security and health), global and regional links, and links to malaria-related organizations. Also provides research-related links, including libraries, a listing of online resources, databases for literature searching, tutorials, and information about various software tools. Further details about this project and its future plans can be found on the MAP website.

1502 **National Information Center on Health Services Research and Health Care Technology (NICHSR).** National Library of Medicine (U.S.). 2002–. Bethesda, Md.: National Library of Medicine, National Institutes of Health, U.S. Dept. of Health and Human Services. http://www.nlm.nih.gov/nichsr/.

Health Services Research (HSR); NICHSR; National Library of Medicine® (NLM®) (427).

NICHSR coordinates NLM's HSR information programs, with links to databases and retrieval services, HSR Information Central (882), presentations, publications, and other information. An alphabetic list (http://www.nlm.nih.gov/hsrinfo/alphahsre.html) and a subject list (http://www.nlm.nih.gov/hsrinfo/hsrsites.html) of related websites, providing a large number of HSR-related links: federal agencies; associations; data sets and data sources; epidemiology and health statistics; evidence-based medicine and health technology assessment; funding; health policy and health economics; informatics; public health; rural health; state resources; disparities, and others.

A related page is NLM's Health Services Research & Public Health Information Programs (822), a website that lists resources from multiple NLM programs.

1503 **National Institute of Environmental Health Sciences.** National Institute of Environmental Health Sciences. 1994?–. Research Triangle Park, N.C.: National Institute of Environmental Health Sciences. http://www.niehs.nih.gov.

RA565

Website of National Institute of Environmental Health Sciences (NIEHS).

Contents: Health and Education; Research; Funding Opportunities; Careers and Training; News and Events; About NIEHS.

Presents information and resources for several user groups, including health professionals, research scientists, teachers, children, and the general public. Includes a list of environmental health topics (i.e., A–Z List of Conditions and Diseases Linked to Environmental Exposures), access to specialized databases and software, resources of the NIEHS Library and Information Services (http://www.niehs.nih.gov/research/resources/library/index.cfm), NIEHS bioethics resources (http://www.niehs.nih.gov/research/resources/bioethics/index.cfm), and other information resources.

1504 National Institute of Mental Health. National Institute of Mental Health (U.S.). 1995?–. Bethesda, Md.: National Institutes of Health. http://www.nimh.nih.gov/.

616.89   RA790.A1

Part of National Institutes of Health (NIH) (470).

Provides funding for research on mind, brain, behavior, and behavioral disorders; for research on the causes, occurrence, and treatment of mental illness; and for mental health services, including major projects such as the Human Brain Project and neuroinformatics research in support of this project. Contains topics useful for the public concerning adult and pediatric psychopathology. Provides extensive information on a variety of mental health topics (http://www.nimh.nih.gov/health/topics/index.shtml), links to NIMH publications and other resources, to other websites (e.g., Getting Help: Locate Services; http://www.nimh.nih.gov/health/topics/getting-help-locate-services/ind ex.shtml), and to mental health information available via MedlinePlus (http://www.nlm.nih.gov/medlineplus/mentalhealth.html) (463). Site index.

1505 National Institute on Drug Abuse (NIDA). National Institute on Drug Abuse (U.S.). 1995–. Rockville, Md.: National Institute on Drug Abuse. http://www.nida.nih.gov.

NIDA is part of the National Institutes of Health (NIH) (470).

Addresses questions and supports research on health aspects of drug abuse and addiction as well as drug addiction treatment. Educational resources and materials on drugs of abuse are presented for several different user groups: students and young adults, parents and teachers, medical and health professionals, and researchers. Includes links to publications and InfoFacts fact sheets (http://www.nida.nih.gov/Infofacts/index.html) with effects of drug abuse, health effects of specific drugs, prevention and treatment, research reports, survey data, and other information.

1506 **National Office of Public Health Genomics.** Centers for Disease
Control and Prevention (U.S.). 2006–. Atlanta: Centers for Disease
Control and Prevention. http://www.cdc.gov/genomics/default.
htm.

The National Office of Public Health Genomics (NOPHG) is a center
within the Centers for Disease Control and Prevention (CDC) (940).

Public health genomics is considered "an emerging field that assesses
the impact of genes and their interaction with behavior, diet and the
environment on population health."—*Main page.* NOPHG promotes the
integration of genomics into public health research, policy, and practice.
Its activities are related to genomics and health, family history, population research, and related areas. Provides a variety of educational links
about genetic research. The Human Genome Epidemiology Network
(HuGENet), for example, is a "global collaboration of individuals and
committed to the assessment of the impact of human genome variation
on population health and information can be used to improve health
and prevent disease."—*HuGENet website* (http://www.cdc.gov/genomics/
hugenet/default.htm).

A related CDC site is Genomics and Disease Prevention (http://apps.
nccd.cdc.gov/genomics/GDPQueryTool/frmA-ZDisease.asp), with access
to Health Topics A–Z, which provides a listing of diseases, outcomes, or
health topics found within the Genomics and Disease Prevention Information System (GDPInfo) database.

1507 **Occupational Safety and Health Administration (OSHA).**
Occupational Safety and Health Administration. 199?–.
Washington: Occupational Safety and Health Administration.
http://www.osha.gov/.

Access to OSHA programs and services. Includes information on OSHA
standards on safety, preventing injuries, and protecting the health of American workers. Provides access to the OSHA/EPA Occupational Chemical
Database (http://www.osha.gov/web/dep/chemicaldata/), jointly developed and maintained by OSHA and EPA, with information from several
different government agencies. Safety and health topics include biological
agents (avian flu, food-borne disease, ricin, etc.), construction (key standards and compliance activities), emergency preparedness (e.g., national
safety and health standards for emergency responders), ergonomics (with
focus on musculoskeletal disorders), hazard communication (e.g., workplace chemical safety programs), maritime industry, and other subjects.
Also links to related resources.

1508 **Pan American Health Organization (PAHO).** Pan American Health Organization. 1990s–. Washington: Pan American Health Organization. http://www.paho.org/.

RA438.A45

Published by World Health Organization (WHO); United Nations.

PAHO is WHO's regional office for the Americas, an international public health agency with the mission to improve health and living standards of the countries of the Americas.

Searchable website, with detailed information about PAHO's governance and mission, links to basic health indicators, core health data, country health profiles, trends and situation analysis, information products, and other related information. Includes, for example, Regional Core Health Data Initiative (http://www.paho.org/english/dd/ais/coredata. htm), including access to PAHO's Basic Country Health Profiles for the Americas (http://www.paho.org/English/DD/AIS/cp_index.htm), which provides mortality statistics for the Americas and health profiles for all countries in North and South America.

Provides access to PAHO electronic books (English and Spanish) at http://www.paho.org/Project.asp?SEL=PR&LNG=ENG&ID=360.

A related title is *Health in the Americas* (959).

1509 **Partners in information access for the public health workforce.** U.S. National Library of Medicine. 2003–. Bethesda, Md.: U.S. National Library of Medicine, National Institutes of Health, Dept. of Health and Human Services. http://phpartners. org/.

"Collaboration of U.S. government agencies, public health organizations, and health sciences libraries which provides timely, convenient access to selected public health resources on the Internet [with the mission of] helping the public health workforce find and use information effectively to improve and protect the public's health."—*Website*

Provides links to the individual partner websites, such as Agency for Healthcare Research and Quality (AHRQ) (733), American Public Health Association (APHA), Association of Schools of Public Health (ASPH), Association of State and Territorial Health Officials (ASTHO), Centers for Disease Control and Prevention (CDC) (940), Medical Library Association (MLANET) (465), National Library of Medicine (427), and several other organizations. Provides extensive information on several public health topics (currently to bioterrorism, environmental health, and HIV/AIDS). For additional information and links see the Partners in Information

Access for the Public Health Workforce fact sheet at http://www.nlm.nih. gov/nno/partners.html.

1510 **Public health image library (PHIL).** Centers for Disease Control and Prevention. [1998]–. Atlanta: Centers for Disease Control and Prevention. http://phil.cdc.gov/Phil/.

Public Health Image Library (PHIL), created by a working group at the Centers for Disease Control and Prevention (CDC) (940); National Library of Medicine (NLM) (427).

Collection of a variety of single images, image sets, multimedia files, etc., with current and historical content about people, places, scientific subjects, etc. FAQ section (http://phil.cdc.gov/Phil/faq.asp) provides detailed information. Useful for public health professionals, scientists, librarians, teachers, and students.

This website also provides links to other CDC and NLM image libraries (e.g., Images from the History of Medicine [352] and Visible Human [502]). Complements other medical image collections such as Health Education Assets Library (HEAL) (458) and ImagesMD (http://www. images.md).

1511 **Public health law materials.** Centers for Disease Control and Prevention (U.S.), Dept. of Health and Human Services. 200?–. Atlanta: Centers for Disease Control and Prevention, Dept. of Health and Human Services. http://www2a.cdc.gov/phlp/lawmat. asp.

Provides access to public health topics, including general public health law and international public health law. Includes emergency preparedness topics (e.g., bioterrorism, disease outbreaks and incidents, natural disasters, and general emergency preparedness). Pt. of the Public Health Law Program (CDC) (940) website (http://www2a.cdc.gov/phlp/) which also provides an A–Z topics list with information on a variety of areas and subjects related to public health law and legal issues, including a list of state public health departments.

1512 **Special populations.** National Library of Medicine (U.S.). 2008–. Bethesda, Md.: National Library of Medicine. http://sis.nlm.nih. gov/outreach/specialpopulationsanddisasters.html.

Part of the National Library of Medicine's Enviro-Health Links (1489).

Contents: Disabled; Seniors; Hearing Impaired; Visually Impaired; Women and Gender; Pregnancy; Children; Diabetes; Native Americans;

Foreign Language Materials; Información en Español; Guidance for Organizations and Governments; Guidance for Employers; Law and Policy; Lessons Learned from Prior Disasters; Searches from the National Library of Medicine.

Additional selected NLM resources for disaster preparedness and response can be found on the Environmental Health and Toxicology home page, http://sis.nlm.nih.gov/pdf/nlmdisasterresources.pdf.

1513 U.S. Dept. of Health and Human Services (HHS). U.S. Dept. of Health and Human Services (HHS). 1997–. Washington: U.S. Dept. of Health and Human Services. http://www.os.dhhs.gov/.

HHS has the mission "to enhance the health and well-being of Americans by providing for effective health and human services and by fostering strong, sustained advances in the sciences underlying medicine, public health, and social services."—*Website*

Overview and links to all HHS offices: Office for Civil Rights; Office of Global Health Affairs; Surgeon General, and many others. Also provides overview and links to the HHS agencies: Administration for Children and Families; Administration on Aging; Agency for Healthcare Research and Quality (AHRQ) (733); Agency for Toxic Substances and Disease Registry (1397); Centers for Disease Control and Prevention (CDC) (940); Centers for Medicare and Medicaid Services (742); Food and Drug Administration (630); Health Resources and Services Administration (877); Indian Health Service (IHS) (1401); National Institutes of Health (NIH) (470); Substance Abuse and Mental Health Services Administration (769). "HHS Acronyms and Abbreviations" at http://www.hhs.gov/acronyms.html. Includes a "Reference Collections" page (http://www.hhs.gov/reference/index.html) which provides an extensive collection of resources, including dictionaries and glossaries, encyclopedias, databases, indexes, and various other reference resources, publications, reports, and statistics. Provides policy information (e.g., science policy issues; Surgeon General priorities; legal information; HHS-related publications and reports).

1514 WISER (Wireless Information System for Emergency Responders). National Library of Medicine (U.S.). 2004–. Besthesda, Md.: National Library of Medicine. http://wiser.nlm.nih.gov.

PDA application designed to assist first responders in hazardous materials incidents, including substance identification support, physical characteristics, human health information, and advice on containment and suppression. Content from TOXNET (1580)'s HSDB (Hazardous Substance Data Bank) (1569). Further information about PDA and desktop/laptop versions available at the website.

Statistics

1515 **DHHS Data Council gateway to data and statistics.** U.S. Department of Health and Human Services. 200?–. Washington: U.S. Department of Health and Human Services. http://www.hhs-stat.net/about.htm.

RA407.3

Provides access to key health and human services data and statistics. Covers information sponsored by federal, state, and local governments. Complements other government resources such as FirstGov (http://www.usa.gov/) and FedStats (519). Links to health and human services surveys and data systems sponsored by Federal agencies. Datafinder leads to websites that contain statistics and data. The MetaDirectory is a comprehensive list and description of the statistical and surveillance systems supported by HHS agencies. Other key resources links lead to additional information.

1516 **European health for all database (HFA-DB).** World Health Organization Regional Office for Europe. 2000s–. Copenhagen, Denmark: World Health Organization Regional Office for Europe. http://data.euro.who.int/hfadb/.

Description based on Jan. 2007 version.

Provides basic health statistics and health trends for the member states of the WHO European Region, with approx. 600 health indicators, including basic demographic and socioeconomic indicators; some lifestyle- and environment-related indicators; mortality, morbidity, and disability; hospital discharges; and health care resources, utilization, and expenditures. Can be used as a tool for international comparison and for assessing the health situation and trends in any European country.

1517 **Faststats A to Z.** National Center for Health Statistics (NCHS). Hyattsville, Md.: U.S. Dept. of Health and Human Services, Centers for Disease Control and Prevention, National Center for Health Statistics. http://www.cdc.gov/nchs/fastats/Default.htm.

Provides topic-appropriate public health statistics (e.g., birth data, morbidity and mortality statistics, and health care use) and relevant links to further information and publications. Includes state and territorial data, with clickable map for individual state data. Also includes data derived from the "Behavioral Risk Factor Surveillance System (BRFSS)," which compiles data for 16 negative behaviors.

1518 Health data for all ages (HDAA). National Center for Health Statistics. 200?–. Atlanta: National Center for Health Statistics. http://www.cdc.gov/nchs/health_data_for_all_ages.htm.

Searchable website presents tables that provide Centers for Disease Control and Prevention (CDC) (940) health statistics for infants, children, adolescents, adults, and older adults. Table topics include pregnancy and birth, health conditions/risk factors, health care access and use, mortality, and others, and topics can be customized with characteristics such as age, gender, race/ethnicity, and geographic location.

1519 Health in the Americas. Pan American Sanitary Bureau. ill. Washington, D.C: Pan American Health Organization, Pan American Sanitary Bureau, Regional Office of the World Health Organization, 1998–.
610.8s; 362.1091812   RA10.P252

Published by Pan American Health Organization (PAHO) (950); "Salud en las Américas."

Title varies: Previously had title *Summary of reports on the health conditions in the Americas* and *Health conditions in the Americas.* Description based on 2007 ed. (2 v.): v. 1, Regional analysis; v. 2, Country-by-country assessment.

Health data, facts, health trends, and related information for Central and South America, with emphasis on health disparities. Provides a vision for the future of health and health challenges in the Americas. Also available online through netLibrary; both print and online versions in English or Spanish.

A complement to this publication is *Health statistics from the Americas*, publ. in print format 1991–98, and now online (2003 ed. http://www. paho.org/english/dd/pub/SP_591.htm and 2006 ed. http://www.paho.org/ English/DD/AIS/HSA2006.htm).

1520 Health, United States. National Center for Health Statistics. 1975–. Rockville, Md.: National Center for Health Statistics. http://purl. access.gpo.gov/GPO/LPS2649.

Description based on the 2006 ed. (30th annual report).

Subtitle of this edition: With Vhartbook on Trends in the Health of Americans with Special Feature on Pain.

"An annual report on trends in health statistics. The report consists of two main sections: a chartbook containing text and figures that illustrates major trends in the health of Americans; and a trend tables section that contains 147 detailed data tables. The two main components are supplemented by an executive summary, a highlights section, an extensive appendix and reference section, and an index."—*NCHS website.* Hyperlinks to tables and graphs. Also provides easy access to other online resources provided by NCHS, for example, Faststats A–Z (518), Healthy People 2010 (530), and other websites.

1521 Healthy People 2010. National Center for Health Statistics (NCHS). Hyattsville, Md.: Centers for Disease Control (U.S.), National Center for Health Statistics. http://www.cdc.gov/nchs/hphome.htm.

RA395.A3

Contents: Healthy people 2010: Understanding and improving health; Healthy people 2010: Objectives for improving health; Appendixes; Tracking healthy people 2010.

Described as a "national initiative of the U.S. Dept. of Health and Human Services [HHS] that brings together national, state, and local organizations, businesses, communities, and individuals to improve the health of all Americans, eliminate disparities in health, and improve years and quality of life. Since its inception in 1979, it has been coordinated by the Office of Disease Prevention and Health Promotion."—*Website.* Represents the third time that HHS has developed ten-year health objectives for the nation. Previous reports include *Healthy people 2000* (http://purl. access.gpo.gov/GPO/LPS3745) and *Healthy people: The Surgeon General's report on health promotion and disease prevention: Background papers: Report to the Surgeon General on health promotion and disease prevention* (Washington, D.C.: Institute of Medicine, 1979). "Healthy People DATA 2010," an interactive database system accessible via CDC WONDER (1399) provides various reports and data. A search interface providing searches for published literature related to the Healthy People 2010 was added to the "special queries" section of PubMed (432).

Also available in print format: *Tracking healthy people 2010: Healthy people 2010* (Washington, D.C.: U.S. Dept. of Health and Human Services,

2000 [Nov. 2000 version]), which supersedes the conference edition, entitled *Healthy people 2010* (Washington, D.C.: U.S. Dept. of Health and Human Services, 2000 [Jan. 2000]).

1522 Healthy women. Centers for Disease Control and Prevention (U.S.); National Center for Health Statistics (U.S.). 2004. Hyattsville, Md.: National Center for Health Statistics, Centers for Disease Control and Prevention, U.S. Dept. of Health and Human Services. http://www.cdc.gov/nchs/datawh/statab/chartbook.htm.

RA408.W65

Title varies: Suggested title for website: Healthy Women: State Trends in Health and Mortality; suggested citation for print version, publ. in 2004 as Women's health and mortality chartbook by K. M. Brett and Suzanne G. Hayes.

Provides access to the PDF version of *Women's health and mortality Chartbook*, developed by NCHS with support from the Office on Women's Health. It describes the health of people in each state in the U.S. by sex, race, and age by reporting current data on critical issues of relevance to women. Because of the large file size, this report has been broken into four accessible PDF files. Users may also download the entire report. Website provides help for using tables.

Other publications in this area include *Women's health data book: A profile of women's health in the United States*, ed. by D. Misra, a collaborative publication by the Jacobs Institute of Women's Health and the Henry J. Kaiser Family Foundation (Kaiser Family Foundation [884]) since 1992, complemented by *State profiles on women's health: Women's health issues*, publ. since 1998.

1523 National vital statistics system (NVSS). National Center for Health Statistics. 2000s–. Hyattsville, Md.: National Center for Health Statistics. http://www.cdc.gov/nchs/nvss.htm.

NVSS is a unit of the National Center for Health Statistics (539), which is responsible for the official vital statistics of the United States: births, deaths (annual mortality data, monthly provisional mortality data, cause-of-death data by age, race, sex, etc.), marriages, divorces, and fetal deaths. Provides access to a vital-statistics information sources portal (http://www.cdc.gov/nchs/about/major/dvs/Vitalstatsonline.htm), with links to publications and information products (http://www.cdc.gov/nchs/products.htm), including Advance Data, Vital and Health Statistics Series (also

referred to as "series reports" and "rainbow series"; http://www.cdc.gov/
nchs/products/pubs/pubd/series/ser.htm), Vital Statistics of the United
States (http://www.cdc.gov/nchs/products/pubs/pubd/vsus/vsus.htm),
and many others that can be identified via a helpful site index at http://
www.cdc.gov/nchs/siteindex.htm or via NCHS Web Search (http://www.
cdc.gov/nchs/search/search.htm).

1524 Statistical record of health and medicine. Gale Research Inc. 2 v.
Detroit: Gale Research Inc. c1995–c1998. ISSN: 1078-6961.

362.10973021   RA407.3.S732

Description based on 2nd ed., 1998.

Compilation of U.S. national, state, and municipal health and medical
statistics from a variety of sources. Provides statistics on health status of
Americans, health insurance, health care costs and expenditures, medical
professions, international rankings and comparisons, etc. Further detailed
notes on scope and coverage in the introduction and the sources from
which the information is drawn. Keyword index.

Can be supplemented by more recent resources, for example, *Chronology of public health in the United Sates* (Jefferson, N.C.: McFarland,
2005), which covers events back to 1796, but mainly since 1900, as well
as various government websites containing health and medical statistics.

1525 WHOSIS. World Health Organization. [1994]–. Geneva,
[Switzerland]: World Health Organization. http://www.who.int/
whosis/.

Published by World Health Organization (WHO).

Provides description and online access to statistical and epidemiological information, data, and tools available from WHO and other sites:
mortality and health status, disease statistics, health systems statistics, risk
factors and health services, and inequities in health. Provides links to several databases: WHOSIS database, with the latest "core health indicators"
from WHO sources (including *The world health report* [559] and *World
health statistics* [560]), which make it possible to construct tables for any
combination of countries, indicators and years, Causes of Death database,
WHO Global InfoBase Online, Global Health Atlas, and Reproductive
Health Indicators database.

1526 Women's health USA. U.S. Dept. of Health and Human Services,
Maternal and Child Health Bureau. 2002–. Rockville, Md.: U.S.

Dept. of Health and Human Services, Maternal and Child Health Bureau. http://purl.access.gpo.gov/GPO/LPS21379.

Part of Health Resources and Services Administration (HRSA) (877), within the U.S. Dept. of Health and Human Services (HHS) (894).

Description based on 5th online ed., 2006.

Contents: Population Characteristics; Health Status; Health Services Utilization; Indicators in Previous Editions; Site Map.

Collection of current and historical data on health challenges facing women, with information on life expectancy and addressing topics such as postpartum depression, smoking, alcohol, illicit drug use, etc. Brings together the latest available information from various government agencies (HHS, U.S. Dept. of Agriculture, U.S. Dept. of Labor, U.S. Dept. of Justice).

National Women's Health Information Center, Womenshealth.gov (http://www.womenshealth.gov/), provides extensive further information.

1527 The world health report. World Health Organization. 1995–. Geneva, [Switzerland]: World Health Organization. ISSN: 1020-3311. http://www.who.int/whr/.

614.405   RA8.A265

Pt. of WHOSIS (WHO Statistical Information System) a guide to statistical information (556). Description based on the 2006 online ed., has subtitle: "working together for health." Also available in print format. 2007 ed. ("promoting international health security") due Aug. 2007.

"Every year. takes a new and expert look at global health, focusing on a specific theme, while assessing the current global situation. Using the latest data gathered and validated by WHO, each report paints a picture of the changing world."—*Website.* Website also provides links to the full-text reports 1995–2005, each with focus on a special theme: 1995, "bridging the gaps"; 1996, "fighting disease, fostering development"; 1997 "conquering suffering, enriching humanity"; 1998, "life in the 21st century: a vision for all"; 1999, "making a difference"; 2000, "health systems: improving performance"; 2001, "mental health: new understanding, new hope"; 2002, "reducing risks, promoting healthy life"; 2003, "shaping the future"; 2004, "changing history"; 2005, "make every mother and child count;" 2006, "working together for health."

1528 World health statistics. World Health Organization. 2005–. Geneva, Switzerland: World Health Organization. http://www.who. int/healthinfo/statistics/en/.

1939/46–96 publ. as World *health statistics annual = Annuaire de statistiques sanitaires mondiales* (print version).

Part of WHOSIS: WHO Statistical Information System (556).

Description based on online 3rd ed., 2007 ed. (http://www.who.int/whosis/whostat2007.pdf).

Contents: pt. 1, "Ten statistical highlights in global public health." Pt. 2, "World health statistics": "Health status: Mortality"; "Health status: Morbidity"; "Health services coverage"; "Risk factors"; "Health systems"; "Inequities in health"; "Demographic and socioeconomic statistics."

"Presents the most recent health statistics for WHO's 193 Member States. collated from publications and databases produced by WHO's technical programmes and regional offices. Selected on the basis of their relevance to global health, the availability and quality of the data, and the accuracy and comparability of estimates. The statistics for the indicators are derived from an interactive process of data collection, compilation, quality assessment and estimation occurring among WHO's technical programmes and its Member States."—*Introd.* Print version also available.

13 > TOXICOLOGY

1529 Dictionary of toxicology. 2nd ed. Ernest Hodgson, Richard B. Mailman, Janice E. Chambers. xii, 504 p., ill. London; New York: Macmillan Reference; Grove's Dictionaries, 2000. ISBN: 033354700.

615.9003   RA1193

Rev. ed. of *Macmillan dictionary of toxicology*, 1988. Title varies.

Designed as an introduction to the field of toxicology for students and for scientists in other disciplines. Most entries relate directly to toxicology, but others provide information that might be needed by toxicologists. For example, contains certain anatomical, biochemical, pathological, and physiological terms. This revised edition includes 800 new and 1,200 revised entries, with structure and CAS number for important toxic chemicals. Provides references to *Hazardous chemical desk reference* (New York: Wiley, 2002) (entries cross-listed as HCDR) and *Toxicological profiles* (Agency for Toxic Substances and Disease Registry [1397], cross-listed as ATSDR). Online access to this edition available via Credo Reference (London; Boston: Credo Reference) as *Macmillan dictionary of toxicology*.

Dictionaries

1530 Dictionary of environmentally important chemicals. D. C. Ayres, Desmond Hellier. xi, 332 p., ill. Chicago: Fitzroy Dearborn, 1999, c1998. ISBN: 1579582060.

TD196.C45.A97

Chemicals included appear on three of the following regulatory agency lists: American Conference of Governmental Industrial Hygienists, European Community Directives of Dangerous Substances, German Commission for Investigation of Health Hazards of Chemicals in the Work Area, International Agency for Research on Cancer, and the United States Environmental Protection Agency list of priority pollutants (1995). Selected additional chemicals included were chosen when considered a risk to the general public. Few synonyms are given, so use of a chemical synonyms dictionary such as *Gardner's chemical synonyms and trade names* (Brookfield, Vt.: Ashgate, 1999) or *Gardner's commercially important chemicals* (Hoboken, N.J.: Wiley-Interscience, 2005) is recommended. Entries vary, but many are a page or two in length. A strength of the dictionary lies in the referrals to additional literature for each chemical. Includes brief glossary of acronyms and abbreviations, brief glossary of medical terms used, and a list of further reading (in addition to those given for individual chemicals).

TOXICOLOGY

689

1531 Dictionary of plant toxins. J. B. Harborne, Herbert Baxter, Gerard P. Moss. xv, 523 p., ill. Chichester, [England, U.K.]; New York: Wiley, 1996. ISBN: 0471951072.

615.95203   RA1250.D53

Provides a comprehensive source with concise entries on phytotoxins, i.e., poisonous substances produced by plants. Each entry mentions common name(s) with synonyms, chemical class and subclass, chemical structure, Chemical Abstracts Service (CAS) registry number, molecular weight, and chemical formula.

References to the primary literature. Includes subject, plant species, molecular formulas, and common plant/common toxin name indexes.

1532 The dictionary of substances and their effects. S. Gangolli Royal Society of Chemistry (Great Britain). [2005]. London: Royal Society of Chemistry. http://www.knovel.com/knovel2/Toc.jsp?BookID=527.

615.9003   RA1193.D53

1st ed., 1992; 2nd ed., 1999 (7 v.).

This edition is the updated electronic version of the seven-volume print edition. Continually updated, with interactive features, contains 5,310 substances. All substances are listed in the searchable interactive table Physical Constants of Chemical Substances, which lists basic properties, toxicity, synonyms, molecular structure, and links to full-text articles. Compounds can be searched and located by their names, synonyms, molecular formulas, occupational exposure limits, and other properties. Available through Knovel (Norwich, N.Y.: Knovel, 2003–).

1533 IUPAC glossary of terms used in toxicology. John H. Duffus, Monica Nordberg, Douglas M. Templeton, National Library of Medicine (U.S.). 2007. Bethesda, Md.: National Library of Medicine. http://sis.nlm.nih.gov/enviro/iupacglossary/frontmatter. html.

International Union of Pure and Applied Chemistry (IUPAC).

Originally publ. (print and online) in *Pure and applied chemistry* 79(7) 2007: 1153–1344.

1st ed., 1993, had title *Glossary for chemists of terms used in toxicology*, publ. (print and online) in *Pure and applied chemistry* 65(9) 1993: 2003–2122 (http://sis.nlm.nih.gov/enviro/glossarymain.html).

This 2nd ed. contains newly coined and redefined terms, with explanatory notes, from many disciplines that contribute to toxicology. Includes many medical terms, a list of abbreviations and acronyms used in the toxicology literature and names of international bodies and legislation, classification of carcinogenicity, and other related terminology. Includes bibliographical references.

1534 Lewis' dictionary of toxicology. Robert A. Lewis. 1127 p. Boca Raton, Fla.: Lewis, 1998. ISBN: 1566702232.

615.9003   RA1193.L48

Alphabetical arrangement. Contains common terms and definitions used in toxicology, environmental sciences, and many related fields. Cross-references for synonyms and related entries. For researchers and students.

Directories

1535 DIRLINE. National Institutes of Health (U.S.). [1983?–]. Bethesda, Md.: U.S. National Institutes of Health, Dept. of Health and Human Services. http://dirline.nlm.nih.gov/.

DIRLINE® (Directory of Information Resources Online), maintained by the National Library of Medicine (NLM) (427).

Online annotated directory of organizations, research resources, projects, databases, and other information resources concerned with health and biomedicine from a variety of sources, including federal, state, and local government agencies, academic and research institutions, and also consumer health-related resources such as self-help groups and health hotlines. Resources are mostly from the U.S. but also include some international resources. Currently contains over 8,000 entries, with topics on most diseases and conditions and health services research and technology assessment. Can be searched using MeSH® (Medical Subject Headings) (575), keywords, or by name and location of a resource. Detailed information on DIRLINE can be found via a fact sheet prepared by NLM: http://www.nlm.nih.gov/pubs/factsheets/dirlinfs.html.

1536 Poisoning and toxicology handbook. 4th ed. Jerrold B. Leikin, Frank P. Paloucek. xlv, 1331 p., ill. Boca Raton, Fla.: CRC Press/ Taylor & Francis Group, 2008. ISBN: 9781420044.

615.9   RA1215.P65

1st ed., 1998; 3rd ed., 2002.

Contents: sec. 1, "Medicinal agents"; sec. 2, "Nonmedicinal agents"; sec. 3, "Biological agents"; sec. 4, "Herbal agents"; sec. 5, "Antidotes and drugs used in toxicology"; sec. 6, "Diagnostic tests/procedures"; appendix; index.

Provides detailed information on approx. 900 drugs and poisons, including environmental toxins, and related special topics and resources. Includes listings of U.S. poison control centers and organizations that offer toxicology and teratology information services.

TOXICOLOGY

691

Encyclopedias

1537 Encyclopedia of clinical toxicology: A comprehensive guide and reference to the toxicology of prescription and OTC drugs, chemicals, herbals, plants, fungi, marine life, reptiles and insect venoms, food ingredients, clothing, and environmental toxins. Irving S. Rossoff. xiv, 1507 p. Boca Raton, Fla.: Parthenon, 2002. ISBN: 1842141015.

615.9003   RA1193.R67

Approx. 6,000 alphabetically-arranged entries on toxic substances that adversely affect or destroy health or cause death. Mainly human data, with data on animals where insufficient data on human toxicity are available. Entries mention synonyms and use, toxic effects, and treatment, where appropriate. An appendix, "Alternative nomenclature," functions as an index.

1538 Encyclopedia of toxicology. 2nd ed. Philip Wexler, Bruce D. Anderson, Ann de Peyster. Boston: Elsevier Academic, 2005. ISBN: 0127453512.

1st ed., 1998.

Contents: v. 1, A–Dib; v. 2, Dib–L; v. 3, M–Ser; v. 4, Sev–Z, index.

Comprehensive survey of toxicology, with approx. 1,150 entries. Provides an introduction to the different areas of toxicology and includes experimental, applied, and regulatory toxicology entries. Contains entries on the Chernobyl and Three-Mile Island incidents, a history of the U.S. environmental movement, and also new areas such as computational toxicology, nonlethal weapons, and others. A–Z arrangement, cross-references, and references to primary and secondary literature. Index. Online edition available via Elsevier ScienceDirect.

1539 Encyclopedic reference of immunotoxicology. Hans-Werner Vohr. xxi, 730 p., ill. (some color). Berlin; New York: Springer, 2005. ISBN: 3540441727.

616.07903   QR180.4.E55

"Immunotoxicology focuses on the undesirable effects of chemicals on the immune system. The exposure of humans to such agents may be intentional (drugs) or unintentional (environment). The side effects may lead to over-activation of the immune system, or equally to immunosuppression. The end points of dysregulation therefore also varies: allergies, cancer, autoimmunity, poor resistance to infection."—*Pref.* Intended for scientists and advanced students. Also available online.

1540 Essentials of medical geology: Impacts of the natural environment on public health. O. Selinus, B. J. Alloway. xiv, 812 p., ill. (some color). Amsterdam, [The Netherlands]; Boston: Elsevier Academic Press, 2005. ISBN: 0126363412.

614.42   RA566.E87

Contents: sec. 1, "Medical geology: Perspectives and prospects"; sec. 2, "Pathways and exposures"; sec. 3, "Environmental toxicology, pathology, and medical geology"; sec. 4, "Techniques and tools"; appendixes: (A) international reference values; (B) Web links; (C) glossary.

Medical geology, considered an emerging discipline, is defined by the International Working Group on Medical Geology as the science dealing with the relationship between natural geological factors and health in man and animals. Chapters address such topics as natural distribution and abundance of elements, uptake of elements from a chemical or biological point of view, geological impacts on nutrition, volcanic emissions and health, radon in air and water, arsenic in groundwater and the environment, fluoride in natural waters, water hardness and health effects, GIS in human health studies, and histochemical and microprobe analysis in medical geology. Reference tables, graphics, and maps. Index. Available online via Knovel (Norwich, N.Y.: Knovel, 2003–) and netLibrary.

1541 Patty's toxicology. 5th ed. Eula Bingham, Barbara Cohrssen, Charles H. Powell. 9 v., ill., maps. New York: Wiley, 2001. ISBN: 0471319430.

613.62   RA1229.P38

Previous editions had title *Industrial hygiene and toxicology*. Now publ. separately as *Patty's industrial hygiene* (1556) and *Patty's toxicology*.

Contents: v. 1, toxicology issues, inorganic particulates, dusts, products of biological origin, and pathogens; v. 2, toxicological issues related to metals; neurotoxicology and radiation metals and metal compounds; v. 3, metals and metal compounds; compounds of inorganic nitrogen, carbon, oxygen, and halogens; v. 4, hydrocarbons, organic nitrogen compounds; v. 5, organic halogenated hydrocarbons, aliphatic carboxylic acids, ethers, aldehydes; v. 6, ketones, alcohols, esters, epoxy compounds, organic peroxides; v. 7, glycols and glycol ethers, synthetic polymers, organic sulfur compounds, organic phosphates; v. 8, physical agents, interactions, mixtures, populations at risk, United States and international standards; v. 9, cumulative indexes, v. 1–8.

Standard reference for occupational health and toxicology professionals, with comprehensive toxicological data for industrial compounds. Entries include CAS numbers, physical and chemical properties, threshold limit values (TLVs), permissible exposure limits (PELs), maximum workplace concentrates (MAK), and biological tolerance values for occupational exposures (BAT) for each compound.

Also available online from Wiley and Knovel (Norwich, N.Y.: Knovel, 2003–).

Guides

1542 Information resources in toxicology. 3rd ed. Philip Wexler, P. J. Hakkinen, Gerald L. Kennedy. xxviii, 921 p. San Diego, Calif.: Academic Press, 2000. ISBN: 0127447709.

615.9007   RA1193.3.I574

1st ed., 1982; 2nd ed., 1988.

Enlarged and updated edition. A selective guide to the major print and nonprint media resources and online sources of information. Contains annotated bibliographies of books by subject and listing of journals, organizations, audiovisuals, and Internet and other digital resources. New chapters have been added and cover, for example, publishers, grants, and other funding opportunities, assessment of physical hazards, patent literature, technical reports, and an overview of international activities. Ch. 1–21 are devoted to U.S. resources, ch. 22–25 to international resources. Appendix 1 is "Glossary of terms used in toxicology," and Appendix 2 provides "Career opportunities in toxicology." Index. Available online via publisher and netLibrary.

Handbooks

1543 Casarett and Doull's toxicology: The basic science of poisons. 7th ed. Louis J. Casarett, Curtis D. Klaassen. New York: McGraw-Hill, 2007. ISBN: 9780071470.

615.9   RA1211.C296

1st ed., 1975, had title *Toxicology: The basic science of poisons*; 6th ed., 2001.

A standard toxicology text, in seven units: (1) "General principles of toxicology"; (2) "Disposition of toxicants"; (3) "Non-organ-directed toxicity (carcinogenicity, mutagenicity, and teratogenicity)"; (4) "Target organ toxicity"; (5) "Toxic agents"; (6) "Environmental toxicology"; (7) "Applications of toxicology."

Detailed contents:http://www.loc.gov/catdir/toc/ecip0715/2007015656.html.

This updated edition covers the latest advances in molecular biology and pharmacogenetics and also includes new content (e.g., on chemical terrorism). Contains a brief history of toxicology, "Recommended limits for occupational exposure to chemicals"; Threshold Limit Values (TLV); and Permissible Exposure Limits (PEL). References include Internet sites. Written for graduate students and research scientists. Available as an e-book.

1544 Clarke's analysis of drugs and poisons: In pharmaceuticals, body fluids and postmortem material. 3rd ed. Anthony C. Moffat, M. David Osselton, B. Widdop, E. G. C. Clarke. 2 v. (xii, 3–564, viii, 567–1935, llxxxiv p.), ill. London: Pharmaceutical Press, 2004. ISBN: 0853694737.

1st ed., 1969–75, and 2nd ed., 1986, had title *Clarke's isolation and identification of drugs in pharmaceuticals, body fluids, and post-mortem material.*

Contents: v. 1, analytical toxicology; methodology and analytical techniques; v. 2, drug and poison monographs (1,737); indexes of analytical and toxicological data.

This revised and expanded edition provides analytical procedures used in analytical toxicology and data for drugs and poisons as well as applications of these techniques in areas such as forensic toxicology, workplace drug testing, drug abuse in sports, pesticide poisoning, and others. Drug and poison monographs provide physical properties, analytical methods, pharmacokinetic data, and toxicity data. Mass spectra are included within the monographs. Indexes of analytical data include CAS numbers, molecular formulas, therapeutic classes, color tests, molecular weights, melting points, thin-layer chromatographic data, gas chromatographic (GC) data, high-performance liquid chromatographic (HPLC) data, ultraviolet absorption maxima, infrared peaks, mass spectral data of drugs and pesticides, reagents, E numbers (i.e., for food additives approved in the European Union), and a medical glossary. Subject index covering both volumes at the end of v. 1 as well as v. 2. Intended for use primarily by forensic toxicologists, pathologists, and other scientists and students in these areas of study. Available online as part of MedicinesComplete (1236).

1545 Comprehensive toxicology. I. Glenn Sipes, Charlene A. McQueen, A. Jay Gandolfi. 14 v., ill. New York: Pergamon, 1997–2002. ISBN: 0080423019.

615.9 RA1199.C648

Contents: v. 1, General principles; v. 2, Toxicological testing and evaluation; v. 3, Biotransformation; v. 4, Toxicology of the hematopoietic system; v. 5, Toxicology of the immune system; v. 6, Cardiovascular toxicology; v. 7, Renal toxicology; v. 8, Toxicology of the respiratory system; v. 9, Hepatic and gastrointestinal toxicology; v. 10, Reproductive and endocrine toxicology; v. 11, Nervous system and behavioral toxicology; v. 12, Chemical carcinogens and anticarcinogens; v. 13, Indexes; v. 14, Cellular and molecular toxicology.

This reference work provides a comprehensive review of toxicology, presenting biological effects of toxicants across the different areas of toxicology, with emphasis on the action of chemicals on human systems. Each chapter contains a listing of peer-reviewed articles, reviews, and related websites.
Also available on CD-ROM.

1546 Environmental toxicants: Human exposures and their health effects. 2nd ed. Morton Lippmann. xvii, 987 p., ill. New York: Wiley, 2000. ISBN: 0471292982.

616.98   RA565.E58

Rev. and expanded edition; 1st ed., 1992.

Contents: ch. 1, "Introduction and background"; ch. 2, "Ambient particulate matter"; ch. 3, "Asbestos and other mineral and vitreous fibers"; ch. 4, "Benzene"; ch. 5, "Carbon monoxide"; ch. 6, "Chromium"; ch. 7, "Diesel exhaust"; ch. 8, "Dioxins and dioxin-like chemicals"; ch. 9, "Drinking water disinfection"; ch. 10, "Environmental tobacco smoke"; ch. 11, "Food constituents, additives, and contaminants"; ch. 12, "Formaldehyde and other aldehydes"; ch. 13, "Indoor bioaerosol contaminants"; ch. 14, "Lead and compounds"; ch. 15, "Human-made ionizing radiation and radioactivity: Sources, levels, and effects"; ch. 16, "Mercury"; ch. 17, "Microwaves and electromagnetic fields"; ch. 18, "Nitrogen oxides"; ch. 19, "Noise: Its effects and control"; ch. 20, "Ozone"; ch. 21, "Pesticides"; ch. 22, "Radon and daughters"; ch. 23, "Sulfur oxides: Acidic aerosols and SO2"; ch. 24, "Trace elements: Aluminum, arsenic, cadmium, and nickel"; ch. 25, "Ultraviolet radiation"; ch. 26, "Volatile organic compounds and the sick building syndrome"; ch. 27, "Perspectives on individual and community risks"; ch. 28, "Reducing risks: An environmental engineering perspective"; ch. 29, "Clinical perspective on respiratory toxicology"; ch. 30, "Industrial perspectives: Translating the knowledge base into corporate policies, programs, and practices for health protection."

Presents information "on the effects of human exposure to selected chemicals and physical agents in nonoccupational environments, exploring such issues as individual and community risk, environmental engineering for risk reduction, pulmonary medicine, and lessons learned in the industrial sector."—*Publ. notes*

1547 Goldfrank's toxicologic emergencies. 8th ed. Lewis R. Goldfrank, Neal Flomenbaum. xxxii, 1981 p., ill. New York: McGraw-Hill, 2006. ISBN: 0071437630.

615.9   RA1224.5.G65

1st ed., 1978, had title *Toxicologic emergencies: A handbook in problem solving*; 7th ed., 2002.

Guide to medical toxicology from a clinical perspective, with coverage of toxicologic emergencies (e.g., various medications, food poisoning, heavy metals, household toxins, toxic envenomations, etc.) and bioterrorism. Detailed information on how toxins affect the body and each organ in the body, with treatment guidelines, including use of antidotes. Includes "preventive, psychosocial, nursing, epidemiologic, research and legal perspectives."—*Table of contents*. Also provides a historical perspective. A website is associated with this edition. Color plates (plants, mushrooms, spiders, snakes, marine life, dermatologic reactions). Includes bibliographical references and index. A condensed version, *Goldfrank's manual of toxicologic emergencies* (New York: McGraw-Hill Medical, 2007), is also available. Various eds. available online via Knovel (Norwich, N.Y.: Knovel, 2003–) and Stat!Ref.

Several other major publications in this area, publ. since 2000, include, for example, *Critical care toxicology: Diagnosis and management of the poisoned patient*, Dart's *Medical toxicology*, Ford's *Clinical toxicology*, and Haddad and Winchester's *Clinical management of poisoning and drug overdose*.

1548   Handbook of industrial toxicology and hazardous materials.
Nicholas P. Cheremisinoff. vi, 914 p., ill. New York: Marcel Dekker, 1999. ISBN: 0824719352.

615.902   RA1229.C472

Provides concise health and safety information for commercial chemicals and the health risks associated with them. For toxicologists, chemists, chemical engineers, and laboratory technicians. Includes information on safe handling and transportation of chemicals, worker protection, and emergency responses to spills. Alphabetically-arranged glossary. Available online via netLibrary.

1549   Handbook of pesticide toxicology. 2nd ed. Robert Irving Krieger. 2 v. (xxxiv, 1908 p.), ill. San Diego, [Calif.]: Academic Press, 2001. ISBN: 0124262600.

615.951   RA1270.P4H36

A major work on pesticide toxicology, with separate volumes on principles and agents. The 88 chapters are equally distributed between the two volumes. Many chapters contain numerous drawings of chemical structures, as well as other illustrations, photographs, and tables. Each chapter has an extensive bibliography. Index. Also available online via publisher.

1550 Handbook of poisoning: Prevention, diagnosis, and treatment.
13th ed. Bev-Lorraine True, Robert H. Dreisbach. viii, 696 p., ill.
Pearl River, N.Y.: Parthenon, 2001. ISBN: 1850700389.

615.9   RA1215.T78

1st ed., 1955; 12th ed., 1987. Description based on 13th ed., 2002. Title varies; also called *Dreisbach's handbook of poisoning: Prevention, diagnosis and treatment.*

Contents: (1) "General considerations"; (2) "Agricultural poisons"; (3) "Industrial hazards"; (4) "Household hazards: Cosmetics, food poisoning, miscellaneous chemicals"; (5) "Medicinal poisons"; (6) "Animal and plant hazards: Reptiles, arachnids and insects, marine animals, plants."

Updated and revised edition, designed as a ready-reference manual. Contains concise information for the diagnosis and treatment of poisoning. Also provides general information about prevention of poisoning and guidelines for consultations with medical toxicologists and regional information centers. For physicians and other health professionals. Bibliographic references contain listings of information resources about poisons and selected references for specific poisons. Also includes substances banned in the U.S. Index.

1551 Handbook of toxicologic pathology. 2nd ed. Wanda M. Haschek, Colin George Rousseaux, Matthew A. Wallig. 2 v., ill. San Diego: Academic Press, 2002. ISBN: 0123302153.

615.9   RA1211.H3196

1st ed., 1991.

Vol. 1, *General toxicologic pathology*, provides an overview of the basic practice and the special techniques employed; also covered are risk assessment, experimental design, and statistical analysis. Contains several chapters on specific classes of environmental toxicants, for example, endocrine disruptors and heavy metals. Vol. 2, *Organ specific toxicologic pathology*, presents information in a standardized format, covering the different organ systems and the effects of toxic injury on a particular system. Available online via ScienceDirect.

1552 Handbook of toxicology. 2nd ed. Michael J. Derelanko, Mannfred A. Hollinger. 1414 p., ill. Boca Raton, Fla.: CRC Press, 2002. ISBN: 0849303702.

615.9   RA1215.C73

Updated and enlarged edition of *CRC handbook of toxicology*, 1995.

Designed to locate basic toxicological information quickly. Organized into 33 chapters, with data arranged by toxicology subspecialty. Each chapter begins with a detailed listing of information presented. Most of the information is provided in tables and figures. This edition has expanded coverage of inhalation toxicology, neurotoxicology, and histopathology and several new regulatory chapters (on pesticides, medical devices, consumer products, and worldwide notification of new chemicals). Also new is the addition of information on ecotoxicology, in vitro toxicology, and basic male and female endocrinology and an overview of the toxicology of metals. Provides information on the care and use of laboratory animals. Bibliographical references and websites for further information. For professionals and students. Includes useful information for nontoxicologists in the areas of health, safety, and the environment. Index.

Available online via netLibrary and CRCnetBase (Boca Raton, Fla.; London: CRC Press; Taylor and Francis).

1553 Handbook on the toxicology of metals. 3rd ed. Gunnar Nordberg. xlvii, 975 p., ill. Burlington, Mass.: Academic Press, 2007. ISBN: 9780123694.

615.9253   RA1231.M52.H36

1st ed., 1979; 2nd ed., 1986.

Comprehensive review of the effects of metals and metallic elements and compounds on biological systems, with emphasis on their toxic effects on human health. Provides access to basic toxicological data and also a general introduction to the toxicology of metallic compounds. Contains chapters on carcinogenicity of metal compounds, reproductive and developmental toxicity of metals, diagnosis and treatment of metal poisoning, principles for prevention of the toxic effects of metals, etc. Includes bibliographical references and index. Considered a standard work for physicians, toxicologists, and biomedical engineers.

1554 Hazardous chemicals desk reference. 5th ed. Richard J. Lewis. xx, 1695 p. New York: Wiley, 2002. ISBN: 0471441651.

604.7   T55.3.H3.L49

1st ed., 1987; 4th ed., 1997.

A compilation of basic hazard data concerning approx. 5,000 chemicals, extracted from *Sax's dangerous properties of industrial materials* (1559). Typical entries, filed alphabetically by compound name, include CAS registry number, molecular formula, molecular weight, synonyms, a "hazard rating" on a scale of 1–3 (where 3 is high hazard) or "D" if the data are insufficient, Department of Transportation (DOT) hazard code and classification, physical properties, indication of availability or consensus reports (such as from the World Health Organization, International

Agency for Research on Cancer, etc.), and a "safety profile" (a summary of reported hazards). Synonyms in English and also in Dutch, French, German, Italian, Japanese, and Polish. CAS number cross-index; synonym cross-index; DOT guide number cross-index.

1555 NLM training manuals and resources. National Library of Medicine (U.S.). 2003–. Bethesda, Md.: National Library of Medicine. http://www.nlm.nih.gov/pubs/web_based.html.

Produced by National Library of Medicine (NLM) (427).

Provides access to online training materials used in conjunction with classes and courses offered by the National Training Center and Clearinghouse (NTCC), e.g., for PubMed (432), NLM Gateway (429), ClinicalTrials.gov (191), TOXNET (1580), Unified Medical Language System (UMLS) (89), and others.

1556 Patty's industrial hygiene. 5th ed. Robert L. Harris, F. A. Patty. 4 v., ill. New York: Wiley, 2000. ISBN: 0471297569.

613.62   RC967.P37

Previous editions had title *Industrial hygiene and toxicology*. Now publ. separately as *Patty's industrial hygiene* and *Patty's toxicology* (1541).

Contents: v. 1, "Introduction to industrial hygiene"; "Recognition and evaluation of chemical agents"; v. 2, "Physical agents"; "Biohazards"; "Engineering control and personal protection"; v. 3, "Law, regulation, and management"; v. 4, "Specialty areas and allied professions."

Standard reference for occupational health and toxicology professionals. Also available online from Wiley (http://www3.interscience.wiley.com/cgi-bin/mrwhome/104554794/HOME) and Knovel (Norwich, N.Y.: Knovel, 2003–).

1557 Poisoning and toxicology handbook. 4th ed. Jerrold B. Leikin, Frank P. Paloucek. xlv, 1331 p., ill. Boca Raton, Fla.: CRC Press/ Taylor & Francis Group, 2008. ISBN: 9781420044.

615.9   RA1215.P65

1st ed., 1998; 3rd ed., 2002.

Contents: sec. 1, "Medicinal agents"; sec. 2, "Nonmedicinal agents"; sec. 3, "Biological agents"; sec. 4, "Herbal agents"; sec. 5, "Antidotes and drugs used in toxicology"; sec. 6, "Diagnostic tests/procedures"; appendix; index.

Provides detailed information on approx. 900 drugs and poisons, including environmental toxins, and related special topics and resources.

Includes listings of U.S. poison control centers and organizations that offer toxicology and teratology information services.

1558 Proctor and Hughes' chemical hazards of the workplace. 5th ed.
     Nick H. Proctor, James P. Hughes, Gloria J. Hathaway. xi, 785 p.
     Hoboken, N.J.: Wiley-Interscience, 2004.

615.902   RA1229.P76

1st ed., 1978; 4th ed., 1996.

Contents: (1) "Introduction: Toxicological concepts"; (2) "The chemical hazards"; (3) "CAS number index"; (4) "Index of compounds and synonyms." Detailed contents at http://www.loc.gov/catdir/toc/ ecip0410/2003024018.html.

Covers the effects on human health of chemicals likely to be encountered in various places of work. Each monograph includes chemical formula, CAS number, Threshold Limit Value, synonyms for the chemical, physical properties, uses, routes of exposure, toxicological information, carcinogenicity, mutagenicity, fetotoxicity, clinical effects of overexposure and treatment, and significant odor characteristics. For health professionals and students. Available online from Wiley (http://www3.interscience. wiley.com/cgi-bin/bookhome/109871799).

Other titles in this area include, for example, *Sittig's handbook of toxic and hazardous chemicals and carcinogens* (Norwich, N.Y., U.S.A: Noyes Publications, 2002) and *Sax's dangerous properties of industrial materials* (1559).

1559 Sax's dangerous properties of industrial materials. 11th ed ed.
     Richard J.; Lewis, N. Irving Sax. 3 v. Hoboken, N.J.: J. Wiley &
     Sons, 2004–. ISBN: 0471476625.

604.7   T55.3.H3L494

1st ed., 1957 had title *Dangerous properties of industrial materials*; 10th ed., 2000.

Contents: v. I, section 1: DOT Guide number cross-index; section 2: CAS Registry cross-index; section 3: Synonym cross-index; section 4: References; v. II, General chemicals: entries A–G; v. III, General chemicals: entries H–Z.

A standard compilation of hazardous properties, covering some 25,962 materials, with 2,597 new in this edition. Vol. 1 includes an introduction explaining the entries, formats, sources, and codes. It also lists full references corresponding to the alphanumeric codes used in the entries. New in this edition are "immediately dangerous to life or health concentrations (IDLHs)" for 1,035 substances. Vols. 2 and 3 contain the entries, alphabetical by substance name; typical entries include synonyms, molecular formula, molecular weight, CAS Registry Number, a "hazard rating" (HR) of 1–3 (or "D" if there is insufficient data), properties, toxicity data with references, references to consensus reports in the literature, a Department of Transportation hazard code, and standards and recommendations from various agencies (OSHA, NIOSH, DOT, etc.) as to toxic concentrations. Most entries are one or two paragraphs; a few, such as DDT, run one or two pages. Available in CD-ROM format and online via Wiley Interscience and Knovel (Norwich, N.Y.: Knovel, 2003–). A related title is *Hazardous chemicals desk reference* (1554).

1560 Sittig's handbook of toxic and hazardous chemicals and carcinogens. 5th ed. Richard P. Pohanish, Marshall Sittig. 2 v. (xxiv, 2854 p.). Norwich, N.Y.: William Andrew, 2008. ISBN: 9780815515.

615.902   RA1215.S58

1st ed., 1981, had title *Handbook of toxic and hazardous chemicals*; 2nd ed., 1985; 3rd ed., 1991, had title: *Handbook of toxic and hazardous chemicals and carcinogens*; 4th ed., 2001 (also available online via Knovel [Norwich, N.Y.: Knovel, 2003–]).

Vol. 1, A–H; v. 2, I–Z.

Contents: "How to use this book"; "Key to abbreviations, symbols, and acronyms"; "Pesticide records A to Z"; bibliography; "General guide to chemical resistance gloves"; appendixes: (1) "Oxidizing materials"; (2) "Carcinogens, confirmed and suspected"; (3) glossary; synonym and trade name index-cross index; CAS number-cross index.

This updated edition presents concise chemical and safety information for approx. 2,100 toxic and hazardous chemicals, giving for each substance a code number, such as CAS (Chemical Abstract Service) number; RTECS number; DOT designation; EC (Commission of the European Communities); synonyms; potential exposure; incompatibilities; permissible exposure limits and determination in water; routes of entry, harmful effects, symptoms, points of attack, medical surveillance, first aid, decontamination, personal protective methods, etc.; suggested disposal method; and references for, about, and to sources of more information. Contains a glossary of chemical, health, safety, medical, and environmental terms used in this handbook. Useful reference for a variety of professions, including emergency response personnel, toxicologists, occupational doctors and nurses, special, technical, and university librarians, and many others (see *Pref.*).

Indexes; Abstract journals; Databases

1561 CCOHS. Canadian Centre for Occupational Health and Safety. 1999–. Hamilton, Ontario, [Canada]: Canadian Centre for Occupational Health and Safety. http://www.ccohs.ca/.

T55

Similar to TOXNET (1580), the CCOHS site makes available a variety of occupational health and safety information. Data collections allow retrieval of aggregated information using simple chemical name searches. Access to the complete search features of CCOHS is by subscription, but much of the data is free of charge.

1562 CCRIS (Chemical carcinogenesis research information system). National Library of Medicine (U.S.). 1990s. Bethesda, Md.: National Library of Medicine. http://toxnet.nlm.nih.gov/cgi-bin/sis/htmlgen?CCRIS.

Part of TOXNET (1580). Developed and maintained by the National Cancer Institute (NCI) (166).

Currently contains approx. 9,000 chemical records with carcinogenicity, mutagenicity, tumor promotion, and tumor inhibition test results. Includes data from studies cited in primary journals, NCI reports, and other special sources. Test results have been reviewed by experts. For additional details, see TOXNET fact sheet at http://www.nlm.nih.gov/pubs/factsheets/toxnetfs.html.

1563 ChemIDplus. National Library of Medicine (U.S.). Bethesda, Md.: National Library of Medicine. http://sis.nlm.nih.gov/chemical.html.

Part of TOXNET (1580).

Database providing chemical synonyms, structures, regulatory list information, and access to structure and nomenclature authority databases used for the identification of chemical substances cited in the various NLM databases. Provides structure searching and direct links to many biomedical resources at NLM and on the Internet for chemicals of interest. More than 349,000 chemical records, of which more than 56,000 include chemical structures; searchable by name, synonym, CAS registry number, molecular formula, classification code, and structure (see TOXNET fact sheet at http://www.nlm.nih.gov/pubs/factsheets/toxnetfs.html).

1564 DART/ETIC (Developmental and Reproductive Toxicology/ Environmental Teratology Information Center database). Institute of Environmental Health Sciences, National Center for Toxicological Research. Bethesda, Md.: National Library of Medicine. http://toxnet.nlm.nih.gov/cgi-bin/sis/htmlgen?DARTETIC.

DART/ETIC is part of TOXNET (1580).

Bibliographic database covering literature published since 1965 on reproductive and developmental toxicology. For additional details, see TOXNET fact sheet at http://www.nlm.nih.gov/pubs/factsheets/toxnetfs. html.

1565 The dictionary of substances and their effects. S. Gangolli, Royal Society of Chemistry (Great Britain). [2005]. London: Royal Society of Chemistry. http://www.knovel.com/knovel2/Toc. jsp?BookID=527.

615.9003   RA1193.D53

1st ed., 1992; 2nd ed., 1999 (7 v.).

This edition is the updated electronic version of the seven-volume print edition. Continually updated, with interactive features, contains 5,310 substances. All substances are listed in the searchable interactive table Physical Constants of Chemical Substances, which lists basic properties, toxicity, synonyms, molecular structure, and links to full-text articles. Compounds can be searched and located by their names, synonyms, molecular formulas, occupational exposure limits, and other properties. Available through Knovel (Norwich, N.Y.: Knovel, 2003–).

1566 GENE-TOX (genetic toxicology). National Library of Medicine (U.S.). 1990s–. Bethesda, Md.: National Library of Medicine. http://toxnet.nlm.nih.gov/cgi-bin/sis/htmlgen?GENETOX.

Part of TOXNET (1580). Created by the U.S. Environmental Protection Agency (EPA).

A database of genetic toxicology (mutagenicity) test results, containing information on approx. 3,000 chemicals. For additional details, see TOXNET fact sheet at http://www.nlm.nih.gov/pubs/factsheets/toxnetfs. html.

1567 Haz-Map. National Library of Medicine (U.S.). 2000–. Bethesda, Md.: National Library of Medicine. http://hazmap.nlm.nih.gov/.

Haz-Map is part of TOXNET (1580).

An occupational toxicology database designed for health and safety professionals and consumers seeking information about the health effects of exposure to chemicals and biological agents at work. For additional details, see TOXNET fact sheet at http://www.nlm.nih.gov/pubs/factsheets/toxnetfs.html.

1568 Household products database. Specialized Information Services, National Library of Medicine (U.S.). Bethesda, Md: Specialized Information Services, U.S. National Library of Medicine, National Institutes of Health, Dept. of Health & Human Services. http://householdproducts.nlm.nih.gov/.

TS175

Part of TOXNET® (1580).

Provides information on potential health effects and composition of chemicals contained in common household products. Includes reference to health effects information contained in Material Safety Data Sheets (MSDS). Products can also be searched by type, manufacturer, product ingredient/chemical name, and by health effects. Additional details concerning this resource can be found via TOXNET fact sheet at http://www.nlm.nih.gov/pubs/factsheets/toxnetfs.html.

1569 HSDB (Hazardous substances data bank). National Library of Medicine (U.S.). 1990s. Bethesda, Md.: National Library of Medicine. http://toxnet.nlm.nih.gov.

Part of TOXNET (1580).

Factual database providing toxicology information relating to approx. 5,000 potentially hazardous chemicals, including information on human exposure, industrial hygiene, emergency handling procedures, environmental fate, regulatory requirements, and related areas. Data are fully referenced and peer reviewed by expert scientists. Further details are provided via the TOXNET fact sheet at http://www.nlm.nih.gov/pubs/factsheets/toxnetfs.html.

1570 IRIS (Integrated risk information system). National Library of Medicine (U.S.). Bethesda, Md.: National Library of Medicine. http://toxnet.nlm.nih.gov/cgi-bin/sis/htmlgen?IRIS.

A database from the U.S. Environmental Protection Agency (EPA). Part of TOXNET (1580).

Toxicology data in support of human health risk assessments for more than 500 chemicals. Focuses on hazard identification and dose-response

TOXICOLOGY

705

assessment. Also includes carcinogen classifications, unit risks, slope factors, oral reference doses, and inhalation reference concentrations. Produced by the U.S. Environmental Protection Agency (EPA). For further details, see TOXNET fact sheet at http://www.nlm.nih.gov/pubs/factsheets/toxnetfs.html.

1571 ITER (International toxicity estimates for risk). National Library of Medicine (U.S.). 2004(?). Bethesda, Md.: National Library of Medicine. http://toxnet.nlm.nih.gov/cgi-bin/sis/htmlgen?iter.

Part of TOXNET (1580). Compiled by Toxicology Excellence for Risk Assessment (TERA).

Contains chemical data in support of human health risk assessments for more than 600 chemical records. Data, produced by the U.S. Environmental Protection Agency (EPA), several international health organizations, and independent peer-reviewed parties, are presented in side-by-side comparisons. Further details are provided in TOXNET fact sheet at http://www.nlm.nih.gov/pubs/factsheets/toxnetfs.html.

1572 LactMed (Drugs and lactation database). National Library of Medicine (U.S.). 2006–. Bethesda, Md.: National Library of Medicine. http://toxnet.nlm.nih.gov/cgi-bin/sis/htmlgen?LACT.

Part of TOXNET (1580).

Database of drugs and other chemicals to which breastfeeding mothers may be exposed. Data on maternal and infant levels of drugs; possible effects on breastfed infants and on lactation; and alternate drugs to consider. For further details, consult TOXNET fact sheet at http://www.nlm.nih.gov/pubs/factsheets/toxnetfs.html.

1573 LexisNexis environmental. LexisNexis. 2002–. Dayton, Ohio: LexisNexis. http://web.lexis-nexis.com/envuniv/.

Indexes a wide range of publications that explore humans' impact on the environment, emphasizing effects on air, water, and noise pollution, solid and toxic waste, radiological contamination, toxicology, population, endangered species, and climate change. Materials abstracted include journals, technical reports, government publications, and conferences. Full text of indexed reports formerly sold separately as the EnviroFiche microfiche collection. Online access available through LexisNexis.

1574 **Micromedex healthcare series.** Thomson Micromedex. [199?–]. Greenwood Village, Colo.: Thomson Micromedex. http://www. micromedex.com/products/hcs/.

Micromedex Healthcare Series; also called Healthcare Series Online.

Intended for clinicians. Includes a variety of resources for finding information on drugs, toxicology, emergency, acute care, and disease data as well as alternative medicine information. Drug resources include DRUGDEX, DRUG-REAX, IDENTIDEX, IV Index, *Index nominum* (Medpharm Scientific, 2004), *Martindale: The complete drug reference* (1182), *Physicians' desk reference: PDR* (1250), POISINDEX, *Red book* (1255), REPRORISK, and *USP DI* (727). Emergency and disease data can be found, for example, in DISEASEDEX and alternative therapies in AltMedDex and other Thomson products. Searchable across either all databases, by specific database(s), and by groups of databases. Drugs can be searched by trade or generic drug name. Specific drug database search and drug topic search provide, for example, a drug evaluation overview, dosing information, pharmacokinetics, contraindications, precautions, adverse reactions, single and multiple drug interactions, IV compatibility, teratogenicity, therapeutic uses, and comparative efficacy.

A matrix of all Micromedex products and versions in this series, with listing of the individual titles, various format options, and indication of whether a particular title is also available in print can be found at http:// www.micromedex.com/support/faqs/plat_matrix.html. Help with citing the various Micromedex versions is provided at http://www.micromedex. com/about_us/legal/cite/.

1575 **NLM gateway.** National Library of Medicine (U.S.). 2000–. Bethesda, Md.: National Library of Medicine. http://gateway.nlm.nih.gov/.

RA11

Allows simultaneous searching of information resources at the National Library of Medicine (NLM). Databases include MEDLINE (425)/PubMed (432) and the NLM Catalog (482) as well as other resources, including information on current clinical trials and consumer health information (MedlinePlus [463]). Currently provides access to 21 databases and other information resources (for a complete list of databases and other details, see http://www.nlm.nih.gov/pubs/factsheets/gateway.html). An overview of the search results is presented in several categories (bibliographic resources, consumer health resources, and other information), with a listing of the individual databases and the number of results within these categories.

1576 **PubMed.** U.S. National Center for Biotechnology Information, National Library of Medicine, National Institutes of Health. 1996–. Bethesda, Md.: U.S. National Center for Biotechnology Information. http://www.ncbi.nlm.nih.gov/sites/entrez/.

PubMed®, developed and maintained by the National Center for Biotechnology Information (NCBI) at the National Library of Medicine® (NLM) (427). It is available via the NCBI Entrez (3) retrieval system. PubMed also provides access to the other Entrez molecular biology resources (*PubMed Overview*). Starting May 23, 2007, NCBI is changing to a new version of Entrez in a phased implementation (cf. Nahin AM. New and Improved PubMed®/Entrez and New URL *NLM tech. bull.*, 2007 May–Jun.; [356]: http://www.nlm.nih.gov/pubs/techbull/mj07/mj07_issue_cover.html).

Provides a search interface for more than 16 million bibliographic citations and abstracts in the fields of medicine, nursing, dentistry, veterinary medicine, health care systems, and preclinical sciences. It provides access to articles indexed for MEDLINE® (425) and for selected life sciences journals. PubMed subsets found under the "Limits" tab are: MEDLINE and PubMed Central®, several journal groups (i.e., core clinical journals, dental journals, and nursing journals), and topical subsets (AIDS, bioethics, cancer, complementary medicine, history of medicine, space life sciences, systematic reviews, and toxicology). "Linkout" provides access to full-text articles.

For detailed information see the PubMed fact sheet at http://www.nlm.nih.gov/pubs/factsheets/pubmed.html. For a brief overview of searching PubMed, see the PubMed Quick Start at http://www.ncbi.nlm.nih.gov/books/bv.fcgi?rid=helppubmed.section.pubmedhelp.PubMed_Quick_Start. For details on the now completed OLDMEDLINE retrospective conversion projects, see http://www.nlm.nih.gov/pubs/techbull/so06/so06_oldmedline_status.html.

1577 **Specialized Information Services (SIS).** National Library of Medicine (U.S.). Bethesda, Md.: National Library of Medicine. http://sis.nlm.nih.gov.

Specialized Information Services (SIS) is a division of the National Library of Medicine (NLM) (427) and is responsible for information resources and services in toxicology (e.g., TOXNET [1580]) and environmental health (http://sis.nlm.nih.gov/enviro/envirohealthlinks.html). Currently includes 17 topics, such as children's environmental health, indoor and outdoor air pollution, and biological warfare, to name a few; chemical information (ChemIDplus [1563] search system with access to nomenclature and structure authority files used for identification of chemical substances cited in the NLM databases); HIV/AIDS resources (e.g., AIDSinfo [447]); (directories [e.g., DIRLINE [208]); and hotlines (e.g., Health hotlines [http://healthhotlines.nlm.nih.gov/]). Each topic has its own website created for a specific audience (the public, researchers/scientists, health professionals, students/educators, and emergency responders), reference tools, listservs, and additional related links. Also provides websites for and about specific populations and specialized topics in minority health (for example, American Indian health, arctic health, and Asian American health). Further detailed information concerning SIS is provided via a fact sheet by Division of Specialized Information Services at http://www.nlm. nih.gov/pubs/factsheets/sis.html.

1578 **TOXLINE.** National Library of Medicine (U.S.). 1990s–. Bethesda, Md.: National Library of Medicine. http://toxnet.nlm.nih.gov/ cgi-bin/sis/htmlgen?TOXLINE.

Part of TOXNET (1580).

"A bibliographic database providing comprehensive coverage of the biochemical, pharmacological, physiological, and toxicological effects of drugs and other chemicals from 1965 to the present. Contains over 3 million citations, almost all with abstracts and/or index terms and CAS Registry Numbers. *Toxline* references are drawn from sources grouped into two major parts, TOXLINE Core and TOXLINE Special, both of which offer a variety of search and display capabilities."—*TOXNET fact sheet* (http://www.nlm.nih.gov/pubs/factsheets/toxnetfs.html).

1579 **TOXMAP.** National Library of Medicine (U.S.). 1995–. Bethesda, Md.: National Library of Medicine. http://toxmap.nlm.nih.gov/ toxmap/main/index.jsp.

RA1190

As part of TOXNET (1580), TOXMAP addresses toxicology and environmental health information needs. Uses maps of the United States to show the amount and location of toxic chemicals released into the environment. Data shown in TOXMAP come from the U.S. Environmental

Protection Agency's Toxics Release Inventory (TRI) and Superfund Programs (http://www.epa.gov/tri or http://www.epa.gov/superfund/), HSDB (Hazardous Substances Databank) (1569), TOXLINE (1578), Agency for Toxic Substances and Disease Registry (ATSDR) (1397), USGS National Atlas (http://www.nationalatlas.gov), and U.S. Census (http://www.census.gov). Users can create their own geographic region or select from a list of predefined regions. Provides various search options and links to other environmental health and toxicology resources, e.g., Environmental Health and Toxicology (http://toxmap.nlm.nih.gov). For further details, see TOXNET fact sheet (http://www.nlm.nih.gov/pubs/factsheets/toxnetfs.html).

1580 TOXNET (Toxicology data network). National Library of
Medicine (U.S.). 1998–. Bethesda, Md.: National Library of
Medicine. http://toxnet.nlm.nih.gov/.

TOXNET: Toxicology Data Network, part of the Specialized Information Services (SIS) division of the National Library of Medicine (NLM) at http://sis.nlm.nih.gov/, responsible for information resources and services in toxicology, environmental health, chemistry, and other specialized topics.

Managed by the Toxicology and Environmental Health Information Program (TEHIP) of the NLM, TOXNET is a group of searchable databases that can be used separately or in combination (TOXNET Multi-File; http://toxnet.nlm.nih.gov/cgi-bin/sis/htmlgen?Multi) to locate toxicology data, literature references, and information concerning environmental health and toxic release of chemicals. It can also identify chemicals that cause specific effects and provides links to PubMed (432).

TOXNET includes the following databases: ChemIDplus (1563), HSDB (Hazardous Substances Data Bank) (1569), TOXLINE (1578), CCRIS (Chemical Carcinogenesis Research Information System) (1562), DART/ETIC (Developmental and Reproductive Toxicology/Environmental Teratology Information Center database) (1564), GENE-TOX (Genetic Toxicology) (1566), IRIS (Integrated Risk Information System) (1570), ITER (International Toxicity Estimates for Risk) (1571), LactMed (Drugs and Lactation) (1572), Toxics Release Inventory (TRI) (1584), Haz-Map (1567), Household Products Database (1568), and TOXMAP (1579).

1581 ToxSeek. National Library of Medicine (U.S.). 199?–. Bethesda,
Md.: National Library of Medicine. http://toxSeek.nlm.nih.gov.

Produced by National Library of Medicine (NLM); NLM Specialized Information Services (SIS).

Subtitle is Meta-search and Clustering Search engine for Environmental and Health Toxicology.

Searches a large number of biomedical and environmental health resources: 15 NLM/SIS TOXNET (1580) databases, nine other NLM databases, two NIH databases, three international databases, and seven other resources. Detailed information about TOXSEEK at http://toxseek.nlm. nih.gov/toxseek/inc/help/abouttoxseek.jsp.

Internet Resources

1582 Agency for Toxic Substances and Disease Registry (ATSDR).
Agency for Toxic Substances and Disease Registry, U.S.
Department of Health and Human Services. 1999–. Atlanta:
Agency for Toxic Substances and Disease Registry. http://www.
atsdr.cdc.gov/.

Agency for Toxic Substances and Disease Registry (ATSDR), part of U.S. Dept. of Health and Human Services (HHS) (894).

Provides health information and takes public health actions to prevent harmful exposures and diseases related to toxic substances (e.g., recent examples: childhood lead poisoning prevention, drinking water concerns, anticipating the health concerns of climate change, etc.). Includes A–Z index by main topic (http://www.atsdr.cdc.gov/az/a.html), information about toxic substances, various data resources (e.g., access to the Hazardous Substance Release/Health Effects [HazDat] database, National Exposure Registry, and others), emergency response information, hazardous waste sites, a toxic substances portal (http://www.atsdr.cdc.gov/substances/index.html), and many other information sources.

1583 Enviro-health links. National Library of Medicine (U.S.). 2005–.
Bethesda, Md.: National Library of Medicine. http://sis.nlm.nih.
gov/enviro/envirohealthlinks.html.

Part of National Library of Medicine's Specialized Information Services (SIS) Environmental Health and Toxicology program.

Contents: American Indian Health; Arctic Health; Arsenic and Human Health; Asian American Health; Biological Warfare; California Wildfires; Chemical Warfare; Children's Environmental Health Information Resources; Dietary Supplements; EdCoTox; Environmental Justice; Health Effects of the Collapse of the World Trade Center; Hurricanes; Indoor Air Pollution; Keeping the Artist Safe: Hazards of Arts and Crafts Materials; Lead and Human Health; Multi-cultural Resources for Health

Information; Outdoor Air Pollution; Pesticide Exposure; Special Populations: Emergency and Disaster Preparedness (Bethesda, Md.: National Library of Medicine, 2008–); Tox Web Links; Toxicogenomics; West Nile Virus: Pesticides Used for Mosquito Control.

Provides selected links to Internet resources on toxicology and environmental health topics and issues. Includes both NLM and outside resources. Guidelines for the selection of resources outside of NLM are spelled out at http://sis.nlm.nih.gov/enviro/envirohealthlinkscriteria.html.

1584 Toxics release inventory (TRI). National Library of Medicine (U.S.). Bethesda, Md.: National Library of Medicine. http://toxnet.nlm.nih.gov/cgi-bin/sis/htmlgen?TRI.

Part of TOXNET (1580).

"A series of databases that describe the releases of toxic chemicals into the environment annually for the 1987–2004 reporting years. *TRI* is mandated by the Emergency Planning and Community Right-to-Know Act and is based on data submitted to the EPA from industrial facilities throughout the U.S. These data include the names and addresses of those facilities, and the amounts of certain toxic chemicals they release to the air, water, or land, or transfer to waste sites. Information is included on over 650 chemicals and chemical categories. Pollution prevention data are also reported by each facility for each chemical."—*TOXNET fact sheet* at http://www.nlm.nih.gov/pubs/factsheets/toxnetfs.html.

1585 TOXMAP. National Library of Medicine (U.S.). 1995–. Bethesda, Md.: National Library of Medicine. http://toxmap.nlm.nih.gov/toxmap/main/index.jsp.

RA1190

As part of TOXNET (1580), TOXMAP addresses toxicology and environmental health information needs. Uses maps of the United States to show the amount and location of toxic chemicals released into the environment. Data shown in TOXMAP come from the U.S. Environmental Protection Agency's Toxics Release Inventory (TRI) and Superfund Programs (http://www.epa.gov/tri or http://www.epa.gov/superfund/), HSDB (Hazardous Substances Databank) (1569), TOXLINE (1578), Agency for Toxic Substances and Disease Registry (ATSDR) (1397), USGS National Atlas (http://www.nationalatlas.gov), and U.S. Census (http://www.census.gov). Users can create their own geographic region or select from a list of predefined regions. Provides various search options and links to other environmental health and toxicology resources, e.g., Environmental Health and Toxicology (http://toxmap.nlm.nih.gov). For further details, see TOXNET fact sheet (http://www.nlm.nih.gov/pubs/factsheets/toxnetfs.html).

1586 TOXNET (Toxicology data network). National Library of Medicine (U.S.). 1998–. Bethesda, Md.: National Library of Medicine. http://toxnet.nlm.nih.gov/.

TOXNET: Toxicology Data Network, part of the Specialized Information Services (SIS) division of the National Library of Medicine (NLM) at http://sis.nlm.nih.gov/, responsible for information resources and services in toxicology, environmental health, chemistry, and other specialized topics.

Managed by the Toxicology and Environmental Health Information Program (TEHIP) of the NLM, TOXNET is a group of searchable databases that can be used separately or in combination (TOXNET Multi-File; http://toxnet.nlm.nih.gov/cgi-bin/sis/htmlgen?Multi) to locate toxicology data, literature references, and information concerning environmental health and toxic release of chemicals. It can also identify chemicals that cause specific effects and provides links to PubMed (432).

TOXNET includes the following databases: ChemIDplus (1563), HSDB (Hazardous Substances Data Bank) (1569), TOXLINE (1578), CCRIS (Chemical Carcinogenesis Research Information System) (1562), DART/ETIC (Developmental and Reproductive Toxicology/Environmental Teratology Information Center database) (1564), GENE-TOX (Genetic Toxicology) (1566), IRIS (Integrated Risk Information System) (1570), ITER (International Toxicity Estimates for Risk) (1571), LactMed (Drugs and Lactation) (1572), Toxics Release Inventory (TRI) (1584), Haz-Map (1567), Household Products Database (1568), and TOXMAP (1579).

1587 Tox town. National Library of Medicine (U.S.). [2002]–. Bethesda, Md.: National Library of Medicine. http://purl.access.gpo.gov/GPO/LPS70098.

Companion to the TOXNET (1580) collection of databases.

An interactive guide that uses graphics, sounds, and animation to identify the types and sources of commonly encountered toxic substances and how they relate to public health and the environment. TOXNET fact sheet at http://www.nlm.nih.gov/pubs/factsheets/toxnetfs.html contains further details. Intended for students, educators, and the general public.

INDEX

Numbers in **bold** refer to entry numbers. Numbers in light face type refer to mentions in annotations of other works.

A

A to Z drug facts, **1204**

AAMC curriculum directory, **177,** 181, **198,** 205

AAMC data book: Medical schools and teaching hospitals by the numbers, 453, **507**

The ABC clinical guide to herbs, **1202**

ABC of nutrition. 4th ed., **1119**

Academy of General Dentistry, **624,** 772, **777**

ACP Center for Ethics and Professionalism, **606**

ADA/PDR guide to dental therapeutics. 4th ed., **795, 1203**

ADEA official guide to dental schools, **787**

AEGiS, **446**

Aerospace medicine and biology, **437**

African American firsts in science and technology, **43, 775, 1025**

AgeLine, **866**

Agency for Health Care Research and Quality (AHRQ), 537, 715, **733, 872,** 886, 889, 893, 906, 975, **1481**

Agency for Toxic Substances and Disease Registry (ATSDR), **1397, 1582**

AGRICOLA, 293, **1141**

AHA guide to the health care field, **199,** 508, **842**

AHA hospital statistics, 199, **508, 895**

AIDSinfo, **447, 695, 734**

AJCC cancer staging manual. 6th ed., **77,** 81

Alternative medicine, **283, 696**

Alternative medicine resource guide, **284**

AMA manual of style: A guide for authors and editors. 10th ed., **561**

American Academy of Family Physicians, **448, 735, 1482**

American Academy of Pediatrics, **449, 736**

American Cancer Society, **1, 450, 737**

American Dental Association, **738, 778, 802, 816**

American dental directory, **788**

The American dentist: A pictorial history with a presentation of early dental photography in America, **803**

American drug index, **1177**

American health care in transition: A guide to the literature, **825, 1405**

American health: Demographics and spending of health care consumers, **509, 896**

American Health Lawyers Association (AHLA), **1004**

The American Heritage medical dictionary, **91,** 107, 108, 117, **641**

American hospital association, **510, 873**

American Medical Association, **451, 607,** 715, **1005**

American Medical Association complete medical encyclopedia, **652**

American Medical Association family
     medical guide. 4th rev. ed., **697**
American Medical Association
     handbook of first aid and emergency
     care. Rev. ed., **653**
American Medical Association, 704
American Medical Association's
     DoctorFinder, 204, 451
American medical bibliography 1639–
     1783, **7**
American medical imprints, 1820–
     1910, **8**
American nursing: A biographical
     dictionary, **1026**
American nursing: A history. 4th ed.,
     1068
American Psychiatric Association
     (APA), 588, **1390**
American Psychiatric Association
     practice guidelines for the treatment
     of psychiatric disorders, **1338**
American psychiatric glossary. 8th ed.,
     1300
American Public Health Association
     (APHA), **1398**
American surgery: An illustrated
     history, **335**, 348, 361
amfAR, **452, 939, 1483**
An annotated catalogue of medical
     Americana in the Library of the
     Wellcome125 Institute for the
     History of Medicine, **363**
Annual bibliography of significant
     advances in dietary supplement
     research, 765, **1097, 1142**
Annual statistics of medical school
     libraries in the United States and
     Canada, **178, 200**
AOA yearbook and directory, **200, 647**
APA dictionary of psychology, **1301**
Application of the international
     classification of diseases to dentistry

and stomatology: ICD-DA. 3rd ed.,
     78, 84, **776**
Application of the international
     classification of diseases to
     neurology: ICD-NA. 2nd ed., **78**
Arabic medical manuscripts of the
     Wellcome Library: A descriptive
     catalogue of the Haddād Collection
     (WMS 401– 487), **364**
ARBA in-depth: Health and medicine,
     9
Assessment scales in old age psychiatry.
     2nd ed., **1339**
Association of American Medical
     Colleges (AAMC), **453**, 507
Association of Cancer Online
     Resources (ACOR), **739**
Atlas of cancer, **294, 511**
Atlas of cancer mortality in the United
     States, 1950–94, **512**
Attorney's illustrated medical
     dictionary, **969**

B
Bailey and Bishop's notable names in
     medicine and surgery. 4th ed., **44**
Barron's guide to medical and dental
     schools. 11th ed., **202**
Basic resources for pharmacy
     education, **1161**
Bender's dictionary of nutrition and
     food technology. 8th ed., **1098**
Bergey's manual of systematic
     bacteriology. 2nd ed., **295**
Best medical schools, **179, 203**
Bibliography of bioethics, **577, 602**
A bibliography of dentistry in America,
     1790–1840, **804**
A bibliography of medical and
     biomedical biography. 3rd ed., **50**
A bibliography of nursing literature
     1859–1960, **1020**

Bibliography of the history of medicine, **10**

Bibliography of the history of medicine of the United States and Canada, 1939–1960, **365**

A bibliography of the writings of Dr. William Harvey, 1578–1657. 3rd ed., **366**

Bibliotheca Osleriana: A catalogue of books illustrating the history of medicine and science, **367**

Bio-bibliographisches Verzeichnis jü discher Doktoren im 17. und 18. Jahrhundert, **57**

The biochemistry of human nutrition: A desk reference. 2nd ed., **1120**

Biodefense and bioterrorism (MedlinePlus), **740, 1484**

Bioethics information resources, **608**

Bioethics resources on the Web, 608, **609**, 620, **1006**

Bioethicsweb, **610**

Biographical dictionary of medicine, **58**

A biographical dictionary of women healers: Midwives, nurses, and physicians, **59**

Biographical memoirs of fellows of the Royal Society, 50, **54**

Biographical memoirs of the National Academy of Sciences, 50, **71**

Biographisches Lexikon der hervorragenden Ärzte aller Zeiten und Völker. 2. Aufl . ed., **60**

BioLaw: A legal and ethical reporter on medicine, health care, and bioengineering, **585, 980**

Biomedical abbreviation server, **112**

The biomedical engineering handbook. 3rd ed., **296**

Biomedical informatics: Computer applications in health care and biomedicine. 3rd ed., **297**

BIOSIS previews, **410**

Bioterrorism and public health: An Internet resource guide, **1439**

Bioterrorism: Guidelines for medical and public health management, **1440**

The bioterrorism sourcebook, **298, 1444**

Blacks in science and medicine, **45**

Black's medical dictionary. 41st ed., **92, 1029**

The Blackwell companion to medical sociology, **849, 921, 1441**

The Blackwell dictionary of neuropsychology, **1302**

The Blackwell guide to medical ethics, **584, 979**

Botanical medicines: The desk reference for major herbal supplements. 2nd ed., **1205**

Bowes and Church's food values of portions commonly used, **1121**

British national formulary, **1178**

The British pharmacopoeia, **1179**

Burger's medicinal chemistry and drug discovery. 6th ed., **1206**

C

CAB abstracts, **1143**

CAM on PubMed, **411**

The Cambridge dictionary of statistics. 3rd ed., **513**

The Cambridge dictionary of statistics in the medical sciences, **514**

Cambridge handbook of psychology, health, and medicine. 2nd ed., **1340**

The Cambridge historical dictionary of disease, **93, 336**

The Cambridge illustrated history of medicine, **389**

The Cambridge world history of food, **1122**

The Cambridge world history of human disease, **337**, 343

Campbell's psychiatric dictionary. 9th
ed., **1303**
Canadian medical directory, **180**
The cancer dictionary. 3rd ed., **132, 642**
Cancer facts and figures, **515**
The cancer handbook. 2nd ed., **299**
Cancer.gov, **438, 454,** 465, 636, **741**
Casarett and Doull's toxicology: The
basic science of poisons. 7th ed., **1543**
Catalog of biographies, **61**
Catalog of human cancer genes:
McKusick's Mendelian inheritance
in man for clinical and research
oncologists (onco-MIM), **300**
A catalogue of printed books in the
Wellcome Historical Medical
Library, **368**
A catalogue of seventeenth century
printed books in the National
Library of Medicine, **11, 369**
Catalog of teratogenic agents. 12th ed.,
1207
Catalogue of Western manuscripts on
medicine and science in the Wellcome
Historical Medical Library, **370**
CCOHS, **1561**
CCRIS (Chemical carcinogenesis
research information system), **1562**
CDC: Emergency preparedness and
response, **1485**
CDC WONDER, 530, 534, **1399**
CDT: Current dental terminology, **779,
796**
Celebrating nursing history, **1021, 1069**
Centers for Disease Control and
Prevention (U.S.), 465, 633, 636,
740, 916, **940, 1486,** 1518
Centers for Medicare and Medicaid
services (U.S.), 723, **742, 874**
A Century of Black surgeons: The
U.S.A. experience. 1st ed., **72**
A century of Nobel prize recipients:
Chemistry, physics, and medicine,
62

A century of psychiatry, **1375**
Chemical Abstracts Service source
index, **34,** 434
ChemIDplus, **1563**
Chiropractic: History and evolution of
a new profession, **390**
Chronicles of pharmacy, **1262**
A chronology of medicine and related
sciences, **371**
Churchill Livingstone's dictionary of
nursing. 19th ed., **1030**
Churchill Livingstone's international
dictionary of homeopathy, **133**
CINAHL, **439,** 440, 441, **867, 1078**
CINAHL. subject heading list:
Alphabetic list, tree structures,
permuted list, 439, 867, **1093**
Citing medicine, **562**
Clarke's analysis of drugs and poisons:
In pharmaceuticals, body fluids and
postmortem material. 3rd ed., **1208,
1544**
Clinical Care Classification (CCC)
system manual: A guide to nursing
documentation, **1051**
Clinical handbook of psychiatry and
the law. 4th ed., **981, 1341**
Clinical manual of psychiatry and law.
1st ed., **967, 1342**
Clinical pharmacology, **1209**
ClinicalTrials.gov, **191,** 328, 471, **648,**
885
A clinician's dictionary of pathogenic
microorganisms, **134**
The clinician's guide to medical
writing, **563**
The Cochrane Library, **412, 868**
Codes of professional responsibility:
Ethics standards in business, health,
and law. 4th ed., **301, 586**
Codex alimentarius, **1094**
The Cole Library of early medicine and
zoology: Catalogue of books and
pamphlets, **372, 478**

A commentary on the medical writings of Rudolf Virchow: Based on Schwalbe's Virchow-Bibliographie, 1843–1901, **373**

Companion encyclopedia of the history of medicine, **338**

Companion to clinical neurology. 3rd ed., **135**

Companion to psychiatric studies. 7th ed., **1343**

The complementary and alternative medicine information source book, **698,** 700

The complete German Commission E monographs, **1210**

The complete guide to medical writing, **564, 1211**

The complete reference guide to medicine and health, **654**

The complete writing guide to NIH behavioral science grants, **302, 565, 1344**

Comprehensive clinical psychology, **1319**

Comprehensive dictionary of audiology, illustrated. 2nd ed., **136**

Comprehensive glossary of psychiatry and psychology, **1304**

Comprehensive handbook of personality and psychopathology, **1345**

Comprehensive handbook of psychopathology. 3rd ed., **1346**

Comprehensive handbook of psychotherapy, **1347**

Comprehensive medicinal chemistry II, **1212**

Comprehensive toxicology, **1545**

Comprehensive tumour terminology handbook, **137**

Concise dictionary of biomedicine and molecular biology. 2nd ed., **138**

The concise dictionary of medical-legal terms: A general guide to interpretation and usage, **970**

Concise dictionary of modern medicine, **94, 1031**

Concise dictionary of pharmacological agents: Properties and synonyms, **1163**

Concise rules of APA style, **1348**

Conn's current therapy, **303**

Consumer and Patient Health Information Section of the Medical Library Association (CAPHIS), **625**

Consumer health: A guide to Internet information resources. 2nd rev. ed., **699**

Consumer health information source book, 698, **700**

A consumer's guide to dentistry. 2nd ed., **701, 794**

Contemporary issues in healthcare law and ethics. 3rd ed., **587, 852, 982**

Coordinating Office for Global Health, 523

Core readings in psychiatry: An annotated guide to the literature. 2nd ed, **1295**

CPT handbook for psychiatrists. 3rd ed., **853, 1349**

CRC desk reference for nutrition. 2nd ed., **1099**

CRISP, **413**

Current medical diagnosis and treatment, **223, 655**

Current practice in health sciences librarianship, **285**

Current procedural terminology: CPT, 451, 607

Current procedural terminology: CPT. Standard ed., **573**

Current psychiatric therapy II, **1350**

D

DailyMed, **626, 1156**

DART/ETIC (Developmental and Reproductive Toxicology/ Environmental Teratology Information Center database, **1564**

The Dartmouth atlas of health care, **875**

De humani corporis fabrica, **485**

Delivering health care in America: A systems approach. 4th ed., **854**

Dental abstracts, **810**

Dental anatomy: Its relevance to dentistry. 6th ed., **797**

Dental bibliography: Literature of dental science and art as found in the libraries of the New York academy of medicine and Bernhard Wolf Weinberger. 2nd ed., **774**

Dental Health (MedlinePlus), **743, 817**

Dental materials: Properties and manipulation. 9th ed., **798**

Dental terminology. 2nd ed., **799**

Dentistry: An illustrated history, **805**

DermAtlas, **455, 486, 744**

Dermatology lexicon project, **139, 487**

Dermatology therapy: A–Z essentials, **140**

Desk reference to nature's medicine, **1213**

The development of medical bibliography, **12, 51**

DHHS Data Council gateway to data and statistics, **516, 897, 1515**

Diagnostic and statistical manual of mental disorders: DSM-IV-TR. 4th ed., 80, **1296, 1351,** 1366

Dictionary for clinical trials. 2nd ed., **141, 1164**

Dictionary of alternative medicine, **142**

Dictionary of American medical biography: Lives of eminent physicians of the United States and Canada, from the earliest times, **74**

Dictionary of American nursing biography, 59, 70, 73, **1027**

Dictionary of biomedical sciences, **95**

Dictionary of cancer terms, **143,** 166, 538, **643**

Dictionary of dentistry English-Spanish, Spanish-English =Diccionario de odontologia Ingles-Espanol, Espanol-Ingles, **780**

Dictionary of developmental disabilities terminology. 2nd ed., **144**

Dictionary of environmental and occupational medicine: Wörterbuch Umwelt- und Arbeitsmedizin, **145, 1411**

A dictionary of epidemiology. 4th ed., **1413**

Dictionary of environmental health, **146, 1412**

Dictionary of environmentally important chemicals, **1530**

Dictionary of ethical and legal terms and issues: The essential guide for mental health professionals, **971, 1306**

Dictionary of existential psychotherapy and counselling, **1307**

Dictionary of eye terminology. 4th ed., **147**

A dictionary of food and nutrition. 2nd ed, **1100**

Dictionary of food ingredients. 4th ed., **1101**

Dictionary of food science and technology, **1102**

A dictionary of genetics. 7th ed., **148**

The dictionary of health economics, **149,** 820, **833**

Dictionary of health economics and finance, **150, 820**

Dictionary of health insurance and managed care, **151, 834**

Dictionary of medical acronyms and abbreviations. 5th ed ed., **113**

Dictionary of medical biography, **63, 73**

Dictionary of medical eponyms. 2nd ed., **152**

Dictionary of medical sociology, **153, 835**

Dictionary of medical syndromes. 4th ed., 154

Dictionary of medicine = Dictionnaire de médecine: French–English with English–French glossary = Français–anglais avec glossaire anglais–français. 2nd rev. ed., 118

A dictionary of natural products: Terms in the field of pharmacognosy relating to natural medicinal and pharmaceutical materials and the plants, animals, and minerals from which they are derived. 2nd ed., 1165

Dictionary of nursing. 5th ed., 1032

Dictionary of nursing theory and research, 1019, 1033

Dictionary of nutraceuticals and functional foods, 1103

Dictionary of ophthalmology, 155

Dictionary of optometry and visual science. 6th ed., 156

Dictionary of pharmacoepidemiology, 1166, 1414

A dictionary of pharmacology and allied topics. 2nd ed., 1167

Dictionary of pharmacovigilance, 1168

Dictionary of pharmacy, 1169

Dictionary of plant toxins, 1531

Dictionary of protopharmacology: Therapeutic practices, 1700–1850, 1263

The dictionary of psychology, 1309

A dictionary of psychology. 2nd ed., 1308

Dictionary of psychology and psychiatry: English–German/German–English/Englisch–deutsch/deutsch–Englisch. 2nd ed., 1310

A dictionary of public health, 1415

Dictionary of public health promotion and education: Terms and concepts. 2nd ed., 1416

Dictionary of scientific biography, 50, **64**

The dictionary of substances and their effects, **1532, 1565**

A dictionary of the history of medicine, **96, 339**

Dictionary of toxicology. 2nd ed, **1529**

Dictionary of visual science and related clinical terms. 5th ed., **157**

Dictionnaire français-anglais anglais-français des termes médicaux et biologiques et des médicaments = French-English English-French dictionary of medical and biological terms and medications, **119**

Dietary guidelines for Americans, 2005, **702, 1095**

Dietary supplements. 3rd ed., **1214**

Dietary supplements labels database, **728, 1144, 1272**

Diets and dieting: A cultural encyclopedia, **1108**

Directories (MedlinePlus), **204, 649, 745, 790**

Directory of American medical education, 177, **181**, 184, 198, **205**, 217, 453

The directory of complementary and alternative medicine, **176**

Directory of deceased American physicians, 1804—1929: A genealogical guide to over 149,000 medical practitioners providing brief biographical sketches drawn from the American Medical Association's Deceased Physician Masterfile, **75, 206**

Directory of health and human services data resources, **1423**

Directory of health library and information services in the United Kingdom and the Republic of Ireland. 11th ed., **187**

Directory of history of medicine collections, 347, **388**

Directory of open access journals, **35**, 39, 431

Directory of special libraries and information centers, **192**

Directory of physicians in the United States, **207**

Directory of the Medical Library Association, **193**

DIRLINE, **208**, **581**, **650**, **791**, **843**, **918**, **974**, **1043**, **1107**, **1316**, **1424**, **1535**

Disaster preparation and recovery (MedlinePlus), **746**, **1487**

Disease and destiny: A bibliography of medical references to the famous, **13**, **52**

DoctorFinder, **209**, 607, **651**, 704, 790

Doctors and discoveries: Lives that created today's medicine, **46**

Doctors, nurses, and medical practitioners: A biobibliographical sourcebook, **53**, **1028**, **1070**

Doctors: The biography of medicine. 1st ed., **47**

Doody's review service, **14**, **286**

Dorland's illustrated medical dictionary. 31st ed., **97**, **1034**

The DOs: Osteopathic medicine in America. 2nd ed., **340**

DRI, dietary reference intakes: The essential guide to nutrient requirements, **1123**

Drug abuse (MedlinePlus), **747**, **1007**, **1157**, **1391**, **1488**

Drug dictionary for dentistry, **781**

Drug discovery: A history, **1264**

Drug facts and comparisons, **1215**

Drug information: A guide for pharmacists. 3rd ed., **1198**

Drug information: Guide to current resources. 3rd ed., **1199**

Drug information handbook. North American ed., **800**, **1052**, **1216**, **1352**

Drug information portal, **729**, **748**, **1273**, **1282**

Drug interaction facts, **1217**

Drug interactions: Analysis and management, **1218**

Drugs@FDA, 770, **1283**

Drugs in pregnancy and lactation, **627**, **1219**

Drugs, supplements, and herbal information (MedlinePlus), **749**, **1284**

Drugs: Synonyms and properties. 2nd ed., **1170**

E

Early American medical imprints: A guide to works printed in the United States, 1668–1820, **15**

Electronic orange book, 770, **1158**

Elsevier's dictionary of abbreviations, acronyms, synonyms, and symbols used in medicine. 2nd, enl. ed., **114**

Elsevier's dictionary of medicine and biology: In English, Greek, German, Italian, and Latin, **120**

Elsevier's dictionary of medicine: Spanish–English and English-Spanish, **121**

Elsevier's dictionary of nutrition and food processing: In English, German, French, and Portuguese, **1104**

EMBASE, **414**

EMBASE list of journals indexed, **36**, 414

EMTREE thesaurus, **574**, **1291**

Encyclopedia and dictionary of medicine, nursing, and allied health. 7th ed., **98**, **1035**

The encyclopedia of addictive drugs, **656**, **1189**

Encyclopedia of aging, **226, 657**

Encyclopedia of aging. 4th ed., **224, 1047**

Encyclopedia of aging and public health, **225, 1428**

Encyclopedia of AIDS: A social, political, cultural, and scientific record of the HIV epidemic, **227,** 247, 670

The encyclopedia of Alzheimer's disease, **228, 658,** 659

Encyclopedia of Alzheimer's disease: With directories of research, treatment, and care facilities, **229, 659**

Encyclopedia of behavior modification and cognitive behavior therapy, **1320**

Encyclopedia of bioethics. 3rd ed., **582**

Encyclopedia of biomaterials and biomedical engineering, **230, 793**

Encyclopedia of biopharmaceutical statistics. 2nd rev. and exp. ed., **1190**

Encyclopedia of biostatistics. 2nd ed., **1429**

Encyclopedia of bioterrorism defense, **1430**

The encyclopedia of blindness and vision impairment. 2nd ed., **231**

Encyclopedia of cancer. 2nd ed., **232**

Encyclopedia of cancer and society, **233, 846**

Encyclopedia of clinical pharmacy, **1191**

Encyclopedia of clinical toxicology: A comprehensive guide and reference to the toxicology of prescription and OTC drugs, chemicals, herbals, plants, fungi, marine life, reptiles and insect venoms, food ingredients, clothing, and environmental toxins, **1192, 1537**

Encyclopedia of cognitive science, **1321**

Encyclopedia of common natural ingredients used in food, drugs, and cosmetics. 2nd ed., **1109, 1193**

The encyclopedia of complementary and alternative medicine, **234, 660**

Encyclopedia of complementary health practice, **235, 661**

The encyclopedia of depression. 2nd ed., **662**

Encyclopedia of diet fads, **664, 1110**

Encyclopedia of dietary supplements, **663, 1194**

Encyclopedia of disability, **236**

Encyclopedia of drugs, alcohol and addictive behavior. 2nd ed., **237**

The encyclopedia of elder care: The comprehensive resource on geriatric and social care. 2nd ed., **665, 1048**

Encyclopedia of endocrine diseases, **238**

Encyclopedia of epidemiology, **1431**

Encyclopedia of family health. 3rd ed., **666**

Encyclopedia of folk medicine: Old world and new world, **239**

Encyclopedia of food and culture, **1111**

Encyclopedia of food science and technology. 2nd ed., **1113**

Encyclopedia of food sciences and nutrition. 2nd ed., **1114**

Encyclopedia of foods: A guide to healthy nutrition, **667, 1112**

Encyclopedia of forensic and legal medicine, **976**

Encyclopedia of forensic sciences, 977, **1322**

Encyclopedia of gastroenterology, **240**

The encyclopedia of genetic disorders and birth defects. 2nd ed., **241, 668**

Encyclopedia of genetics, **242**

Encyclopedia of genetics, genomics, proteomics, and bioinformatics, **243**

Encyclopedia of gerontology. 2nd ed., **244**

Encyclopedia of global health, **919**

Encyclopedia of health and aging, **245, 669**

Encyclopedia of health and behavior, **246, 1432**

Encyclopedia of health care management, **847, 920**

The encyclopedia of HIV and AIDS, 227

The encyclopedia of HIV and AIDS. 2nd ed., **247, 670**

Encyclopedia of hormones, **248**

Encyclopedia of human nutrition. 2nd ed., 682, **1115**

Encyclopedia of immunology. 2nd ed., 2

Encyclopedia of infectious diseases. 3rd ed., 249

Encyclopedia of infectious diseases: Modern methodologies, **249, 1433**

Encyclopedia of life sciences, **251,** 278

Encyclopedia of life sciences. 2nd ed., **250**

Encyclopedia of medical anthropology: Health and illness in the world's cultures, **252**

Encyclopedia of medical devices and instrumentation. 2nd ed., **253**

Encyclopedia of medical genomics and proteomics, **254**

Encyclopedia of medical history, **342**

Encyclopedia of medical organizations and agencies: A subject guide to organizations, foundations, federal and state government agencies, research centers, and medical and allied health schools, **210**

Encyclopedia of medical sources, **374**

Encyclopedia of mental health, **671, 1323**

Encyclopedia of molecular cell biology and molecular medicine. 2nd ed., **255**

Encyclopedia of neuroscience. 3rd rev. and enl. ed., **256**

Encyclopedia of nursing research. 2nd ed., **1019,** 1033

Encyclopedia of nutrition and good health, 682

Encyclopedia of obesity, **258, 673, 1434**

Encyclopedia of obesity and eating disorders. 3rd ed., **257, 672, 1324**

Encyclopaedia of occupational health and safety. 4th ed., **1427**

Encyclopedia of pain, **259**

Encyclopedia of plague and pestilence: From ancient times to the present. 3rd ed., **343**

Encyclopedia of primary prevention and health promotion, **1435**

Encyclopedia of psychology, **1325**

Encyclopedia of psychotherapy, **1326**

Encyclopedia of public health, **1436**

Encyclopedia of respiratory medicine. 1st ed., **260**

Encyclopedia of science, technology, and ethics, **583**

Encyclopedia of statistical sciences. 2nd ed., **517**

Encyclopedia of statistics in behavioral science, **1327**

Encyclopedia of stress. 2nd ed., **261, 1328**

The encyclopedia of the brain and brain disorders. 2nd ed., **674**

Encyclopaedia of the history of science, technology, and medicine in non-western cultures, **341**

Encyclopedia of the human brain, **262**

Encyclopedia of the neurological sciences. 1st ed., **263, 1329**

Encyclopedia of toxicology. 2nd ed., **1538**

Encyclopedia of women's health, **264**

The encyclopedia of women's health. 5th ed., **265, 675**

Encyclopedia of women's health issues, **266, 676, 1437**

Encyclopedic reference of cancer, **267**

Encyclopedic reference of genomics and proteomics in molecular medicine, **99**

Encyclopedic reference of immunotoxicology, **268, 1539**

Encyclopedic reference of molecular pharmacology, **1195**

Encyclopedic reference of traditional Chinese medicine: [a manual from A–Z, symptoms, therapy, and herbal remedies], **304, 1171, 1220**

Entrez, **3, 6,** 347, 415, 427, 432, 471, 605, 608

Enviro-health links, **1489, 1583**

Environmental toxicants: Human exposures and their health effects. 2nd ed., **1546**

The enzyme reference: A comprehensive guidebook to enzyme nomenclature, reactions, and methods, **305**

The essential guide to aging in the twenty-first century: Mind, body, and behavior. 3rd ed., **306**

Essential nursing resources, **1022**

Essentials of managed health care. 5th ed., **855**

Essentials of medical geology: Impacts of the natural environment on public health, **1438, 1540**

Ethics, **588, 1353**

Ethics and health [Internet resource], **611, 1008**

ETHXWeb, 577, 602, **603,** 604, 618

European health for all database (HFA-DB), **953, 1516**

The European multilingual thesaurus on health promotion in 12 languages, **836, 1417**

European pharmacopoeia, **1180**

The evolution of surgical instruments: An illustrated history from ancient times to the twentieth century, **344**

F

Fact sheet, access to audiovisual materials, **28, 345**

Facts and comparisons 4.0 online, **1159**

The Facts on File encyclopedia of health and medicine, **677**

Facts on file library of health and living series, 228, 234, 241, 662, 668, 670, 671, 672, **678**

The family practice desk reference. 4th ed., **307, 1053**

FAQ, **1285**

FAQ international drug information, **1286**

Faststats A to Z, **518,** 529, 534, 539, **898, 1517**

FDI World Dental Federation, **773,** 792

FedStats, 516, **519**

Fenaroli's handbook of flavor ingredients. 5th ed., **1124**

Fennema's food chemistry. 4th ed., **1125**

Find a library (MedlinePlus), **182, 211**

Finding and using health statistics, **520, 954**

First aid manual. 2nd American fully rev. and updated ed., **308, 628**

The 5-minute herb and dietary supplement consult, **629, 1221**

Food additives data book, **1126**

Food and drug administration, **630**

Food and Nutrition Information Center, **631, 1096**

Food chemicals codex. 5th ed., **1127**

Food safety: A reference handbook, 1129

Food safety handbook, **1128,** 1129, **1445**

Food Safety Research Information Office at the National Agricultural Library, **933, 1129, 1446, 1472**

The founders of neurology: One hundred and forty-six biographical sketches by eighty-eight authors. 2nd ed., **65**

Fragments of neurological history, **391,** **1376**
FREIDA online, **212,** 213, 451, 607
French's index of differential diagnosis: An A–Z. 14th ed., **269**
The Freud encyclopedia: Theory, therapy, and culture, **1330**

G
Gabbard's treatments of psychiatric disorders. 4th ed., **1331,** **1354**
The Gale encyclopedia of alternative medicine. 2nd ed., **270,** **679**
The Gale encyclopedia of cancer: A guide to cancer and its treatments. 2nd ed., **271,** **680**
The Gale encyclopedia of childhood and adolescence, **1332**
The Gale encyclopedia of children's health: Infancy through adolescence, **681**
The Gale encyclopedia of diets: A guide to health and nutrition, **682,** **1116**
The Gale encyclopedia of genetic disorders. 2nd ed., **272,** **683**
The Gale encyclopedia of medicine. 3rd ed., **273,** **684**
The Gale encyclopedia of mental health. 2nd ed., **685,** **1333**
The Gale encyclopedia of neurological disorders, **686**
The Gale encyclopedia of nursing and allied health. 2nd ed., **1049**
The Gale encyclopedia of psychology. 2nd ed., **1334**
The Gale encyclopedia of surgery: A guide for patients and caregivers, **687**
Gale's Health and Wellness Resource Center, 698
Gen-Bank, 327, **415**
General Dental Council, **818**

General residency training and subspecialties in psychiatry, **1317**
The genesis of neuroscience, **392,** **1377**
GeneTests, **194,** **309,** **416,** **456**
Genetics home reference, **703,** **750**
GenETHX, 577, 602, 603, **604,** 616, 618
Genetics home reference, 608, 885
GENE-TOX (genetic toxicology), **1566**
Genomic Resource Centre, **612,** **1009**
German dictionary of medicine: Wörterbuch Medizin Englisch. 2nd rev. and exp. ed., **122**
The global burden of disease: A comprehensive assessment of mortality and disability from diseases, injuries, and risk factors in 1990 and projected to 2020, **521,** 522, **955**
Global burden of disease and risk factors, 521, **522,** 524, **956**
Global health, **934,** **1473**
Global health atlas, **941,** **957,** **1490**
Global health library, **943,** **1492**
Global health statistics: A compendium of incidence, prevalence, and mortality estimates for over 200 conditions, 522, **524,** **958**
Global Index Medicus, **417,** **1474**
Globalhealth.gov, **523,** **942,** **1491**
Goldfrank's toxicologic emergencies. 8th ed., **1547**
GPO access, **31**
Graduate medical education directory, **213,** **451,** **607**
The greatest benefit to mankind: A medical history of humanity. 1st American ed., **393**
Grey literature report, **16,** 475, 481, **1406**
Guardians of medical knowledge: The genesis of the Medical Library Association, **394**

Guide to Canadian health care facilities: Guide des établissements de santé du Canada, **183**

Guide to libraries and information sources in medicine and health care. 3rd ed., **188**

A guide to pharmacy museums and historical collections in the United States and Canada, **1265**

Guide to popular natural products. 3rd ed., **1222**

Guide to the code of ethics for nurses: Interpretation and application, **589, 1054**

Guides to the evaluation of permanent impairment. 6th ed., **79, 310**

H

Handbook for health care ethics committees, **590**

Handbook of bioethics and religion, **591**

Handbook of bioethics: Taking stock of the field from a philosophical perspective, **592**

Handbook of clinical child psychology. 3rd ed., **1355**

Handbook of clinical health psychology (Boll et al.), **1357**

Handbook of clinical health psychology (Llewlyn and Kennedy), **1356**

Handbook of contemporary neuropharmacology, **1223, 1358**

Handbook of eating disorders. 2nd ed., **1359**

Handbook of environmental health. 4th ed., **311, 1447**

Handbook of epidemiology, **1448**

Handbook of health behavior research, **312**

Handbook of industrial toxicology and hazardous materials, **1548**

Handbook of medicinal herbs. 2nd ed., **1224**

Handbook of neurologic rating scales. 2nd ed., **313, 1360**

Handbook of non-prescription drugs, **722, 1225**

Handbook of nutraceuticals and functional foods. 2nd ed., **1130**

Handbook of nutrition and food. 2nd ed., **1131**

Handbook of pesticide toxicology. 2nd ed., **1549**

Handbook of pharmaceutical excipients. 5th ed., **1226**

Handbook of poisoning: Prevention, diagnosis, and treatment. 13th ed., **1550**

Handbook of psychiatric education, **1361**

Handbook of psychiatric measures. 2nd ed., **1362**

Handbook of psychology, **1363**

Handbook of research methods in clinical psychology, **1364**

Handbook of research on informatics in healthcare and biomedicine, **856**

Handbook of the psychology of aging. 6th ed., **1365**

Handbook of toxicologic pathology. 2nd ed., **1551**

Handbook of toxicology. 2nd ed., **1552**

Handbook of vitamins. 3rd ed., **1132**

Handbook on injectable drugs, **1227**

Handbook on the toxicology of metals. 3rd ed., **1553**

Hardin MD (Hardin meta directory of Internet health sources), **457, 488,** 710

Harty's dental dictionary. 3rd ed., **782**

The Harvard guide to psychiatry. 3rd ed., **1366**

The Harvard Medical School family health guide. 1st Free Press trade paperback ed., **688**

The Hastings Center, **613**

Hazardous chemicals desk reference.
  5th ed., **1554,** 1559
Haz-Map, **1567**
Health and British magazines in the
  nineteenth century, **375, 1465**
Health and healthcare in the United
  States: County and metro area data,
  525, 899
Health and human rights: Basic
  international documents. 2nd ed.,
  983
Health and psychosocial instruments
  (HaPI), **1292**
Health and wellness resource center,
  632, 1079
Health care almanac: Every person's
  guide to the thoughtful and practical
  sides of medicine. 2nd ed., **704, 850**
The health care crisis in the United
  States: A bibliography, **826**
Health care defined: A glossary of
  current terms, **837, 972**
Health care policy and politics A to Z.
  2nd ed., **848**
Health care reform around the world,
  857, 922
Health care resources on the Internet: A
  guide for librarians and health care
  consumers, **705, 851**
Health care standards: Official
  directory, **844, 975**
Health care state rankings, **900**
Health care systems around the world:
  Characteristics, issues, reforms, **858,**
  923
Health care systems of the developed
  world: How the United States'
  system remains an outlier, **859, 924**
Health care terms. 4th ed., **821**
Health data for all ages (HDAA), **526,**
  901, 1518
Health education assets library
  (HEAL), **458,** 461, 493, 499, 819

Health Fraud (MedlinePlus), **751,**
  1010
Health in the Americas, **959, 1519**
Health information for international
  travel, **633, 916, 1449**
Health of Black Americans from post
  reconstruction to integration, 1871–
  1960: An annotated bibliography of
  contemporary sources, **376, 1407**
Health on the Net Foundation
  (HON), **4, 489, 634**
The health professional's guide to
  popular dietary supplements. 3rd
  ed., **1133**
Health professionals style manual, **566,**
  1055
Health professions career and education
  directory, **214,** 451, 607
Health professions education standards,
  215
Health reference center, 228, 234, 241,
  660, 662, 668, 670, 671, 672, 674,
  678, **689, 1080**
Health reference center—academic,
  418, 632
Health reference series (Omnigraphics,
  Inc.), **707**
Health Resources and Services
  Administration (HRSA), **877, 1494**
Health science books, 1876–1982, **17**
Health services cyclopedic dictionary:
  A compendium of health-care and
  public health terminology. 3rd ed.,
  838, 973, 1418
Health services research and public
  health information programs, **822,**
  1400
Health services research methodology
  core library recommendations,
  2007, **827, 878, 1408, 1495**
Health Services Technology
  Assessment Texts (HSTAT), **419,**
  828

Health Statistics (MedlinePlus), **528, 960**

Health statistics: An annotated bibliographic guide to information resources. 2nd ed., **527**

Health System (MedlinePlus), **752, 879**

Health, United States, **529,** 539, **902, 1520**

Healthcare Cost and Utilization Project (HCUP), **876**

Healthfinder, 222, 465, 636, 651, **706**

HealthMap, **944, 1493**

HealthSTAR (Ovid), **440,** 441, **869, 1475**

Healthy People 2010, 222, 529, **530, 880, 903, 1496, 1521**

Healthy women, **531, 881, 904, 1522**

Healthy work: An annotated bibliography, **1409**

Heinemann dental dictionary. 4th ed., **783**

Herbal drugs and phytopharmaceuticals: A handbook for practice on a scientific basis. 3rd ed., **1228**

Herbal medicine: Expanded Commission E monographs, **1229**

Herbal medicines: A guide for healthcare professionals. 3rd ed., **1200, 1230**

An historical account of pharmacology to the 20th century, **1266**

Historical anatomies on the Web, **490**

A historical dictionary of psychiatry, **1311**

Historical dictionary of the World Health Organization, **917, 930, 1466**

Historical encyclopedia of nursing, **1050, 1071**

Historical statistics of the United States, **532**

History and bibliography of artistic anatomy: Didactics for depicting the human figure, **18, 491**

The history and influence of the American Psychiatric Association, **1378**

History of AMA ethics, **593**

The history of American homeopathy: The academic years, 1820–1935, **395**

A history of chiropractic education in North America: Report to the Council on Chiropractic Education, **396**

A history of dentistry from the most ancient times until the end of the eighteenth century, **806**

History of medicine, **346,** 347, **397**

History of medicine (NLM), **347**

A history of medicine. 2nd rev. and enl. ed., **398**

History of medicine in the United States, **399**

History of neurology, **400, 1379**

A history of nursing, from ancient to modern times: A world view. 5th ed., **1072**

History of periodontology, **807**

The history of pharmacy: A selected annotated bibliography, **1267**

A history of public health. Expanded ed., **1467**

The history of psychiatry: An evaluation of psychiatric thought and practice from prehistoric times to the present, **1380**

A history of psychiatry: From the era of the asylum to the age of Prozac, **1381**

History of science, technology, and medicine database, **377**

The history of surgery in the United States, 1775–1900, **348,** 361

The history of the health care sciences and health care, 1700–1980: A selective annotated bibliography, **378, 829**

History of the health sciences. 2nd rev. ed., **379**

History of the health sciences World Wide Web links, **349,** 379

A history of the National Library of Medicine: The nation's treasury of medical knowledge, **350**

HIV InSite knowledge base, **314,** 465, 636, **1497**

Homoeopathy in the United States: A bibliography of homoeopathic medical imprints, 1825–1925, **380**

Hospital and health administration index, **441, 870**

Household products database, **635, 1568**

How to report statistics in medicine: Annotated guidelines for authors, editors, and reviewers. 2nd ed., **533, 567**

How to write and publish a scientific paper. 6th ed., **568**

HSDB (Hazardous substances data bank), **1569**

HSR information central, 822, **882, 1498**

Human anatomy: From the Renaissance to the digital age, **492**

Human Genome Project information, **459, 614**

I

The ICD-10 classification of mental and behavioural disorders: clinical descriptions and diagnostic guidelines, 78, **80, 1297**

An illustrated Chinese materia medica, **1231**

Illustrated dictionary and resource directory of environmental and occupational health. 2nd ed., **1419**

Illustrated dictionary of immunology. 2nd ed., **158**

Illustrated history of medicine, **401**

The illustrated history of surgery. 2nd rev. and up. ed., **351**

Illustrated manual of nursing practice. 3rd ed., **1232**

Images from the history of medicine, **352**

Incunabula scientifica et medica: Short title list, **33**

Index medicus, 13, **420,** 425, 430, 813

Index nominum, international drug directory = Internationales Arzneistoff- und Arzneimittelverzeichnis = Repertoire international des substances médicamenteuses et spécialités pharmaceutiques. 18th ed., **1233**

Index to dental literature, 425, **811,** 813

IndexCat, **479**

Index-catalogue of the library of the Surgeon General's office, 13

Indian Health Service (IHS), **1401**

Information resources in toxicology. 3rd ed., **1542**

Information sources in the history of science and medicine, **353**

Injury data and resources, **534, 1402**

Institute of Medicine (IOM), **19, 460, 1392**

Intellectual disability: Definition, classification, and systems of supports. 11th ed., **1298**

International bibliographic information on dietary supplements (IBIDS) database, 765, **1145**

International classification of diseases for oncology: ICD-O. 3rd ed., 77, 78, **81, 84,** 776

International classification of diseases, ninth revision, clinical modification, **82,** 539

International classification of functioning, disability, and health (ICF), 79, **83,** 539

International classification of functioning, disability and health problems (ICD-10), 83, 84

International clinical trials registry platform search portal (ICTRP), **935**

International dictionary of psychoanalysis = Dictionnaire international de la psychanalyse, **1312**

International digest of health legislation = Recueil international de législation sanitaire, **936, 998, 1476**

International guidelines on HIV/AIDS and human rights, **594, 925, 984**

International health (MedlinePlus), **946, 1011, 1499**

International health data reference guide, **535, 945, 961**

International health regulations (2005), **926, 985, 1450**

International nursing index, 867, **1081**

The International pharmacopoeia: Pharmacopoea internationalis. 4th ed., **1181**

International research centers directory, **195**

International travel and health, **708**

International clinical trials registry platform search portal (ICTRP), **421**

International nursing index, 425, 439, 813

International pharmaceutical abstracts, **1274**

International statistical classification of diseases and related health problems, **84**

International Travel and Health, 633, **1451**

Interpretation of diagnostic tests. 8th ed., **315,** 318, 319, 325, 334, **709,** 753

Interpreting the medical literature. 5th ed., **316, 1056**

Introduction to health services. 7th ed., **823**

Introduction to health sciences librarianship, **317**

Introduction to health services research, **830, 883**

Introduction to reference sources in the health sciences. 5th ed., **287**

An introduction to the history of dentistry: With medical & dental chronology & bibliographic data, **808**

An introduction to the history of medicine: With medical chronology, suggestions for study and bibliographic data. 4th rev. and enl. ed., **402**

IRIS (Integrated risk information system), **1570**

ISI web of knowledge, **422**

ISI web of science, **423**

ITER (International toxicity estimates for risk), **1571**

IUPAC glossary of terms used in toxicology, **1533**

J

Jablonski's dictionary of syndromes and eponymic diseases. 2nd ed., **159**

Jonas and Kovner's health care delivery in the United States. 8th ed., **824**

K

Kaiser Family Foundation, 531, **884,** 893, **947, 1500**

Kaplan and Sadock's comprehensive textbook of psychiatry. 8th ed., **1396**

Kennedy Institute of Ethics' National Reference Center for Bioethics Literature [NRCBL], 608

Kidshealth®, 465, 636

Krause's food and nutrition therapy.
   12th ed., **1134**
Kremers and Urdang's History of
   pharmacy. 4th ed., **1268**

L

Lab tests online, **319,** 325, 334, **753**
Laboratory tests and diagnostic
   procedures, 315, 319, 325, 334, 709
Laboratory tests and diagnostic
   procedures. 4th ed., **318,** 753
LactMed (Drugs and lactation
   database), **1572**
Law and risk management in dental
   practice, 595, **801**
The law and the public's health. 7th ed.,
   860, 987, 1452
Law and risk management in dental
   practice, **986**
Law, liability, and ethics for medical
   office professionals. 4th ed., **595,** 801,
   988
Lawyers' medical cyclopedia of personal
   injuries and allied specialties. 5th
   ed., **978**
Legal and ethical issues for health
   professionals. 1st ed., **596, 989**
Legal, ethical, and political issues in
   nursing. 2nd ed., **1057**
Legal medicine. 7th ed., **990**
Lewis' dictionary of occupational and
   environmental safety and health,
   160, 1420
Lewis' dictionary of toxicology, **1534**
Lexi-Comp online, **812, 1082, 1275**
Lexicon of psychiatric and mental
   health terms. 2nd ed., **1313**
Lexicon of psychiatry, neurology, and
   the neurosciences. 2nd ed., **1314**
LexisNexis congressional, **999**
LexisNexis environmental, **1573**
The Life Sciences Search Engine, 444,
   575

The Lippincott manual of nursing
   practice. 8th ed., **1058**
List of journals indexed for
   MEDLINE, **37,** 38
List of registered medical
   practitioners, **189**
List of serials indexed for online users,
   37, **38**
Lister Hill National Center for
   Biomedical Communications, **885**
Literature, arts, and medicine
   database, **424**
Litt's drug eruption reference manual
   including drug interactions. 10th
   ed., **1234**
LocatorPlus, 28, 38, 347, 471, 479,
   480, 618

M

Macmillan encyclopedia of death and
   dying, **274**
Magill's medical guide. 3rd rev. ed.,
   690
Malaria atlas project (MAP), **948,**
   1501
The managed health care dictionary.
   2nd ed., **161, 839**
A manual for writers of research
   papers, theses, and dissertations:
   Chicago style for students and
   researchers. 7th ed., **569**
A manual of orthopaedic terminology.
   7th ed., **162**
Martindale: The complete drug
   reference, **1182,** 1574
Mayo Clinic family health book. 3rd
   ed., **691**
MayoClinic.com, **710**
Measuring health: A guide to rating
   scales and questionnaires. 3rd ed.,
   320, 1367, 1453
MedEdPORTAL, 453, **461, 493, 819**
MedHist, **354**

Medical abbreviations and eponyms. 2nd ed., **115**

Medical and health care books and serials in print, **20**

Medical and health information directory, **216,** 632

Medical dictionary: English, Spanish, Portuguese = Diccionario de medicina: español, inglés, portugués = Dicioná rio de termos médicos: português, inglês, espanhol. 2nd rev. and exp. ed., **123**

Medical dictionary in six languages, **124**

Medical dictionary (MedlinePlus), **100, 644, 1036**

The Medical directory: London, provinces, Wales, Scotland, Ireland, abroad, Navy, Army & Air Force, **190**

Medical discoveries: Who and when; a dictionary listing thousands of medical and related scientific discoveries in alphabetical order, giving in each case the name of the discoverer, his profession, nationality, and floruit, and the date of the discovery, **355**

Medical encyclopedia (MedlinePlus), **275, 494, 692**

Medical ethics: Codes, opinions, and statements, **597**

Medical firsts: From Hippocrates to the human genome, 355, **356**

Medical/health sciences libraries on the Web, **196,** 211, 457, 488

Medical images and illustrations, **462, 495**

The Medical Library Association consumer health reference service handbook, **711**

The Medical Library Association encyclopedic guide to searching and finding health information on the Web, **288, 712**

The Medical Library Association guide to cancer information: Authoritative, patient-friendly print and electronic resources, **713**

The Medical Library Association guide to managing health care libraries, **321**

Medical meanings: A glossary of word origins. 2nd ed., **163**

Medical phrase index: A comprehensive reference to the terminology of medicine. 5th ed., **101**

The medical practitioners in medieval England: A biographical register, **66**

Medical records and the law. 4th ed., **598, 861, 991**

Medical reference works, 1679–1966: A selected bibliography, **289**

Medical reference works, 1679–1966: A selected bibliography. Supplement, 289, **290**

Medical response to terrorism: Preparedness and clinical practice, **1454**

Medical school admission requirements, U.S.A. and Canada, 177, 181, **184,** 198, 205, **217,** 453

Medical statistics from A to Z. 2nd ed., **536, 1421**

Medicare handbook, **723, 862, 992**

Medicinal plants of the world: An illustrated scientific guide to important medicinal plants and their uses, **1235**

Medicinal plants of the world: Chemical constituents, traditional and modern medicinal uses. 2nd ed., **1160**

Medicine: A bibliography of bibliographies, **21**

Medicine: An illustrated history, **357**

Medicine, health, and bioethics: Essential primary sources, **22, 578, 1410**

Medicine in America: A short history, **358**

Medicine in Great Britain from the Restoration to the nineteenth century, 1660–1800: An annotated bibliography, **381**

Medicine in quotations: Views of health and disease through the ages. 2nd ed., 5

Medicine, literature and eponyms: An encyclopedia of medical eponyms derived from literary characters, **276**

MedicinesComplete, **1236,** 1544

Medieval science, technology, and medicine: An encyclopedia, **359**

MEDLINE, 38, 100, 227, 322, 347, **425,** 427, 430, 440, 441, 463, 471, 575, 602, 608, 619, 626, 638, 710, 714, **813, 1082**

MEDLINE: A guide to effective searching in PubMed and other interfaces. 2nd ed., **322**

MedlinePlus, 222, 324, **463,** 464, 465, 471, 494, 528, 608, 619, 626, 636, 638, 644, 649, 692, **714,** 725, **754**

MedlinePlus go local, **755**

Melloni's illustrated dictionary of medical abbreviations, **116, 1037**

Melloni's illustrated dictionary of obstetrics and gynecology, **164, 1038**

Melloni's illustrated dictionary of the musculoskeletal system, **165**

Melloni's illustrated medical dictionary. 4th ed., **102**

Men's health (MedlinePlus), **464, 756**

Mental disorders of the new millennium, **1335**

Mental health in America: A reference handbook, **1368, 1455**

Mental health, United States, **905, 1395**

The mental measurements yearbook, **1369**

MEPS Medical Expenditure Panel Survey, 509, **537, 886, 906**

The Merck index: An encyclopedia of chemicals, drugs, and biologicals. 14th ed., **1237**

The Merck manual of diagnosis and therapy, **323**

The Merck manual of medical information. 2nd rev. home ed., **693**

Merck Manuals, 323, **324,** 693, **724**

Merriam-Webster's medical dictionary. Enl. print ed., **103**

MeSH, 38, 208, 427, 461, 471, 480, 493, 574, **575,** 577, 791, 819, 843, 974

Meyler's side effects of drugs: The international encyclopedia of adverse drug reactions and interactions, **1196**

Micromedex healthcare series, 710, **1084, 1276, 1574**

The MIT encyclopedia of communication disorders, **277**

The MIT encyclopedia of the cognitive sciences, **1336**

MLANET, **465, 636,** 644

Modern nutrition in health and disease. 10th ed., **1135**

Morton's medical bibliography: An annotated check-list of texts illustrating the history of medicine (Garrison and Morton). 5th ed., **382**

Mosby's dental dictionary. 2nd ed., **784**

Mosby's dental drug reference. 8th ed., **645, 785, 1172**

Mosby's dictionary of medicine, nursing and health professions. 7th ed., **104, 1039**

Mosby's drug consult, **1238**

Mosby's manual of diagnostic and laboratory tests. 2nd ed. 315, 318, 319, **325,** 334, 709, 753, **1059**

Multilingual glossary of technical and popular medical terms in nine European languages, **125**

N

NANDA, NOC, and NIC linkages: Nursing diagnoses, outcomes, and intervention. 2nd ed., 87, **1060,** 1062

National academies press, **23, 466**

National Bioethics Advisory Committee, 608

National Cancer Institute, **166, 467, 538,** 644, **757,** 1562

National Center for Biotechnology Information, **6,** 327, **426,** 432

National Center for Complementary and Alternative Medicine, **468**

National Center for Environmental Health, **1456**

National Center for Health Statistics, 509, 512, 525, 534, 535, **539,** 545, 553, 557, **1403**

National Center for Injury Prevention and Control of the U.S. Centers for Disease Control and Prevention, 557

National drug code directory, 770, **1183**

National guideline clearinghouse, **326, 715**

National Human Genome Research Institute, **469,** 616

National Human Genome Research Institute (U.S.), **615, 1012**

National Information Center on Health Services Research and Health Care Technology (NICHSR), **887, 1502**

National Information Resource on Ethics and Human Genetics (NIREHG), 604, **616**

National Institute of Environmental Health Sciences, **617, 1503**

National Institute of Mental Health, **1393, 1504**

National Institute of Nursing Research, **758, 1088**

National Institute on Drug Abuse (NIDA), **1505**

National Institutes of Health (NIH), 463, 468, **470,** 616, 620, 714

National Library of Medicine, **427,** 432, 463, 581, 729, 843, 1577

National Library of Medicine guide to finding health information, **291, 716**

National Library of Medicine (NLM), 30, 364, 468, 470, **471,** 528, 577, 605, 608, 650, 714, 755, 791, 827, 974

National Library of Medicine publications catalog, **32**

National Library of Medicine's History of Medicine, 12, 369

National Network of Libraries of Medicine (NN/LM), **472**

National Office of Public Health Genomics, **1506**

National Organization for Rare Disorders, Inc., 329, **428, 473,** 476, 717, **759,** 766

National Patient Safety Foundation (NPFS), **760, 888, 1089**

National Quality Measures Clearinghouse, 326, 715, **889**

National Reference Center for Bioethics Literature (NRCBL), 577, 604, 616, **618**

National vital statistics system (NVSS), **540, 1523**

National Women's Health Information Center, **474, 761**

Natural medicines comprehensive database, **637, 1239**

Natural standard, 710, **1277**

Nature encyclopedia of the human genome, 278

NCBI Entrez, 432, 605, 731

The NCBI handbook, **327**

NCI visuals online, **496**

NetAnatomy, **497**
The Netter Collection of medical illustrations, **498**
Neurological eponyms, **167**
The new dictionary of medical ethics. New ed., **580**
The new Walford guide to reference resources: Volume 1: Science, technology, and medicine. 9th ed., **292**
New York Academy of Medicine Library online catalog, 16, **475, 481**
NIH Office of Dietary Supplements, 468
NIH Office of Rare Diseases, 329, 428, 759
NLM Catalog, 471, 480, **482,** 602, 608, 618, 619, 638
NLM classification, **85,** 427, 471
NLM Gateway, 328, 427, **429,** 430, 440, 471, **619, 638, 730, 814, 890, 949, 1013, 1085, 1146, 1278, 1387, 1477, 1575**
NLM training manuals and resources, **86, 328, 1555**
Nobelprize.org, **67**
NORD guide to rare disorders, **329,** 428, 473, 476, **717,** 759, 766
Novy˘ı anglo-russki˘ı meditsinski˘ı slovar': Okolo 75 000 terminov = New English-Russian medical dictionary: Approx. 75,000 terms, **126**
Nurse practitioner's legal reference, **993, 1061**
Nurse-midwifery: The birth of a new American profession, **1073**
Nursing, a historical bibliography, **1074**
Nursing history resources, **1023, 1075, 1090**
Nursing home compare, **762**
Nursing Interventions Classification (NIC). 5th ed., **87, 1062**

Nursing studies index, **1086**
Nursing, the finest art: An illustrated history. 2nd ed., **1076**
Nutraceuticals: A guide for healthcare professionals. 2nd ed., **1240**
Nutrients A to Z: A user's guide to foods, herbs, vitamins, minerals and supplements. 3rd rev. ed., **1105**
Nutrition: A reference handbook, **1136**
Nutrition abstracts and reviews series A, **442, 1147**
Nutrition and diet therapy reference dictionary. 5th ed., **1106**
Nutrition and well-being A to Z, **1117**
The nutrition desk reference. 3rd ed., **725, 1137**
Nutrition diagnosis and intervention: Standardized language for the nutrition care process, **1138**
Nutrition (MedlinePlus), **763, 1151**
The nutrition source, **764, 1152**
Nutrition.gov, **718, 1118, 1150**

O
Obituary notices of fellows of the Royal Society, 50
Occupational Safety and Health Administration (OSHA), **1507**
OECD health data, **541, 907, 962**
Office of Dietary Supplements, **765, 1153**
Office of Rare Diseases, 473, **476,** 717, **766**
The Official ABMS directory of board certified medical specialists, **218**
Official guide to graduate nursing programs, **1044**
Official guide to undergraduate and graduate nursing programs. 2nd ed., **1045**
OLDMEDLINE data, **430**
OMIM, 327, **330**
OncoLink, **477,** 767, **1091**

150 years of caring: A pictorial history of the American Pharmaceutical Association, **1261**

One hundred years of American psychiatry, **1382**

Online bioethics resources, 469, 615, **620, 1014**

Ophthalmic drug facts: ODF, **1241**

Ophthalmic eponyms: An encyclopedia of named signs, syndromes, and diseases in ophthalmology, **168**

Organic-chemical drugs and their synonyms. 9th ed., **1173**

The Oxford companion to the body, **279**

The Oxford companion to the mind. 2nd ed., **1337**

Oxford desk reference: Clinical genetics, **331**

Oxford dictionary of medical quotations, **169**

The Oxford dictionary of sports science and medicine. 3rd ed., **170**

The Oxford handbook of bioethics, **599**

The Oxford illustrated companion to medicine. 3rd ed., **280**

P

Pan American Health Organization (PAHO), **950, 1508**

Partners in information access for the public health workforce, **891, 1509**

The path we tread: Blacks in nursing worldwide, 1854–1994. 3rd ed., **1077**

Patient Information Section of the Medical Library Association, 636

patientINFORM.org, **639**

Patients' rights in the age of managed health care, **726, 863, 994**

Patty's industrial hygiene. 5th ed., 1541, **1556**

Patty's toxicology. 5th ed., **1541**

PDR drug guide for mental health professionals, **1242, 1370**

PDR electronic library, 795, 1064, **1243**

PDR for herbal medicines, **1244**

PDR for nonprescription drugs, dietary supplements, and herbs: The definitive guide to OTC medications, **1245**

PDR for nutritional supplements, **1246**

PDR guide to drug interactions, side effects, and indications, **1247**

PDR medical dictionary, **105**

PDR nurse's drug handbook, **1064, 1248**

PDRhealth, **768**

PEP archive, **1293**

Peterson's graduate programs in business, education, health, information studies, law and social work, **185, 219**

Peterson's nursing programs. 10th ed., **1046**

Pharmaceutical Excipients, 1226

Pharmaceutical medicine dictionary, **1174**

Pharmacopoeia of the People's Republic of China. English ed., **1184**

Pharmacopoeias and related literature in Britain and America, 1618–1847, **1185, 1269**

Pharmacy in history, **1270**

Physician characteristics and distribution in the U.S., **542**

Physician compensation and production survey, **543, 908**

Physicians' desk reference for ophthalmic medicines, **1249**

Physicians' desk reference: PDR, **1250,** 1574

Phytochemical dictionary: A handbook of bioactive compounds from plants. 2nd ed., **1251**

Plagues and politics: The story of the United States Public Health Service, **1468**

Plarr's lives of the fellows of the Royal college of surgeons of England, **55**

Poisoning and toxicology handbook. 4th ed., **1252, 1536, 1557**

PolicyFinder, 451

POPLINE, **443, 937, 1000, 1478**

Portrait of health in the United States. 1st ed., **544, 909**

A practical dictionary of Chinese medicine. 1st ed., **127**

A practical guide to global health service, **927, 1425, 1442**

Praeger handbook of Black American health: Policies and issues behind disparities in health. 2nd ed., **1457**

President's Council on Bioethics, **621**

Proctor and Hughes' chemical hazards of the workplace. 5th ed., **1458, 1558**

Professional guide to signs and symptoms. 5th ed., **332, 1065**

Profiles in science, **48**, 347, 885

The progressive era's health reform movement: A historical dictionary, **171, 360, 840**

PsychiatryOnline, 721, **1294**

Psychodynamic diagnostic manual (PDM), **1253, 1299**

Psychologists' desk reference. 2nd ed., **1371**

PsycINFO, **1388**

PubChem, **444**

Public health image library (PHIL), **499, 1469, 1510**

The public health law manual. 3rd ed., **995, 1459**

Public health law materials, **1015, 1511**

Public library of science (PLoS), **39**, 40, **431**, 433

Publication manual of the American Psychological Association. 5th ed., **1372**

Publications from the National Center for Health Statistics for the period 1898–2004 on DVD, **545, 910**

PubMed, **6**, 38, 227, 293, 322, 327, 328, 347, 427, 430, **432**, 438, 440, 441, 454, 463, 467, 471, 530, 575, 577, **605**, 608, 619, 626, 638, 714, 725, **731**, 754, **815, 871, 938, 1001, 1087, 1148, 1279, 1389, 1479, 1576**

PubMed Central (PMC), 39, **40**, 431, 433

Q

Quackwatch, **622, 719**, 751, **1016**

Quality Tools, 326, 715, **892**

The quotable Osler, **505**

R

Rational phytotherapy: A reference guide for physicians and pharmacists. 5th ed., **1254**

Recent dissertations in the medical humanities, **24, 383, 579, 831, 1024, 1162**

Red book, **1255**, 1574

Remington: The science and practice of pharmacy, **1197**

Repertorium commentationum a societatibus litterariis editarum, **25**

Research centers directory, **186, 220**

Resources for nursing research: An annotated bibliography. 4th ed., **1066**

Resources on the history of psychiatry, **1383**

The review of natural products, 1222, **1256**

The rights of patients: The authoritative ACLU guide to the rights of patients. 3rd ed., **600, 720**, 726, **996**

The roll of the Royal College of Physicians of London: Comprising biographical sketches of all the eminent physicians whose names are recorded in the Annals. 2d rev. and enl. ed., **56**

S

The SAGE handbook of health psychology, **333, 1373**

Saunders nursing drug handbook 2008, **1067**

Sax's dangerous properties of industrial materials. 11th ed., **1559**

Say it in Spanish: A guide for health care professionals. 3rd ed., **128, 1040**

Science and technology in medicine: An illustrated account based on ninety-nine landmark publications from five centuries, **403**

Science.gov, **293**

Scientific style and format: The CSE manual for authors, editors, and publishers. 7th ed., **570**

SciFinder, **434**

Scirus, **435,** 436

Scopus, **436**

Secondary data sources for public health: A practical guide, **546, 911, 1443**

Secondary sources in the history of Canadian medicine: A bibliography, **384**

SEER Cancer Statistics Review, 166, 515, 538, **547**

A select bibliography of medical biography, 50

A select bibliography of medical biography: With an introductory essay on medical biography. 2nd ed., **68**

A short history of neurology: The British contribution, 1660–1910, 400, **404, 1384**

Sir William Osler: An annotated bibliography with illustrations, **385**

Sittig's handbook of toxic and hazardous chemicals and carcinogens. 5th ed., **1560**

Slee's health care terms. 5th ed., **172, 841, 1422**

Sloane's medical word book: A spelling and vocabulary guide to medical transcription. 4th ed., **106**

SNOMED CT, **88**

Source book in bioethics, **601, 997**

A sourcebook of dental medicine: Being a documentary history of dentistry and stomatology from the earliest times to the middle of the twentieth century, **809**

The Sourcebook of medical illustration: Over 900 anatomical, medical, and scientific illustrations available for general re-use and adaptation free of normal copyright restrictions, **500**

Southwestern medical dictionary: Spanish-English, English-Spanish. 2nd ed., **129**

Spanish-English, English-Spanish medical dictionary =:Diccionario médico español-inglés, inglés-español. 3rd ed., **130**

Special populations, **1512**

Specialized Information Services (SIS), **1577**

SPORTDiscus, **445**

Standard acupuncture nomenclature, **131, 173**

State cancer legislative database program (SCLD), **732, 1002, 1480**

State medical licensure requirements and statistics, 451, **548,** 607, **1018**

State snapshots, **893**

Statistical abstract of the United States, **549, 912**

Statistical handbook on infectious diseases, **550, 1460**

Statistical methods for health care research. 5th ed., **551, 913, 1092**

Statistical record of health and medicine, **552, 1524**

Stedman's medical abbreviations, acronyms and symbols, 4th ed., 107, 108, **117, 1041**

Stedman's medical dictionary. 28th ed., **107,** 117

Stedman's medical dictionary for the dental professions: Illustrated. 1st ed., **786**

Stedman's medical dictionary for the health professions and nursing. 6th ed., 107, **108,** 117, **1042**

Stedman's medical eponyms. 2nd ed., **109**

STINET, 293

Stockley's drug interactions: A source book of interactions, their mechanisms, clinical importance and management. 7th ed., **1257**

Substance Abuse and Mental Health Services Administration (SAMHSA), **769, 1318, 1394**

Surgery: An illustrated history, 348, **361**

T

Taber's cyclopedic medical dictionary, **110**

Terminology of communication disorders: Speech-language-hearing. 5th ed., **174**

Thesaurus ethics in the life sciences, **576**

THOMAS, **1003**

Thornton's medical books, libraries, and collectors: A study of bibliography and the book trade in relation to the medical sciences. 3rd rev. ed., **26**

Three hundred years of psychiatry, 1535–1860: A history presented in selected English texts, **1385**

Tietz clinical guide to laboratory tests, 315, 318, 319, 325, **334,** 709, 753

Tox town, **1587**

Toxics release inventory (TRI), **1584**

TOXLINE, 626, **1578**

TOXMAP, **1579, 1585**

TOXNET (Toxicology data network), 328, 471, 627, 635, 1561, 1562, 1563, 1564, 1566, 1567, 1568, 1569, 1570, 1571, 1572, 1578, 1579, **1580,** 1584, 1585, **1586,** 1587

ToxSeek, **1581**

Traditional medicine (WHO), **1287**

Turning the pages online, **362, 501**

Two centuries of American medicine, 1776–1976, **405**

Tyler's honest herbal: A sensible guide to the use of herbs and related remedies. 4th ed., **640, 1258**

U

Unified medical language system (UMLS), **89,** 328, 471, 885

Uniform requirements for manuscripts submitted to biomedical journals, **571,** 572

The United States pharmacopeia. 20th rev. ed., **1186**

U.S. Dept. of Health and Human Services, 222, 769, **894, 1017, 1513,** 1582

U.S. Food and Drug Administration home page, **770, 1271, 1280, 1288**

The U.S. health care delivery system: Fundamental facts, definitions, and statistics, **864, 914**

U.S. health law and policy, 2001: A guide to the current literature, **832, 968**

U.S. National Library of Medicine, 479

USDA nutrient data laboratory, 765, **1139, 1149, 1154, 1155**

Using the pharmaceutical literature, **1201**

USP (U.S. Pharmacopeia), **1188**

USP DI, **727, 1187,** 1574

USP dictionary of USAN and international drug names, **1175**

V

The value of health: A history of the Pan American Health Organization, **931, 1470**

Videos of surgical procedures (MedlinePlus), **29, 771**

Visible Human Project, 471, **502,** 885

W

Wallace/Maxcy-Rosenau-Last public health and preventive medicine. 15th ed., **1461**

Webster's new world medical dictionary. 2nd ed., **111, 646**

Wellcome bibliography for the history of medicine, 11, **386**

Wellcome Images, 483, **503**

Wellcome Library for the History and Understanding of Medicine, 354, **483**

The Western medical tradition: 800 B.C.–1800 A.D., **406**

The western medical tradition: 1800 to 2000, **407**

Western medicine: An illustrated history, **408**

What your patients need to know about psychiatric medications, **721, 1259, 1374**

WHO child growth standards, **553, 1140, 1462**

WHO drug information, **1289**

WHO family of international classifications, 83, 84, **90**

WHO global infobase, **554, 963**

WHO historical collection, **387, 932, 1470**

WHO mortality database, **555**

The whole brain atlas, **504**

WHOLIS, **484**

Who's who in medicine and healthcare, **76, 221, 845**

The who's who of Nobel Prize winners, 1901–2000. 4th ed., **69**

WHOSIS, **556,** 559, 560, **964, 1525,** 1527, 1528

Wiley encyclopedia of biomedical engineering, **281**

Wiley encyclopedia of molecular medicine, **282**

Wiley handbook of current and emerging drug therapies, **1260**

Wiley's English-Spanish and Spanish-English dictionary of psychology and psychiatry = Diccionario de psicología y psiquiatría inglés-español español-inglés Wiley, **1315**

WISER (Wireless Information System for Emergency Responders), **1281, 1290, 1514**

WISQARS: Web-based Injury Statistics Query and Reporting System, 534, **557, 1404**

Women and medicine. 3rd ed., **49**

Women, health, and medicine in America: A historical handbook, **409**

Women in medicine: A bibliography of the literature on women physicians, **27**

Women in medicine: An encyclopedia, 59, **70**

Women's health USA, **558, 915, 1463, 1526**

The words of medicine: Sources, meanings, and delights, **175**

World directory of dental schools, 773, **792**

World directory of medical schools, **197**

World health and disease. 3rd ed., **928, 1464**

World Health Organization (WHO), 844, 930, 932, 940, **951**

World Health Organization's International Classification of Functioning, Disability, and Health (ICF), 310

The World health report, 556, **559, 965,** 1525, **1527**

World health statistics, 556, **560, 966,** 1525, **1528**

World health systems: Challenges and perspectives, 865, **929**

World history of psychiatry, **1386**

World list of pharmacy schools, **1176**

World list of scientific periodicals published in the years 1900–1960. 4th ed., **41**

World Medical Association Ethics Unit, **623, 952**

World medical periodicals: Les périodiques médicaux dans le monde. Perió dicos médicos del mundo. Medizinische Zeitschriften aller Länder. 3rd ed., **42**

World of health, **694**

Writing and publishing in medicine. 3rd ed., **572**

Www.health.gov, **222, 1426**

Y

The Yale book of quotations, **506**

You may also be interested in

ALA GUIDE TO ECONOMICS AND BUSINESS REFERENCE
American Library Association

Focusing on print and electronic sources that are key to economics and business reference, this is a must-have for every reference desk. Readers will find information on business law, electronic commerce, international business, management of information systems, market research, and much more.

PRINT ISBN: 978-0-8389-1024-5
528 PAGES / 6" x 9"

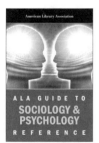

ALA GUIDE TO SOCIOLOGY AND PSYCHOLOGY REFERENCE
AMERICAN LIBRARY ASSOCIATION
ISBN: 978-0-8389-1025-2

FUNDAMENTALS OF REFERENCE
CAROLYN M. MULAC
ISBN: 978-0-8389-1087-0

THE ALA BIG BOOK OF LIBRARY GRANT MONEY, 8E
EDITED BY ANN KEPLER
ISBN: 978-0-8389-1058-0

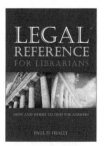

LEGAL REFERENCE FOR LIBRARIANS
PAUL D. HEALEY
ISBN: 978-0-8389-1117-4

ALA GLOSSARY OF LIBRARY AND INFORMATION SCIENCE, 4E
EDITED BY MICHAEL LEVINE-CLARK AND TONI M. CARTER
ISBN: 978-0-8389-1111-2

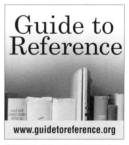

GUIDE TO REFERENCE ONLINE
AMERICAN LIBRARY ASSOCIATION
GUIDETOREFERENCE.ORG

Order today at **alastore.ala.org** or **866-746-7252!**
ALA Store purchases fund advocacy, awareness, and accreditation programs for library professionals worldwide.